Psychology of Ageing

by the same author

Dictionary of Psychological Testing, Assessment and Treatment
2nd edition
Ian Stuart-Hamilton
ISBN 978 1 84310 494 0
eISBN 978 1 84642 657 5

An Asperger Dictionary of Everyday Expressions
2nd edition
Ian Stuart-Hamilton
ISBN 978 1 84310 518 3
eISBN 978 1 84642 578 3

The Psychology of Ageing
An Introduction
5th Edition

Ian Stuart-Hamilton

Jessica Kingsley *Publishers*
London and Philadelphia

This edition published in 2012
by Jessica Kingsley Publishers
116 Pentonville Road
London N1 9JB, UK
and
400 Market Street, Suite 400
Philadelphia, PA 19106, USA

www.jkp.com

Library of Congress Cataloging in Publication Data
Stuart-Hamilton, Ian.
The psychology of ageing : an introduction / Ian Stuart-Hamilton. -- 5th ed.
p. cm.
Includes bibliographical references and index.
ISBN 978-1-84905-245-0 (alk. paper)
1. Older people--Psychology. 2. Aging--Psychological aspects. I. Title.
BF724.8.S78 2012
155.67--dc23
2011050951

British Library Cataloguing in Publication Data
A CIP catalogue record for this book is available from the British Library

ISBN 978 1 84905 245 0
eISBN 978 0 85700 577 9

Printed and bound in Great Britain

To the memory of my late father,
Charles Alfred Hamilton
(1928–2011)

Contents

Preface

The first edition of this book appeared in 1991. Thus, since the appearance of the fourth edition in 2006, it has under UK law reached its majority. It can accordingly vote, order drinks in a public house and marry without its parents' permission. In another few months it can stand as a candidate for Parliament. The book's conception was at the end of a rather surreal Thursday. I was attending a research conference at a Cambridge University college.[1] During the day I was offered a lecturing post I didn't know I had applied for. Over lunchtime, I had retreated into the college gardens for a quiet read of a P.D. James detective novel and found myself reading a description of a person sitting reading one lunchtime – in the same college gardens and indeed in the very same seat where I was now sitting reading. Then, at the evening drinks reception laid on by a consortium of academic publishers, a publisher's rep asked me if there were any gaps in the existing range of books. It is inadvisable to drink on an empty stomach, in my case doubly so, since I have no head for alcohol. My recollection is that I gave an erudite explanation of why there was a need for a basic introductory text on the psychology of ageing. What I actually sounded like I dread to think, but I vaguely recall writing down my contact details. A few days later I was amazed to find a letter from Jessica Kingsley Publishers, inviting me to put forward a book proposal and sample of text. The sample was duly sent (curiously, practically none of it appeared in the printed version) and met with approval. I was then invited to visit the Jessica Kingsley headquarters.

My knowledge of publishers at that time was based almost solely on the scurrilous gossip in *Private Eye*. I accordingly expected Jessica Kingsley to be a chain-smoking harridan who had already polished off a half bottle of whisky before I arrived for my mid-morning appointment. Instead, I found an utterly charming and erudite lady who listened to my blather as if I were an interesting person and offered me invaluable advice that quietly corrected some of my more insane ideas and steered me through to a workable proposal. Jessica is, I know, hugely admired by fellow publishers and has patiently and kindly guided a vast cohort of authors

---

1   In keeping with the unusual sequence of events described here, this has since changed its name.

into producing readable and sensible prose. It has been my great privilege to have enjoyed her support and friendship over these past 20 years.

The first edition was largely written in a flurry of activity over the summer of 1990. Somehow during this same period I got married and wrote the lecture notes for three modules of an undergraduate degree course as well. Critics were immensely (and I think inexplicably) kind about the first edition. Very little of the text from it has survived into this latest edition. Largely this reflects the updating of information and similar, but also, over the years, I have become less satisfied with the slightly earnest tone I adopted in that first version. The one exception to this is the final chapter of the book – my vision of the future of the psychology of ageing. I wrote this chapter in two hours from start to finish. I wrote it longhand (when typing up, deciphering my handwriting, never easy at the best of times, was particularly trying, I recall). It was a very hot sultry day, the windows were open and my writing was accompanied by the sounds of Radio 1 being played very loudly by the sunbathing teenager next door. Reading it back now evokes for me strong memories of early 1990s' pop music. I have decided to keep the chapter more or less as it is.[2] Not for the sake of personal nostalgia (the early 1990s was hardly a vintage period for pop), but simply to illustrate the fallibility of predicting *anything* about the future directions of research.

When I was writing the first edition of the book, I obviously had to do preparatory reading, and I was recommended to try the then new-fangled method of performing an electronic database search. Incredible as it now seems, this involved making an appointment with a specialist librarian, who performed the task for me (I supplied the keywords). The resulting print-out (on tractor-feed paper, a term that will have anyone under 40 scratching their heads) ran to under 100 pages. Today, a computer search of *PsycINFO* or *Medline* will produce a larger print-out for just a single specialist topic within the psychology of ageing. The subject has mushroomed in size. This is not just a personal observation. Colleagues have noted the same thing, and in support I can cite one of the pre-eminent figures in the field, Professor Tim Salthouse:

> As recently as a decade ago an author could attempt to survey the field [...] and hope to be reasonably comprehensive by focusing primarily on articles published in three or four major journals. However, now such an effort would represent only a small fraction of the relevant literature because research [...] is published in journals based in the disciplines of psychology, neuroscience, neurology, radiology, health psychology, psychopharmacology, epidemiology, public health, endocrinology, and more. (Salthouse, 2010, pp.vi–vii)

It is worth noting that Salthouse is talking purely about the psychology of ageing from the viewpoint of a cognitive psychologist or a neuropsychologist. If we factor

---

2   For those wanting to follow up particular threads, I have included a couple of recent references, but it is otherwise unchanged.

in the rest of the psychological disciplines, the extent of the issue can be readily appreciated.

Excluding the issue of the inconvenient burden placed on authors doing preparatory reading, such an expansion in research reports should be a good thing. More activity should mean that we are learning more and more in greater depth about the subject. However, note the use of the word 'should' in the previous two sentences. In theory, more research is good. In practice, a very large quantity of this research has tediously picked over the same small patches of ground, examining research topics that were often not very interesting in the first place to see if a new and better way can be found to examine the same issue. As has so often happened with psychology in the past, the phenomenon that was being examined has given way to turf wars over who has the best experimental or analytical method to prove the same point. Thus, in writing this fifth edition, the net result of a depressing proportion of my reading has been to retain essentially the same text as in the fourth edition, simply updating the references to support the same arguments.

This does not mean that there has been no progression in the field, nor that this state of affairs is an excuse for outright cynicism about the subject. Many of the findings, regardless of how many people examine them, are important (e.g. the issue of the causes of intellectual decline in later life). In other instances, progress has been made and new topics are being uncovered that are worthy of attention. For example, the new area of molecular psychology could in the future be immensely informative about psychological changes in later life. My personal belief is that we are on the verge of a radical shift in geropsychology, and in the last days of the traditional views, dominated as they are by cognitive psychology paradigms. But, as noted earlier, predictions are a risky business. As with the previous edition, therefore, I have included a chapter criticising the research methods and approaches currently used. While being critical and alerting the reader to issues in the current literature, I have as far as possible tried to remain neutral in the main body of chapters. However, the chapter of criticisms is unashamedly partisan. Readers are invited to accept or reject it as they please, but I wanted to make the point that not all in the garden is rosy and that there are strong grounds for questioning the current research methods and the assumptions behind them.

One thing I have attempted to amend in this book is to move away, at least a little bit, from the doom and gloom air that previous editions have (unintentionally) had. I am now in my fifties, and some of the topics I so airily discussed in the first edition, such as presbyopia and difficulties remembering people's names, are now things I am experiencing at first hand. It was never my intention to present a gloomy view of ageing, but describing everything that can go wrong does rather create that sort of mood. It was summarised for me a couple of years ago when one of the students on my geropsychology course asked at the start of a lesson, 'What's going to go wrong with us this week?' Therefore, while not adopting a Pollyanna approach to things (which would be both foolish and patronising), I have attempted where appropriate to stress that findings on decline are relative and not absolute. The impression that can be gained from a lot of research, particularly that based on cognition and psychometrics, is that older adults 'fail' when their scores decline. As will be noted at various points throughout this book, getting lower scores on a laboratory test of limited practical applicability should rarely be anything to get worked up about. In addition, I have explored issues surrounding lifestyle in later life, and the positive aspects of this, in greater depth.

It seems perverse to follow this statement by saying that I have also added a new chapter, on death, dying and bereavement. Quite simply, some books on the psychology of ageing have such a chapter, some do not. Until now I have resisted the temptation, because I am not wholly convinced that the subject matter is best seen in terms of ageing. In many parts of the world, death is still something that most often happens to people *before* they reach old age, and in industrialised countries the odds on drawing an old age pension are far less good than one might suppose. However, a lot of students over the years have expressed an interest in studying this topic, and not all of them were dressed as goths. Therefore, I have included it.

I should like to finish as always by thanking my long-suffering family and colleagues for enduring my happy, patient and content mood when writing this book.

Ian Stuart-Hamilton
Professor of Developmental Psychology
University of Glamorgan

CHAPTER 1

What is Ageing?

In this first chapter, some key background information is provided that sets the rest of the book in context. Thus, it deals with aspects of ageing that, while not directly psychological, have an impact on aspects of the psychology of ageing: issues such as how we define ageing, population changes, biological changes in ageing, and so forth. The chapter is only intended as an introductory gloss. Suggested key items for further reading are presented at the end.

Definitions of ageing

Our age is measured is years – in other words, how many times the earth has been round the sun since we were born. This is often termed **chronological age**, but, if we want to know something about what an individual person is like based solely on this, it is not a totally reliable measure. This is because people of the same chronological age vary in their physical and mental state, and this becomes more pronounced the older the person concerned. For example, we can think of 70-year-olds who look like stereotypical older people (grey hair, wrinkled skin, etc.), but we can also recall 'well-preserved' individuals who lack these features (**agerasia**) and, indeed, younger adults who look 'prematurely old'. In very rare cases, this is grossly exaggerated. For example, in **progeria** (or **Hutchinson-Gilford syndrome**) the patient begins to age rapidly in early childhood and typically dies in early teens, and in **Werner's syndrome** patients begin to look prematurely old in their teens, typically dying in their forties. Whether these conditions are caused by genuinely accelerated ageing or simply resemble ageing coincidentally is open to debate (see Bergeman, 1997; Hayflick, 1994). However, even excepting these unusual cases, chronological age by itself is a far from infallible indicator.

But, for all that chronological age is unreliable, people still set great store by it. This is best illustrated by **social age**, or what is considered to be socially acceptable behaviour at a particular chronological age. We thus do not expect grandparents to play on skateboards, any more than we expect teenagers to need walking sticks. Social age even shapes appropriate inter-generational behaviour, with a sexual relationship in which there is a large age gap between the partners being frowned upon. Chronological age, unreliable measure or not, thus brings with it a heavy baggage of expectations. Not least of these is the pervasive idea that old age is qualitatively different from earlier life. This concept is deeply rooted in many cultures. For example, of great antiquity is the idea that a long life is the reward for pious behaviour (Minois, 1989; Thane, 2000). Two of the most common manifestations of this are the **antediluvian ageing myth** and the **hyperborean ageing myth** – the beliefs that in ancient times or in a far distant land, respectively, there was a race of virtuous people with incredibly long lifespans. Modern industrialised societies take a slightly different view. Later life is seen as a time of leisure after a lifetime of work. This is neatly symbolised by the traditional retirement present of a gold watch, which is intended to signify the time served in work and the 'golden years' that lie ahead. However, more cynically, later life can be seen as a time of enforced removal from paid work. In many countries, retirement from employment is mandatory at a particular age, or in effect is made so by assorted constraints.

The idea of a pensioned retirement in which practically everyone is legally entitled to at least a state-provided pension is so ingrained in the consciousness of industrialised nations that it comes as a surprise to many to learn that pensions of this sort are a late nineteenth century German invention that rapidly spread to other countries through the early decades of the twentieth century.[1] Prior to this, the concept was largely unknown (Thane, 2000). However, the idea of a state pension is less philanthropic than it might first appear. The pension was a useful way of forcing older workers (*inter alia*, perceived as less strong and less easy to retrain) out of the labour force, making way for younger people. In addition, when the schemes were first introduced, relatively few people lived long enough to collect their pension (see later in this chapter) so contributions in the form of taxes and similar more than paid for the scheme (see McDonald, 2011).

A state pension scheme brings with it a need to define an age of retirement. Fortunately for the early policy-makers, the age at which old age begins had already been established. Adolphe Quetelet's *Sur l'Homme et le Développement de Ses Facultés, ou, Essai de Physique Sociale* (Quetelet, 1836) was an attempt to identify the characteristics of the average person. It was based on statistical measures of a wide range of human characteristics and was an early attempt at anthropometry. Among the wealth of objective facts were some rather more dubious interpretations, including the assertion that from 'sixty to sixty-five years of age viability loses much of its energy, that is to say, the probability of life then becomes very small' (Quetelet, 1836, p.178). This is, to say the least, questionable (though by delicious irony, Quetelet himself had a stroke when he was 59 that limited his activity thereafter). However, Quetelet's contemporaries tended to take this assertion as fact, and by the 1840s the idea that old age begins at around 60–65 years of age was widely promulgated (Mullan, 2002).

---

1   State pensions were introduced by Bismarck, essentially to undermine the appeal of a burgeoning
     socialist movement (see Steinberg, 2011).

Fortunately for us, although Quetelet's reasoning was wrong (as we shall see, there is no evidence for the catastrophic loss he described), the choice of age was nonetheless a reasonably good one. There is no sudden moment when people 'become' old. But as shall be seen, at around 60–65 years of age, in the majority of people there are significant (if not dramatic) changes in mental and physical functioning that mean that 60–65 is a reasonable choice of age of onset or **threshold age**, and is the one used by most modern **gerontologists** (people who study ageing: e.g. Bromley, 1988; Decker, 1980; Kermis, 1983; Rebok, 1987; Stuart-Hamilton, 2011; Ward, 1984).

Some commentators further divide older adults into **young elderly** people and **old elderly** people (or 'young old' and 'old old'). The precise ages involved in this categorisation vary between writers, however. Some feel that 'young elderly' describes anyone between 60 and 75, and 'old elderly' anyone older than this, but others take different spans under the same terms (e.g. 60–80, 65–80 or 65–75 for the young elderly group). Caution in reading reports using these terms is thus advised. A variant on this theme by Burnside, Ebersole and Monea (1979) proposed categories of 'young old' (60–69), 'middle-aged old' (70–79), 'old old' (80–89) and 'very old old' (90+). This seems simply to introduce new and unnecessary synonyms for 'sixties', 'seventies', 'eighties' and 'nineties'. Another method divides the over-65s into the **third age** and the **fourth age**. The 'third age' refers to active and independent lifestyle in later life, and the 'fourth age' to a (final) period of dependence on others. The terms have met with some favour, since they do not have the pejorative overtones some people perceive in words such as 'old' or 'elderly'. However, this is a moot point, since terms such as 'third age' in effect classify people according to how much help they need from others. It should also be noted that the terms used by gerontologists are not necessarily the ones employed (and by implication, liked) by older people (e.g. Midwinter, 1991).

Another approach to classifying later life has been to consider **functional age**. Definitions of this term vary widely, but essentially it means the average chronological age at which a particular level of skill is found. The concept has been in use for over a century in child psychology, where it is a useful and instantly comprehensible guide to a child's development (e.g. if a child is 12 but has a mental age of 8, then he or she clearly has intellectual problems). However, the term sits less comfortably in dealing with older adults. For example, it is known that some older adults' intellectual skills decline to a level on a par with children (see Chapter 2). In principle, we could label these older people as having the functional age of a child. In one sense this is accurate, but it brings with it an unwelcome set of associations about 'second childhood' and similar that question whether the use of functional age in these circumstances is appropriate. In addition, it seems contradictory to create a new method of classification intended to supplant chronological age and then use chronological age as a key part of the definition (i.e. functional age is basically the mean chronological age at which a skill is shown at a particular level).

Arguably there is more mileage in defining performance in terms of a scale of measurement independent of age considerations (e.g. longest list of numbers that can be remembered, highest frequency note that can be heard), but this in effect is doing nothing more than advocating the use of test scores to grade people. A refinement of this is to argue that anyone passing a set threshold of ability can be held to be functional in that particular activity (e.g. remembering lists longer than a particular length, hearing sounds higher than a particular frequency), but ultimately this is simply paraphrasing measures of everyday competence used all the time by clinicians and nurses. Also, the concept does not necessarily extend well into measuring everyday activities outside a clinical setting, where, apart from all other considerations of whether a simple accurate test can be devised, there is the issue of compensatory strategies (see Chapter 2) that might negate the effects of a decline in some skills.

Other measures of ageing have eschewed considerations of chronological age and have, for example, examined it in terms of the processes affecting a person as he or she has developed. These can be divided into relatively distant events (e.g. lacking mobility because of childhood polio) known as **distal ageing effects**, and those more recent (e.g. lacking mobility because of a broken leg) known as **proximal ageing effects**. Again, ageing can be defined in terms of the probability of acquiring a particular characteristic of later life. **Universal ageing** features are those that all older people share to some extent (e.g. wrinkled skin), while **probabilistic ageing** features are likely but not universal (e.g. arthritis). These terms may be contrasted with the similar concepts of **primary ageing** (age changes to the body) and **secondary ageing** (changes that occur with greater frequency, but are not a necessary accompaniment). Some commentators add a third term – **tertiary ageing** – to refer to the rapid and marked physical deterioration immediately prior to death. These are all useful measures in their place, but the problem with them is that they are not as widely applicable as (for all its flaws) chronological age is. There are only limited instances, for example, where describing people in terms of their number of primary and secondary ageing characteristics will produce a meaningful grouping for the purposes of describing age differences.

Arguably, there is no method of codifying old age that is universally successful. All have the capacity to describe the mainstream experience of ageing, but none can be said to be all-embracing. This is not really surprising. Ageing by definition is a continuous process and definitions attempt the impossible in trying to codify this into static lumps. It is like trying to decide at which point a stream becomes a river. Whatever measure is decided upon it is to all intent and purposes arbitrary – if we say that at point x the river begins, that does not mean that the water on either side of our imaginary line changes in any way; the flow is continuous and our division has no effect on this. But nonetheless, for all that attempts at categorisation might appear foolish when considered from this angle, there is reason behind them. If we look at the tiny trickle of water that is the source of a great river, there is a demonstrable distinction between it and the river as it flows into the sea. Likewise, for all that ageing is continuous, there are demonstrable differences between a person in their teens and their eighties. Therefore, it is not unreasonable to want to group a continuous variable such as age into discrete units, even though, when looked at closely, the dividing line might be somewhat arbitrary.

Therefore, adopting Quetelet's precedent (no matter how flawed his initial reasoning) we shall for most of this book assume that old age 'begins' at roughly 60–65 years of age. But it is important to stress that: (1) there is no single point at which a person automatically becomes 'old'; and (2) chronological age is in any case an essentially arbitrary measure.

Prevalence of ageing – the greying population

Ageing is not unique to the modern times, but it is only in the past hundred years that it has become commonplace. It is estimated that in the prehistoric era old age was extremely rare, and even up to the seventeenth century probably only about 1 per cent of the population was over 65. By the nineteenth century, this proportion had risen to approximately 4 per cent (Cowgill, 1970). In Britain today, about 11 million (c.16%) of the population is aged 65 or older. Put in another perspective – in 2007, for the first time in recorded history, there were more older people than under-18s living in the UK (www.statistics.gov.uk). There are similar figures for other industrialised nations (OECD, 1988; see also www.oecd.org). Nobody disputes that old age is now a commonplace experience (hence the phrase the **greying population** is an accurate one), but the full story is nonetheless not as simple as these broadbrush stroke figures might make it appear.

First, it is important to identify what is meant by 'living longer'. This is generally measured by **life expectancy**, which in itself can be a misleading figure. 'Life expectancy' simply means how much longer a person can expect to live, which is straightforward enough. However, the way it is measured is not. Depending upon which person is doing the measuring, it is either the mean time left for all the people in a person's age group, or the median time left for the same people. Although this definition usually gets statisticians annoyed, the mean is to all intent and purposes the average. The median is the 50 per cent mark – half the numbers in the data set in question are bigger than the median, half are smaller. Thus, life expectancy is either the average amount of time a person can expect to carry on living, or the amount of time before half the people in his or her age group have died. This means that life expectancies calculated by the mean and the median method can differ, but there is a greater concern than this. Namely, life expectancy calculated by either method can give the illusion that people are living longer when it would be more accurate to say that fewer of them are dying when very young.

The above statement initially seems nonsensical, but it is mathematically valid. To explain why, let us consider some data on life expectancy for people born in the

UK in 1400, 1841 and 1981. In 1400, it is estimated that the life expectancy was 35 years; by 1841, this had risen to 40 years, but, by 1981, it had skyrocketed to 71 years (i.e. over double the 1400 figure). To the unwary, these figures seem to indicate that in 1400 it was almost impossible to grow old since most people died before they reached 35. Indeed, the irresistible mental image for some is that in 1400 'old age' must have been in the forties. This is wrong. The reason for the lower life expectancy in 1400 is because a lot more people died in infancy and childhood than they do today. If a lot of people die at a very young age in a sample, then this drags down the group's mean or median score very dramatically; but this does not mean that if you survived childhood your *remaining* life expectancy would be as bad. To illustrate this point, consider the life expectancy figures for people who have already reached the age of 60. In 1400 their life expectancy was 69, in 1841 it was 73, and in 1981 it was 76. The difference between the 1400 and the 1981 figures has shrunk from 36 years at birth to 7 years at age 60. This clearly illustrates the prime reason for differences in life expectancy figures over historical time – namely, fewer people die in childhood, not that people who reach adulthood live vastly longer lives.

Of course, this argument can be taken too far. Although a person aged 60 in 1981 could expect to live 'only' seven years longer than a person of the same age in 1400, seven years is still an appreciable difference. Again, in the period 1911–1915, British people aged over 75 died at the rate of 137 deaths per thousand per year. In 2006–07, that rate of death had fallen to 83/1000 (www.statistics.gov.uk). Thus, as we move through history, extra surviving life expectancy is being provided in all parts of the lifespan – it is not that medical science is 'failing' to create additional life expectancy in older people. But nonetheless, in historical terms, the biggest changes have been in the early years of life.

The reasons for improved life expectancy over historical time are legion. Some concern the combating of disease and injury after they have occurred – antibiotics and other pharmaceutical products, better surgery (enhanced by better anesthesia), etc. Others concern the prevention of disease in the first place – inoculation is perhaps the most obvious example, but also the advent of clean water supplies, better food hygiene and storage, better quality housing and similar have all played their part. However, most of these changes have occurred over the last 150 or so years, exactly the same period that has seen the biggest increase in life expectancy. If we look at the historical life expectancy figures cited earlier, we can see that the improvement from 1400 to 1841 is extremely modest compared with the huge rise seen between 1841 and 1981. Considerations such as these led Oeppen and Vaupel (2002) to examine **best practice life expectancy**. This is simply the highest life expectancy figure to be found in any country in the world at a particular point in time. Oeppen and Vaupel found that this figure has risen linearly (i.e. a graph would show a steady straight line) from 45 years in Sweden in 1840 up to 85 years in Japan in 2000. Given such a steady rate of increase in life expectancy of approximately 3 months each year for 160 years, it is tempting to conclude that this is a highly reliable trend that will presumably continue into the future. In other words, life expectancy could carry on growing and growing. This is just what Oeppen and Vaupel argue and they are not alone in this – note the popular media that regularly regale the public with tales of how, in the future, the majority of us will live into our nineties or beyond.

The thought of ever-increasing lifespans is an attractive one, but regrettably it is not guaranteed. The growth rate of 3 months per year for 160 years is beguiling, but it is largely based on the decreases in infant mortality as we have seen; although there has also been an increase in remaining life expectancy for older adults, it is far too modest to account for this growth rate (see Post and Binstock, 2004). The biggest changes to our collective health over the past 160 years have been in combating infectious disease, and it is readily apparent why children would be the biggest beneficiaries of these changes – infectious diseases nearly always strike for the first time in childhood, and the various factors mentioned earlier will all help combat or prevent these. But eventually, the capacity to preserve life in childhood is bound to reach its limit and, when it does, the seemingly inexorable rise in life expectancy will also decline from its current impressive rate, unless the ability to prolong life in older adults improves. Perhaps this will happen, but, if it does not, then best practice life expectancy cannot possibly continue to rise at the same rate.

In fact, there are additional grounds for being uncertain about future life expectancy figures. Their derivation from historical data is laborious, but mathematically speaking the process is simple enough. All the data are already there (i.e. we already know how long people lived), and 'all' that the researcher has to do is feed the numbers into the computer and run the programme. The same cannot be done with life expectancy figures for groups of people who are still alive. When it is reported that a baby born today will have a life expectancy of, for example, 85 years, there is no possible way of knowing with absolute certainty that this figure is accurate. The figure is produced by extrapolating from known historical data and projecting the effects of predicted changes in health care and similar onto these. However, such figures are only as accurate as the predictions built into the model. Accordingly, researchers usually allow for a margin of error in their calculations – they will give what they feel is the most likely outcome, but also indicate their margin of error, producing upper and lower estimates (it is often one of these extreme figures that news media report when they wish to sensationalise an otherwise dull story on statistics). The problem is that we have no reliable way of judging the effects of several key factors on future life expectancy. On the one hand, there are the long-term effects of obesity – a higher proportion than ever before of people in industrialised countries are overweight. Coupled with this, people take less exercise and have less physically demanding jobs and daily lives than in the past (www.statistics.gov.uk). The long-term effects of this are not certain, but it will almost undoubtedly have a negative effect on life expectancy (Olshansky et al., 2005). But counterbalancing this, there is a potential explosion in the effects of gene therapy and similar that could eradicate many key health problems. How do we predict the balance of the effects of the two? The simple answer is that it is extremely difficult to do so. This means that the predictions of future life expectancy for the population are more uncertain than previously. If we were to draw line graphs of projected life expectancies produced by different predictive models, we would see that the lines diverge from each other (i.e. they fan out) the further into the future the figures are extrapolated. Thus, the further this **longevity fan** spreads into the future, the less certain we can be about the proportion of older adults within the population (see Dowd, Blake and Cairns, 2010). Echoing research in other countries, in the UK, the Continuous Mortality Investigation, which advises actuaries, has advised caution in projecting future life expectancies and, with it, a host of related financial products such as pensions and similar (Continuous Mortality Investigation, 2006a, b).

Predicting future life expectancy is thus problematic, and it is tempting, because of this uncertainty, to dismiss the whole issue as too nebulous. However, even allowing for doubt, the majority opinion still favours an increase in the proportion of older adults in the population. Some estimates argue that the number of older people will peak at approximately 17 million (c.25% of the total population) in 2060, before various demographic changes cause a relative decline (Shaw, 2004). Within these figures, the most notable increase in the developed world will be among the 'oldest old' – those aged 85 years and older. For example, in the UK, the number in this group has increased from 0.66 million in 1984 to 1.4 million in 2009, and is projected to be 3.5 million (or 5% of the total population) by 2034. Small wonder then that the median age of the total UK population is predicted to rise from 35 years in 1984 to 42 years by 2034 (Office for National Statistics, 2010a). Put another way, about 70 per cent of today's Western population can expect to live past 65, and 30–40 per cent past 80. By 2050 it is predicted that almost half the population will live past 85. Although, as seen, we should be cautious about a too literal faith in some of these figures, it is almost certain that things will be better for future generations of older adults. In 1900, only about 25 per cent of the population could even hope to reach their sixty-fifth birthday (Brody, 1988; Sonnenschein and Brody, 2005). In broad terms, this means that we are moving from a **pyramidal society** to a **rectangular society**. Since in the modern world increasingly equal numbers of people are alive in each age decade (i.e. equal numbers of 0–9-year-olds, 10–19-year-olds, etc.), a histogram plotting numbers alive against age decade appears (with a little artistic licence) like a rectangle. By comparison, a population graph from 1900 looks like a pyramid (lots of people in the youngest age decade, progressively fewer in the older ones).

The figures presented so far are for the hypothetical typical person within the UK population (though the data for any other industrialised country will be very similar). However, there are considerable variations in figures introduced by gender, occupation and social class, culture and similar. These shall be examined in the next section.

Prevalence of ageing – variations

The largest differences in life expectancy tend to be between industrialised/high income countries and developing/low income countries. For example, in 2010, life expectancy at birth was an average of 69 years for the world. In industrialised/ developed countries, mean life expectancy was 77 versus 67 in less developed nations and 55 in the least developed. North America had a life expectancy of 78, Latin America of 74, Europe of 76 (with EU countries alone, the figure was 79), Asia of 70 – and Africa of 55 (Population Reference Bureau, 2010). In the main, this can be attributed to differences in infant mortality and (strongly related to this) the prevalence of infectious diseases (often associated with levels of vaccination and public hygiene). It also means that the principal cause of death in the developed world is increasingly chronic (i.e. long-term) illness, such as cancer and long-lasting cardiovascular and pulmonary problems. Lopez, Mathers, Ezzati *et al.* (2006) estimate that these will form circa 90 per cent of the burden by 2030. However, in developing countries, they will only form circa 54 per cent. In contrast, the health burden of communicable diseases and health problems resulting from nutrition and perinatal issues, which it is projected will form only 3 per cent of the burden in developed countries, will form 32 per cent of the burden of developing countries. This has important ramifications for life expectancy projections. Once these latter issues are brought under control in developing nations, life expectancy should skyrocket, based on the historical experience of developed countries. Indeed, there are already clear signs that this is happening. In many developing countries, it is projected that up to 2050 the number of people aged over 65 will increase at more than double the rate of developed countries (United Nations Economic and Social Council, 2006). However, although there is cause to rejoice in these figures, it should be noted that in developing countries where AIDS/HIV has taken its toll (particularly sub-Saharan Africa) it is unlikely that anything resembling these figures will be seen (United Nations Economic and Social Council, 2006).

Although there are striking differences between countries, it should be remembered that even within the same country there can be considerable regional variations in life expectancy (Blake, 2009). Within the UK, the regional group with the lowest life expectancy at birth is, at the time of writing, the North East of England (76.8 years), the highest the South West of England (79.2 years). If we consider smaller areas of the country, the differences become more startling, with Kensington and Chelsea (a very prosperous area of London) recording the highest male at-birth figure of 84.4 years, compared with, at the other end of the scale, Glasgow City (71.1 years). This is a gap of 13 years – equivalent to comparing best practice life expectancy figures 50 years apart. Reasons for such differences are not explored in the UK Government source that provided these data (Office for National Statistics, 2010b) but it is readily apparent that the higher life expectancy areas of the UK (Kensington and Chelsea, Westminster, Epsom and Ewell, *et al.*) have on average far higher mean incomes and financial assets than those areas with the lowest expectancy figures (Glasgow City, West Dunbartonshire, Inverclyde, etc.). This accords with reports from other countries that found similar regional differences, also largely associated with socio-economic status (see Griffiths and Fitzpatrick, 2001). Essentially, the less affluent the social group is, the lower its life expectancy and prospects of a healthy life (e.g. Kawachi and Kennedy, 1997; Luo and Waite, 2005; Macintyre, 1994; Mackenbach *et al.*, 2008; Marmot, 2001; Roberge, Berthelot and Wolfson, 1995; Schwartz *et al.*, 1995; Singh and Siahpush, 2006). Many reasons have been suggested for this phenomenon, not least of which are levels of stress, nutrition and access to health care services. The differences between groups need not be very pronounced for there to be a difference in life expectancy. Marmot and Feeny (1997) studied UK civil servants and found that even within this occupational group (where nearly all could be described as at least financially comfortable), life expectancy significantly rose the higher the income of the sub-group being considered.

However, it would be misleading to attribute all differences in life expectancy to wealth. Other lifestyle factors that are not particularly wealth-dependent also play a role. A striking illustration of this is the **Roseto effect** (see Egolf *et al.*, 1992). This is named after an Italian-American community in Roseto, Pennsylvania, whose members' susceptibility to heart disease increased as it became more 'Americanised'. The instinctive reaction is to assume that this was a dietary issue because Italian food is often seen as adhering to the 'Mediterranean diet' ideal of few saturated fats. Nothing could be further from the truth – the regional variant favoured by the Roseto community included seemingly artery-clogging quantities of saturated fats (the people also drank and smoked). The reason for the greater resistance to heart disease was ascribed to the Roseto community itself: wealth was not flaunted, people supported each other and social life was family-centred. However, as time progressed, members of the community moved away from this communal view to a more individualistic one. A study of Roseto at the point when this transition was becoming apparent predicted that there would be a concomitant rise in heart disease (Lynn *et al.*, 1967) – alas, this prediction proved all too accurate. However, it should be noted that the effect on the inhabitants of Roseto was not a uniform one – younger men and older women were disproportionately more badly affected (Egolf *et al.*, 1992).

Roseto is not quite unique – several other immigrant communities have been found that also have longer life expectancies (see Leader and Corfield, 2007). There is no doubt that cohesive supportive societies can in some instances improve life expectancy. However, it is improbable that this is the total explanation. For every supportive community resembling the town in *It's a Wonderful Life*, there are arguably many more close-knit places that are snooping, judgmental and, accordingly, stressful. Presumably, sometimes the right balance of support and interference is attained, but this seems to be a hard thing to achieve, given the rarity of places like Roseto (the town was originally selected for study precisely because it was so unusual). And whether a longer life spent in a town where individuality is repressed and everyone knows their place is a blessing or a curse is a debatable point. This is not to deny the principal findings from Roseto *et al.* – undoubtedly community support can prolong life expectancy under certain circumstances. But nor can the findings be accepted uncritically.

At this point it is probably worth mentioning studies of small communities claiming to have long-living citizens that, unlike Roseto, have turned out to be based upon bogus or downright fraudulent data. The best known of these is a group of people in Georgia (in the former USSR) where a disproportionate number of centenarians were found. Various explanations were offered (many involving health foods and abstinence), but the prosaic truth is that there were no centenarians. The older adults, to avoid conscription into the Soviet Army, had used their parents' birth certificates, thereby adding 20 or 30 years to their real ages. This draft dodging had backfired because, in later years, the Soviet authorities had seized upon the 'well-preserved' older people and used them as a tourist attraction and propaganda vehicle. Detailed medical examinations debunked the story. Other cases of long-lived communities in Pakistan and Ecuador are explained by the simpler reason that high local levels of illiteracy coupled with poor population records had led to calculations of ages that were, to say the least, fraught with errors (see Schaie and Willis, 1991). Although a few commentators still rather touchingly believe that these older people are indeed very old, the majority of evidence points to there being no 'magical' society in which people live significantly longer then elsewhere.

Nonetheless, the idea of there being ways of remaining youthful still has a powerful effect on most people's imaginations. It is commonplace for sociologists and social psychologists to deconstruct cosmetics adverts that promise 'youthful looks', to banish wrinkles, grey hair and to firm up parts of the body that are heading south for the winter. Such messages play on a far older myth of the **fountain of youth** – the belief that somewhere there is a special foodstuff or drink that will keep a person perpetually young. This concept appears in nearly every culture's mythology in one form or another, and regularly appears as a theme in modern popular entertainment (e.g. the book *Lost Horizon* and the movies *Death Becomes Her* or *Star Trek: Insurrection*). And it is a rare week when a newspaper does not carry at least one item on how our diet/exercise regime can make us look younger and live longer.

We want to live longer. But not, it must be said, at any price. This can be demonstrated with two very old tales. The first comes to us from Ovid (though he was in turn probably relating an older myth), concerning Philemon and Baucis. They were a married couple who, uniquely among members of their village, showed hospitality to the gods Zeus and Hermes when they were disguised as peasants. As a reward, the gods made Philemon and Baucis's humble home into a magnificent temple (while the rest of the village – villagers included – was flattened). Philemon and Baucis were also granted a long life but, interestingly, they added a request that, when one of them eventually died, the other should die also. Thus, long life can be seen as desirable provided it is free from suffering such as that induced by bereavement. This idea of old age being desirable only if suffering-free is amplified in the ancient Greek myth about Tithonus, a mortal who was made immortal by the gods – but only in the sense that he grew ever older, but could never die. This was seen as a terrible fate, and the **Tithonus myth** is a phrase sometimes used to denote the (erroneous) belief that gerontologists and medical experts want to prolong life at any price, regardless of the cost in suffering. Thus, we only want to cheat ageing and death on very specific terms.

How, then, can we prolong life in a pleasant and pain-free way? There are two answers: first, have the right lifestyle; and second, choose long-living ancestors. Though not absolutely necessary, it also greatly helps to be a woman.

With regard to choosing the right lifestyle, the answer seems to lie in the things a lot of people hate: namely, taking more exercise, eating and drinking less, and smoking not at all. For example, it is estimated that the root cause of 35 per cent of all deaths in the USA in this century are attributable to indolence, poor diet and smoking (Centers for Disease Control and Prevention, 2007). Findings such as these have led to recommendations to increase the level of exercise, stop smoking and eat more sensibly, such as the Healthy People 2010 scheme in the USA (US Department of Health and Human Services, 2000) and Live Well in the UK (National Health Service, 2011). These general recommendations are well supported by research evidence and are not seriously disputed (Ostwald and Dyer, 2011).

However, this does not mean that the details are so clear-cut. To demonstrate this, consider the oft-cited **Harvard Alumni Study**. It found that in their sample of ex-students from Harvard University, exercise was strongly equated with longevity. Nobody disputes this overall finding. However, the relationship is not consistent across all conditions. For example, regular exercise burning up between 1000 and 2000 kilojoules (kJ) per week significantly reduced the risk of stroke. There was a further reduction in risk if the exercise rate was between 2000 and 3000 kJ burnt per week. However, exercise beyond this point did not seem to confer any additional reduction in risk (Lee and Paffenbarger, 1998). In contrast, Sesso, Paffenbarger and Lee (2000) reported that the risk of getting coronary heart disease decreased with more vigorous exercise (i.e. burning 4000 kJ per week conferred on average more protection than burning 2000 kJ per week in exercise). Generally, regular exercise throughout the week seems best for longevity, but the Harvard Alumni researchers also found that 'weekend warrior' behaviour (in which an individual crams their exercise into one or two brief, rather intense periods of exercise) can also be beneficial, provided there are no underlying risk factors (Lee et al., 2004). Overall, the findings of the Harvard Alumni Study 'provide some support for current recommendations that emphasize moderate intensity activity; they also clearly indicate a benefit of vigorous activity' (Lee and Paffenbarger, 2000, p.293). As already noted, almost all studies that have looked for it similarly find a strong association between exercise and health and, although there may be some dispute over what constitutes the right level of exercise (see Lee and Paffenbarger, 2000), there is little doubt that exercise is a good thing.

However, in our eulogy to the life-giving properties of exercise, there is a danger in overlooking confounding factors. For example, someone with an underlying fatal condition may be predisposed not to exercise even though medical tests can find no sign of a disease waiting to strike. Similarly, those who have the leisure time to engage in exercise are also likely to be financially better off, and so forth. These counter-arguments do not create a couch potato's charter to carry on doing nothing (though anyone starting serious exercise after a long period of sloth should consult a qualified person before beginning), but they do indicate that exercise might not be *quite* as beneficial as it may first appear.

Not surprisingly, smoking (of any amount) and heavy drinking can reduce life expectancy by a decade of more. For example, excessive alcohol consumption is associated with raised blood pressure and other life-threatening conditions (e.g. Huntgeburth, Ten Freyhaus and Rosenkranz, 2005), and the strong link between smoking and numerous fatal illnesses such as lung cancer and heart disease is very well documented. However, the evidence on eating is more equivocal. Although obesity is known to reduce life expectancy (e.g. Olshansky *et al.*, 2005), discussions of what should be eaten and how much of it are open to debate. For example, it has been known since the 1930s that deliberately restricting calorific intake significantly increases the lifespan of many animal species (e.g. Masoro, 1988, 1992). However, this statement must be qualified. First, a restricted diet is only effective after a certain age – if begun too early, then ageing will be accelerated, not retarded (Aihie Sayer and Cooper, 1997; Gage and O'Connor, 1994). Second, the most reliable results are from studies of rodents and fruit flies: evidence on humans is more circumspect. Third, restricted diet varies in its effects between species and sub-species – it is not universally beneficial (see de Magalhaes, 2011).

Some variations of diet have also been suggested as 'life prolonging'. For example, an increased consumption of nuts has been proposed as a prophylactic against ischemic heart disease (Sabate, 1999). Again, vegetarians live slightly but significantly longer than their omnivorous neighbours, probably because they are less prone to some common forms of illness, notably heart disease and some forms of cancer (see Dwyer, 1988). However, it is probably not a complete absence of meat that accounts for this. Similar results can be claimed for an omnivorous diet in which the proportion of meat is (by most Western standards) drastically lowered, though not completely removed (see Dwyer, 1988; Nestle, 1999). Perhaps more pertinently, if we dispense with specialist diets and consider what people actually eat, there is worrying evidence that only a minority of older adults eat sensible balanced meals. For example, Ervin (2008) found that lower than a third of older US adults ate their recommended quantities of meat, grain, fruit and vegetables, etc. Indeed, overall, only a small minority of older adults eats what is nutritionally sound (Ostwald and Dyer, 2011).

For those who reject the idea of exercise and a limited-calorie diet of lettuce leaves and tofu, and hope instead that medical science will provide anti-ageing treatments, there might be a long wait. Ageing involves changes in multiple biochemical processes, and treating one without the others is unlikely to be particularly beneficial (an analogy might be replacing the window frames of an old house while the unusable floor boards, wiring and utility supplies are left untouched). Thus, even if there is a breakthrough tomorrow in one area of anti-ageing research, researchers are still likely to have to wait for other areas to catch up before an effective treatment can be created (see Rose, 1999, for an excellent review of the issues involved). And if a 'cure' for ageing is found, this may create more problems than it solves, not least of which is that, if everyone can avoid ageing, overpopulation to an unprecedented degree seems inevitable. In this case, anti-ageing treatments will be either rationed or banned, both of which will in turn create the possibility of serious social unrest (see Chapter 9).

However, it is worth noting that environmental and lifestyle factors alone are probably not a complete explanation. In spite of some of the claims that gain wide circulation in the media, many of the strategies for prolonging life are largely speculative and based on extrapolations from laboratory studies rather than real-life observation (see Bernarducci and Owens, 1996). Furthermore, other aspects of lifestyle may affect matters. For example, we have already seen how certain communities like Roseto can offer protection against some types of heart disease. Again, Giles et al. (2005) followed a group of 1500 older adults for ten years and found that those who at the start of the study reported having five or more friends were a quarter less likely to die over the period of the study than those who did not. This also means that considering factors in isolation, such as a single index of physical health, can be an unwise policy – put simply, we need to see the bigger picture. Potentially someone with a worse medical history may survive an apparently healthier person, perhaps because their social life ensures they have less stress. Again, findings on differing life expectancies illustrate trends across whole groups – they do not automatically dictate the fates of individuals within those groups. Not everyone who leads a healthy lifestyle will reach older age; not everyone who lives in a deprived environment will die young. The **Winston Churchill argument** can be raised here – namely, that some individuals live long lives in spite of seemingly doing everything that modern medical advice would say is wrong. Churchill was overweight for most of his life, smoked, drank too much, had a history of cardiovascular illness and had what could be reasonably described as a stressful job in stressful conditions. Yet he survived into his nineties (compare and contrast this with Adolf Hitler, a vegetarian teetotal non-smoker). Most people can think of similar examples (e.g. in the author's case, his two grandmothers who single-handedly could keep the sweet shops of Barrow-in-Furness in business and who both lived to their late eighties), but this is not a reason personally to adopt such a lifestyle since, first, it is possible that such people would live even longer by adopting a healthier lifestyle, and, second, for the majority, an 'unhealthy' lifestyle will almost certainly reduce their life expectancy.

In addition to environmental factors, life expectancy is to some extent determined by genetic inheritance. The most obvious manifestation of this is that longer-lived individuals tend to produce longer-lived offspring (Murphy, 1978). Again, there is evidence from studies of identical twins (who of course have the same genes) that there is a strong genetic influence on both mortality and susceptibility to many diseases (Iachine *et al.*, 1998; see also Korpelainen, 1999). It is clear how genetic inheritance might influence life expectancy through relatively 'obvious' factors such as a congenitally weak heart, but other effects may be less apparent, such as the finding that height may influence longevity (generally, shorter people have longer lives than tall people, possibly because of lower blood pressure; see Samaras and Elrick, 1999).

A high proportion of genetic research on longevity has concentrated on a limited number of species: fruit flies, mice, certain species of worms, and yeast. These are chosen largely because they are small and reproduce quickly, thereby making it easy to see the effects of genetic changes when they are passed down the generations. It can be logically argued that a fruit fly is not much like a human being, making extrapolations difficult, but in fact these species have a surprisingly high proportion of genes in common with humans. Within these species, over 500 genes have been discovered that are involved in determining life expectancy (de Magalhaes, 2011). These genes work in several ways, but a significant number control the hormonal operations of a growth factor known as the IGF1 pathway (Kenyon, 2010). These findings do not automatically apply to humans, but nonetheless, progress is being made (see de Magalhaes, 2011). However, just as with the evidence on environmental effects, some caution must be sounded. Not least is that teasing apart the effects of environment and genetics in determining what causes increases in longevity is notoriously difficult (see Yashin *et al.*, 1999).

Thus, there is evidence that differences in ageing are attributable to both lifestyle and genes. Readers new to the area may by now have a feeling of imminent doom, since it appears that anything pleasurable is bound to lower life expectancy, while anyone with short-lived relatives may feel that no matter what they do the Grim Reaper is going to call before too long. However, it is worth stressing once again that such matters are relative. A good lifestyle generally only extends time spent in old age, and even then only by a small proportion of overall lifespan relative to an average person – there are no immortal non-smoking teetotal fitness-fanatic vegans.

Another major influence on life expectancy is gender. In peaceful societies (i.e. where heavy war casualties do not distort the figures), the balance of men and women is roughly equal until about 45 years. Thereafter, men die at a faster rate so that, by 70, there are approximately six women for every five men and, by 80, this ratio has moved to 4:1. Many reasons for the earlier deaths of men have been suggested. A popular conception is that it is because men have traditionally led physically more strenuous lives. However, this seems at best a marginal explanation, since comparisons of men and women matched for levels of physical industriousness still show a strong sex difference in mortality rates. It had been assumed that this sex difference is seen across many animal species besides humans (e.g. Shock, 1977), implying that differences lie at a chromosomal rather than an environmental level. However, more recent research disputes this (Austad, 2006). Other biological explanations have been suggested, including gender differences in the IGF1 pathway, but no explanation appears to be overwhelmingly convincing (Austad, 2006). Other research has identified a complex interaction of physical and environmental factors and differences in social behaviour (such as higher risk-taking and preference for poorer diet among males) that may also play a key role (see Lang, Arnold and Kupfer, 1994; Zhang, Sasaki and Kesteloot, 1995). Tangential to this, Tsuchiya and Williams (2005) argue that part of the gender difference may be due to unequal treatment of older men and women. They point out that the life expectancy of women from poor socio-economic groups is about equal to that of men from the richest socio-economic groups. Perhaps the most sensible conclusion that can be drawn from the current evidence is that several explanations might each account for part of the difference.

Thus, variations in life expectancy are dependent upon a multitude of factors – not only in which country a population is based, but which region of the country, socio-economic status, level of community support, and, at an individual level, lifestyle, genes and gender also play roles. However, while all this is a valid conclusion at a general level, nonetheless findings are still too scant for more detailed arguments to be made.

So far, extending life expectancy has been regarded as a desirable thing. However, living longer is not necessarily an unalloyed pleasure, as we shall see in the next section.

The cost of living longer

Increased life expectancy appears to be such a wonderful thing that it would be idiotic to question its utility. However, it is not the universal benefit that it might at first seem to be. First, it must not be supposed that the added life many modern people experience is necessarily blissful. Wilkins and Adams (1983), working from Canadian actuarial tables, calculated that for older adults about 75 per cent of this 'extra time' is spent suffering from one or more physical disabilities and hence discomfort. Brattberg, Parker and Thorslund (1996) cite a similar figure of 73 per cent of Swedish adults in their late seventies reporting mild or severe pain. These considerations give rise to the concept of **active life expectancy**. This has been described as 'the expected remaining years of functional well-being, in terms of the activities of daily living, for noninstitutionalized elderly people' (Katz et al., 1983, p.1218) – in other words, the average number of years remaining in which people can expect to lead a reasonably active life. Unsurprisingly, active life expectancy gets shorter the older the person being considered (Katz et al., 1983). From birth, the average citizen of an industrialised country can expect to spend at least the final 10 per cent of their life suffering an appreciable disability (World Health Organization, 2004). And if this is not depressing enough, serious chronic illness (i.e. enough to impinge significantly on quality of life, if not immediately to disable) will probably appear several years prior to this (World Health Organization, 2004).

However, it should be noted that not all commentators and researchers agree with this rather gloomy outlook (sometimes called the **expansion of morbidity theory**, or, loosely, that on average people 'buy' extra life by suffering more). It is tempting to see this as vindication of the Tithonus myth – namely, that people are being given extra life expectancy, but only at the price of suffering. However, things are not necessarily as gloomy as they seem. Commentators such as Fries (e.g. Fries, 2000) propose the **compression of morbidity theory**. This argues that advances in medical science mean that many previously fatal illnesses have been eradicated or brought under control, and thus the range of diseases or conditions people can die from has been reduced. Thus, probabilistically speaking, in the future, people will have on average to live longer before they develop something that medical science cannot cure. Additional to this, many of the incurable diseases can be staved off with appropriate prophylactic measures such as sensible diet and exercise. Thus, with the right intervention, it is possible to avoid entering into a disabled state until very late in life. Although a final fatal illness cannot of course be prevented, Fries and others have argued that the period of severe disability and suffering can be compressed into a shorter time frame than has been known by previous generations.

Arguably the expansion of morbidity theory represents the (undesirable) current state of health for many older adults, while the compression of morbidity theory represents what should be the norm in the future. Fries presents strong evidence that the goals are attainable, and this argument is supported by the observations of researchers who have noted that the proportion of reported severe disability among older patients has significantly declined (e.g. Gorin and Lewis, 2004; Laditka and Laditka, 2002). In addition, in a USA-based study, the proportion of remaining life expectancy that will also be active life expectancy has increased over recent decades and is projected to increase (Manton, Gu and Lamb, 2006; Manton, Gu and Lowrimore, 2008). However, in a study of German older adults over roughly the same time period, Unger (2006) observed that active life expectancy estimates are dependent upon what is meant by the term. By only considering very serious barriers to active life, active life expectancy can appear to increase in leaps and bounds, whereas if moderate limitations are included (that compromise but do not completely remove an active lifestyle), then improvements in lifestyle are less spectacular. But nonetheless, and in spite of some studies that have found less positive evidence (e.g. Hubert et al., 2002), overall the findings point towards a compression of morbidity, at least in industrialised countries.

Notwithstanding the above comments, the shift in the balance of older people in the population creates potential economic and social problems. If the proportion of older adults increases, then by definition the proportion of younger adults decreases. This means that a smaller fraction of the population is working and hence paying direct taxation (i.e. income tax, National Insurance and similar). Such taxation forms the backbone of funding for welfare support schemes such as state pensions and (in most countries) national health care. Older people are of course pensioners and also, along with children, the main beneficiaries of national health care. Thus, a 'grey shift' will create an increase in demand for services that are principally funded by a workforce diminishing in size. A simple method of expressing this is the **old age dependency ratio**, which is the number of people of pensionable age divided by the number of people of working age. This currently stands at about one-fifth for most industrialised nations, but is expected to rise to one-third or more by 2040. In the case of the UK, the current figure is circa 27 per cent and is expected to rise to circa 50 per cent by 2050 (OECD, 2004). This is an instance of the **demographic time bomb** – the major and potentially catastrophic financial burden on the economies of the coming decades created by a greying population.

How this problem is to be dealt with is currently a key preoccupation of most governments. The full story is too lengthy to be dealt with here. In any case it falls well outside the scope of this book and at the time of writing is changing so rapidly that a detailed account would be almost instantly out of date. However, in essence, governments need to deal with a huge increase in pensions and health and welfare provision. One way to do this is to increase the age of retirement. This is being done in many countries (e.g. UK from 65 to 68 by 2044; Germany from 65 to 67 by 2031; USA from 65 to 67 by 2027), though not always without protest. For example, in France in 2010, the pensionable age for state workers was raised from 60 to 62, and the age for receiving a full state pension from 65 to 67, resulting in nationwide protests and strikes. Another method of dealing with the problem is to make current pension schemes less generous (e.g. by no longer linking them to final salary levels) – financially sound, but morally reprehensible for those workers who have already invested in a pension scheme in good faith and are now nearing retirement. A further method is to make new pension schemes less generous. This is a good solution – but will only have its full effect decades from now when these workers retire. A further method is to increase current pension contributions; but then this is asking employees to pay more at a time when wage rises are being kept low and prices are nonetheless rising. And the final and possibly worst problem of all is the perilous state of the stock market. Pension funds rely very heavily on investments in stocks and bonds. Poor returns on these mean in turn there is less money for pensions. The financial crisis resulting from the collapse of several important banks from 2008 onwards resulted in appallingly poor investment conditions at the very time when a financial boom was needed.

However, although the demographic time bomb and the pensions crisis are serious problems, it is important to put things into perspective. First, the costs of health care of older adults may be exaggerated by current accounting methods, and the real cost may turn out to be significantly lower (Sanderson and Scherbov, 2010; Seshamani and Gray, 2004; Yang, Norton and Stearns, 2003). Second, the discussions so far have dealt with industrialised nations. It is a sobering thought that for developing countries the figures for 1900 are more appropriate, with infant mortality being commonplace rather than the tragic rarity it is in developed countries (World Health Organization, 2004). In addition, the old age dependency ratio is projected to vary enormously across nations, so that by 2050 the ratio is expected to be 1 in Japan, 3 in the USA and at the other end of the scale, 19 in Niger (United Nations Population Division, 2009). However, it is also worth reiterating the warnings of the longevity fan set out earlier – quite simply, we might have seriously over-estimated the proportion of older people in the future population in many industrialised countries. Or, on the other hand, seriously under-estimated. The only way of seeing the future accurately is with hindsight.

A third and final point is that reactions to increasing pensionable age are based on the erroneous assumption that pensions are an inalienable right. First, as has already been noted, pensions are in historical terms a recent invention. The state pension was originally intended to provide basic sustenance to workers in the last handful of years of their lives. It was never intended to fund the leisure time of a significant proportion of the population for two decades or more. As life expectancy has increased, increasing the pensionable age is not unreasonable in this light. Second, in any instance, the arbitrary nature of what constitutes pensionable age can be seen in the French example, mentioned earlier, where the age of retirement is being raised to 62 – that is, three years less than the existing British retirement age (small wonder that the protests met with little popular sympathy in the UK). French wrath was thus being directed at something they saw as a right, but which in the UK would be seen as early retirement. Thus, what constitutes the 'correct' age to retire, like the concept of old age itself, is to some extent arbitrary.

So far in this chapter we have examined how we measure ageing and life expectancy, and some of the pitfalls that these measurements can create. In addition, we have examined how increasing life expectancy is not without potential problems in terms of both personal and financial cost. However, these issues beg the question of *why* we age at all. What are the processes that determine this, why do they exist, and what are their physical effects? The remainder of this chapter will be spent addressing these issues.

Causes of biological ageing

The term 'biological age' refers to the body's state of physical development/ degeneration. Generally, the term is used loosely to describe the overall state of a person's body. However, several more specific exemplars are sometimes used. These include **anatomical age** (the relatively gross state of bone structure, body build, etc.); **carpal age** (the state of the wrist [carpal] bones); and **physiological age** (the state of physiological processes, such as metabolic rate). In the instances cited in this section, the general term is usually implied.

Ageing is the final stage of development that every healthy and accident-free individual experiences. However, one must be careful not to overextend the word 'development' to imply that ageing necessarily involves an improvement. Indeed, one commentator emphasises this point by classifying later life as **post-developmental**: 'all the latent capacities for development have been actualized, leaving only late-acting potentialities for harm' (Bromley, 1988, p.30). Although compression of morbidity theory states that the effects of this harm should eventually be minimised, nonetheless, without medical intervention, ageing is a time characterised by physical weakness and decay.

Why should these changes occur? A great many theories have been proposed – Medvedev (1990) estimated there were over 300 of them, and today's figure is undoubtedly higher than this. The full intricacies of the competing models need not concern us here because they fall outside the scope of this book. However, a brief overview is required, since biological changes in the body, and the reasons for them, have a profound impact on psychological functioning.

The first point to establish is that the body's cells are not immortal – over a period of about seven years, most of them die and are either replaced by new cells or lost. Cell loss becomes a notable feature from early adulthood onwards, with most bodily systems showing a decline of 0.8–1 per cent per annum after the age of 30 (Hayflick, 1997). The course of this loss is very slow and, as most bodily systems have over-capacity built into them, it is only in about the sixth decade of life that the change is first apparent to the casual observer. Botwinick (1977) notes that the decline is greater in complex than in simple functions. This is probably because the simpler functions have each only declined slightly, but, when used together in a more complex action, the total effect becomes multiplicative. As shall be seen, this disproportionate loss of complex over simple functions manifests itself repeatedly in both the ageing body and the ageing mind.

But of course not all cells by any means are totally lost. Many of them are replaced. However, over time the cell replacement process becomes less efficient, so that cells are replaced by inferior copies (the **somatic mutation theory of ageing**). A loose analogy is that the process is like photocopying a complex diagram, throwing away the original, then photocopying the copy, then copying the copy, and so forth. The copies will become weaker and less distinct simulations of the original until eventually they become useless and have to be thrown away with no further copying being possible (see Holliday, 2007). Certainly it is known that older animals have a higher proportion of damaged DNA in their cells (Bohr and Anson, 1995).

Arguably theories such as these describe rather than explain what happens in the ageing body. Other theories have attempted to explain the causes of these changes. These are varied and in the main could each account for some aspects of the ageing process without necessarily contradicting each other (see de Magalhaes, 2011;

Hayflick, 1994; Holliday, 2007). For example, the **autoimmune theory of ageing** argues that ageing might be attributable to faults in the body's immune system. Another argument (the **cellular garbage theory**) is that ageing occurs because of toxins produced as by-products of normal cellular activity. A variant of this is the **free radical theory** (Harman, 1956), which argues that the damage is caused by chemical by-products of cells' metabolic processes. Disease, although not seen as a cause of ageing *per se* (see de Magalhaes, 2011) might nonetheless exaggerate or accelerate some ageing processes (see Birren *et al.*, 1963; Botwinick, 1977; Kermis, 1983). Likewise, long-term exposure to toxins and stress might have similar effects.

These theories assume that the body ages because it cannot adequately cope with an onslaught of harmful chemicals. Another approach is to argue that the body's cells are themselves pre-programmed to die. The best evidence for this is the evidence of a limit to the number of times a cell can be replaced. The **Hayflick phenomenon** (named after its discoverer: see Hayflick, 1985, 1994, 1997) states that living cells taken from the body and raised *in vitro* will only reduplicate themselves a limited number of times before dying (the **Hayflick limit**). In other words, cells seem to be pre-programmed to die. Why this happens is open to debate. One plausible explanation currently in great favour concerns the **telomere**, a sequence of DNA located at the end of chromosomes. The analogy frequently made is that, if the chromosome is a shoelace, the telomere is the plastic bit at the end that prevents the shoelace fraying. The analogy is an appropriate one, because it is felt that telomeres are a key component in maintaining the structural integrity of chromosomes (see Cong, Wright and Shay, 2002).

In the previous edition of this book, the role of the telomere seemed to be relatively straightforward. It appeared that each time a cell duplicated itself, the telomere shortened, and when it got too short the cell died. The reason it did this was simple – if the cell did not die but instead carried on replicating itself, the genetic information in the cell would get so distorted that eventually cancerous growths would be created. The telomere was thus a safety mechanism that reduced the risk of contracting cancer – but with the heavy price of causing cell loss and thus many of the most obvious signs of ageing (Stuart-Hamilton, 2006). Since then, the published research has tended if not to refute this theory, at least to question whether the telomere's role is quite that simple, and although it is highly probable that the telomere plays a central role, what that is has yet to be determined (see de Magalhaes, 2011; Holliday, 2007).

Taking a rather different approach, evolutionary theorists have argued in effect for a **programmed senescence** theory, which argues that ageing is caused by evolutionary forces, and is in essence designed to happen (readers who are Creationists are advised to skip this section). The evidence for this argument is at first sight plausible. Perhaps the best-known version of this theory is that bodies have an inbuilt programme to decay and die in order to make way for younger members of the species, and thus prevent the problem of overcrowding. Other versions include the concept that individuals grow weaker so that they become easier targets for predators, thereby preventing younger species members (still capable of breeding) from being chosen as targets. Such arguments are still accepted uncritically by a few commentators, but they are undermined by one simple fact: very few animals in their natural habitat reach old age. Accordingly, because older animals are so rare 'in the wild', it is unlikely that evolutionary pressure has created a method of 'self-culling' a species – predators, disease and accident do a satisfactory job in themselves (see Hayflick, 1998; Kirkwood, 1988; Medawar, 1952).

A more plausible argument is the **mutation accumulation theory** (Medawar, 1952), which argues that ageing effects happen because they are not selected against by evolutionary forces. Let us suppose that there is a genetic predisposition to die if exposed to sunlight, and that this manifests itself at birth. It is highly unlikely that anyone born with such a gene would survive into adolescence and breed. Thus, such a gene would not survive and would not be handed down the generations. However, suppose the 'killer sunlight' gene only took effect when a person was in their sixties? For the overwhelming majority of human existence, the chances are extremely high that most people would be dead before they reached 60, so first, the gene would rarely appear, and second, if it did, it would have very little effect on survival rates. Therefore, genetic mutations that only take effect in later life can accumulate without any strong evolutionary pressure stopping them.

The **antagonistic pleiotropy theory** (Williams, 1957) bears some similarities to the mutation accumulation theory in that it too argues that harmful later life changes have been created by evolutionary pressure because too few members of a species live long enough to experience them. The theory adds the additional argument that some genes can confer an advantage in early life and a disadvantage in later life, and might be favoured by natural selection even though they will cause harm in later life. Thus, suppose that in younger life there was a gene creating an abundance of testosterone and an easy capacity to gain weight. This would be advantageous in a male trying to establish dominance through aggression and physical strength. But in later life, such attributes would greatly increase the risk of cardiovascular problems and might lead to an unavoidable death. Until very recent times, the downside of the deal would not have been evident. Because most animals die relatively young, the effects of the gene in later life would be rarely observed and would have little effect on breeding success (since, *inter alia*, by the time they appeared, the animal would probably be past breeding age). As proof of the antagonistic pleiotropy theory, there are a lot of experiments on fruit flies. If an advantage in early life is met by a disadvantage in later life, then manipulating a genetically controlled aspect of early life should affect later life. In one such study, it was found that creating a disadvantage in early life (breeding fruit flies that took longer to reach sexual maturity) was met with an advantage in later life – namely, increased life expectancy (Rose, 1984).

A further permutation of these arguments is the **disposable soma theory of ageing** (Kirkwood, 1988). Modern evolutionary theory argues that an organism is driven to reproduce as much as possible, and this takes precedence over the organism's personal survival. What matters is that the genes the organism carries survive (and which body they are in is of secondary importance). Thus, according to this theory, it would be better for a man to die at 20, having sired 30 children, than to die childless at 100 (see Dawkins, 1976). The disposable soma theory takes this argument and adapts it as follows. Body cells die and have to be replaced constantly. If they are not replaced, then the body parts concerned decline in number and efficiency. However, it is not possible to replace all cells equally effectively. The disposable soma theory argues that the best evolutionary strategy is to maintain the reproductive organs in top condition at the expense of the somatic (non-reproductive) body parts. Accordingly, the greater the energy invested in reproduction, the greater the bodily decay. Taken to extremes, this theory sounds like a Victorian homily, but at a subtler level the argument is persuasive, and Kirkwood (1988) provides strong supporting proof, to which the reader is referred.

The theories outlined here provide explanations of ageing based on evolutionary theory. Although distinct, their focus on evolution and their shared assumption that old age would have been rarely seen before the advent of the developed world gives them a kinship. Arguably all could be correct in different scenarios. If one accepts the theories, then it follows that later life is not 'planned' by natural selection to the extent it is earlier in the lifespan. In other words, when we consider an older person, it is difficult to argue that a particular change in behaviour or bodily function is 'designed' to happen. Wrinkled skin, more brittle bones, lowered memory span or lowered response speeds may never have been deliberately planned – they have arisen because there was no evolutionary pressure to prevent them (mutation accumulation theory), because they are the reverse side of processes that were advantageous in earlier life (antagonistic pleiotropy theory) or because investment in earlier life was centred on reproduction (disposable soma theory). Most individuals in 'natural' surroundings are dead before these characteristics can ever manifest themselves (see Zwaan, 1999). It is both the curse and the privilege of modern life to see evolution cheated in this way.

Hayflick (1994) makes the useful analogy of the life course being, in evolutionary terms, like a satellite sent on a mission to survey a distant planet. Once a satellite has done its mission and sent back pictures of its target, it carries on into space, continuing to send back signals until eventually accident or simple decay terminate its activities. In a similar way, individuals, once they have accomplished their target of producing viable offspring, continue to live until accident or illness kills them. However, the life of the satellite after sending back the photos of the target, or of the individual after breeding, is coincidental. Enough 'over-engineering' has to be built into the system to ensure that the job can be accomplished with something to spare. We interpret this extra life afforded by the over-engineering as a 'natural' part of the lifespan, but in fact in evolutionary terms it is an accidental gift, not a right. However, in another sense the argument that old age 'defeats' evolution is inaccurate – what is being shown in effect is what evolutionary pressure thinks of old age.

Namely, it is a time when in evolutionary terms the usefulness to species survival is at an all-time low, and thus it can act as a repository for all types of decay that will strike those who have 'failed' to die having successfully reproduced their genes.

The ageing body

The general picture of changes to the ageing body is not an attractive one. For example, at the level of tissue, the skin and muscles become less elastic; at the cellular level, there is a loss in the efficiency of the mitochondria (which generate energy within the cell); and at a molecular level, the somatic mutation theory of ageing and the research on telomeres have already been mentioned. Not surprisingly, these changes have a deleterious effect upon the functioning of bodily systems. For example, the urinary system becomes slower and less efficient at excreting toxins and other waste products. The gastrointestinal system is less efficient at extracting nutrients. There is a decline in muscle mass and the strength of the muscle that remains. The respiratory system can take in less oxygen. The cardiovascular system receives a double blow – the heart decreases in strength while simultaneously a hardening and shrinking of the arteries makes pumping blood around the body more energy-consuming. The result is that the average 75-year-old person's cardiac output is approximately 70 per cent of the average 30-year-old's (Aiken, 1989; Holliday, 2007; Kermis, 1983).

These changes have a disadvantageous effect on the functioning of the brain and hence on psychological performance. Cardiovascular illness, in addition to normal senescent decline, will also have a detrimental effect on brain functions (Kermis, 1983), and the link between physical health and indices of cognitive functioning are well established (e.g. Deary *et al.*, 2006; Renaud, Bherer and Maquestiaux, 2010). *In extremis*, the most notable example of this is the **stroke**, where blood supply to a section of the brain is interrupted, causing death of the affected brain tissue. At a less severe level, some older people may have an oxygen supply so constricted that they fall asleep after meals, because the energy required by the digestive processes deprives the brain of sufficient oxygen to remain conscious. Changes in other systems may have more subtle effects. For example, a decline in the urinary system may mean a high level of toxins accumulating in the body, in turn affecting the efficiency of neural functioning. If an older person is receiving drug therapy, then failure to excrete the drug from the system with sufficient speed may lead to overdosing problems, including **delirium** (see Chapter 6). A decline in the gastrointestinal system can have similar far-reaching consequences. If the decline has the effect of lowering an older person's interest in food, then malnutrition can result. This is especially serious from a psychological viewpoint if the person develops a deficiency of vitamin B12, since this can trigger dementia-like symptoms.

Another effect of ageing bodily processes is that it can cause people to re-evaluate their state of being. This is not necessarily serious. Being aware that bones are becoming more brittle and muscles less strong may create a reluctant but pragmatic sense of caution. However, in others, these physical signs can lead to depression (Raskin, 1979). Weg (1983) and others have argued that the majority of older people still have ample *capacity* to deal with the demands of everyday life. However, whether they *do* is another matter.

The ageing sensory systems

The senses are the brain's means of contact with the surrounding environment and, accordingly, any decline in them directly impinges on the workings of the mind. Age-related declines in perception deprive the brain of a full experience of the world, but it would be unrealistic to assume that such a loss begins in later life. Like many aspects of age-related decline, the changes often start in early adulthood, and it is important to bear this in mind when reading the sections that follow.

Vision

It is a frequent complaint of older people that their sight 'isn't what it used to be'. This is usually true: aside from relatively simple problems of long- and short-sightedness, about a third of people aged over 65 have a disease affecting vision (Quillan, 1999). A common problem is the decline in **accommodation** (the ability to focus at different distances), leading to **presbyopia** ('old sight' – 'presby-' indicates 'old'), characterised by long-sightedness. This is probably due to the ageing lens losing some of its elasticity and hence focusing power. The most serious visual disability most people suffer is a loss of **acuity** (variously defined as 'ability to see objects clearly at a distance' or 'ability to focus on detail'). Bromley (1988) estimates that about 75 per cent of older adults need spectacles, and many will not have full vision even with this aid. Holden *et al.* (2008) estimate from multiple population surveys that in 2005 there were circa 1.04 billion people with presbyopia, of whom 517 million had no spectacles or spectacles unfit for the purpose. Of this 517 million, circa 80 per cent could not perform tasks that required near sight, effectively blocking them from a large range of daily necessary activities. As with so many of these situations, there is a vast cross-national difference, with an estimated 94 per cent of all those needing spectacles living in the developing world.

An interesting feature of acuity is the interaction between image size and image contrast, expressed in the **contrast sensitivity function (CSF)**. The principle of this is that a tiny image might be invisible if it is presented in low contrast (e.g. a black image on a dark grey background) but the same image can be seen if it is in high contrast (e.g. a black image on a white background). From this, the smallest detectable image dependent upon different lighting conditions and contrast can be calculated. It is well established that problems older people face in detecting small visual items can be offset by increasing the contrast in luminance of the display (e.g. Corso, 1981) and that doing this can restore near-youthful levels of vision (Haegerstrom-Portnoy, Schneck and Brabyn, 1999). But of course the real world is not always optimally lit, and poor CSF has been linked to many problems older people face, including a significantly raised risk of falls (Lord, Smith and Menant, 2010; Pijnappels *et al.*, 2010). Again, on average a person in their sixties requires three times the brightness that a person in their twenties does to read everyday printed materials (Beers and Berkow, 2000). It would appear that CSF is also a key gauge of general visual health. For example, Schneck *et al.* (2004) followed a group of older participants over a four-year period. They found that out of a range of measures of eyesight (e.g. glare recovery, flicker sensitivity), ability to detect low contrast patterns was the only measure significantly to predict visual acuity loss circa four years later. For every doubling of the pattern size necessary to make the pattern visible to an observer, there was a greater than doubling of the chance of significant sight loss four years later.

Beyond considerations of CSF, practically all other aspects of vision worsen in later life (Haegerstrom-Portnoy *et al.*, 1999). This leads to serious questions about the format that sight testing should take to ensure that an older adult is safe to perform visual tasks such as driving. Certainly, measuring changes in acuity alone is not sufficient (see Bohensky *et al.*, 2008). For example, the visual threshold (the dimmest light that can be seen) *increases* with age – in other words, older people cannot see lights as dim as younger people can see (Elias, Elias and Elias, 1977; McFarland and Fisher, 1955). Similarly, the rate at which people can adjust to low-level lighting conditions (dark adaptation) decreases with age (Domey, McFarland and Chadwick, 1960). The converse – ability to recover from glare – is also reduced, sometimes by several hundred per cent (Carter, 1982). This clearly has practical implications (e.g. for night driving). Images become mildly distorted in later life because of changes in lens shape (Athaide, Campos and Costa, 2009). Another important consideration is the change in colour perception: older adults perceive the world as being yellower. Colours at the yellow end of the spectrum (red, orange and yellow) are identified reasonably well, but greens, blues and purples become harder to discriminate between (note that this problem does not typically manifest itself before people are in their eighties). Many commentators have argued that this is due to the lens yellowing with age, but this cannot be the full explanation. Some unfortunate individuals who have had a lens surgically removed still perceive the world as having a yellow tinge. The reason is thus probably due to changes in the nervous system (Marsh, 1980; see also Jackson and Owsley, 2003). The size of the visual field also diminishes. A relatively minor problem is that older people cannot move the eyeball as far up as younger adults, with the result that older people have to move their heads to see some object above them which younger adults can see with eye movements alone. A more serious problem is a loss of peripheral vision (i.e. how 'wide' the field of view is). Onset of this decline occurs in middle age, but becomes far more pronounced in the over-75s (Jaffe, Alvarado and Juster, 1986).

These problems can be serious and annoying for older people. Some visual changes might be of sufficient magnitude to stop key activities such as driving, but they are not necessarily totally incapacitating. In addition, many of the problems in vision arise prior to later life, in some instances as early as the mid-thirties (Corso, 1987). In other words, it is misleading to see visual problems in later life as being purely an ageing issue. However, that is not to deny that age-related problems with eyesight do not pose problems. The issues of increased incidences of falls and of driving problems have already been mentioned. Thankfully rarer is **Charles Bonnet syndrome**, a disorder characterised by visual hallucinations in people otherwise devoid of any symptoms of mental illness. The syndrome increases in frequency with age and typically occurs in older adults with visual impairments (e.g. Rovner, 2006). Teunisse *et al.* (1995) estimate that about 11 per cent of people with impaired vision have the syndrome, and it is also more likely to occur in older than in younger adults. The syndrome is almost certainly currently under-reported (Schadlu, Schadlu and Shepherd, 2009). Reasons include clinicians not being alerted to look for the problem, and sufferers possibly avoiding reporting symptoms for fear of being considered mentally ill. However, prevalence of reported cases is likely to increase in frequency with the greying of the general population (Rovner, 2006).

It is pertinent to remember that about 7 per cent of 65–74-year-olds and 16 per cent of people over 75 are either blind or severely visually impaired (Crandall, 1980). In the UK, circa 20 per cent of over-75s and 50 per cent of people in their nineties have severe sight loss (Royal National Institute for the Blind, 2011). The principal causes of this are **cataracts** (where the lens becomes opaque); **glaucoma** (where excess fluid accrues in the eyeball, and the resultant pressure permanently destroys nerve and receptor cells); **macular degeneration** (where the macula or 'yellow spot' on the retina, which has the greatest acuity of vision, degenerates; see Sunness *et al.*, 1999); and **diabetic retinopathy** (damage to the blood vessels of the retina as a result of diabetes). These illnesses are not confined to later life, but they are certainly much commoner then (Corso, 1981; Pelletier, Thomas and Shaw, 2009). It should be noted that they can also be either prevented, or at least the worst effects can be tempered, if they are identified early enough (see Pelletier *et al.*, 2009). For example, the longer the time since last visiting an eye specialist, the worse a discovered case of glaucoma is likely to be (Fraser, Bunce and Wormald, 1999).

Hearing

Hearing loss is a stereotypical problem of older adults and the subject of much ageist humour. Difficulties with hearing, such as detecting faint sounds that younger people can hear distinctly, affect many people by the age of 50 (Bromley, 1988) and the problems become more pronounced thereafter. Attempts to place a firm figure on the extent of hearing loss within the population tend to vary according to how 'loss' is defined. If we consider very severe hearing loss (where the person is deaf or will typically require a hearing aid for even basic hearing to be possible), then under 2 per cent of people in their twenties and thirties fall into this category, versus about a third of people in their seventies and eighties (Stephens, 1982) and about half of people in their eighties and older (Herbst, 1982). If we consider age-related hearing loss (**ARHL**), also known as **presbycusis**, then an estimate that 50 per cent of people over 65 years have some degree of ARHL is not unreasonable (Gordon-Salant et al., 2010). However, other researchers, using more permissive criteria, argue for a figure between 70 and 80 per cent (Sprinzi and Riechelmann, 2010). Regardless of the exact size of the proportion (which is heavily dependent upon the threshold value of hearing loss that the individual researcher considers is problematic), there is little doubt that presbycusis/ARHL is the single most common sensory disorder found in older adults (Someya et al., 2010).

It is important to stress that hearing loss is not simply a matter of not being able to hear quiet noises. For example, presbycusis has several forms (Cohn, 1999; Schuknecht, 1974) but is characterised by proportionately greater loss in perception of high frequency sounds. At first reading this can appear to mean simply that the world will sound a little muffled, rather like the effect of turning down the treble on a hi-fi system. However, it is a far more serious problem than this. Many of the key differences in speech sounds are in the high frequencies, and thus the ability to tell what people are saying becomes markedly impaired. In addition, other auditory skills, such as sound localisation (the ability to detect where a sound is coming from) are impaired (see Rakerd, Van der Velde and Hartmann, 1998). These problems can have a disproportionate effect on ability to process auditory information. For example, Tun, McCoy and Wingfield (2009) demonstrated that when asked to remember a spoken list of words while conducting another mental task simultaneously, older adults with presbycusis were disproportionately disadvantaged. It appears that the extra mental effort people with presbycusis need to process auditory information means they lack sufficient 'mental capacity' to cope with remembering words and performing a simultaneous task as efficiently.

The causes of hearing loss are legion. People often assume that a lifetime of working in a noisy environment is the cause. Although this is a significant factor (see Ohlemiller, 2008; Sekuler and Blake, 1985), there are many others, including genes (Van Eyken, Van Camp and Van Laer, 2007), diet (Houston et al., 1999; Someya et al., 2010), free radicals (Someya and Prolla, 2010), cardiovascular (Hull and Kerschen, 2010) and general health (Huang and Tang, 2010). Gender also has an effect. Men's hearing declines at a faster rate (Chao and Chen, 2009) but sensitivity to low frequencies (<1000 Hz) remains better (though there is considerable individual variation in patterns of loss: Pearson et al., 1995). It has been supposed that this is because men have tended to work in noisier places than women. However, evidence indicates that even among people in 'quiet' occupations, there is still a gender difference (Pearson et al., 1995).

Working from the outside of the ear inwards, an assortment of age-related changes may be noted. One of gerontology's more esoteric findings is that ageing ear lobes increase in size by several millimetres (Tsai, Chou and Cheng, 1958). The functional significance of this remains unclear. The elderly ear canal can get blocked with wax more easily, causing hearing loss, though this is easily treated. Changes in the middle ear are more severe and usually less easily solved. The bones of the middle ear – the hammer, anvil and stirrup (or malleus, incus and stapes) – tend to stiffen with age, through calcification or arthritis (see Moon and Hahn, 1981). This affects the transmission of sound, most particularly for high frequencies. The problem may be compounded by changes in the inner ear, where cell loss is usually concentrated in the receptors for high frequency sounds. Leading from the inner ear to the brain is the auditory nerve. This bundle of nerve fibres diminishes in size with age. The atrophy is probably due to a combination of loss of blood supply, and bone growth restricting the channel for the fibres (Corso, 1981; Park, Back, Park *et al.*, 2010; Someya and Prolla, 2010).

Because presbycusis has so many identified causes, several treatments will be required if cures are to be found. Although there is little feasible available yet, progress is being made (see Bielefeld *et al.*, 2010; Sprinzi and Riechelmann, 2010). However, it is important to note that there is compelling evidence that even if cures for all the problems cited earlier are found, that will not be the end of the matter, since some measures of auditory skills, such as the ability to detect silent gaps between auditory signals, appear to be affected by the age of the participant, rather than their level of hearing loss (Fitzgibbons and Gordon-Salant, 2010). Since temporal resolution is a key component in speech perception, this could have a significant effect on everyday communication. Thus, level of hearing loss in and of itself does not account for all the changes in auditory skills found in later life (see Gordon-Salant *et al.*, 2010 for a further review). It should also be remembered that presbycusis is not the only hearing problem in later life. There is a worsening of pitch discrimination, sound localisation and in perceiving timing information (see Marsh, 1980; Schneider, Speranza and Pichora-Fuller, 1998; Strouse *et al.*, 1998). Also, up to 10 per cent of older adults suffer from **tinnitus**, or what is commonly (if slightly inaccurately) known as 'ringing in the ears' (Eggermont and Roberts, 2004; Lasisi, Abiona and Gureje, 2010). This can block out other auditory signals as well as causing suffering in its own right.

A further problem with hearing in later life is that the decline appears to be another manifestation of the **age × complexity effect**. Generally, the more complex the speech signal, the more older people are disadvantaged relative to younger adults (Corso, 1981). For example, this can be the case when detecting signals played against a background of noise or competing signals compared with a silent background (e.g. Bergman *et al.*, 1976; Dubno, Dirk and Morgan, 1984; Pichora-Fuller, Schneider and Daneman, 1995). However, when signals are familiar phrases or ones expressing familiar concepts, there is no or little age difference (Hutchinson, 1989). Again,

Orbelo *et al.* (2005) found that comprehension of the emotional content of speech, although impaired in older adults, is unrelated to level of hearing loss (or for that matter cognitive decline – the report's authors attribute it to an ageing-related deficit in the right hemisphere).

It should also be noted that hearing loss often carries an emotional burden. Herbst (1982) observes that most societies have held a grudge against deaf people since the start of recorded time. To the Ancient Greeks, the word 'deaf' was synonymous with 'stupid', while to the early Christian, deafness was a curse because, in preliterate societies, it blocked the person from holy teachings. In modern times, this bias has continued. The word 'dumb' is used to denote someone of limited intellect. Deaf charities tend to receive fewer donations than those for the blind because, Herbst argues, while blindness cuts one off from things, deafness cuts one off from people. This is perhaps rather too tenuous an argument to be wholly supported, but it is nonetheless not without some validity.

Taste

The tastes humans perceive can be divided into four primary types: bitter, sour, salty and sweet. Researchers have generally found a decline in sensitivity to these, but the details are inconsistent between studies. For example, Engen (1977) reported a general decline, but increased sensitivity to bitter. However, Schiffman *et al.* (1995) found a *loss* in sensitivity to bitter, while Cowart, Yokomukai and Beauchamp (1994) found decreased sensitivity to some bitter-tasting substances but not to others. Weiffenbach, Baum and Berghauser (1982) found a decline in sensitivity to bitter and salty tastes, but no change in sweet and sour sensitivities (though detection of sweet and sour may decline in centenarians; see Receputo *et al.*, 1996). To further muddy the waters, Mojet, Heidema and Christ-Hazelhof (2003) found that, although there is no age-related loss in ability to judge which concentration of a primary taste was stronger than another, the ability to grade how strong a taste was on an individual basis was impaired in older adults. However, Nordin *et al.* (2003) found a significant worsening of taste intensity discrimination for some substances. Watanabe, Kudo, Fukuoka *et al.* (2008) found no decline in saltiness detection. But Fukunaga, Uematsu and Sugimoto (2005) found declines in ability to detect all the taste primaries. The reason for the marked variability in findings is probably the result of several factors – for example, where on the tongue the tests are applied (different parts of the tongue have different levels of sensitivity) and possibly cultural differences (a lifetime of eating a particular set of flavourings might affect taste sensitivity). However, overall, there seems general agreement that ability to detect primary tastes declines.

The data on detection of complex tastes are (thankfully) more clear-cut, with older people showing a marked decline in detection of many everyday food items (see Bischmann and Witte, 1996; Murphy, 1985; Ng *et al.*, 2004; Schiffman, 1977), and in detecting a primary taste when presented in a mixture of other tastes (Stevens, 1996). And irrespective of what older people can or cannot taste, they are in some instances bad at either choosing or metabolising a healthy diet. For example, a study by Clarke *et al.* (2004) found that 5 per cent of their sample of 65–74-year-olds had a vitamin B12 deficiency, and this proportion rose to 10 per cent for their sample of people aged 75 and over. Although the full details are as yet not mapped out, it is apparent that nutrition plays a key role in maintaining cognitive status in later life (see Ordovas, 2010).

Smell

Sense of smell appears to show relatively little change in *very healthy* older adults (e.g. Corso, 1981). However, since most older adults experience illness in one form or another, it would be more demographically representative to argue that most older adults will show at least some decline (see Doty, 1990; Finkelstein and Schiffman, 1999). Various studies have linked changes in olfactory abilities to changes in dietary habits (see Drewnowski and Shultz, 2001). Furthermore, declines in sense of smell are linked with cognitive decline in typically ageing older adults (Swan and Carmelli, 2002; Wilson *et al.*, 2006) and profound loss is found in people with dementias such as Alzheimer's disease (e.g. Moberg *et al.*, 1997; Murphy, 2008; Weilge-Lüssen, 2009). At least in non-dementing older adults, the olfactory-cognitive link appears to be genetically mediated, since identical twins show markedly similar patterns of change in this respect (Finkel, Pedersen and Larsson, 2001).

Touch

Older adults have higher touch thresholds (i.e. firmer stimulation of the skin is required before it is detected: see Saizano *et al.*, 2010; Stevens and Patterson, 1996; Thornbury and Mistretta, 1981) and, similarly, sensitivity to the temperature of objects decreases (see Heft and Robinson, 2010). The touch sensors are housed in the skin and, accordingly, it is tempting to link the decline in sensitivity to the obvious thinning and wrinkling in an older person's skin. This may be a partial explanation, and there is evidence that at least part of the decline is due to a decrease in the number of touch sensors in the skin (Gescheider *et al.*, 1994).

Pain

Some researchers have reported an increase in the pain threshold of older people: in other words, they can endure more extreme stimuli without perceiving them as painful (e.g. Benedetti *et al.*, 1999; Gibson and Farrell, 2004; Lasch, Castell and Castell, 1997). This might be readily explained by a decline in the number of sensory receptors in later life. However, other researchers have found no age difference (see

Bromley, 1988), not even in facial expressions when experiencing a painful stimulus (Kunz *et al.*, 2008). Whether an age difference is found or not might in part depend on where on the body the pain is inflicted, but it should also be borne in mind that for obvious ethical reasons the intensity and duration of a painful stimulus is strictly limited, and this might affect the ability to extract realistic and meaningful findings. Notwithstanding these considerations, the prevalence of pain-providing conditions increases markedly in later life (Hill-Briggs, Kirk and Wegener, 2005). It is possible that the emotional meaning of pain may differ between ages. For example, older adults tend to be less distressed about the lessening of mobility through the pain of an illness, because they may generally have lower expectations of what they can or 'should' do at their particular age (see Williamson and Schulz, 1995). Also, a study by Yong *et al.* (2001) found that older adults were more reticent about reporting pain and less willing to label an aversive stimulus as being painful. Added to this is the problem that nursing staff might also have significant gaps in their knowledge of pain management (e.g. Zwakhalen *et al.*, 2007).

Overview

The clear message from this brief survey of the ageing senses should be readily apparent: the information reaching the brain from the surrounding environment is constrained in its range, is less detailed and, given the general slowing of the nervous system, takes longer to arrive. This hardly bodes well for the ageing intellect (see Glisky, 2007; Lindenberger and Baltes, 1994); nor indeed for the personality if an elderly person's self-image is affected (it is known that illness is linked to level of depression in older people; see Williamson and Schulz, 1992). However, it should be noted that the ageing brain is in turn not making the best use of the incoming sensory information. A notable pattern of decline in the ageing perceptual processes is that the older mind is less adept at integrating several strands of sensory information into a cohesive whole (e.g. complex versus simple tastes, complex versus simple auditory signals). As mentioned earlier in this chapter, the principal age deficits appear to occur when several simple processes must be operated in tandem.

Neuronal changes in later life

Discussions on the psychological effects of neurological changes in later life are scattered through the rest of this book. However, it is useful if a brief overview is presented here. For those unfamiliar with neuroanatomy, a short introduction is provided in Appendix I.

It has long been known that the brain decreases in volume in later life, even in healthy, well-functioning individuals. Early measures, which relied on the relatively crude measure of weight of brains, found that there was a decline of 10–15 per cent in the course of typical, dementia-free ageing (Bromley, 1988). More recent studies, using magnetic resonance imaging (MRI) scans, have found that the brain diminishes in volume while the ventricular system (the pockets of fluid within the brain) increase. These changes are not uniform, with the biggest losses found in the temporal and frontal cortex, and also the putamen, thalamus and accumbens. On average, the loss is between 0.5 and 1 per cent per annum (Fjell and Walhovd, 2010). It is intuitively tempting to see this decrease as being due to loss of neurons and other cells, but in the main it is attributable to shrinkage of the neurons and lowering of the number of interconnections between neurons. However, it is worth noting that there is considerable variability between individual people in how their brain changes in later life (Caserta *et al.*, 2009). Generally, declines in intellectual skills in later life are correlated with decreased brain volume (Caserta *et al.*, 2009; Fjell and Walhovd, 2010). This can be interpreted as meaning that physical decline will produce a reduction in mental skills, but it can also be argued that the brain is more plastic than this (i.e. it can physically change in response to inputs) and that changes in brain volume might be the result of less demand being made of neural processes because of changes in behaviour and lifestyle. In other words, the brain physically declines because it is not being exercised enough (see Mahncke, Bronteone and Merzenich, 2006). The degree to which the elderly brain causes unavoidable changes in intelligence versus the extent to which behaviour and practice can stave off decline is considered in greater depth in later chapters.

In addition to changes in brain volume, there are also changes in patterns of functioning in later life. For example, functional magnetic resonance imaging (fMRI), which measures not only the structure of the brain but also its level of activity, identifies that many memory tasks are less lateralised (i.e. showing bias towards one hemisphere) in older adults (Cabeza, 2001). Again, Hedden (2007), in a review, notes that changes in prefrontal cortex function are a key explanation of many ageing changes in cognitive abilities. The influence of brain function, particularly in the frontal lobes, is explored in more detail in later chapters.

The brain thus changes in both volume and function and these changes are linked to alterations in intellectual functioning. One possible reason – lack of mental practice of skills – has already been given. Another potential cause is decreased cerebral blood flow, leading to neurons starving of oxygen and thus dying. Alternatively, reduced blood flow may lead to neuronal function being severely compromised because of reduced supply, particularly at times when there is a need for intense activity (see Riddle, Sonntag and Lichtenwalner, 2004). Another explanation is that many older people suffer from miniature strokes or **infarcts**, where a minute portion of the brain atrophies because of the demise of the local blood supply. The older person is unaware of this happening, and it is worth stressing that usually the number of infarcts is small, and can be regarded as symptomatic of normal ageing. However, in some individuals they dramatically increase in numbers, giving rise to **vascular dementia** (see Chapter 6). A third explanation is that the cerebral blood supply, when operating efficiently, filters out possible toxins in the blood before they reach the brain, by a mechanism called the **blood–brain barrier**. If ageing causes this to decline, then the brain might be exposed to potentially damaging toxins (see Bouras *et al.*, 2005) and a decline in the effectiveness of the blood–brain barrier has been linked to, *inter alia*, dementia, cognitive decline and diminished ability to recover from strokes (see Zeevl *et al.*, 2010). Generally, ageing-related declines in metabolism and cardiovascular problems mean that, even if their death is not caused, the neurons are less well supplied with oxygen and blood glucose and cannot operate as efficiently (see Farkas and Luiten, 2001; Meier-Ruge, Gygax and Wiernsperger, 1980; Woodruff-Pak, 1997).

As stated earlier, these issues will be returned to throughout this book. However, it is important to note from the start that, given the ageing declines in the physical brain, the sensory systems that inform it of the surrounding environment, and the body that supports it, it would be extraordinary if there were not changes in psychological function resulting either directly or indirectly from these.

Suggested further reading

An excellent text on ageing populations and the ageing body is *Brocklehurst's Textbook of Geriatric Medicine and Gerontology* (Tallis and Fillit, 2003). It should be noted that, at the time of writing, the current hardback edition retails at circa £130 (thus, for many this may be a book for borrowing from a library). For those on less generous budgets, Bromley (1988) is still often cited. It is a general textbook, comparatively inexpensive, well written and provides a solid (if now slightly dated) overview. And if readers are not already fed up with the present author, then a book edited by him called *An Introduction to Gerontology* (Stuart-Hamilton, 2011) is quite readable and indeed excellent if you skip the chapters written by him. For those interested in a more technical discussion of evolution and ageing, Gavrilov and Gavrilova (2002) is recommended. Jackson and Owsley (2003) provide a good overview of ageing changes in vision. For a review of pain assessment and management in older adults, see Hadjistavropoulos, Hunter and Dever Fitzgerald (2009). Fjell and Walhovd (2010) provide a solid review of brain anatomy changes in later life. For those interested in the history of ageing, then Thane (2000) is warmly recommended. In addition to being scholarly and informative, it is also an engrossing read. Although the book concentrates on the history of ageing and later life in England, many of the findings will be applicable to other cultures. There is an excellent later text by Thane and Parkin (2005) that is also recommended. For discussions of population change and its effects on policy, it is difficult to recommend a particular source for fear of it being immediately out of date. Government websites such as National Statistics Online (www.statistics.gov.uk) and the Population Reference Bureau (www.prb.org) are useful for basic up-to-date figures and often produce (surprisingly readable) summary reports. Wait (2011) gives an excellent review of the basics of policies on ageing and the issues facing policy-makers.

CHAPTER 2

Measuring Intellectual Change in Later Life

Introduction

It is well established that intelligence changes across the lifespan. For example, consider a simple measure of intellectual skills – the number of questions correctly answered on an intelligence test, sometimes called the **raw score**. Suppose we find the mean raw score for groups of different ages, from children through to older adults (e.g. mean score for 6-year-olds, mean score for 7-year-olds, etc. through to mean score for 80-year-olds, 81-year-olds, etc.). We then plot these mean scores on a graph. Unless our study defied over a hundred years of research experience, we would find the **classic ageing curve**. Basically, the mean raw score would rise through childhood and adolescence, reach a plateau in the late teens, and then at some point in adulthood the line would decline. In other words, just as surely as there will be a rise in the mean raw score throughout childhood and the teen years, there will be a decline in intelligence in later life.

This fundamental argument is not particularly disputed. Alas, this is where the certainty ends. Numerous supplementary questions may be asked, and each and every one creates a new set of caveats. For example:

- How is the age change best measured?
- When in adulthood does the decline start?
- Is the change equally true for all types of intellectual skill?
- Will all individuals show the same pattern of change?
- What causes these changes?
- How does this affect everyday intellectual skills?

In this chapter we shall attempt to examine these and further questions.

Measuring age changes in intelligence

If we wish to look at age differences in intelligence (or indeed any other measurement), we have a simple choice. Either we measure people when they are young and then measure them again when they are older (the **longitudinal study**) or we compare young and old people on the same measure at the same point in time (the **cross-sectional study**). The answer to this at first seems blindingly obvious. It is severely impractical to run a longitudinal study since it takes (literally) a lifetime to run. For example, if we wished to know the difference between 20- and 70-year-olds on the performance of a task, we would have to wait 50 years for the result. Nobody has that sort of time on their hands.

Therefore, cross-sectional studies seem to be the only practical solution. Many of the early studies (*c.*1900–1930) of the classic ageing curve used cross-sectional methods, and they argued that raw scores began to decline from their plateau around a person's thirtieth birthday, though verbal skills were typically unaffected (see Rebok, 1987; Thompson, 1997). However, we pay a heavy price for the cross-sectional studies' convenience. Suppose that we run a cross-sectional study, in which we compare groups of 20- and 70-year-olds and we find that the younger group is significantly better than the older group at whatever test we have chosen. The immediate assumption is that this is because the 20-year-olds are younger and, therefore, chronological age explains all. However, that is not necessarily the case. Yes, the 20-year-olds are younger, but they also differ from the older group in many other respects. For example:

- The older adults will almost certainly have had less formal education (particularly at degree level).

- The younger adults will almost certainly have had healthier childhoods (remember that antibiotics and indeed many types of immunisation were unknown when the 70-year-olds were born).

- The younger adults will have had access to a far wider range of cultural inputs through television, the Internet, and different styles of formal education.

The list can be expanded practically *ad infinitum*. However, the point is clear – older and younger adults differ not only in age but in the way that they were brought up and their lifetime experiences. How certain can we therefore be that if, in a cross-sectional study, we find an age group difference, it is due to age and not another factor? A difference due to generational differences in background and upbringing rather than ageing *per se* is called a **cohort effect**.

There are several ways of compensating for the cohort effect. One of these is to match the groups on the cohort measures you feel could distort the findings of your research. These measures are called **confounding variables**. For example, suppose you run an experiment in which you want to compare older and younger adults on how well they can do an intelligence test. You believe that education level and physical health are confounding variables, and thus you match the older and younger age groups on these measures so that you can then argue that, if you find an age group difference, it cannot be due to education level or physical health, because participants were matched on those. The problem with this approach is that for practical reasons it is often extremely difficult to match groups of people in this way (e.g. you have a 25-year-old man with a degree in town planning who has had his appendix removed; now find a 75-year-old man with the same attributes).

To get round this problem, it is generally easier to measure all the variables you are interested in and then by statistical means cut out the effects of the confounding variables. Thus, in our example, we would take measures of education level, physical health and intelligence test score. We would first see if there was an age difference in intelligence test score and then statistically remove the amount of this age difference that was due to the coincidental effects of education and health. There are three possible outcomes of this procedure – either there will be no change in the finding (i.e. education and health have no influence on the difference in test scores); or the difference is removed (i.e. the age group difference was coincidental: it was all due to differences in education and health levels); or the difference is lessened, but a significant (if smaller) difference remains (i.e. education level and health account for some of the age group difference, but not all of it).

It has been known for several decades (e.g. Ghiselli, 1957; Latimer, 1963) that when confounding variables are controlled for in cross-sectional studies the age difference is typically diminished but not removed (see Stuart-Hamilton, 1999b). This will be considered in detail in Chapter 7, but for the moment it is sufficient to note that at least some of the age difference found in a cross-sectional study will almost inevitably be due to cohort effects. And what is more, although attempting statistically to remove cohort effects from a study can be effective, it is practically impossible to remove all of them, simply because some of those that have an effect cannot be measured. These include different historical and cultural experiences (e.g. how do you match the experiences of rationing and bombing held by people who lived through World War II?). So in short, cross-sectional studies always leave a lingering doubt that, even when some confounding variables are controlled for, there could be others that weren't measured that could account for a supposed 'age' difference.

It is for reasons such as these that longitudinal studies can appear to be worth the wait, because at a stroke they remove many of the problems of cohort effects. Suppose we test our 20-year-olds, wait 50 years, and then retest them when they are 70. Any difference between them surely must be due to ageing alone, because it's the same group of people we are comparing at the two test sessions. Longitudinal studies thus appear to be a fairer system. This seems to be borne out by a comparison of cross-sectional and longitudinal study findings. Cross-sectional studies tend to find that intellectual skills start to decline in early adulthood. When early longitudinal studies were run, raw scores were usually found to be preserved until at least middle age, and typically far longer (e.g. Bayley, 1968; Owens, 1959; Purdue, 1966; Schaie and Hertzog, 1986). Salthouse (2009) cites several highly respected researchers in the field who have argued, based on longitudinal studies, for a relatively late onset of decline in intelligence. Thus, Aartsen *et al.* (2002) argue for a decline in middle age that does not become marked until the seventies; Albert and Heaton (1988) for a decline starting in the fifties; Plassman *et al.* (1995) for a decline in the sixties; and Schaie (1989a) for a decline in the sixties/seventies. In previous editions of this book, this has been presented as the consensus view. However, recent research seems to have tipped the balance towards a different conclusion.

The argument begins with the observation that longitudinal studies are not as pure and accurate as they first appear. First, because they *are* prone to cohort effects if used in a simplistic manner. For example, if you ran a longitudinal study on people born in 1920, this would tell you a great deal about ageing – for people born in 1920. You would not know if what was found for the 1920 cohort applied to people born in other times. To get round this problem, a refinement of the basic longitudinal study is required. This is often called the **overlapping longitudinal study**. This essentially involves testing several age cohorts on one occasion, then retesting them at regular intervals thereafter. To take a simplified example, suppose that at the first test session there are groups of people who are 50, 57, 64 and 71 years old. They are tested, and their performances at Session 1 can be compared in the manner of a traditional cross-sectional study. At regular intervals thereafter (for the sake of argument, let us say every seven years), the participants are retested. Thus, at Session 2, the 50-year-old group is now 57, the 57-year-old group is now 64, and so forth. The age groups at Session 2 can once again be compared in a cross-sectional manner, but, in addition, the members of each group can be compared with their younger selves, as in a longitudinal study (e.g. the people who are 71 at Session 2 can be compared with their 64-year-old selves at Session 1).

Table 2.1   A conceptual table illustrating the overlapping longitudinal study

	Session 1	Session 2	Session 3	Session 4	Session 5
Cohort 1	50	57	64	71	78
Cohort 2	57	64	71	78	85
Cohort 3	64	71	78	85	92
Cohort 4	71	78	85	92	99

However, there are further advantages to the overlapping longitudinal method beyond simply combining cross-sectional and longitudinal methods. Consider Table 2.1, which conceptually represents this imaginary study. As can be seen, as the study progresses, the younger cohorts will become the ages the older cohorts were earlier in the study. For example, at Session 4, Cohort 1 will become the age Cohort 4 was at Session 1. Armed with such information, it is possible to gauge and control for cohort effects. Take the following (intentionally simplified) example. Suppose that at Session 4 it is found that Cohort 1 has scores 20 per cent higher than Cohort 4. Does this mean that ageing from 71 to 92 will result in a 20 per cent loss in ability, or is this change due to a cohort difference? To answer this, we can consult Cohort 4's scores on Session 1, when they were the same age as Cohort 1 is at Session 4. Suppose we find that Cohort 4 when aged 71 had scores only 5 per cent lower than when aged 92. We now have two measures of ageing decline – the longitudinal method says the change is 5 per cent, the cross-sectional method says the change is 20 per cent. Armed with such information, it is possible to tease apart how much of ageing change is due to ageing *per se*, and how much is due to cohort differences.

Adopting this design (though in a more complex and erudite form – the previous example is a simplified illustration), Schaie and colleagues conducted the **Seattle Longitudinal Ageing Study** (e.g. Schaie, 1983, 1994, 2005). In 1956, a group of people aged between 20 and 70 were tested and then retested at seven-yearly intervals thereafter (i.e. in 1963, 1970, 1977, and so forth). Periodically new participants have been added. By cross-checking the figures in a manner conceptually similar to the earlier example, Schaie has demonstrated that part of the difference between age groups is due to cohort effects. For example, the earlier born participants have significantly lower scores when matched for age with people born later (e.g. people who were tested when aged 60 in 1970 will have lower scores than a group of 60-year-olds tested in 2000). Thus, some of the lowered scores in later life might simply be because older people were born at a time that did not favour intellectual skills as well as later times did.

But this does still not mean that longitudinal studies, even in the overlapping longitudinal design, are necessarily accurate measures of intellectual change. This observation arises from a very simple fact – namely, that many volunteers drop out of longitudinal studies. This drop-out is not random. A significant proportion of participants who leave a longitudinal study do so for motivational reasons. Quite simply, if they think they did badly on the tests, they don't come back for more. No matter how hard researchers try to explain to the contrary, most participants in experiments seem to regard psychological tests as a competition. Therefore, volunteers who perceive themselves to be worsening in intellectual performance will be less willing to be retested. This means that, as a longitudinal study progresses, the 'declining' participants drop out, leaving a rump of 'well-preserved' volunteers (the **drop-out effect**). For example, Riegel and Riegel (1972) demonstrated that people who refused to be retested in a longitudinal study had significantly lower test scores than those who remained, a finding echoed by Siegler and Botwinick (1979). It should be noted that the size of the drop-out effect among older participants can be *very* large. Salthouse (2010, p.173), in a review of percentage attrition from longitudinal studies, finds figures varying from 26 to 92 per cent. Singer *et al.* (2003b) found that if only those participants who attended several sessions of a longitudinal study (in this case, the **Berlin Ageing Study**; see Baltes and Mayer, 1999) were considered, then their performance on longitudinal and cross-sectional comparisons was very similar. But if all the participants were considered (i.e. including those who dropped out), then the cross-sectional comparisons showed significantly bigger age changes than the longitudinal comparisons. This implies that longitudinal studies might be under-estimating ageing decline to a very marked degree.

This problem is compounded by a **practice effect** – namely, that those participants who remain in a longitudinal study often significantly improve in their performance on the tests employed (Salthouse, 1992b). To rebut the obvious criticism, this is not because the participants remember the answers from the last time they did the test (at different sessions they are usually given 'parallel versions' of the test, which use different questions while having the same general format and level of difficulty). Instead, the problem is probably due to several factors, but the main problem is that participants might become **test wise**: in other words, they are increasingly at ease with the test procedures (and hence perform better), have increased general awareness of the ways in which psychological tests operate, and so forth. For whatever reason they occur, the result of these flaws is that the longitudinal method might under-estimate the effects of ageing (while the cross-sectional method probably exaggerates them). For example, Rabbitt et al. (2004) found that practice effects were significantly masking the rate of decline in their 17-year-long longitudinal study of older adults. Practice effects were even noticeable when there was a seven-year gap between test sessions. However, Rabbitt et al. (2008b) note that the gains from practice decrease with age (though, to further muddy the waters, the researchers also noted that performance improved significantly more across test sessions in people with higher intelligence test scores). Similarly, Ferrer et al. (2004) found that practice effects caused longitudinal changes to be under-estimated. Furthermore, the researchers noted that practice effects were stronger for some tests than others (in the case of Ferrer et al.'s study, memory-based tests showed a larger practice effect than measures of speed of response). This means that especial caution needs to be employed in interpreting results, since practice effects may not be uniform across all types of test.

Verhaeghen (2011) notes that, when these considerations are taken into account, the key longitudinal studies (e.g. Seattle, **Duke Longitudinal Study**, Berlin Ageing Study) find that there is decline in some intellectual skills across most of the adult lifespan. A reasonable consensus figure for a mean age group change is that by the age of 75 the mean test score on a measure of intelligence such as the **Wechsler Adult Intelligence Scale** is approximately 1 standard deviation (see page 58–59) lower than the young adult mean (Miller et al., 2009). Another approach is to note that the classic ageing curve has a very short plateau – after reaching a peak in the late teens/early twenties, a decline starts in the late twenties (Salthouse, 2009). It thus seems that the earliest studies of the classic ageing curve probably got it right after all, even if they did use flawed tests. It also means that old age is not an especial time of decline – our intellectual degradation occupies almost the whole of our adult lives.

However, demonstrating that there is a decline across the lifespan in raw scores is not automatically the gloomy news it at first appears. It cannot help but be noticed that each new wave of research papers claiming a new finding on ageing decline appears to rely upon more and more complex statistical analysis. Nobody ever seems to prove a point about cognitive decline in later life using a simpler, more direct analysis. To some extent this is of course to be expected as part and parcel of the research process. However, people with a lingering suspicion that the changes are increasingly the product of statistics rather than reality might not be quite as ignorantly wrong as would first appear. As will be seen in the next section, Salthouse and other researchers make strong claims for the magnitude of intellectual decline (particularly fluid skills) over the lifespan. These sound impressive, but they are based on paper and pencil tests in a laboratory. If older adults really behaved in the same way in real life, they would, to all intent and purposes, behave like younger adults with severe intellectual disabilities. That clearly is not the case. The original interpretations of longitudinal studies, which showed some decline in later life but relative preservation prior to this, accord far better with everyday experience in this respect.

There are further important caveats that must be made. First, it should be noted that this decline, although seen in the group averages, does not follow the same pattern in all individuals (Verhaeghen, 2011). In addition, the decline is only seen in *some* measures of intellectual skill (see the next section on fluid and crystallised intelligence). A further caveat is also needed, but this requires a little more explanation. The research we have been discussing is based on the *raw scores* on intelligence tests (i.e. how many answers a person gets right). However, the raw score is not the same thing as the **intelligence quotient (IQ)**. The IQ is calculated by converting the raw score into a measure of how intelligent a person is *relative to the rest of his or her specific age group*. In practice, this means calculating what percentage of an age group get a score less than a particular raw score. Let us create a hypothetical case in which it is known that on a particular intelligence test 50 per cent of 80-year-olds get a raw score of less than 45. In this case, an 80-year-old woman who gets a raw score of 45 is average, since we know that 50 per cent of people in her age group get a score less than this, and the other half get a higher score. In many instances, test scores are presented in this **percentile** format (i.e. in terms of percentage with higher or lower scores). In other cases, largely for historical reasons, the percentile scores are converted to an IQ scale, with 100 representing average, scores below 100 representing below average and, conversely, scores above 100 representing above average.

Generally, an individual remains at *roughly* the same level of IQ relative to his or her age peers throughout the lifespan. For example, if a person starts life as a young adult of average IQ, he or she will probably end life as an older person of average IQ. This has been demonstrated in numerous studies, including one by Deary *et al.* (2000). In 1931, ten-year-old children attending school in Scotland were given an intelligence test in (predictably enough) a survey of intelligence levels among Scottish children born in 1921. By curious coincidence, some of this same group had been gathered together in the 1990s in a medical study of people born in 1921 and resident in Aberdeen, Scotland. Even more remarkably, the records of their test performances in 1931 were intact, and so the opportunity was taken to retest this group of now elderly people on the same test papers they had first sat as ten-year-old children in 1931, and their scores then and now were compared. It was found that, with only a few exceptions (in one case alas attributable to the onset of dementia), their child and older adult scores were very much the same. A study of a similar Scottish survey conducted in 1947 of children born in 1936 provided similar findings (see Deary, Whalley and Starr, 2009; Deary *et al.*, 2004a, b).

This at first can seem confusing. If IQ stays relatively the same across the lifespan, why do raw scores follow the classic ageing curve? The answer lies in how the IQ is calculated. As was stressed earlier, IQ is a measure solely of how well an individual performs *relative to his or her age group*. But at different ages the raw score needed to attain the same IQ will vary. For example, in our hypothetical test mentioned previously, a raw score of 45 gives an IQ of 100 in a group of 80-year-olds. However, as we have seen, the average raw score for age groups declines in later life. Overall, a group of 20-year-olds will have higher scores, and perhaps, in this hypothetical example, to be bang in the middle of the younger adult group (i.e. to have an IQ of 100), an individual might have to have a raw score of 60 on the same test. Thus, individuals of different ages can have the same IQ but radically different raw scores. However, note also that it has been stated that IQ remains *relatively* constant: there can still be some variability. The correlations between test scores in childhood and old age are in the 0.7 region (Deary *et al.*, 2004a). These are solid respectable correlations, but still leave room for a lot of unexplained variance. Nonetheless, the fact that IQ remains even fairly constant throughout life indicates that there is a degree of stability to intellectual change across the lifespan that is often overlooked by researchers.

Measuring intelligence changes is thus fraught with problems and no single method seems to be perfect in practice. Cross-sectional studies are inevitably riddled with cohort effects, while longitudinal studies are prone to drop-out and practice effects. And there is a further criticism – studies such as these mask the great complexity and variability of the changes that are taking place in later life. In the next section of this chapter, we will examine the relative changes in different types of intellectual skills.

Fluid and crystallised intelligence

Most people, if asked to describe the effects of ageing on intelligence, would judge that stereotypical older adults have more knowledge but are slower at thinking things through. In short, ageing is popularly characterised as an increase in wisdom at the expense of a decrease in wit. For example, Berg and Sternberg (1992) found that, when asked to describe exceptionally intelligent adults of different ages, participants tended to emphasise 'ability to deal with novelty' in younger people and stress 'competence' in older adults. This reflects the finding that young and middle-aged adults have a greater tendency than older adults to associate 'wisdom' with later life (Clayton and Birren, 1980). A problem with attitude studies is that it is sometimes difficult to judge if everyone is using the same mental models in making their judgements (e.g. is the 'very intelligent' older person what the hypothetical very intelligent younger person will turn into?).

A more revealing insight into everyday concepts of ageing and intelligence is perhaps to be gained from studies of works of art. For example, painters and sculptors have conditioned people to accept that a depiction of a healthy older man looking pensive is automatically a representation of the epitome of wisdom, be it temporal or spiritual. It is very difficult for anyone raised in a Western culture to think of a philosopher as anything other than an older man (long white beard optional). Paradoxically, older people are simultaneously portrayed as being slow thinking and dull witted. The elderly person, doddery of mind and body, has been the butt of jokes from Chaucer to television situation comedy. Dogberry's famous adage in *Much Ado About Nothing* that 'when the age is in, the wit is out' expresses the guiding spirit for centuries of ageist humour. This conflicting view is neatly encapsulated in **Dewey's paradox of ageing**, which states that 'we are...in the unpleasant and illogical condition of extolling maturity and depreciating age' (Dewey, 1939, p.iv). However, popular opinion is not necessarily synonymous with scientific fact. Is there any proof that different aspects of intelligence are differentially preserved?

So far intelligence has been considered principally as a sort of global measure of intellectual ability, otherwise called **general intelligence**, or **g**. But psychologists have long argued that *g* is simply a composite measure of a set of sub-skills, each responsible for a different type of intellectual activity (see Appendix II for further information). One commonly used classification is to categorise intellectual skills into those involving **fluid intelligence** (ability to solve novel problems) and **crystallised intelligence** (pre-existing knowledge). These concur remarkably well with popular notions of 'wit' and 'wisdom' respectively. The very widely accepted view is that in later life fluid intelligence declines, while crystallised intelligence rises or at least remains stable. An often-cited study by Horn and Cattell (1967) supports this argument; in their comparison of older and younger adults, they found that there were significant age differences in fluid intelligence test scores, but not crystallised intelligence test scores. Schaie's Seattle study used a **test battery** (i.e. a collection of tests with a common theme – in this case intelligence – although each test measures a different facet of the skill). He found that components of the battery that were crystallised remained relatively unaffected by ageing, while fluid skills began to decline appreciably in the mid-sixties (see Schaie, 2008). Subsequent studies have almost universally supported Schaie (even if they have disputed exactly when the decline in fluid skills starts). For example, Cunningham, Clayton and Overton (1975) demonstrated that younger people had significantly higher scores on a common test of fluid intelligence (**Raven's Progressive Matrices**) than did older people, while age differences on a crystallised test of vocabulary were relatively insignificant. Hayslip and Sterns (1979) found similar results using a battery of fluid and crystallised tests. So did Rabbitt *et al.* (2004), who in their longitudinal study found accelerated decline in fluid intelligence, but no significant decline in the crystallised intellectual measure of vocabulary. Singer *et al.*'s (2003b) findings echo those of Rabbitt *et al.*, at least until the participants were in their nineties. Other longitudinal studies have similarly found crystallised skills are maintained or even rise, while fluid skills decline (Salthouse, 2009; Verhaeghen, 2011). Furthermore, these changes are prone to more effects than simply ageing. For example, Blelak *et al.* (2010) tested a group of older adults (aged 64–92 years) four times over three years. When people re-do tests, they rarely score exactly the same each time. The researchers found in their study that, within individuals, the scores on fluid intelligence tasks varied significantly more over the time period than did crystallised task scores. This variability increased the lower the cognitive performance.

It is important to note that the age-related changes in fluid intelligence test scores are often very considerable. Salthouse (2009) estimates that, after allowing for confounding variables, adults under 60 decline by between -0.02 and -0.03 **standard deviations** every year. The standard deviation is a measure of variability in a normally distributed population. The normal distribution, drawn as a graph, looks a bit like the cross-section of a bell (hence it is often called the 'bell curve'), and a huge number of everyday things have a normal distribution – height and weight being two of them. Intelligence tests also are usually normally distributed. If you know that a measure is normally distributed, and you also know the mean and standard deviation (s.d.) then you can calculate what percentage of the sample will have a particular range of scores on the measure. For example, if you take the range of scores between the mean minus 2 s.d.s and the mean plus 2 s.d.s, you will know that roughly 95 per cent of all the measures you will take are likely to fall between these two values. For a variety of reasons, scores that are more than 2 s.d.s away from the mean take on almost sacred meaning to some psychologists, and are often seen as indicating something exceptionally out of the ordinary. For example, for many educational psychologists, scoring more than 2 s.d.s below the mean on a test of intellectual skills indicates a potentially serious problem, probably one leading to remedial education or at least being labeled as having intellectual disabilities.

Therefore, when researchers in psychogerontology make statements about large declines in performance in terms of falls in s.d., this raises some interesting questions. This may be illustrated by considering a classic study by Salthouse (1992a). He reviewed a number of studies of performance on fluid intelligence tests, and re-tabulated the scores of the older participants. He found that, compared with younger adults, the older people were an average of 1.75 s.d.s below the mean of the younger group (figures extrapolated from Salthouse, 1992a, pp.175–6). In other words, the *average* older person by this reckoning is 0.25 s.d.s off the 2 s.d.s borderline. Put another way, were the average older adult several decades younger, he or she would be a strong candidate for special education. And this is just the *average* older adult. Some of those just slightly below average have, by the younger adults' scale of things, intellectual abilities on a par with the very severely intellectually disabled person. This point is a dramatic one, and is surprisingly infrequently aired in the research literature (possibly because the majority of leading psychogerontologists are not from developmental or educational psychology backgrounds; see Birren and Schroots, 2000). We shall return to it in Chapter 7. However, what can be legitimately asked here is why, if older adults are really showing the enormous declines that have been cited, they do not act in a commensurate way in everyday life? But it is important to state two caveats at this point. First, the studies used by Salthouse are largely cross-sectional. Therefore, part of this considerable age gap may be due to cohort effects (though elsewhere Salthouse seems willing to defend cross-sectional studies; see Salthouse, 2009). Second, different studies using the same test have produced rather variable results. For example, considering Salthouse's data set, the **Primary Mental Abilities (PMA) Test** (a commonly used test battery) has, in different researchers' hands, yielded effects ranging from -1.62 s.d.s to -5.19 s.d.s. Accordingly, these findings must be treated with caution: something might not be quite the robust phenomenon it appears if there is such large variability in scores.

It is also important to stress that confounding variables can exaggerate measurements of age differences. For example, Storandt (1976) tested older adults on a component of a widely used intelligence test battery called the **Wechsler Adult Intelligence Scale**, or **WAIS**. The particular measure she used was the **digit-symbol test**. This requires participants to match up digits to printed symbols according to a preordained code (e.g. if one sees a square, write a 2 underneath it, and, similarly, a triangle equals 3, a rectangle equals 4, etc.). There is a time limit of 90 seconds, during which the participant must match up as many symbols as possible. There is little doubt that changes in performance of such a task can be a useful measure of perceptual processing (e.g. MacDonald *et al.*, 2003) and that there is an age decline. However, the absolute size of the decline that can be attributed to psychological change alone is open to question. The test clearly is centred on the ability to remember and use a coding system, but because of the time constraint it also requires rapid writing. However, older people are generally slower at writing because of physical problems (e.g. arthritis, rheumatism, simple general weakening of muscles and joints). Thus, they may perform relatively badly at the task, not because of a failure of mental processing, but because they cannot write down the answers quickly enough. To see how much time older people were losing through writing, Storandt measured how many symbols people could copy within 90 seconds, and took this as the index of writing speed. This was compared with the performance on the test itself, and Storandt was able to demonstrate that about half the age difference was due to writing speed. This clearly demonstrates that physical limitations may exaggerate psychological differences, but it should be noted that a psychological difference nonetheless remained (a finding echoed in a similar study by Tun, Wingfield and Lindfield, 1997). Indeed, even when given as long as they wanted to perform a fluid intelligence test (Storandt, 1977), or increasing the test print size to overcome eyesight problems (Storandt and Futterman, 1982), older people still performed significantly worse then younger controls.

To further confuse matters, performance on crystallised intelligence tests is not as immune to ageing as it may first appear. For example, Core (unpublished, cited in Rabbitt, 1984) found that older adults took significantly longer to respond to questions on a crystallised intelligence test (the **Mill Hill Vocabulary Test**). Had a time limit been imposed on the test (significantly, crystallised intelligence tests are generally not against the clock), then older people would have performed significantly less well than younger controls. Hence, to a certain extent, the absence of an age difference on a crystallised intelligence test is because researchers have decided not to put a stopwatch to the task. Again, Botwinick and Storandt (1974) demonstrated that, although there was no age difference in performance on the WAIS vocabulary subtest, the answers given by older people were less precise. However, the test marking criteria were sufficiently lax for this difference to go unchecked. Other researchers, using different crystallised tests, have found an age decline without any revision of marking scales (e.g. Kaufman and Horn, 1996). Again, although general studies of younger age groups find a better correlation between knowledge and crystallised than fluid intelligence (Beier and Ackerman, 2001), Ghisletta and Lindenberger (2003) found that in older old (70–103 years) participants changes in knowledge levels were, to use the authors' phrase, 'dominated' by fluid intelligence (note the same group found a decline in knowledge levels in the over-nineties in a longitudinal study of their participant group; see Singer et al., 2003b). Therefore, crystallised intelligence is not as immune to ageing as might at first be supposed.

There are further examples in this chapter (and in Chapter 4) where crystallised skills can be shown to decline with age. This general theme is supported by Meacham (1990) who argues that 'the essence of wisdom is not in what is known but in how that knowledge is held and put to use' (p.188). This implies that once one moves beyond a straightforward recital of stored information to any form of *interpretation* then a decline is at least possible. However, it cannot be concluded from this that crystallised skills are fluid intellectual skills in disguise. There is considerable evidence that the two behave in different ways. For example, as Horn and Cattell originally argued, fluid intelligence tests are more strongly correlated with physical condition (e.g. pulmonary function; see Emery et al., 1998). Again, decline in crystallised skills, where observed, has tended to be far less severe than for fluid skills (see Lindenberger and Baltes, 1997), and longitudinal changes in the variability between people's crystallised test scores tend to be less than for fluid scores (Christensen et al., 1999). Longitudinal data also show that different factors underlie changes in crystallised and fluid test performance (Finkel *et al.*, 2007). Furthermore, in at least the early stages of dementia, certain crystallised skills may be preserved (thereby giving a reasonable indicator of pre-illness level of intellectual functioning) when fluid skills have already severely deteriorated (see Carswell *et al.*, 1997; Raguet *et al.*, 1996). Crystallised skills might not be ageing-proof, but they are rather more resistant than fluid skills.

A word of caution should be raised here. It has been argued that the 'true' size of a decline may be different from what has been measured. This is a common theme in psychological studies – since researchers cannot open up the brain and see thought taking place, everything has to be inferred from behaviour and this inevitably means that some error creeps in. However, an admission of measurement error can lead the unwary into making an unfortunate mistake. Occasionally a student reads that, for example, differences between young and old test scores are partly due to a cohort effect and therefore assumes that the 'real' difference between young and old is in reality smaller than the test score implies. So for example, if the difference between the test scores of a group of younger and older adults is 20 points, and it is known that half this difference is due to a cohort effect, then the 'true' difference is ten points. This is wrong – the true difference is still 20 points. In discussing cohort effects and similar, what is being debated is the *cause* of the difference, but this does not refute the existence of the difference. As has been argued elsewhere (Stuart-Hamilton, 2003), it is like being mugged. On one level it matters little whether the mugger is a hardened criminal or someone who, had they been brought up differently would have been a nice person and thus is not 'truly' a criminal. The fact remains that the victim feels the same level of pain and loss regardless of what the 'true' cause was. Similarly, the size of the difference between younger and older adults remains the same, no matter what the cause. However, the degree to which these findings have any bearing on real life is not necessarily resolved.

Variability in intellectual change

The crystallised-fluid intelligence distinction shows that different intellectual skills do not all decline in the same way and that there is variability between skills. Generally speaking, the more reliant a skill is on crystallised ability, the less it declines (though in a sense this is of course a circular argument; see Rabbitt, 1984). Schaie (e.g. Schaie, 2005) often divides intellectual tasks into six sub-skills: *inductive reasoning* (ability to work out rules governing newly encountered data), *spatial reasoning, perceptual speed* (essentially, speed to respond to basic stimuli such as flashes of light), *numeric ability, verbal ability* and *verbal memory* (in effect, ability to remember words). Verbal ability shows little or no age-related decline. This is unsurprising, since many of the verbal ability tasks used in studies are also used to assess crystallised intelligence! However, the other measures to a greater or lesser extent show a decline as people grow older (e.g. Jenkins *et al.*, 2000; Verhaeghen *et al.*, 2002; see also Verhaeghen, 2011).

These results describe what happens to a *group* of people as they grow older. However, on an individual level, the pattern of change can be radically different. It has been said by several researchers that no two people age in precisely the same way. Taken at a detailed level this is a truism of no value (because of course anyone, if looked at in enough detail, is unique). At a broader level it is hyperbole (it is nigh-on impossible that, out of the billions of people on the planet, no two individuals could not have the same pattern of scores as they grow older). However, if the argument is toned down slightly, so that it states that people vary enormously in how they age, there is a great deal of merit in what is being said. Group mean scores are not necessarily representative of what individual people are doing. The example that is always produced at this point is the '2.4 children' argument. A few years ago, the average number of children per household was 2.4. Taken at face value, this implies that every household contained two intact children and a very unfortunate individual with 60 per cent of his or her body missing. Of course, this is nonsense, but it neatly illustrates that the mean can at times represent the population without having the remotest relevance to any real-life individual. In a similar manner, a decline in group mean scores over the years does not mean that everybody in the group is declining exactly in the same pattern as the group. For example, suppose that over two test sessions the group mean goes from 100 to 50. If every individual in the group performed just as the group mean suggests, then at the first test session every individual scored 100 and at the second session every individual scored 50. But of course many other combinations of individual scores could yield means of 100 and 50. Perhaps on the first occasion half the group scored 95 and the other half scored 105 – that would give a group mean of 100. On the second occasion, perhaps half the group scored 100 and the other half all scored zero – that would give a group mean of 50. So group means are not totally reliable indices of how an individual within the group performs.

This argument that group means could mask individual variability is borne out by the research findings. Schaie noted that the rates of change within subtypes of intelligence varied considerably between individual participants (2005). Thus, one person might show a decline in skills *A*, *B* and *C*, while showing preservation of skills *D*, *E* and *F*. For another individual, the reverse might be true. Another individual might show a relative decline in *A*, *C* and *E* but not in the other skills, and so on. In a six-year longitudinal study by Wilson *et al.* (2002), a group of older participants were tested annually. It was found that there was considerable variation between individuals in the pattern of decline they showed. Although decline in one sub-skill was likely to be met with a decline in another, this was not inevitable, and level of performance at the start of the study was not an indicator of the rate of decline in skills as the study progressed. Other longitudinal studies have likewise found considerable individual variability (see Verhaeghen, 2011).

If there is individual variation in scores, this suggests that, leaving considerations of dementia aside, some individuals decline more than others. The fact that people's

IQs remain relatively constant means that there is a limit to this variability (since individual people remain more or less at the same percentile point within their age group, they cannot decline *too* much out of step with others). However, some individuals do seem to retain relatively youthful levels of performance for longer than others. Estimates of the percentage of 'well-preserved' people were at one stage supposed to be relatively high, but Salthouse (1992a) argued that only a very small proportion were, and recent research tends to support this argument. Notwithstanding this, there is considerable variability between individual older people's test scores. Rabbitt (e.g. Rabbitt, 1993) and others (e.g. Barton *et al.*, 1975) have demonstrated that variability in test scores is greater for older than for younger people on a variety of cognitive measures, such as reaction times (see later) and measures of memory. The longitudinal study by Rabbitt *et al.* (2004) likewise demonstrated that variability increased with the age of the participants. A literature review by Morse (1993) also records similar findings on changes in variability in later life. This means that, among themselves, older adults differ more in their performance than do younger people and hence, in this context, it is harder to justify talking about a 'typical' older person than it is to talk about a 'typical' younger person. It should also be noted that individuals can vary in performance considerably between test sessions. For example, Nesselroade and Salthouse (2004) found that in a study of perceptual-motor performance:

> the magnitude of between-session variability was found to average between 25 per cent and 50 per cent of the between-person variability and was equivalent in magnitude to the variation that was apparent across an age range of 12 to 27 years in cross-sectional comparisons. (p.49)

It is worth adding to this that it can be reasonably surmised that the size of the variability may have varied considerably had the participants been given other tasks. This serves only to muddy the waters further.

Another aspect of variability in performance is **dedifferentiation**, otherwise called **reintegration**. At its most basic, the issue is relatively straightforward. Early researchers on intelligence (e.g. Garrett, 1946) argued that in childhood all intellectual sub-skills were strongly related with each other. In effect, if you knew how well a child performed on a **visuo-spatial** task, it was a reasonably safe bet that they performed in the same way on other sub-skills. However, as children develop into adults, the sub-skills become less related to one another. To continue our example, the same individual, when grown to be a young adult, might be tested again on a visuo-spatial task. However, we could not be anywhere near as certain of how this individual would perform on other intellectual tasks as we could be when they were a child. This is the essence of the differentiation hypothesis – the belief that intellectual sub-skills become less related in childhood and early adult development. However, other researchers (e.g. Balinsky, 1941; Lienert and Crott, 1964) argued that in later life the process reverses itself, and the skills become more related to each other once again, a process known as dedifferentiation.

The abiding research question is whether dedifferentiation truly exists. There are a plethora of papers arguing for and against it (see Tucker-Drob and Salthouse, 2008). For example, Deary *et al.* (2004a) found evidence of dedifferentiation in their longitudinal study of former schoolchildren in the Scottish Mental Surveys of 1932 and 1947. Ghisletta and Lindenberger (2004) also found evidence for it in their analysis of data from the Berlin Aging Study and a Swiss longitudinal study (SWILSO-O). So did de Frias *et al.* (2007). In a cross-sectional study, Carp *et al.* (2010) found evidence for dedifferentiation in changes in neural activation in older adults, as did another paper by the same research team (Park *et al.*, 2010, who also found it especially influenced a decline in fluid intelligence). However, Hale *et al.* (2011) found no evidence for dedifferentiation when working memory skills were considered in their cross-sectional study. Sims *et al.* (2009) found no evidence of dedifferentiation in their study. Interestingly, the Sims *et al.* research was unusual in that it studied African American participants, and it is possible that this reflects an as yet untapped cultural difference. Tucker-Drob (2009) and Tucker-Drob and Salthouse (2008) found that, by varying the statistical analytic methods used and using plausible alternatives, no support for dedifferentiation was found. This is an area of research that is clearly in flux. As things stand, it appears that demonstrating the existence (or not) of dedifferentiation depends upon the specific skill, participant group and analytic method used. It is possible that a useful and informative model underlies all of this that will provide greater insights into psychological ageing, but as yet this model arguably has yet to be discovered.

Wisdom

The stereotypical view of ageing as being a time of declining wit but increased wisdom was stated earlier in this chapter. It is tempting to see wit as equivalent to fluid intelligence and wisdom as being the same as crystallised intelligence. This would not be wholly inaccurate. Crystallised intelligence is in effect the knowledge that has been gained through experience and, by extrapolation, we can reasonably argue that wisdom must be part and parcel of this. However, it is important to note that **wisdom** has been studied in its own right. There is some dispute about how 'wisdom' should be defined in a research setting (see Coleman and O'Hanlon, 2004; Shea, 1995; Sternberg, 1996). To some, it is more or less synonymous with crystallised intelligence. However, many definitions centre on the concept that wisdom involves producing a pragmatic rather than a purely logical answer. In other words, a pragmatic solution might not be logically watertight, but it is more likely, by integrating emotional considerations into the equation, to appease people and/ or maintain a sense of social order. It thus allows for a bending of the rules that a purely logical solution could never do. However, it should be noted that measures of wisdom often are based on realistic moral dilemmas (e.g. a terminally ill friend wants to commit suicide – what would you say?), and accordingly this tends to favour producing pragmatic responses. An example of this is a research technique used by Baltes and colleagues (e.g. Baltes and Staudinger, 2000; see also Kunzmann, 2007). Participants are asked a realistic problem akin to the suicide example, and then have to think out loud about the problem. This is then graded on various measures, such as how factually accurate the response is, how much attention is paid to social considerations, etc. To score well on such a test, participants must be aware of social considerations, and indeed it can be argued that wisdom is to some considerable extent a social skill rather than 'intellectual' in the conventional sense (see Staudinger, Kessler and Dorner, 2006). Skills such as wisdom, which build on 'pure' measures of intelligence, are often termed examples of **assembled cognition**.

There have been various approaches to assessing wisdom. At one level, there have been attempts to define it in terms of psychometric parameters. For example, Sternberg has attempted to correlate it with various essentially intellectual traits (see Sternberg, 1996, 1998), and he predicates his model of wisdom on the concept that it is essentially about finding balance between conflicting forces. Coming from a radically different research tradition, psychoanalytic approaches have attempted to link it with a lifetime of experiences of personal conflicts and resolutions (see Shea, 1995). Again, there have been attempts based on questionnaires and interviews that have met with varying degrees of success (see Coleman and O'Hanlon, 2004). Baltes and Smith (1990) define wisdom in terms of sagacity of judgements about real-life problems (see also Baltes and Staudinger, 2000). Chandler and Holliday (1990), based upon interviews with members of the public, synthesise a similar view of providing good advice, with the additional considerations of being competent and socially skilled in doing this.

Empirical evidence on wisdom generally finds a reasonably strong correlation with intelligence, tempered by personality traits, but with a significant proportion of measurement independence (e.g. Staudinger, Lopez and Baltes, 1997; Staudinger *et al.*, 1998). In other words, although wisdom is in part a product of a person's personality and intelligence (which, given its definition, would not be surprising), it is also in part independent of these factors (i.e. it is not just another way of describing *g*). Predictably, researchers have also found that wisdom is a beneficial ability, and is strongly related to, *inter alia*, life satisfaction in older people (Ardelt, 1997, 1998) and very old people (Ardelt and Jacobs, 2009) and preparation for death (Ardelt, 2008). But, most interestingly, wisdom is *not* found to be a preserve of old age. Adults of any age can score highly (or badly) on measures of wisdom. There is no indication, however, that in general, older people are significantly wiser than other adult age groups (see Ardelt and Jacobs, 2009; Baltes and Staudinger, 2000). However, recent research by Ardelt (2010) suggests that older adults score more highly on affective (pertaining to emotion) and reflective aspects of considering problems. Therefore, although the basic skill of wisdom might not be particularly age-dependent, older adults might nonetheless show greater skill in some aspects of wisdom-related issues.

Health, intelligence and the terminal drop model

So far, discussion of intellectual change in later life has centred on what happens to intelligence test scores as people grow older. However, an equally pertinent point is *why* these changes in test score occur. One prominent theory is that physical fitness and health are correlated with intelligence in older adults. This can be readily demonstrated, because it is well established that physical exercise can improve certain aspects of ageing intellectual performance. For example, Hawkins, Kramer and Capaldi (1992) demonstrated that a ten-week exercise programme resulted in a significant improvement in attention tasks, and that in some instances this was disproportionately greater for older than younger participants. Powell (1974) found cognitive improvements in older institutionalised patients given an exercise regime. Again, people who maintain a reasonable level of physical fitness appear in general to change less over time on indices of intellectual performance, particularly fluid intelligence (Bunce, Barrowclough and Morris, 1996; Emery *et al.*, 1998).

There are many reasons why physical exercise might have a beneficial effect on the intellect. For example, exercise is beneficial to the cardiovascular system and it is known that cardiovascular health is correlated with cognitive skills in older adults (e.g. Elwood *et al.*, 2002; Fahlander *et al.*, 2000; Izquierdo-Porrera and Waldstein, 2002). Again, sensible levels of exercise and diet are useful in staving off old-age diabetes, which is associated with a lowering of intellectual skills (Bent, Rabbitt and Metcalfe, 2000). A healthy body is likely to function more effectively and, as was seen in Chapter 1, a healthy body can enhance neural and hence intellectual functioning. Again, an older person who feels fit and healthy is also more likely to have greater confidence in what he or she is doing, and therefore have a higher motivation to do well at mental tasks. Aside from considerations of fitness, it can be easily demonstrated that many indices of health are correlated with aspects of intellectual functioning, such as blood rheology (essentially, the efficiency of blood flow – Elwood, Pickering and Gallacher, 2001); body mass index (though this could be an index of prior ability and socio-economic status; see Corley *et al.*, 2010); level of B vitamins (Bunce, Kivipelto and Wahlin, 2005; Calvaresi and Bryan, 2001); levels of urinary peptides (Lopez *et al.*, 2011); levels of apolipoprotein E (Raz *et al.*, 2009; Seeman *et al.*, 2005) and genotype (Raz *et al.*, 2009).

However, the weight that can be placed on these findings is harder to judge than would first seem apparent. For example, suppose that it is known that a deficiency in chemical X is associated with a reduction in intelligence in later life. The apparent solution is to increase levels of chemical X, sit back and watch the intelligence test scores rise. However, there are several reasons for arguing that this may not be the case. First, there is the argument that the horse has already bolted – in other words, once the damage has been done, it is irrecoverable. Second, it is possible that the wrong horse is being backed – i.e. the lowered level of X is a symptom not the cause. Thus, a lowered level of X may be caused by a general decline in bodily functions, and treating X alone may be like offering an arts festival to a country where the population is starving – it may do some momentary good, but when it is over the situation will be as before. A third reason is that, to return to the equine metaphors, the wrong horse has been backed. It is possible that the lowered levels of X are a product of the lowered intelligence levels. For example, people with an impaired understanding of things may be less good at looking after themselves, and indeed there is some evidence for this (e.g. intellectual status when a child is a strong predictor of health status in later life: Starr et al., 2000). A fourth reason is also worth noting: namely, that aside from considerations of health, in nearly all instances studies that have looked for it have found strong effects of socio-economic status (e.g. Elwood et al., 1999; Starr et al., 2000). Lower education levels are probably also associated (Bosma et al., 2003). Therefore, although health is an important issue in and of itself, its role in ageing cognitive change is less easily defined.

However, what occurs when health catastrophically fails in later life, and a person enters into a terminal decline? Some older people display a very rapid decline in scores in the months before they die. This phenomenon has the moribund title of terminal drop (Kleemeier, 1962; Riegel and Riegel, 1972). The **terminal drop model** argues that individuals maintain the same level of performance until a few months or years before death, when their abilities plummet, as if their minds suddenly 'wind down' in preparation for death. These precipitous drops, when averaged out, appear as a smooth curve when the age group averages are considered, along the same averaging out principles described earlier. It is also worth noting that many models of cognitive ageing do not factor terminal drop into their calculations, with the result that they may over-estimate the size of 'normal' (i.e. non-terminal phase) ageing (Bäckman and MacDonald, 2006).

Kleemeier (1962), working on longitudinal data, found that if, on retesting, a participant showed a large drop in intellectual performance, then there was a high probability that he or she would be dead within a short space of time. Similar evidence was provided by Riegel and Riegel (1972). They tested a group of middle-aged and older volunteers, and then retested them 10–20 years later. The researchers found that the volunteers who had died before they could be retested had had significantly lower scores at the initial test session. Every longitudinal study has similarly reported the terminal drop phenomenon (Jarvik, 1983), although the magnitude of the effect varies from study to study and to a certain extent is dependent upon the method of statistical analysis used (Bäckman and MacDonald, 2006; Palmore and Cleveland, 1976). The phenomenon is thus not really in doubt. What are debated are the details.

It is already well established that intellectual skills decline in later life. Therefore, a simple measure of decline is unlikely to be an especially good predictor of death, since this applies to both those about to die and those who will survive. Therefore, Jarvik and colleagues introduced the concept of **critical loss** (e.g. Jarvik, 1983; Jarvik and Falek, 1963). This essentially argues that, whereas some intellectual measures can decline without predicting anything in particular, changes in some specific indices are far more likely to indicate that death is imminent. However, different studies have identified radically different measures as being the indicators of critical loss:

- Decline in ability to detect verbal similarities greater than 10 per cent (Jarvik, 1983).

- Any decline in vocabulary size (Blum, Clark and Jarvik, 1973).

- Worsening abilities on paired associate learning (remembering which items have been previously seen together) and psychomotor skills (very loosely, mental skills with a physical skill component) (Botwinick, West and Storandt, 1978).

- Declining verbal skills (Siegler, McCarty and Logue, 1982).

- Decline in total score on the WAIS (Reimanis and Green, 1971).

- Decline in most cognitive skills (e.g. Bäckman *et al.*, 2002; Johansson *et al.*, 2004; Small *et al.*, 2003).

- Decline in fluid intelligence greater than 10 per cent (with a further increase in probability of death if the loss was greater than 20 per cent) (Rabbitt *et al.*, 2008b).

- Decline in vocabulary score and level of depression (Rabbitt *et al.*, 2002).

- Decline in the digit-symbol task (Hall *et al.*, 2009; see also Duff, Mold and Gidron, 2009).

- Decline in general decline in intelligence (van Gelder *et al.*, 2007; Wilson *et al.*, 2007).

- Level of life satisfaction (Gerstorf *et al.*, 2008).

- Decline in verbal and spatial abilities, with spatial decline starting 15 years before death (Thorvaldsson *et al.*, 2008).

Further examples can be given, but the point is surely apparent – while everybody is agreed on terminal drop being a phenomenon, researchers find it hard to agree on *what* must drop for it to be a harbinger of death. The problem in part is because different studies have used radically different measures, different forms of statistical analysis, different participant groups, and so forth. The findings of older studies might differ from more recent ones in part because of these considerations and also perhaps because of marked changes in medical care over the last few decades. Again, some studies have used more statistical controls than others (though a consistent finding is that terminal drop exists after education has been controlled for; see e.g. Gerstorf *et al.*, 2008; Wilson *et al.*, 2007).

In a further muddying of already murky waters, several studies have argued that terminal drop seems more prevalent among younger older adults, with the oldest old showing a gentle decline (e.g. Berkowitz, 1964; Jarvik, 1983; Riegel and Riegel, 1972; White and Cunningham, 1988). Other studies (e.g. Gerstorf *et al.*, 2008) argue that decline in their measure of critical loss (life satisfaction) was *more* pronounced in the oldest of old adults, or is unaffected by age but may nonetheless show considerable individual variation (Wilson *et al.*, 2007). Intuitively, it might be supposed that the type of illness a person dies from might affect the rate of decline, but in fact deaths from different illness types are not preceded by appreciably different patterns of psychological change (e.g. Rabbitt *et al.*, 2002; Rabbit, Lunn and Wong, 2008a; Small *et al.*, 2003).

It is tempting to look at the confusion that besets research on the *details* of the terminal drop model and assume that we can therefore reject the entire concept. However, it is important to reiterate that the general concept of terminal drop does have considerable weight of proof behind it. Furthermore, a point not often stressed is that it clearly demonstrates that successful cognitive ageing (i.e. retaining mental abilities) is a good augur of physical health and longevity (Yaffe *et al.*, 2010). Thus, there is a strong link between health and intelligence. This creates mental images of physical exercise being beneficial for cognitive ageing. But what of *mental* exercise?

Disuse theory

A commonly used expression is 'use it or lose it'. The more refined psychological term is **disuse theory** – the belief that age-related declines are attributable to a failure to use skills, so that eventually they fall into a decline (see Milne, 1956). The theory is not easy to prove or disprove. Finding that older people practise a skill less, and that the level of performance on that skill is lowered, is ambiguous. The skill might be worse because of lack of practice. However, the skill might have worsened because of unavoidable physical decay, causing the older person to lose the motivation to continue practising it (motivation is known to adversely affect older participants in a variety of tasks – see Perlmutter and Monty, 1989). Or, the skill could have worsened by itself, in spite of practice or motivation. Studies of older very well-practised individuals have almost always found that there is a decline in at least some related skills in spite of regular practice. For example, architects and airline pilots have shown age-related declines on spatial tasks in spite of using spatial skills every day of their working lives (Salthouse, 1992a). Before readers panic that older architects are therefore unsafe to design buildings or older pilots unsafe to fly, it should be stressed that these declines are relative to younger architects or pilots – in absolute terms, their skills are still high.

In another approach to the problem, Salthouse, Berish and Miles (2002) examined the effects of intellectual stimulation on level of cognitive skills. They began by arguing that if disuse theory is correct then three predictions can be made. The first is that the older the person, the lower their level of intellectual stimulation. This is on the grounds that we know that older people have lower intellectual skills. By the disuse theory's reasoning that level of skill is due to level of practice/ exposure to intellectual stimulation, this means that older adults should have lower levels of intellectual stimulation. Salthouse *et al.* conducted a survey of adults aged 20–91 and found that this was indeed the case – older adults had lower levels of intellectual stimulation than younger adults. This seems like proof for the disuse theory, but Salthouse *et al.* still had two further predictions that they said must be fulfilled. The second prediction was that there should be a positive correlation between level of stimulation and level of functioning. In other words, the more intelligent the person, the more intellectual stimulation he or she would report in his or her life. However, this was not found to be the case. The third prediction was that there should be an interaction between age and level of stimulation in predicting intellectual functioning. This is a rather complex point, but essentially it is arguing that, if practice is helping to stave off ageing effects, then it should be especially beneficial to older people, and this would show in this analysis. However, the data collected did not support this prediction. This appears to be a heavy blow to the disuse theory, but it should be borne in mind that level of intellectual stimulation was principally gauged by an activity inventory. This is a rather unsubtle instrument that cannot detect all the incidental stimulation that can be received in daily living. A large amount of learning can take place in everyday life without the person being consciously aware of being intellectually stimulated (Schliemann, 2000). Again, in a longitudinal study involving following up men who had participated in a World War II intelligence testing programme, Potter, Helms and Plassman (2008) found that people of relatively low intelligence, who in their youth had been placed in cognitively demanding jobs, displayed higher cognitive skills in later life, indicating that in effect enforced cognitive practice *can* have long-term benefits in old age. Therefore, the Salthouse *et al.* (2002) study might be overlooking key parts of the equation. In addition, it is worth noting that a study by Schooler and Mulatu (2001) found a positive correlation between the intellectual complexity of leisure activities and the intelligence of their participants aged 40–80.

The experiments just cited use relatively abstract laboratory tests. If one considers more realistic situations, then the age difference is often less. Although older people may be slower and less accurate at some 'basic' skills, their experience may be able to compensate for this. For example, Charness (1981) studied older chess players and found that they were able to play chess as well as younger adults. However, what was remarkable was that the older players often showed quite serious declines in skills that should be essential to good chess playing, such as memory. Charness found that the older players compensated for this loss by having a greater fund of experience. Because they had played (literally) thousands more games than younger opponents, they were able to tap a greater store of knowledge. Thus, when faced with practically any sort of game, they had probably been in the same situation many times more often than younger players. Greater experience thus compensated for loss of more basic skills. The same researcher found analogous results in an earlier study of habitués of bridge (Charness, 1979). More recently, Masunaga and Horn (2001) demonstrated that players of go (a Japanese board game of strategy) maintained relatively high-level skills relevant to the game, even if more generally their intellectual skills (such as fluid intelligence) showed a decline. Similarly, Salthouse (1985) compared older and younger typists. He found that the older typists generally had slower finger movements and reaction times, but showed no difference in typing speed. This was because the older typists planned longer sequences of finger movements than younger typists (with less experience) could manage. Thus, although it took an older typist longer to move a finger to a key, the move towards that key started earlier because they looked further ahead (in essence, younger typists were starting later in their sequences of finger movements and then catching up with the older typists). Bosman (1993) adds that this only applies to older typists who regularly practise their skill. A caveat to this is provided by a study by Westerman et al. (1998) of older and younger participants who were all practised in word processing. The researchers found evidence for a compensatory strategy, but also noted that, among the more skilled older participants, their abilities were associated with possession of high levels of basic cognitive capacities rather than integration of sub-skills into an overall strategy. This implies a bigger role for basic skills than other compensation studies have suggested, but it should also be noted that Westerman et al.'s sample was of people who had 'over 100 hours of experience in using a word processor' (p.583) as opposed to the years or decades of experience of participants in some other studies.

In another study of compensatory strategies, Hoyer and Ingolfsdottir (2003) conducted an ingenious experiment on medical laboratory technicians. They showed the participants microscope slides with the task of identifying target structure on them. Anyone other than a biologist who has seen slides of cells and similar will readily appreciate that the difference between such slides and random blobs of ink can seem fairly minimal, and the task is a demanding one. Hoyer and Ingolfsdottir found that the older technicians (in their late forties) took significantly longer over the task than younger technicians (in their twenties) if just presented with the slide images. However, if they were given contextual information (i.e. orienting them to what was expected) before they started, then the age difference disappeared. In other words, given the capacity to use a compensatory strategy (20 years' greater experience of looking at slides), the age decline in basic visual search skills could be overcome.

Practice may not only preserve existing skills, but also revive supposedly lost or declining ones. For example, Plemons, Willis and Baltes (1978) demonstrated that training in taking fluid intelligence tests could boost the test scores of older participants. Furthermore, this seemed generally to enhance performance on intellectual tests, suggesting that the training made participants more test wise. These findings are echoed by other researchers (e.g. Kermis, 1983; Rebok, 1987; Tranter and Koustaal, 2008). Salthouse (1992a) criticises these studies because often there have been inadequate control groups, and/or the success of the training has been judged on too narrow a range of tests (though some recent studies would seem to belie these criticisms; for further discussion, see Salthouse, 2010). Again, he (and other commentators) have suggested that training may not affect the root skill, which remains in decline, but instead may offer new strategies to cope with the problem. This is analogous to taking a painkiller to mask the pain of toothache – it does not cure it, but it enables one to cope. A summary of Salthouse's recent views on the subject can be found in Salthouse (2010). He presents a concise survey of the literature, arguing that many of the findings on intellectual change in later life cannot be attributed to confounding variables, in the main because either allowing for them does not remove sufficient of the age differences, or they might not be measuring what they claim.

From a practical viewpoint, this argument may seem relatively unimportant (why worry if it helps older people cope?), but the theoretical considerations are of course not trivial. More recently, Mireles and Charness (2002) have conducted computerised simulations of the effects of knowledge on factors likely to influence chess-playing skills (in this instance, memory span for sequences of moves). The researchers found that knowledge appears to protect against increased neural noise (see Chapter 1), but not cell loss. This perhaps helps explain the work of Rothermund and Brandstädter (2003), who in a longitudinal study found that compensatory strategies were increasingly used by their participants until they were circa 70 and then use decreased.

Thus, there is evidence that compensation can have its uses (see Hertzog and Jopp, 2010 and Vahia, Cain and Depp, 2010 for recent reviews). However, even in its full flowering, it might not be totally effective. For example, Charness et al. (2001) conducted a study in which young, middle-aged and older typists who were either novices or experienced were given the task of learning a new word-processing application. In the case of the novices, the younger participants were faster to learn and retained more information at the end of the training course. In the case of the experienced participants, the older group differed only minimally from the younger groups in what was learnt and retained. Thus, there is evidence that experience acts to compensate for age-related decline. However, the older group had a significantly slower learning rate. Lindenberger et al. (2008) found that older graphic designers given training in a memory improvement technique (the **method of loci**) showed a significantly greater *relative* improvement in memory scores than age-matched controls or younger graphic designers. However, in absolute terms, the older graphic designers still had poorer memory scores than the younger participants, even after training.

Therefore, compensation through practice has its limits. However, even if it cannot fully compensate for cognitive changes in later life, that does not mean in practical terms that it is a bad thing. Even one of the sternest critics of disuse theory has argued that there are considerable personal benefits to keeping up mentally demanding exercise and having faith in the idea that it staves off at least the worst of the decline (see Salthouse, 2006). Compensation can also be seen in the broader, whole lifespan terms of the **SOC model** (e.g. Baltes and Baltes, 1990; Freund and Baltes, 2007). 'SOC' stands for selection, optimisation and compensation. The theory argues that we develop in adulthood by first selecting what to specialise in doing, then optimising by practice, and, in later life, protecting against decay of skills through compensatory strategies.

Another facet to the concept of compensation is the argument that, as the brain ages, neural mechanisms alter to make best use of dwindling resources, such as slower neural transmission, fewer synapses, greater neural noise, and so forth (see Chapter 1). This is an area of research still in its relative infancy, but there is already strong evidence for such processes. For example, even if older and younger adults perform the task to the same level of ability, recent research in neuroimaging indicates that the neural processes taking places in older and younger adults' brains are significantly different (Phillips and Andres, 2010). One way in which this can occur is simply that the older people's brains apparently work harder. More accurately, brain imaging shows neural activity is higher in older people (Reuter-Lorenz and Cappell, 2008; see also Schneider-Garces et al., 2010).

There are many ways in which these changes can occur. One is to make use of a **cognitive reserve** (see Garrett, Grady and Hasher, 2010; Stern, 2009). This is in effect a 'buffer' against loss that is possessed by people with a higher level IQ and/or level of education. At its most basic, people with a higher level of intelligence can afford to lose more before a decline in their intellectual performance on many tasks becomes noticeable. There is some evidence for this (e.g. Stern, 2009) though doubts have been raised (e.g. Tuokko et al., 2003) and the effects might not be as clear-cut as first supposed (Garrett et al., 2010). Another explanation argues that, as many neural mechanisms decline, these are offset by increased use of the prefrontal cortex. This leads to the **scaffolding theory of ageing and cognition (STAC)**, which in effect argues that declining mental mechanisms are 'propped up' by greater reliance on the workings of the prefrontal cortex (Park and Reuter-Lorenz, 2009). The available evidence suggests that this scaffolding is strengthened through rehearsal of skills, thereby strengthening the traditional compensation model. This reflects a similar proposal by Cabeza (2002) who argued that the prefrontal cortex in older adults tends to be less lateralised (i.e. the left and right sides of the brain are more equally involved). This leads to the **HAROLD (hemispheric asymmetry reduction in older adults)** model. Cabeza argues that the model might be an example of compensation, or it could be evidence for dedifferentiation (see also Zhihao *et al.*, 2009). Greenwood (2007) has suggested a model of neurological change concerning the **plasticity** (basically, ease with which neurons can change their connections and thus functions) of neurons both within the prefrontal cortex and the surrounding areas of the brain. And for those readers interested in how these changes might occur at the level of the individual neuron, Kumar and Foster (2007) provide a useful review.

An objection to such models might reasonably be that differences in activation might reflect nothing more than general differences in functioning that have been misinterpreted. However, it can be established that age differences in mental functioning can be very specific. For example, Fischer, Nyberg and Bäckman (2010) measured brain function (using functional magnetic resonance imaging or fMRI) while participants were attempting to memorise faces. The faces were either emotionally neutral or fearful. When looking at fearful faces, the young adult participants showed greater activation of the right amygdala and bilateral hippocampus compared with the older participants, who showed greater relative activation in the left insular and right prefrontal cortices. However, neither the old nor young participants showed similar neural activation when looking at neutral faces. Similarly, Addis *et al.* (2010) demonstrated old-young adult differences in brain activity when encoding emotionally positive information but not when encoding emotionally negative information. These findings indicate that neural changes in later life can be very precise and are not just a blanket change in level of activation.

The concept of neurological compensation thus looks fruitful. It also points to the possibility of computerised cognitive intervention that could directly stimulate the appropriate areas of the brain, thus further enhancing neurological compensatory mechanisms (Cruz-Jentoft *et al.*, 2008). However, the area is not yet as clear-cut as some advocates would like to suppose (see Mast, Zimmerman and Rowe, 2009) and also it is not the only neurological explanation of intellectual change in later life. Of the alternatives, one of the most prominent is often set up as the opposite of the traditional 'use it or lose it' disuse theory. In its strongest form, it argues that practising skills is a largely fruitless exercise: ageing decline is due to an inexorable biological process of the slowing of bodily functions that in turn leads to a slowing and lowering efficiency of mental processes. To understand this argument fully, we first need to take a step back and consider how this slowing can be measured.

Reaction times and the general slowing hypothesis

The **reaction time (RT)** is the time taken to respond to a stimulus. It is measured as the time between the stimulus first appearing and the person making a response. In the most commonly used measure, the stimulus is an image on a computer screen, which is responded to by pressing a particular key on the computer keyboard.

However, there are many permutations of this basic experiment – participants can, for example, be required to speak an answer into a microphone (which is set up to stop a response timer), press a button with their feet, etc. Likewise, the stimulus can be in another sensory modality, such as sound. However, all have the same basic purpose – to measure how quickly a person can respond. Thus, the *lower* the RT, the *faster* the response.

Aside from the above considerations, RT studies come in two basic flavours:

- **Simple reaction time (SRT)** measures speed of response when there is only one stimulus and only one response allowed (e.g. pressing a button every time a light flashes).

- **Choice reaction time (CRT)** measures speed of response when there are different stimuli requiring different responses (e.g. press button *A* if a red light flashes, *B* if a green light, or *C* if a blue light).

Because CRT experiments require more decision-making than SRT experiments, response times on CRT are longer, and as the number of stimuli that have to be chosen between increase, so does the mean response time.

It is very well established that reaction times get slower as people get older. According to a review by Birren and Fisher (1995, p.329), it is 'one of the most reliable features of human life' (see also Lindenberger, Mayr and Kliegl, 1993; Rabbitt, 1996). Furthermore, the age difference gets proportionately larger the more choices that must be discriminated between in a choice reaction time task (see Botwinick, 1973; Deary and Der, 2005; Kermis, 1983; Salthouse, 1985). The simple explanation for these phenomena is that older people's nervous systems are slower and less efficient at conducting signals, and the disadvantage imposed by the extra choices is another manifestation of the age × complexity effect (see Chapter 1). The principal exception to this rule is if people are allowed to practise different versions of a choice reaction time task for several days. After *lots* of practice, the age difference becomes a constant across all conditions (Rabbitt, 1980). So, if at the start of the practice older adults get disproportionately slower than younger adults the more choices have to be made, by the end of the practice they are still slower than younger adults, but by the same amount on each condition. This implies that a significant proportion of the age difference may be due to 'settling in' to the task. Once it has become sufficiently rehearsed to be automatic (in psychological terms, this generally refers to a skill rehearsed to the point where it requires no conscious control), then age differences are less important than when the task requires conscious monitoring. Hasher and Zacks (1979) argue that automatic processes are relatively unaffected by ageing (see also Wishart *et al.*, 2000), although some commentators (e.g. Burke, White and Diaz, 1987; Myerson *et al.*, 1992) have found some instances where this is not the case.

A further consideration is that many researchers have only considered age difference in *mean* reaction times. Rabbitt (1980, 1988, 1998) argues that this is misleading, since it presents the impression that older people are incapable of the fast responses of their youth. In fact, if the distribution of response speeds is considered, then the fastest reaction times of older and younger people are the same. The age differences lie elsewhere. In part they are because older adults make fewer very fast responses. They are also due to older people making a much wider variety of response speeds, which increases the mean reaction time. This is particularly the case when reactions to errors are concerned (an error occurs when, e.g. in a choice reaction time task, the participant presses button *B* when the correct response was *A*). Participants are usually aware they have made a mistake, and respond by slowing down on the next trial. Younger adults then pick up speed relatively quickly, while older people take several more trials to return. This means that, relatively speaking, younger adults 'shrug off' their mistakes quickly, while older adults are over-cautious. Younger adults thus can find an optimal response speed (i.e. as fast as they can go without making too many mistakes) and stick to it, while older people seem to lack this level of control and oscillate far more. When the average performances are considered, this age difference expresses itself more simply as a difference in mean response times. In a more recent study, Smith and Brewer (1995) have provided similar evidence. It should also be noted that increasing the preparation interval (i.e. the time gap before the start of the next trial in a reaction time experiment) also disproportionately aids older adults' reaction time performance (Bherer and Belleville, 2004).

However, why is the study of reaction times relevant to intelligence? The simple answer is that it is well established that reaction times correlate with measures of intellectual performance (e.g. Ferraro and Moody, 1996). Rabbitt and Goward (1986) found that if groups of older and younger adults are matched for intelligence test scores, then there is no difference in their choice reaction times. Hertzog (1991), Salthouse (1991a) and Schaie (1989b) similarly report that, when the effect of speed of response is statistically controlled for, differences between age groups on intellectual tasks are significantly lowered, or disappear altogether. How do we explain this link between speed of response and intelligence? Essentially, reaction times measure the speed with which neurons send messages; intelligence tests measure what is done with those messages. This implies that slowing reaction times are measuring the *cause* of declining intellectual skills (e.g. Eysenck, 1985; Salthouse, 1985). If older people have slower reaction times, then they have slower neural processing and thus slower mental processes, and this in itself could explain much of the decline on timed intelligence test scores. However, there is more to this issue than just simple speed. In tandem with the slowing comes a lowering of the general accuracy and efficiency of the system. In part this is because some mental processes may have to be executed within a certain number of milliseconds or they decay beyond recovery – a slower system means that some processes will take longer to complete than this critical limit, and so a particular mental process cannot be completed (see Salthouse, 1996). Again, a decline in speed is the result of the general physical decline of the nervous system, such as a depletion in the number of interconnections between neurons, lowered efficiency of neurotransmitters, increased neural noise (see Kail, 1997), and so forth. The reaction time may thus be not only gauging the speed of transmission, but also giving a general indication of the efficiency and health of the nervous system.

A further aspect of reaction times concerns the consistency of responses by older adults. If a person is given a reaction time task, it makes intuitive sense that they will not respond at exactly the same speed on every trial. For example, they are more likely to have responses over five successive trials of, for example, 500, 478, 520, 431 and 576 msecs than they are to have responses of 500, 500, 500, 500 and 500 msecs. Such variability in scores is to be expected. However, in older adults this variability increases, and (purely as descriptive shorthand) this is sometimes described as 'unreliable' performance. Hultsch, MacDonald and Dixon (2002) found that the more 'unreliable' the participant, the lower their cognitive test score. Rabbitt et al. (2001) argued that this apparently capricious behaviour may in fact be a stable characteristic, and were able to demonstrate that the level of unreliability an individual displayed remained remarkably consistent over a study in which older adult participants attended 36 weekly test sessions to perform a variety of reaction time tasks (an heroic accomplishment in itself). Furthermore, the more 'unreliable' a person, the lower their intelligence test score. Thus, in addition to speed of response, the pattern of response in a reaction time study may also be revealing of cognitive status.

Returning to studies of speed of response, the attribution of an ageing decline in intellectual skills to a slowing in the speed of neural transmission (and all the related phenomena this implies) is known as the **general slowing hypothesis** (or, rather confusingly, the **speed hypothesis**). At a general level, this argument is not greatly disputed: low speed typically equals low test scores and, across time, changes in speed of processing correlate significantly with changes in fluid intelligence (Zimprich and Martin, 2002). Instead, the debate is principally about the degree to which general slowing alone predicts intellectual performance. At first, there seemed to be a major problem with the general slowing hypothesis – namely, the issue of the age × complexity effect (to reiterate: as the task gets harder, so older adults become disproportionately more disadvantaged). For various reasons, it was difficult to explain how general slowing could explain why the age difference gets proportionately bigger the harder the version of the task being performed. But then researchers (notably Cerella, 1985, 1990, following earlier research by Brinley, 1965) found a way of describing the phenomenon that made it easily explicable by a general slowing model.

Let us explain this using a hypothetical example. A typical graph showing the age × complexity effect is shown in Figure 2.1. As can be seen, the younger group has a line rising less steeply than that of an older group. However, what if we plot the response times for older and younger adults on the same tasks against each other? In other words, each point on the graph represents the mean time taken by the old group on a particular task plotted against the time taken by the young group on the same task. What we will usually find is illustrated in Figure 2.2, and is known as a **Brinley plot**. What we see is a straight line. In other words, the traditional age × complexity graph in Figure 2.1 is misleading us. Although old and young groups seem to go further apart the harder the task, the reality is that the difference between them is linear. To those who are non-mathematically minded, this might create an understandable reaction of 'so what'? However, this is a very important finding. Showing a linear relationship means that the difference between old and young people can be represented by a straightforward mathematical relationship that remains the same across different conditions of a reaction time task. So in other words, the age × complexity effect can be explained by a simple difference in basic processing speed – no more elaborate explanation is necessary. This was of great value to researchers, who had been tying themselves up in knots trying to account for the old–young difference increasing with task complexity. It means, *inter alia*, that complex formulae used to predict changing age differences across different levels of complexity (see Rabbitt, 1996) can be jettisoned; instead, all age differences can be expressed by a simple formula – find the mean reaction time of a younger adult on a task, multiply it by a constant, and that will be the mean reaction time for older people on the same task. For those not mathematically minded, what this means is that the apparent disproportionate difference between older and younger people illustrated in Figure 2.1 is illusory; older adults *appear* to be disproportionately disadvantaged the more complex the task, but in fact they are not – the real underlying difference remains the same size.

Because of the beguiling simplicity of this theory, the general slowing hypothesis has understandably attracted a lot of attention. It has been established that the phenomenon is widespread: across a wide variety of tasks, where average older and younger response speeds can be compared, a linear relationship has been found (e.g. Cerella, 1990; Lindenberger *et al.*, 1993; Maylor and Rabbitt, 1994; Ratcliff, Thapar and McKoon, 2001; Sliwinski *et al.*, 1994; Verhaeghen and De Meersman, 1998; Verhaeghen, 2006). Myerson *et al.* (1992, p.266) make the important point that, within a particular domain, 'the term *general slowing* would appear to capture the fact that the degree of slowing does not appear to depend on the nature of the task or the specific cognitive processing components involved'. In other words, slowing must involve something more basic, such as changes at a neural level (Cerella, 1990).

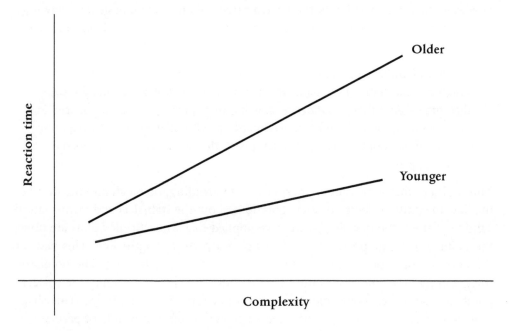

Figure 2.1 Illustration of the age × complexity effect

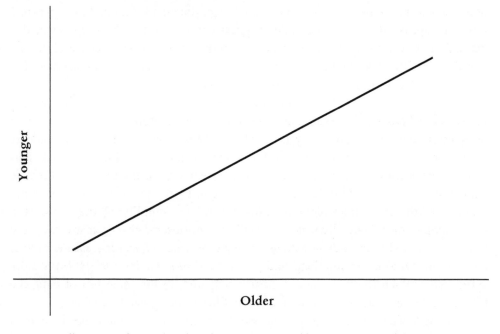

Figure 2.2 Illustration of a Brinley Plot, plotting younger v. older means on same data as Figure 2.1

However, there are several important caveats that limit the extent of general slowing's applicability. For example, it does not stop the old–young speed relationship being influenced by other factors, such as compensatory strategies by older people:

> Because of the compensatory effects of lifelong knowledge accumulation, for instance, some domains of cognitive functioning may be less affected by slowing than others. And there is evidence showing that slowing is less pronounced in tasks requiring lexical decisions as compared with analogous tasks requiring nonlexical decisions which is consistent with this assumption. (Lindenberger *et al.*, 1993, p.207)

This indicates that some caution must be taken in reading too much into the shape of the line. In addition, there are some questions about the statistical and mathematical validity of the technique. So far, we have implied that when Brinley plots are done, the points on the graph set themselves up in a perfect straight line. This was for the purposes of explanation, and in reality they do no such thing. The points on the graph go in a general upward direction, but a line literally joining the adjacent points to each other would more often than not form a zig-zag shape. This shape is attributed to experimental error – measurement mistakes, a couple of participants having an 'off day' and similar could distort the findings away from their 'true' form of a straight line, and so statistics are used to determine if the line between points would really be a straight one if these experimental errors had not occurred. Generally speaking, a technique called **regression** is used. For the purposes of this discussion, we can say that the regression technique measures whether a straight line best describes the data. And it is this regression technique that has demonstrated that Brinley plots of straight lines best describe the data.

However, the regression techniques used are not as reliable as they first appear. For example, Perfect (1994) suggests that similar linear relationships can be generated using essentially random data. Again, Rabbitt (1996) notes that, when data increase in variability with task complexity, a linear relationship can still be obtained. This is a mathematically difficult argument, but it essentially means that a considerable amount of the young–old difference may be due to more than just a simple slowing process, and that the Brinley plot is masking this by 'over-simplifying' the relationship into a simple linear one. Sliwinski and Hall (1998) observe that in many cases the statistical method used to demonstrate Brinley plots (the *ordinary least squares multiple regression*, or OLS) is too simplistic and that a *hierarchical linear model* (HLM) is more appropriate. When the two techniques are compared on the same sets of data, the OLS produces Brinley plots, while HLM identifies rather greater variability.

The evidence thus seems to pull in two directions. On the one hand there are a lot of studies that demonstrate the validity of Brinley plots and yet there are others that say Brinley plots can be flawed. The most parsimonious explanation of these findings is that Brinley plots apply in some situations and not others. Thus, there are some processes that genuinely do show a linear pattern of slowing, while in other instances this model simply cannot apply. Even within studies where Brinley plots have been shown to be sound measures, it now appears that slowing can be at two broad rates – in some instances older people are slower than younger adults by about 20 per cent, while in other studies they are slower by circa 80 per cent (Verhaeghen, 2011). Findings such as these do not mean that the general slowing hypothesis is 'wrong' – simply that it is not quite as universal an explanation as might have been first assumed.

If proof for the slowing hypothesis is sought away from Brinley plots, the evidence is similarly equivocal. For example, Salthouse and Czaja (2000) produced a plausibly argued and technically complex case that, if a study shows no evidence for general slowing, this is because in effect it has been taken out of context (more technically, by studying some variables in isolation their shared variance with other variables – which would indicate a common factor, such as general slowing – is overlooked). As proof of this, the authors demonstrated the presence of a common factor explaining impressively large proportions of the variance in two separate data sets of older adults' intellectual performance (see also Salthouse, 2001). However, this plea to look at the bigger picture was short-lived because the following year Allen et al. (2001) re-analysed Salthouse and Czaja's data and found that by using a different (and arguably superior) statistical technique, although a common factor could be found, it explained less of the variance than previously claimed and, furthermore, other significant explanatory factors were present, thus denying a single factor explanation (a finding echoed in studies by Anstey, Hofer and Luszcz, 2003; Anstey, Luszcz and Sanchez, 2001; Schmiedek and Li, 2004). Allen et al. demonstrated similar problems with other published studies supporting a single factor case, and, as a coup de grâce, showed that if simulated data sets were used (i.e. where the underlying structure was deliberately created), the statistical methods used by the single factor supporters were difficult to falsify. In other words, a single factor was likely to be produced regardless of whether it was the best fit for the data.

An assortment of disparate findings have further indicated that general slowing may not be as strong a predictor as was first assumed (see Bashore, Ridderinkhof and van der Molen, 1997, for a review). A few are listed as follows:

- Sliwinski (1997) reports that cognitive slowing did not seem to be a good predictor of counting speed in tasks of different levels of complexity. Instead, different counting tasks seemed to be mediated by different mechanisms.

- Salthouse (2000) reported that in a survey of responses to individual items on a variety of tests, a common age-related factor correlated across all these, but in addition there appeared to be a second factor (also related to age) that was correlated only with performance on the most difficult individual items.

- Salthouse and Ferrer-Caja (2003) found 'at least 3' factors underlying performance of adults (aged from their teens to their nineties) on a range of cognitive tasks.

- Shimamura *et al.* (1995) demonstrated that a decline in skills might be offset by use of what is in effect compensation in some individuals.

- The use of reaction times as an index of mental processing has also been criticised, on the grounds that it is essentially a simplification of what are probably a series of complex and very rapid mental processes, and may thus overlook important subprocesses (Bashore *et al.*, 1997).

- In perceptual comparison tasks, general slowing is a key, but not sole, factor determining age differences (McCabe and Hartman, 2008).

- Vance *et al.* (2010) claim that speed of processing can be manipulated through training, thereby questioning how inevitable and 'fundamental' such changes are (see also Goldstein *et al.*, 1997; Vance, 2009).

- Deary, Allerhand and Der (2009) found in a longitudinal study that reaction times did not predict future fluid intelligence test scores, suggesting that processing speed might not be the root cause of intellectual change.

- Deary, Johnson and Starr (2010), using the longitudinal study of Scottish schoolchildren mentioned earlier, found that intelligence test performance at 11 years was a better predictor of 70-year-old participants' intelligence test performance than measures of processing speed (with the exception of inspection time).

However, saying that speed of processing is not as universal a predictor as first assumed does not mean that it has no role in cognitive ageing. There is abundant evidence that speed of processing is strongly related to many aspects of ageing change in intelligence. For example, in an impressive meta-analysis of the research literature (172 studies, with a total of over 53,000 participants), Sheppard and Vernon (2008) demonstrated a reliable, significant correlation between speed of processing measures and cognitive ability. So general slowing almost certainly *does* play a role. The follow-up question concerning the *size* of this role is less easy to answer. As we have just seen, there seem to be many exceptions where speed of processing is not central to an ageing change. And when it is, the size of the effect can at first sight seem surprisingly small. For example, Salthouse (1985) found an average correlation of 0.28 between age and simple reaction times and 0.43 between age and choice reaction times. For those unfamiliar with statistics, this means that ageing can only account for about 8 per cent of the variability in simple reaction times and about 19 per cent in choice reaction times. This seems to indicate that the interest in reaction times is unmerited given that they have a relatively peripheral role to play. However, this would be an inaccurate conclusion. Salthouse has provided an ingenious, if mathematically complex, rejoinder, which demonstrates that changes in intellectual skills are *mediated* by the decline in processing speeds (Salthouse, 1985, 1991b, 1992b). In a similar manner, the chains connecting the carriages of a railway train are relatively unimportant in comparison with the power of the engine – but try pulling a train without the chains. For further consideration of this issue, see Salthouse (1992b).

Brain volume and intellectual skills

The relationship between reaction time and intellectual performance is a complex one, but nonetheless, and despite the caveats, a relationship exists. However, reaction times are only one possible gauge of neural health and efficiency, and it follows that other neural measures might also correlate with intelligence. For example, it is well established that the brain loses volume with age, though there have been disputes about the precise size of the decline (e.g. Coffey et al., 1999; Burgmans et al., 2009, and reply by Raz and Lindenberger, 2010). The same phenomenon has been observed for many subsections of the brain, such as the hippocampus, parahippocampal region and the amygdala (e.g. Jack et al., 1997; Kaye et al., 1997). We also know that there is greater loss for the cortical region controlling the non-dominant hand (Bonilha et al., 2009). Given such findings, one might reasonably expect ageing changes in the brain's structure to have psychological correlates, and such is the case. As will be noted in Chapter 6, the severe loss of brain tissue in dementia has a catastrophic effect on mental functioning. However, links can also be noted in normal ageing. For example, Deary et al. (2003) used magnetic resonance imaging (MRI) scans to examine the brains of participants in the follow-up to the 1932 Scottish Mental Survey described previously (see page 64). They found that circa 14 per cent of the variance in cognitive skills was attributable to abnormalities in the **white matter** of participants' brains. White matter takes its name from a substance called myelin that covers the nerves. Essentially, it is the part of the nervous system responsible for transmitting information – as opposed to **grey matter**, which is the cell bodies, synapses, etc., responsible for processing information. Other studies have found that white matter increases in volume through early adult life, before declining in middle-aged and older adults (e.g. Westlye et al., 2010), and this echoes the findings of the classic ageing curve of intellectual change. Martin et al. (2010) demonstrated that a pronounced decline in brain volume (more specifically, the anterior medial temporal lobe) in younger older adults is a significant predictor of the onset of **mild cognitive impairment (MCI)** (this is dealt with more thoroughly in Chapter 6, but in essence is a decline in intelligence greater than expected in typical ageing, but less severe than found in dementia). Furthermore, subsequent decline in brain volume is far commoner in older adults with MCI than in typically ageing individuals, who show less or even no further decline (Schuff et al., 2010).

The evidence is thus strong that there is a link between brain volume and intellectual performance in later life. But once again, caution must be exercised. First, a *lot* of physical and mental measures decline in later life. Finding that some measures decline in tandem is not all that surprising. Although there are logical grounds for assuming that a change in brain structure will have an effect on psychological abilities and thus giving credence to the correlations found in brain volume studies and similar, there *could* be confounding variables that simply have not been taken account of. This is a rather tenuous argument, but it cannot be totally dismissed. In any case, the size of the correlation between brain and performance changes is not necessarily overwhelming, with studies reporting correlations accounting for, for example, 19 per cent of the variance (Charlton, Barrick, Markus and Morris, 2010) and circa 25–26 per cent (Bergfield *et al.*, 2010). These are far from paltry figures, but nonetheless the correlation sizes leave room for plenty of other variables to also influence ageing change.

A second caveat reinforces this argument. Reading reports of ageing changes in the brain can easily give the impression that brain scans produce very clear pictures (literally as well as metaphorically) of changes in brain structure. In fact, the whole process is very complex, and measurements often have to be gleaned from advanced statistical analysis, rather than being immediate and face valid evident. A lot of brain structure research is still in its relative infancy; there are still considerable gaps in our knowledge and some debate exists over the best techniques for measuring change (e.g. Fjell *et al.*, 2009). However, what we cannot do is simply assume that, because different measures show a decline and are correlated, there is automatically a causal connection between them. To take a specific example: Rabbitt, Scott *et al.* (2007) examined white matter lesion prevalence, or WMLP (basically, the extent of damage/cell loss within white matter) in relation to a set of measures of mental ability. The researchers found that using basic correlations (which fail to account for complex interrelationships between the variables being measured) gave radically different findings from when more complex statistical techniques were used (which arguably give a more accurate analysis because they control for confounding variables, etc.). Using the optimal analysis available, Rabbitt *et al.* found that WMLP accounted for the age-related variance on measure of speed of processing but not the age-related variance of intelligence test performance. Analogous results were found in a later study by the same team (Rabbit, Mogapi *et al.*, 2008). These findings undermine a simplistic reading of the speed of processing hypothesis, suggesting that the reason for the relationship between speed of processing and fluid intelligence might simply be that they are fellow travelers, and both symptomatic of a more deep rooted and probably very complex set of ageing changes in neural processes. Further studies by the same research team have found similarly complex results – for example, that changes in brain volume were related to fluid intelligence test performance, but not several measures of memory (Rabbitt, Ibrahim *et al.*, 2008).

A third, and rather less tangible caveat is that the overwhelming impression that is gained from reading the brain volume literature is that we are doomed to an unavoidable mental decline because brain changes are unstoppable and seemingly inevitable. However, this is not quite the whole truth. First, as has already been noted, the correlations between brain volume and mental skills are not so large that room is not left for other influences as well. Second, research findings also indicate that lifestyle can to some extent offset ageing changes in brain volume. For example, Rovio et al. (2010) demonstrated that grey matter volume in later life was positively correlated with level of physical exercise in middle age (i.e. the more exercise, the more grey matter), but there was no relationship with white matter. Grey matter differences were notably concentrated in the frontal lobes. Again, Debette, Belser and Hoffmann (2010) demonstrated that level of excess body fat is associated with lower brain volume in middle-aged adults – in other words, eat too much and your brain is likely to shrink, with all the consequences this will have for intellectual functioning in later life (see also the commentary by Handel, Disanto and Ramagopalan, 2010).

The frontal lobe hypothesis

Changes in brain structure are not uniform, but tend to be concentrated in some areas more than others. We know from a range of studies (e.g. Shan et al., 2005) that a region affected particularly badly is the **frontal lobes** (see Appendix I). Changes in frontal lobe function in later life are well documented (see Band, Ridderinkhof and Segalowitz, 2002; Rabbitt, 1997; Shan et al., 2005). The frontal lobes are heavily involved in many forms of complex thought processes, particularly those involving planning sequences or remembering the order in which events occurred. In many instances, brain activity on a specific task produces several potential responses, and a principal function of the frontal lobes is to inhibit those responses that are not needed, allowing the correct response to be made. In other instances, several responses may be produced that need to be given in the correct sequence, and the frontal lobes ensure that it is this sequence that is given and that other possible sequences are inhibited. For this reason frontal lobe activity is often referred to as **inhibitory functioning** or similar. Evidence that older people show a decline in skills known to involve the frontal lobes is considerable (e.g. Chao and Knight, 1997; Friedman, 2003; Geraci, 2006; Isingrini and Vazou, 1997; McFarland and Glisky, 2009; Persad et al., 2002; Sanchez-Benavides et al., 2010).

However, once again, some caveats are needed. It is certainly true that frontal lobes are important, though early claims such as general intelligence being 'largely a reflection of the control functions of the frontal lobe' (Duncan et al., 1996, p.257) are now questionable. One key reason is because many 'frontal' effects are anything but 'frontal'. Some are confined to specific areas of the frontal region (MacPherson, Phillips and Della Sala, 2002; Phillips and Della Sala, 1998), and in any case, many of the 'frontal' deficits found in older people are qualitatively distinct from those seen in patients with frontal lobe damage (Phillips, 1999). Also, although frontal lobe problems play a key role in age differences on many cognitive tasks, they are rarely the sole area of the brain that is significantly involved (Foster et al., 1997; Robbins et al., 1998; Whelihan et al., 1997). On top of this, Rabbitt, Lowe and Shilling (2001) note that failing to account for differences in the statistical reliability and validity of different frontal lobes tests may lead to inaccurate estimates of loss of function. Parkin and Java (1999) demonstrated that a considerable degree of the difference supposedly due to frontal lobe deficits was removed if the scores on a digit-symbol substitution test and a fluid intelligence test (the AH4) were taken into account. Removing the influence of scores on crystallised tests had relatively little effect. In other words, much of the frontal lobe deficit may be a manifestation of a general change in fluid intelligence-related skills. This may apply not just to the frontal lobes but to many supposedly 'localised' effects. Salthouse, Fristoe and Rhee (1996) studied age changes in skills associated with the frontal, parietal and temporal lobes, and found that an average of '58 per cent of the age-related variance in a given variable was shared with that in other variables' (p.272). In other words, although different areas of the brain may each contribute something unique to the patter of age-related decline, a great deal of what they do is in tandem with other ageing changes.

However, these findings must be put in perspective. Arguing that frontal lobes do not have the overwhelming influence that researchers initially supposed does not deny the existence of frontal lobe problems. There are still many research papers being produced that identify frontal lobe dysfunction as being a prime cause of age differences in cognitive functioning. The distinction is that identifying an *important* cause does not mean that it is the *sole* cause. To make an analogy, a naturally clumsy man might break his leg. Seeing him struggling to get around on crutches may be ultimately part of the manifestation of his clumsiness, but that does not mean that the specific problems associated with a broken leg have gone away. In other words, whether frontal lobe problems are a cause of age-related decline, an effect, or a bit of both, does not stop them being a significant factor in considerations of ageing decline in intellectual skills.

Sensory changes and intelligence

Reaction times are not the only potential gauge of neurological decline in later life. Another useful measure is sensory abilities – in other words, quality of hearing, sight, touch, etc. It is well established that sensory abilities are positively correlated with intelligence test scores in older adults (i.e. the worse the sensory acuity, the lower the intelligence test score). For example:

- Lindenberger and Baltes (1997) found that, under certain conditions, measures of sensory and sensorimotor skills predicted the majority (59%) of variance in intelligence test scores in older adults. This relationship appears to grow stronger through adulthood.

- Baltes and Lindenberger (1997) found that the variability in intelligence test scores explained by the status of sensory functioning (as measured by auditory and visual acuity) rose from 11 per cent in a group of adults aged under 70 to 31 per cent in adults aged 70–103. In both age groups, sensory functioning was correlated with fluid intelligence. Dulay and Murphy (2002) found similar results.

- Finkel, Pedersen and Larsson (2001) found a strong correlation between olfactory and cognitive skills in a sample of middle- and older-aged identical twins. The authors concluded that a significant proportion of the relationship was genetically mediated.

- Marsiske, Klumb and Baltes (1997) found that older people's perceived level of basic competence and the degree to which they participated in social activities were both correlated with their sensory acuity (and particularly their vision).

- Clay et al. (2009) found that controlling for vision and processing speed removed age differences in fluid intelligence test scores.

The findings thus echo the arguments made earlier in this chapter that intelligence in later life is, to at least some degree, dependent upon physical health. At a simplistic level, the effect of sensory decline can be explained away in terms of poor sensory input leading to the mind having lower quality of materials to work with – thus, garbage in, garbage out. However, Lindenberger, Scherer and Baltes (2001) demonstrated that simply reducing sensory acuity in middle-aged people to the level of an average older person (using special glasses, muffling hearing, etc.) did not reduce cognitive performance to an older person's average level. Therefore, sensory change is about more than simply making input harder to see or hear. In any case, the finding that olfactory skills are related to intelligence makes a 'compromised input' argument implausible, since intelligence tests never assess or need olfactory skills. The explanation therefore lies at a deeper level, and must reflect a general ageing change that affects both cognitive and sensory processes to the same extent (see Li and Lindenberger, 2002; Scialfa, 2002; Stankov, 2005). In other words, we have returned to the general slowing hypothesis in another guise, and as with the general slowing hypothesis, although the basic findings are not in dispute, caution must be exercised in interpreting the results.

Arguably the biggest single problem is that although sensory decline correlates significantly with cognitive changes, the size of the correlation is sufficiently small to indicate that other factors probably also play a key role. For example, Dulay and Murphy's study cited earlier found that, although sensory and cognitive skills were correlated, there was additional variance accounted for by chronological age, implying that the sensory deficit explanation does not account for all ageing-related changes in cognitive skills. Lövdén and Wahlin (2005) reported analogous findings. Again, Lindenberger and Ghisletta (2009) in a thorough analysis of longitudinal data found that, although cognitive and sensory declines correlated with each other, the size of the relationship was only 'moderate'. Even when relatively strong correlations are found, there is some debate about whether sensory measures are correlated with all types of cognition. Several studies (e.g. Anstey *et al.*, 2002) have found correlations between some cognitive skills and sensory acuity, but not others. In Anstey *et al.*'s case, there were significant correlations between visual acuity and fluid intelligence (even after statistically removing the effects of age) but visual acuity could not statistically 'explain' performance on a face recognition task. The finding that sensory measures only correlate with some cognitive measures and not others (and studies do not necessarily agree on which skills correlate) raises uncomfortable thoughts of the early studies searching for critical loss in the terminal drop (see earlier in this chapter). Again, not all researchers have found a relationship: Hofer, Berg and Era (2003) found no correlation between sensory acuity and cognitive change, suggesting that whether it is found or not may depend upon the technique of analysis used (they used narrower age bands in their study).

Sensory changes thus appear to be a useful index of change but only at a relatively general level, with much of the variance left unexplained (and often thus labeled as a **general ageing effect**, which means that the effect is known to be linked to ageing, but its precise nature is unknown).

Another (and complementary) possibility is that older people with high IQs are likely to be better at looking after their health (e.g. going for regular eye tests) and may have had occupations that did not expose their senses to potential damage (e.g. working in a quiet office rather than on the factory floor). For example (with tongue only slightly in cheek), good senses and high IQ may be part and parcel of a more general factor of good self-preservation skills – and this returns us to the world of disuse theory ('use good self-preservation skills or lose your intelligence'). Newson and Kemps (2005) report that, in their six-year study of older adults, they found a significant correlation between sensory acuity and cognitive skills. However, a large amount of the variance could be accounted for by lifestyle activities. Therefore, a link between acuity and lifestyle may not be as frivolous as it may first appear.

Intelligence with everything?

So far this chapter has mainly examined intelligence in fairly broad terms – namely, what happens to general intelligence or intelligence as it is commonly divided up by psychometricians (fluid intelligence, crystallised intelligence, and so forth). In the remainder of this chapter, we shall examine the effects of ageing on a couple of specific *intellectual* skills, but, before doing this, one final comment is required. An often-repeated finding is that any change in intellectual skills in later life is highly correlated with changes in general intelligence (see Horn, 1982). For example, the following are all very strongly correlated with intelligence, and all show an age-related decline: memory for word lists; identifying briefly presented visual images (Walsh, Williams and Hertzog, 1979); pattern recognition (Walsh, 1982); finding solutions to anagrams (Witte and Freund, 1995); everyday problem solving (Diehl,

Willis and Schaie, 1995; Sorce, 1995); and speed of planning a driving route (Walker et al., 1997). This is merely the very tip of a massive iceberg, and the list could be continued for the rest of the book. The ubiquitous decline in any skill with a heavy reliance on intelligence led one noted researcher to state the following: 'Such changes in intellectual competence as may occur with ageing are much better picked up by a simple, brief, timed test of general intelligence, than by any single specific cognitive measure we have yet explored' (Rabbitt, 1984, p.113).

Pat Rabbitt is probably deliberately overstating the case, but certainly most intellectual changes in later life are strongly tied to, if not uniquely explained by, the decline in intelligence.

This raises a serious problem for some researchers. Suppose that an experiment discovers that older adults are significantly worse at mental arithmetic, and suppose also that this is explained by a general fall in intelligence. If one is interested in discovering what makes older and younger people different from each other, then this finding is dull, because it tells one nothing *new* about ageing – the drop in arithmetic skills has been shown to be nothing more than yet another manifestation of a general decline in intelligence that is already thoroughly documented. It is about as earth shattering as the finding that elephants have big toenails.

However, this is just one viewpoint, and there are grounds for doubting just how ubiquitous general intelligence is. First, the correlations between intelligence and other intellectual skills are not perfect. The variance in performance on the latter is not *only* explained by intelligence test performance – other factors must also play a role. Second, the fact that intelligence test performance correlates with other, mainly laboratory-based, measures should not surprise us; they are all arguably measuring the same skill of how well people perform in lab-based tasks. And as we have already seen, such measures do not necessarily reliably correlate with the real world. Third, Phillips (2005) neatly describes the superfluity of the whole issue with the following argument:

> If a researcher wishes to statistically predict age differences on a range of psychological measures, using indices of fluid intelligence will on average provide a useful way of mopping up a reasonable portion of the age-related variance. But this does not necessarily provide a useful theoretical mechanism to understand aspects of process. A cognitive neuropsychologist might argue: so what if an intelligence test which measures a complex mix of cognitive processes predicts variance in lots of other cognitive tasks? Does this provide any kind of theoretical advance? In contrast a psychometrician may argue: so what if tweaking an inhibition task influences the effects of ageing? Do these executive tasks have predictive validity? Both methods may have their place in understanding cognitive ageing, but they address different types of research question. (Phillips, 2005, pp.236–7)

Again, even if the correlation between general intelligence and a specific skill were 100 per cent, this does not mean that the experiment is of no value at all. In our example, the researchers may be able, from their results, to construct a detailed model of how ageing affects mental arithmetic (i.e. explain *why* the changes take place). If the findings are not used for model building, then the study might still be of value from a practical viewpoint. Thus, the study might lead one to exhort older adults to use a calculator when they go shopping.

Notwithstanding these comments, throughout this book there are examples of tests of intellectual ability, many of which demonstrate that the decline in a skill is attributable to general intellectual decline, and their value must be weighed against the consideration that they are really just an unremarkable facet of a well-documented phenomenon (an elephant's toenail, if you like). There are a variety of ways in which the effect of general intelligence on performance can be assessed. The two simplest are **matching** and **partial correlation**. The former involves comparing groups of people who are known to have the same level of ability at a certain skill. Thus, any difference between the groups cannot be due to that skill. For example, suppose younger and older people with the same intelligence test scores are compared on a task, and an age difference is found. This cannot be due to differences in intelligence. Matching is a useful technique, but it is often difficult to get good matches between people, especially in different age groups. In such circumstances, partial correlation may provide a solution. This is a statistical technique that is quite complex to perform, but relatively easy to explain. It assesses whether the relationship between two variables is due to the common influence of a third. To take a standard example, suppose some strange passion drove a researcher to measure schoolchildren's foot sizes and to compare these with their scores on a maths test. It is highly probable that there would be a good **positive correlation** between the two measures – that is, on average, the bigger the foot size, the bigger the test score. There is obviously not a causal connection between the two measures, so why the correlation? The answer lies in a third factor – age. Older children have bigger feet and also will perform better on maths tests. Therefore, the feet–maths correlation is the coincidental effect of the influence of a third variable (i.e. age). This can be demonstrated mathematically using the partial correlation technique. The children's foot sizes, test scores and ages are fed into the equation, and the coincidental effect of age is removed mathematically – that is, age is said to be **partialled out**. If, after this has been done, there is no longer a significant correlation between foot size and test scores, then it is valid to assume that the effect was attributable to the coincidental effect of age. The partial correlation technique is an important one in gerontology, because it enables researchers, among other things, to test if an ageing decline on an intellectual skill is solely due to the coincidental effect of a general fall in g. Further information about the mathematical rationale behind the method can be found in any general statistical textbook.

Attentional deficits in ageing

Attention is the ability to concentrate on and/or remember items, despite distracting stimuli (which may have to be simultaneously mentally processed). The frontal lobes (see earlier) are often cited as being involved in attentional processes. Attention manifests itself in several forms. The ability simply to concentrate on the task at hand without being distracted is known as **sustained attention**. A typical test of this might be to require a participant to respond every time a particular letter appears in a continuous stream of letters presented on a computer screen. Ability on sustained attention tasks is known to be quite well preserved in later life (Salthouse, 1982). However, there is some loss (e.g. Mani, Bedwell and Miller, 2005). Gauging the extent of 'true' loss is extremely difficult, however, because different measures introduce different confounding variables. For example, in some instances, decline may be a product of the test stimuli being hard to detect by older participants under any conditions rather than a failure of attention *per se* (see Giambra, 1993). It is also notable that older adults prefer visual attention tasks to occupy a small rather than wide visual field (Kosslyn, Brown and Dror, 1999). Carriere *et al.* (2010) compared different measures of sustained attention and noted that different measurement methods yielded different patterns of ageing change.

Selective attention refers to the ability to concentrate on the task at hand while there are other distracting stimuli present. A popular method of testing this is the **visual search task**. Participants are shown a display of (for example) letters, and are told to find a particular letter. Another is the **Stroop task**, in which participants must identify one feature of a stimulus while ignoring other features. In the basic version of this task, participants must identify the colour of a printed word. This is relatively easy, unless the printed word is the name of a different colour (e.g. the word 'red' printed in blue ink, and the participant is required to answer 'blue').

As with sustained attention studies, the degree of ageing decline in selective attention appears to be dependent upon the experimental method in question (e.g. Gamboz, Russo and Fox, 2002; Kramer and Strayer, 2001; Rogers, 2000; Walsh, 1982). Researchers have also found contradictory findings. For example, Rabbitt (1979) showed that older people did not take advantage of a feature of an experiment in which the target appeared more often in some positions than others. This was not because older people were unaware of the phenomenon: at the debriefing after the test session, they could accurately identify where the target was most likely to appear. Hence, they could accrue the information but not act upon it. Furthermore, repeated practice did not seem to improve their performance (Rabbitt, 1982). Other researchers, however, have failed to replicate Rabbitt's findings. For example, Gilmore, Tobias and Royer (1985) found that older people can use information conveyed by a visual array, and Nissen and Corkin (1985) showed that, in their experiment, older adults responded relatively faster to a target appearing repeatedly in the same position. McCrae and Abrams (2001) demonstrated that older adults retain information about position relatively more efficiently than visual aspects of a target (see also Madden *et al.*, 2004). Also, older adults' ability to ignore distracting information at fixed positions is preserved (see Einstein, Earles and Collins, 2002). Other studies have shown that the presence or absence of an effect depends upon relatively peripheral features of the experimental design, such as the size, shape and brightness of the stimuli (Albert, 1988).

Again, Maylor and Lavie (1998) gave participants the task of identifying a **target** contained within a set of letters presented in the centre of a visual display. In the periphery was a **distracter**. It was found that, relative to younger adults, the older participants were more affected by the distracter when there was a small number of letters to choose from than when there was a large number. This seems an interesting finding, but a subsequent study by Madden and Langley (2003) failed to find an age effect by altering perceptual load.

The research literature on selective attention contains many more examples of how using a slightly different test method or even re-analysing the data in a different manner can yield significantly different results (e.g. Cornelissen and Kooijman, 2000). A critical review by Guerreiro, Murphy and Van Gerven (2010) concluded that older adults became increasingly disadvantaged when some general conditions were employed (e.g. the target and distractor were in the same sensory modality). Changes can often be relatively mild and yet yield considerable changes. For example, Ben-David and Schneider (2010) presented younger adults with two versions of the Stroop task – one in 'normal' colours and one with desaturated colours (imitating the colour vision of older adults). The desaturated condition made younger adults perform in a manner that mimicked older adults. Measures of selective attention are thus very prone to experimental artifacts.

However, there is a danger that, because we can find problems in measuring selective attention, a decline in selective attention in later life is illusory. This is not the case. There is more than ample evidence that older adults display a decline in selective attention (e.g. McDowd and Filion, 1992; McLaughlin *et al.*, 2010; Watson and Maylor, 2002; Watson, Maylor and Manson, 2002). The debate is over the *size* of the change, not its existence. It is also important to note that the influence of selective attention, like the other forms of attention, extends beyond tasks that are very obviously centred on an explicit attentional task. We use attention in a vast range of everyday tasks (for example, it would be impossible to read this sentence without being able to attend to what is printed on the page rather than the visual surroundings). Thus, research in attention is about more than how participants perform in laboratory tasks (even if, after several hours of reading about the topic, this is all it seems to be to a less than fanatical observer). For example, Viskontas *et al.* (2004) demonstrated that attentional skills are strongly correlated with other cognitive skills in older adults. What happens in attention is often a guide to the general level of intellectual performance in older people.

Divided attention refers to the ability to attend simultaneously to and process more than one source of information. Many **working memory** tasks (see Chapter 3) fall into this category. However, there are many other ways of measuring divided attention, but the evidence in all cases almost invariably finds an ageing-related decline. Consider the case of **useful field of view (UFOV)**. This is in effect a measure of how much 'tunnel vision' people have in particular situations, and a person's UFOV can change according to the task they are doing. UFOV is measured by getting participants to fixate on a symbol presented in the middle of a computer monitor. Stimuli are presented at various distances away from this symbol, and the participants' ability to detect these is measured. The further towards the periphery the stimuli that are detected, the wider the person's UFOV. Older adults have smaller UFOVs, and the size of their UFOVs is correlated with their likelihood of having car accidents (e.g. Ball *et al.*, 1993). The problem becomes compounded in a divided attention task. When older adults have to attend to two types of information at once, their UFOVs shrink significantly more than younger adults' (Ishimatsu, Miura and Shinohara, 2010).

Another method of assessing divided attention is the **dichotic listening task**. Using stereo headphones, the participant is presented with a different message in either ear. Typically, the participant must report what he or she heard in either ear separately. Many researchers have shown that older people are bad at this task (e.g. Horn, 1982; Salthouse, 1985). More generally, researchers have found that there is an ageing deficit on tasks requiring the sharing of attention between two or more sources (e.g. Lajoie *et al.*, 1996; Vaneste and Pouthas, 1999).

A further set of studies measure balance or gait while performing mental tasks. It might be thought that maintaining one's balance while doing a mental problem is a relatively easy task, but it can be demonstrated that a person standing upright will shift their balance more markedly when performing a mental task. Older adults, who are poorer at balance, will make larger compensatory muscle movements (Fraser *et al.*, 2007). In dual tasks of this type, where the participant is attempting to do two things at once, people typically tend to pay relatively more attention to one task over the other. In general, older adults attempt to preserve walking/balance performance, whereas younger adults tend to invest more attention in the mental task (Cho, Gilchrist and White, 2008; Verhaeghen, 2011). This probably reflects an entirely rational fear of falling.

Conceptual organisation

The ability to treat items at an abstract level, in order to uncover basic rules and principles, is called **conceptual organisation**. It is often measured by using shapes and symbols where the rules that classify the groupings have been decided by the experimenter and it is the task of the participant to uncover these rules (e.g. 'shapes are grouped by colour irrespective of size and shape' or 'all shapes are grouped by colour and by shape', etc.). Researchers have shown that, in many instances, older people have difficulty in doing these sorts of tasks (see Filoteo and Maddox, 2004). Another test of conceptual abilities is the '20 questions' type of task. This is a version of the parlour game in which the participant is told that the experimenter is thinking of an object, and, by a series of questions to which the experimenter can only answer 'yes' or 'no', the participant tries to elicit the name of the object. Clearly, the optimal strategy is to narrow down the field by asking questions that progressively constrict the choice of alternatives (e.g. 'Is it an animal?', 'Is it a mammal?', 'Is it a household pet?'). This is called a **constraint seeking strategy**, because the choice of possibilities is increasingly constrained by each question. Eventually, when the list is down to a small number, it is best to switch to a **hypothesis scanning** question, where a specific item is named (e.g. 'Is it a dog?'). If a hypothesis scanning question is asked when the list is still large, then this is a foolish strategy, because the chances of hitting on the right name are too remote (e.g. asking 'Is it a dog?' having only established that the animal is a mammal).

Denney and Denney (1974) found that older people are far less efficient at the '20 questions' task. They had to ask more questions before getting the right answer, largely because they asked fewer constraint seeking questions. Older people are disadvantaged in an analogous fashion when they are given a range of items and asked to divide them into groups. Clearly a good strategy would involve the grouping of items into superordinate categories (e.g. 'animals', 'items of furniture'). However, older participants tend to produce more groupings where the linkage between items is illogical to an observer (Denney and Denney, 1973). It might be argued that the decline in categorisation skills is due to an artefact of declining memory (i.e. older adults cannot simultaneously keep in mind everything they need to sort through). However, varying the memory load by varying the number of items to be categorised has no appreciable effects on performance (see Rebok, 1987). Neither can differences in education level provide a total explanation (Cicirelli, 1976; Laurence and Arrowood, 1982). Nor again can a cohort difference in knowledge of how to deal with this sort of task, since even after being shown the best strategy older adults failed to use it as extensively as younger controls (Hybertson, Perdue and Hybertson, 1982). Maddox *et al.* (2010) found that, where older adults could learn the formal rules of a categorisation task, they nonetheless were worse than younger adults at integrating the information necessary to use the rules (i.e. they knew what to do in principle but in practice were less adept). These processes were underpinned by inhibition and working memory skills (see Chapter 3), which are known to be especially ageing-sensitive.

Some of the categorisation errors made by older adults can be qualitatively different. For example, Laurence and Arrowood (1982) found that, in a sample of older hospitalised (but not dementing) older adults, 42 per cent of them used **sentential grouping** to place items in the same category. For example, it might be assumed that 'rabbit' belongs in the category of 'animals' and 'carrot' in 'vegetables' but, in sentential grouping, rabbit and carrot can belong together because they can be used in the same phrase ('the rabbit ate the carrot'). This seems like a failure to think in abstract terms, and not seeing rabbits and carrots at a more abstract level of belonging to different semantic categories. Arguably a similar problem besets understanding many colloquial phrases such as proverbs. Taken at face value, the adage that people in glass houses shouldn't throw stones implies rather obvious advice to greenhouse owners. However, it might be intuitively assumed that knowledge of what proverbs mean is part and parcel of crystallised intelligence and thus relatively resistant to ageing decline. However, Albert, Duffy and Naeser (1987) found that older people were worse at interpreting the meaning of proverbs. This applied whether participants were left to provide their own answers unaided, or were given a multiple choice test. Furthermore, Arenberg (1982), in a longitudinal study, showed that younger participants' performance on a conceptual formation task improved on subsequent test sessions, while the older participants got worse.

Errors in conceptual organisation might thus be indicative of a deeper rooted problem with abstract thought. We shall return to this concept in the discussion of Piagetian task performance later. However, it may be observed that, when people make 'errors' in a classification task, they are only 'wrong' because their classifications do not conform with what the experimenter wanted. Grouping a carrot with a rabbit is perfectly sensible; although, in a wider scheme of things, it is not the most elegant solution, it is perhaps more fun (that participants might seek amusing solutions does not seem to occur to many experimenters). Denney (1974) argues that older people make grouping mistakes, not because of any 'decline' but because they forget the accepted 'correct' way of grouping things as defined by educational practice, and instead adopt an arguably more 'natural' method of grouping. This may be coincidentally related to education level and intelligence, because higher educated and higher intelligence people tend to enter professions and have leisure activities more demanding of formal grouping practices, and thus maintain these methods longer than other people.

Critics might argue that the studies reported here are relatively 'gentle' classification tasks. Where there is added difficulty (e.g. being required to transfer between categorising items in one way to categorising them in another), then age differences become more pronounced, and there is good evidence that this is attributable to differences in frontal lobe functioning (e.g. Kramer et al., 1995; Levine, Stuss and Milberg, 1995). However, these more difficult tasks may also be more demanding of other cognitive processes, and it is doubtful if they are testing the same genre of skill. It should also be noted that age differences are more pronounced if people try some categorisation techniques rather than others. For example, Filoteo and Maddox (2004) found that, if categorisation was based around rule-based learning, then age differences were less than if categorisation was based on integrating information. Similarly, Rousseau and Rogers (2002) demonstrated that there was little difference between younger and older adults who formed hypotheses about categories and tested them out, while for those who tried to 'form an impression' age differences were larger. This implies that, if people stick to tried and tested working methods, age differences are likely to be minimised.

Creativity in later life

Running in tandem with general intelligence is **creativity**. Researchers are divided on how best to describe the skill, but most would agree that for an act to be creative it must be novel, and it must be appropriate to the situation. The best way to demonstrate what is meant by this is to consider a typical creativity test. The participant is presented with a house brick and is asked to think of as many uses for it as possible. There are two types of response that are classified as being 'uncreative'. The first is appropriate but conventional (e.g. 'Use it in building a house'). The second is novel but inappropriate (e.g. 'Use it to cure insomnia by knocking yourself out with it'). A creative answer would be something like 'Scrape the surface of the brick to make rouge' (i.e. something both novel and feasible). People who produce a lot of creative answers are said to be good at divergent thinking (i.e. given a simple situation they can produce answers that diverge from mainstream thought).

Studies have found that older people are poorer at divergent thinking tasks, producing fewer answers and/or at a lower rate (Foos and Boone, 2008), peaking in their scores about the age of 40 (McCrae, Arenberg and Costa, 1987). It might be argued that this is because the older also have depleted intellectual skills in general. However, the age difference persists even when older and younger participants are matched for intelligence and education level (Alpaugh and Birren, 1977; McCrae, Arenberg and Costa, 1987). Among individuals who have always been very creative, this difference may be lessened or even absent (e.g. Crosson and Robertson-Tchabo, 1983). Again, Sasser-Coen (1993) has argued that divergent thinking becomes generally less important in the creative process as people grow older, with greater emphasis placed on items generated from personal experience. An important caveat to the findings of the these studies is raised by Simonton (1990) and separately by Hendricks (1999), which is simply that the applicability of divergent thinking tests, along with other psychometric measures, is debatable, and that they may not be reliable indicators of 'real-life' creative abilities in all cases.

Another way to consider creativity is the biographical approach. By this method, the lives of acknowledged leaders in fields of activity where originality of thought is highly prized are examined, to see what made or makes them 'better' than others. Some generalisations can be gleaned from such studies. Artists and musicians tend to display their talents early in life (e.g. Mozart), while scientists are usually in their twenties before they show signs of outstanding ability. In addition, scientists are often competent, but not outstanding students, until the area of specialisation in which they will become pre-eminent grips their imagination (Hudson, 1987). Charles Darwin was a classic example of this. Thereafter, most eminent persons make their major contributions to their field before the onset of old age. Most have a peak of creative output before they are 40. This applies to disciplines as diverse as mathematics, chemistry and musical composition. It is important to note that 'great' and 'routine' pieces of work tend to be produced in tandem. In other words, in a prolific period, a creative person will produce the same ratio of good to indifferent work as he or she will during relatively unproductive periods – thus, the **quality ratio** stays fairly constant (Simonton, 1990). Creativity has for *most* people relatively declined by their sixties (see Rebok, 1987). Although there have been several studies claiming that creativity continues to rise throughout life (e.g. Reed, 2005), it is notable that these often rely on self-report and self-perception, not on more objective measures. However, this is not *universally* true, and Butler (1967) has made a spirited counterattack to this view, citing numerous masterpieces produced late in their creators' lives. Titian, for example, continued to paint into his nineties, and most critics agree that his later work far surpasses his earlier output. However, Butler cites notable *exceptions*. For the majority of creative people, ageing is associated with a decline.

It can be argued that the sensory and physical declines of ageing will affect creative people especially badly, because above all others they need a precise, accurate and untiring view of the world (Rebok, 1987). Undoubtedly in some creative fields, where physical fitness is *de rigeur*, this is true. Opera singers and ballet dancers are never at their peak in old age (but equally, there are few ballet dancers over 35 who still perform on the stage). However, for the majority of creative persons, another explanation must be sought, since there is a long list of innovative people who have succeeded in spite of, or even because of, physical incapacity (e.g. Beethoven was deaf when he wrote many of his greatest works). Similarly, attribution for the effects of ageing cannot be laid upon a general intellectual decline, for two main reasons. First, because, as was seen from Alpaugh and Birren (1977) cited previously, age differences in creativity exist even when intelligence levels are matched. Second, intelligence is in any case a poor predictor of creativity (Hudson, 1987). Therefore, another explanation must be sought.

One possibility is that creative people are victims of their own success. Scientists who achieve pre-eminence in their field are likely to find themselves quickly elevated to headships of departments or research groups. Once in this position, much of the running of experiments and 'hands on' experience is passed on to research assistants, while the head of department finds him- or herself embroiled in an increasing quantity of administrative duties. Thus, the eminent scientist's reward for success at a particular endeavour may be to have his or her future activities in the field restricted, thus causing a decline in creative output. A different set of values probably applies to people pre-eminent in the arts. First, far more than scientists, artists (of any type) rely for their success on critical and public opinion. Accordingly, the worth of an artist depends upon what is fashionable at the time, and to be considered creative the artist must be seen as a leading interpreter of the fashion and/or to have been the creator of that fashion. A second consideration is that few artists are able to support themselves if their craft does not pay. Accordingly, if they do not achieve success in early life, they are likely to withdraw from full-time creative activity and seek other employment. It follows from these two premises that the creative person usually becomes noticed for being a skilled exponent of a current fashion at an early stage in his or her career. Obviously, the artist seeks to capitalise on this, and accordingly becomes increasingly identifiable with that fashion. However, opinions change, and almost inevitably the artist becomes a representative of a movement that is now unfashionable. The more successful he or she was, the more strongly he or she is now identified as being unfashionable. In short, successful artists are hoisted by their own petard (for a brilliant fictional account of this, see the shamefully under-regarded novel *Angel* by Taylor, 1957). The only solution for most artists is to move with the fashion. Since this probably involves a radical change of style, their output is likely to suffer. The speed at which these changes occur vary from discipline to discipline. Anyone with any knowledge of pop music will know that a cycle such as the one described occurs every three or four years. However, in any field, there are very few artists who produce 'timeless' works that rise above the mercurial changes of fashionable opinion. For example, a quick perusal through a second-hand bookshop or a musical dictionary will readily reveal how many 'geniuses' of literature and music from previous generations are now completely forgotten. Thus, the reasons behind the changes in creative output across the lifespan may be due far more to the lifestyles and job demands of the gifted than to ageing *per se*. Older people may have 'lost' their creativity because they were too good at their job earlier in life.

The above arguments apply to people who are outstanding in their field, but they do not deny a role for creativity in everyday life. It is important to note that, even where studies have found creativity scores to be lower in later life, nobody has argued that creativity is non-existent. This argument is not just a simple justification for older adults to pick up their paint brushes. It also counteracts the claims of some creativity advocates that mainstream psychology has claimed older adults are over the hill and lack creative powers. This is not the case – on objective measures, creative acts usually *decline* in later life. Nobody has said that they *stop*, nor that older adults should be barred from creative acts. In fact, there is considerable evidence that engaging in creative activity (e.g. painting, writing, and so on) is of considerable value to older participants, and is reported as enhancing feelings of well-being and general self-esteem (e.g. Hickson and Housley, 1997; Weisberg and Wilder, 2001).

Piagetian conservation

Papalia (1972) demonstrated that older people are bad at some of the **Piagetian conservation tasks** (named after their inventor, Piaget). This is a surprising finding, because most seven-year-old children can successfully perform them. The tasks in question test participants' knowledge that two items of equal volume remain of equal volume even when one of them changes shape. The participant is shown two balls of modelling clay of equal size and shape, and agrees that each is composed of the same amount of clay. The experimenter then rolls one of the balls into a sausage shape, and asks the participant if the two pieces have the same amount of clay in them, to which of course the answer is 'yes' (pedants note that one ignores the minuscule amount lost on the hands and table surface during rolling). It is surprising that ageing should cause people to fail what appears to be such a simple task (and indeed, Piaget thought it impossible). The decline is not limited to conservation of matter. For example, McDonald and Stuart-Hamilton (2002) conducted a replication of another of Piaget's studies, in which participants were placed at a table on which was a model of three mountains, each with a distinct feature (one had a snow cap, one had a house on it, etc.). The participants were shown a range of pictures showing views of the model from various positions around the table. Asked to select their own viewpoint, they could do this faultlessly. However, if now asked to select a picture representing what a doll positioned at another location around the table could 'see', participants made errors. Some of these were simple errors of spatial judgement (i.e. they chose a view that was close to that of the doll's, but nonetheless inaccurate). However, circa 15 per cent of older participants chose a view that was their *own*. This type of error – called an egocentric error – is illogical and is only otherwise seen when the task is given to younger children (typically aged 8 years or younger). There are similar surprising failings on other Piagetian tasks, such as moral reasoning (McDonald and Stuart-Hamilton, 1996), correctly drawing the water level in a tilting glass or bottle (Tran and Formann, 2008) and animism – the erroneous belief that some inanimate objects are alive (McDonald and Stuart-Hamilton, 2000; Parry and Stuart-Hamilton, 2009). Certainly, older people who fail Piagetian tasks are not incapable of performing them, since they can be easily retrained to do them correctly (Blackburn and Papalia, 1992).

Hooper, Fitzgerald and Papalia (1971) suggest that skills necessary to perform Piagetian tasks may be lost in the reverse of the order in which they were acquired during childhood, and may also be strongly linked with changes in fluid and crystallised intelligence. However, research by McDonald and Stuart-Hamilton (e.g. Stuart-Hamilton and McDonald, 1996, 1999, 2001) suggests a more complex tale. If older people's performance on a wide variety of Piagetian tasks is measured, then it is possible to create a 'Piaget score' (i.e. the total number of tests correctly performed). This is a better predictor of participants' ages than their intelligence test scores (Stuart-Hamilton and McDonald, 1996). In turn, the best predictor of Piagetian score is a personality measure called **need for cognition** (Stuart-Hamilton and McDonald, 1999, 2001). This is a measure of the drive a person feels to pursue intellectually demanding tasks as part of their lifestyle, as opposed to their actual level of intelligence. Overall, this implies that the changes in Piagetian performance may reflect an older person's level of involvement with intellectual tasks and (for want of a better expression) an 'intellectual lifestyle'. As a person gets older, he or she may become less committed to certain intellectual pursuits, and his or her methods and styles of thinking shift (no value judgement is implied in this – see Chapter 7). Such changes will correlate reasonably well with performance on intelligence test scores, but this is in part coincidental.

To some extent this echoes the argument by Labouvie-Vief (1992), who proposed a concept of **postformal thought**. This is a stage of intellectual development, which, it is argued, occurs in adulthood, after the stage of **formal operations** (the final stage of Piaget's theory of development in which people begin to think in genuinely abstract terms). Formal operations is very systematic and relies on logical processes. However, it can reasonably be argued that people do not spend their lives being logical, and that many important decisions are made by not only cold logic but also considerations of emotions and other subjective feelings. Accordingly, 'postformal thought' refers to this ability to weigh up and balance arguments created by logic and emotion, and is similar in some respects to the discussion of wisdom earlier in this chapter. However, while this is a useful operational distinction, it is debatable whether formal and postformal thought are intrinsically different, since arguments created from an emotional source and arguments created from a logical source can be combined logically, without the need for a 'new' kind of thinking. A cynic might argue that a further danger is that the theory might be used to excuse some age-related declines in intellectual performance by relabelling failures to perform tasks as examples of alternative strategies. It is also hard to justify a stage of postformal thought when there is evidence that a significant proportion of older adults are jettisoning earlier stages of Piagetian development. More probably, some older adults lose skills because they are no longer important in their lives (see Chapter 7 for further discussion of this point). This raises potentially awkward questions for more general studies of intellectual change in later life. Many studies have assumed that participants, both younger and older, are using the same set of mental skills, albeit with varying efficiency. However, if a significant proportion of older adults are using different logical systems, then is such a comparison fair or meaningful?

Summary – the bumblebee flies

There is an urban myth that states that, according to the best calculations of scientists, it is impossible for the bumblebee to fly. This is usually used as an illustration of 'What do scientists know?' and like most urban myths is a means to justify a cherished prejudice. The origins of this nugget of misinformation are uncertain, but a plausible explanation is that it was a misunderstanding of a mathematical model illustrating the limitations of a particular calculation technique (see McMasters, 1989). For our purposes, the story illustrates a different point. We can judge if bumblebees can fly simply by observing real life. This is an example of the acid test of much of science and social science – does what is modeled actually resemble or explain what is around us? In the case of ageing and intelligence, a lot of the findings are not in dispute at a general level. Finding that older people on the whole have a lowered level of intellect is not too hard to believe. The arguments for the effects of health (and *in extremis*, terminal drop) and exercise (mental and physical) are feasible. The problem arises when we start making claims for the *size* of some of these changes. A significant proportion of laboratory studies claim that the decline in intellect is very big indeed – so big that a sizeable proportion of older adults are at or below the level of a younger adult with intellectual disability. This raises three key possibilities.

First, that the models and observations are simply wrong. This seems improbable: quite simply, there is too much evidence that decline in these tests is real.

Second, perhaps the age changes are *exaggerated* by current calculations (particularly in the recent re-evaluations of the longitudinal data), as we have already considered, but nonetheless there are changes, and these have a central bearing on everyday life, not just laboratory conditions. But if there are changes of this magnitude, then clearly older adults do not show them in everyday life. Although older people might be stereotyped as being slower of wits and a little more forgetful, nobody has argued that many an older non-dementing adult is intellectually on a par with a young adult with very severe intellectual disabilities. Therefore, compensation must be playing a larger role in real life than has hitherto been appreciated. Interestingly, some of the most ardent supporters for there being very large changes in the 'true' scale of ageing decline are also the ones most likely to diminish the role of compensation. However, the greater the decline that is demonstrated in laboratory tasks, the greater becomes the case for there being compensation in real life.

To escape the conundrum presented by the second argument, a third possibility is that models are measuring a genuine change, but it is in skills that have limited relevance to real life. Many of the measures that have shown large ageing declines are either psychometric tests of intelligence or laboratory-based studies with tightly controlled conditions. At first such studies appear to be beyond reproach – they are rigorously standardised and/or run in conditions where confounding variables are kept to a minimum. Alas, this is part of the problem. A key aim of psychological measures is that they should be **culture fair** (i.e. accessible equally by people from all backgrounds). Thus, any elements of a test that could have much bearing on real life are often rigorously expunged, lest one group of people is unfairly advantaged by having greater experience of the real-life situation in question. The net result is that tests often lack direct relevance to the real world, and numerous researchers have noted the relatively poor correlations between standardised intelligence test scores and real-life abilities across a wide variety of conditions (e.g. Duckworth and Seligman, 2005; Estes *et al.*, 2010; Gould, 1981).

Thus, much of the study of intellectual changes in later life might be compromised by the simple fact that they are based on tests that have limited applicability to the world that real people (as opposed to test participants) live in. A case in point is that many factors that we know have an effect on everyday life, such as education, have little effect on the tightly controlled studies of psychometric intelligence test performance (Salthouse, 2010, p.109). This is presented by many researchers as proof that their measures are 'pure' and unsullied by cultural effects such as level of education. To quote one such example:

> It is also possible that although experience may not prevent decline, it could serve to obscure some of the manifestations of the decline. That is, age-related decline might occur among people at every level of experience or expertise, but if more experience is associated with higher levels of cognitive performance, then the greater experience often accompanied by increased age may functionally offset some of the declines associated with ageing. (Salthouse, 2010, p.153)

The revealing phrase here is 'obscure some of the manifestations of the decline'. With tongue in cheek, it is tempting to ask, 'How dare real life hide the true state of affairs as defined by a psychology laboratory?' What seems to be said is that studies of compensation and similar, that examine real-life skills, are 'obscuring' decline on measures conducted in a laboratory. In one sense, this argument is of course sound. But it is predicated on the assumption that the laboratory measures are more central and real than everyday behaviour, and this is far less certain. This is not the end of the possible criticisms of testing older adults, and we shall return to this subject in Chapter 7.

It should also be noted that some areas of debate in this area now rely more or less totally on statistical interpretation. Of course, statistical analysis has always been a lynchpin of this area, but increasingly it is turning from being used to confirm findings that everyone can see to analysing data sets that are essentially ambiguous. For example, many conventional 'old school' studies demonstrate that one group has a higher score than another or that one score is related to another score. Statistics in these instances simply show whether the difference or relationship in question is significant. In other words, the probability of it being a chance result is so low that we can assume that the same result would be found if we repeated the study, and thus what was found is representative of the whole population. Permutations of this (e.g. where we control for some confounding variables) are still essentially a case of what you see is what you get. However, the debates over, for example, the extent to which longitudinal studies are distorted by drop-out effects and similar, arguably move beyond this to a point where the issues have become one of mathematical interpretation rather than simply testing the validity of empirical observations. This is not necessarily wrong – complaining that an area of research has got a lot of mathematics in it is foolish. But for this author at least, there is a distinctly uneasy feeling that arguments about what is taking place in the real world are being increasingly decided by who has the most persuasive mathematical analysis. The danger with this approach is twofold. First, it is unverifiable by real-life observations.

The raw data are still the same, the real-life behaviour is just the same. But we are asked to take on trust that the mathematical model that in effect wins the most votes from other researchers best describes our lives. Second, the analyses used are statistical. Thus, they work, in essence, by claiming that they account for the greatest quantity of variability in the data. But this is not the same as a cut and dried and essentially logically watertight mathematical proof that can stand or fall on its own internal logic. We are being asked to take on trust that the statistical method chosen is the best available. And the problem with this is that successive waves of researchers have produced successive statistical models that claim just this – flip-flopping from one argument to another in the process. There is nothing to stop further attempts to duke it out with the best of the current models. Thus, the argument can continue *ad infinitum*. But the raw data and real-life experiences of the people involved still remain obstinately the same, no matter what interpretation is put on them.

Notwithstanding these considerations, older people have traditionally been seen as retaining crystallised skills and increasing their wisdom, while showing a decline in fluid intelligence. Research has generally backed this conclusion, but only at a relatively broad level. *Inter alia*, it should be noted that the size of the difference is in part an artifact of the experimental and analytical methods used, and part of the 'preservation' of crystallised intelligence relies on tests not being timed and/or marked rigorously. Where an age change is noted, it can be considerable. However, in all of the cases discussed, the cohort effect exaggerates it. Longitudinal studies lessen age differences, but they are also error-ridden, expensive and (obviously) time consuming to run. There is some evidence that, in older people, a sudden decline in intellectual abilities is a harbinger of death. Various models of ageing change have been proposed, including the disuse theory (that skills decline because they are insufficiently practised) and the general slowing hypothesis (that the changes are due to a slowing in neural conduction). The former has some validity (particularly through the related issue of compensation), but has difficulty in explaining why certain well-practised older people still display a worsening of skills. The latter theory is backed by some intriguing evidence (particularly Brinley plots), but evidence also suggests that at least some variability in skills is left unexplained. Declines in more specific intellectual skills, such as attention, conceptual organisation, creativity and Piagetian task performance, have all been well documented. However, in all instances, cohort effects or lifestyle changes may strongly colour the results. Indeed, in general, it would appear difficult if not impossible to decide how much of ageing change is due to cohort effects rather than 'pure' ageing.

Suggested further reading

Perhaps the best (and most readable) summary of the study of intelligence and how it is tested is provided by Deary (2001); although a short book, it covers a lot of ground and is very readable. More advanced texts covering a lot of the areas addressed in this chapter in much greater depth are Craik and Salthouse (2008) and Perfect and Maylor (2000). Readers should be cautioned that, although very erudite, these books require a high level of prior knowledge of advanced psychological and statistical techniques. The same caveat applies to Hertzog and Nesselroade's (2003) excellent critical review of methodological problems in testing older adults. There is a good review of attention and ageing by Kramer and Madden (2008). Salthouse (2010) provides a concise overview of his model of ageing and intelligence. These works remain required reading for anyone hoping to come to grips with mainstream psychological research on ageing and cognitive skills. Some of the classic journal papers and book chapters on the psychology of ageing, particularly cognitive ageing, can be hard to find without using an inter-library loan or similar. Lawton and Salthouse's (1998) edited collection, *Essential Papers on the Psychology of Aging*, contains many of the widely cited papers and is warmly recommended. A more critical consideration of problems with testing older adults is provided by the present author in Chapter 7 of this book and in another work (Stuart-Hamilton, 1999b).

CHAPTER 3

Ageing and Memory

Introduction

The study of the psychology of memory has generated a large number of concepts and technical terms, and a brief survey of at least some of these is necessary before an examination of the effects of ageing on memory skills can begin. A belief held by many lay people is that memory is a homogeneous skill: that is, everything is memorised in the same way. This is erroneous, simply because physiological research has demonstrated that different types of memories (e.g. for words, pictures, physical skills) are stored in anatomically different sections of the brain. Furthermore, psychologists have found that these memory systems also behave in different ways. Accordingly, when researchers talk, for example, of 'verbal' or 'visual' memories, they can be confident that they are discussing anatomically and functionally distinct systems.

One of the simplest ways of categorising memories is by the length of time over which they are retained, and this usually means a division into **short-term memory (STM)** and **long-term memory (LTM)**. Short-term memory is the temporary storage of events and items perceived in the very immediate past: that is, events and items that occurred no more than a few minutes ago, and usually a much shorter period (i.e. the last few seconds). The classical test of STM requires the experimenter to read out a list of letters, numbers or words, and get the participant to repeat it back. The longest length of list of these **to-be-remembered (TBR)** items that can be repeated back reliably is called the participant's **span**. Spans vary according to the nature of the TBR items and, thus, there is usually a prefix denoting the materials used in the test. Hence, **digit span** denotes memory for numbers, **word span** memory for word lists, and so forth.

One of the problems with the classical span experiment is that it is not very realistic: people simply do not spend very much of their time learning arbitrary lists. Another point is that STM is impermanent: unless an especial effort is made, the memory fades within a brief time. A popular explanation of why there is a short-term store, and how it might function, is provided by Baddeley and Hitch's (1974) working memory model. Working memory is defined as 'the temporary storage of information that is necessary for such activities as learning, reasoning, and comprehension' (Baddeley, 1986, p.324). Thus, typical tasks involving working memory 'are those in which the person must hold a small amount of material in mind for a short time while simultaneously carrying out further cognitive operations, either on the material held or on other incoming materials' (Morris, Craik and Gick, 1990, p.67).

This is a form of STM that most people can intuitively appreciate that there is a need for. For example, in listening to speech, it is necessary to keep in mind what a person has just said in order to make sense of what is currently being said. Another example of working memory in action is mental arithmetic. All the figures of the sum have to be retained (in the right order) while the arithmetic transformation is performed on them. Note that in both these instances something has to be remembered while another mental operation takes place.

Full details of how the working memory model is presumed to operate are still far from finalised. However, in its basic form the system is said to be controlled by the **central executive**. This is in part a memory store (though with a limited capacity) and in part a controller of several **slave systems**. These have larger memory capacities than the central executive, and each specialises in only one type of memory. Thus, there are separate systems for verbal material, pictures and spatial position. The verbal material system is called the **phonological loop** (in some older texts it is called the **articulatory loop**). This deals with words in the broadest possible sense, and thus not only memorises letters and words but also numbers. The central executive controls the depositing and retrieval of memories to and from the slave systems. When **concurrent processing** is required (i.e. maintaining a memory and doing another attention-demanding task at the same time), the central executive helps to co-ordinate these. It is important to note that, if there are too many TBR items to fit in the slave systems (i.e. the slave systems by themselves cannot remember everything sent to them), then some or all of the items can be transferred to LTM (see Baddeley, 2010), which thus acts as a back-up.

Memory traces quickly fade from STM for the simple reason that the vast majority of information taken in is only of value at the time, and afterwards is highly redundant. To return to the example, remembering the numbers in a mental arithmetic problem is necessary at the time, but to keep remembering them afterwards would be both an irritation and a waste of memory space. However, there is obviously some information that *does* need to be remembered more permanently, and this is the role of long-term memory.

Long-term memory seeks to be a permanent store of information. Whether it has a maximum capacity and how much information is lost from it are unanswerable questions. However, it is certainly the case that, for people not suffering from amnesia, 'essential' and 'everyday' information is never lost. For example, people do not forget their native language, their names, the name of the capital of France or toilet training. In all probability, this is because such information is either very important to them and/or it is frequently **rehearsed** (i.e. the memory is recalled and thus 'practised') so that they form strong, unshakeable **memory traces**. Some information *is* lost from LTM, however (e.g. old addresses, telephone numbers, etc. tend to be forgotten when friends move). These lost memories tend to be information that either is now irrelevant and has been superseded, or is unimportant, so it is infrequently rehearsed. The classical test of LTM is the same as the STM 'span' procedure, except that the participant is required to hold the TBR items in memory for a longer time (typically, anything from 30 minutes up to several days). If the reader is wondering why participants do not forget the TBR items as with the STM experiment, the simple answer is that the participants are encouraged to rehearse them.

Another method of categorising memory is into **episodic** and **semantic memories** (Tulving, 1972). Episodic memories are of personal experiences (a deceptively similar concept is **autobiographical memory**, referring to memory for events specific to one's personal life). Semantic memory is for items independent of personal experiences and is a store of facts, such as general knowledge or academic learning. A further system divides memory into **explicit** and **implicit memories** (Graf and Schachter, 1985). This refers to the distinction between a memory that is consciously sought (e.g. trying to recall the date of the Battle of Waterloo) and one that can be gleaned from memory, but which has not been deliberately stored. For example, one method of testing implicit memory is to expose a participant to a list of words in the guise of a psychological task (e.g. grading words for the level of visual images they provoke). At a later time, the participant is given a **word completion task**, in which a word must be provided, having been given its first letter or letters (e.g. 'complete FOR_ _ _'). The participant is more likely to provide a word he or she has encountered in the previous list (e.g. 'FOREST' rather than 'FORGET'), even though he or she may be unaware that these memories are being drawn upon. In other instances, implicit memory may refer to inferences which may be drawn from memories, even though the inferences themselves have not been explicitly stored. For example, people can readily answer the question 'Does Elton John have two legs?' by extrapolating the information from the memory that Elton John is a pop singer, pop singers are humans and humans are bipedal. In short, people can have a 'memory' that Sir Elton has two legs, even though it is not stored as an explicit statement of fact.

Tangential to these domains of memory are the skills of planning and overseeing. One of the commonest uses of memory is to remember to do something in the future, or **prospective memory**. Conceptually related to this is **metamemory**, which is knowledge about one's own memory – what its capacity is, how best to remember things, and so forth.

Memory systems can also be considered in terms of how they work: for example, how memories are created for storage (**encoding**) and how they are retrieved. There is a considerable debate within psychology as to whether memories are lost through inefficient coding or inefficient retrieval. The inefficient coding hypothesis can be likened to a library where an incompetent librarian puts books on the wrong shelves, so that when a search is made for a book it cannot be found in its rightful place. Similarly, memories that are inefficiently encoded will be lost because they cannot be retrieved. The inefficient retrieval argument is that memories are lost because, although they are stored properly, the search for them is inefficient. To return to the library analogy, it is as though a person with severe dyslexia were sent to find a book. This issue is of especial importance in discussing the memories of people with dementia (see Chapter 6).

Memory can be tested in a variety of ways. The commonest distinction is between **recall** and **recognition**. The former requires a participant to report as much as possible of a list of TBR items. In an **ordered recall** task, the participant is only marked correct if all TBR items are repeated in their exact order of presentation (e.g. if TBR items are *17654*, the participant must recall *17654*; *71546*, for instance, is not sufficient). In a **free recall** task, the order of recall does not matter (thus, *71654, 71546, 56147*, or any other permutation of these numbers would be equally acceptable). A recognition task is considered to be easier than a recall task. Both begin with a presentation of the TBR items. However, in a recognition task, the participant's memory is tested by having to select the items he or she has seen (the *targets*) from a list that also includes items that were not on the original list (the *distracters*). Participants tend to remember more items in a recognition than in a recall task, because the memory load is lighter (it is also worth noting that the recognition and recall processes are almost certainly controlled by different mental mechanisms). In a **cued recall** task, the participant is in effect given a hint about the answer (e.g. he or she might be given the first letter or letters of the TBR word).

Having thus briefly considered some of the technical terms, theories and techniques employed in memory research, attention will now shift to how ageing affects memory.

Ageing and short-term memory

If a basic short-term memory span test is administered (where the participant simply repeats back what the experimenter has just said or shown), then several studies have demonstrated a statistically significant but nonetheless rather small decline in later life (Craik and Jennings, 1992; Craik *et al.*, 1995). However, when any extra demands are placed on participants, then age effects generally become very much more pronounced (Cohen, 1996; Craik, 1986). Bopp and Verhaeghen's (2005) meta-analysis of research data found a mean span of 7.6 for younger adults compared with 7.1 for older adults. This difference grew the more complex the task became (for the records: backwards span was the next most complex, followed by working memory). The authors used a Brinley plot to reduce this pattern of differences to a single linear relationship (see Chapter 2).

One method of making a short-term memory task more complicated is the **backward span** procedure, where the participant is required to repeat the items back in reverse order of their presentation (e.g. TBR items are *75123*; participant must reply *32157*). This is clearly harder than straightforward recall, since participants must keep in store the items in their correct order while simultaneously working out what they are in reverse (in essence, this is a test of working memory). Bromley (1958), among others, has shown that older people are significantly worse at this task. A curious exception to this rule is the **Corsi Blocks Test**, where the backwards and forwards spans are the same, though this might be due to a specific feature of the test design (see Kessels *et al.*, 2008).

Several causes have been suggested for older people's relatively poorer backwards span. One is that, because the items in the forward and reverse lists are identical, it is easy to confuse the two, and thus form a garbled amalgam. This implies a failure of planning of mental materials and thus problems with frontal lobe functioning (see Thompson-Schill *et al.*, 2002). Thus, just as a decline in frontal lobe functioning may have a significant influence on other cognitive tasks (see Chapter 2), so might it do in memory. This failure to distinguish between irrelevant and necessary information is sometimes described under the heading of the **inhibitory deficit hypothesis** (see Hasher, Zacks and May, 1999). The hypothesis can also be demonstrated in working memory tasks in which older participants are disproportionately disadvantaged on later trials of the experiment, because the accrued earlier lists of TBR items have not been properly 'flushed out' and thus interfere with memory of the new TBR items (Bowles and Salthouse, 2003). Hedden and Park (2001) similarly demonstrated that older adults have an especial difficulty in distinguishing between items from earlier TBR lists and items in a current TBR list. The inhibitory deficit hypothesis has been applied to other mental processes besides memory. For example, Morrone *et al.* (2010) ingeniously demonstrated its role in discriminating between metaphors and literally false statements. Butler and Zacks (2006) used the theory to explain why older adults are significantly impaired relative to younger adults in suppressing a previously highly practised response (in this instance, eye movements). Evidence from brain scans indicates that the phenomenon can be attributed to a failure by older brains to inhibit activity associated with irrelevant stimuli (e.g. Alain and Woods, 1999; Gazzaley *et al.*, 2005).

The inhibitory deficit hypothesis is widely cited but, as with many other models of psychological ageing, it is not universally found in all memory conditions. For example, Aslan, Baumi and Pastotter (2007) did not find evidence of an ageing- related deficit in **retrieval-induced forgetting** in episodic memory. If older adults have an especial problem with inhibition in all types of memory, then this should not be the case. However, it should also be noted that finding behavioural measures and techniques that are exactly equivalent across different types of mental process is a very difficult task (see Alain and Woods, 1999), so finding lack of evidence for the hypothesis might simply reflect a problem with experimental procedure rather than the theory. Of course, the converse of this is that the theory thus becomes unfalsifiable, since not finding evidence for the theory can then always be attributed to a fault in the study. We should also be wary of the inhibitory deficit hypothesis for a further reason. What it is arguing is that older adults have poorer abilities at inhibiting irrelevant stimuli. But a relative failing of inhibition is unlikely to occur by itself in older brains – it is also likely to be associated with a large number of other declines in both brain structure and mental processing. It is thus rather akin to the frontal lobe hypothesis (see Chapter 2). In other words, how much of the effect is down to pure inhibition and how much to a general ageing effect has arguably not yet been established. This does not deny a role for the inhibitory deficit hypothesis, but it does raise a question mark over the uniqueness of its contribution.

Moving to the effects of ageing on working memory, Baddeley (1986) cited the central executive as the prime cause of this age-related decline in short-term memory. Given that the central executive is felt to be anatomically centred on the frontal lobes (see Baddeley, 1995; Dahlin *et al.*, 2009; Tays *et al.*, 2008), this makes intuitive sense. Although something of a simplification, what is being argued is that memory span is relatively unaffected by ageing – the principal deficit is in organising the material that is to be remembered and in juggling different tasks when doing something more complex than simply remembering a list of items. For example, it can be readily demonstrated that increasing the complexity of the distracting task in a working memory task disproportionately affects older people's recall (e.g. Mitchell *et al.*, 2000; Morris, Gick and Craik, 1988; Verhaeghen, 2011; Zeintl and Kleigel, 2010). Note that the distracting task does not have to be overtly cognitive. For example, Lindenberger, Marsiske and Baltes (2000) found that walking whilst memorising was sufficient to impair memory in older people, and the more complex the path to be walked, the disproportionately greater the decline in older adults' memories. Again, Maylor, Vousden and Brown (1999) present an ingenious model linking STM for serial order to a combination of frontal decline and response slowing. Findings such as these thus support the argument that a principal component of age-related decline in short-term memory is in the processing of information, rather than the storage *per se*. Given this finding and the argument that both memory and other aspects of cognition both appear to be strongly influenced by the state of frontal lobe functioning, it is fairly predictable that ageing changes in short-term memory ability are strongly correlated with fluid intelligence (Salthouse, 1991b), speed of processing (Bryan and Luszcz, 1996; Byrne, 1998; Fisk and Warr, 1996; see also Rabbitt *et al.*, 2007) and, more broadly, with other indices of central nervous system functioning, such as visual acuity (Salthouse *et al.*, 1996). To this extent short-term/working memory decline may be seen as little more than part and parcel of general intellectual ageing. It is thus not surprising to find that the decline in ability to inhibit is held by many commentators to be a key factor in ageing memory decline. However, as with the frontal lobe hypothesis in Chapter 2, we should be cautious about over-applying the theory. Bowles and Salthouse (2003) found it does not explain all the variance in memory scores (see also Robertson, Myerson and Hale,

2006), and Burke, Mackay and James (2000) note that inhibition can be difficult to define accurately. Maylor and Henson (2000) found that the **Ranschburg effect** was greater in older than in younger adults on a task requiring participants to recall letter lists in their correct order. The Ranschburg effect is the deterioration in memory performance when items are repeated in a list of TBR items (e.g. that ATYABF would be harder to recall than ATYMBF). It is argued that this is because inhibitory processes tend to act against repeating items. If inhibition is failing in older adults, one would expect the Ranschburg effect to be less pronounced but, as Maylor and Henson demonstrated, the reverse is true. Thus, although inhibition is a good predictor of ageing memory performance, it is not the sole predictor (see also Maylor, Schlaghecken and Watson, 2005).

Thus, short-term memory tasks such as backwards span and working memory paradigms present compelling evidence of an age-related decline. However, there is an important caveat to these findings. Some researchers use the difference between forward and backward spans as a 'benchmark' gauge of ageing decline. However, Ryan, Lopez and Paolo (1996) argue that this is too variable between test sessions to be of value, whilst Gregoire and Van der Linden (1997) go further and argue that there is no age difference in the size of the effect (a finding echoed by Myerson *et al.*, 2003).

However, this is not the only problem besetting older people's short-term memory skills. A study by Belmont, Freeseman and Mitchell (1988) suggests that older people may encode information in STM using less efficient strategies. This concerns a memory process called **chunking**. Given a long string (>4) of TBR items, a better strategy than trying to remember them as one long string is to think of them as a series of groups of three or four items. For example, instead of trying to remember *345172986142* as *345172986142*, a better strategy would be to think of it in chunks of three as *345 172 986 142*. Precisely this principle is used in the presentation of credit card and telephone numbers. Belmont *et al.* demonstrated that older people are less likely than younger people to chunk long digit lists when trying to encode them. However, it is worth noting that some older participants *did* chunk, and their spans were as good as the best of the younger participants. Other researchers have also noted that older people do not arrange TBR items and that, without prompting, they do not pay as close attention to them. In other words, they do not process the items 'deeply' enough (e.g. Craik and Rabinowitz, 1984). Furthermore, older adults may at a broader level change their memory strategies. For example, Brébion, Smith and Ehrlich (1997) argue that, when given a working memory task in which a set of TBR items had to be remembered in tandem with performing a sentence comprehension task, the older participants tended to place greater emphasis on the comprehension than the memory task. This echoes the findings on attentional tasks cited in Chapter 2, where older adults will tend to invest relatively more attention to walking and balance than to concurrent mental problem solving.

However, not everybody has found evidence for different use of strategies explaining age differences. For example, Bailey, Dunlosky and Hertzog (2009) found that although different strategies did have an effect on working memory task performance, this accounted only for differences between individual participants (regardless of age). When age differences were specifically looked at, these were best described by differences between old and young adults' processing speeds – their strategy use did not greatly differ. In other words, although strategy use can account for some of the difference between age groups, when this is controlled for, a strong age difference remains. This does not mean, however, that strategy use is ineffective in and of itself. It can be readily established, for example, that training in techniques to improve working memory aid older and younger adults (e.g. Carretti, Borella and De Beni, 2007; see also Lemaire, 2010). One method is to train older people in the **method of loci** technique. This involves memorising a series of mental pictures of familiar scenes, such as the rooms in one's house. Each TBR item is mentally placed in a scene, and then the list is recalled by making an imaginary journey, recalling what was stored in each picture. Suppose that one was given the list *15794* to recall. One might imagine entering one's house. A *1* is sticking through the letter box, a *5* is in the umbrella stand. Entering the living room, *7* is sitting on the sofa, whilst next door *9* is helping himself to a large drink. Going into the kitchen, *4* is peeling potatoes. The purpose of the technique is to make each image as vivid as possible and, accordingly, more memorable. Smith *et al.* (1984, cited Rebok, 1987) using native Berliners as participants, found that they could increase their digit span by using familiar Berlin street scenes as loci. Herrman, Rea and Andrzejewski (1988) have also reported improvements in the memory of older participants after training, but noted that training only aided the particular memory task involved – the advantages did not transfer to other forms of memory. Improving digit span, for example, does not automatically aid recall of pictures. This effect has been noted in all age groups (i.e. it is not just a phenomenon of ageing).

It must also be borne in mind that the method of loci technique is also used more efficiently by younger than older adults. For example, Lindenberger, Kliegl and Baltes (1992) found that older participants performed less well than younger controls on a method of loci task, even in comparisons of older experienced graphic designers (with good spatial skills) and younger people with no especial spatial skills. Singer, Lindenberger and Baltes (2003a) reported at best very modest gains in memory performance in older old people (75 years+) following training in mnemonic techniques. However, for younger older adults, memorisation training can be effective and retained (at least over eight months, as shown in a study by Derwinger, Neely and Bäckman, 2005), and generally training is reported as efficacious (e.g. Cavallini, Pagnin and Vecchi, 2003). In a meta-analysis of memory training studies, Verhaeghen, Marcoen and Goossens (1992) concluded that training was beneficial, resulting in a net gain of about 0.3 standard deviations in performance (though younger adults' performance improvement was even greater). Similar conclusions were reached by Ball *et al.* (2002).

Ageing and long-term memory

As mentioned in the Introduction, the 'basic' LTM and STM tasks are identical, save that the time gap between presentation of the TBR items and the request for their recall differs. Whereas the age differences in basic STM tasks are significant but quite small, there is a very pronounced effect in the case of LTM (Albert, 1988). This may not be very surprising, since much of the information passing into LTM must first be processed by STM, and any defects in STM may be magnified over the time items are stored in LTM prior to recall. Much of the recent work on ageing, however, has moved beyond the rather arid 'laboratory studies' of long-term retention of arbitrary lists of words and digits to more realistic everyday memory tasks, and this chapter will concentrate on these.

For example, it is also known that, when compensatory strategies can be used in a realistic situation, the age difference diminishes. Castel (2005) demonstrated that, if a range of groceries were priced ludicrously cheaply or expensively, older adults were less able than younger adults to remember these unrealistic prices. However, if the groceries were priced realistically, older and younger adults recalled the prices equally well.

Remote memory

Remote memory is for non-autobiographical events that occurred within a person's lifetime. It is usually tested by giving participants a list of names and/or descriptions of events that have been 'in the news' over the past 50 or so years, and asking them to indicate which they can remember. One such example is the **Famous Names Test**, or **FNT** (Stevens, 1979), which comprises a list of names of people. Participants simply have to indicate which names they recognise. The list comprises:

- groups of names of people who were briefly famous in the 1970s (e.g. John Conteh, a boxer), 1960s, 1950s, 1940s or 1930s (e.g. Reggie Whitcombe, a golfer)

- a group of very famous names (e.g. Winston Churchill), whose non-recognition might indicate dementia

- a group of fictitious names.

The names are presented in a scrambled order and participants are warned that some of the names are fake (thus preventing them from cheating by claiming that they recognise every single name on the list).

Stuart-Hamilton, Perfect and Rabbitt (1988) tested participants aged 50–80 on the FNT and found that, for all ages, memory of recent names was better than for distant ones. This phenomenon has been observed by many other researchers (e.g. Craik, 1977; Perlmutter, 1978; Poon et al., 1979), and contradicts the once popular

Ribot's hypothesis (Ribot, 1882). This argues that, in older people, memory for recent events should be worse than for remote ones. A useful analogy is to think of the brain as a long deep tank, into which memories, in the form of water droplets, are deposited. Obviously, it takes a long time for the tank to fill, but, when it does, water starts to flow over the edge of the tank and is lost. This overflow is likely to be composed of recently deposited water that is lying on or near the surface: the older deposits deeper in the tank are unlikely to be much disturbed and hence are not lost. In a similar manner, Ribot's hypothesis argues that recently deposited memories are more likely to be displaced because they are not sufficiently 'bedded in'. However, experimental evidence indicates that it is the remote, not the recent, memories that are lost.

In terms of the number of names correctly recognised, the FNT is a rare example of a psychological test in which older participants outperform the younger. Having acknowledged this, there are problems in accurately interpreting what the findings mean. The most serious difficulty is that the youngest participants in the Stuart-Hamilton *et al.* (1988) study were in their fifties when the experiment was run (*c.*1987), and thus would be hard-pressed to remember the earliest names on the FNT (from the 1930s). In a second experiment in the same paper by the authors, 20-year-olds, who could not possibly know the older names except as 'historical' figures, were given the FNT. However, they could still accurately recognise about 25 per cent from each decade group (the participants correctly rejected all or most of the false names, so they were not simply guessing). This means that a proportion of items on remote memory tests are probably recognised from semantic memory rather than as genuine 'only experienced at the time' remote memories. In short, remote memory tests may in part assess remote memory, but the answers are heavily contaminated with recollections from a store of general knowledge. Furthermore, the relative likelihood of a particular name on the FNT being recognised was relatively similar for participants of different ages. In other words, if 'Miss X' were the tenth most recognised name amongst participants in their seventies, she was likely to be at or around tenth position amongst those aged 60, 50 or 20 (Stuart-Hamilton *et al.*, 1988). This suggests that supposedly 'remote' names may be rather more frequently aired in the media than researchers suspect, and the similar 'league tables' of popularity for different names implies that the impact of media coverage is remarkably consistent for different age groups.

This argument is supported by research by Basso, Schefft and Hamsher (2005), which found that in very old (90 years+) participants, scores on the Presidents Test (a measure of knowledge of the temporal order in which the last eight US presidents had held office) are significantly worse. The same researchers also found that education level was positively correlated with remote memory (a finding echoed by Lalitha and Jamuna, 2006). These results support the argument that remote memory tests might reflect exposure to the news media, since we would expect more highly educated people to read more and be more aware of recent history, and we might also hypothesise that very old people might find themselves less exposed to news media and similar through deteriorating senses.

Thus, whilst remote memory may exist, testing it remains fraught with difficulties, and measuring it in a 'pure' form, uncontaminated by general knowledge, is probably impossible. However, the measure can be useful in assessing patients with dementia (see Chapter 6), since notable errors can occur relatively early in the illness. For example, Storandt, Kaskie and Von Dras (1998) found that (American) participants' scores on the Presidents Test was impaired in demented patients even in the early stages of the illness. However, the area of ageing and remote memory remains under-researched (Basso et al., 2005).

Eyewitness testimony

As the title suggests, eyewitness testimony refers to the ability to remember information about an incident that has been seen once. In 'real life', eyewitness memory forms the basis of many legal cases, and experimental measures of eyewitness testimony have tended to present participants with an enacted incident (either 'in the flesh' or on video tape). Generally, older people are found to be as good as younger adults at remembering the main points of an incident, but show some worsening of recall of relatively minor points, such as details of the clothing of the protagonists (e.g. Adams-Price, 1992). For example, if a simple 'score' of overall information recalled is made, then there is an appreciable age difference (e.g. Yarmey and Yarmey, 1997). This does not bode particularly well for the credibility of older adults as eyewitnesses.

Such a feeling is not enhanced by the findings of Coxon and Valentine (1997). They directly compared the responses of older and younger adults and children to a series of misleading and non-misleading questions about a crime video they had witnessed. It was found that both the older adults and children performed less well than the younger adults. A study by Karpel, Hoyer and Toglia (2001) found that older adults were more susceptible to misleading information surrounding a vignette depicting a theft. Not only did they subsequently report more pieces of misinformation as 'fact', but their level of certainty that the misinformation was real was significantly higher than in younger adults. This is echoed in a study by Dodson and Krueger (2006). They found that when older adults were most confident of their memories, they were also *most* likely to commit suggestibility errors. For younger adults, the reverse applied. Aizpurua, Garcia-Bajos and Migueles (2009) produced analogous findings. Again, in a review of the literature, Cohen and Faulkner (1989) note that older people are more prone to believing that an interpretation of an event is the actual memory of the event (see also Kensinger and Schachter, 1999). This means that there may be a greater danger of the memory of an event being distorted to fit a subsequent interpretation, thereby removing the objectivity of an eyewitness account. Overall, therefore, the view is a pessimistic one (see LaVole, Mertz and Richmond, 2007) and is plausibly linked to a decline in frontal lobe processing failing to suppress irrelevant information (Roediger and Geraci, 2007).

Although this section presents a rather gloomy picture, it should be stressed that the effects reported are only *average* and not applicable to *all* older adults (see Mueller-Johnson and Ceci, 2007). In part, the problems of older people's eyewitness memories may be perceptual deficits. Certainly, when these are controlled for, then at least some age differences are reduced or removed (see Searcy, Bartlett and Memon, 1999). However, in real-life situations, these sensory deficits cannot of course be compensated for. Brimacombe *et al.* (1997) found that if people read statements in which the age of the witnesses had been manipulated (i.e. there were statements that were really by younger adults ostensibly provided by older adults and vice versa) then judgements of accuracy tended to go with the perceived accuracy of the statement rather than the perceived age of the witness. In other words, it is the *content* rather than the stereotype of older people's eyewitness accounts that may provoke a negative judgement. But nonetheless, in real life, it is the older person who is producing these lower rated statements.

Such considerations paint a grim picture of the status of an older person as a witness in a courtroom. Even if they are correct in the main points of their testimony (which arguably may be all that matters), a lawyer may quickly discredit this by playing on weaknesses over (what are after all irrelevant) recall of details (thereby reducing the older person's self-esteem as well). It is small surprise to find that older eyewitnesses' testimony is rated as being less credible (e.g. Kwong See, Hoffman and Wood, 2001). This is in spite of the fact that older people are generally perceived as being more honest (Kwong See *et al.*, 2001; Moulin *et al.*, 2007).

Text recall

Because recall of text is strongly linked with linguistic skills, this topic is dealt with in detail in Chapter 4. A summary of the findings is that, essentially, there are no or relatively few age differences in the recall of the main points of a story (the 'gist' of the text) but that memory for details may worsen, especially in older people who are also low scorers on intelligence tests. However, there are a number of occasions when this rule breaks down, and interested readers should consult the appropriate section in the next chapter.

Semantic memory

Semantic memory might be expected to survive ageing in a fairly robust state, because memory for facts and information is part of the definition of crystallised intelligence, which is known to be relatively age-invariant (see Chapter 2). Indeed, this appears to be the case – in general, older adults are as good as, if not better than, younger adults at recalling facts and information held in semantic memory (e.g. Camp, 1988; Fozard, 1980; Sharps, 1998). In part this might be attributed to the fact that semantic memories appear to be distributed across the cortex rather than located in one specific region (Eichenbaum, 2003). This makes them more resistant to ageing change because, if they are not all concentrated in one specific area, decay has less chance of destroying them than if they were concentrated in one area and thus easier to damage with one concerted attack. Recent evidence suggests that size of semantic memory in older adults is best correlated with size and preservation of grey matter (see Glossary) (Taki *et al.*, 2011). However, it should also be noted that semantic memory is rather different from many other types of memory:

- It is different from an episodic memory in that it does not have to have a time and location attached to it. It is quite sufficient to remember that Tchaikovsky wrote the *1812 Overture* – you do not have to remember where or when you learnt that information. And freedom from this constraint means that you can be reminded of this information again and again throughout your life without needing to learn where or when each new learning experience took place. All that you need remember is the same basic fact.

- It is different from digit span tasks in that you have had years (possibly decades) in which to rehearse much of your semantic memory. Meeting the same fact repeatedly over the years (e.g. it is wildly unlikely that, if you encounter the *1812 Overture* once, you will never hear of it again) gives rehearsal of a quality lacking in other types of memory.

- Much of semantic memory is supported by a huge 'memory infrastructure' – it fits into well-established knowledge bases and cultural values, so that it is more easily assimilated than other, rather more arbitrary types of TBR items, like word lists.

In other words, semantic memory tasks might well be intrinsically easier for older adults. If we look at instances where older adults are asked to retrieve relatively specific rather than relatively general, or relatively recently acquired rather than often-rehearsed, information from semantic memory, then age-related differences become apparent. For example, Craik *et al.* (1995) in a review of the literature concluded that, whilst this is true for existing memories, storage of new semantic memories might be somewhat worse. A more recent review by Luo and Craik (2008) notes that the preservation of semantic memory is strongest in frequently used areas of information; very specific information (e.g. people's names) is far less well preserved (see also Hough, 2006). Again, ability to retrieve items from memory might not be as fluent in later life. For instance, Kozora and Cullum (1995) found that producing examples of particular semantic categories was less efficient in older adults. In a similar vein, it was noted in Chapter 2 that many older people's definitions of words, whilst correct, were less exacting. Furthermore, Hultsch *et al.* (1992), in a three-year longitudinal study, found a significant decline in general knowledge for world events (along with declines in other memory and intellectual measures). However, this may in part have been a cohort effect.

Episodic memory

Episodic and semantic memory are often compared with each other – not only because of their shared origins in theoretical models, but also because the relative preservation of semantic memory is explicitly compared with the relative decline in episodic memory. Episodic memory has already been defined as memory of personal experiences. This encompasses not only memories of everyday experience but also the relatively artificial laboratory-based tasks such as remembering lists of words over periods of time (i.e. the LTM tasks mentioned at the start of this section). There is overwhelming evidence that there is a significant ageing decline in such tasks (e.g. Naveh-Benjamin *et al.*, 2004; Plancher *et al.*, 2010; there is also an age difference when participants are ordered to *forget* information – see Titz and Verhaeghen, 2010). Indeed, when we turn to possible causes of episodic memory decline, there is arguably *too* much information. The following are but a few of the many hundreds of factors identified as being linked to changes in episodic memory in later life:

- An input of glucose can significantly improve memory performance (Riby, Meikle and Glover, 2004).

- Education level (Angel *et al.*, 2010).

- Possession of the ApoE allele 4 (a gene variant also associated with dementia) significantly mars episodic memory performance (Wisdom, Callahan and Hawkins, 2011).

- Level of activity in the thalamus (Ystad *et al.*, 2010).

- Level of activity in the hippocampus (Doeller, King and Burgess, 2008).

- Preservation of white matter (Charlton *et al.*, 2010).

- *Aides memoire* (e.g. providing the initial letters of the TBR word at the time of retrieval) generally improve episodic recall (see Thomas and Bulevich, 2006) but whether older adults are differentially aided in this relative to younger adults is a moot point (Craik, 2000).

These form but the tip of the iceberg. A basic computerised search of papers published between 2005 and 2011 alone found several hundred papers identifying factors linked to episodic memory decline. Of course there is overlap in subject matter between many of these studies, but nonetheless there are a lot of varied findings. And unfortunately, much of this research has not proved particularly satisfactorily that there is a causal link. Episodic memory declines so markedly in old age that practically any other measure known to change in later life is likely to have at least *some* correlation with it, simply through a general ageing effect.

Episodic memory is almost certain to show significant ageing effects because, by its very nature, it is more complex and prone to distortion than semantic memory.

People are being asked to recall facts for once-only events (not like semantic memory where the same information might be encountered on numerous occasions), and must nail down what, where, when, and often also by whom, things were said or done (again, not something required of semantic memory). There is far more information that needs to be remembered, and, therefore, far more that can go wrong. It is therefore not surprising that a key failing in the episodic memory abilities of older adults is what amounts to a failure to remember sufficient details surrounding the TBR items. Often this concerns the issue of **source memory** (essentially, remembering the context in which something was learnt). For example, McIntyre and Craik (1987) gave participants the task of remembering a new set of 'facts' (in reality false but plausible snippets of general knowledge). Over a week, the older adults showed little deficit in memory for the facts themselves, but were far worse than younger participants at remembering where they had first learnt the information (i.e. at the previous test session). Again, Simons *et al.* (2004) found that older adults were significantly worse at remembering specific source information (which of four people said a TBR item) and partial source information (the gender of the person who said a TBR item). The evidence collected by Simons *et al.* implies that memory for partial and specific information is equally affected.

In a related theme, older people also show a significant impairment in **destination memory** (i.e. remembering who has already told or been told the same information), with older adults impaired in both remembering to whom they have already told the same piece of information and in remembering who told them a piece of information (Gopie, Craik and Hasher, 2010). Another related finding is that older adults are similarly poor at editing out irrelevant information. In a technique they named 'externalised free recall' Kahana *et al.* (2005) gave participants a free recall task, but during the recall phase told participants to produce not only the TBR words but also any other words that 'appeared in the head' (i.e. distracters). Participants were instructed to press a button indicating if they knew a word to be a distracter. Whilst older and younger adults produced distracters, the older participants were significantly worse at identifying distracters. Even allowing for older adults being poorer at doing concurrent tasks such as button pressing and recalling words, the findings of Kahana *et al.*'s study further indicate that older people's episodic memory is seriously hampered by a failure to organise and keep in check.

It follows from studies such as these that, if older adults are less able to recall contextual information and more willing to accept distracters as targets, they are also more prone to false memories – and that generally appears to be the case, at least in laboratory studies (see Dehon and Brédart, 2004). This, *inter alia*, raises further concerns for the reliability of older adults' eyewitness memory. It is known, perhaps not surprisingly, that false memory production is related to level of executive functioning (Plancher *et al.*, 2010) and, as in other instances reported in this chapter, older people are more likely to be (erroneously) confident that these false memories are in fact true (Shing *et al.*, 2009). Episodic memory thus shows patterns of decline not all that different from other memory types, and indeed researchers have noted that episodic memory changes are part and parcel of general cognitive ageing decline (see Lövdén and Wahlin, 2005). Indeed, changes in episodic memory are a good guide to general changes in cognitive skills and other memory processes such as working memory (Hertzog *et al.*, 2003). This leads to the noteworthy finding that, although semantic and episodic memory are often contrasted with each other, in fact, the two skills are correlated with each other and might even become more strongly related in later life. In a longitudinal study over five years, Lövdén *et al.* (2004) found that although episodic memory performance fluctuated over time more than semantic (a finding echoed by Nyberg *et al.*, 2003), the two types of memory were strongly correlated, and this relationship tended to increase over time. However, although episodic and semantic memory are associated with each other, there is still room for each to have unique properties (Allen *et al.*, 2002).

Implicit memory

Evidence on implicit memory points to there being no significant age difference, or, at worst, only a slight decline (e.g. Fay, Isingrini and Clarys, 2005; Fleischman *et al.*, 2004; Mitchell and Bruss, 2003; Mitchell and Schmitt, 2006). This phenomenon continues into very old age (Spaan and Raaljmakers, 2011).

A limited number of manipulations of implicit memory tasks do induce age differences, however. For example, Harrington and Haaland (1992) gave participants the task of performing various hand movements. These were either performed in a repetitive set sequence or done in random sequences. It was anticipated that the regular repetition should aid implicit memory far more than the random sequences. The researchers found that this was true for younger participants, but older adults showed no difference between the two conditions. This implies that older people are less able to make use of implicit information. However, the finding is possibly limited to very specific circumstances. For example, Rowe *et al.* (2006) found that implicit memory for distracters used in an earlier memory experiment was significantly better in older than in younger participants. Again, McEvoy *et al.* (1992) found an apparent worsening of ability to *use* implicit information. In one of their experiments, they gave participants a set of words to remember, and then tested recall using cues (in this case, words related in meaning, e.g. if the TBR word was 'butter' then the cue might be 'bread'). For the younger participants, recall was worse if the TBR word had a lot of potential associates (e.g. 'car' has lots of associates, 'basilisk' very few). This was also true for the older participants, but the size of the effect was significantly diminished. This, it is argued, indicates that older people are less able to make use of implicit associations. It is probable, however, that the older participants took longer to respond (no response latencies are recorded by McEvoy *et al.*). Therefore, the effect of the implicit associations may be diluted by the extra processing time.

Again, a more recent study by Geraci and Hamilton (2009) found no age difference in a general knowledge test based on implicit memory.

Park and Shaw (1992) argue that in studies that have found an age difference, it has not been established if the younger participants had realised that they were taking part in a memory test, and so deliberately concentrated harder on the TBR items. Park and Shaw cite the work of Light and Albertson (1989), which found that, if aware participants were excluded from the analysis, an age difference in implicit memory performance disappeared.

Autobiographical memory and ageing

Several major problems beset autobiographical memory research. The most often cited of these is the issue of reliability. For example, an older participant may reminisce about a picnic in 1936, held with her now-dead parents. How can one possibly verify the accuracy of this recollection? This is not to say that the participant is deliberately lying, but usually reminiscences have been recalled many times over a person's lifetime and, with each retelling, details often alter to improve the flow of the narrative (Bartlett, 1932). Thus, the recounting of a story five years after the event in question may have the same basic plot as a retelling 50 years on, but the details of the two narratives are likely to be different. This argument is supported by the findings of a longitudinal study by Field (1981). Comparing reminiscences of the same events 30 and 70 years on, there was a reasonably high correlation for points in the basic plot ($r = 0.88$), but only a 16 per cent concordance for recall of more peripheral details ($r = 0.43$). This finding is echoed in a study by Dijkstra and Misirlisoy (2009), who found that accuracy of identifying altered transcripts of autobiographical memories a year after their telling was high for main details but low for peripheral information.

Another serious methodological flaw concerns how the memories are elicited. One general problem is that participants might censor their memories. It is a reasonable assumption that, human nature being what it is, people's most vivid memories include a largish proportion of sexual experiences. Curiously, these seem to be rarely mentioned by participants. Again, asking people to produce autobiographical memories by prompting them with cues generally produces memories linked by being from roughly the same time period in a person's life. Asking people to produce an autobiographical memory and then recording any further memories that arise from the initial one produces memories linked conceptually rather than from the same period of a person's life (see Talarico and Mace, 2010). Also, the cueing method is sensitive to the choice of cues. For example, asking participants for their most *vivid* memories produces a glut of reminiscences from the early part of their lives. So does giving participants a cue word, and asking them to produce a reminiscence associated with it (e.g. jam – 'Oh yes, I remember helping my mother make jam when I was a child'), provided the participant has to put a date to each memory after producing it. However, if the participant is allowed to produce a whole list before any dating of memories is done, then the bias shifts in favour of a preponderance of memories from the recent past (Cohen, 1989). To further muddy the waters, words that are rated highly in imagery-provoking properties tend to generate older memories (Rubin and Schulkind, 1997b).

Thus, how the participant is asked determines the age of memories produced, and there is certainly no evidence to support the cliché that older people live in the past. Indeed, several studies have shown that younger and older adults produce equal numbers of reminiscences from childhood (e.g. Cohen and Faulkner, 1988; Rubin and Schulkind, 1997a). This is not necessarily due to participants wallowing in nostalgia. Rabbitt and Winthorpe (1988) found that, when memories are divided into 'pleasant' and 'unpleasant', reminiscences from early life fall predominantly into the latter category. Berntsen and Rubin (2002), using a different technique for eliciting memories, found a higher proportion of happy memories, but unpleasant memories were nonetheless reported in appreciable numbers.

Related to this, most studies of autobiographical memory have in effect examined **involuntary memory**. In other words, participants are asked to produce memories that they would not have produced at that point in time. However, in real life, far more autobiographical memories are examples of **voluntary memory** – in other words, they are spontaneous recollections that appear unbidden or are prompted by an association with something encountered in the immediate present. Research on this potentially interesting topic is scarce, but the available evidence indicates that voluntary memories are less frequent in older people. The memories also tend to be more specific and positive in mood than involuntary memories (see Schlagman, Kvavilashvili and Schulz, 2007). Interestingly, voluntary memories are more likely to be cued by abstract thoughts than a specific sensory input such as a taste or smell (Mace, 2004). Although this does not discount Proust's famous account of the *madeleine* that kick starts *Remembrance of Things Past*, it indicates that this oft-cited memory cue is a less common source of reminiscence than might be supposed.

However, this does not mean that taste and smell have no effect on autobiographical memory. Almost everyone has experienced unexpectedly strong memories stirred by a scent or taste. This is probably because scent and taste cannot be easily rehearsed and mentally revived in the memory – what is needed is the genuine article, and so presumably the awakening of memories by smell/taste is so much the stronger because they are unexpected and less often encountered. Maylor, Carter and Hallett (2002) found that, for both younger and older adults, presenting a cue word in combination with an odour attached to the word (e.g. the word 'rose' in combination with the smell of rose oil) doubled the number of memories produced. The finding is interesting in its own right, but it also questions whether other autobiographical memory tests have accidentally biased results by the smell of the test room, scent worn by the researcher, etc. Again, Chu and Downes (2000) demonstrated that autobiographical memories elicited by smell cues came from significantly earlier in life than memories evoked by word cues. Thus, the 'Proust phenomenon' exists, even if it is not the principal source of voluntary reminiscence.

Notwithstanding these considerations, the **reminiscence peak** (a.k.a. **reminiscence bump**) has been reported by many researchers. This is the phenomenon that, when due allowance is made for testing methods, most autobiographical memories for relatively distant events (as opposed to the immediate past) are likely to come from the period when the individual was between 10 and 30 years old (e.g. Berntsen and Rubin, 2002; Rubin, Rahhal and Poon, 1998; Webster and Gould, 2007). This is not surprising, since this is the time when most of the key life events (first forays into sex, employment, exams, marriage, parenthood, and so forth) usually occur (see Jansari and Parkin, 1996). Several researchers have argued that the reminiscence bump only applies when just positive life event memories are concerned – there is no similar bump for negative memories (e.g. Leist, Ferring and Filipp, 2010). In contrast, autobiographical memories from the very early years are scarce or non-existent (**childhood amnesia**). Freud and his followers believed that this was due to suppression of unpleasant memories and psychoanalytic conflicts, but it is now felt to be because young children lack the mental facilities to encode retrievable autobiographical memories.

An issue related to what is remembered is the vividness of the recall. Introspection shows that some memories are clearer than others, and, generally, earlier memories are perceived as 'dimmer' than later ones (Cohen and Faulkner, 1988). This was also demonstrated by Nigro and Neisser (1983), who found that distant memories are usually perceived as if watching the events taking place as a bystander (i.e. as though watching oneself), while more recent events are remembered from one's viewpoint at the time. Furthermore, the reasons why an event is perceived as vivid change across the lifespan. Cohen and Faulkner (1988) found that younger and middle-aged adults were affected by how emotionally charged the event was – the greater the feelings, the greater the vividness. For older adults, the biggest cause of vividness was how often they had thought about the event subsequently. Cohen and Faulkner suggest that, because ageing blunts the vividness of memories, it is only by rehearsing them that their details can be retained (rather like taking pieces of silverware out of the cupboard to polish them, to prevent them tarnishing).

Rabbitt and Winthorpe (1988) found that older people gave poorer quality responses in autobiographical memory tests (and were also generally slower to produce reminiscences). For example, they provide vague rather than specific answers (e.g. 'I remember going on a picnic when I was a child' as opposed to 'I remember going on a picnic on Salisbury Plain on my seventh birthday'). However, Rabbitt and Winthorpe (1988) demonstrated that this was not due to ageing *per se*, but to the coincidental decline in fluid intelligence and working memory (which is used to keep track of what has been said and what needs to come next in the narrative). In a subsequent study by the researchers, it was found that detail in the reminiscences was determined by age, fluid intelligence and crystallised intelligence (Holland [née

Winthorpe] and Rabbitt, 1990; Phillips and Williams, 1997; both studies report analogous results). This was interpreted as meaning that, although the ageing process and the fall in fluid intelligence cause a decline in reminiscence skills, the age-invariant crystallised skills may to some extent compensate for this. These findings are complemented by more recent research by Levine *et al.* (2002). They found that younger adults provided details specific to the memory being recalled, whereas older adults tended to recall general semantic information that could be applicable across many situations. This phenomenon persisted even after the participants were probed for further details. Again, Piolino *et al.* (2010) demonstrated that the more detailed the type of autobiographical memory, the greater the age deficits, a phenomenon the researchers linked to changes in executive functions and working memory. It should also be noted that, even if older and younger adults are compared on similarly vivid memories, there are still age differences, with older adults producing reminiscences that are more likely to be positive, less intimate and more concerned with a social occasion than are younger adults (Webster and Gould, 2007).

There is growing evidence that brain activity during autobiographical memory production involves the hippocampus (e.g. Maguire and Frith, 2003; Viard, Piolino *et al.*, 2007; Viard, Lebreton *et al.*, 2010), an area known to be badly affected by ageing, and this might account for some of the perceived differences in vividness as well as differences in detail. Frontal lobe functioning has also been associated (McKinnon *et al.*, 2008), another region known to be badly affected in later life and associated, *inter alia*, with planning and sequencing of memories. Interestingly, temporal remoteness of memories does not seem to produce radically different age differences in neural activity (Donix *et al.*, 2010).

Moving away from consideration of quantities and qualities of autobiographical memories, there is the issue of their function. A plausible argument is that they are a key component in forming a sense of identity (see Cohen-Mansfield *et al.*, 2010). A study by Cappeliez and O'Rourke (2002) identified a link between production of autobiographical memories and personality type. Using the five-factor theory of personality (see Chapter 5), they found production of autobiographical memories to be correlated with extraversion, neuroticism and openness to experience. Perhaps unsurprisingly, extraversion was associated with producing memories for use in conversations and neuroticism with ruminating about unpleasant past events. Openness to experience was correlated with seeking a meaning for both life and death. Because of its association with finding meaning in life, reminiscence has been used in therapeutic contexts. Many commentators believe that 'reminiscence therapy' for older people should be encouraged, since it enables them to come to terms with their lives (see Kermis, 1983; Pasupathi and Carstensen, 2003). There is also evidence that eliciting autobiographical memories can be an effective component in the treatment of older adults' depression for roughly the same reason (Serrano *et al.*, 2004). However, for many older people, reminiscence may simply be a response to boredom: 'Older people may experience an increasing contrast between an unmemorable present and an eventful past. Remote events may be more often researched and rehearsed in memory as the theatre of the mind becomes the only show in town' (Rabbitt and Winthorpe, 1988, p.302).

Prospective memory

One of the principal functions of memory is not to remember the past but to plan for the future. In part this means learning from one's experiences and mistakes in order to cope better with situations when they next arise. This can be considered as part of wisdom/crystallised intelligence. Another, more literal aspect is prospective memory, or the ability to remember to do something in the future. It might be supposed that prospective memory is simply another form of LTM, since it involves retaining information over a long time period. However, there is ample evidence to disprove this notion. First, on theoretical grounds the two memory types are distinct. In retrospective memory, it is sufficient to recall an item or event for the action to be considered a success. In prospective memory, however, the item can be recalled any number of times, but it is only successful if the person remembers to do it at the right time and acts upon it (West, 1988). A second consideration is that the memory types are empirically distinct, with little correlation either in accuracy or in types of mnemonic strategies used (Jackson, Bogers and Kersthold, 1988; Kvavilashvili, 1987; Wilkins and Baddeley, 1978).

Methods of recall in prospective memory vary greatly between individuals, but, broadly speaking, they can be divided into two classes – **internal** and **external cues** or strategies. External cues are such familiar things as entries in a diary or the knot in the handkerchief. In other words, prompts that the person places in the external environment. Some experiments test use of these strategies through **event-based tasks** (where the participant must retrieve and act on a memory when given a particular prompt). Internal cues, on the other hand, are purely mental strategies, where the person hopes to prompt him- or herself at the appropriate time. This may be measured through **time-based tasks** (the participant must respond at a particular point in time). This division is not as clear-cut as some commentators seem to suppose, however. For example, a common strategy is to remember to do something in conjunction with a familiar daily routine, such as the habitual breakfast coffee (Maylor, 1990a, Appendix A). Is this an internal strategy (simply remembering to add another action onto the end of a familiar sequence) or an external one (the sight of the coffee acting as an *aide memoire*)? Similarly, an external cue such as a diary entry requires an internal strategy to remember to look in the diary. Therefore, the functional distinctions between the mnemonic methods are blurred, and certainly are too ambiguous to bear deep analysis. Therefore, for the rest of this section, internal and external methods will be treated purely as practical strategies, avoiding the question of how they work.

In certain kinds of prospective memory tasks, there is either no age difference or even an ageing superiority. For example, a 'traditional' prospective memory task requires participants to remember to phone the experimenter at prearranged times. Poon and Schaffer (1982, cited in West, 1988) and Moscovitch (1982) found that older participants remembered to phone more often and they were more punctual. However, this could in part be a cohort effect. Older people might lead more sedate lives and thus have less to distract them from making phone calls. Again, older people might have been brought up to place greater emphasis on punctuality and keeping appointments than younger people and thus were more motivated to make the calls. This latter supposition is supported by Poon and Schaffer's finding that increasing the monetary reward for making a call improved the older people's performance, but not the younger people's. Again, Altgassen, Kliegel, Brandimonte and Filippello (2010) found that when a prospective memory task had an attached social importance (as opposed to being simply part of a typical unrealistic laboratory experiment), older adults performed significantly better relative to younger adults. Kvavilashvili et al. (2009) report that when asked to report real-life memory lapses, older participants were more likely to report a failure to remember an event in the past than a failure of prospective memory, whereas the reverse was true for young adult participants.

One method of minimising the cohort effect is to take participants in their fifties as the younger adult group. This age group will still intellectually perform more or less on a par with adults in their twenties (the age of a typical 'younger adult' group) but are more similar to older adults in their upbringing. Maylor (1990a) did this, and furthermore selected participants who had similar lifestyles. The participants had to phone once per day for five days, either at a specific time (the 'exact' condition) or between two specified times (the 'between' condition). Maylor found no significant difference between age groups in punctuality nor in number of calls made. She also found no age difference in the cues used to remember to make the calls. This contradicts earlier findings that older adults tend to use more external cues (e.g. Jackson et al., 1988; Moscovitch, 1982). Possibly this reflects a cohort effect. Studies other than Maylor's have often used as younger participants students who may be forced to take part in experiments as part of their degree programme (much psychological research takes place under the guise of practical classes). Given the typical undergraduate enthusiasm for practicals, the younger participants may be apathetic, and they may use internal cues because it is less effort than creating external reminders. Maylor's study used younger participants who were all active volunteers in an ongoing large-scale programme into the effects of ageing, and thus they were probably more motivated.

Maylor did find an age effect, however, in the efficiency with which participants used external and internal cues. Namely, internal cue users who made errors were significantly older, and external cue users who made errors were significantly younger. Thus, those participants who continue to rely solely on their memories worsen, whilst those who turn to external aids improve (probably because they become more practised). However, to some extent participants use strategies according to the task at hand. Maylor found that the 'between' condition generated greater use of external cues than did the 'exact' condition. She suggests that this is because of the perceived difficulties of the two tasks (i.e. the condition thought to be harder demands a more positive response in the shape of preparing an external cue). West (1988) has reported similar links between cue use and task demands.

However, under other circumstances, considerable age differences in prospective memory can be found. For example, Cockburn and Smith (1988) found that older participants were worse on tests of remembering an appointment and remembering to deliver a message. Again, West (1988) demonstrated that older participants were significantly worse at remembering to deliver a message during a test session. Indeed, in general, if participants must remember to do something as part of other measures, then there is an age difference. Furthermore, age declines tend to increase with the increased complexity of the task (e.g. Einstein, McDaniel and Guynn, 1992) and/or its attentional demands (Einstein *et al.*, 1998). Why older people should be better at some prospective memory tasks than others remains an open issue. It has been suggested that older adults are better at event-based tasks than time-based tasks. However, ignoring the criticism of this classification presented earlier, the findings of several studies militate against a simplistic interpretation of this. For example, Maylor (1998) found significant age differences in a task requiring participants to identify pictures of famous people, with a prospective memory component requiring participants to identify those people wearing spectacles. Thus, the experiment provided strong event-based cues, but there was an age difference. Again, Park *et al.* (1997) have plausibly argued that, under some circumstances, time-based tasks may be measuring time monitoring rather than memory *per se*. And finally, Henry *et al.* (2004) demonstrated that younger adults significantly outperform older adults on both time- and event-based tasks (and the age difference on the latter significantly increases if the processing demands are increased).

Perhaps a more satisfying explanation is derived from Craik *et al.*'s (1995) observation that prospective memory tasks tend, perversely enough, to be most prone to age differences over relatively short time frames. Thus, if asked to do something as part of a fairly complex ongoing task, this is more likely to be forgotten than, for example, remembering to do a single act in a week's time. It is questionable whether the relatively long-term and naturalistic and relatively short-term and laboratory-based paradigms are assessing the same types of prospective memory. For example, suppose a person is asked to play a particularly taxing video game of the 'shoot 'em up' variety, and told that every time they shoot a red monster they should shout out 'bananas'. If they forget to call out every time they kill a red monster, is this due to forgetting to do something in the future or a lapse in performing just another component of the ongoing task (akin to forgetting that, for example, shooting the yellow monsters gets double the points of shooting the blue monsters?). In comparison, forgetting to phone the experimenter at a particular time on a particular day is more likely to be a memory lapse rather than distraction by a large number of demands competing for the participant's attention at *precisely* the same moment in time.

It should be noted that the demands of the short-term prospective memory tasks need not (in subjective terms) be onerous to induce an age difference. For example, Maylor's (1998) task could not exactly be described as difficult. Again, Maentylae and Nilsson (1997) found older people were significantly less likely to remember to do the even simpler task of asking an experimenter to sign a paper at the end of a two-hour test session. Nonetheless, older adults are less adept at prospective memory tasks the more distracting/noisy the environment is (Knight, Nicholls and Titov, 2008) and a meta-analysis by Kliegel, Jager and Phillips (2008) demonstrated that the more focal (i.e. 'in-your-face obvious') the cue, the better older participants perform. Another consideration is that longer-term tasks, such as remembering to phone someone on a particular day and time can be integrated into the general routine of daily life and thus become part of a well-practised procedure. However, doing concurrent tasks or delivering messages during meetings with researchers is not something at which older adults have had much practice. This argument is supported by Bailey *et al.* (2010) who found that, if a standard laboratory-type measure of prospective memory were conducted in a naturalistic setting, older people's performance significantly improved. The authors suggest that this is because in a naturalistic or real-world setting older adults are able to 'act on intentions during everyday activities, but have difficulty in prospective remembering during experimenter-generated ongoing tasks' (Bailey *et al.*, 2010, p.646). In other words, if older people are working at their own pace in their own world, and not trying to follow essentially unrealistic commands in an unrealistic world over which they have little control, then their memories perform better.

In short, current research on prospective memory in ageing may be encompassing two rather different phenomena under a blanket heading. 'Prospective Memory I', used in a naturalistic setting, is remembering a future appointment or responsibility. This is almost inevitably tested under realistic conditions. 'Prospective Memory II' is the ability to remember to perform an action during concurrent processing of other tasks. This is almost inevitably tested under laboratory conditions. This difference appears to be borne out by a meta-review of the research literature by Henry *et al.* (2004). They found that whilst older adults outperform younger adults on naturalistic tasks, the reverse applies for laboratory-based tasks. Intelligence, however, is not a particularly strong predictor for either type of study (Cockburn and Smith, 1988; Maylor, 1998), though the decline in type II prospective memory resembles that found in working memory (Logie and Maylor, 2009).

Zollig, Martin and Kliegel (2010) found that older adults, adolescents and younger adults all had distinct patterns of brain activity during a prospective memory task, implying that the neural mechanisms involved in prospective memory might change over the lifespan (see also West and Bowry, 2005). McFarland and Glisky (2009) found that prospective memory test performance (on a time-based task) was strongly related to level of frontal lobe functioning. In addition, an interesting study by Livner, Wahlin and Backman (2009) suggests that thyroid functioning level might affect prospective memory performance. Individuals who do not have thyroid problems might nonetheless vary in the level of thyroid functioning, and it is known that this can affect certain aspects of frontal lobe functioning. Livner *et al.* found that older adults with relatively high levels of thyroid-stimulating hormone (TSH) had significantly better prospective memory test scores. However, the effect of thyroid functioning is not clear-cut (e.g. there is not a linear relationship between concentration of TSH and memory test score: not all thyroid hormones have the same effect) and further research is needed.

Metamemory and ageing

To what extent can older people gauge their mental abilities? There is little effect of ageing when judging relatively abstract features of memory, such as deciding on which types of TBR items are easiest to remember and the best mnemonic strategies to use (Perlmutter, 1978). However, other aspects of metamemory generally *do* show an age-related decline. Principally, age differences occur when: (1) judgements are asked on a memory act that is incomplete, or (2) global judgements on past and future performance are required. Furthermore, as will be seen later, methodological problems with the test of the latter in any case make much of the research literature uninterpretable.

One method of gauging one's own memory abilities is **metaknowledge**, or **feeling of knowing (FOK)**. A typical FOK experiment might require participants to look at a question and then declare how confident they are that their answer is correct (typically using a numerical scale). We have already seen that older adults can be quite spectacularly poor at judging accuracy in areas such as eyewitness testimony (see also Perfect and Hollins, 1999). The same applies to other memory types, such as episodic memory (Dodson, Bawa and Krueger, 2007), and prospective and retrospective memories (Reese and Cherry, 2006). An exception to this is straightforward semantic recall, where most studies report no or very little age difference in FOK accuracy (e.g. Allen-Burge and Storandt, 2000; Fozard, 1980; Perlmutter, 1978). More generally, self-estimates of memory ability can even predict memory test performance six years later (Valentijn *et al.*, 2006). Souchay *et al.* (2007), in a comparison of FOK in different memory types in the same participants, found a significant age difference in episodic but not in semantic memories.

Thus, although there are many instances of ageing decline, metamemory for some types of memory can be accurate in later life. However, although this may be the case, older people do not necessarily believe it. For example, Camp (1988) reported that older adults thought their semantic memory had declined. In other instances, FOK may be related to the level of confidence in the subject matter being memorised.

For example, Marquié and Huet (2000) demonstrated that older participants' FOK levels were only lower than younger adults' for information about computing, but were not significantly different on general knowledge items. Arguably this is part of a larger trend of age-related pessimism, since researchers have long reported lowered self-confidence in older participants (e.g. Botwinick, 1967). Certainly, if given more exposure to TBR items in an episodic memory task during encoding, FOK scores increase in magnitude, indicating greater confidence, presumably created by greater exposure (see Hertzog, Dunlosky and Sinclair, 2010).

However, FOK changes are not just the result of pessimism, and factors such as lowered executive functions have also been cited (see Bouazzaoui *et al.*, 2010; Juncos-Rabadan *et al.*, 2010; Perrotin *et al.*, 2006), as have poorer skills at using contextual information (Thomas, Bulevich and Dubois, 2011). In addition, Dodson *et al.* (2007, p.122) note that 'age-related memory impairments are due to older adults' vulnerability to making high-confidence errors when answering questions that require memory for specific details about recently learned events'. In other words, if a person has an incomplete memory, then the memory might be so poor that the person also does not know it is poor. They are therefore doomed to make a poor metamemory judgement because by definition they are basing it on incomplete information. A neural processing deficit might explain this. Chua, Schacter and Sperling (2009) noted that, when processing items for which they had a high level of confidence, younger adults showed increased neural activity in the medial temporal lobes. Older adults in the same situation did not show this pattern. It is possible, therefore, that changes in neural activity in later life undermine the ability to make as clear and delineated a set of judgements as people were capable of making when they were younger.

A prime example of an incomplete memory act is the **tip of the tongue (TOT)** state (for readers pursuing matters further, note that some commentators classify TOT as part of semantic memory rather than metamemory; see also Schwartz and Frazier, 2005). This is a familiar experience for most people. The word or name one is searching for cannot quite be recalled, yet one can remember some features of it, such as the first letter, the number of syllables, words that sound like it, and so forth. Brown and McNeill (1966) were the first to investigate this phenomenon intensively, by giving participants definitions of obscure words and asking them to provide the words. Often, participants either knew the word or simply had no idea, but on some occasions a TOT state was generated. Typically, participants could indeed provide details of the word (e.g. 57% of the time they could identify the first letter). The TOT state is nothing more than an annoyance when confined to defining rare words. However, if it creeps into everyday speech, then it is a potential disability. Burke, Worthley and Martin (1988) decided to study the TOT state in older people, in part because older volunteers in a study the experimenters were running had complained about it being a problem. Indeed, in general older people can be bad at remembering words, and especially names (Crook and West, 1990; James, 2006).

Burke *et al.* asked their participants to keep diary records of all TOTs over a four-week period. They were asked to record all the details of the word they could remember whilst in the TOT state, and whether they ever discovered what the word they were searching for actually was (i.e. whether the TOT resolved itself). Burke *et al.* found that the older participants reported significantly more TOTs, although there was no age difference in the proportion of resolved TOTs (over 90% of the time both age groups eventually found the word they were looking for). However, whilst in the TOT state, the younger participants could report significantly more details of the word (a finding echoed by Maylor, 1990b). Subsequent research has indicated that younger people's TOTs contain more information and are closer to the recognition threshold than older people's. For example, White and Abrams (2002) found that, if participants were asked general knowledge questions that generated the occasional TOT state, a phonological prime (e.g. the initial sound of the word the participants were searching for) would resolve the TOT state for younger but not older adults. Priming words drawn from different grammatical categories can also differentially affect resolution of TOT states in participants of different ages (Abrams, Trunk and Merrill, 2007).

In a similar study to Burke *et al.*'s, Cohen and Faulkner (1986) had participants complete a two-week diary of TOTs for proper nouns (i.e. names). Surprisingly, the majority of these (68%) turned out to be for names of friends and acquaintances. Perhaps, as Cohen (1989, p.104) notes, 'there are more opportunities to forget names that are in frequent use' (though it seems unlikely that memory for names is *disproportionately* disadvantaged in later life, as a careful analysis by Maylor, 1997 demonstrates). It should also be noted that in general older adults are significantly and disproportionately worse than younger adults at remembering new names than new details about people, such as their occupation (James, 2004), probably due to a lowered efficiency of mental processing (simplistically, it is easier to remember a semantic category such as 'farmer' than the precise name 'Mr Farmer'). Again, older people seemed to rely on a strategy of waiting for the name to 'pop up'. Given these findings, one can surmise that older people have a problem with retrieving faint memory traces. This can be seen in the facts that they have more TOT states and that, when in a TOT state, they have fewer details of the word. Because they lack many details of the target word, it is probably not worth their while to search for it on the basis of the little information they have available (the product of a metamemory strategy?). Conversely, younger people, who can identify more about the word in a TOT state, and thus have more information to act upon, will probably find it worthwhile to indulge in a search of their memories. Neurologically speaking, evidence suggests that TOT states are associated with loss of grey matter and lower activity levels in the left insula, an area of the brain known to be involved in phonological processing (see Shafto *et al.*, 2007, 2010). In addition, activity in the prefrontal region differs in older adults in a TOT state, implying an ageing change in neural processing (Galdo-Alvarez, Lindin and Diaz, 2009).

Summary and overview – how does ageing affect memory?

Alas, the familiar complaint of many older people that their memories 'aren't what they used to be' seems in the main to be justified. Memory *does* decline in later life, and despite a few areas of relative preservation (e.g. 'basic' STM span and some aspects of prospective memory and metamemory) the outlook is downwards.

Some commentators have suggested that having a positive image of ageing may offset memory loss, and this is a not wholly implausible idea. Earles *et al.* (2004) found that imposing tight time constraints or making the task harder led to a disproportionate decline in older adults' performance. This was attributed by the researchers at least in part to induced anxiety and lowered self-image. In contrast, Yoon *et al.* (2000) considered a group of Chinese Canadians with very positive images of ageing and found no evidence for the argument, beyond a higher level of recall of items that were strongly related to Chinese culture (which may be attributable to a specific cohort effect). Rahhal, Hasher and Colcombe (2001) argued that perhaps older people's negative images of their memory skills pre-set them to perform badly on memory tasks. The researchers manipulated the instructions given at the start of a memory task so that the memory aspects of it were emphasised or were underplayed. Where memory instructions were explicit, there was a significant difference between younger and older participants; where no emphasis on memory was made, there was no significant age difference. This implies that many studies of ageing and memory may have exaggerated the size of memory loss. What was being examined was not the genuine memory skills of older adults, but rather the degree to which manipulating older people's self-esteem can mar their performance.

Murphy *et al.* (2000) found that the performance of younger adults in memorising items under noisy conditions was functionally similar to that of older adults memorising under quiet conditions, leading to the argument that perhaps part of the decline in ageing memory is attributable to degraded sensory input (basically, because the TBR items lack sensory fidelity, and mental effort that could have been spent on memorising has to be diverted to basic perception). Other physical changes in the body can also have an effect. For example, West *et al.* (2002) found that the time of day of testing can also have an effect on memory performance. Older adults tend to report being relatively more alert in the morning, younger adults in the evening. Testing at the 'wrong' time of day can accentuate age differences.

However, for all these caveats, there would still appear to be a tangible age difference in memory. It has already been noted on several occasions that there is a strong link between memory and general ageing decline. At a neural level, it is readily apparent that there must be a link between memory performance and the structure of the brain, from the structure of the brain down to the level of the individual neuron. It can be easily demonstrated that neural structure and memory are correlated. In addition to the specific instances already cited in this chapter, the following might be considered:

- The significant correlation between white matter integrity (i.e. how much white matter [see Glossary] remains intact) and working memory performance (Charlton *et al.*, 2008).

- The significant correlation between frontal lobe activity and working memory performance (Dahlin *et al.*, 2009; Rypma *et al.*, 2001; Stebbins *et al.*, 2002; Tays *et al.*, 2008).

- The significant correlation between brain volume and long-term memory (Charlton *et al.*, 2010; McArdle *et al.*, 2004).

- Semantic memory is distributed across the cortex, making it less susceptible to ageing decline than, for example, episodic memory, which is more reliant on the hippocampus (Eichenbaum, 2003) and a declining dopaminergic system (see Bäckman and Nyberg, 2010).

A danger with studies of neural change is that finding a correlation between physical and mental changes in later life should not be difficult, since both could be manifestations of the same general ageing effect (see Chapter 2) and thus the links found might be pure coincidence. This might be the case in some instances, but in others the relationship between the physical and mental declines is too specific for this argument to fit comfortably. For example, in the Charlton *et al.* study cited earlier, a correlation was found between long-term memory changes and decline in overall brain volume. But correlations with some specific parts of the brain, such as the hippocampus, were non-significant. The same applies to almost all the other studies cited here – the relationships are very specific. This implies that we are looking at the effects of specific neural damage rather than general ageing effects. Although a confounding variable explanation still cannot be ruled out, these findings make this explanation far more implausible.

Turning to specific models of neural change, the memory decline in later life has been attributed by some researchers to a permutation of the dedifferentiation hypothesis (see Chapter 2) – namely, that neural representations of mental states become less distinctive in later life, leading to, *inter alia*, badly stored memories. A refinement of this is **Compensation-Related Utilisation of Neural Circuits Hypothesis (CRUNCH)** (Reuter-Lorenz and Cappell, 2008). This argues that neural representations are *more* distinctive in older adults when there are relatively low task demands, but they then become *less* distinctive when task demands are high. The reasoning behind this is centred on brain cell loss (see Chapter 1) and changes in the surviving neurons to cope with this loss. Such changes in neural structure were once felt to be relatively unlikely, but it is now known that brain structure can be quite plastic (i.e. malleable) even in later life. For example, Lövdén *et al.* (2010) demonstrated that given extensive training in memory tasks (101 one-hour sessions over 180 days) resulted in growth in white matter in the corpus callosum (see Appendix I) in young and old adults to the same extent. This indicates that experience-dependent plasticity (i.e. changes in brain structure in response to changing mental practice) survive into old age. Thus, the brain's neural structure is far from rigidly fixed in later life (though research by Dahlin *et al.*, 2008 suggests that younger adults are still likely to be more adept at generalising what they learn in one task to similar situations).

The CRUNCH model argues that, as the ageing brain loses cells and interconnections between the surviving cells diminish, so more neurons have to be activated to handle a basic task, relative to younger adults. However, as task demands increase, the older neurons lack the numbers and processing power to cope as effectively. Hence there is the shift in distinctiveness. The experimental findings largely support this (Schneider-Garces *et al.*, 2010). Using **multi-voxal pattern analysis**, Carp, Gmeindl and Reuter-Lorenz (2010) found proof of both dedifferentiation *and* CRUNCH during a working memory task with varying task loads. Relative to younger adults, the sensory cortex of an older participant showed signs of dedifferentiation, whilst the prefrontal lobes showed greater distinctiveness during low task demands, but less distinctiveness when task demands increased. Analogous results were reported by Cappell, Gmeindl and Reuter-Lorenz (2010).

Thus, memory changes in later life might be the result of the ageing brain compensating for loss as best it can by drawing as many resources as it can muster. This will work adequately (perhaps more than adequately) at lower task loads, but there will still not be enough forces when task demands increase. Reuter-Lorenz and Park (2010) pursue this argument a step further by proposing a complementary **scaffolding theory of ageing and cognition (STAC)**. This argues that in order to offset the neural decline the brain recruits help from other sources – social engagement with others, compensation and similar. This theory thus brings together many of the models of ageing neural processes that have been considered in various forms within geropsychology (e.g. the general slowing hypothesis) and combines them with other models (e.g. compensation; see Reuter-Lorenz and Cappell, 2008) into an integrated theory that promises to describe much of cognitive ageing. However, the model is different in that it is flexible – no section of functioning is necessarily the most important, since the process works as an interactive whole, and, indeed, the relative importance of different components might well vary considerably between individuals (see Kennedy, 2010). However, the theory at the time of writing is still in its relatively early days, and more research is still required.

However, persuasive as neural models can appear, there is a very big caveat to these arguments. Finding a neurological explanation for memory does not provide the sole 'answer' to research on memory and ageing. Of course finding the neural mechanisms is fantastically important, but, regardless of the cause of memory change, the nature of the memory change still has to be dealt with in everyday life. So, in one sense, explaining the origins of ageing memory change in neural processes is like discovering that budgerigars are originally Australian birds. This is useful information in many respects, but it does not in any way, shape or form affect how we deal with budgies in everyday life.

Another reality check

This chapter makes depressing reading if taken at face value. Memory defines us – besides mundane things like remembering shopping lists and appointments, it reminds us of who we are and locates us in time and space. These sound high-flown, almost pretentious words, but all we have to do is think of books or movies based on a person having amnesia to appreciate just how disorienting a loss of memory would be. In addition, severe loss of memory is synonymous with dementia, and, accordingly, memory loss has both a stigma and a fear attached to it. It is not surprising, therefore, that evidence of memory loss can be depressing.

However, we need to put things in perspective. Although we often use the term 'memory *loss*', it is far more accurate to use the term 'memory *decline*'. We do not lose our memory ability, it simply gets a little bit worse. Of course this is deeply annoying, even upsetting at times. But we should be careful of over-dramatising this change. Put simply – our memories never have been perfect (see Baddeley, Eysenck and Anderson, 2009). They have always been easily distorted and prone to error. Age simply makes our fallibility a little more fallible. But it is NOT the same as the catastrophic loss seen in dementia. Most of us have encountered an older person who tells you how bad their memory is these days and gives a lengthy anecdote of how they forget things. But their memory must still be working well if they are able to remember in detail examples of how they forget things.

We live in a literate world. One of the great advantages of this is that we no longer rely on memory for storage of information, be it historical or more immediate (e.g. shopping lists). We should not be afraid of making use of this literacy, and indeed, given the fallibility of even the best memories, we would be foolish to do so. How many people would trust someone with a very good memory to get a weekly shopping list absolutely right? But this should not be an excuse for complacency. Maintaining good intellectual and memory functioning through mental exercise (augmented by regular physical exercise) is still a wise policy, as we have seen.

Suggested further reading

Baddeley (1983) provides an immensely readable introduction to the general psychology of memory, and the book is warmly recommended. Baddeley (1995) and Baddeley *et al.* (2009) are more advanced texts, but still reasonably accessible to a non-specialist. A useful briefer survey of ageing and memory is provided by Old and Naveh-Benjamin (2008). There are good reviews of semantic memory in ageing by Luo and Craik (2008) and Peraita (2007). For a review of episodic memory, see Craik (2000) and Smith (2006). There is an excellent introduction to the topic of brain ageing and the CRUNCH model by Reuter-Lorenz and Lustig (2005).

CHAPTER 4

Ageing and Language

Introduction

Linguistic skills encompass the production and comprehension of speech and writing.

For those readers unfamiliar with basic psycholinguistic terms, it is advisable to read Appendix III before continuing.

Although each section that follows is reasonably self-contained, researchers do not devise their work with the express aim that it can be neatly compartmentalised under sub-headings in textbooks, so there is some overlap. Indeed, it is fair to say that studies of ageing and linguistic skills provide a more disjointed picture than, for example, intelligence or memory. In all sections it should be noted that research has almost always used cross-sectional studies. Where longitudinal research has been conducted on linguistic changes, then, as with measurements of cognitive performance (see Chapter 2), it has generally found smaller scale changes than have cross-sectional studies (e.g. Connor *et al.*, 2004). To take a more specific example, in a cross-sectional study of vocabulary size, Alwin and McCammon (2001) found that differences within an age group were significantly greater than differences between age groups (probably reflecting radical differences in educational experiences and other cohort effects). Thus, some caution should be exercised in interpreting data from cross-sectional studies. It should also be noted that the interaction between different skills involved in reading is very complex and still far from understood, and considerable portions of variance in ability may be specific to a particular situation, person or group (see Stine-Morrow *et al.*, 2001).

The degree to which changes are identified also to some extent depends upon the level of focus. Burke *et al.* (2000) argue that age-related decline in reception of language is practically non-existent in comparison with problems in the production of language. In overall and relative terms this is arguably true, but it can give the impression that reception of linguistic information is totally unaffected by ageing, and that is not the case.

The sections that follow begin with general considerations of reading – as part of lifestyle and in conjunction with general cognitive change. Then different aspects of linguistic skills are considered in a (loosely) hierarchical manner, beginning with word recognition and proceeding 'up' to comprehension.

It is worth stressing once again, however, that as with intelligence and memory the changes we will examine are *relative* and not, repeat *not*, absolute. Discussion of a decline in speech comprehension and similar can lead to the misguided but understandable impression that researchers have conclusively proved that older people are incapable of understanding a single thing beyond the most elemental and simple of concepts. This is not the case. Although under certain laboratory conditions, older people will perform less well, such situations are often far from realistic and simply demonstrate what happens *in extremis*. Such scenarios are sometimes necessary to discover how a particular process operates, but they might have little bearing on everyday experience. In a similar way, sometimes an engine's performance is only truly tested by pushing it to its limits, but this has little bearing on the performance of the same engine in a family car consigned to the school run and weekend shopping. In most situations corresponding to normal everyday life, older people's comprehension and use of language in all its manifestations operate within acceptable bounds (see Whitbourne and Whitbourne, 2011).

The role of reading in older people's lifestyles

Reading can be used for various media. We tend to think of it in terms of books, magazines and newspapers, but it can also include mundane everyday items such as posters and timetables, as well as relatively recent innovations such as text on a computer screen. With regard to book reading, the percentage of people who read a book for pleasure declines slightly from a peak in middle age, but is still higher in older age groups than in many younger age groups (e.g. National Council on Aging, 1975; National Endowment for the Arts, 2007). Regarding other types of print reading, particularly newspapers, in the USA at least, a higher percentage of older adults read these than many younger adult age groups (National Endowment for the Arts, 2007). Furthermore, these figures have remained relatively stable in recent years for older adults, whilst the figures for younger adults have shown a decline (National Endowment for the Arts, 2007). It should also be noted that the Internet and other digital media are increasing as a source of reading material for older adults. For example, in the USA, although they are the smallest by percentage consumers of digital media, almost a quarter of older adults claim to have accessed digital media in the past day as a source of news (Pew Research Center, 2010). It should also be noted that, although there are similarities, the precise pattern of reading activity between cultures can vary somewhat (e.g. Chen, 2008).

Reading in later life appears to be beneficial. For example, Verghese, Lipton, Katz *et al.* (2003) found that reading was a leisure activity (along with playing board games or musical instruments and dancing) that was correlated with a lower risk of developing dementia. Lachman *et al.* (2010) found that reading, as part of a package of cognitive activities (the others were writing, word games and lecture attending), appeared to offset some indices of cognitive decline. Again, Dellenbach and Zimprich (2008) demonstrated that reading was a key predictor of level of **typical intellectual engagement (TIE)**, a measure of willingness to engage in cognitively demanding activities (a concept akin to the need for a cognition measure cited in Chapter 2). These examples might be seen as further proof of the disuse theory (see Chapter 2) since reading is mental exercise and thus presumably keeps the mind and brain active. In contrast, Ackerman, Kanfer and Calderwood (2010) found that giving older adults extra reading tasks for a month produced no discernible transfer effects through changes to cognitive test performance (a month of training on the Wii computer game similarly had no effect). However, it could be legitimately questioned whether a mere month of extra reading is a realistic intervention treatment.

Reading can play a greater role than simply being a type of mental exercise, since it is a principal means of deriving information. For example, in the USA, Medicare is a key means of providing health insurance for older citizens. Time per week spent reading is correlated with level of knowledge about Medicare, even after statistically controlling for level of education (Bann *et al.*, 2006). Jacobs *et al.* (2008), using a longitudinal study, found that reading was correlated with survival eight years later, even after controlling for various health and social measures. Evidence almost overwhelmingly supports the argument that **health literacy** (the ability to access and constructively use health care information) is beneficial both in reducing mortality and increasing quality of life (see Perlow, 2010). However, this is not a simplistic scenario in which if people read more about their health they will act on the advice and get better (see Sudore *et al.*, 2006). There are probably several key mediating factors that determine whether the advice is read, understood and/or heeded, such as self-efficacy (Kim and Yu, 2010). Put simply, if a person feels that they cannot change their own lives for the better, then reading about health matters will have negligible impact. Care needs also to be taken with health literature design, because apparently minor changes in semantic content can significantly alter comprehension levels, particularly for people with low verbal ability (see Liu, Kemper and Bovaird, 2009).

Again, when reading is found to be a predictor, it is often one of several factors cited as having a significant influence on health behaviour (e.g. Baker *et al.*, 2000; Scazufca, Almeida and Menezes, 2010). Also, reading as an activity will only improve health literacy if it is directed at reading health literature. This might seem an obvious point to make, but, if older adults direct reading only towards, for example, reading for entertainment, then its efficacy might be blunted (see Fisher, 1990). Nonetheless, there are occasions where, even if it is only part of the problem, a reading difficulty is still a serious issue. A case in point is the finding by Beckman, Parker and Thorslund

(2005) on older people's ability to dose themselves correctly with medicine. Nearly 10 per cent of their participants (aged 77+ and demographically representative) *could not even read the instructions on a sample medicine container.* That is worrying enough – but an even higher proportion could not comprehend the instructions they had read. Factor in physical issues such as difficulties undoing the safety cap on a pill bottle and similar, and two-thirds of the participants tested had at least one problem that limited their competence to dose themselves correctly with medicines. Banning (2007) reviews the implications of poor patient comprehension in older adults in the UK population and points to some serious practical shortcomings that can result, not only in health dangers to the older people themselves, but also in the gross waste of resources that could easily be prevented by increasing the ease of comprehension and similar.

If solely those older adults who are active readers are considered, then there are some intriguing differences between them and their younger counterparts. The older active readers spend more time reading (e.g. Rice, 1986a), but significantly more of this time is spent on newspapers and magazines (e.g. Ribovich and Erikson, 1980; Rice, 1986a). This means that the reading 'practice' older people obtain may be of a poorer quality, because the content of newspapers may be facile compared with the demands of, for example, a 'heavyweight' novel. In the same manner that failure to train strenuously reduces an athlete's performance, so a failure to read sufficiently demanding texts may cause a decline in reading skills. Why this change in reading habits should occur is open to debate. Reduced mental resources may mean that some older people no longer have the intellectual rigour to plough through works by Dostoevsky or similar authors. Alternatively, when old age is reached, many people may feel that they have read most of the fiction they wanted to read, and have no desire to reread works for which they already know the plot. A more cynical view is that older people feel that there is too little time left to waste it on wading through tedious 'classics'. Younger adults may read 'heavy' works to 'improve' themselves. Older people perhaps no longer have this competitive urge. For whatever reason, older people select 'easy' reading over 90 per cent of the time, be it periodicals, newspapers or 'light' fiction. Furthermore, they appear to get the same level of enjoyment out of reading as do younger adults (Bell, 1980; Rice, 1986a).

Physical constraints

As was noted in Chapter 1, the eyesight of most older people worsens, and visual acuity ('focusing power') is reduced. Even in older adults with relatively normal sight, diminishing text size within a range easily visible by younger adults will cause a decline in older people's reading skills (Hasegawa *et al.*, 2006). One study (Bell, 1980) estimates that about 23 per cent of community resident older people are incapable of reading normal print. A solution to this problem is to print books in a larger typeface (for the technically minded, 18–20 point, which is about the size of the main chapter titles in this book). Perhaps the best-known example of this in the UK is the Ulverscroft series. The larger print makes easier reading for those with poor sight, but a study has shown that in the UK at least there are disadvantages. The first arises from the fact that large print books have a relatively small market. Younger visually impaired adults tend to use magnifying equipment, enabling them to cope with normally sized print. Therefore, the principal market is older people. This is further restricted by the fact that few readers buy large print books – most borrow from the local library. These considerations mean that publishers tend to stick to fairly 'safe' lightweight fiction that will appeal to the largest readership, such as that by James Herriot, Agatha Christie, Catherine Cookson, and so forth. Whilst there is nothing wrong with these authors *per se*, this policy means that an older person with eyesight problems is restricted in his or her choice to texts that are unlikely to stretch his or her reading abilities. An additional consideration is that many older people are limited in the amount they can read. Large print books are heavy, and older people may take fewer books home from the library than when they were younger, simply because they cannot carry more (Bell, 1980). Furthermore, there is some evidence that, while large print size may increase the rate at which words can be read aloud, it may decrease the speed with which they are read silently (Bouma *et al.*, 1982). However, Lovie and Whittaker (1998) found limited evidence that print size had an effect on reading rate. As noted in Chapter 2, adjusting print size of intelligence tests lessened, but did not remove, age differences (Storandt and Futterman, 1982), whilst Rosenstein and Glickman (1994) found increased print size had no effect on performance of a personnel selection test. The font face used can also affect reading speed (Vanderplas and Vanderplas, 1980), although note that Cerella and Fozard (1984) found that making print harder to read did not differentially affect older people relative to younger people. For a recent review of the practical options available to older adults with vision problems, see Dunning (2009).

Considerations about print size may eventually become outmoded because of the rise in availability of talking books. For example, Bouchard Ryan *et al.* (2003) observed that older adults with visual problems such as macular degeneration (see Chapter 1) were more likely to change from reading newspapers and magazines (which typically have small print and poor contrast) to listening to talking books. The authors also noted that circa a quarter of their sample used computer technology to enlarge print. However, although talking books offer a solution to people with sight difficulties, they are not, as is commonly supposed, a direct substitute for reading. Three reasons can be cited. First, the narrator will almost certainly place emphases upon what is being read out that may not match what the listener would emphasise were he or she reading for themselves. Second, listening to a talking book involves hearing every word. As noted earlier, reading does not involve reading every word (studies of eye movements in reading show that necessary but predictable words such as 'the' and 'and' are usually skipped over). Third, in reading it is easy to move back over a passage of print just read, or to skim read through a section of prose. This is either very difficult or impossible to do when using a talking book.

It should be noted that many older people are unaware that they have problems with their vision. Holland and Rabbitt (1989) noted that all participants from the age of 50 onwards gave near-identical subjective ratings of their vision, though in reality there was a marked deterioration in the older participants. A decline in perceptual abilities does not just mean that older people need larger print and/or hearing aids, however. A sensory loss can directly affect the efficiency with which information is processed. For example, Rabbitt (1989) noted that older people with mild hearing loss (35–50 dB) had great difficulty remembering lists of spoken words, even though they were earlier able to repeat them all perfectly as they were spoken to them. It appears that hearing impaired older people can perceive words, but it takes greater effort to do this, leaving fewer mental resources to encode and remember them. That there is nothing especially wrong with their memories can be shown by the fact that, if the participants were shown *printed* lists of words, then there was no difference between their and normal hearing controls' performance (i.e. the effect was confined to when hearing was part of the processing chain). Again, Cervera *et al.* (2009) demonstrated that age differences in speech recognition and memory tasks were eliminated when hearing ability was partialled out of the equation.

Similarly, Schneider (1997) demonstrated that cochlear degeneration and relatively small changes in the fidelity of signal transmission can have much broader effects on, for example, following conversations in a noisy environment or rapidly spoken prose. Schneider *et al.* (2000) found that older adults only demonstrated a failing of memory for discourse (both in terms of the details and the gist of what had been heard) when differences in hearing levels were not controlled for. If volume levels of the stimuli were presented at what was appropriate for the individual participant's hearing abilities, then older and younger participants could recall aspects of discourse equally well both with and without background noise (only in a very high background noise condition did the younger participants show an advantage in recall of details). Schneider, Daneman and Murphy (2005) found that altering parameters of the speech signal that minimised its auditory degradation likewise removed age differences. Thus, peripheral changes in hearing can account for a large proportion of the ageing decline in linguistic skills involving auditory input. However, this does not mean that absolutely everything is preserved. For example, when asked to perform a task and memorise spoken words at the same time, older adults were significantly worse at the task, even when the words were amplified to overcome the effects of hearing loss (Tun, McCoy and Wingfield, 2009).

The voice also undergoes changes. The obvious superficial alterations, in a raising of pitch and a weakness of projection, arise from a variety of factors, including muscle wastage and a reduction in lung capacity. Other changes may result from relatively modern phenomena, such as (ill-fitting) dentures and smoking (Thompson, 1988). However, whatever the reason, vocal output is generally poorer in older people (Xue and Deliyski, 2001). This loss of vocal efficiency also shows itself in a slowing of articulation rate for normal impromptu speech, reading a passage of prose and reaction times to pronouncing words (e.g. Laver and Burke, 1993; Oyer and Deal, 1989; Ryan, 1972). However, it should also be noted that slower speech rate correlates significantly with memory span (Multhaup, Balota and Cowan, 1996), implying a cognitive connection as well.

Handwriting undergoes changes (see Miller, 1987), largely tied to physical deterioration. Aside from the effects of conditions such as the early stages of dementia (Slavin et al., 1999) and Parkinson's disease (e.g. Contreras-Vidal, Teulings and Stelmach, 1995), 'normal' ageing too presents its problems. For example, fine control over the spatial co-ordination of finger and wrist movements involved in handwriting declines in later life (Contreras-Vidal, Teulings and Stalmach, 1998) and generally older writers are less efficient in using visual feedback (Slavin, Phillips and Bradshaw, 1996). However, not all age differences are necessarily due to physical factors. For example, it is worth noting that many older adults who are 'naturally' left-handed use their right (i.e. less efficient) hand for writing, simply because until relatively recently, many schools forced all children to write with their right hands (see Beukelaar and Kroonenberg, 1986). This may distort findings on some age differences in handwriting skill. The effects of these changes, other than in the aesthetic appearance of the writing itself, are mixed. Dixon, Kurzman and Friesen (1993) found that, overall, writing speed decreases with age across a wide variety of writing tasks. However, to some extent this is shaped by the level of familiarity of the tasks: the more familiar the task, the less the age difference. In addition, the more tasks were practised, the less the age difference became (recalling Rabbitt's findings on the effect of practice on reaction times reported in Chapter 2).

General cognitive constraints

Given the findings reported elsewhere in this book, it might be intuitively supposed that anything that increases processing load or otherwise makes a linguistic task 'harder' will be disproportionately disadvantageous for older adults. However, the results are surprisingly mixed. For example, Smiler, Gagne and Stine-Morrow (2004) found that reading speed was unaffected by a concurrent load placed by having to perform another distractor task simultaneously. An analogous finding was reported by Stuart-Hamilton and Rabbitt (1997b), who found that manipulating aspects of text (e.g. syntactic complexity and/or amount of the text that could be seen at any one time) did not affect the reading speed of older adults relative to younger adult controls.

With regard to eye movements, Kemper, Crow and Kemtes (2004) found relatively few age differences in eye movements except that older adults tended to look back over ambiguous text (e.g. to use one of the authors' examples, *The experienced soldiers warned about the dangers conducted the midnight raid*) more than did younger adults.

This implies that older adults can process less information in a single 'bite' and thus need to re-check complex text more often than younger adults. Analogous findings were reported by Rayner *et al.* (2006). They examined eye movements in reading text that was varied in various ways, including predictability and frequency of words used. The researchers found that older readers tended to 'skip' their eyes over words far more than younger readers did. Rayner *et al.* concluded that older adults have slower processing speeds than younger adults and compensate for this by taking more chances and skipping over words whose identity is highly predictable, thereby increasing the speed at which they can get through a passage of text. This explains why the researchers found that their older participants were significantly more affected by predictability and frequency of the text.

Supporting evidence for Rayner *et al.*'s conclusions comes from Christianson *et al.* (2006), who gave participants an assortment of **garden path sentences**. These are sentences that appear to be saying one thing but at a certain point it becomes obvious that another meaning is intended (e.g. *While John brushed the dog scratched for fleas*). When given comprehension questions later, participants sometimes gave answers that were only correct if just the first bit of the sentence is taken into account (e.g. answering 'yes' to the question *Did John brush the dog?*). Christianson *et al.* found that older adults gave more of these 'good enough' answers (which are of course errors), and they argue that this is because in later life people become more dependent upon heuristics to compensate for declines in basic skills. It is worth making a caveat here that many garden path sentences can be made easier to understand when spoken, and prosody (i.e. how something is said) is taken into account. Hoyte, Brownell and Wingfield (2009) gave participants sentences whose interpretation was ambiguous and whose intended meaning could only be determined by the prosodic pattern (e.g. *The doctor said the nurse is thirsty*). Aspects of the prosody were systematically varied (namely, pitch, amplitude and timing), but, for old and young adults alike, timing variation had the most significant effects. The findings of Christianson *et al.* are echoed in a study by Abada, Baum and Titone (2008). They found that where a target word was made phonologically ambiguous (e.g. it sounded as if it might begin with either a 'g' or a 'k' sound), older adults were far more easily biased by context into identifying the target as a word that fitted the context.

Kemper, McDowd and Kramer (2006) examined eye movements in readers when a distracter word (printed in italics or a red font) was placed in a display of target text (i.e. participants were meant to be reading the text on the screen, but a word that was not meant to be there would also sometimes appear). The researchers found that younger and older participants had similar eye movements when processing the distracting word. However, the younger adults read faster and could answer more questions correctly about the target text. This finding argues against the **inhibitory deficit hypothesis**. This hypothesis states that, because of age-related declines in inhibition (see Chapters 2 and 3; also Morrone *et al.*, 2010), this will cause specific problems with any mental process where inhibition has been used – in this case, processing the distracter. It should also be noted that the effect of distracters on older adults is not simply a matter of differences in eyesight. Mund, Bell and Buchner (2010) presented a distraction task in which participants were told to read only those words in italics and to ignore distracters printed in conventional font. The researchers found that, even if the younger participants' eyesight were altered to resemble the acuity of older people or if the younger and older participants were matched for acuity, there was still a significant age difference. This indicates that reading problems experienced by older adults in these circumstances cannot be simply attributed to changes in visual acuity. This the researchers attributed to age changes in inhibitory mechanisms.

Some other manipulations produce rather more straightforward ageing effects. For example, Speranza, Daneman and Schneider (2000) presented participants with sentences to read that were obscured by an overlying pattern of 'visual noise'. The researchers found that the older adults needed a significantly lower level of noise in order to perform at the same level as younger adult readers. However, older readers were disproportionately advantaged over younger readers when the sentences offered semantic facilitation (thus echoing the findings of other studies; see page 147). Again, measurements of EEG responses by older and younger participants engaged in reading whilst attempting to ignore distracters demonstrate that older adults' mental processes are significantly more disrupted by the extraneous stimuli (Phillips and Lesperance, 2003).

Kemper, Herman and Lian (2003) provided participants with the task of giving spoken responses to questions whilst engaged in another activity (walking and finger tapping). The researchers found that older participants produced less fluent and syntactically less complex speech than younger participants, thus supporting the argument that older adults have a lowered working memory span (see Chapter 3). Interestingly, the researchers also found that younger adults adopted a different strategy from older participants – namely, they used grammatically simpler and shorter sentences, whereas the older adults slowed their speech rate. Kemper, Schmalzried, Hoffman and Herman (2010) found analogous results when they examined language production by adults as they conducted a simultaneous task (the **pursuit rotor task**; see Glossary). Unsurprisingly, as the pursuit rotor task was made more demanding, linguistic skills deteriorated. Kemper *et al.* found that participants with higher levels of vocabulary and working memory capacity showed less deterioration in linguistic skills, and this effect was more pronounced for older than for younger adult participants. Conversely, faster processing speeds were associated with a lesser linguistic decline in younger more than in older adults.

Other effects are more complex and not uniform across all types of linguistic activity. For example, Gilchrist, Cowan and Naveh-Benjamin (2008) measured recall of spoken sentences with various structures. The researchers found that, although older participants recalled fewer words than younger participants, there was no age difference in the percentage of complete clauses accessed. Gilchrist *et al.* concluded that older adults simply recall fewer chunks (see Glossary) in verbal recall tasks. DeDe *et al.* (2004) found that working memory's influence varied according to which aspect of reading skills was being considered. The paper is very difficult to summarise, but, in essence, using structural equation modelling, the researchers found that the mediating effect of working memory shifted from a marginal role to central importance depending upon the specific reading task being considered.

Thus, although there are instances where linguistic skills are affected by general cognitive decline and a lowering of cognitive capacity, the effects are not always clear-cut, with some skills apparently largely immune to these effects. This is something of a recurrent theme in ageing and language, with some instances of decline that fit with the general findings of intellectual and memory changes and others where there is a surprisingly well-preserved skill that goes against intuitive expectations. So far no overarching theory has been devised to explain these dichotomies, but, as noted earlier, linguistic skills tend in any case to be multi-faceted and surprisingly resistant to reduction to basic explanations. It must also be stressed that most of the studies considered earlier are not of normal reading but of an artificial situation. Like the majority of reading studies, it is difficult to say with absolute certainty that what is being observed is analogous to normal reading conditions and thus the findings could to some extent be an artifact of the research method used. This issue of the realism of laboratory reading tasks will be returned to later.

Word recognition

There are a variety of ways to test the ability to read single words, but two of the commonest are the **lexical decision** and the **naming latency** tasks. The former requires participants simply to decide if a group of letters forms a word (note that the participants do not have to identify what the word 'says'). A naming latency task measures how quickly a participant can read a word aloud. Generally, older people are no worse at these tasks than younger adults when the task is presented in its conventional form (e.g. Bowles and Poon, 1985; Cerella and Fozard, 1984). Duñabeitia *et al.* (2009) gave participants a lexical decision task. In the condition of interest here, participants were shown compound words (i.e. words made up of two or more individual words such as *bookshop*) preceded by a priming word, which was either the first word within the compound word, the second word, or an unrelated word (e.g. if the word is *bookshop*, the primes would be *book*, *shop* and, for instance, *house* respectively). Duñabeitia *et al.* found that there was no difference in priming effects for younger and older adult participants, implying that **morphological processing** (the processing of word structure) remains intact in later life.

However, if the tasks are made harder or more complex, then often an age decrement appears. For example, Ratcliff *et al.* (2004) found that in two lexical decision tasks older adults were slower but more accurate than younger participants. This was accounted for using the **Ratcliff diffusion model**, which argued that older adults were slower at some aspects of processing but adopted more conservative decision criteria.

Bowles and Poon (1981) found further evidence of age-related decline when they gave participants a modified lexical decision task. Participants had to judge pairs of letter groupings, both of which had to form real words for a 'yes' response to be given. Allen *et al.* (1993) manipulated the difficulty of the words used in a lexical decision task in ways likely to strike at relatively peripheral (such as altering the ease with which stimuli could be encoded) and relatively central (such as word frequency) aspects of processing. The researchers concluded that age differences tend to arise in peripheral rather than central mental processes (e.g. there were no age differences induced by word frequency). This is echoed in the findings of Madden (1992) who found age differences were greater when the visual appearance of the words (likely to be a fairly peripheral effect) was manipulated. Evidence of lack of differences at a central level is provided by, amongst others, Karayanidis *et al.* (1993), who found no differences between the EEG patterns of older and younger adults during a lexical decision task (though there were some differences when encountering words seen earlier, this is essentially a memory rather than word recognition effect). Spieler and Balota (2000) found that in a naming latency task older adults made significantly greater relative use of word frequency information, whereas younger adults made significantly greater use of orthographic features of the word. The authors concluded that this denotes an age-related shift from primary reliance on features within the word to features of the word itself.

Generally, as lexical decision task difficulty increases, then so does the size of the age difference. Myerson *et al.* (1997) found that this can be reduced to a Brinley plot – in other words, the general phenomenon may be explained in terms of the general slowing hypothesis (for further discussion, see Chapter 2). However, Allen *et al.* (2004) found in a study of older and younger adults' lexical decision speeds that Brinley plots for errors and response times were significantly different and in effect contradicted each other. Using a very complex mathematical technique (for those interested – error values were converted into entropy and then response speeds predicted from these transformed data), the authors demonstrated that components of the response associated with peripheral processes were significantly affected by ageing, but those associated with central processes were relatively unaffected – thus, by a circuitous route, supporting the earlier findings cited in this chapter. However, another study by Allen *et al.* (2002) points to a rather more complex state of affairs. Participants were given a lexical decision task in which the words were either conventionally printed all in the same case (e.g. 'same case'), or were mixed case (e.g. 'MiXed CaSe') and in either instance could be printed in one colour or in several colours. It was predicted that conventionally printed words would be processed faster since the mind would process them holistically (basically, they primarily would be processed by shape and outline with relatively little reliance on the more laborious method of reading letter by letter). On the other hand, mixed case words present unusual outlines, and thus cannot be processed holistically, but instead must be processed analytically (in essence, letter by letter). It was thus predicted that processing of mixed case words would be slower. It was felt that use of different colours would have no effect on holistic processing of words but it would speed up processing of mixed case words (because they could be more easily distinguished from each other). The researchers found that these predictions were borne out by the performances of young adult participants, but older participants had a different pattern of responses, suggesting that ageing does not affect holistic processing, but causes a decrement in analytic processing. This is reflected in a study by Logan and Balota (2003). They gave participants the task of studying a group of words and then doing a task in which they had to complete a word from a fragment of it. If the word fragment was preceded by a blocking word that was orthographically related (loosely, had a lot of letters in common), then older participants were disproportionately disadvantaged and were more likely to complete the fragment by erroneously using the blocking word. The authors concluded that this was because older adults may have problems in suppressing activity of rival (but inaccurate) alternatives in processing words. This recalls the research on frontal lobe deficits discussed in Chapter 2.

In **semantic facilitation** experiments (see Appendix III), older people are generally slower (as with many reaction time experiments; see Chapter 2). This can be demonstrated at a neurological level. Federmeier and Kutas (2005) found that the brain activity of older adults to these harder-to-predict phrases was slower and weaker in older adults. However, older participants gain a disproportionately greater advantage from this, when compared with recognising words seen in isolation (Laver and Burke, 1993; Myerson et al., 1992; though note that earlier commentators, such as Craik and Rabinowitz, 1984, found no difference). At one level the explanation for this phenomenon is simple – 'a slow horse will save more time than a fast horse when the distance is reduced by a constant amount' (Laver and Burke, 1993, p.35). If one horse runs at 40 kilometres per hour, and another at 20 kilometres per hour, then cutting the race distance from 40 to 20 kilometres will save 30 minutes for the faster horse and an hour for the slower one. In a similar manner, if older people are reacting less quickly, then facilitation (which in effect decreases the computational 'distance') will be of greater benefit to older participants (see also Bennett and McEvoy, 1999).

So far, word recognition has been examined largely in terms of printed words, but of course word recognition can also be auditory. There are also age differences in this process. Robert and Mathey (2007) examined memory for words in older and younger adult French speakers. The words used either were spelt in a similar fashion to other words in more common usage (e.g. *loupe* is spelt similarly to the more commonly occurring words *soupe* and *coupe*) or had no 'orthographic neighbours' (e.g. there are no particularly common words in French that are spelt in a similar manner to *taupe*). Robert and Mathey found that younger adults were significantly affected by orthographic frequency (i.e. if there were similarly spelt words, recall was worse) but older adults were not. The researchers concluded that this is because, with increasing age, the activity level in lexical processing is lowered, and thus the alternative words are not activated to the same extent and hence cannot interfere with recall. Harris *et al.* (2009) measured brain activity whilst participants attempted to identify spoken words presented with different levels and kinds of background noise. Unsurprisingly, the older participants were significantly worse at this task. However, of especial interest was that the poor performance could at least partly be attributed to differences in volume of grey matter in a specific area of the brain (the anreomedial Heschl's gyrus/superior temporal gyrus region).

Spelling

Spelling skills in later life might be supposed to experience the same fate as word recognition. Knowledge of spelling rules is a crystallised skill, and as such should be relatively immune from ageing effects. However, there is evidence that this is not always the case. Certainly it is generally true that, when participants are simply asked to judge if a word is correctly spelt, there is relatively little effect of ageing (see Shafto, 2010). However, there are (as is inevitably the case in psychogerontology) exceptions to this rule. For example, MacKay, Abrams and Pedroza (1999) observed that older participants were as adept as younger participants at detecting misspellings in a list of words. However, there was an age difference involved in being able subsequently to retrieve the correctly and incorrectly spelt words from memory. Abrams, Farrell and Margolin (2010) found that, if *solely* older adults were considered, who were then grouped into age decades (60s, 70s and 80s), the two oldest groups were both slower and less accurate at detecting misspellings when reading sentences in which words were presented one at a time.

When *production* of words is considered, generally an ageing decline is observed. For example, MacKay and Abrams (1998) found that misspellings increased in later life, as did Stuart-Hamilton and Rabbitt (1997a). These age-related deficits are not directly attributable to general slowing, crystallised intelligence or education level. Stuart-Hamilton and Rabbitt found fluid intelligence to be a good predictor of spelling skills, whilst MacKay and co-researchers link the decline to a more specific linguistic coding deficit (see MacKay *et al.*, 1999). In part it is predicated on the **transmission deficit hypothesis** (MacKay and Burke, 1990), which argues that concepts are stored in interconnected 'nodes'. Ageing weakens these connections and the ease with which nodes may be activated, though this can be compensated for by regular practice, and/or stimulation by more prompts. Hence, *inter alia*, new pieces of information are more prone to inefficient processing than older pieces, and recognition is easier than recall. Further support for this argument is provided in a more recent study by Shafto (2010).

Tip of the tongue states

These have already been mentioned in Chapter 3, which addressed memory. Tip of the tongue states (TOTs) describe the familiar experience of remembering a number of features of a word (what it sounds like, etc.) without being able to bring the word to mind. The study of TOTs is often treated as a memory issue, but of course it is also of considerable interest in psycholinguistics, since it can inform us of the processes by which words are produced. Generally speaking, psycholinguists are interested in TOTs for what they can tell us about retrieval from memory, whilst cognitive psychologists are generally more interested in the 'phenomenological experience' of having a TOT state (Schwartz and Frazier, 2005). However, this is a generalisation and there are plenty of exceptions. See Chapter 3 for further discussion of TOTs.

Pronunciation

Knowledge of pronunciation of words might also be expected to be preserved in later life, and indeed this would appear to be generally the case (though note that the *speed* with which words can be pronounced may decrease – see earlier). Typically, pronunciation is tested by presenting participants with a list of irregularly spelt words (e.g. *yacht, dessert*), and asking them to say them out loud. Because the words do not obey conventional spelling rules, their pronunciation cannot be calculated from first principles. For example, pronouncing *dessert* by conventional spelling rules would yield the spoken presentation of *desert* (and vice versa). Those readers who have already read Chapter 2 will appreciate that pronunciation abilities are therefore seen as part and parcel of crystallised intelligence (loosely speaking, general knowledge), which is largely ageing-proof. It follows from this that pronunciation ability should remain stable in later life.

Nelson and O'Connell (1978) examined the pronunciation abilities of 120 adults aged 20–70 years, and found no significant correlation between test score and chronological age (Nelson and McKenna, 1973). This word list was developed into the **National Adult Reading Test**, or **NART**. A subsequent study by Crawford *et al.* (1988) found a slight negative correlation between age and NART score, but this disappeared when either length of education or social class was partialled out of the equation. Hence, concluded the authors, 'age has little or no effect on NART performance' (p.182). Because of such arguments, the NART has become widely used as a quick assessor of crystallised intelligence (see Deary, Whalley and Starr, 2009), particularly where older participants with dementia or some other kinds of brain damage have retained the ability to read whilst being incapable of some other intellectual tasks (e.g. Brayne and Beardsall, 1990; Carswell *et al.*, 1997; Starr and Lonie, 2007). The NART is not necessarily a totally accurate guide, however. When words from the NART are placed in the context of a sentence, then performance generally improves (Conway and O'Carroll, 1997, who developed this format into a new test – the Cambridge Contextual Reading Test, or CCRT; see Beardsall, 1998).

In other instances, the NART may over-estimate intelligence levels (Mockler, Riordan and Sharma, 1996), whilst researchers using an American version of the NART (called, not surprisingly, the American NART or AMNART or ANART) found somewhat different patterns of results within groups of White American and African American older people who were either non-demented or suffering from dementia (Boekamp, Strauss and Adams, 1995). There are also question marks about the general advisability of using reading tests across groups of older people in multiethnic and multilingual groups (see Cosentino, Manly and Mungas, 2007). It is difficult to get a clear overall picture from these and similar studies simply because different samples of people have been used (e.g. some have dementia, some have not; amongst studies of dementia, different grading criteria have been used, and so forth). The general conclusion of many researchers is that the NART is a fair *general* predictor of intellectual status (and breakfast consumption: cereal eating and test score are positively correlated; Smith, 1998), even if the shortened (and quicker) format arguably lacks accuracy (Bucks *et al.*, 1996) and the full test is not absolutely precise (see Law and O'Carroll, 1998).

Semantic processing

In addition to recognising words and knowing how they are spelt and pronounced, it is also necessary to know what the words mean. In Chapter 2, it was demonstrated that knowledge of word meaning is the key component of many measures of crystallised intelligence, and it is known that, although age does not affect crystallised intelligence (and thus knowledge of word meanings) as much as, for example, tasks heavily based on fluid intelligence, nonetheless there is a decline in later life. Principally, older adults are slower to produce responses, and definitions offered are likely to be less precise than younger people's. For example, McGinnis and Zelinski (2000) gave participants the task of providing definitions of unfamiliar words that could be gleaned from the context in which they were presented. The researchers found that older adults picked up fewer of the available pieces of information available in the text, and produced more vague generalised definitions. In a second experiment, McGinnis and Zelinski provided four definitions for each unfamiliar word and asked participants to choose the correct definition. One definition was rigorously correct; one was more generalised (thus, not quite 'wrong' but certainly vague); one was a generalised interpretation of the story; and one was irrelevant. Younger adults relatively favoured the exact definitions, whilst the oldest old participants (those aged 75 years and over) were more likely to select the generalised definitions. In a follow-up study, the authors gave participants the task of reading a passage of prose that contained an unfamiliar word. Whilst reading, the participants were asked to 'think aloud' about what they were reading, and afterwards were asked to rate a set of definitions derived from the passage for accuracy (McGinnis and Zelinski, 2003). The researchers found that the older participants produced more generalised comments about the passages whilst thinking aloud, and rated generalised and irrelevant definitions more highly. Overall, McGinnis and Zelinski concluded that older adults have appreciable problems processing the relatively complex information required to extract meaning from context. More specifically, they fail to think at a sufficiently abstract level and thus fail to draw adequate inferences (however, see Madden and Dijkstra, 2010). This echoes the findings of Albert *et al.* (1987) cited in Chapter 2, in which it was noted that older adults have especial problems providing definitions of sayings and proverbs. It might also be noted that older adults take significantly longer than younger adults to distinguish between metaphors and literally untrue statements (Morrone *et al.*, 2010). This failure too can be seen as a reduced ability to see beyond the literal to the underlying symbolic structure. At a neurological level, this has been attributed to a decline in frontal lobe functioning (Uekermann, Thoma and Daum, 2008).

It should be noted, however, that semantic processing almost invariably is predicated on the use of other skills, and thus age differences may be the result of a wide variety of potential factors. It is rather like judging the worth of different brands of flour in cake recipes. Whilst a reasonable estimate of differences may be gauged, the influence of the other ingredients will always be there and will vary from recipe to recipe. Similarly, whilst semantic skills can be measured, participants have by definition to use other skills (e.g. phonological processing) to perform a semantic task. Thus, the field is wide open for other variables to have an effect. For example, Taylor and Burke (2002) presented participants with pictures of objects. The participants had to name these objects, whilst distracting words were read out. In some instances, the object was a homophone (i.e. had more than one meaning – the authors cite the example of *ball*). If the participant was looking at a picture of an item and a word semantically related to its other meaning was spoken (e.g. the participant sees a picture of a ball and hears the word 'dance' spoken) then this aided the response times of younger participants, but not older participants. Other distracters generally did not differentially affect the responses of the age groups. Taylor and Burke use this finding to develop an interesting and rather complex connectionist model in which ageing has an asymmetric effect on phonological and semantic mechanisms.

In contrast, Mayr and Kliegl (2000) gave participants the task of producing members of either (1) the same semantic category or (2) a member of one semantic category alternating with a member of another semantic category (i.e. a member of category *A*, then a member of category *B*, then a member of category *A*, then *B*, etc.). The researchers used the parameters of the experiment to estimate performance at semantic retrieval itself and performance at the peripheral skills necessary for semantic retrieval to take place. Mayr and Kliegl concluded that semantic retrieval was relatively intact – it was the peripheral factors that showed a significant decline.

Interesting as the findings of Taylor and Burke and Mayr and Kliegl are in their own right, of concern here is the fact that, under different circumstances, semantic processing in older adults can be made to appear good, bad or indifferent according to the experimental design used. In addition, what is meant by 'semantic processing'? Relatively basic semantic processes appear to be age-resistant. For example, Lahar, Tun and Wingfield (2004) demonstrated that filling in a missing word in a sentence where the answer can be gauged from the context appears to be relatively unaffected by ageing (though there may be differences in EEG activity; see Federmeier and Kutas, 2005). Again, presented with the relatively uncomplicated task of providing a definition of a new word just encountered in a passage of prose, older adults produced more complete definitions (Long and Shaw, 2000). It is only with more complex semantic skills that the evidence is more circumspect. However, if the 'mugging analogy' made in Chapter 2 is recalled, it may be argued that, no matter what the 'real' state of something is after all extenuating variables have been accounted for, at the end of the day it is how a skill presents itself for immediate inspection that is usually of paramount concern.

Syntactic processing

Relatively little research has been conducted on semantic or syntactic processing independent of the concurrent considerations of text recall. However, one notable exception is a series of excellent papers and articles by Susan Kemper on changes in syntactic processing in older people. Kemper (1986) requested younger and older adults to imitate sentences by creating new ones with the same syntactic structure. She found that the older participants could only reliably imitate short sentences: long sentences, particularly those containing embedded clauses, were the hardest to imitate. Baum (1993) likewise found that increasing the syntactic complexity of sentences resulted in age group differences in a sentence repetition task; this also occurred when the sentences were used in a lexical decision task. Obler *et al.* (1991) found similar effects of syntax on sentence comprehension. This syntactic decline is also reflected in spontaneous everyday language. Kynette and Kemper (1986) noted that the diversity of syntactic structures declines with age, whilst there is an increase in errors such as the omission of articles and the use of incorrect tenses. In a similar vein, Kemper (1992) found that older and younger adults had the same number of sentence fragments in their spontaneous speech. However, the younger adults' fragments tended to be of 'better quality', being false starts to statements, whereas older adults tended to produce these incomplete statements as 'filler' during a pause.

Kemper and Rush (1988) reported other examples of this decline. For example, the average number of syntactic clauses per sentence fell from 2.8 for those aged 50–59 to 1.7 for those aged 80–89. The researchers also assessed the **Yngve depth** of the syntax. This is a fairly complex technique that gives a syntactic complexity 'score' to a phrase or sentence (the higher the score, the more sophisticated the construction). Yngve scores declined with age but, more intriguingly, they correlated well ($r = 0.76$) with digit span. Thus, the better the memory, the better the syntax. There is an attractively simple explanation for this finding. Syntactically complex sentences are almost invariably longer than simple ones and, to construct or comprehend them, greater demands are placed on memory. Or, put simply, more words have to be remembered at one time. This general principle is illustrated in a study by Stine-Morrow et al. (2010). The researchers examined the issue of **wrap up** in text processing. It is well documented that when a reader reaches a syntactic boundary (basically, where one grammatical phrase ends and another begins), the reading rate slows down. This is termed the 'wrap up' and the more complex the phrase, the bigger the slowing down becomes. It is argued that this occurs because the reader is attempting to process the syntactic phrase just read, and the more complex it is, the greater the processing time that has to be allocated to it. Stine-Morrow et al., examining, inter alia, the eye movements of younger and older participants, demonstrated that older adults use wrap up in effect in a more exaggerated form. However, some other measures of reading (such as regulating processing time to different parts of the reading task) showed little age difference, indicating that older readers make use of the exaggerated wrap up to compensate for other factors.

This is a plausible explanation of why older people simplify their syntax – they know that their cognitive skills are declining, so sentences are simplified and shortened, more time is taken etc., to cope with this. The advantage conferred on older adults when they are in effect given back their processing time is demonstrated in a study by Dupuis and Pichora-Fuller (2010). The researchers presented participants with spoken prose in which the emotional content of the prose and the emotional tone in which it was read out either was congruent or incongruent (e.g. a happy story read in a happy voice versus a sad story read in a happy voice). Older adults were relatively poor at the incongruent condition. However, if they were allowed to repeat the sentences they had heard before responding, the age difference in performance was eliminated.

Comparable results are reported by Gould and Dixon (1993). They asked younger and older married couples to describe a vacation they had taken together, and analysed their descriptions for linguistic content. The general finding was that the younger couple produces a greater amount of detail. The researchers attributed the older couples' 'failure' to do this to a decline in working memory. However, they also acknowledge it is possible that the age-related change is due to a shift in attitude – 'the younger couples...may have given less consideration to being entertaining than did the older couples' (Gould and Dixon, 1993, p.15). Arbuckle, Nohara-LeClair and Pushkar (2000) argue that off-target verbosity is indicative of poor processing skills (e.g. poor inhibition; see Chapter 2). They identified people who had particularly high levels of off-target verbosity and found that they were significantly worse at providing accurate descriptions (in this instance, in a task where they were required to provide a description of an abstract figure to a listener) even when they did not stray off-target. A further study by the same research group (Pushkar *et al.*, 2000) also noted that being high in off-target verbosity generally brought less satisfaction to those listening to it. However, the same study also found that verbosity was unrelated to age or cognitive level, thereby arguing against the case that verbosity necessarily reflects an age-related decline.

Related to Gould and Dixon's findings is a study by Adams (1991), which noted that, compared with a group of younger controls, older adults' written summaries of stories tended to interpret the text at a more abstract level, and placed emphasis on a *précis* of the story's structure. This qualitative difference may arise because of a loss of processing capacity. For example, if the older participants cannot remember as much about the story, then talking about it in abstract terms might be a wise option. Kemper and Anagnopoulos (1993) likewise argue that older people may use various discourse strategies to circumvent deficiencies or discrepancies in their syntactic processing skills. Pasupathi, Henry and Carstensen (2002) also note that, in telling a narrative, older adults are more likely to emphasise positive emotional aspects of the story (i.e. there may be more than simply a cognitive change at work).

Kemper (1987a, b) examined six diaries kept by people for most of their adult lifespans. Drawn from museum archives, the diaries commenced between 1856 and 1876, and finished between 1943 and 1957. Kemper found that the language used became simpler over the writers' lifespans. Sentence length decreased, as did complexity of syntax. For example, the number of embedded clauses declined, and there was an increase in the failure of **anaphoric reference** (e.g. referring to 'he' without adequately specifying which of two previously cited males is meant). At the same time, the sophistication of the narrative declined, and increasingly events were described as a catalogue of facts rather than as a 'story' with a plot and a conclusion. In a similar vein, Bromley (1991) gave participants aged 20–86 years the task of writing a description of themselves. Analysing the results, he found that the syntactic complexity and breadth of vocabulary exhibited in the writing was related to the participant's age, but that other factors, such as word length and readability, were affected by the participant's educational level and level of vocabulary (as measured by the Mill Hill test, a common crystallised intelligence measure; see Chapter 2). Interestingly, fluid intelligence did not play a significant role.

There are other grounds for assuming that a decline in writing cannot automatically be attributed to an intellectual failing. As anyone who has kept a diary for some time will know, writing it can be a chore. Thus, the older they got, the less motivated the writers may have felt to write a 'story' (or perhaps less happened in their lives that might have motivated them to describe it in more elaborate prose). Again, rereading their attempts at creative writing might have so embarrassed the writers that they decided to resort to a less florid style. Furthermore, the purpose of the journal may change over years and become, for example, a method of empowerment at a time of changes in self-perception (see Brady and Sky, 2003). This might also necessitate a change in writing style. It may be the case too that, as the writers grew older, general attitudes to writing styles relaxed, and thus a simpler style was deliberately adopted (e.g. when the diaries began, the massive Victorian novel was in its heyday and, when they ended, F. Scott Fitzgerald and Hemingway were contemporary figures). Indeed, Kemper (1987b) could identify a cohort difference even within her small sample. The writers born earliest in her group used significantly more infinitives ('to go', 'to do', etc.) than did the younger ones.

However, more recent research tends to support the argument that writing changes reflect a decline in ability rather than a stylistic shift. For example, an ingenious study of the letters of King James VI/I by Williams *et al.* (2003) demonstrates a cognitive-related decline that furthermore can be correlated with well-documented bouts of illness that can be reasonably assumed to have had deleterious intellectual effects on the king. In a slightly more prosaic format (no pun intended), Kemper, Thompson and Marquis (2001) conducted a longitudinal study of the writing of older volunteers. Annual samples of language were taken and cognitive tests were also administered. The researchers demonstrated an age-related decline (particularly after the mid-seventies) in grammatical complexity and propositional content, and this was linked to cognitive changes. Kemper and Sumner (2001) demonstrated that grammatical complexity was linked to working memory, and sentence length to verbal intelligence (see also Kemper, Herman and Liu, 2004). Kemtes and Kemper (1997) found that processing of syntactically complex sentences was correlated with working memory performance both at the 'on-line' level of reading the text and the 'off-line' level of comprehending the text (see also Waters and Caplan, 2001). Thus, although there may be stylistic and cohort effects to account for some syntactic changes in later life, the principal factor would appear to be general ageing intellectual decline.

A related argument concerns how the changes in older people's language can be linked to linguistic usage in childhood. In other words, do older people regress to a childlike linguistic state? This is known as the **regression hypothesis**. The argument in a strong form does not seem plausible, because the grammatical usage of older people is still far more sophisticated and varied than that of children (see Kemper, 1992). Although language may in some sense be simplified in later life, it does not simplify itself *that* much. At a weaker level, the theory is more plausible, since *some* linguistic usage may be superficially similar to children's language, in that both use simplified forms; but this does not prove much beyond the fact that older people at times use simpler language (Hemingway used simpler language than Thomas Hardy, but nobody thought Hemingway had regressed). However, beyond general considerations such as this, it is difficult to make very firm statements.

From these arguments, it is plausible to link syntactic change to alterations in the general intellect. However, there is also evidence that the effects are confounded by crystallised skills, cohort effects and possibly a deliberate change in linguistic style (though whether this is a response to a lowered mental processing capacity is a moot point). Thus, as with much in research on ageing and language, the results are not totally clear-cut.

Story comprehension

The basic 'story comprehension' paradigm is simple – a participant listens to or reads a short passage of text (usually 300–400 words long) and then in one form or another either repeats back as much as possible or is given a multiple-choice recognition test. Most studies have shown that older people remember less (e.g. Byrd, 1985; Light and Anderson, 1985; Petros *et al.*, 1983 in cross-sectional studies; Zelinski and Burnight, 1997; Zelinski and Stewart, 1998 in longitudinal studies) and may generalise more (e.g. Zelinski and Hyde, 1996). However, whilst this is a general finding, it is not a universal truth, and varying the types of experimental participants and/or test materials can have a crucial effect.

Studies using 'old' participants who are in their sixties have often found no difference with young adults (e.g. Mandel and Johnson, 1984). Age differences are only reliably found when the 'old' participants are in their mid-seventies or older (Meyer, 1987). Also, participants with a high verbal ability generally show no age difference (e.g. Taub, 1979). The findings on prior experience are more complex. Soederberg Miller (2003) gave participants various texts to read, some of which related to cookery. The readers varied in cookery expertise, and the greater their knowledge (not surprisingly) the greater their encoding and memory of cookery-related items. However, the age of the participants had no effect on this phenomenon. In contrast, Soederberg Miller (2009) performed an experiment in which participants of various ages differed in their level of knowledge about cookery. She measured 'reading efficiency', defined as time spent reading divided by quantity of information recalled from each passage read. When reading prose passages about cookery, younger adults' reading efficiency was unaffected by their prior knowledge of cookery. However, for older adults, efficiency rose the greater their prior knowledge. An analogous result was found when participants were classified by working memory ability. Those with a high level of working memory were unaffected by cookery knowledge, whereas those with a low level of working memory performed better if they had a high prior knowledge of cookery.

This provides evidence for a compensatory strategy, often termed within reading research an **allocation policy**, which, it is argued, can be very consistent across time and tasks (Stine-Morrow, Soederberg Miller and Hertzog, 2006). In effect, older adults cut their suit according to their cloth. Stine-Morrow, Soederberg Miller, Gagne and Hertzog (2008) demonstrated that if, for example, participants had lower working memory span, then greater resources were allocated to word processing (i.e. simply working out what the individual words mean). In contrast, those with higher verbal abilities diverted more resources into processing the meaning of the text. A further example of allocation policy can be seen in the findings of Crowley, Mayer and Stuart-Hamilton (2009). They tested children and younger and older adults on a series of measures of general reading (as measured by word recognition), spelling, phonological processing skills (e.g. identifying the reason why two words sound similar because of a shared phoneme) and measures of fluid and crystallised intelligence. The researchers found that, in children and younger adults, reading and spelling were best predicted by phonological test performance (echoing the finding of Majeres, 2005). However, older adults' reading and spelling abilities were best predicted by fluid intelligence and chronological age. These findings suggest that as we age there can be considerable shifts in our reliance on specific sub-skills involved in the reading and spelling processes.

The study by Crowley et al. assumes readers and spellers of relatively equal ability. However, individual differences in ability can have different effects across the lifespan. For example, Margolin and Abrams (2007), in a comparison of older and younger adults, demonstrated that for good spellers there were no age differences in performance. However, for poor spellers, the older adults were significantly poorer at a range of spelling-related skills. This finding indicates that ageing changes in spelling might well contain a considerable factor of individual differences.

The choice of intended listener can also make a difference. Adams et al. (2002) gave older and younger women the task of remembering a story that they were told had to be repeated to either an adult or a child. Although both younger and older adults simplified the story and did more elaborations of key points when retelling the story to a child, older adults did this to a greater extent. When an adult was the listener, the retelling was more 'sophisticated' and younger adults produced a significantly higher proportion of propositions from the original story. This does not necessarily indicate a superiority of older adults in the child as listener condition (arguably it is easier and the additional elaboration may represent a different level of pragmatic awareness rather than a cognitive superiority). However, as Adams et al. point out, it does mean that social context may be a confounding variable of some importance in this area of research, and researchers should be careful over choice of the 'listener' when participants are recalling stories and other information.

In connection with this, it is also worth noting that there may be a further cohort effect in many studies. Ratner et al. (1987) observed that many studies compare a group of younger adults recruited from students with older adults recruited from a broader demographic base. The researchers found a group of non-student younger adults matched for verbal ability with a group of students and compared the two groups with a group of older people on a prose recall task. The students performed better than the other two groups (the non-student younger and older adults performed reasonably similarly to one another). This implies that a considerable part of the age difference in many studies of story recall and comprehension may be attributable to using younger participants who not only are different in age but also radically different in skill at memorising and interpreting text.

Choice of presentation of materials has an even more profound effect upon outcome than choice of participants. Even an apparently simple procedure, such as examining prose comprehension following simplification of the text, has met with nebulous results. For example, Walmsley, Scott and Lehrer (1981) found that simplifying a passage of prose improved comprehension when the simplification was done by the subjective opinion of experienced writers. However, more objective measures, such as simplifying according to a readability formula, had no significant effect on recall.

It might be anticipated that given the findings already reported in this chapter, older adults would be significantly worse at comprehending spoken as opposed to written text. However, the findings are not clear-cut. Cohen (1981) found that older people were significantly worse at recalling spoken than written materials, whilst for the younger participants there was no difference (Zacks *et al.*, 1987). Tun, Benichov and Wingfield (2010) found that even when older adults with hearing loss could answer comprehension questions about auditory passages of prose, the latency with which they responded got significantly longer the quieter the speech and the more complex the prose that was used. Much (though not all; see Petros *et al.*, 1983; Tun *et al.*, 1992) of the early research literature reported that speech comprehension decreases significantly more for older than for younger adults when the speed of the speech is artificially increased (e.g. Wingfield, 1996). This is often explained as being due to general slowing.

However, as Schneider *et al.* (2005) noted, sped-up speech is often degraded in quality (e.g. the speech rises in pitch or the experimenters remove segments from the speech, so a sentence is delivered in a shorter time but the pitch of the speech remains the same). Schneider *et al.* found that, if speech was speeded up but without artificially distorting its acoustic qualities, no age difference in comprehension was found. This implies that a key problem is auditory processing rather than general cognitive slowing. It should also be noted that varying the speed of presentation of a *written* story has yielded mixed results. Where participants are free to read at their own speed, usually no age difference is reported, but there have been exceptions (Meyer, 1987).

Attempts to manipulate the presentation of the story itself have met with variable results. Some alterations have no effect. For example, requiring participants to read aloud versus reading silently does not affect the quantity of information recalled (Taub and Kline 1978), nor does giving people the choice of subject matter for the to-be-read text (Taub, Baker and Kline, 1982). Margolin and Abrams (2009) found that older and younger adults were slightly but significantly slower and less accurate in comprehension tasks when sentences were in a negative form (e.g. 'he did not do it' versus 'he did do it'). Overall, younger adults had higher comprehension test scores, but the two age groups were relatively affected to the same extent by negation.

Some other manipulations of text have an effect. For example, Connelly, Hasher and Zacks (1991) gave participants short passages of prose to read. Interspersed in the to-be-read prose were segments of distracting prose, printed in a different font, which the participants were told to ignore. Both younger and older participants read the passage more slowly and correctly answered fewer comprehension questions, but the older group were disproportionately disadvantaged. Again, Dywan and Murphy (1996) found that when sections of italicised to-be-ignored text were interleaved with to-be-read text, older adults were more likely to make false starts and read out bits of the italicised text (before correcting themselves), and were also more likely to miscomprehend the to-be-read text by erroneously incorporating information from the italicised text. However, when later tested, younger participants were better able to recognise words from the italicised text, in spite of apparently being better at ignoring it. This implies that the younger adults were better at shutting out *responses* to the text rather than not reading it. It also implies that there is a difference in the degree to which readers of different ages are able to control the early stages in the reading process. This is supported by the findings of Stine-Morrow, Loveless and Soederberg (1996) that in reading text for subsequent recall younger readers place relatively greater emphasis on the immediate features of the text, whilst older readers put greater store in contextual information.

Generally, and as with much else in psychogerontology, complexity increases the age difference. For example, Byrd (1985) found older people were impaired on straightforward recall of a passage of text, but were disproportionately disadvantaged when asked to *summarise* it. In other words, when the passage had to be simultaneously remembered and processed, older people were at a severe disadvantage. Again, Hamm and Hasher (1992) found that older people had greater difficulty in drawing inferences from ambiguous stories in which the text began by implying one thing before finally resolving itself in a different direction from the one initially anticipated. They attributed the age-related decline to a lessening ability to process information in working memory (i.e. to keep the initial story 'in mind' whilst resolving the contradiction introduced at the end of the story). Light and Albertson (1988) found that ability to draw inferences from sentences was only marred when the sentences were complex and/or concurrent processing of another task was required. Cohen and Faulkner (1984) demonstrated that older participants were especially disadvantaged at a recognition task when they had to integrate separate facts gleaned from the story to answer correctly. Smith *et al.* (1989) tested memory for prose of three types: 'standard' (self-explanatory), 'scrambled' (sentences with no coherent links) and 'interleaved' (two or more stories alternating with each other sentence by sentence). The older and younger participants performed qualitatively the same for the standard and the scrambled texts. However, for the interleaved condition, the younger participants treated it qualitatively as they had done for the standard prose, and the older participants treated it qualitatively as they had done for the scrambled prose. In other words, the younger participants had sufficient processing capacity to untangle the interleaved prose and treat it as a standard text, whilst the older participants could not do this.

It is tempting to ascribe the above changes to a decline in the memory skills of older people. Certainly, under some circumstances the age difference in memory does seem to play a significant role. De Beni, Borella and Carretti (2007) tested young (18–30), young-old (60–75) and old-old (75+) on a series of measures, including metacomprehension (understanding of how comprehension processes work) and working memory. All participants showed an equivalent level of comprehension for text when it was in a narrative format (e.g. 'first x happened, then y', etc.). However, when expository text (i.e. text intended to explain and present a series of facts and arguments, not necessarily in chronological or other sequence) was used, there was a significant age difference. Furthermore, this age difference was attributable to levels of metacomprehension and working memory, not chronological age.

But the memory difference argument can be overplayed, and there is a considerable older body of research that found a poor correlation between text recall and other memory measures, such as digit span (Light and Anderson, 1985). Other, more linguistic, factors may also contribute. For example, Kemper and Rush (1988), reviewing their own and others' studies, found that the quantity of information recalled varied directly with the syntactic complexity of the to-be-remembered passage. Given the evidence on syntactic changes presented earlier in this chapter, this is not a surprising finding.

An oft-reported finding is that older participants remember as many main points of a story as younger adults, but that they are significantly worse at remembering details (Cohen, 1989). For example, Jeong and Kim (2009) found that recall of content of text was significantly better in younger adults. However, there was no age difference in ability to *interpret* the text. McGinnis (2009) compared young and young-old and old-old participants. She found that, although the old-old group performed significantly the worst on comprehension measures, they also scored the highest marks on measures of generalised and elaborative inference. Therefore, 'comprehension', as traditionally measured by psychologists, might only be tapping one type of skill and not all of the factors that would be understood by a layperson to constitute 'comprehension'.

Furthermore, many of the changes in comprehension that are often attributed to old age might start earlier in adult life. In a study by Ferstl (2006), young, middle-aged and older adult participants showed no age difference on the ability to judge the pragmatics of two sentences, but the ability to recognise words that had appeared in test materials declined steadily with age. Of key interest here is that Ferstl demonstrated that decline was notable in *middle-aged* participants. Studies of age changes have typically compared 'young' adults in their twenties with people in their sixties or older, with middle-aged people largely ignored. Therefore, a research literature has developed where it is almost tacitly assumed that decline begins in old age. However, Ferstl's study demonstrates that change might occur far earlier in some skills than is often realised.

It is perhaps worth noting that in many studies of comprehension the young adult participants are students – a cohort that perhaps more than any other has been drilled to note everything and not just the superficial details. Finding that younger adults have better memory for story details is not surprising, since older people probably have less processing capacity to note and encode details having memorised the main points (Cohen, 1988; Holland and Rabbitt, 1990). But could there also be a cohort effect? If we ask someone what a book or a movie is about, we just want the bare outline, not the details. Many people might learn to give 'just the facts' and ignore the details as an irrelevance. It is often only students who have a mindset of noting as much as possible.

The possibility of a cohort effect raises its head again in considering a specific aspect of this issue – namely, humour comprehension (in other words, understanding jokes). Mak and Carpenter (2007) found that older adults appeared to have a lower comprehension of humour (verbal and non-verbal). The researchers found that this correlated with a decline in cognitive skills. Similar findings were reported by Uekermann, Channon and Daum (2006), who found older adults were significantly worse at selecting the punchline to a joke in a multiple choice task.

As has been often noted, nothing kills a joke more effectively than trying to explain it. The simple fact is that either you comprehend a joke or you do not. A large part of humour relies upon the joke teller and the recipient having a shared culture and often a shared set of common responses to the same events. Take the following cartoon the author once saw in a student magazine, which shows a young man in the 1920s driving along in an open-top sports car. Out of his head there is a thought bubble, which reads, *I know, I'll get Isadora a scarf for her birthday.* Now, if you get the reference to Isadora Duncan, then you will understand the joke (which, it should be said, is in appallingly bad taste, as anyone who has just looked up 'Isadora Duncan' on Google will have found out). But unless you have the requisite knowledge shared with the joke teller and can make the logical connection to an oblique reference, then the joke will make no sense.[1] Humour comprehension is thus about having the cognitive skills to make the connections, but also about having the shared experiences and assumptions of the joke teller. Older people, from a different cohort, will therefore possibly not have sufficient shared culture to appreciate the same humour as younger adults. The study of age differences in humour comprehension is potentially a rich field of research and it is regrettable that relatively little has been done in this area. As Mak and Carpenter acknowledge, the full picture is as yet far from clear.

---

1   Take another example: Comic Sans walks into a bar and the bartender says, '*Sorry, but we don't serve your type here.*'

These findings on comprehension have to be weighed against the argument that the experiments reported here lack ecological validity (in other words, they are not very realistic). The standard story recall test – of reading a passage of 300–400 words and then attempting to regurgitate it whole – is hardly an everyday activity. Rice (1986b) observes that the only activity where anything approaching this skill is required is studying for exams, an activity which few older people indulge in. The experience is probably more central to the younger participants, thus creating an experimental bias. However, even in hardened exam takers, attempts at verbatim recall do not consist of attempting to learn 300–400 words in one reading. A far saner strategy would be to learn such a length of prose sentence by sentence (and evidence for age differences in this activity is more equivocal; e.g. Hannon and Daneman, 2009). In short, the text recall paradigm is unrealistic, and much of the age difference may be a cohort effect. In this context it is also worth noting a study by Bonini and Mansur (2009), who found that older adults had a near-perfect comprehension of radio news items. In other words, in a very naturalistic task, older adults did not show the same sort of deficit found under 'laboratory tasks'.

Another consideration is the length of the prose passage used. Experimenters have usually chosen items of about the same length as magazine or newspaper articles – the most common items read by older people (Rice, 1986b). However, they do not accord with other reading experiences. Meyer (1987) observes that a 'very long text' used in only a minority of studies is about 1600 words. Given that a moderately sized novel is circa 60,000 words, even the longest texts currently being used in standard experiments fall well short of a realistically long piece of prose. The reason for this observation is that, as librarians know to their cost, older adults are often appallingly bad not only at remembering the plots of books, but also *which* books they have read before. Clive James, the writer and television presenter, once worked as a librarian and describes the phenomenon thus:

> I ran out of answers for the little old ladies who wanted to know if they had already read the books they were thinking about taking out. The smart ones used personalised coding systems… There were hundreds of them at it all the time. If you picked up a book by Dorothy L. Sayers or Margery Allingham and flicked through it, you would see a kaleidoscope of dots, crosses, blobs, circles, swastikas, etc. (James, 1983, p.243)

The phenomenon seems to be widespread. The author has spoken to a number of librarians who practically gave a paraphrase of Mr James's observations. However, this shining failure of recall for lengthy passages of prose seems to have escaped researchers' attention.

Neural compensation

Reference has been made throughout this chapter to compensatory strategies by older adults, analogous to the compensation discussed in Chapters 2 and 3 on intelligence and memory. Such strategies might be performed more or less unconsciously, but there is no reason to assume that older adults might not also be consciously aware of changing needs and thus have developed metacomprehension strategies as well. This argument is supported by Champley *et al.* (2008) who interviewed a group of 96 older participants, and found that they used a wide variety of strategies in reading.

There is a burgeoning body of literature indicating that in part this compensation is due to neurological changes in the brain, with new areas being brought into use as areas used since childhood deteriorate in later life. It can be readily established that neurological changes occur in the parts of the brain concerned with auditory and speech perception as we get older. For example, it is known that older adults have problems following a speaker when there is background noise. This problem appears to begin in middle age, when speakers with no apparent hearing difficulties subjectively report difficulties following conversation in a noisy situation such as a party. Wambacq *et al.* (2009) demonstrated that this is probably due to changes in neural responses to incoming auditory signals. Specifically, a key part of listening to a person involves identifying their spatial position, and this is done by mentally processing the time difference between the sound of the voice reaching the two ears (e.g. in simple terms, a sound that reaches the right ear before the left indicates someone speaking on your right). Wambacq *et al.* demonstrated that middle-aged adults' neurons fire differently in performing this calculation, for reasons as yet not fully understood, but probably reflecting a slowing in the speed of response by the neurons concerned (indeed, a frequent finding is that older brain cells take longer to respond to stimuli; see e.g. Matilainen *et al.*, 2010). However, note that certain other processes, such as 'basic' neural processing of sound duration are relatively unaffected by ageing (Ross *et al.*, 2009).

However, there is evidence for neurological compensatory strategies that attempt to ameliorate age-related changes by bringing other areas of the brain into use. For example, Wingfield and Grossman (2006), using functional magnetic resonance imaging (fMRI) scans, found that in older adults additional areas of the brain became activated when comprehending syntactically complex sentences. Thus, older people make use of the brain's elasticity to recruit new areas to assist in mental processing. Again, Richardson *et al.* (2010) found that grey matter in one area of the brain (the left posterior supramarginal gyrus) was positively correlated with vocabulary knowledge in teenagers. There was no such correlation in adults but the quantity of grey matter in another specific area (the left posterior temporal region) was positively correlated with vocabulary knowledge throughout the lifespan.

Findings from neuroimaging studies also provide support for changes in allocation. For example, Wong *et al.* (2009) found that older adults increase activity in some brain areas to compensate for lowering operational efficiency in other brain areas in processing speech. More specifically, a decrease in activity in the auditory cortex was offset by increased activity in other areas of the brain associated with working memory and attention (mainly in the prefrontal region). The more activity of this kind was recorded, the better the performance, implying that this is evidence of a compensatory strategy. However, note that Peelle *et al.* (2010) found slightly different results when they examined brain activity during a speech comprehension task. They noted that areas of the brain known to be involved in speech comprehension were less activated in older people, and co-ordination between different brain areas was less successful. The authors concluded that this might explain why older people have especial difficulties with tasks such as speech comprehension when listening conditions are impaired.

Geal-Dor *et al.* (2006) measured brain activity (**event related potentials** or **ERPs**) as participants listened to various auditory stimuli. When listening to speech, on some measures of ERP, younger adults showed relatively greater neural activity in the left hemisphere, but in older adults this balance shifted to relatively greater activity in the right hemisphere. Middle-aged adults' performance lay between the older and younger groups. Tyler *et al.* (2010) also reported a relative shift towards right hemisphere activity in a speech comprehension task.

The full mechanisms and structure of these processes is far from fully understood, but it is clear, even from these early studies, that brain structure and function do not remain static. For example, there are even differences in pupillary response (i.e. changes in pupil size) between younger and older adults when listening to sentences for later recall (Piquado, Isaacowitz and Wingfield, 2010). The range of processes involved in mental tasks is wide and surprisingly disparate.

Summary

The study of language changes in older people is currently fragmented. Some areas have been covered in depth, whilst others have barely been touched upon. Because of this, interpretations must be guarded.

It should first be noted that declines in sight and hearing will affect linguistic skills. More generally, a decline in physical health may generally lessen access to the 'outside world', and with it conversational opportunities, library visits, and so forth. Within the home, reading habits change, with a general shift towards 'lightweight' reading materials. Whether this is due to declining intellectual skills or changing motivation is a moot point, but nonetheless for many older people there is an appreciable alteration in the practice of reading and other linguistic skills. This may in part account for the more general changes in language. However, the usual suspects of general slowing and intelligence must also be cited (though, surprisingly, crystallised intelligence may not play a particularly major role).

Concentrating on specific skills such as word recognition, syntactic processing and story recall, it can be seen that there are age-related declines. However, the magnitude of any age differences is probably inflated by experimental artifacts such as the types of test materials used, cohort effects, and so forth. Perhaps the biggest criticism is that many reading tests are unrealistic – people do not normally spend their time learning very short stories verbatim, pronouncing obscure words or deciding if a string of letters on a computer screen forms a word or not. Thus, a loud note of caution needs to be sounded over these results, since the measures used probably do not directly match real-life experiences.

Suggested further reading

There are surprisingly few textbooks that deal specifically with language and ageing that are specifically targeted at the general reader. Light and Burke's (1988) edited collection of papers on ageing linguistic skills is probably still the most comprehensive review of this type currently available. A more recent book by De Bot and Makoni (2005), though more directed towards multilingual issues, may also be of interest. Although outside the remit of this book, there is a useful sociolinguistic study of older people's language by Coupland, Coupland and Giles (1991), which some readers may find of interest. For those interested in reading more about psycholinguistics, Aitchison (2007) is recommended.

CHAPTER 5

Ageing, Personality and Lifestyle

Introduction

So far, most of the topics addressed in this book have principally concerned the internal mental world of the older person. How people think, how people memorise, and so forth all largely address how the brain and mind process information. In this chapter, we will consider psychological factors that are largely concerned with how older people interact with the world around them, through their personality and lifestyles. We will also consider related issues, such as how older people view themselves, lifestyle choices, and the attitudes of others towards older people and ageing.

Trait models of personality

There have been numerous attempts to define 'personality', but a useful general definition is 'the individual characteristics and ways of behaving that, in their organization or patterning, account for an individual's unique adjustments, to his or her total environment' (Hilgard, Atkinson and Atkinson, 1979, p.364).

However, paradoxically, psychologists have usually not been as bothered about what makes each of us unique. Instead, they have typically been interested in patterns of behaviour that we hold in common. A prime example of this is the study of the **personality trait**. Personality traits are sets of related behaviours that everyone possesses, but the strength with which traits manifest themselves vary from person to person. This concept becomes easier to understand if we consider an example. A commonly-measured trait is **extraversion–introversion**, often shortened to the single letter **E**. This trait describes the degree to which a person is outgoing and assertive. A person with a high E score is thus very outward going and likely to be what is often called the life and soul of the party. Somebody with a low E score, on the other hand, will be very shy and retiring. Most people tend to be towards the middle of the E scale – in other words, neither very outward going nor very quiet and withdrawn. However, *everybody* can be measured on this same single scale – we all possess the same trait; all that differs is the strength with which this trait is held.

Of course, one trait by itself cannot tell us everything about a person's personality. Therefore, several traits need to be taken in combination to get anything approaching a rounded psychological portrait of an individual person. However, if *too* many traits are used, then it becomes very difficult for people to integrate the information into a coherent picture that carries any meaningful information. For this reason, psychologists typically attempt to limit the number of traits used to as small a number as possible. This creates a trade-off: measuring personality using a small number of traits will give a broad outline of a person's personality, but, inevitably, details are going to be missed. However, if the choice is this or an unfeasibly large number of traits that might describe a person if only anyone could understand the figures, then parsimony seems the better option.

An early study of personality traits in later life was conducted by Hans Eysenck (Eysenck, 1987; Eysenck and Eysenck, 1985). Eysenck argued that personality could be adequately summed up using just three traits: the aforementioned extraversion–introversion, plus **psychoticism (P)** and **neuroticism (N)**. These measure the degree to which a person is emotionally 'cold' and antisocial, and the extent to which a person is anxious and emotionally unstable, respectively.[1] Eysenck argued that E, P and N alter as people get older, and gender also has an important influence. P declines with age, but the rate of decline is much greater for men than women. At 16 years, male P scores are almost double those of females, but by the age of 70 this difference is practically non-existent. More curious is the change in E. Both men and women become more introverted as they get older. Males in their late teens are more extraverted than females, but thereafter their extraversion declines at a much greater rate, so that by their sixties males are more *introverted* than females (the crossover point, where the two sexes are equally introverted, occurs in the forties). The changes in N are less spectacular. There is a decline in neuroticism for both sexes, but at all ages female scores remain higher than male scores (Eysenck, 1987; Eysenck and Eysenck, 1985). Eysenck (1987) argues these findings predict that older people should be less prone to violent swings of mood and hence calmer. Note that Eysenck was not arguing that older people should necessarily be happier in later life. If anything, people should become more indifferent about the world, with only relatively small swings in mood in either direction. At an ideal best, such indifference might be cultivated into calmness and serenity, but, equally, an undesirable apathy or sloth might be produced. Eysenck argued that personality changes across the lifespan are primarily the result of physiological changes altering levels of excitation within the nervous system. This argument is disputed by many other psychologists and a plausible case can be made for changes in lifestyle being the prime cause of shifts in E, P and N.[2] For example, older people may become more introverted, not because of changing levels of neural excitation, but because, as they

---

1   High scores on the P and N scales do not necessarily mean that a person is mentally disturbed, but rather that under stress they are likely to display psychotic or neurotic characteristics.

2   In fairness to Eysenck, recent genetic studies indicate that neuroticism and extraversion are linked to genetic causes that could interact in complex physiological ways; see Terracciano *et al.* (2010).

age, society becomes less geared to their needs. This causes older people to withdraw in upon themselves, and this in turn engenders feelings of reserve and hence increased introversion. Because men more than women define themselves by their role in society (see later), men will show a disproportionately bigger loss of assertiveness as they age, reflected in their declining E score.

Other researchers have tended to use a broader range of personality traits than the three used by Eysenck. A very popular choice is the **Big Five** model (a.k.a. five-factor personality model) by Costa and McCrae (see Costa and McCrae, 1980, 1982). This is predicated, as its name implies, on the assumption that personality is best described using five basic personality traits – conscientiousness (how reliable a person is), agreeableness (how compliant with others' wishes) and openness (how willing to cope with the unfamiliar), extraversion, and neuroticism (see Stuart-Hamilton, 1999a for further discussion).[3] The results of studies using the Big Five and other personality trait measures point to a rather less cut-and-dried picture than the one Eysenck presented, possibly because different tests were used, but perhaps also because different measurement methods were applied. In particular, several studies based on longitudinal data are now available.

Generally, early longitudinal studies found little alteration in personality test scores, even though participants often felt they had changed dramatically (Perlmutter and Hall, 1992). However, later studies have often found greater changes. For example, in a longitudinal study of Dutch people, Steunenberg et al. (2005) found a mild decrease in N between the mid-50s and 70 and then a slight rise. Field and Millsap (1991) found that extraversion declined slightly in a longitudinal study of older adults. Again, Mroczek and Spiro (2003) conducted a longitudinal study on a group of 1600 men (initially aged 43–91) over a 12-year period. They found considerable variability in E and N scores over this time. They also found that significant life events (e.g. death of spouse) were related to these changes.

Roberts, Walton and Viechtbauer (2006) conducted a meta-analysis of 92 longitudinal studies of personality and found that overall there was evidence for cumulative change in many traits. The picture they present is complex, because not all the studies they analysed used exactly the same tests. However, overall, there appeared to be relative stability in some personality attributes such as sociability, whilst traits such as conscientiousness and agreeableness increase in later life. However, openness to experience (essentially, level of mental flexibility) declines in old age (thus perhaps providing an explanation for the stereotype of hidebound older adults).[4] Allemand, Zimprish and Hendriks (2008), using a cross-sectional study, similarly found that agreeableness and conscientiousness increased in later life.

---

3   Sometimes referred to as *emotional stability*, since emotional stability and neuroticism form opposite ends of the same continuum, akin to extraversion and introversion.

4   Though note the changes are *relative* and not absolute. Thus, a decline in openness means a person is slightly less flexible, not that they suddenly become a complete curmudgeon, clinging with limpet-like tenacity to old ideas and practices.

Overall, these findings seem to point to some traits remaining relatively stable, some (e.g. neuroticism) showing a slight rise, others showing a bigger rise (e.g. agreeableness and conscientiousness). However, it is difficult to know how much weight to put on many of the findings on personality traits. First, there is the problem of variability. Put simply, scores on many measures of traits fluctuate across the lifespan. For example, a longitudinal study by Specht, Egloff and Schmukle (2011) found that personality is most variable in early and late life, with relative stability in the middle-aged years. A significant proportion of this change was attributable to changes in lifestyle, indicating that personality can change in response to changing demands in one's personal life. This reflects the findings of an earlier review by Kogan (1990), who noted that many of the significant shifts in personality were commensurate with major changes in lifestyle. Thus, personality can be a capricious thing.[5] Life events, sometimes unpredictable, can cause personality measures to fluctuate. And findings of variability across the lifespan have been extensively reported (e.g. Lucas and Donellan, 2009; Ojha and Pramanick, 2010).

Just to muddy the waters a bit further, it should also be noted that through all these fluctuations the relative positioning of an *individual* within their cohort remains remarkably constant. It was noted in Chapter 2 that, although raw scores on intelligence tests fluctuate, the IQ of the individual participant remains relatively stable. The same applies to individuals' personality test scores – although their raw scores on tests fluctuate, relative to their age group, they remain on roughly the same percentile relative to the rest of their age group (Kogan, 1990; Roberts and DelVecchio, 2000).

A further point is that there is evidence that personality traits have shifted towards being more flexible and accommodating across birth cohorts in the twentieth century (see Schaie and Willis, 1991; also Mroczek and Spiro, 2003). This might in part also explain the stereotype that older adults become more conservative and hidebound. It is not ageing *per se* that makes someone hidebound – rather, older groups belong to less tolerant cohorts. But more importantly for the argument being presented here, if there are cohort effects, then comparisons of scores between age groups are not necessarily comparing just on age – there could be a significant cohort effect colouring the analyses.

A final point is that the overwhelming majority of research on trait personality relies on test scores. However, an ingenious study by Noftie and Fleeson (2010) suggests these findings might at times be misleading. When real-life personality measures were taken of a group of adult test participants,[6] it was found that the patterns of change were typically more pronounced in real life than in test measures

---

5   Though in the very long term a pattern might emerge – for example, Allemand, Zimprich and Martin (2008) found that over several test sessions of their longitudinal study significant correlations emerged between scores on all the trait scores (except for neuroticism).

6   By getting participants to record their current behaviour at multiple sampling points throughout the day over a one- or two-week period.

of traits. Thus, trait measures might not be measuring personality as it is expressed in everyday life.

In conclusion, therefore, we must be extremely cautious in interpreting findings on age changes in trait test performance for several reasons, including:

- Studies are not uniform in what they have analysed. Whilst most studies have used the Big Five, others have not, and there is no overwhelming evidence that the Big Five measure is automatically better than other trait measures.

- Increased variability has been noted in later life test performance, but, paradoxically, individual performance relative to age cohort remains fairly stable.

- Studies are not unanimous in their conclusions about which traits change in later life and how they alter. However, there is a general consensus that agreeableness and conscientiousness improve.[7]

- However, there is also evidence that cohort effects might be colouring results, and, in any case, trait measures might not be an accurate reflection of everyday personality.

Although studies of general personality change across the lifespan yield somewhat conflicting and confusing results, other aspects of research on personality in later life have produced more substantial findings. A key example is the study of the effects of neuroticism. It is intuitively plausible that a person who worries a lot and has brooding preoccupations is unlikely to enjoy a healthy lifestyle. The worrying in itself might raise blood pressure, whilst attempts to alleviate the worry (e.g. drink, drugs, over-eating) will further worsen the neurotic person's health. Furthermore, once a person becomes ill, then excessively worrying about the illness will only make matters worse. This is not only intuitively plausible, because a plethora of studies have supported these suppositions. For example:

- Wilson, Mendes de Leon et al.'s (2004) longitudinal study found a strong correlation between neuroticism and mortality, with those with the top 10 per cent of N scores having double the risk of dying compared with the scorers with the lowest 10 per cent of N scores.

- Lauver and Johnson (1997) demonstrated that higher levels of neuroticism were disadvantageous in coping with chronic pain in later life.

- Spiro et al.'s (1995) longitudinal study found neuroticism to be correlated with high blood pressure.

- People with high N scores are significantly more likely to have memory failures on days with high stress levels (Neupert, Mroczek and Spiro, 2008).

---

7   Though Jackson et al. (2009) argue that conscientiousness can be broken into sub-traits, some of which increase, some of which do not.

- Steunenberg *et al.* (2007) found that level of neuroticism was significantly related to recovery from depression in later life.

- Shipley *et al.*'s (2007) 21-year longitudinal study found that high levels of neuroticism were significantly associated with greater risk of death from cardiovascular illness (though this was mediated by other factors, such as socio-economic status).

- Generally, neuroticism is inversely related to general health status in older people (Kempen, Jelicic and Ormel, 1997; Mroczek, Spiro and Turiano, 2009).

It is thus readily apparent that a high level of neuroticism is disadvantageous in later life for a whole host of reasons. However, it would be unwise to assume that neuroticism is the *sole* personality trait that is at fault. Several studies report that, although N scores have a major influence, either an appreciable amount of variance is unaccounted for (e.g. 60 in the study by Mroczek *et al.*, 2009) or other factors are of near-equal importance (e.g. physical health in the study by Steunenberg *et al.*, 2007). Again, in some situations, neuroticism ceases to be a valid predictor when a broader range of confounding variables are controlled for (e.g. Dong *et al.*'s 2011 study of self-neglect in older people).

Research on extraversion has yielded findings of various levels of predictability. The discovery that extraversion is related to likelihood of doing voluntary work in later life (Okun, Pugliese and Rook, 2007) is perhaps not all that unpredictable.[8] Again, a higher level of extraversion appears to be advantageous in recovering from a stroke (Elmstahl, Sommer and Hagberg, 1996) and more generally in maintaining a high level of morale (Adkins, Martin and Poon, 1996), feeling of well-being (Francis and Bolger, 1997), and having a more positive outlook on future health (Chapman *et al.*, 2006; see also Jerram and Coleman, 1999). These are perhaps not too surprising, since we often perceive the outgoing personality as being more robust and thus healthy. However, researchers often report that extraversion has no correlation with other factors of interest, even when it might be intuitively expected. For example, Iwasa *et al.* (2009) found that E scores did not significantly predict older people's participation in health check-ups. Nor is it correlated to future health care plans in older adults (Sorensen *et al.*, 2008). In other instances, although E scores at other ages are significantly related to the measure in question, by later life they are not. For example, Gomez *et al.* (2009) found that, although extraversion scores were significantly correlated with subjective well-being (SWB) in young adults, they were not a significant predictor of SWB in older people. Finally, in some rare instances, extraversion has been reported as being actually disadvantageous. For example, one study found a negative relationship between E scores and driving performance in older people (Adrian *et al.*, 2011).

---

8   In fairness to Okun *et al.*, a key theme of the paper is the pattern of the relationship and the effects of social capital.

Openness to experience is correlated with a range of measures, including risk of developing Alzheimer's disease (Duberstein *et al.*, 2011) and ability at creativity tests (Shimonaka and Nakazato, 2007). The link with greater creativity and imagination possibly accounts for the association some researchers have found between openness and successful or at least more contented ageing (see Gregory, Nettlebeck and Wilson, 2010). Sometimes openness is related to other measures in combination with other traits. For example, awareness of future care needs is linked to openness, but it is also linked to levels of neuroticism and agreeableness (Sorensen *et al.*, 2008). Along with conscientiousness, openness is a significant predictor of active coping behaviours (basically, over-exerting to gain a better lifestyle, though at cost to one's health) in African Americans (Whitfield *et al.*, 2010). It is also, along with agreeableness, *negatively* correlated with **executive function** (the ability to plan and control mental processes) in older adults (Williams, Suchy and Kraybill, 2010).[9] In older adults, openness is related to activity in the orbitofrontal region in both sexes. In men, there is additional activity in the anterior cingulate region, whereas in women there is additional activity in the prefrontal cortex (Sutin, Beason-Held, Resnick and Costa, 2009). However, like extraversion, there are also measures where openness has no significant predictive role (e.g. medication adherence; see Jerant *et al.*, 2011).

The role of agreeableness has already been partly addressed. A lowered level of agreeableness (including, one assumes, a willingness to endure unpopularity when necessary) has been shown, along with a higher level of extraversion, to increase older people's use of hospital emergency departments for treatment (Chapman *et al.*, 2009). Conversely, a high level of agreeableness has been associated with more effective regulation of responses to saddening events and images (Pearman, Andreoletti and Isaacowitz, 2010). Research on conscientiousness shows similarly piecemeal results, with relationships found between disparate measures such as lower overall effect of multiple simultaneously occurring illnesses and conditions (Chapman, Lyness and Duberstein, 2007), increased life expectancy (Terracciano *et al.*, 2008) and decreased incidence of mild cognitive impairment (Wilson *et al.*, 2007; see also Chapter 6). As with other traits, it is also often linked with several other measures. Examples have been given earlier in this chapter.

It can thus be concluded that, although the manner in which traits change over the lifespan is open to question, traits nonetheless can be significantly related to other key indices of health and activity. The role of neuroticism is probably the most unremittingly negative. High N scores have almost always signified poorer prognoses on a wide variety of health and life expectancy measures. However, we must be careful not to overplay this argument. Although measures such as neuroticism do indeed appear to have an effect, it is rarely an effect that accounts for all the observed variability. Often traits are found to multiply correlate with another measure, or

---

9   However, conversely, the researchers found that neuroticism was positively correlated with executive function.

much of the variance is unexplained. And when a trait is found to have an effect, its impact can be lessened or magnified by other factors, such as socio-economic class. Also, there might be a cohort effect – older participants may be less 'open' about their responses than younger people, not because of their personalities *per se*, but because they wish to be 'polite' (Stokes, 1992).

Psychoanalytic and type models of personality

Some of the earliest attempts to codify the ageing personality came from **psychoanalysis**. It is difficult to give a concise definition of this term. In its usual sense, it means any treatment regime based upon an integrated theory of the subconscious and its effects on behaviour. However, the term sometimes applies (particularly with later practitioners) to broader based models that, whilst having roots in psychoanalysis, also integrate findings from the behavioural sciences. Often psychoanalytic theories are named after their author (e.g. 'Freudian' after Sigmund Freud, 'Jungian' after Carl Jung). Strictly speaking, psychoanalysis is not part of mainstream psychology (see Stuart-Hamilton, 1999a), and many psychologists have questioned its efficacy (e.g. Eysenck, 1952). However, from an historical viewpoint at the very least, a brief examination is necessary. The founding father of psychoanalysis, Sigmund Freud, was sceptical about the value of therapy being administered to older patients, because they had relatively little remaining life in which to enjoy the benefits of treatment (generally, the treatment of older people has been a minority subject within the psychoanalytic literature, though this position has changed in recent years – see Gorusch, 1998; Mallick, 1982; Settlage, 1996). The crux of Freud's theory is that personality is made up of a mixture of three components – the **id**, **ego** and **superego**. The id describes basic appetitive urges, the ego people's rational selves, and the superego a set of moral dictums (often unrealistically harsh). For reasons too complex to describe here, Freudian theorists felt that the id's efficiency and strength were drawn from the state of a person's smooth (i.e. involuntary) muscle, whilst the ego's strength was dependent on the state of the central nervous system (CNS). Because the CNS declines more rapidly in later life than does smooth muscle, the ego becomes relatively weaker than the id. A tenet of Freudian theory is that the ego strives to keep the id in check. To prevent the id getting the upper hand, the ego starts to conserve its energy by rationalising resources. In psychoanalytic terms, this means adopting a relatively unvarying and conservative set of attitudes and responses, even though they may not be entirely appropriate to the situations older people find themselves in. This perceived inflexibility of older people is specious, however. For example, Pratt *et al.* (1991) found no age differences on measures of moral reasoning. Again, as we have seen in the section on traits, although older people are less open to new experiences, this is a *relative* change – older people are not utterly inflexible. It is also worth noting that, although he did little formal work on ageing, in his private life and correspondence Freud appears to have had a very melancholy and illogical attitude towards the subject (Woodward, 1991).

Erikson (1963, 1982; see also Wolf, 1997) felt that personality developed throughout the lifespan – unlike other psychoanalysts who felt that it was essentially determined by childhood habits. He argued that at different ages different conflicts had to be resolved. For example, in infancy, individuals must resolve the conflicting impulses to trust or to mistrust by developing a sense of trust. There are eight of these conflicts to resolve, of which only the final one occurs in later life. The goal of this stage is **ego integration** – the acceptance that earlier goals have been satisfied or resolved, and there are no 'loose ends'. A person who feels that not everything has been achieved can feel a sense of despair because, with death approaching, it is too late to make amends. Thus, the person comes to fear death, and he or she ends life feeling anxious and depressed.

The **Rochester Adult Longitudinal Study (RALS)** has examined several cohorts of students from Rochester University in the USA, using Eriksonian measures. The study has found that adults change in a consistent fashion on these measures in the directions predicted by the theory (see Krauss Whitbourne and Whitbourne, 2011). However, not everyone proceeds along an identical path. Whitbourne (2010) argues that individuals can be grouped into five pathways of development:

- *Authentic road* – adopted by people keeping their mind open to challenges and continued development.

- *Triumphant trail* – adopted by people who are resilient in the face of adversity.

- *Straight and narrow way* – for those adopting a rigid course of development, resisting change; may feel constrained because of this.

- *Meandering way* – for those lacking a clear sense of identity who have not taken firm decisions about key choices.

- *Downward slope* – taken by those who have made poor choices and have a self-deprecating or self-destructive behaviour.

It is important to note that these pathways are not deep ruts from which there is no escape, and changes can be made (see Krauss Whitbourne and Whitbourne, 2011). However, a genuine fulfilment in the Eriksonian model still requires individuals to resolve a series of conflicts, and Hannah *et al.* (1996) present evidence that ego integration is usually only attained by people who have successfully resolved the earlier Eriksonian stages of conflict. In other words, personality in later life is as much a product of early behaviour as the current situation. Happily, a large proportion of the participants in the RALS study appear to be on the authentic road and will thus attain fulfilment (see Whitbourne, 2010). However, participants in the RALS study are not necessarily demographically representative of the population of the USA, let alone other countries, and whether other populations can enjoy an equally rosy future is open to question. A criticism of Erikson's theory might be that, taken simplistically, it portrays ageing as a passive preparation for death. However, this is not what Erikson intended. He viewed the final stage of development as a learning process, and in 'such final consolidation, death loses its sting' (Erikson, 1963, p.268).

Peck (1968) expanded on Erikson's theory, and argued that in later life three conflicts need to be resolved. The first of these is **ego differentiation versus work-role preoccupation**. Many working people (particularly men) establish their status and self-concept through their work. Thus, a professional person may develop a high self-esteem simply because he or she has an occupation that society regards favourably. However, when a person retires, this status disappears with the job. Thus, retirees must find something in themselves that makes them unique or worthy of an esteem previously conferred on them by a job title. The second conflict is **body transcendence versus body preoccupation**. For most individuals, ageing brings a decline in health and general physical status. If an older person overemphasises bodily well-being in extracting enjoyment from life, then disappointment will almost inevitably result. Successful ageing involves an ability to overcome physical discomfort, or at least finding enjoyable activities where bodily status is unimportant. The third of Peck's conflicts is **ego transcendence versus ego preoccupation**. This essentially means that a person comes to terms with the fact that he or she will inevitably die. This is obviously an unpleasant thought, but Peck argues that, by attempting to provide for those left after a person has died, and continually striving to improve the surroundings and well-being of loved ones, an overweening concern for the self and the self's fate can be overcome.

Levinson's view of ageing is akin to Erikson's and Peck's but concentrates rather more on the role of the older person in family and society (e.g. Levinson, 1980). Changing physical and occupational status means that in the early to mid-sixties (the **late adult transition**) people must come to terms with the fact that they are no longer the prime movers in either work or in family life (this may be affected by the lowering of typical retirement age; see Settersen, 1998). To remain content, older people must therefore learn to shed leadership and take a 'back seat' (other researchers have reported similar conflicts; e.g. Settersen and Haegestad, 1996). This does not mean that all cares and duties can be avoided, since, aside from assuming the role of wise counsellor to family and younger friends, older people must come to terms with their past (in a manner similar to that described by Erikson). Levinson refers to this process as the '**view from the bridge**'.

Research has tended to support psychoanalytic descriptions, at least in broad terms. We have already seen the RALS study in support of the Eriksonian model. Reichard et al. (1962) interviewed 87 American men aged 55–84, half of them in retirement, and half in full- or part-time employment (note that for some jobs in the USA there is no compulsory retirement age). Many points raised by Reichard et al. support the psychoanalytic theories. For example, participants approaching retirement seemed to be particularly 'on edge' and self-deprecatory, indicating that the period in question was perceived as being one of change and of anxiety. Overall, five main **personality types** were identified. In the first section of this chapter, we saw that trait models of personality assume that people share personality attributes in common – what makes us different from each other is the relative strength with which we have these attributes or traits. Personality type models take a different viewpoint. They assume that we are best described by grouping us into distinct categories.

The five types identified by Reichard were as follows. **Constructiveness** is akin to the optimal resolution envisaged by Erikson's and Peck's theories – people possessing this trait had come to terms with their lives, and were relatively free from worries, while striving to interact with others. The **dependent** or 'rocking chair' type created some contentment, but individuals were dissatisfied with products of their own efforts, and relied on others to help or serve them, regarding later life as a time of leisure. The **defensiveness** or '**armoured approach**' type is essentially neurotic. Participants possessing it carried on working or were engaged in a high level of activity as if to 'prove' that they were healthy and did not need other people's help. The fourth type – **hostility** – involves blaming others for personal misfortune. Participants unrealistically attributed failures throughout their lives to factors other than themselves. In part this sprang from a failure to plan adequately. The final type identified by Reichard *et al.* was **self-hatred**. The self-hating individuals were akin to the hostile type possessors, except that they turned their hatred and resentment inwards. Reichard *et al.* found that people possessing the first three types were well adjusted towards later life, whilst those possessing one of the latter two were less successful. However, given that the researchers' personality descriptions contain implicit value judgements of quality of lifestyle, this is not surprising.

Reichard *et al.* also observed that people's personalities had developed long before the onset of later life. In other words, the types are not the result of 'being old' *per se.* It follows from this that, in order to enjoy later life, one must prepare for it. This argument is somewhat supported by the findings of a longitudinal study reported by Haan (1972). Participants were studied from their teens to the onset of middle age. Various personality types were identified, but these can be principally divided into: the stable and secure; those akin to Reichard *et al.*'s defensive personalities; and the insecure who blamed others for their misfortunes and who often had disorganised lifestyles. These types are remarkably similar to those found in studies of older people, and it is reasonable to conclude that those found in later life are probably those that have been there since early adulthood (Kermis, 1986).

Another study of types was by Neugarten, Havinghurst and Tobin (1961, 1968), who studied a sample of people in their seventies. Four principal personality types (with subdivisions) were identified, which bore great similarity to the traits uncovered by other studies already mentioned. The most desirable type was the **integrated personality**. People in this category were either: **reorganisers** (as one activity became physically impossible, another was found); **focused** (activities were limited to a small set of feasible and highly rewarding ones); or they were **disengaged** (the deliberate abnegation of many responsibilities). Another major type was the **armoured-defensive** personality. People in this category were either **holding on** types who felt that they could stave off decay by maintaining a high level of activity; or they were **constricted** and dwelt on what they had lost as a result of ageing. The armoured-defensive individuals were less satisfied than those with integrated personalities. A third group possessed **passive-dependent** personalities. Like Reichard *et al.*'s dependent/'rocking chair' types, such people relied on others to help them (the **succourant seeking**), or they withdrew from interaction with others as much as possible (the **apathetic**). The fourth and final group comprised the **disorganised** personalities. These unfortunate people had serious problems (possibly early dementia?) and could not be classified as functioning conventionally.

It is interesting to note that some personality types may be better adapted to early rather than late adulthood and vice versa. **Type A personalities** are very hard-edged, competitive types who find it difficult to relax – in eighties' parlance, they are ideal 'yuppie' material. **Type B personalities** are the opposite – easygoing, carefree, and so forth. It might be expected that Type As will be best suited to early adulthood when there are perhaps the greatest chances to exhibit competitiveness in career chasing, sport, and so on. Later life should not suit Type As because of its emphasis on a sedentary lifestyle. For Type Bs, the reverse should hold true. Strube *et al.* (1985) measured the psychological well-being of a group of people aged 18–89, and found that in general Type A and B personalities fulfilled this prediction, although the results were mediated by factors such as the social environments of individuals. Again, Shimonaka, Nakazato and Homma (1996) found Type B personalities to be more prevalent amongst centenarians.

A notable feature of type models is that they show relatively little change across the lifespan, or show a predictable pattern of change from one outlook to another. Why should type models find relatively little change when traits alter considerably? The reason is largely an artefact of the measurements used. People can vary in the strength with which they show a particular set of behaviours and still remain within the same broad category of personality. On the other hand, traits are a scale and thus *any* change is registered. However, this does not mean that there is absolutely *no* change in types over the lifespan. In a review of the literature, Aiken (1989) noted that, while some of the more stable personality types may not alter greatly over the lifespan, the less stable types may be more labile in response to age changes. A more recent longitudinal study by Cramer (2003) echoes this. Various psychoanalytic theories, such as Vaillant's (1992) model, argue that, as we mature, our ego defence mechanisms (loosely, how we defend and justify ourselves) develop in tandem, so we leave behind (or *should* leave behind) flouncing out of rooms and similar in favour of standing our ground and resolving conflicts in a rational, reasonable manner. Cramer demonstrated that many adults mature in a desirable manner, but those who cling to immature defence mechanisms are significantly more likely to face a range of psychological problems as they grow older.

As has been noted, there is much similarity between the various type studies. There is more than one way to age successfully, but all essentially involve accepting limitations and renouncing responsibilities without suffering a feeling of loss. A slightly less successful strategy is to maintain a fear of the ravages of ageing, and to fight them by keeping as active as possible. However, as this involves a failure to come to terms with ageing, it is ultimately less satisfying. The worst option is to have no strategy at all and to blame all the wrong factors for one's present state. Many commentators have arrived at the same general conclusions, as has already been noted (see also Aiken, 1989; Kermis, 1983, 1986; Turner and Helms, 1987; Whitbourne, 1987). However, the argument presented is a generalisation and a potentially misleading one. Successful ageing involves accepting limitations and abnegating responsibility, but this might be because of societal pressure to hand over the reins of power. Accepting this change willingly might be akin to surrendering gracefully to a stronger opponent on the principle that if one is going to lose, one may as well do so with the minimum of hurt. In other words, the 'successfully' aged older person has not gained a philosophical insight as much as grasped a point of pragmatics. Another important consideration is socio-economic class. The 'unsuccessful' aged person might rant and rail about external forces precisely because their social position has yielded them fewer privileges and 'lucky breaks' (often researchers note that such individuals are downwardly socially mobile). In contrast, someone who has had an emotionally and materially successful life will be more likely to have a relaxed view of things. Accordingly, the older personality might be as much a product of social and economic circumstances as of any internally motivating factors. This consideration does not refute the theories described, but one should be careful not to consider personality as a purely internally driven entity.

However, this is perhaps too bleak a conclusion to draw. There is a grave danger that we can see personality as something that, because it is shaped by earlier life, is irredeemably fixed. But it is not. The longitudinal studies presented in this section show that personality types are categorically *not* set in stone, and, though it is difficult to move from one type to another, it is not impossible. Arguing that because of previous experiences a poor conclusion is inevitable might describe what typically happens, but it should never be an excuse to avoid attempting to change if the person wants to. There is a rather trite cliché that when you drive a car, which turnings you take are dependent on your steering now, not where you have chosen to drive in the past. In recent years, a popular belief (promoted amongst others by some religious groups) has arisen that deeply hoping and wishing and praying for something desirable will make it happen. This has led to understandable mockery by many scientists, only too willing to trumpet the cause of rationalism over faith. However, assuming a positive outlook and setting one's resolve is far from stupid – *provided a person changes their behaviour to match their changing attitudes.* Consider the following:

- Whitbourne (2010) demonstrated that adults lagging behind in Eriksonian developmental stages can and do catch up and even overtake others in later life. The current situation thus does not totally dictate the future self.

- McMamish-Svensson *et al.* (1999) demonstrated that subjective health is a significantly better predictor of life expectancy than formal medical diagnosis. This does not mean that one can wishfully think oneself a longer life, but a robust attitude will certainly not be harmful.

- As was demonstrated in Chapter 2, taking up even moderate exercise can and does significantly improve cognitive skills. Altering lifestyle and behaviour does make a difference.

- Measures of personality are variable and not totally accurate predictors. Performance on formal psychological tests are not in and of themselves utterly accurate prophets of future performance and behaviour.

Thus, personality measures are only a guide – they are not a life sentence.

Dependency

Not all studies of how people interact with the world around them are concerned with personality. A significant body of research concerns facets of social behaviour and how old age affects these. A key instance of this is dependency. This is essentially the degree to which a person is capable of performing routine daily activities without the necessary assistance of others. Put another way, the more a person relies on others to do things for them, the more dependent they are.

One of the features of old age is a loss of the means to be totally independent. Physical ailments can impede an older person's mobility to the point where they can no longer easily walk, and require a wheelchair to move more than a few steps. Worsening vision can cause a person to stop driving. The onset of marked cognitive decline can lead a person to stop cooking (e.g. for fear of them forgetting to turn off the heat under a pan, leading to a fire). There are many reasons why an older person might have to abnegate a routine activity that they once took for granted. However, these routine activities still need to be performed: housebound older people still need to visit places (even if it is just their doctor's or dentist's), older people barred from cooking still need to eat, etc. And in order to perform these activities, older people become dependent on the help of others.

The issue of dependency is loaded with value judgements. If an adult is dependent on others for basic daily tasks (e.g. meal preparation, transport to other places), then in many societies (particularly Western ones), this is seen as demeaning (see Cordingly and Webb, 1997). Individualism and 'standing on one's own feet' are measures of societal approval. Thus, an older person in need of assistance might be seen as having a lowered status. There is, however, another side to this issue. There are many welfare organisations (e.g. local and national government agencies, charities, etc.) whose specific purpose is to offer assistance to older people in need. This can be tending to people living in the community or in residential homes, sheltered accommodation and similar. If older people do not use these services, this can be seen not in terms of older people trying to preserve their independence, but a 'failure' of older people to make use of all that the organisations are generously offering. For example, Baltes and Wahl (1996) found that older people's requests for help tend to be met, whilst independent behaviour is ignored.

Baltes (1996) examined the issue of dependency in detail and argued that it can be both good and bad, depending upon the type of dependency and the circumstances in which it is acquired. Bad dependency might result from bad motives. Thus, an institutional environment in which older residents are denied any autonomy is a clear example of this. However, bad dependency can also be produced from good intentions. For example, a social worker might provide an older person not just with the specific help they need, but then swamp them with lots of other forms of assistance (even though the older person has neither asked for them nor needs them), because they are seen as a generous aid package. Of course at one level they are, but this largesse is also forcing an older person to become dependent on a system to a much greater extent than they need. However, not all dependency is bad. Baltes notes that increased dependency can be good, if, for example, it liberates an older person from trivial cares or tasks which are too problematic. It should also be noted that bad dependency can be reversed or at least lessened through intervention. Thus, dependency is in itself neither good nor bad – it is how and why it is used that matters. Fiori, Consedine and Magai (2008) found a complex interrelationship between what might be termed good and bad dependency and other factors. For example, they found that what they termed 'healthy dependency' was related to higher levels of self-reported health. A 'dysfunctional dependency' was, on the other hand, related to an increased probability of being on medication for hypertension, and 'over-dependency' to a higher level of depression.

However, not all the research literature has addressed dependency in quite the same way as Baltes. Often the term is used in the sense of care dependency, or the amount of work required to look after dependent older adults.[10] Various measures are available to measure this (see Boggatz et al., 2009; Gardner and Helmes, 2007). Many researchers have found that increased dependency is predictive of subsequent illness (e.g. Willis et al., 1997). For example, a higher number of dependencies is associated with a poorer recovery from acute illness in older patients (Boyd et al., 2008). These findings are not necessarily surprising – dependency arises from frailty and, therefore, finding that physical health and dependency are well correlated might

---

10   Thus, in this context it often means dependency on non-family aid or aid that is not paid for out
     of the pocket of the older person themselves.

be taken as read. But this does not mean that the health–dependency relationship can be dismissed. In a sense practically all older people are dependent, because of their reliance on pensions and other financial welfare provisions. Hence why the **dependency ratio** is a term often used by economists and similar to refer to the ratio of older people to adults of working age within the population. However, the crucial issue in the future might not be the proportion of people who are simply old, but their state of health and thus the level of dependency that they have (Goodman, 2010). Changing demographics and improved survival rates mean that not only are more people going to reach old age (thereby altering the ratio) but the proportion of older people with significant physical and psychological dysfunctional problems is also going to increase (see Lin *et al.*, 2011; Sanderson and Scherbov, 2010). Shah (2011a) observes that, after controlling for confounding variables, there is a significant correlation between national suicide rates and dependency ratios across countries. This implies that the stress created by dependency (both amongst older people *and* their younger carers) could have greater effects than have hitherto been suspected. Further research is needed, however.

Boggatz *et al.* (2010), studying an Egyptian sample of older adults, found that care dependency was highest in the lowest socio-economic groups. This group was also the one least likely to be able to pay, thereby calling upon voluntary groups, who often lack adequate training. The need for adequate training, including an ability to appraise the level of actual need, is a point raised by many researchers (e.g. Mendes-Chiloff *et al.*, 2009). The association between low socio-economic status and higher dependency is also found in other cultures (see Lucchetti *et al.*, 2009).

The issue of dependency is not just simply a matter of the impact of physical ailments and welfare provision, however. There is also a significant psychological component to the process and an older person's responses and attitudes can play a significant role. For example, Coudin and Alexopoulos (2010) demonstrated that a stronger belief in negative stereotypes about ageing is associated with a higher level of dependent behaviour (e.g. seeking out the help of health care services). MacDonald *et al.* (2010) examined the factors determining economic dependency in a sample of very old (octogenarian and centegenarian) people. To quote from the authors directly:

> Past life style, gender, ethnicity, socio-economic status, functional health, and coping were not related to economic dependency. With the exception of the number of types of care, centenarians were not more dependent than octogenarians. Cognitive ability had the strongest effects for medical care and caregiving services. (MacDonald *et al.*, 2010, p.100)

Thus, as for personality, matters are not firmly fixed. The attitude adopted by the older adult can make things better than they might otherwise be.

Attitudes to ageing

Attitudes to ageing shape the way in which we treat and regard older adults. It is therefore not encouraging to find that overall they are regarded less favourably than younger adults (e.g. Catterall and Maclaran, 2001; DePaola *et al.*, 2003). This is undesirable on many levels. First, such attitudes are damaging to older people themselves. We have already seen in the earlier section on personality that failing to sustain a positive self-image can have serious repercussions for health and longevity in later life. It is well established that older people have an aversion to being called 'old', with only a fifth of people in their sixties and a half of those in their seventies being content with this label (Ward, 1984). The author of the study that produced this finding noted that, ironically, older people are often hoisted by their own petard, since when they were younger they formed the illogical stereotypes of ageing that now haunt them. Stereotyping seems to affect older people's confidence and, generally, the more older people believe in stereotypes, the lower their self-esteem (Ward, 1977). Indeed, the majority of studies find that self-image declines in later life in most people (Aiken, 1989).

This argument was reinforced in a study by Ryff (1991). She asked younger, middle-aged and older adults to rate their past, present and future selves and well-being. She found that the younger and middle-aged adults tended to see themselves on a path of self-improvement – they were better than their past selves, and in the future would get even better. The older participants, on the other hand, saw the best behind them and a decline in front of them. Graham and Baker (1989) examined two groups of (Canadian) participants: a group of older people (mean age 67 years) and a group of younger adult students. Participants were asked to grade imaginary people of different ages (e.g. '40-year-old man') for their level of status within society. The researchers found that, for both groups of participants, children were graded at a low level, status then rose through the teens, twenties and thirties, and then began to decline once again, so that 80-year-olds were perceived to have roughly the same status as 5-year-olds.

A subsequent study by Garstka *et al.* (2004) indicated that this was even more damaging than first thought. Younger people who are denigrated in this way tend not to feel discriminated against because they feel it is a temporary state of affairs they will (literally) grow out of, whereas for older people this is seen as a permanent state. Returning to Graham and Baker's study, although older participants gave the same relative balance of judgements as the students, the difference between the highest and lowest ratings was significantly less. Thus, although different generations have the same general pattern in their view of ageing and status, the researchers argued that older people are apparently 'slightly more egalitarian than the young' (Graham and Baker, 1989, p.255). This finding was echoed in a study by Laditka *et al.* (2004), which found that older participants were more likely to rate older adults positively (though arguably this could be through self-interest). Gluth, Ebner and Schmiedek

(2010) similarly found that negative comments were more likely to be made by the young against the old than vice versa. Gluth *et al.* also noted that mood and personality could play a key role, with extraverts who were not depressed being significantly less likely to make negative comments about older people.

Less egalitarianism was found in a study by Igier and Mullet (2003). They asked participants of different ages to describe how well different age groups epitomised each personality trait of the Big Five model. The researchers found that the older adults were seen as more conscientious, less open, not markedly neurotic, and moderately introverted and agreeable. The ratings are not particularly anti-ageing, but of interest is that across the whole study the age of the person being graded accounted for circa two-thirds of the total variance, whilst the age of the participant accounted for only circa one-tenth. Studies on level of self-esteem across the lifespan tell a similar tale with regard to ageing. Robins *et al.* (2002) found that self-esteem was high in childhood, dipped during adolescence, then rose again, only to decline in old age. These findings applied across gender, socio-economic and national groups. Likewise, whilst younger adults felt that the future would bring an increase in their subjective well-being, older adults saw only further decline (Staudinger, Bluck and Herzberg, 2003). Overall the evidence implies that most people have a consensus of opinion about what constitutes 'typical' signs and status of ageing.

Such generally negative attitudes occur even when considering nursing and medical staff, who have a professional duty of care towards older adults, but still are often found to have ageist attitudes on a par with the general population (Duerson, Thomas, Chang and Stevens, 1992). This can lead to the phenomenon that, even when presenting with identical symptoms, older and younger patients were diagnosed and treated completely differently (Duerson *et al.*, 1992). Again, Helmes and Gee (2003) found that, when presented with a (fictional) description of a patient presenting with symptoms of depression, both psychologists and counsellors were significantly less optimistic about the prognosis for the patient if they were described as 'elderly'. Peake and Thompson (2003) followed the progress of circa 1600 patients diagnosed with lung cancer. They found that treatment was directed more intensively towards the younger patients, even when other health factors were equal. For example, one commonly used surgical treatment was given to 37 per cent of younger patients versus only 15 per cent of patients aged over 75 years. Six months after diagnosis, the mortality rate for patients aged under 65 was 42 per cent versus 57 per cent in those aged over 75, a difference that arguably cannot be accounted for simply by differences in other health indices. Negative attitudes about older patients amongst clinicians are nothing new. We saw earlier in this chapter that Freud was unwilling to consider psychotherapy for older clients, and, in a similar vein, psychiatrists have sometimes regarded treatment of older adults as unwarranted because they have too little remaining life to benefit from therapy (James and Haley, 1995). In addition, the negativity surrounding geriatric care can deter practitioners from specialising in the area (see Ferrario *et al.*, 2008; Goncalves *et al.*, 2011). This is at a time when specialists in ageing are needed as never before (see the persuasive account by Lun, 2011).

In part, this inequality of attitude might reflect an ignorance of the full facts about ageing and the attitudes of practitioners. For example, Knapp, Beaver and Reed (2002) found that church ministers and students for the ministry were surprisingly unaware of very basic facts about ageing and later life. Nurses are similarly often lacking in knowledge about ageing and the specific needs of older people (see Alsenany, 2009; Wells *et al.*, 2004), although specialists in nursing older adults will probably outscore other student groups (Flood and Clark, 2009). A further study demonstrates that, even when exposed to situations that should increase knowledge and awareness of older adults, this might not occur. Hakamies-Blomqvist *et al.* (2002) examined Swedish and Finnish general practitioners' (GPs') knowledge of ageing and driving. Under Finnish law, older adults must be assessed by a GP before they are allowed to drive. The same is not true in Sweden. It might therefore be assumed that Finnish GPs would be more knowledgeable about ageing and driving than their Swedish counterparts, but this is not the case. The authors suggest that this may be because of undue complacency by Finnish doctors, convinced of the efficacy of their screening procedures, but it seems remarkable that little additional knowledge seems to have been acquired during repeated exposure.

Some comfort can be gathered from the argument that negative attitudes can be changed. For example, Guo, Erber and Szuchman (1999) demonstrated that exposing participants to positive reports about ageing can improve subsequent judgements of older people's skills. Likewise, Schwartz and Simmons (2001) reported that positive experiences of older adults (rather than simple frequency of meetings) was a significant determinant of younger adults' positive opinions of older people. In a similar vein, Stuart-Hamilton (2000) found that altering a set of five questions at the beginning of a questionnaire on attitudes from neutral to very slightly negative (the latter questions drew attention to the financial problems of some UK pensioners) was sufficient to create a significantly more negative set of judgements about older people in the latter group. Again, Polizzi and Millikin (2002) found that asking participants to rate the characteristics of people aged '70–85 years of age' resulted in significantly more favourable ratings than when asked to rate the characteristics of 'old' people. Deltsidou *et al.* (2010) studied Greek nursing students over the three years of their college course, and found that their attitudes significantly improved (and interestingly, were more positive towards ageing than their tutors'). Similar findings were reported by Ferrario *et al.* (2008) when participants in a training course were given greater exposure to the concept of successful/healthy ageing as part of their training, and by Eskildsen and Flacker (2009) when an intensive week-long module on geriatric medicine was introduced into a clinical medicine course. Encouraging self-reflection amongst students might also be beneficial in this regard (Del Duca and Duque, 2006).

The ease with which views can be manipulated implies that to some extent negative views of ageing might be a product of experimental design. Certainly in the studies that have found strongly negative views of ageing, participants have been asked to more or less make a direct comparison between an older and a younger person (Stuart-Hamilton, 2000). Under such circumstances, older people will be almost inevitably regarded in a negative light. It is not being ageist to say that on average older people have more physical and psychological problems than younger people, any more than it is sexist to say that on average women are shorter than men. However, such statements can easily predispose a person to ageist or sexist views. Thus, if participants are asked to compare younger versus older adults, the older adults will almost certainly come off the worse. This is indicated by Stuart-Hamilton (1998), who conducted a (UK) nationwide survey of women's attitudes to ageing. Women of all ages were questioned, and were simply asked what they thought of older people on their own terms (in other words, without comparisons being drawn with younger adults). The responses were much more positive about ageing than those in many other studies. Therefore, at least some of the negative view of ageing is probably a result of how the questions have been asked.

However, how deeply these attitudes are profoundly changed by such manipulations, and the degree to which they express true opinions is open to question. The measure of attitudes used in the studies discussed here addresses **explicit attitudes** – in other words, the expressed attitude of a person who has had time to prepare their answer. However, even under very rigid conditions of anonymity, such attitudes are prone to self-presentational bias (Goffman, 1959; Jones and Pittman, 1982). There are thus sound grounds for questioning whether explicit attitudes are expressions of what a person 'really' thinks. Instead, they are arguably a measure of how far a person is prepared to express his or her true opinions. This implies that there could be more than a hint of impression management in the responses of participants to many attitudes to ageing studies, and there is some evidence for this.

For example, Harris and Dollinger (2001) found that students taking a course on the psychology of ageing improved their knowledge of ageing but their own anxieties about growing old had not significantly altered. In short, training had improved *knowledge* of ageing, but had not really affected underlying emotions or opinions on the subject. Stuart-Hamilton and Mahoney (2003) conducted a study in which younger adult participants (employees of a local government district in the UK) were given a half-day training session intended to increase awareness of ageing and older adults. Prior to the session, participants were given two questionnaires – one measured attitudes to ageing (the **Fraboni Scale of Ageism**; see Fraboni, Saltstone and Hughes, 1990) and the other knowledge of ageing. Two months after the training session, participants were given the same tests again. Not surprisingly, it was found that knowledge of ageing improved following training. However, attitudes to ageing and older adults remained unaffected, except for an increased awareness not to use ageist language. This is a potentially worrying finding. Many studies of anti-ageism training use a measure of knowledge of ageing as a gauge of whether training has been successful (see Stuart-Hamilton and Mahoney, 2003). However, just as with the Harris and Dollinger study, *knowledge* can change without significant changes in the underlying *attitudes* (in the same way that an army general in battle can learn a great deal about the state of the opposing forces without changing his or her dislike for them). Indeed, Stuart-Hamilton and Mahoney found that knowledge and attitude scores did not correlate significantly, a finding echoed by Cottle and Glover (2007). The degree to which attitudes can truly change is therefore still open to question, and it may therefore be assumed that anti-ageing stereotypes are still strong in many instances, despite whatever the measures of explicit attitudes claim to show.

Indeed, ageist stereotypes appear even when views are not directly measured by questionnaire. For example, Hummert, Garstka and Shaner (1997) found that participants attributed significantly fewer positive attributes to pictures of older people (there is also an interesting rebuttal of Graham and Baker's claims of egalitarianism cited earlier, since photos of very old people were rated significantly less positively by older participants). A later study by the same group (Hummert *et al.*, 2002) further reinforced this, finding that implicit associations about older adults and ageing were often less ageing-positive than overt statements. Again, participants giving instructions to people of different ages tended to 'talk down' to older people, and, although this was done less if it was emphasised that the older person was 'competent', nonetheless, speech was still different from when providing instructions to a younger adult (Thimm, Rademacher and Kruse, 1998).

Note that these are the findings from studies where participants have at least some conscious control over what they are saying. What then might attitudes to ageing be like if we could identify what people think *before* they have had time to impose conscious control and, in effect, impose a layer of impression management onto their opinions? This leads to the study of **implicit attitudes**. These have been defined by Greenwald and Banaji (1995, p.8) as 'introspectively unidentified (or inaccurately identified) traces of past experience that mediate favourable or unfavourable feeling, thought or action toward social objects'. They are in effect the very first reaction a person has before they have had time to think about whether their thought is socially acceptable or accords with their other beliefs. It is tempting to see implicit attitudes as a measure of what the person 'really' thinks, but, although this is plausible, it cannot definitely be proved. For example, it is also possible that a person might have a 'knee-jerk reaction' to a phenomenon, but, because this does not accord with genuinely held values, it is amended.

There are various ways of measuring implicit attitudes, but the most widely used is probably the implicit attitudes test, or IAT (Greenwald and Banaji, 1995). The IAT is based on the well-established premise that the more strongly two items are associated together, the faster a person responds to them. For instance, people will associate the words *bread* and *butter* with each other faster than, for example, *bread* and *razor*.

If people are implicitly ageist, then it follows that they should associate unpleasant words faster with older people and pleasant words faster with younger people. These are what are termed the 'congruent conditions'. Conversely, ageist people should be relatively slower at associating pleasant words with older people and unpleasant words with younger people. These are called the 'incongruent conditions'. However, if people are *not* ageist, then they should associate the words in the congruent and incongruent conditions at equal speed. Over several blocks of trials, participants are shown pairings in different combinations. Before each block begins, participants are told to press one response button if one type of pairing appears, and another button if another pairing appears. The full procedure is laborious to describe, but in short, when the test is over, it is possible to measure the difference in mean response times to congruent and incongruent pairings – the larger the difference, the stronger the implicit attitude.

Although the IAT has been widely used to examine implicit attitudes to a range of things (see Baron and Banaji, 2006), studies of attitudes to ageing and old people are at the time of writing relatively rare (though there is a large literature on tacit cultural acceptance of ageist values; e.g. Levy and Banaji, 2002; Zebrowitz and Montepare, 2000). Jelenec and Steffens (2002) demonstrated pronounced ageist attitudes using the IAT, a finding more recently replicated by Turner and Crisp (2010). These researchers found that implicit attitude scores were less prejudicial the greater the contact the participants had with older people. This should bode well for many nursing and medical situations, since it implies that people who work regularly with older adults will have more positive implicit attitudes. However, it is important to bear in mind that all the researchers found was a *relative* lessening of prejudice, not necessarily an absence of it. Older people were still seen negatively even by those with the greatest contact with them. A study by Nash, Stuart-Hamilton and Mayer (2009) demonstrated a further worrying trend. Nursing students with regular exposure to older patients had negative implicit attitudes, but their *explicit* attitudes were positive. In short, the students appear to pay lip service to explicit support for older adults whilst their implicit attitudes are ageist. These students were followed over a year, during which time this situation did not significantly change in this regard. Furthermore, performance on the implicit and explicit measures did not correlate significantly. Studies of implicit attitudes towards ageing and older adults are still in their relative infancy, but the existing findings indicate that many measures of explicit attitudes might be the expressions of very shallow beliefs.

Cross-cultural differences

So far, a high proportion of the research discussed has been conducted in industrialised nations with Western cultures. This is not wilful bias, but a simple reflection of the fact that this is where a lot of the research has been conducted. Generally, this is of little concern: age changes in working memory are likely to be reasonably similar from Austria to Zambia, and the same applies to nearly all cognitive ageing. There are exceptions (e.g. some relatively minor differences in the way stories are recalled; see Hosokawa and Hosokawa, 2006), but in the main this argument probably holds. However, in studies of how older people present themselves to the outside world, clearly culture could potentially have an impact. If a country is generally accepting and supportive of old age, then a person might have different attitudes and behaviours compared with a person living in a more ageist environment.

In practically any discussion of attitudes to ageing in the popular media, a sharp contrast is drawn between attitudes in the East and West. A visual cliché of documentary makers is to contrast shots of an impoverished pensioner in a British planning blight apartment block with serene octogenarians doing communal Tai Chi exercises. Certainly, there are East–West differences to be found. For example, older people in Hong Kong have a higher proportion of immediate family members and lower proportion of acquaintances in their social circle with increasing age. The reverse applies to older people in Germany (Fung *et al.*, 2008). Generally in the Far East, later life *is* revered to a greater extent than in the West. However, this is a generalised statement. First, it is usually active old age that is prized, where the older adult can still make a contribution (see Okamoto and Tanaka, 2004). A later life of infirmity and reliance is regarded less positively. Again, as globalisation continues its seemingly inexorable progress, there are signs of some change towards Western values in Eastern countries – in other words, views about ageing are becoming more negative (see Ingersoll-Dayton and Saengtienchai, 1999). However, there is potentially a culture × age interaction in this: older people in China have been found to be less extreme in their opinions than older people in the USA (Blanchard-Fields *et al.*, 2007).

Eastern cultures are sometimes treated by Western observers as homogeneous, but in reality not all Eastern cultures have the same strengths of attitude. For example, Levy (1999) reports that Japanese people tend to have less negative attitudes towards older people than do Chinese. Also, note that even at best the view of ageing is still often negative in absolute terms – it is merely the *strength* of the view's expression that differs between cultures. And nor in East-West comparisons does the difference in every attitude and behaviour go in the expected direction. For example, Fu *et al.* (2006) found that Australian men and women had better mid-life quality of life scores (see below) than Taiwanese men and women. A study by You, Fung and Isaacowitz (2009) found that older Americans had a higher level of **dispositional optimism** (the tendency to expect positive rather than negative outcomes) than younger Americans, whereas for Hong Kong Chinese people the reverse applied (i.e. it was the younger adults who had the higher level of dispositional optimism). However, it should be noted that studies of dispositional optimism have been known to produce capricious findings (see You *et al.*, 2009).

A final caveat is that arguably too much stress can be placed on East-West differences, since it implies that Western cultures are all very similar to each other, and ditto for

Eastern cultures. However, as we have just seen, this is not true for Eastern cultures, and nor is it true for Western. For example, Clarke and Smith (2011) demonstrated that American older adults have a significantly higher sense of personal control than British older adults. Again, differences in the representation of ageing have been found between Italian and Brazilian participants (Wachelke and Contarello, 2010). But these cultural differences are not a consistent finding and other permutations of differences are also possible. For example, a comparison of Brazilian and American participants of various ages showed a nationality difference on the Iowa Gambling Task (a measure of gambling decision-making), but no age difference. Cultural differences with regard to age are not fixed in a single set pattern (see Bakos et al., 2010).

Discussion of cross-cultural differences thus presents a rather confused picture – cultures certainly differ, but the differences are not always where expected nor necessarily in the direction that might be intuitively supposed. However, it is nonetheless important that we are aware of what these differences are. A key measure of well-being in many older people is **quality of life (QOL)**. This is essentially a gauge of how contented a person is with his or her lifestyle and day-to-day experiences. However, different cultures have different expectations of what constitutes the good life, so what a typical person in one culture considers to be a barely adequate and thus unsatisfying existence might be seen by a person in another culture as living in the lap of luxury. This means that comparisons of quality of life in different cultures can be fraught with difficulty if due allowance is not made for cultural differences (Bowling and Stenner, 2011). In addition, as noted in Chapter 1, the ageing population is increasing in proportion and with it will come a concomitant rise in probabilistic diseases of later life such as many of the cancers, cardiovascular and respiratory complaints, etc. Over time, the rise in these diseases plus other demographic variables means that quality of life will be in flux and present challenges to care providers (de Mendonca Lima, Leibing and Buschfort, 2007).

Tangential to this, in general, non-industrialised and developing societies have a higher regard for later life, according it a special status. This may be because later life is relatively rare in such groups, and, in peoples lacking a written language system, older people may be especially valued for their memories of the past. However, as with many Eastern countries, the very elderly and physically and mentally infirm are often regarded far less favourably (see Perlmutter and Hall, 1992). It is also important to recognise that within developing countries, just as with the East, attitudes to ageing are not in stasis. For example, Aboderin (2004) has identified significant shifts in attitudes to ageing amongst urban Ghanaians, with an increasing expectation that older adults show self-reliance rather than (as was traditional) relying on younger members of the family to provide a high level of support. Aborderin attributes this sea change in attitudes to the increasingly materialist culture of Ghana.

Ethnic minority groups within industrialised countries tend to have a higher regard for, and more inclusive treatment of, older adults. This may in part be attributed to a higher proportion of multigenerational households, and closer-knit families (for majority culture Europeans, the social support systems in different countries are broadly similar; Wenger, 1997). Even where the traditional family unit is becoming less common, a support system may still remain in place that leaves older adults satisfied with the level of support from younger family members and their social network (e.g. Cornman *et al.*, 2004). In addition, for some ethnic minorities (e.g. African Americans) the church may play a greater role in providing social and unifying support (Jackson, Antonucci and Gibson, 1990) and specific cultural expectations and practices may significantly shape interactions and their success (e.g. the outcomes of caring for a sick older relative; see Dilworth-Anderson, Goodwin and Wallace Williams, 2004).

However, it is dangerous to overgeneralise such arguments and assume that cultural differences are uniquely the product of particular cultures and are fundamentally different to the core. Almost inevitably there are confounding factors, such as the fact that ethnic minorities tend to have a lower socio-economic standing and thus may be forced to be more inter-reliant through economic necessity, and these are difficult to tease apart from other factors (see Rosenthal, 1986 for a discussion of the methodological implications of ethnicity research). For example, Fung, Lai and Ng (2001) demonstrated that the life expectancy of an ethnic group can significantly shape matters. In comparing social preferences of older Taiwanese people against those of typically shorter-lived mainland Chinese people, statistically controlling for differences in life expectancy also removed cultural differences. In addition, studies across different ethnic/cultural groups have found common themes and expectations, such as recognising the importance of mutual assistance and reciprocity between generations, even if the relative emphasis placed on individual factors within the system varies between groups (e.g. Becker *et al.*, 2003). Furthermore, level of education is a consistent predictor of health and health change across Eastern and Western cultures (Chiu *et al.*, 2005; Farias *et al.*, 2011).

Notwithstanding these comments, older people within an ethnic minority face what has been termed **double jeopardy** – the problem that not only will they be treated prejudicially because they are older, but also because of their ethnic identity. It is certainly true that older people from ethnic minorities under-use health and social care programmes (e.g. Gallagher-Thompson *et al.*, 1997). Norman (1985) states the case more strongly, and argues that many older members of ethnic minorities are in fact faced with a **triple jeopardy** because, in addition to the aforementioned problems, they also, through the prejudice of others and often through communication problems, cannot get the help they need and deserve from the local or state authorities (other commentators, such as Paz and Aleman, 1998, have identified the three factors as age, poverty and ethnicity, but the import of the term is the same). Norman makes a strong case based on the practical problems faced by older ethnic minorities in claiming services and amenities.

What evidence is there for double/triple jeopardy? In other words, are older people in ethnic minorities significantly disadvantaged? Findings that older people from minority groups have poorer health cannot be taken at face value, since minority groups often have lower socio-economic status, and this, as we have seen, can be a powerful confounding variable. Many early researchers were thus sceptical about how genuine a problem was there, and gave the concept of double jeopardy equivocal support (see Perlmutter and Hall, 1992). However, more recent studies, which have adjusted data for socio-economic variables, have found that older people from ethnic minorities are physically unhealthy significantly more often than majority culture older people, and, furthermore, this difference is significantly larger in older than in younger adults from the same cultures (Carreon and Noymer, 2011). The research literature is packed with further examples. The following list is intended as illustrative rather than in any way exhaustive:

- Nielsen *et al.* (2011) demonstrated that dementia is under-diagnosed in older adults from ethic minorities, but, conversely, it is *over*-diagnosed in people aged under 60. Nielsen *et al.* attribute this to several factors, including problems in using the health care system and seeking assistance.

- Warner and Brown (2011) found that some ethnic minority groups display different patterns of change in their levels of physical disability (though similarities between other ethnic groups were noted).

- White-Means (2000) found that older African Americans are less likely to use various medical services, and this explanation holds even after financial differences have been accounted for (see also Dunlop *et al.*, 2002).

- August and Sorkin (2011) found similar differences in level of exercise and use of a health diet amongst Californian residents (see also Waters *et al.*, 2011).

- Likewise, Hardy *et al.* (2011) found differences between ethnic groups in use of hospice care.

- Levine *et al.* (2011) found that, amongst American stroke patients, Mexican and African American patients had received less specialist after-care and had access to fewer drug treatments (because of the relative poverty of these groups). This in turn heightened the risk of further strokes.

Thus, although the findings on cultural differences in later life are at times mixed, one thing that is very clear is that ethnic minorities often face appreciable health problems. The argument that in part this is due to the confounding effects of socio-economic class is important for researchers, but in moral terms it does not excuse failure to rectify this problem. However, it is important to note that, although ethnic minorities as a group might experience problems, this cannot be automatically said of every individual member of any cultural group, and there is a wide variability in individual scores in many studies (see Whitfield and Baker-Thomas, 1999). Thus, discussions of ethnic minority problems are descriptive, not prescriptive. A further caveat is that it can be seen that the experiences of older adults can, all the recent qualifications notwithstanding, be strongly influenced by their culture. This means that, in many respects, the lifestyle and quality of life of older people is not set in stone and can be varied. Once more, therefore, we have evidence that we are not doomed to follow one inevitable life course.

Retirement

Although some people think about retirement in terms of a set 'retirement age', this is often inaccurate. As noted in Chapter 1, the idea of a formal pensionable age is largely a phenomenon of the twentieth century, and, even then, it was not obeyed rigorously or indeed at the same age in all countries. For example, the formal retirement age for many public sector workers, such as school teachers, varies from the late-fifties to the mid-sixties, depending upon the country in question. In addition, not everyone waits for the formal retirement age to retire. Companies wishing to shed surplus workers often find it financially easiest to offer early retirement packages to the oldest workers.[11] In addition, the advent of more humane employment laws means that early paid retirement through chronic ill health is on the rise.[12] Conversely, other people choose to work past retirement age (if their country's laws permit it) and, in the case of self-employed people, there is almost always no legally defined age at which a person must retire. This means that retirement, although probabilistically an experience of old age, is not automatically so, and the precise age of retirement, and the reasons for it, can vary widely (see McDonald, 2011). It is therefore not totally surprising that a study by Settersen (1998) found that for many people age was now an irrelevant criterion on which to judge retirement. It should also be noted in passing that over the past 40 years the proportion of men still working from those aged 55–65 has significantly declined, whilst the comparable figures for women have risen (McDonald, 2011).

It is possible to see retirement from various angles, such as sociological, economic, etc. For reasons of space, discussion here will be restricted to a brief overview of psychological issues concerned with retirement. Some researchers have treated retirement as one stage or factor in a larger model of ageing or lifespan development, and such models are dealt with elsewhere in this chapter.[13] Other researchers have

---

11 If common office folklore is to be believed, early retirement is also a useful way of getting rid of the most inefficient/most work-shy individuals, a consideration that does not seem to have been examined by many researchers. Conversely, widespread early retirement amongst some skilled professions, such as medicine, lead to significant economic and social problems (see Heponiemi *et al.*, 2008).

12 At times of high unemployment, depression-related early retirement cases can also rise; see Lamberg *et al.* (2010). Other psychiatric conditions such as personality and anxiety disorders also greatly increase the probability of early retirement (Korkeila *et al.*, 2011).

13 For example, Erikson's model, described earlier, or disengagement theory (see page 209).

examined the specific process of retirement or individual issues relating to the retirement process. From this research, two recurring questions have emerged. First, what determines the nature of retirement? In other words, how happy people will be once retired, and what they do. Second, how do people plan for retirement?

With regard to the first of these questions, the answer has often focused on the degree to which people feel they have controlled their retirement for themselves. Swan, Dame and Carmelli (1991) reported in their study of American retired persons that those who felt that they had been 'forced' to retire had generally lower levels of well-being, and (perhaps not surprisingly) that people with Type A personalities were more likely to complain that they had retired against their will. However, it is difficult to exclude the possibility that such people would have suffered problems and complained in any case. Sharpley (1997) identified three factors – missing work, health, and relationships – and, once again, it is tempting to argue that the latter two problems might have arisen regardless of retirement. A longitudinal study by Gallo *et al.* (2000) found significant negative effects on mental and physical health of being involuntarily retired (in contrast, older workers made redundant and then fortunate enough to be re-employed showed a marked improvement in mental and physical health, independent of how long they had been out of work). These findings applied even after prior health and socio-economic status were controlled for (see also Szinovacz and Davey, 2004). De Vaus *et al.* (2007), studying a sample of Australian retirees, found that amongst a range of possible factors the most salient seemed to be the level of control the retirees felt they had over the retirement process. For example, if they could plan the timing of their departure and the way in which it was done, well-being was higher, even three years after the event. This finding was echoed by Calvo, Haverstick and Sass (2009). Similarly, van Solinge (2007) found, in a study of Dutch workers, that the type of job that was being retired from did not have a significant effect on self-reported health, but being forced to retire did. Also of interest in this regard are the findings of Price and Balaswamy (2009), who found that amongst the key predictors of women's satisfaction in retirement were self-esteem and mastery. Also, Herzog, House and Morgan (1991) studied older adults who were working or in semi-retirement. They found that well-being was not related to how much work they did but to whether the work was what they wanted to do. This finding was the same for a group of slightly younger workers (aged 55–64 years).

These findings demonstrate that retirement satisfaction is shaped to a significant extent by the degree to which retirement is voluntary and a person feels in control of his or her own life, but this does not mean that other factors do not play a part. The evidence on some factors, such as whether it is better to go from working one day to being fully retired the next, or to retire by gradually working less and less each week, is somewhat equivocal (see de Vaus *et al.*, 2007), with some authors being largely dismissive of any difference (e.g. 'what matters is not the type of transition [gradual retirement or cold turkey] but whether people perceive the transition as chosen or forced'; Calvo *et al.*, 2009, p.112). However, other factors do seem to play a significant role. For example, Price and Balaswamy (2009) found that financial status, though not as important as some other factors, was still a significant predictor. In a study of British civil servants (basically, government officials) opting for early retirement, Mein *et al.* (2000) found that the principal reasons were high income (i.e. could afford to retire early on a good pension), ill health or dislike of the job. Older workers who had material difficulties (e.g. debts) usually felt compelled to carry on working. Again, van Solinge and Henkens (2007) found that, whilst degree of choice over when to retire was a key consideration, so were other measures such as the social environment the retirees lived in. Body satisfaction and perceived health are also key predictors of retirement satisfaction (Stephan, Fouquereau and Fernandez, 2008a; van den Berg, Elders and Burdorf, 2010).

Given the apparent mania for linking personality traits to every behaviour under the sun, surprisingly little research has addressed the relationship between the Big Five (see page 168) and retirement. An exception to this is the work of Robinson, Demetre and Corney (2010). They found that each trait in the Big Five was related to an aspect of retirement: neuroticism correlated with the extent a person viewed the events leading up to retirement in a negative fashion. Neuroticism and extraversion correlated with life satisfaction in individuals approaching retirement, whilst conscientiousness was related to what people aspired to achieve in retirement. Agreeableness (along with neuroticism and conscientiousness) correlated significantly with life satisfaction in people who were already retired.

In couples with traditional gender roles, marital satisfaction is higher where the husband is working and the wife is retired than in the reverse situation (Myers and Booth, 1996; Szinovacz, 1996). Perhaps not surprisingly, marital satisfaction can be improved by retirement from a stressful occupation, but health problems may cause a worsening (Myers and Booth, 1996). Unsurprisingly, perhaps, retirement through ill health is associated with a lowered level of leisure activity relative to physically healthier retirees (Scherger, Nazroo and Higgs, 2011). This echoes earlier findings of an increase in satisfaction among very healthy retirees (e.g. Parnes, 1981). Some studies report that white collar workers tend to enjoy retirement more than blue collar workers, but this can probably be attributed to better health and finances (Bengston and Treas, 1980; Ward, 1984).

A related method of examining retirement effects is to place them in the context of larger models of lifespan development. **Role theory** argues that, as people grow older, they play various societal roles, including that of the retired person. Since this is less prestigious than that of the working person, retirement is potentially a psychologically damaging time. In contrast, the **continuity theory of retirement** (Atchley, 1989) sees retirement as a continuation of the same sense of identity as before, and thus not as a stressful period (see Krauss Whitbourne and Whitbourne, 2011 for further discussion).

The effects of retirement on health are often hard to gauge. Since retirees are also generally in old age, this means that many of the health changes that occur post-retirement are probably age rather than retirement related. Fonseca (2007), studying Portuguese retirees, argued that many people find retirement itself relaxing and pleasurable (absence from stress and 'being your own boss' were often cited). Many of the negative factors surrounding retirement are, Fonseca argued, the product of ageing, rather than retirement *per se*. Hult *et al.* (2010) studied a group of retired Swedish construction workers, comparing how early they had taken retirement. The researchers found that there was no link between mortality and age at retirement. Although some early retirees died earlier than the norm, the researchers concluded that this was due to the underlying physical health of the worker, rather than retirement *per se*. The effects of retirement on weight gain have been discussed in the literature, but recent studies suggest that the effect is slight. For example, Chung, Domino and Stearns (2009) found that retirement was marked by a small but nonetheless significant weight gain (0.24 BMI) though this is about a fifth of the total weight gain shown by people between the ages of 50 and 60 (1.30). Forman-Hoffman *et al.* (2008) only found a significant weight gain in women who had been in blue-collar occupations and who were normal weight at time of retirement.

It can thus be seen that a wide variety of factors shape the enjoyment of retirement. Furthermore, the full picture may be complicated by individual differences and circumstances (Moen, 1996). As an illustration of this, van Solinge and Henkens (2005), examining Dutch people approaching retirement, found that a combination of several factors (length of time in the same full-time job, degree of control over when and how to retire, level of anxiety and expectations about the process of retirement, level of self-efficacy) predicted success at adjusting to retirement, and that these factors varied considerably between individuals. Kim and Moen (2002) make a similar case for observing a wide variety of factors. In addition to this, there are possible cultural/national differences. The majority of research on retirement appears to have been conducted in countries with reasonably advanced state welfare provision, such as national pensions. However, even within countries with seemingly similar welfare provision there can be differences in retirement behaviour. For example, in the Netherlands, early retirement is relatively common compared with Denmark, where it is relatively rare. The effect seems to be explained by a complex collection of different cultural practices and social mores (see van Oorschot and Jensen, 2009).

To turn to the second question raised earlier (*how do people plan for retirement?*), the answer is again a multifaceted one. It is clear that retirement is seen as a deeply desirable thing by most people. European readers of this will have witnessed the furore in many countries that greeted proposals to increase the pensionable age. The right to retire and enjoy the fruits of one's labours is seen as an inalienable right, even though, as we have seen, state pensions are a relatively new invention. Be that as it may, surveys of attitudes to working past retirement age are typically met with extreme opposition in many workers (e.g. Davies and Cartwright, 2011). Generally, workers want to retire sooner rather than later. Zappala *et al.* (2008), interviewing a sample of Italian workers, found there was on average a preference to retire three years earlier than the statutory age. However, such attitudes were reported as malleable and could, for example, be shaped by more age-friendly company policies and similar.

People approaching retirement often have a rose-tinted view of what retirement years will be like. A key interest is often the prospect of taking up a new hobby. In reality, the uptake of interests in retirement is subject to many factors. Stephan, Fouquereau and Fernandez (2008b) found that reasons for engaging in post-retirement activities within a university-run organisation were intrinsic, such as desire for increased knowledge, rather than extrinsic pressures, such as the expectations of others. However, this is only one type of activity and does not necessarily universally apply to all types of activity. Hopkins, Roster and Wood (2006) categorised (American) retirees according to the attitude they took to retirement. They found that expenditure was increased on more outward-looking activities if the individuals concerned regarded retirement either as a 'new start' or a 'disruption'. On the other hand, if retirees saw retirement as the 'continuation of life' or 'onset of old age', then expenditure tended to increase on inward-looking activities.

Other popular dreams of retirement are the prospect of long life and a pleasant place to live. These seem utterly reasonable wishes, but people often fail to examine the issues in sufficient depth. Ayalon and King-Kallimanis (2010) posed the following question to their (American) participants: whether they would prefer fewer years of remaining life in perfect health or more years of life in imperfect health. Those participants already in imperfect health tended to prefer fewer years of perfect health; white participants preferred fewer years of imperfect health, whilst black participants preferred more years of imperfect health; people with lower levels of education preferred more years of imperfect health. As we shall see in Chapter 8, these answers echo the findings of cultural differences in supporting extending life in terminal illness at the expense of quality of life.

The conundrum presented by Ayalon and King-Mallimanis is one to which arguably there is no correct answer. However, in other instances, planning for the future does involve more definitely right and wrong decisions. Advanced financial planning is clearly important. A study of Dutch participants by van Rooij, Lusardi and Alessie (2011) demonstrated that the greater the financial literacy of the participant, the more likely they were to have planned for retirement. This is perhaps not very surprising, since an awareness of retirement planning is part and parcel of financial literacy. However, a key issue raised by this and similar studies is the necessity for financial education to begin early – planning for retirement takes decades of saving. Another key issue is provision of key amenities. Retirement advisors often talk despairingly of the 'roses round the cottage door' phenomenon – in other words, retirees who entertain an over-romanticised dream of living in a quiet country cottage miles from anywhere. Such places might be bearable when young and with reliable transport, but are much less convenient when older, in need of frequent visits to the doctor/hospital, but without a car and with sporadic (at best) public transport. The great nineteenth century wit, the Reverend Sydney Smith, once complained that, stuck in a country parish in Yorkshire, he was 12 miles from the nearest lemon. This is often taken as being a whimsical joke but, like much of Smith's wit, there is a serious point to it. Rural locations are often the very worst places to live without adequate access to modern amenities. And yet, retirees often head with seemingly lemming-like determination to what is pretty rather than practical. This is neatly summed up in a study by Oishi *et al.* (2009), who studied retirement location choices of retirees and non-retirees in Korea and the USA. Non-retirees assumed that places with nice weather and plenty of cultural amenities were the best choice.[14] However, retirees who had gone for the practical (easy access to medical services and routine daily amenities) were significantly happier than other retirees.

In summary – retirement is not necessarily a time of problems, perpetual ill health and misery. However, it does need to be carefully planned for, and that planning (particularly the financial) needs to start in early adulthood.

Bereavement

This is addressed more fully in Chapter 8 in the sections on bereavement and widowhood. The experience is typically described in terms of relatively short-lived extreme distress followed by a prolonged and generally societally sanctioned period of grieving. There are considerable cultural differences in this experience, indicating that what seems to be an intensely personal experience is in fact strongly shaped by societal forces. However, the cultural argument can be overplayed, since it cannot be assumed that if a person is from a particular culture they 'must' always behave in a particular way. There is still considerable scope for individual variability in bereavement responses.

Well-being

The issue of well-being has already been partly addressed in the earlier section on life satisfaction in retirement, since the vast majority of retired people will by definition be in old age. However, not all older people have, strictly speaking, 'retired', since they have never had a full-time paid job and have spent their entire lives as a homemaker or similar. Thus, many studies of well-being in old age do not consider the issue of retirement in their analysis.

---

14 However, the assumption that urban equals better provision than rural does not always hold true. For example, Peterson and Litaker (2010) demonstrated that health care provision was equally unmet in urban and rural settings in poverty-affected regions.

It is generally acknowledged that chronic features of ageing can take their toll on life satisfaction. For example, insidious physical changes, from the relatively minor (e.g. greying hair) to the more serious (e.g. arthritis) can all cause a revaluation of self-concepts (Ward, 1984). Some studies have found that health and concomitant changes in mobility are the biggest predictors of satisfaction in later life, but others have failed to replicate this (e.g. Bowling, Farquhar and Grundy, 1996) and findings might depend upon what measures the health gauge is weighed against (the research on retirement has also produced equivocal findings on this subject).

If a single factor affecting life satisfaction is sought, the issue of monetary worries figures large in most researchers' lists. In probabilistic terms, this is not surprising, since older people, and particularly older women, are disproportionately more likely to suffer financial hardship than other groups (Gillen and Kim, 2009; see also Foster, 2011). In the USA, for example, almost half of all older people will have at least one year of poverty during old age (Rank and Williams, 2010). Krause, Jay and Liang (1991) demonstrated that financial problems (common in many older people) are a prime factor in reducing feelings of self-worth and in increasing depressive symptoms (see also Choi and McDougall, 2009). This is true of many cultures. Krause et al.'s study found the same basic phenomenon in samples of both American and Japanese older people. Zhang *et al.* (1997) found financial problems to be a major negative factor amongst older people in China. Ferraro and Su (1999) similarly found financial problems increased psychological distress in participants from three different cultures (Fijian, Korean and Philippino, though note that Malaysian participants were an exception). However, the authors also noted that the level of social and family support can at least ease some of these problems. This is reflected in a longitudinal study by Russell and Catrona (1991), who found that the less the social support the older person experienced at the start of the study, the higher his or her depressive symptoms were one year later (and the greater his or her experience of 'daily hassles'). Again, personality factors may play an important role. For example, a well-integrated individual can cope with stress far better than someone who is disorganised. Conversely, a person in bad health and with poor finances may be better able to cope with the declines of health and wealth because they are already used to it (Ward, 1977, 1984). It is also worth noting that, in addition to personality types, other psychological factors such as intellectual changes can dent self-esteem. For example, in Chapter 3 it was noted that a high self-report of memory lapses is correlated with level of depression. Perlmutter *et al.* (1987) note that this may create a vicious circle – an older person who perceives his or her performance on a memory task to be poor may suffer a lowering of morale, which may further hamper his or her abilities.

However, although financial problems are a significant cause of negative feelings for many older adults, they are not universal and they do not dominate every older person's life even when lack of funds is an issue in an individual's life. For example, MacDonell *et al.* (2010) found that financial problems were just one of several factors of roughly equal importance, a finding echoed by Rurup *et al.* (2011). It should also be noted that financial difficulties might be associated with other potentially poor conditions, such as living in rundown neighbourhoods with poorer amenities. This can create a vicious circle, since people living in poorer neighbourhoods are also likely to be more hostile and thus less likely to help each other (Krause, 2011). And it is also known that unmet needs make a significant contribution to depression in older adults (Choi and McDougall, 2009). Again, the presence of other factors can affect the impact of financial difficulties. For example, Krause (2010) found that many of the depressive effects of financial difficulties were ameliorated in older people who preferred to suffer in silence. In short, mental attitude can shape the impact of other problems.

It is also important to note that episodes in a person's past can impinge on their attitudes to later life. Obviously, decisions about careers, relationships, whether to have children, and so forth, have a direct impact. Stallings *et al.* (1997) found that negative events in a person's life tend to affect the negative aspects of the mood of a person and positive events the positive aspects with minimal crossover influences (supporting the so-called **two-factor theory of well-being**). Taking a different approach, Caspi and Elder (1986) examined feelings of life satisfaction in a group of older women who in their thirties had experienced the American Great Depression. Middle-class women who endured hardship at this time now had demonstrably higher ratings of life satisfaction as a result. However, the reverse applied to working-class women in the same situation – they had a lower life satisfaction. Perhaps this is because the middle-class women had demonstrably 'won through' to a better material lifestyle, while the working-class women perceived themselves as being still 'at the bottom'. In an analogous manner, people rated as high in wisdom and who experienced the Great Depression had better psychological health in later life than people rated low in wisdom (Ardelt, 1998). However, regardless of background, women on the whole demonstrate a lower level of subjective well-being, as a meta-analysis of the research literature by Pinquart and Sörensen (2001) demonstrated.

Other factors also may contribute to life satisfaction. For example, Cook (1998) found that participating in organised group reminiscence sessions improved the level of life satisfaction amongst older women in a residential home. This should not be taken as support for the stereotype that older people long to live in the past. Although there is evidence that at least some groups of older people would like their past achievements and status to be recognised more (Ghusn *et al.*, 1996), when asked the question 'Looking back, what period of your life brought you the most satisfaction?', the most common response from older people was 'right now' (Field, 1997). Generally, and perhaps unsurprisingly, social activities and friendships have been found to be beneficial by almost all researchers (though in the case of friendships, it is probably quality rather than quantity of friendships that is more important; Pinquart and Sörensen, 2000). Gleibs *et al.* (2011) found that offering members of residential homes gender-based groups (i.e. separate ladies' and gentlemen's clubs) that met fortnightly produced a marked psychological improvement. Women showed evidence of maintaining well-being and identification, whilst men showed a significant decrease in symptoms of depression and anxiety, whilst also increasing their level of social identification with other residents.

An interesting twist on this is provided by Greenwood (1999), who found that, where there are problems in a changing social life in later years, men are less likely to report decreased satisfaction, because in general they may have lower expectations of interpersonal relations than women. Again, it is not sufficient to group older people together and expect satisfaction to increase as a result. For example, in a telling phrase, Kovach and Robinson (1996) reported that being given a roommate in a residential home 'predicted life satisfaction only for those who talked to their roommates' (p.627). Participation in exercise activities or non-energetic leisure activities also is correlated with greater life satisfaction (and health). The authors of one study (Menec and Chipperfield, 1997) attribute this to an enhanced feeling of being in control of events (see also McConatha et al., 1998). However, although sociable activities are undoubtedly beneficial, pastimes do not necessarily have to be gregarious to enhance life satisfaction. For example, Sherer (1996) demonstrated that being allowed access to personal computers had a beneficial effect on the self-esteem and life satisfaction of older nursing home residents and day patients (it is perhaps worth noting in passing that the women in the study tended to use educational software, whilst the men played video games). Generally speaking, purposeful activity is beneficial to life satisfaction (Madigan, Mise and Maynard, 1996). Many of the studies mentioned earlier have been based in residential homes and have centred on psychological issues, assuming they are of maximum importance in determining an older resident's psychological state. This on the face of it is a reasonable assumption. However, a recent study by Rioux and Werner (2011) suggests that many earlier studies might have missed the key role in residential care of the physical nature of the residential home itself – its features, its proximity to services, the pleasantness of the local neighbourhood, etc. Psychological and other factors might be less important when a wider view is taken. Oswald et al. (2011) found analogous results for older adults living in their own homes. At the time of writing, it appears that the role of the broader environment is beginning to be a more important factor than earlier research suggested.

These findings suggest that a rich tapestry of factors determine later life satisfaction. In part, this may be because many studies have an air of 'seek and ye shall find' about them. By asking a limited set of questions or focusing on a narrow range, then some factors can be made to appear more important than they perhaps are. For example, using a more qualitative interview technique, Glass and Jolly (1997) found that their sample of participants did not raise good health or finance as key factors contributing to life satisfaction. Not all studies are equally 'guilty' of this selectivity, but it is difficult to move beyond a fairly general statement that intuitively obvious factors such as health, finance, bereavement, environment and retirement have some influence on both self-esteem and general life satisfaction, but these are undoubtedly not the only factors, and all of these may interact with each other and be mediated by personality variables. Unfortunately, this statement is not far removed from what a non-psychologist might produce if asked for an intuitive summary of the issue.

Psychosocial factors and health

Psychosocial factors such as personality, social environment, etc. are all related to health and health is linked to feelings of well-being (more so than age *per se* – see Kunzmann, Little and Smith, 2000).[15] Indeed, we have already seen how personality traits are related to health in an earlier section of this chapter. However, as has also already been seen, there is rarely a simple one-to-one link between things in real life, and many aspects of health are influenced by multiple factors.

Governments across the world are keen that people pursue a 'healthy' lifestyle, and thus live a longer healthier life without being a burden to the health services and thus the taxpayer. The links between smoking, diet, exercise and health, and health/ life expectancy are too well known to need reiterating here, and it may be assumed that a healthy lifestyle is a good thing. How, though, can older adults be persuaded to adopt one if they are not already? Certainly some of the signs are not propitious. For example, several studies have noted that older adults have poorer eating habits (e.g. Quandt and Chao, 2000; Quinn *et al.*, 1997; Souter and Keller, 2002), though there are exceptions (e.g. older Greek people – see Kossioni and Bellou, 2011). In addition, avoiding weight gain might involve greater cognitive restraint in older than younger adults (Flint *et al.*, 2008). Other factors may have roots much further in a person's past. People rarely take up 'bad habits' in later life (e.g. older smokers have usually been abusing their bodies for several decades) and, accordingly, attempts to make older people change their ways may in some instances be fighting decades of maladaptive behaviour (see Keranen *et al.*, 2009).

Self-motivation is a key factor in initiating and maintaining an exercise regime (e.g. Thogersen-Ntoumani and Ntoumanis, 2006). Therefore, any factor that lowers motivation is a marked impediment to taking up exercise. For example, older adults might be more reluctant to take up exercise because they fear the risks outweigh the benefits, such as having a heart attack through over-exertion (O'Brien Cousins, 2000; Wilcox *et al.*, 2003). This is not helped by the finding that older adults have fewer people to encourage (or nag) them about their health-related behaviour (Tucker, Klein and Elliott, 2004). Again, the status of the person recommending a healthier

---

15   Note that Siedlecki *et al.* (2008) found that, when negative affect was controlled for, self-reported health had very little additional effect on well-being (the researchers found that a more consistent influence was level of neuroticism). But, health was measured using a self-report measure on a group of people who were generally healthy, and that, accordingly, a more objective measure, using a more representative cross-section of people, might yield a different finding.

lifestyle also needs to be considered. Hicks *et al.* (2009) found that an overweight nurse invoked less confidence than a nurse of ideal weight. Thus, obstacles lie in the way of older adults adopting healthier living. However, once past this barrier, numerous studies, across many diverse cultures, have found that health improves following the adoption of a more healthy lifestyle (e.g. Bookwala, Harralson and Parmelee, 2003; Elias, Elias and Elias 1990; Park *et al.*, 2011; Rana *et al.*, 2010; States *et al.*, 2006). However, it should be noted that studies using people's self-reports of health generally produce higher correlations than when objective measures of physical health are taken (e.g. Whitbourne, 1987). Note also that the strength of the relationship tends to weaken in the oldest of older people (Pinquart, 2001).

The adoption of a healthy lifestyle can thus lead to better health. This is not surprising. However, what of correlations that are found between general healthiness of lifestyle and health? What causes what? At the most simplistic, we can ask: does having the right personality/lifestyle make a person healthy? Or does being healthy make a person be healthy? Both these simple questions have evidence in their favour. For example, it can be demonstrated that certain psychological characteristics affect physical health. We have already seen from studies of personality traits that possessing some traits to a marked degree in early life predicts health in later life. Again, Kermis (1986) argues that depression and/or stress can cause a worsening of health (e.g. by suppressing the immune system). In a seven-year longitudinal study, Ostir, Ottenbacher and Markides (2004) found that positive affect was associated with a significantly lowered risk of frailty amongst older Mexican Americans. Exposure even to subliminal presentations of negative stereotypical statements about older adults and ageing can raise blood pressure and other physiological measures of stress in older participants (Levy *et al.*, 2000). Therefore, over the long term, exposure to persistent negative comments about ageing and older people may have a deleterious effect on health (thus refuting the adage about sticks and stones). Conversely, there is evidence that physical health affects psychological functioning. For example, Druley *et al.* (2003) found that the more severe the response to the physical pain of osteoarthritis in older married women, the greater the negative impact on both their and their husbands' behaviour. Again, we have just seen that changing lifestyle for the better improves health.

However, it would be naïve to assume that such an issue as this can be explained simply in terms of 'A causes B' or 'B causes A' arguments. A far more probable explanation is that the effects are multidirectional, and that in effect 'vicious circles' of maladaptive functioning can be created (e.g. physical decline causes a rise in stress and depression, which makes the physical decline worse, which in turn...etc.). A case in point is falls in older adults. A fall is unpleasant at any age, but it brings with it increased health risks in later life. This is principally because more brittle bones mean that breaks of the hip and leg bones are a distinct possibility, and, if not these, then other unpleasant injuries are likely; one study found that an older person has a one in three chance of suffering a functional decline following a fall (Stel *et al.*,

2004). Older people who have fallen over once are understandably unwilling to repeat the experience, but the added caution this feeling engenders may perversely make matters worse. A longitudinal study by Delbaere *et al.* (2004) found that older adults who had fallen were more frightened of falling again and had lower levels of daily activity. But this greater fear and lower activity were the best predictors of having a fall in the subsequent year (on a more positive note, methods for reducing fear of falling are available; see Li *et al.*, 2005). Findings such as this must be treated with some degree of caution because it is possible that an underlying physical cause may be causing people to fall, and it is not difficult to find evidence of physical causes of falls (see Vassallo *et al.*, 2003). However, on *a priori* grounds, the vicious circle argument must hold true for at least some instances of fall behaviour. Nor can it be denied that a fear of falling can have negative consequences not only for quality of life but also general health if mobility is unduly restricted (Li *et al.*, 2003).

It would also be unwise to assume that a relationship between psychosocial and physical factors need be purely causal. In many instances factors appear to alter the strength of expression of another factor rather than simply causing it to be present or absent. For example, Bailis and Chipperfield (2002) argue that, if an older person has a strong sense of social identity, this may cushion (but not remove) the negative effects of a decline in physical health when there is little the individual can do about preventing the decline itself happening. A complex statistical regression analysis of 1200 older female patients supported this hypothesis. Femia, Zarita and Johansson (2001) found that psychosocial factors mediated the impact of illness on the ability of old-old people's daily living activities. Indeed, in general the presence of a support network appears to enhance health in older adults. Kempen *et al.* (2001) found that individuals who reported a high level of social support also showed significantly better recovery from fall-related injuries both at five and twelve months after the injury. Again, Duke *et al.* (2002) found that size of social support network was related to the probability that a person forced to give up one activity because of illness or disability would take up another to replace it (see also Rodin *et al.*, 2009). Socio-economic factors can also have an effect. The most striking examples of this are arguably the social class and regional differences in life expectancy noted in Chapter 1. However, there are other notable instances. For example, Melzer *et al.* (2001) found that education level is a significant predictor of mobility disability in later life, with people with a low level of education (six years or fewer) being circa 1.7 times more likely to be movement disabled that people with over 12 years of education.

A related topic is that of **hostility** and ageing. Hostility has already been mentioned above as a personality type, but it can also be defined as 'a negative orientation toward others that has cognitive, affective and behavioral manifestations' (Barefoot, 1992, p.52). Some studies have reported higher levels of hostility amongst younger adults and older elderly people, with a drop in hostility between these two ages (see Barefoot *et al.*, 1993). This may in part be adaptive, because a healthy cynicism is arguably a useful tool for both younger adults first finding their way in the world and older people in increased dependence on health and social welfare services. Comijs *et al.* (1999) found that hostility was also associated with being mistreated. However, as many commentators have argued, it can also be disadvantageous, because high hostility levels are associated with an increased risk of heart disease (see Meesters, Muris and Backus, 1996; Schott *et al.*, 2009) and other illnesses (see Ranchor *et al.*, 1997). It is also correlated with level of cognitive function (i.e. the higher the hostility, the lower the cognitive skills) but not the rate of decline of cognitive skills in later life (Barnes *et al.*, 2009). It should also be noted that hostility is one of a host of similar traits grouped together as examples of negative affect, and not all studies of hostility have included the other negative affect traits as well. Therefore, it is quite possible that some of the sins visited specifically upon hostility might, if a broader range of tests were used, be found to be more accurately seen as products of a generally negative affect (see Ready *et al.*, 2011).

However, it is also possible to over-estimate the relationship between physical health and psychosocial factors. For example, a good predictor of physical health in later life is physical health in earlier life. Almost 40 years ago, Maas and Kuypers (1974) observed that many illnesses of later life are preceded by related physical complaints earlier in life. In turn this may be related to socio-economic status – low childhood socio-economic status is significantly related to lower health status in later life. In part this is because of the long-term effects of childhood illness, but also because of lower income and living standards in adult life (Luo and Waite, 2005). Again, Krause, Shaw and Cairney (2004) found that suffering trauma in early adulthood is strongly correlated with worse health in later life. This means at the very least that, if there is a change in personality in response to illness, it may not just be the illness in later life that is causing this – it could be an effect accumulated across the lifespan. However, the links between illness and personality can be exaggerated. For example, the Type A personality has been associated with a significantly higher heart attack rate. However, a review by Elias *et al.* (1990) observes that, whilst this may be true for younger people, having a Type A personality *after* the age of 65 does not increase the risk of coronary problems (the finding cannot be simply attributed to most people with Type A dying before they reach this age).

It should also be noted that throughout this section much of the discussion has centred on quantitative methods of research that emphasise reducing complex data to an underlying numerical pattern. However, although it can appear a trite cliché, we should remember that it is the health and suffering of *individuals* that is ultimately the focus of these studies. Research by Black and Rubinstein (2004) examined older adults' experience of illness, and noted that many of their findings can only be treated at an individual level, and defy simple reductionist techniques. Therefore, global statements about this topic potentially overlook important details.

Marriage

Generally, older married couples are found to be as happy or even more content than younger married adults (Cunningham and Brookbank, 1988) and usually report a reduction in negative interactions with increasing age (see Akiyama *et al.*, 2003). This may in part be due to reduced work and parenting responsibilities (Orbuch *et al.*, 1996).[16] Levenson, Cartensen and Gottman (1993) assessed younger (40–50 years) and older (60–70 years) married couples on a variety of measures. They found that the older couples displayed greater equanimity of aims and sources of pleasure (and fewer sources of disagreement) and also tended to have more equal standards of health (and the more egalitarian and less 'gender role traditional', generally the happier the marriage – Kaufman and Taniguchi, 2006). These results are encouraging, in that it would appear that older married people are not simply clinging to the wreckage because the prospect of living apart is financially and/or emotionally too awful to contemplate. In another sense, the results are uninformative, because they do not indicate whether happily married older couples have always been happily married or whether today's happiness is the result 'of a process in which old wars are diminished' (Levenson *et al.*, 1993, p.312) to the point where a truce has been called. In the USA at least, people who are in a current marriage tend to live longer, and having been in a marriage at some point (even if now divorced) is predictive of longer life expectancy than having never been married (Kaplan and Kronick, 2006).

Other research suggests a rather less cosy picture. For example, Chipperfield and Havens (2001) observed older adults over a seven-year period and noted changes in life satisfaction for those whose marital status remained unchanged over the period versus those for whom there had been a marital change (principally, loss or divorce of a partner). The basic finding of the study was that men benefited more from marriage than women. Thus, if there was no change in marital status, women's life satisfaction tended to diminish, whilst men's remained relatively stable. Loss of a partner affected both genders badly, but men more than women. If a couple married, then the man's satisfaction tended to rise, whilst the woman's was unaffected. Reasons for the relative levels of satisfaction may be dependent on a number of factors. For example, the degree to which each partner relies on the other for support. Gurung, Taylor and Seeman (2003) found that older husbands relied principally on their wives for emotional support, whilst wives were more likely to use friends and close family members. As older friends die and families move further apart, it is easy to see how women could lose many of their sources of support. De Jong Gierveld *et al.* (2009) note that, in circa 20 per cent of marriages of older couples, a partner has significant symptoms of loneliness. Emotional loneliness is relatively stronger in

16 It might be supposed that adults in their fifties and sixties would be more willing to consider marriage/remarriage because of the potential material gains and lack of parental responsibilities, but this group is significantly less willing to marry/remarry than younger adults, even allowing for factors such as religiosity, child dependents, etc. (Mahay and Lewin, 2007).

women in second marriages, whilst social loneliness is relatively more frequent in men with disabled wives. Perhaps unsurprisingly, having a smaller circle of friends, a marriage marked by general poor communication and/or arguments also increased the sense of loneliness.

The study by de Jong Gierveld *et al.* indicates that changes in marriages can occur in response to changed circumstances and attributes of the spouse. Similar findings have been reported by other researchers. For example, Hoppmann, Gerstorf and Hibbert (2011) found that a functional decline in one spouse can be met by an increased level of depression in the other. Other researchers have found such relationships between spouses, but they are sometimes a little more complex. For example, Strawbridge, Wallhagen and Shema (2011) conducted a five-year longitudinal study. They found that the husbands' cognitive function at the start of the study was related to the wives' subsequent cognitive function, but only if the couple reported having marital problems. However, the wives' cognitive function at the start of the study had no effect on the husbands' subsequent cognitive function. This sounds as if wives are more responsive to their spouses than husbands are. However, Strawbridge *et al.* were only looking at one aspect of psychological functioning. Walker, Luszcz, Gerstorf and Hoppmann (2011) addressed subjective well-being and found a reverse pattern. The subjective well-being of the wives predicted the subsequent subjective well-being of the husbands,[17] but not vice versa. Thus, changes in status of spouses can influence changes in the other spouse, but often in a complex fashion.

Discussion so far has concentrated on married couples. It might be tempting, given today's social mores, to assume that the findings will be true for cohabiting couples as well. Research on older cohabitees is still in its relative infancy (see Brown and Kawamura, 2010). Some research indicates that there is little difference between married and cohabiting couples (e.g. Brown and Kawamura, 2010). However, other research suggests that marriage is often more advantageous. For example, Brown, Roebuck Bulanda and Lee (2005) found that the male partners in cohabiting couples had significantly higher levels of depression than husbands in married couples, even after controlling for socio-economic factors, health and levels of social support.[18] In the case of same-sex marriages, the opportunity to be a married couple is a relatively new phenomenon. Interviews of older same sex couples (aged 56–73) by Lannutti (2011) found that couples felt that marriage made them feel more secure, more 'recognised' – but at the same time the couples had misgivings about same-sex marriages. However, it is at the time of writing early days of same-sex marriages, and the future might bring with it changed attitudes.

---

17   The higher the wives' subjective well-being, the relatively shallower the decline in the husbands' subjective well-being.

18   Comparing Canadian marrieds versus singles, married men were found to be less likely to be depressed than unmarried men, whilst the proportion of depressed women was similar in married and unmarried women (St John and Montgomery, 2009).

Sexuality and ageing[19]

It is a commonplace observation that the media portray sex as being for the young and slim, and ageist humour dictates that older people wanting a sex life are either 'dirty old men' or ugly and desperate (see Nay, McAuliffe and Bauer, 2007; Scherrer, 2009; Walz, 2002). Even those older people whom the media have labelled 'sexy' are chosen because, generally, they do not 'look their age' (see Walz, 2002). Accordingly, older people do not receive support from everyday sources that wanting a sex life in later adulthood is normal and healthy. It is therefore unsurprising to find that people's professed interest in sex decreases after the age of 50 (Arias-Castillo et al., 2009; Segraves and Segraves, 1995; see also Bauer, McAuliffe and Nay, 2007) and in part this is attributed to negative societal views (though illnesses and medical treatments affecting sex drive are also major contributors). There is also a gender difference. Waite et al. (2009) studied a sample of people aged 57–85, and found that men at all ages were more likely to have a partner (unsurprising, given the longer life expectancies of women; see Chapter 1) and were also more likely to be sexually active and have more permissive sexual views. There is potentially a cohort effect involved, since the groups questioned were amongst the last where women were less likely to be outwardly sexual in their behaviour.

Perversely enough, the lowering of sexual activity and expectations of the same might not be altogether bad. Some loss of sexual opportunity is almost inevitable in later life due to death of partners, loss of physical functioning, etc. A stereotype that informs older adults that less (or even no) opportunity for sex in later life is to be expected may therefore act as a comfort. Examinations of older adults' reactions to a loss of sexual functioning and/or partner show that the negative effects may be lessened or negated by the expectation that this is part of 'normal ageing' (Gott and Hinchliff, 2003). This does not mean that older adults should be discouraged from an enjoyable sex life (far from it), but arguing too vociferously that sex is an automatic right might be misinterpreted by those who lack the opportunity (or physical means) that they have 'failed'.

There are a variety of problems associated with studying sexuality in the later years. The first concerns the general reticence most people feel about discussing their sex lives. Castelo-Branco et al. (2010) found that women aged between 45 and 64 were far more frank about their sexual activities in anonymous questionnaires than in interviews.[20] For example, the questionnaire group was twice more likely to admit to having what the authors termed 'occasional or unconventional partners'. This

---

19 This section deals with ageing rather than middle age, but the related issue of the menopause is clearly of importance (see e.g. Dennerstein, Alexander and Kotz, 2003; Palacios, Tobar and Menendez, 2002). It also is, *purely* for the sake of space, devoted to majority heterosexual practices. For an excellent survey of gay behaviour and ageing, see Heaphy, Yip and Thompson (2004).

20 Though note that even anonymous questionnaires can be prone to impression management responses – see the section on attitude testing earlier in this chapter.

reticence might easily be magnified further by a cohort effect – older people were brought up in less permissive times, and are not accustomed (and indeed might lack the vocabulary) to talk about sexual issues. Surveying the history of studies of sexual activity in later life, Gibson (1992) observed that the more recent the study, the more often older people admit to having sexual relations. Therefore, older groups might provide less information, not because they have sex less often, but because they are less willing to talk about it.

Another problem often cited by researchers concerns what constitutes 'sex'. If penetrative intercourse is taken as the only measure of sex, then older people might show a greater decline in activity than if a wider range of activities is considered. But older adults in many cultures might in reality still engage in sexual activity of other kinds such as caressing, kissing and hugging and in effect 'renegotiate' what 'sex' means to them.[21] However, this is not true for all cultures. For example, older Chinese people tend to restrict the definition of sex very rigidly to penetrative heterosexual intercourse (Yan et al., 2011). It is worth noting, however, that sexually active older people generally report great satisfaction in whatever activity they indulge in (see Gott, 2004; Matthias et al., 1997; Skoog, 1996).

A further problem facing older adults is one of opportunity. Since women on average live longer than men, it follows that there are a lot more older women than men. Thus, older women's opportunities for heterosexual contact are diminished, and activity might cease not because of lack of capability or willing, but because of lack of a suitable partner. For those older people who attempt to find sexual contact through higher risk behaviours, such as using prostitutes, there is an increased risk of contracting sexually transmitted diseases, including AIDS (Gott, 2004). For example, a study of circa 800 Swiss people aged over 45 found that they had behaviours presenting an increased risk of contracting AIDS compared with younger adults (Abel and Werner, 2003). A more recent study by Kott (2011) found that 34 per cent of older (aged 50+) HIV-positive adults had recently had unprotected sex. This was significantly correlated with drug use and loneliness. An additional factor is that the 'baby boomers' generation, which was arguably the first to embrace substance abuse on a widespread scale, has shown less reluctance to drop their habits as they have grown older, relative to previous generations of substance abusers (Topolski et al., 2002). Continued intravenous drug use of course drastically raises the risk of HIV/AIDS, but, in addition, the lifestyle associated with substance abuse is also probabilistically linked to a higher level of risky sexual practices, such as those identified by Kott (2011). Another key risk factor is level of self-esteem – the lower this is, the higher the probability of engaging in (or being persuaded/coerced into) risky sexual behaviours, such as unprotected sex (Jacobs and Kane, 2011). Older adults are no less vulnerable than any other age group when it comes to infection by

---

21 A similar renegotiation of what constitutes 'sex' occurs in the relationships of people with cancer (see e.g. Gilbert, Ussher and Perz, 2010).

AIDS – as proof of this, in the USA, circa 15 per cent of all HIV/AIDS cases are in people aged over 50 (Emlet, 2004). Similarly, 14 per cent of male deaths from HIV in the UK are in men aged over 65 (Office for National Statistics, 2011).

A final problem to be mentioned here is the relative under-treatment by health professionals, who may undervalue or ignore older people's sexuality (see Elias and Ryan, 2011; Gussaroff, 1998; Mayers and McBride, 1998) and may be unaware of the prevalence of HIV/AIDS in older adults (Emlet, 2004); generally, a high proportion of cases of sexual dysfunction in older adults remains untreated (see Godschalk, Sison and Mulligan, 1997). In many instances, there is a clear and pressing need for health care professionals to become far better versed in issues surrounding sexuality and sexual behaviours in later life (see Sharpe, 2004).

Generally, in addition to limitations of physical health, the level of sexual activity is dependent upon the level of activity in early adulthood (e.g. Martin, 1981). This implies that, once again, the state of one's later life is determined by one's earlier behaviour. However, it is worth remembering that sexual drives differ markedly between individuals (e.g. Masters and Johnson, 1966). In later life, a key determinant of sexual activity is the level of importance of sex to the individual (DeLamater and Sill, 2005). Although this may to some extent be a circular argument (e.g. if a person cannot have sex, then arguably it may become less important, especially with a stereotype that loss of libido is 'normal' in later life), it cannot *all* be circular. Put simply, it is wrong to assume that there is a 'correct' level of sexual activity, or indeed, that sexual activity is necessary at all, for successful ageing to occur.

Disengagement and activity theories

It has been tacitly acknowledged in various parts of the research literature that part of ageing is a preparation for death. Nowhere is this made more explicit than in the **disengagement theory** by Cumming and Henry (1961), based on a large study of residents in Kansas City. This argued that, as people get older, their contact with the world lessens. At a social level, the loss of spouses and friends, and other social estrangements such as retirement, cause older people to disengage from contact with others. This was seen by Cumming and Henry as a rational process, initiated by older people and aided and abetted by societal conventions. It is as if older people are preparing to die by shedding their links with the physical world.[22] The theory can be criticised (and indeed was) for presenting the behaviour of passively waiting for the Grim Reaper as a good role model for older people. This is perhaps being a little harsh on Cumming and Henry, who were talking about relative rather than total disengagement. In addition, as Coleman and O'Hanlon (2004) observe, the prevailing societal attitude (in the USA at least)

---

22 The process of physically 'downsizing' when moving into a smaller home in later life and disposing of larger possessions is examined by Ekerdt *et al.* (2004).

was that old age 'should' ideally be like middle age – therefore, old age was seen as an unhealthy decline from the norm.[23] Rather than denigrating later life, Cumming and Henry were in fact making a vigorous stand celebrating the separate identity of later life and in effect empowering people in senescent decline as undergoing a natural rather than aberrant experience.

In any case, later evidence indicated that disengagement was largely confined to individuals who were always reclusive (e.g. Maddox, 1970b) or in some cases to people who had loneliness thrust upon them by force of circumstances, though younger adults do appear to show some constriction of expectations of future activities in the wake of subjective health decline (see Kooij and Van De Voorde, 2011). In other instances it was linked to level of economic hardship. For example, Magai et al. (2001) found that the greater the hardship, the greater the isolation, and this in turn was probabilistically related to racial grouping (African Americans were on average poorer and more isolated than European Americans). It has also been argued that people who disengage from society have probably been doing so for most of their lives – in other words, it is not purely a response to ageing (Maddox, 1970a). This is supported by a longitudinal study by Barnes et al. (2004), which found that such behaviour was present before participants entered old age. Stalker (2011) similarly found that level of engagement in activities is dependent on a large number of factors including not only age but also, for example, ethnicity and socio-economic status. Culture probably plays a big role too: disengagement is a very rare phenomenon in many developing countries, where older people are kept in an active role in the community (e.g. Merriman, 1984). In other words, the phenomenon may be a 'natural' extension of a particular personality type and/or the result of both general circumstances and specific events. It is not a universal feature, or even a product of ageing.

Researchers and commentators responding to Cumming and Henry's work argued that the best policy for older people is to keep as active as possible. Their argument is roughly as follows. Older people usually want to keep active, and life satisfaction is found to be greatest in those with an active involvement (see earlier in this chapter, and also Nimrod, 2007). In addition, greater social involvement (or, at least, a more supportive social network) appears to lessen the impact of negative social exchanges (Rook, 2003) and be associated with a lower level of cognitive decline (Holtzman et al., 2004). This is echoed in Hao's (2008) American and Wahrendorf and Siegrist's (2010) European longitudinal studies of engagement in voluntary community work by older adults, which produced similar findings (though Hao noted that the volunteers also started the study with higher mental health scores). It is important to stress that 'activity' in this context does not have to be physically demanding – the term refers to any sort of behaviour with a social component. Thus, in US assisted living facilities, the simple act of getting together with other people at mealtimes

---

23   This echoes a criticism of current 'successful ageing' models (see Chapter 7).

and enjoying friendly relations with staff and residents constitute 'activity' and can be demonstrated to promote well-being (Park, 2009). Indeed, some researchers have argued that the activity itself is of little consequence – what matters is the social interaction that comes with the activity. For example, Litwin and Shiovitz-Ezra (2006) demonstrated that after accounting for quality of social interaction during an activity, the length the activity went on for had no significant effect on well-being.

Thus, greater social involvement is associated with beneficial things, and it is not surprising that a theoretical stance that older people should be encouraged to be socially active developed. However, in its extreme form this **activity theory** is as unattractive as the argument it tried to replace. The image of hordes of social workers forcing older people to mix with others 'for their own good', with compulsory whist drives and so forth, is not a pleasant one. Nor is it necessarily effective. Social activity is often confounded with level of health (i.e. an older person has to be relatively healthy in order to engage in social activities, so the finding that older adults who engage in social activities are also the healthiest may not be surprising). Lennartsson and Silverstein (2001) found that, when health was statistically controlled for, the most beneficial activities with regard to older people's further life expectancy were solitary activities.

The modern consensus is that disengagement and activity theories describe the optimal strategies for some but not all older individuals, and which is better depends on a variety of factors, such as: financial circumstances (e.g. can one afford an active lifestyle?); health (e.g. does one still have the vigour for some hobbies?); and personality types (e.g. introverts may hate a socially active lifestyle). To some extent, level of activity in later life is explained by behaviour in earlier life. For example, in a longitudinal study, Holahan and Chapman (2002) found that level of purposiveness at age 40 predicted the goals being actively sought from activities at age 80. It is also worth noting that a number of studies have found increased social involvement only appreciably improves well-being in lower income groups (e.g. Caspi and Elder, 1986; Larson, 1978). However, it should also be noted that disengagement can also be indicative of encroaching illness and is correlated with mortality level (e.g. Bennett, 2002). Hence, although caution should be exercised in labelling particular behaviours as undesirable, withdrawal may in some instances be an early warning of serious health problems.

The role of the family

In Western nations at least, most older people, given the choice, would like to live independently, but to have family close by. And traditionally, in about 80 per cent of cases, older parents lived within 30 minutes' travel of at least one of their offspring (Bengston and Treas, 1980).[24] The family can have distinct advantages. For example,

---

24 For an overview of residence patterns across cultures, see Bongaarts and Zimmer (2002).

the effects of hardship can be at least partly offset by family factors (e.g. Ferraro and Su, 1999; Zhang *et al.*, 1997). However, does the family have to actually be *physically* close? In the past, families had to be close together because the children of the aged parents had to be nearby to provide financial and practical assistance. However, in a modern world, with far better communications and transport, this is not as necessary. Financial assistance can be sent electronically, payment for cleaning services and similar can also be done at a distance, etc. For example, in Thailand, many older people living in rural areas have witnessed all or some of their children leaving the village to earn more money in the cities. Traditionally, the elders relied on younger family members to support them, but now that the children can send financial assistance from the city back to the village with ease, at least financial care is possible even if they are physically absent. Abas *et al.* (2009) found that migration of children from urban areas was not, on the surface, associated with depression in the older parents left behind. More remarkably, after confounding variables had been controlled for, older adults with migrated children were actually *less* depressed than other older villagers.

The danger with studying the effects of family on older adults is that most readers come armed with a set of assumptions. High amongst these is the **golden age myth** – the idea that, in the past, extended families were the norm, with multigenerational families living in joy amidst the squalor, as described in some of the more glutinously sentimental passages in Dickens. In reality, the fate of many older people who were too poor to care for themselves was the workhouse, and the extended family (where three generations live under the same roof) was the exception rather than the rule in pre-twentieth century Europe (e.g. Laslett, 1976). In short, there has never been a golden age (see Thane, 2000). However, regardless of reality, there is often a temptation amongst non-experts to assume that there is a traditional duty to care for elderly parents by housing them in the family home, and anything short of that is a 'failure'. Another common assumption is that some cultures take much greater care of older adults than others. We have already seen in the earlier section on cultural differences that this is not entirely accurate. Willis (2008) found that, with the exception of black Caribbean families (who provided less), all cultural and ethnic minority UK groups were as likely as white British people to support older members of their own families. Nor, in spite of the saccharin images of doting grandparents so beloved of the popular media and numerous pieces of fiction, can it be assumed that the state of the rest of the family is necessarily all that older people live for. For example, Sener *et al.* (2008) found that, for older women, health and education made the highest contribution to life satisfaction, whilst for older men it was solely health. For both sexes, the influence of family relationships was relatively minor. Likewise, older adults' views on the ability of their adult children to provide for them are often ambivalent (Radermacher *et al.*, 2010). It is perhaps not surprising that some researchers argue we should move away from regarding family relationships as bonds of blood and upbringing to regarding them as different levels of social units (see Pinazo-Hernandis, 2010).

These caveats indicate that the role of the family in older people's lives is not as cut and dried as might have been initially supposed. However, that does not mean it is unimportant. Family members recognise the importance of harmonious relationships. In a masterly review of the literature up to that time, Bengston and Treas (1980) observed that, while family members were the usual and preferred source of comfort and help in a crisis, older people were more depressed the greater their expectations of assistance from their relatives. In other words, expect too much and disappointment will almost inevitably follow, indicating that people clearly have expectations that family relationships 'should' work. This is further supported by a study by Bengston and Kuypers (1986) who found that, when a crisis occurs and help is needed, this may damage familial relations because family members may feel that they have not adequately coped. This supports the findings of a more recent Japanese study, which demonstrated that older adults with poor family relations have a 31 per cent chance of being sent to a nursing home compared with a 12 per cent chance for older adults with good family relations (Kodama et al., 2009). In other words, family relationships are not simply based on blind obedience to rules (e.g. 'your aged parent is frail, you must take them into your house') – there is a dynamic relationship present. However, taking a parent into the family home will not necessarily change the nature of the relationship – typically, family relationships before and after this event takes place correlate significantly with each other (Kodama et al., 2007).

Family intervention at times of crisis in an older person's life, such as moving to different accommodation, has created several models that are, in the main, descriptive. A detailed analysis of family intervention is provided by McCubbin and Patterson's (1982) **double ABCX model**, where A is the event causing the crisis, B the familial resources for coping, C the familial perception of the crisis and X the perceived stress. Variations in A, B, and C will determine the overall level of stress the family and older person experience. Bailey and Letiecq (2009) used the model to describe the coping strategies used by grandparents rearing grandchildren (see also Clark, 1999). Gatz, Bengston and Blum (1990) created a similar model, comprising a sequence of *event-stressor-appraisals-mediators-outcomes*. The *event* is the crisis, and the *stressor* the deleterious effect of the event. *Appraisals* refers to the process whereby the family caregivers decide the degree to which they feel they can control the situation, and the *mediators* are the available aid and caring skills. The *outcomes* process refers to the degree to which the family feel stressed and/or adapted to the change in the situation. Di Rosa et al. (2011) have developed a typology of seven caregiving situations, each with a different set of critical indicators. Davies and Nolan (2006), in a qualitative study, describe self-perceived roles of family caregivers of older relatives moving into and living in a care home. A caveat to these observations is that the majority of caregiving duties fall on the spouses or offspring of older people (Qureshi and Walker, 1989) – thus, most caregivers are themselves older or middle-aged.

Accordingly, caregivers themselves may experience physical problems in nursing sick patients, and increased incidences of ill-health and accidents in caregivers have (unsurprisingly) been reported (see Ekwall, Sivberg and Hallberg, 2007; Gatz *et al.*, 1990; Hartke *et al.*, 2006).

In addition, perceptions of family harmony seem to be greater the smaller the family – a study by Fingerman and Birditt (2003) found that people who cited a smaller number of family members tended to rate these relatives as being 'closer' and the incidence of problematic relationships to be lower. Interestingly, older adults were less likely to report problematic relationships than were younger members of the same family. It is possible to offer a cynical interpretation of these results – namely, that the smaller the family, the more obliged members feel to get al.ong, and, simultaneously, the older one gets, the more oblivious one becomes to problems within the family. However, this is perhaps an unduly bleak view. It should also be noted that, in the case of childless older adults, where there may be no younger generation to interact with, greater psychological stress is not inevitable but may depend on specific circumstances (e.g. men without a living partner had higher levels of loneliness and often depression, but men with a living partner did not; see Zhang and Hayward, 2001).

Religion and ageing

The role of religion in a time of crisis is something known to many people, and its beneficial nature is well documented.[25] For example, it is known that strength of religious faith is negatively correlated with depression (see Braam *et al.*, 1997; Lee, 2007) and faith is of value in lessening the negative effects of caregiving for an elderly sick relative with, for example, dementia. Similarly, religious attendance is inversely correlated with anxiety (Ellison, Burdette and Hill, 2009). More generally, religiosity is strongly correlated with well-being even after controlling for gender, birth cohort and socio-economic group (Wink and Dillon, 2003). However, men appear to gain more mental health benefits from religious practice than women (McFarland, 2010). Religiosity may also be associated with better physical health, possibly through the intermediary step of increasing optimism and thereby presumably lowering stress (Krause, 2002).

Researchers and non-researchers often make a distinction between religion and spirituality. In very general terms, 'religion' applies to religious belief that is expressed by regular religious practice, such as visits to a place of worship. 'Spirituality' is a more nebulous concept. It can indicate level of sensitivity to spiritual/religious issues

---

25 To the best of the author's knowledge, the majority of research on religious practice and ageing has looked at the Christian faith as practised in industrialised nations, and particularly in the USA. No offence is intended to other belief systems by the concentration of discussion on Christianity in the following section.

and imply an awareness of a deity that embraces all religious practices. However, it can also be used to describe any vaguely religious or mystical feelings, without any adherence to established religious practice. It would appear that many older people think of religion as being formal practice and spirituality as a rather wider concept (Schlehofer, Omoto and Adelman, 2008). For religion to be beneficial in earthly terms, regular formal practice and observance appears to be required. Sullivan (2010) found that amongst various Christian worshippers in the USA regular church attendance was associated with lower mortality levels, even after confounding factors had been accounted for. People with strong religious beliefs might argue that this proves the power of faith. However, it is possible that particular psychological processes that make a person particularly faithful to religious practice might also have other life-prolonging properties.[26] Currently, this question is unanswered. However, it must not be assumed that spirituality (as opposed to religion) is without value in terms of physical health and well-being. For example, Kirby, Coleman and Daley (2004) found that level of spirituality helped lessen the effects of illness and physical frailty on the well-being of very old adults.

Integrating religious belief into cognitive-behaviour therapy can bring significant improvement in depression and anxiety in older patients (Paukert *et al.*, 2009; see also Maltby *et al.*, 2010). At the end of life, religion is often supposed to provide comfort, but relatively few empirical studies have been conducted (for obvious ethical reasons). One of the few studies to examine the issue found that dying people who had religious belief were comforted by, *inter alia*, the promise of an afterlife and the concept of death being part of a larger cosmic order (see Pevey, Jones and Yarber, 2009).[27] A longitudinal study by Idler, Kasl and Hays (2001) found that level of religious feeling remained stable or even increased in the last year of life, even though attendance at religious services declined (perhaps because of physical limitations). Religion is also reported as providing comfort for the bereaved (Chapple, Swift and Ziebland, 2011). Ultimately, what is important is that either the application of religious belief to everyday life or (more probably) a correlate of this brings with it greater life satisfaction to some people.

Summary

The findings of research on personality and lifestyle are varied. There is not a personality type unique to later life, nor do personality traits necessarily follow a predictable pattern. On the other hand, some types of personality enable people to cope with later life better than others. However, all these arguments must be weighed against the considerable criticisms of personality testing and research

---

26 Though curiously, 'women with greater religious commitment and men with greater religious application had greater odds of under-estimating their body weight' (Kim, 2007, p.121).

27 For further discussion of the process of dying, see Chapter 8.

methodologies. Again, it should be noted that many personality taxonomies incorporate implicit value judgements. For example, a successfully ageing person is held to have a placid and almost stoic attitude towards life. However, this conforms to the stereotype that older adults should be quiet wisdom-dispensing archetypal grandparent figures. Or, in other words, people who make little fuss and make themselves available to others. The relationship between lifestyle and well-being is similarly more complicated than it may first appear, however. Socio-economic class, ethnicity, widowhood, familial relations, finances and many other factors interact to provide a complex web of events and pressures whose effects are far from fully mapped.

However, the final words in this chapter must go to another reality check. Much of what is discussed in this chapter is *relative*. Anybody's life can be seen to be miserable if you set high enough standards. Someone reading this book might think themselves impoverished and leading a dull life compared with the stereotypical rich banker or hedge fund manager. But equally, a typical reader, living in a typical modest three-bedroomed house on a typical modern housing estate is living at a level of material comfort beyond the dreams of avarice for a high proportion of the world's population and beyond credence to their forebears in the nineteenth century. Of course, material possessions are far from everything, as we have seen. And there is abundant evidence that many older adults have a strong sense of well-being in spite of material or emotional problems — what is sometimes referred to as the **paradox of well-being** (Mroczek and Kolarz, 1998). Even when people are faced with issues that money cannot solve, such as many relationship and health problems, these issues are rarely omnipresent. The existence of problems in later life does not mean that they dominate to the exclusion of everything else. Or if someone is that burdened with problems, they are almost certainly very neurotic, and for such individuals, even if a solution to a problem is found, another problem will be immediately found to take its place (Hoyer and Roodin, 2003).

Suggested further reading

An excellent overview of many of the issues covered in this chapter (particularly psychoanalytic theories) is provided by Coleman and O'Hanlon (2004). An overview of personality research in general is provided by Caspi, Roberts and Shiner (2005). A more detailed discussion of the level of dependency exhibited by older people is in an excellent book by the late Margaret Baltes (Baltes, 1996). Gibson (1992, 1997) provides an intelligent overview of sexual and emotional changes (see also Schlesinger, 1996). Krauss Whitbourne and Whitbourne (2011) provide a readable survey of many of the topics covered in this chapter and their book as a whole is an intelligent and thoughtful survey of the psychology of ageing and midlife adulthood. McDonald (2011) provides an excellent overview of issues surrounding retirement from a broader academic perspective.

CHAPTER 6

Mental Health in Later Life

Introduction

Older people are less likely to suffer from mental health problems than any other age group (Smyer and Qualls, 1999). All conditions, other than cognitive impairment, are at a lower level. This does not of course mean that mental health issues in later life can be dismissed. They are a serious problem at any age, but in older people may be compounded by generally poorer health and lowered intellectual skills. The number of chronic conditions an average person suffers from increases over the lifespan, and the problem is greater the lower the socio-economic group being considered (House *et al.*, 1992). When further problems, such as double jeopardy (see Chapter 5) and declining intellect and memory are added into the equation, it can be appreciated that the problems facing older adults with mental illness may be considerable. Not surprisingly, there is a considerable literature on mental health in later life (e.g. Smyer and Qualls, 1999; see Woods, 1996, 2011 for more detailed discussions). In the present chapter, an overview will be presented of some of the key types of illness and disability.

Mild cognitive impairment

This condition is what many commentators justifiably describe as a 'grey area'. It undoubtedly exists, but defining it in precise terms is difficult. In Chapters 2 and 3 of this book, we saw that older people often have significantly worse memories and other cognitive skills than younger adults. For most older people, this has little real impact on everyday life. Being a little slower to learn how to use a new mobile phone or retrieve the name of an infrequently encountered person is irksome, but that is all. However, for a not inconsiderable proportion of older people, the problem is worse than this without being totally handicapping. These individuals do not have dementia, but their worsening memories and/or cognitive skills are sufficient for them to have noticed a decline in everyday life. However, the decline is not so large that normal functioning is stopped – memory loss is far from total, and cognitive changes are not halted as much as slower and less efficient. Such loss is often termed

mild cognitive impairment (MCI). There is no precise definition for this, and to further confuse matters, many other similar terms have been used. Woods (2011, p.19) cites the following: benign senescent forgetfulness (BSF); mild dementia; very mild cognitive decline; questionable dementia; limited cognitive disturbance; minimal dementia; age-associated memory impairment (AAMI) (Dawe, Procter and Philpot, 1992); and age-associated cognitive decline (AACD) (Cullum *et al.*, 2000). Another commonly used phrase is **cognitive impairment, not dementia (CIND)**. At the time of writing, a distinction is being drawn between MCI and CIND by some researchers, who argue that CNID describes *all* cases where there is a distinct cognitive impairment on laboratory tests, regardless of whether or not the individual has sought medical attention for it, with MCI being reserved for those individuals who can be objectively measured as having a cognitive impairment *and* who have sought medical attention on the matter (see Chertkow *et al.*, 2009).

Regardless of the niceties of definitions, MCI and related conditions are of great interest to clinicians. Although at times irksome, MCI by definition does not affect a person's daily life. And happily, for many people, that is how things stay. They develop MCI and remain slightly forgetful and occasionally confused, but their cognitive abilities are still sufficiently intact that they can enjoy the rest of their days. However, for some individuals, the mild symptoms of MCI worsen until dementia develops (see Chertkow *et al.*, 2009). The likelihood of developing dementia from MCI is uncertain because different researchers have often used different measurement systems, but Woods (2011) cites a conversion rate of between 10 and 20 per cent. Other researchers have been more pessimistic. For example, Plassman *et al.* (2011) found that new CIND cases outnumber dementia cases by about 2:1.[1] However, over a near six-year period in Plassman *et al.*'s longitudinal study, approximately two-thirds of the people with CIND went on to show symptoms of dementia.

Whatever the final correct figure turns out to be, the current evidence suggests that MCI and other related conditions come in two forms. The first is where MCI is in reality dementia in its **prodromal** (early stage) phase. The second is where MCI is the product of illness or injury and is unlikely to develop further. Numerous causes have been suggested. For example, in a study of origins of CIND, identified causes included hip fractures and taking multiple drug treatments (Monastero *et al.*, 2007). It would greatly help matters if a **smoking gun symptom** could be found. This is a symptom that unambiguously indicates one illness and one illness only. In this instance, if a symptom could be found in people with MCI/CIND that is only present in people who will then develop dementia, this would be fantastically useful as a diagnostic tool. However, so far such a symptom has not been found, although Ritchie and Tuokko (2010) noted that a pronounced failure of memory retrieval was a good (but not perfect) predictor of developing dementia.

---

1   At 60.4 cases per 1000 patient-years versus 33.3/1000 for dementia. For explanation of 'patient-years', see Glossary.

Dementia

Dementia may be defined as widespread deterioration of intellectual functioning resulting from atrophy of the central nervous system. Most authorities argue that the decline in intellectual functioning must include a decline in memory plus at least one other cognitive skill (Woods, 2011). To distinguish dementia from MCI and related conditions, there is typically a requirement that the deterioration is sufficient to interfere with daily activities. To distinguish it from conditions that cause temporary deterioration, there is a further requirement – namely, that the deterioration occurs in the absence of intoxication or other factors that could cause a temporary confused state. There are three common misconceptions about dementia:

- It is a disease that only old people get.

- It causes memory loss.

- It is synonymous with Alzheimer's disease (AD).

All three of these assumptions are only partially correct. First, it is not solely a disease of old age. Cases of **early-onset dementia (EOD)**, where the first symptoms present themselves before the age of 60 are well documented in the research literature (e.g. Garre-Olmo *et al.*, 2010). However, cases of dementia in younger adults are very rare. For example, Garre-Olmo *et al.* (2010) found that, in the age group 30–49 years, the incidence of EOD was circa 5 cases per 100,000 person-years. In the UK, it is estimated that only about 2 per cent of all dementia cases are EOD (Alzheimer's Society, 2007). As age increases, the probability of developing dementia increases. The rate of expansion appears to be a doubling of cases roughly every five years (Corrada *et al.*, 2010; Hestad, Ellersten and Klove, 1998; White *et al.*, 1986), and this is consistent across the world (Ziegler-Graham *et al.*, 2008). Thus, dementia is not totally a condition that occurs in old age – it is simply far more *probable* that if a person develops dementia it will be in late rather than early adulthood. Second, although dementia causes memory loss, it is not *solely* a matter of memory loss. We shall examine this more later. Third, dementia is not synonymous with Alzheimer's disease. Most commentators argue that Alzheimer's is the commonest form of dementia but it is not the sole type of dementia. At least 50 types of dementia have been identified (Haase, 1977), although admittedly a lot of these are extremely rare.

Dementia is a significant problem both in health and economic terms. *Dementia UK* (Alzheimer's Society, 2007), a report produced by the London School of Economics and the Institute of Psychiatry for the charity, the Alzheimer's Society, calculated that at the time of publication there were circa 680,000 people with dementia[2] in the UK alone – or, 1.1 per cent of the population. By 2051, this number could have conceivably swelled to 1,735,087. This increase of 154 per cent

---

2   *Dementia UK* estimated that roughly two-thirds of people with late onset dementia lived at home, and a third in care homes. Living in a care home rose with age of patient and severity of illness.

is not because there is an 'epidemic' of dementia as such, but simply because more people are living into old age. The cost to the UK alone of extra care, etc. needed for people with dementia is over £17 billion p.a. – and this figure is going to carry on rising (see Alzheimer's Society, 2007). However, it is important to note that not everybody will have dementia to the same level of severity. Approximately a half of all cases of dementia are in the early and relatively mild stage; about a third have a moderate level, and the remainder have severe dementia. It should also be noted that severe dementia becomes more common the older the patient being considered, rising from circa 6 per cent in people aged 65–69 to circa 23 per cent for those aged 95 and older (Alzheimer's Society, 2007). Reading between the lines, it is clear that, cold comfort as this is, a considerable proportion of older people die before they enter the moderate or severe stages of the illness.

Functional impairment

An early step in diagnosing dementia is to discover the extent of the disability suffered by patients when they first seek help. As seen earlier, dementia is often heralded by relatively minor changes in cognitive function that in themselves do not impinge upon daily functioning to any appreciable extent. Because dementia often develops gradually, the stage in the illness when the patient first presents for medical help can vary greatly. Perhaps not surprisingly, younger adults are likely to go to a medical practitioner much sooner (McMurtray et al., 2006), because memory loss and other signs of intellectual decline are considered atypical in their age group. In older adults, the symptoms might have reached a more pronounced stage, simply because the early symptoms of decline, which are treated with alarm by younger adults, are dismissed as being no more than 'typical' age-related loss (see Roe et al., 2008).

Once the patient's problem has been noticed, there are a number of basic measures of intellectual functioning to provide a rough guide to the degree of impairment. A widely used British test of this type is the **Blessed Dementia Scale (BDS)** (Blessed, Tomlinson and Roth, 1968). In the USA, the equivalents are the **Mental Status Questionnaire** or **MSQ** (Kahn et al., 1960) and the **Mini-Mental State Examination (MMSE)**. These ask the patient such memory questions as 'Who is the current prime minister/president?', 'What is the day today?' and 'What is your name?' In short, these are questions that no non-demented person should get wrong. The more questions the patient answers incorrectly, the greater the degree of impairment and the more pronounced the illness is held to be. In addition, a questionnaire on the patient's behaviour may be given to a caregiver. This determines the extent to which the patient is still functionally independent, by asking questions such as the degree of help he or she requires in getting dressed. This has the dual advantage of not only giving a further gauge of the patient's degree of impairment but also judging the level of nursing care the patient requires. Scales such as the

Blessed and the MSQ can also be used as the illness progresses, to keep a useful check on the general status and needs of the patient.

A more detailed method of describing the level of functioning of the demented patient is provided by Reisberg et al.'s (1989) Functional Assessment Stages, or **FAST**. The method was originally devised to describe the functional status of Alzheimer's disease patients (see later in this chapter). Patients are placed into one of seven categories, with Stages 6 and 7 divided into sub-stages. Stage 1 describes normal functioning. In Stage 2, there are subjective feelings of loss of intellectual power, although these are not perceived as serious by other people. In Stage 3, intellectual impairment (particularly in memory) is evident in complex tasks that previously posed no problems, and in Stage 4 this has extended to relatively complex everyday tasks (e.g. 'ability to handle finances'). Stage 5 is defined as 'deficient performance in choosing the proper clothing to wear', and in Stage 6 the patient is no longer able to dress him- or herself or properly attend to personal hygiene (this stage is divided into five hierarchical sub-stages, ranging from problems with dressing through to faecal incontinence). Stage 7 describes the loss of motor and speech skills (with six sub-stages, beginning with the loss of speech through to 'loss of ability to hold up head'). The authors also place estimates of the length of time a patient is likely to remain in a particular stage if he or she does not die during it (Stage 3 = 7 years; 4 = 2 years; 5 = 18 months; 6 = 2 years 5 months; 7 = 6 years+). A slightly simpler assessment is provided by the **Clinical Dementia Rating (CDR)**, which is a checklist of level of functioning on a variety of tasks (e.g. memory, orientation, behaviour in the home). Based on the scores, the patient is graded as having no dementia, or 'questionable', 'mild', 'moderate', or 'severe' forms of the illness (Berg, 1988). The American Psychiatric Association periodically produces a taxonomy of mental illnesses, which is highly influential. The most recent edition of the **Diagnostic and Statistical Manual of Mental Disorders (DSM-IV)** (American Psychiatric Association, 1994) indicates that, in addition to perceptual, intellectual and/or memory impairment sufficient to interfere with daily activities, these must be present when the patient is fully awake and with no evidence of intoxication (from alcohol or drugs). The illness is graded by its functional effect: *mild* (no supervision necessary), *moderate* (some supervision necessary) or *severe* (constant supervision required).

It is also worth noting that incidences of **agitation** increase in demented individuals (c.60% of all demented patients exhibit it; Eisdorfer, Cohen and Paveza, 1992). Although there is widely agreed definition (Bidewell and Chang, 2011), the term is generally taken to describe a group of symptoms drawn from a large set of agitated behaviours, including aggression (physical and verbal), lack of co-operativeness, shouting, grabbing, restless behaviour, etc. Level of cognitive impairment appears to be a principal predictor (Vance et al., 2003). Cohen-Mansfield (2007) found that in most cases agitation increases from waking through to circa 4.00 p.m. and then decreases. However, about a quarter of those observed in Cohen-Mansfield's study showed increased agitation later in the day. Several methods of reducing the level of agitated behaviour have been suggested. For example:

- Training caregivers to respond in an appropriate way (see Roth *et al.*, 2002), including offering positive verbal responses.

- Involving institutionalised dementing patients in an indoor gardening project (Lee and Kim, 2008).

- Bright light therapy (Burns *et al.*, 2009).

- Acupressure and Montessori[3]-based activities (Lin, Yang, Kao *et al.*, 2009).

- Increased physical activity (Scherder *et al.*, 2010).

- Listening to favourite music and hand massage (Hicks-Moore and Robinson, 2008).

However, no single method appears to be totally effective (see Kong, Evans and Guevara, 2009) and some patients appear to be resistant to behavioural intervention, in which case drug therapy might be the only plausible solution (Brown, 2010; Lee *et al.*, 2007; Selzman *et al.*, 2008).

The different types of dementia (sometimes called dementias of different **aetiologies** or **etiologies**) all have the general characteristics described earlier. However, within this general decline, each has a unique pattern of dysfunction. We shall now consider the principal forms the illness takes.

Alzheimer's disease (AD)

This condition was first diagnosed in 1907 by Alois Alzheimer in a case study of a 51-year-old woman. The condition is now known by many variants of the basic term, including **senile dementia of the Alzheimer type (SDAT)**, **primary degenerative dementia (PDD)** as well as **dementia of the Alzheimer type (DAT)**. For the sake of convenience, Alzheimer's disease or AD is principally used in this book.

Early symptoms include the following:

- Severe memory failure well beyond the scope of everyday experience. This may include forgetting very simple lists or instructions, or getting lost in familiar surroundings, such as a local shopping centre or streets around the home. Standardised memory tests will typically show a gross failure to remember new information for more than a few minutes or even seconds, and short-term memory (STM) measures for digit span and similar may also show a decline (see Terry *et al.*, 2011).

---

3   Montessori was an educational researcher who advocated allowing pupils to discover for themselves with minimal guidance/facilitation from teachers.

- **Apraxia**, the inability to perform skilled movements (see Capone *et al.*, 2003).

- **Visual agnosia**, the inability to recognise by sight (see Giannakopoulos *et al.*, 1999).

- Impoverished verbal skills: patients may have difficulty in producing the appropriate words (see Clark *et al.*, 2009), and may fail to comprehend abstract phrases, such as proverbs (see Chapman *et al.*, 1997; Rapp and Wild, 2011).

- Patients' responses to their symptoms vary. Some are depressed, others apathetic and unconcerned; others are aware of a problem, but either discount it or under-estimate its severity. Others develop a paranoia that people are deliberately hiding things or stealing from them (see Burns, 1995; Murayama *et al.*, 2009).

As the illness progresses, so the severity of these symptoms increases, though there is considerable variability in the rate and order in which the symptoms appear (see Stopford *et al.*, 2008, Wilson *et al.*, 2000):

- Memory for new items is now severely curtailed, often even for items in STM.

- Memory for remote events, learnt before the onset of the illness, also worsens.

- Recognition declines, even to the point of being incapable of recognising friends and family (which obviously causes great distress).

- Language worsens considerably, and **aphasia** (language failure) becomes a key feature of the latter stages of AD. The patient can have problems producing speech (**Broca's aphasia**), understanding speech (**Wernicke's aphasia**), or both. Speech can be reduced to a few words and a series of garbled speech-like sounds, or can consist of recognisable words produced in a nonsensical order (see Whitworth and Larson, 1988).

- Sometimes the ability to read aloud is remarkably well preserved, with proper observation of punctuation and intonation (see Raymer and Berndt, 1996). However, patients have typically very poor recall of what they have read (**demented dyslexia**).

- The external appearance of the patients reflects their inward decline. Without the aid of dedicated helpers, the patients' grooming and general demeanour inevitably worsen.

- Movement begins to appear crabbed and awkward. A shuffling gait, characteristic of **Parkinsonism** (see Glossary) becomes commonplace.

In the terminal stages of the illness:

- The patient usually falls into an uncommunicative state.

- Incontinence becomes habitual.

- Often patients display **Kluver-Bucy syndrome**. This is a set of behaviours, including **hyperorality** (the urge to put everything seen into the mouth) and the associated problem of **bulimia** (the urge to eat vast quantities of food). The other symptoms of Kluver-Bucy syndrome are visual agnosia, **hypermetamorphosis** (the compulsive urge to touch everything) and a loss of **affect** (emotion).

For further discussion of the middle and late stages, see Burns (2006).

Death typically occurs about five years or more after the appearance of the first 'major' symptoms (though note there are huge variations between studies, depending on what is counted as a 'major symptom', etc.). Certainly, length of survival after being admitted to institutional care has increased since the 1960s (Wood, Whitfield and Christie, 1995), probably reflecting improvements in general medical care. Death is most commonly ascribed to respiratory failure, presumably exacerbated by the relative immobility of patients in the later stages of the disease (see Burns, 1995).

As noted earlier, there is considerable variability between patients in the severity of their symptoms, the relative sparing of individual functions, and the length of time patients remain in each stage of the illness. However, an AD patient who reaches the terminal phase of the disease will at some stage endure all the listed stages. A diagnostic test, specifically designed for AD, is provided by the **NINCDS-ADRDA criteria**. The initials refer to the 'National Institute of Neurological and Communicative Disorders and Stroke' and the 'Alzheimer's Disease and Related Disorders Association of America', the two bodies that jointly devised the scheme. It provides three levels of certainty about the diagnosis: 'probable', 'possible' or 'definite'. The final judgement can only be given when there is physiological proof from a biopsy or autopsy, so most researchers content themselves with a 'probable' diagnosis. This requires, amongst other factors, proof of functional disability (as measured by the Blessed Dementia Scale and similar), memory loss, 'deficits in two or more areas of cognition', an absence of indicators of other causes, such as tumour, delirium (see page 234), and so forth. In other words, this is diagnosis by default (see McKhann *et al.*, 2011): the measures used do not diagnose AD as much as rule out the possibility that no other disease better fits the symptoms. This can create problems, as shall be seen later.

Some older textbooks restrict the use of 'Alzheimer's Disease' to cases arising before the age of 60 and use the term **senile dementia** to describe those occurring after this age. However, this use has in recent years been largely outmoded (see Lezak, 1995; Sulkava, 1982; Sulkava and Amberia, 1982). This does not mean that there are no differences between early- (pre-60) and late- (post-60) onset AD. For example, early-onset patients generally have a higher mortality risk (Koedam *et al.*, 2008) and are considerably more likely to have close family members who also have the disease (McMurtray *et al.*, 2006). Generally, in early-onset AD, symptoms are more pronounced (particularly in linguistic deficits; Seltzer and Sherwin, 1983) and progress at a faster rate (Reisberg *et al.*, 1989). However, early- and late-onset AD are still considered to be fundamentally the same disease (see Miyoshi, 2009 for an overview).

Those unfamiliar with neurophysiology are advised to consult Appendix I before proceeding.

At a cellular level, the brains of people with AD typically have two key characteristics. The first is a large number of **senile plaques**. Plaques are tiny lumps of a protein called beta amyloid, and they are found lying in between neurons. Almost all older people have some senile plaques, but in people with AD they are found in much greater numbers. The second is **neurofibrillary tangles**. Axons in part keep their structure thanks to a protein called **tau**. In AD, tau becomes distorted, leading to the axons becoming distorted and forming neurofibrillary tangles. The tangles mean that communication between the affected neurons is lost (for some excellent illustrations of tangles and plaques, see Hyman *et al.*, 1993). Researchers are unclear as yet about whether plaques and tangles are the root cause of the symptoms found in AD or whether they are by-products of a deeper process. However, it is known that plaques and tangles correlate with some psychological symptoms. For example, the number of plaques correlates significantly with the level of depression in AD patients at the time of their death, irrespective of how severe their dementing symptoms were (Meynen *et al.*, 2010). Again, researchers using a PET scan tracer ([18F]FDDNP)[4] known to be sensitive to plaques and tangles found that tracer activity correlated with cognitive performance in older adults with no dementia, MCI, and AD (Braskie *et al.*, 2010).

Cell loss in AD is concentrated in specific areas of the brain: the cortex (though the occipital region remains relatively undamaged) and some subcortical regions, principally the amygdala, the hippocampus and the brain stem (Moss and Albert, 1988; Braskie *et al.*, 2010). It is worth noting that some areas of the central nervous system are often spared, notably the basal ganglia, cerebellum and spinal cord (Petit, 1982). Death of nerve cells leads to an especial loss of neurons in the cholinergic system.[5] It has long been known that neurotransmitter systems other than the cholinergic are severely depleted in AD (Rossor and Iversen, 1986), so what makes the cholinergic system especially worthy of attention? The simple answer is that it is known that deliberately suppressing cholinergic activity impairs memory, and hence the **cholinergic hypothesis** argues that damage to this particular pathway has a disproportionate role to play in AD.[6] Certainly, there is ample evidence that

---

4   Full name: 2-(1-{6-[(2-[F-18]fluoroethyl)(methyl)amino]-2-naphthyl}ethylidene)malononitrile. The abbreviation doesn't seem quite so bad now, does it?

5   In other words, that use the neurotransmitter acetylcholine.

6   Though again, it has long been known that other neurotransmitters must also play a role (see Gottfries, 1996; Moss and Albert, 1988). The issue here is one of relative importance.

cognitive decline in AD is correlated with cholinergic system functioning (e.g. Bohnen *et al.*, 2005). Craig, Hong and McDonald (2011) propose that a key role for the cholinergic system is in effect to cushion the brain against accumulated damage by helping to maintain neural plasticity. If the cholinergic system is damaged, a disproportionate decline in cognitive skills results. This leads to the argument that, if neural damage cannot be repaired, perhaps pharmacologically stimulating what is left of the cholinergic system will be beneficial. Some of the so-called 'anti-dementing' drugs work in this manner and, although they do not cure or even stop the course of the disease, they can reduce symptoms and retard the disease's development (Sabbagh and Cummings, 2011).

Thus, in AD patients, as cell death increases, intellectual performance decreases. This has been an established general truth since the earliest studies in this field (e.g. Tomlinson, Blessed and Roth, 1968). However, as with much else in ageing research, we must sound a note of caution. Although plaques, tangles and similar indices correlate with psychological symptoms in AD, plaques *et al.* can be found in older adults with *no* signs of dementia (Erten-Lyons *et al.*, 2009; Katzman *et al.*, 1988; Mahley and Huang, 2009; Roe, Xiong, Miller and Morris, 2007). So therefore, the link between cellular abnormalities and behavioural manifestations cannot be a simplistic one of 'greater cellular damage = more symptoms'; otherwise, many more people would have the disease.

Furthermore, other factors can disrupt the rate at which the disease manifests itself and develops. For example, an oft-cited case is the effect of education. Older adults with more education are likely to present for treatment at an earlier age than older adults with less education. Furthermore, those with less education are likely to have more pronounced symptoms when they first present for treatment (Roe *et al.*, 2008). The explanation for this is straightforward. People with a higher level of education are also likely to be more intelligent and to be engaged in more 'intellectual' activities. Thus, the effects of dementia are likely to be recognised as being atypical much sooner.[7] Older adults with less education might lack the knowledge to distinguish between normal ageing and early dementia, and thus be unconcerned about the symptoms until they become far more pronounced. However, a stronger claim for the beneficial effects of education can be made than this – namely, at death, older people can be found who have the neurological symptoms of AD but in their lifetime had no cognitive deficits (Roe, Xiong, Miller and Morris, 2007). Roe *et al.* attribute this to cognitive reserve – in other words, the higher the education, the greater the surplus processing power. This in turn means that far more decay is required before this extra reserve is used up and psychological effects become noticeable. It is also possible that more educated individuals have more heuristics to help them deal with cognitive tasks, thereby

---

7   This also explains the finding that subjective memory complaints are significantly more likely to be the harbinger of AD the higher the education level of the person concerned (van Oijen *et al.*, 2007).

further lessening the difficulty of tasks and keeping the effects of dementia at bay longer. In other words, more education allows a person to mask the problem (see Gilleard, 1997).

Whatever the reason, most studies have found that education level has a beneficial effect in at least the early stages of AD (see also Bruandet et al., 2008; Perneczky et al., 2009; Sando et al., 2008a). Wajman and Bertolucci (2010) noted that having an intellectually demanding occupation added further protection. It should be noted, however, that some studies have not found an education effect (e.g. Lupton, Stahl, Archer et al., 2010). In the case of the Lupton et al. study, this might be attributed to limited variability in the sample.[8] Also, any advantageous effects from education are absent by the time the late stages of AD are reached (Koepsell et al., 2008). Koepsell et al. suggest that in the early stages of the illness greater test-taking skills or cognitive reserve might account for differences, but by the final stages of the illness such skills have long since decayed.

Beyond the effects of cellular loss and the protective effect of education, there is the question of the origins of AD. In short, what is the prime cause of AD? There is occasional mention in the media of a 'dementia gene' but this is potentially misleading. What is known with certainty is that possession of some genes greatly increases the risk of developing AD. Early research in this area (e.g. Schweber, 1989a; St George-Hyslop et al., 1987) found a flawed structure in chromosome 21, at a location close to that of the damage found in patients with Trisomy 21, the most common cause of Down syndrome. Many commentators have noted that a significant proportion of Down syndrome patients develop AD-like symptoms in middle age, and that the neuropathology of the patients' brains is very similar to that of AD patients (e.g. Schweber, 1989b). More recently, several more precise genetic factors have been identified. For example, the **Apolipoprotein E (ApoE)** gene based on chromosome 19 has attracted considerable attention. More specifically, a variant of ApoE known as ApoE e4[9] appears to confer a significantly greater risk of developing late onset DAT, and even in non-dementing people is associated with a significant worsening of memory in later life (see Hofer et al., 2002; Sando et al., 2008b; Small et al., 2004; van der Vlies et al., 2007). However, note that ApoE does not account for the majority of late onset AD cases. Several genetic links to early onset AD have been found: **amyloid precursor protein (APP)**, a gene located on chromosome 21; **presenilin-1**, a gene located on chromosome 14 and **presenilin-2** located on chromosome 1 (see Bekris et al., 2011; Bertram and Tanzi, 2004; Boeras et al., 2008; O'Brien and Wong, 2011).

Finding genes that are strongly associated with AD implies that the disease has a genetic cause. However, this is simply not true. This is for the simple reason that, if one of a pair of identical twins develops AD, the other twin has a raised chance

8   This is a quite a complex statistical argument, but basically, if the scores do not vary much between the people tested, then it is difficult to find many differences.
9   Or epsilon 4.

of developing the disease, but it is far from certain that he or she will *ever* develop it (Alzheimer's Society, 2007; Scheinin *et al.*, 2011). Furthermore, if they do develop it, the age of onset can vary hugely (e.g. 4–18 years in the study of such twins by Brickell *et al.*, 2007). Since identical twins have an identical genetic structure, clearly more than just genes must cause the disease to occur. The most likely explanation is the **threshold model of dementia**, which states that a person's genetic make-up may predispose them to develop DAT, but it requires something in the environment to trigger the onset of the disease (see Virta *et al.*, 2008).

A number of candidates for this lurking menace in the environment have been suggested. Dodge *et al.* (2011) found that vascular disease can increase the risk of developing AD by circa 10 per cent, and there is at least tentative evidence that a decline in death rates from stroke and heart disease in the USA is being met by a decline in dementia and mild cognitive impairment (Rocca *et al.*, 2011). In recent years, aluminium has been suggested as a likely cause of AD. This is because brain cells in AD patients have been found to contain tiny grains of the metal, and it has been known for over a hundred years that aluminium poisoning produces symptoms very akin to AD (Tomijenovic, 2011). Some worried people stopped using aluminium cooking utensils and similar; probably a futile gesture, since aluminium is a very common element, present in a great many 'natural' things and foodstuffs. Why AD patients are especially vulnerable to aluminium is still something of a mystery. It is possible that the aluminium uptake is a symptom rather than a cause of the decline. For example, dying cells within an AD patient's brain may just happen to absorb aluminium, rather than the aluminium causing the cells to die. This is illustrated by the finding that attempting to restrict aluminium uptake into the brains of AD patients does not affect the progression of the illness (Shore and Wyatt, 1983). However, more recent studies suggest that aluminium has a role in the formation of neurofibrillary tangles (Walton, 2010). As yet there is no firm conclusion to be drawn, and a vigorous debate continues (e.g. Exley, 2007; Takashima, 2007). Another proposal is that the illness is caused by a slow-acting virus. It is known that some dementing illnesses such as **Kuru** (which affects a few native tribes in Papua New Guinea) can be caught by handling diseased nervous tissue. A severe blow to the head might trigger *some* cases of AD. However, generally the evidence on causes of AD is inconclusive (Mahley and Huang, 2009; Mondragon-Rodriguez, Basurto-Islas, Lee *et al.*, 2010) and the search continues (see De la Torre, 2011).

Vascular dementia

Vascular dementia (VaD) is an umbrella term referring to dementia caused by damage to the blood vessels within the brain. This may be due to a blood vessel becoming blocked by the formation of a clot (**thrombosis**); a detached clot lodging in an artery (causing an **embolism**); or a rupture in the wall of a blood vessel (a

haemorrhage) causing damage to the surrounding tissue. The damage in turn causes the surrounding brain tissue to die, the dead tissue being called an **infarct**. Dementia can result from a single infarct (**single infarct dementia**), but more commonly it results from multiple infarcts, each in itself too tiny for the patient usually to notice its effects (**multi-infarct dementia**, or **MID**). The majority of cases of VaD are MID.[10] In total, VaD is probably the second most common type of dementia after AD. Note that it is relatively rare in its 'pure' form, where only symptoms of VaD and no other type of dementia are present (accounting for circa 10% of all cases of dementia). However, VaD also occurs reasonably frequently in conjunction with symptoms of AD, where it is termed a **mixed dementia** (see later). Distinguishing between AD, VaD and mixed dementia can be done by means of neurological indices such as preponderance of neurofibrillary tangles (Gold *et al.*, 2007).

In most cases, the infarcts in VaD can be anywhere in the brain and relatively random. In some cases, however, they are concentrated in particular regions of the brain. In **cortical atherosclerotic dementia (CAD)** the damage is largely in the cortex, whilst in **subcortical arteriosclerotic dementia (SAD)** the damage is principally in the subcortical regions. As might be predicted, CAD is associated with greater intellectual impairment and SAD with movement disorders (see Holtz, 2011; Metter and Wilson, 1993; Tomimoto, 2011). Two common forms of SAD are **lacunar strokes** and **Binswanger's disease**, which have similar symptoms though their origins are in damage to different subcortical areas.

The causes of VaD are not fully known. Not surprisingly, patients often have a history of cardiovascular (**CV**) problems, fatty diets and smoking, and there may also be some familial tendency to VaD or stroke (Funkenstein, 1988; Holtz, 2011; Ronnemaa *et al.*, 2011; Qiu *et al.*, 2010). However, these are only risk factors, and finding a definitive set of causes appears to be as remote as for AD (see Stephan and Brayne, 2008). The illness is extremely rare before the age of 55, with average onset at 65. A common method of testing for VaD is the **Hachinski Ischaemic Score (IS)**, after its inventor (Hachinski *et al.*, 1975). This awards points to the patient based upon the number of symptoms he or she displays, with particularly salient symptoms being weighted to reflect their greater importance.

Because infarcts often occur randomly, the course of the illness is often difficult to predict, and symptoms can vary greatly between patients although, as with AD, memory is often an early victim. Also as with AD, the simple quantity of brain tissue destroyed by VaD bears little relationship to the symptoms produced (see Metter and Wilson, 1993). To quote one researcher, 'there are few findings that can be considered consistent with a diagnosis' (LaRue, 1992, p.236). This is because the areas of the brain controlling different mental functions may decay at different rates (according to where the infarcts most frequently strike). To take

---

10   Note that older texts tend to refer to *all* cases of vascular dementia as MID or arteriosclerotic dementia.

an example: suppose that there are areas of the brain called *A, B, C, D* and *E*, controlling abilities *X, Y, Z, P* and *Q* respectively. One VaD patient may show a decline in areas *A, B* and *C*, and thus in abilities X, Y and Z. Another patient may have well-preserved areas A and B, but show decline in areas *C, D* and *E*, and thus in abilities Z, P and Q. Thus, two patients with the same basic complaint may have radically different symptoms. It will have not escaped some readers' notice that, because infarcts can occur relatively randomly, in some instances the damage they inflict can by chance mimic the effects of dementias of other aetiologies, and thus misdiagnosis and reported cases of VaD closely mimicking another type of dementia are common in the literature (e.g. Alzheimer's Society, 2007; Marianetti *et al.*, 2010).

Nonetheless, there is a characteristic of VaD that makes it distinguishable from other dementing disorders – namely, that decline tends to take place in a stepwise fashion: the VaD patient generally shows a relatively sudden decline; then there is no change or even some recovery of function. Then there is another sudden decline, followed by no change or recovery, and so forth *ad infinitum*. This is not a totally infallible diagnostic tool, since some patients (especially Binswanger's disease patients) display a steady decline. However, the majority of texts cite stepwise decline as a cardinal feature of VaD.

Other dementias

Although AD and VaD between them account for most cases of dementia, as mentioned earlier, there are nearly 50 other known causes. Of these, the following are perhaps the most often encountered.

Frontotemporal dementia, as its name implies, first affects the frontal and temporal regions of the cortex (see Mariani *et al.*, 2006). Frontotemporal dementias are very rare. There is an ongoing debate about how many subtypes there are (e.g. Boxer and Miller, 2005; Whitwell *et al.*, 2009). However, the commonest subtype is generally agreed to be **Pick's disease** (named after its discoverer), also known as **behavioural variant frontotemporal dementia (bvFTD)**. This is not commonly a disease of later life, with the average age of onset in the late forties. Atrophy begins and is concentrated in the frontal lobes. At a cellular level, neurons often degenerate into **Pick's bodies**, which have a characteristic swollen appearance (though some patients can have the same *general* pattern of atrophy as Pick's disease, but lack Pick's bodies). The patient usually first presents with problems expected of frontal lobe damage, such as loss of planning skills, ability to think in the abstract, and so forth. Kluver-Bucy syndrome usually manifests itself early in the course of the illness (as opposed to the late stages of AD). It may also incorporate compulsive sexual behaviour, often without regard for social propriety. As the disease progresses, dementing symptoms akin to AD begin to manifest themselves. Often language is more impaired than memory, but this is not an infallible rule. Pick's patients are also more prone to **confabulating** (essentially, making up stories or implausible explanations to cover up gaps in memory or other skills), something rarely seen in VaD or AD patients. In the terminal stages, the patient is reduced to a vegetative state. Death is typically about four years after the onset of the first symptoms. Another form of frontotemporal dementia is **semantic dementia**, also known as **temporal variant frontotemporal dementia (tvFTD)**. In this subtype, the initial symptoms result from atrophy beginning in the temporal lobes. Atrophy in the left temporal lobe causes language skills to deteriorate, whilst atrophy in the right temporal lobe causes loss of facial recognition and the ability to recognise emotions. Atrophy on one side of the brain eventually leads to atrophy on the other side. Symptoms then develop further in a manner akin to Pick's disease.

Creutzfeldt-Jakob disease (CJD) is a very rare illness, affecting approximately one in a million people. The illness typically manifests itself first as a movement disorder before intellectual deterioration begins. The illness is atypical of dementias in two main respects – first, death is usually swifter (c. one year after onset of symptoms), and second, it is known that it is contracted via an infection. CJD is of especial interest because a new variant of the disease (vCJD)[11] was discovered in the 1990s. There is strong evidence that the infection source may be beef contaminated with **bovine spongiform encephalopathy (BSE)**, an infective agent that produces symptoms similar to CJD in cattle. Stories in the news media in the early 1990s were often dramatic in their predictions of the number of victims vCJD would claim. However, so far an epidemic has not happened. By 2010, only 17 new cases of BSE were reported worldwide, indicating the disease had practically been eradicated. So far, there have been circa 170 deaths from nvCJD, with a mean age of victim of 28 years. Susceptibility to the disease seems to be dependent upon the genotype of the victim. The genes in this instance are only two – M and V, meaning that an individual is either MM, VV or MV. All people who have so far contracted vCJD have been MM, which is the gene variant of circa 37 per cent of the population. We know that in kuru most people who contract that disease are also MM, but a smaller proportion with MV contract the disease later in life (Collinge et al., 2008). This can lead to inevitable speculation that we might begin to see cases of vCJD in people with the MV variant and perhaps ultimately with the VV variant as well (Coghlan, 2011). However, there are grounds for doubting this. First, MV cases of kuru are relatively rare relative to cases of MM. Since MM cases of vCJD are rare within the population, this might mean that MV cases will be incredibly scarce, and VV cases simply not arise. Certainly no MV cases of vCJD have yet been found (Coghlan, 2011). Second, if vCJD is going to be a persistent problem, then we should expect a rising or at least consistent number of cases. But the available evidence shows a rise, peak and fall of cases, far more consistent with a brief outbreak. Of course continued vigilance is required, and the rarity of vCJD does not in any way lessen

---

11 Otherwise known as new variant CJD or nvCJD.

the sympathy that should be extended to the bereaved families of victims. But an attitude of sensible caution, rather than scaremongering stories of a lurking menace waiting to claim us all, is arguably the sensible approach.

Huntington's disease (a.k.a. Huntington's chorea) is not considered to be a dementia by all commentators. Like CJD, it is relatively rare, but it tends to cluster in families, indicating a strong genetic component. Also like CJD, the early symptoms of the illness are disturbances of movement, often taking the form of writhing and twitching. Subsequently, patients develop dementing symptoms, although the decline can also mimic schizophrenia (Kermis, 1986). Patients with Huntington's disease tend to last longer than patients with other dementias, typical life expectancy after the appearance of the first symptoms being circa 15 years. The illness can strike at any age, but onset in middle age is the most common.

Parkinson's disease (PD) is also chiefly characterised by movement disorders, including a characteristic shuffling gait and tremors. However, there is a higher than average risk that PD patients will also develop dementia (c.10–15%: Lezak, 1995; Moss and Albert, 1988). It should be noted that many AD patients develop PD-like symptoms as their illness progresses. The most salient difference between PD and AD patients is that linguistic skills are usually considerably better preserved (or even unaffected) in PD (LaRue, 1992).

Dementia with Lewy bodies (DLB), also known as **Lewy body dementia (LBD)**, is a subtype not without controversy. **Lewy bodies** are tiny balls of protein found inside affected nerve cells. The presence of Lewy bodies was well documented by the 1960s, but it was not until the advent of more sensitive laboratory techniques in the 1990s that researchers discovered that Lewy bodies were more prevalent in some cases of dementia than had previously been realised (Mrak and Griffin, 2007). However, there is a problem. Lewy bodies are found in the basal ganglia in Parkinson's disease patients. In DLB, they are found not only in the basal ganglia but elsewhere in the brain. Does DLB constitute a distinct subtype of dementia, or is it simply a variant of Parkinson's disease? Considering the symptoms of DLB does not help matters, because they are a combination of dementia and PD. In brief, onset of DLB is relatively rapid and hallucinations are a common (but not universal) symptom. Movement problems similar to PD might be present. Cognitive skills can be impaired, but memory impairment is rarely a notable early symptom (Woods, 2011). Some researchers treat DLB as a distinct type (e.g. Alzheimer's Society, 2007; Woods, 2011), whereas others argue that PD and DLB are essentially the same (see Nestor, 2010; Revuelta and Lippa, 2009).

Dementia can also appear as a symptom of other illnesses, such as **normal pressure hydrocephalus** (where cerebrospinal fluid gets trapped in the brain instead of draining away, putting destructive pressure on the brain tissue), brain tumours and AIDS; and also as a result of long-term exposure to toxic chemicals and chronic alcohol abuse.

Cortical and subcortical dementias

Some commentators prefer to categorise dementias according to whether the principal atrophy is in the cortex (the **cortical dementias**) or in the subcortical regions (the **subcortical dementias**). By this reckoning, the commonest cortical dementias are AD and Pick's disease, and the commonest subcortical dementias are PD and Huntington's disease (with types of VaD belonging to either group, depending upon the particular form in question). Since the cortex is principally concerned with higher intellectual functions and the subcortex with the control of movement, emotion, and so forth (see Chapter 1), there should be a functional division between the two groups, and this is what is typically found. Thus, cortical dementias manifest themselves most strikingly as disorders of thought, memory and language, with some movement disturbances as relatively minor symptoms, whereas subcortical dementias are very much characterised by problems with movement (for this reason amongst others, some commentators have argued that subcortical dementias are not 'true' dementias). Subcortical dementias also tend to strike before the onset of later life. There is an excellent review of the issue by Peretz and Cummings (1988).

Illnesses that can be confused with dementia

An assortment of conditions can give the appearance of dementia but in fact have other causes. The two most common are both treatable, unlike the dementias, and for this reason are sometimes called the **reversible dementias**. The first of these is **pseudodementia**. This can arise in some older people who suffer severe depression (see below). In becoming depressed, the patient loses motivation and this is reflected in very poor scores on tests of memory and intellect. This, and their general lack of interest in their surroundings, can provide an excellent imitation of dementia. Indeed, some commentators argue that the impersonation is so good that the term 'pseudodementia' is misleading and that the illness should be classified as a form of 'true' dementia. However, there are several key differences between pseudodementia and the genuine article. First, pseudodemented patients are usually well orientated in time and space; for example, they know where they are, what day of the week it is, why they are being tested, and so forth. Second, they are also typically aware that they are performing badly on memory and intellectual tests. Third, pseudodemented patients' intellectual performance typically fluctuates in tandem with their level of depression, and improves as their depression is treated (Jenike, 1988; LaRue, 1992).

However, it would be misleading to suppose that depression and 'genuine' dementia have no connection. Between 20 and 30 per cent of patients with dementia also have some symptoms of depression (e.g. Marsden and Harrison, 1972; see also Boland *et al.*, 1996; Carlson, Sherwin and Chertkow, 2000). Again, it is salient to note that one study found that 57 per cent of older patients referred for treatment for depression subsequently developed dementia (Reding, Haycox and Blas, 1985). Subsequent research by Vinkers *et al.* (2004) and Brommelhoff *et al.*

(2009) demonstrated that, for a significant proportion of patients, depression is a symptom of the early stages of dementia, rather than being a precursor or risk factor. In other words, severely depressed older people may display pseudodementia, but, equally, a high proportion of 'genuinely' demented patients may also display depression. For this reason, some researchers and clinicians are unwilling to use the term 'pseudodementia' because often there is a real dementia present.

The other major impersonator of dementia is **delirium**, also known as **acute confusional state (ACS)**. Delirium is typically rapid in onset (usually a matter of hours or days). The age groups most at risk are children and older adults. There are many possible causes, including fever, infection, (legally prescribed) drug intoxication, stroke and inadequate diet (see Lin *et al.*, 2010). Most cases of delirium are cured by treating the underlying causes. Delirious patients display poor intellectual and memory skills, and also tend to be either excessively languid (**hypoactive delirium**), agitated or anxious (**hyperactive delirium**), or a mixture of both (**mixed delirium**). It is also possible for the patient to exhibit no 'obvious' behavioural symptoms. However, generally, rambling or incoherent speech is also a common feature. To this extent, a patient with delirium can resemble, for example, a demented patient, a depressed patient or a very anxious patient, and misdiagnosis is relatively common (see Foreman and Milisen, 2004). This can have serious consequences. For example, a hyperactive delirium patient may have a serious underlying physical condition that needs urgent treatment; mistaking this for a severe anxiety attack and sedating the patient could be life threatening. However, a major difference between delirium and dementia, other than the rapid onset of the former, is that many delirious patients suffer from **illusions** (distorted perceptions of the world around them). Illusions are relatively rare in dementia, in spite of some popular misconceptions on this subject. In addition, attention span in delirium is limited, whereas (surprisingly) it is often reasonably well preserved in demented patients. Various diagnostic tests, which act as a checklist of symptoms (e.g. the **Delirium Rating Scale**) are available (see Wong *et al.*, 2010 for a review). Note, however, that delirium can, and does, occur in demented patients (see Cole, 2004; Marengoni, Calíbrese and Cossi, 2004) and, because of their weakened cognitive state, might be more easily contracted and be of greater severity (Voyer *et al.*, 2011). Delirium in an older adult indicates a higher probability of serious illness and imminent mortality. For example, Pitkala *et al.* (2005) found that older patients suffering from delirium had an almost 75 per cent greater chance of dying in the subsequent year than did non-delirious controls.

Incidence rates for subtypes of dementia

There is considerable variability in the estimates of how prevalent each subtype of dementia is. For example, Plassman *et al.* (2011) found in their test sample that Alzheimer's was four times more common than VaD. On the other hand, Yamada *et al.* (2008) found that *their* sample had an AD:VaD ratio of 1.7:1. Taking AD cases as a proportion of *all* types of dementia, estimates in the research literature vary from 40 to 80 per cent or more (see Alzheimer's Society, 2007; Cohen and Dunner, 1980; Hestad *et al.*, 1998; Smyer and Qualls, 1999). There are several reasons for this variability:

- Diagnosis on a living patient is almost always by means of examining behaviour. However, dementia subtypes can produce very similar behaviour patterns.

- Figures on incidences are often drawn from multiple clinics, so differences in diagnostic methods (and skill) can introduce distortion as can differences in educational level and intelligence of relatives providing patient histories (Wancata *et al.*, 2007; Wilson *et al.*, 2011). For example, patients with higher levels of intellectual and/or linguistic skills are less prone to dementia, or perhaps just better able to hide it, at least in the early stages (see Hestad *et al.*, 1998; Snowdon *et al.*, 1996).

- Clinicians often look for 'pure' dementias – in other words, dementias that have only one cause. However, subtypes of dementia can often co-exist in the same patient. For example, reporting on a large collection of post-mortem findings, Jellinger (2006) noted that AD accounted for about 80 per cent of cases, but only half of these had pure AD – the other half had AD plus one other dementia (often termed **mixed dementia**). Pure VaD accounted for under 10 per cent of cases.

- Clinicians can miss cases of dementia (particularly in the early stages) with surprising ease. For example, Löppönen *et al.* (2003) found that a sample of Finnish doctors responsible for primary health care had failed to identify *over half* of the cases of dementia amongst the patients in their care.

- Clinicians might disagree on diagnoses in the same patients (see Gurland and Toner, 1983; Lezak, 1995; Roth, 1979).

- Diagnosis by default will only exaggerate these differences further. For example, presented with a mixed dementia of AD and VaD, a clinician might decide on a diagnosis of AD simply because the symptoms of the VaD happened to mimic those of AD. Conversely, the clinician might decide to classify the dementia as pure VaD because there was evidence of a stepwise deterioration.

It is therefore very hard to make a firm estimate of incidence rates for subtypes of dementia, and the waters are muddied yet further by the consideration that there are gender differences and the proportions of subtypes change with the age of the patient. However, a consensus estimate for cases of dementia in the over-sixties (**late onset dementia** or **LOD**) is provided by the *Dementia UK* report, shown in Table 6.1.

Table 6.1 Estimated percentage of types of dementia, stratified by gender

	Male	Female	Total
Alzheimer's Disease	55	67	62
Vascular Dementia	20	15	17
Mixed	11	10	10
Lewy Body Disease	6	3	4
Fronto-Temporal Dementia	2	1	2
Parkinson's	3	1	2
Other	3	3	3

Extrapolated from data in Alzheimer's Society (2007) Dementia UK London: Alzheimer's Society

As can be seen, AD is by far the most common dementia, but it is also more common in women than men. Men are more likely to have VaD. Also, whilst the proportion of subtypes remains relatively constant in older women, in older men AD becomes more common the older the person considered (whilst VaD shows a relative decline in frequency of occurrence).

From a researcher's viewpoint, the lack of accurate diagnoses means that it is very difficult, if not downright impossible, to assemble a group of patients and know for certain that they are all suffering from the same form of dementia. Thus, finding a difference between a group of patients suffering from AD and another suffering from VaD on a particular test may mean there is a genuine difference between AD and VaD patients on the skill measured by that test. However, this conclusion must be weighed against the consideration that at least some of the AD group may be suffering from VaD and vice versa, or that there are a significant proportion of cases of mixed dementia. Another problem is in matching patients with different forms of dementia. It is not really sufficient to assemble a group of AD patients, a group of VaD patients and compare them, without also considering how long the patients in each group have been diagnosed as suffering from their respective illnesses. If, for example, the VaD patients have had the illness longer than the AD patients, how can we be sure that any difference between the groups is not due simply to the length of having the illness rather than any intrinsic difference between AD and VaD? Again, are the groups of the same average age – if not, any difference might be due simply to ageing rather than the illness. Conversely, if the groups are of the same average age, are they typical of their illness groups? For example, suppose that on average dementia *A* strikes at 60 years of age, and dementia *B* at 70. If we test an *A* group and *B* group, and both have an average age of 70, how can we be sure that there is not something slightly unusual about the *A* group (in other words, is it truly representative?). To take yet another possible problem, suppose that it is found that patients with, for example, AD, are very bad at remembering spoken words. It might be supposed that this indicates poor verbal memory. However, dementia, and particularly AD, is Murphy's Law applied to intellectual functioning – in other words, whatever can go wrong *will* go wrong. Thus, finding a failure of verbal memory may mean there is a decline in verbal memory, but perhaps a decline in linguistic skills meant that the patient simply did not understand the test instructions.

None of these problems is necessarily insurmountable, but they do indicate that extreme caution must be taken in interpreting the results of studies of dementia. Certainly it is nearly always unwise to pursue points in any great detail, simply because the initial diagnosis and the problems of accurately comparing different patient groups are too problematic for more than fairly general statements to be made with any certainty.

Memory changes in dementia

The majority of research on memory changes in dementia has been focused on patients with AD. This is hardly surprising, since, as we have seen, this is the most common subtype of dementia. However, as has also been noted, misdiagnosis of subtypes of dementia is common, and many studies have been based on patients whose diagnosis have not been confirmed by *post mortem* examination. This means that any conclusions about the features of a specific subtype must be extremely guarded, since a set of findings on patients who, for example, supposedly have AD, could very easily be findings on a group with some people with pure AD, plus a significant proportion who have mixed dementia, pure VaD or indeed another subtype entirely. This same note of caution applies to studies of all other psychological features of dementia as well.

Readers unfamiliar with psychological models of memory are advised to read the first few pages of Chapter 3 before proceeding.

Since a key feature of dementia is memory loss, it is unsurprising to note that many studies have found general deterioration of memory in patients with dementia, and that, generally, the more advanced the disease, the worse the memory. Indeed, many researchers have argued that appreciable memory loss is indicative of the pre-clinical stages of dementia (Liu *et al.*, 2007; Sliwinski *et al.*, 2003). This argument was refined by Saculu *et al.* (2009) who argued that a global pattern of poor cognitive skills indicated the imminent arrival of dementia, whilst poor memory in isolation predicted the onset of dementia in the longer term.

AD patients' performance on STM tasks worsen the harder the memory task set (e.g. Nebes, 1992). The causes are severalfold. First, there is a deficit in encoding. For example, Kopelman (1985) found that AD patients could retain memories as well as non-dementing participants, provided they were given (a lot) more opportunities to rehearse the to-be-remembered (TBR) items. Thus, if information can get into a long-term store in AD patients' memories, then there is a reasonable possibility that it will be retained. Further evidence for this assumption comes from Becker *et al.* (1987), who found that, within 30 seconds of being given a set of TBR items, AD patients had forgotten far more than non-dementing controls. However, those items that *were* remembered after 30 seconds had the same probability of being remembered 30 *minutes* later as did items that non-dementing control participants remembered after 30 seconds (see also Hulme, Lee and Brown, 1993).

It has long been known that AD patients, just like non-dementing people, are affected by phonological similarities in TBR lists[12] (e.g. Morris, 1984), and the majority of evidence points to the phonological loop (and the visuospatial sketchpad) being unscathed in the early stages of the disease (Huntley and Howard, 2010; though see Caza and Belleville, 2008). However, as AD progresses, the phonological loop becomes more impaired (Collette *et al.*, 1999). Similar problems are found in Huntington's disease patients (Martone *et al.*, 1984). Perhaps not surprisingly, patients with pseudodementia behave like non-dementing older participants, though with an overall lower memory span (e.g. Gibson, 1981; Miller and Lewis, 1977).

Baddeley (1986) and other commentators have argued a key deficit is in the central executive. There is considerable evidence that, when given an STM task and a simultaneous distracting task, AD patients' memory spans get disproportionately worse (MacPherson *et al.*, 2007; Morris, 1986; Sebastian, Menor and Elosua, 2006). This strongly indicates a deficit in the central executive, since one of its main functions is to control and co-ordinate intellectual and memory tasks (Baddeley *et al.*, 1991; Morris, 1994; Morris and Kopelman, 1986). The central executive is felt to be anatomically based in the frontal lobes (Baddeley, 1986), an area known to be badly affected in AD (e.g. Ihara *et al.*, 2010; Sjobeck and Englund, 2003),[13] though note that other areas of the brain such as the hippocampus and temporal lobes have also been implicated in memory loss (e.g. Berlingeri *et al.*, 2008).

Remote memory is also affected by dementia. Although it is sometimes popularly supposed that demented patients have no memory for yesterday but a pin-sharp recall of events from their childhood, this is not the case (except in the very early stages of the illness when the memory problem may be for new information alone). Formal laboratory studies have demonstrated that remote memory for famous names and events is significantly worse than for non-dementing older people (e.g. Corkin *et al.*, 1984; Meeter, Eijsackers and Mulder, 2006), and declines at a greater rate than autobiographical memory (Greene and Hodges, 1996).

---

12 For example, a list of words that sound similar (*cat, rat, bat*) are harder to remember than dissimilar sounding words (e.g. *cat, ran, hug*). This is probably because words are encoded onto a sound-sensitive memory mechanism called the phonological loop, which is poor at distinguishing between similar-sounding words (see Baddeley, 1986).

13 Frontal lobe symptoms generally get worse as the disease progresses in AD and Dementia with Lewy bodies, but, after being pronounced at an early stage, generally remain more stable in people with frontotemporal dementia (Aries *et al.*, 2010).

Autobiographical memory recall in patients with AD can involve a high volume of false memories (see Meeter *et al.*, 2006) and the level of loss is correlated with lowered awareness of actual level of memory skills (Naylor and Clare, 2008) and sense of self (Fargeau *et al.*, 2010). Perhaps not surprisingly, AD patients have impoverished **autonoetic consciousness** (essentially, awareness of oneself in memories and the ability to 'travel' back in time through memories and to experience memories) (Irish *et al.*, 2011). Whether there is a **temporal gradient** (i.e. memories from one time of life are remembered better than others) is uncertain, since studies have produced conflicting findings (Leyhe *et al.*, 2009).[14] However, regardless of this uncertainty, performance on an autobiographical memory task seems to be a reasonably sensitive diagnostic tool in measuring the severity of a patient's dementia (Dreyfus, Roe and Morris, 2010). Greene, Hodges and Baddeley (1995) attributed decline in autobiographical memory in AD patients to a retrieval problem, in turn linking this to a failure of the central executive, a conclusion echoed by Meeter *et al.* (2006). Anxiety might also have an effect: Irish *et al.* (2006) found that playing soothing music lowered anxiety levels and gave a disproportionate and significant increase in AD patients' recall in an autobiographical memory task.

These studies raise the question of whether demented patients' memory problems can be alleviated. Certainly some commonsense procedures seem to help. For example, priming the patient with the first letter of a TBR item produces a disproportionate improvement in the memory performance of demented patients (e.g. Davis and Mumford, 1984; Miller, 1975). However, priming has to be fairly unsubtle to be efficacious. For example, priming with a word semantically related to the TBR item, or giving lists of words semantically related to each other, has no advantageous effect on dementing patients, though non-dementing older adults are advantaged by this (e.g. Davis and Mumford, 1984). Massimi *et al.* (2008) describe a novel case study in which a patient with AD was provided with an ambient display in their home of scenes, music and narratives from the patient's earlier life. The treatment led to an improvement in apathy and self-identity scores, but did not significantly influence autobiographical memory, general cognitive skills, or anxiety and depression levels. In contrast, De Leo, Brivio and Sautter (2011) report a study in which a patient with AD (at FAST stage 4) carried a smartphone on a lanyard for twelve hours a day for four weeks. The phone was programmed to take a picture every five minutes. The pictures were then made into a slideshow, which was shown to the participant. It was found that the slide show improved recall of autobiographical events. There are clearly practical limitations to the adaptation of Massimi *et al.*'s study, and photographing activities on a regular basis raises issues of personal privacy. However, the ideas are interesting ones and might in the future develop into more workable memory aids.

---

14 This information is taken from the literature review in the introduction to Leyhe *et al.*'s paper. The study reported by the authors found that their sample of AD patients had better memories for distant than recent events.

Linguistic skills

One of the most common measures of linguistic skills[15] is a simple naming task in which the patient must identify pictures of common objects. Failure to name objects (**anomia**) is a common first symptom of AD, and patients are notably disadvantaged when compared with not only non-dementing controls but also patients with Huntington's disease, and PD and VaD patients (Bayles and Tomoeda, 1983; Chan et al., 1995; Schram, Rubert and Loewenstein, 1995). Furthermore, although there are some studies that point to the reverse,[16] it seems probable that verbs are harder to name than nouns, probably because verbs are semantically more complex and thus harder to process (Druks et al., 2006). Ability to name an object from its sound has been found to be significantly harder than naming it from its visual appearance (Brandt, Bakker and Maroof, 2010) and, furthermore, the ability to name from auditory sources correlates better with other measures of dementing decline (Miller et al., 2010). There can be considerable variability between AD patients in the types of names that are hard to retrieve (Cuetos et al., 2008). However, researchers have argued that, qualitatively speaking, the overall pattern of change in naming skills in AD is no different from in non-dementing people of the same age (Gale et al., 2009). It has been known from the relatively early brain scan literature that linguistic skills are associated with brain atrophy (see Harasty et al., 1999; Hirono et al., 1998; Keilp et al., 1999), and more recent evidence indicates that a key problem is a decline in the integrity of the medial temporal region of the brain (Venneri et al., 2008).

Linguistic problems are not confined to anomia and related semantic problems, however, and, generally, linguistic skills worsen as AD progresses. An early victim is said to be comprehension of non-literal language such as proverbs and metaphors, though firm empirical evidence for loss of comprehension in the later stage of dementia is sparse (see Rapp and Wild, 2011). More broadly, Grossman et al. (1995) found that AD patients were significantly poorer on a wide range of linguistic tasks (sentence–picture matching, judgements of the grammatical acceptability of sentences, sentence completion), which was not explicable by memory deficits nor indeed the supposed severity of the illness (though note that linguistic deficits in AD do not appear with the same severity at the same stage in all patients). Common symptoms include **intrusions** (inserting inappropriate words or phrases), **perseverations** (repeating the same phrase, word, or part of a word) and **circumlocution** (talking around the subject). Note, however, that Waters and Caplan (2002) found no especial problems in syntactic processing in their study of AD patients in very early stages of the illness.

---

15 There is a considerable research literature on semantic dementia, but it is largely concerned with psycholinguistic theory rather than the psychology of ageing *per se*, and thus falls outside the ambit of this book. For further discussion of linguistic problems in semantic dementia, see Reilly and Peelie (2008).

16 As with most areas of psychology, arguments are occasionally raised that the method of measurement is distorting the results (see e.g. Nebes, 1992; Nebes and Brady, 1990; Nicholas et al., 1996).

However, syntactic deficits are found as the illness develops and are associated with loss of white matter and declining executive control of memory (Giovannetti et al., 2008).

Not all linguistic skills will decline at the same rate, however. For instance, **phonology** (awareness of speech sounds, as shown e.g. in correct pronunciation), and **morphology** (knowledge of the roots of words) are generally well preserved in AD (e.g. Appell, Kertesz and Fisman, 1982). Again, reading (at least of single words) is assumed to be relatively well preserved in at least the early stages of AD. So much so that the NART (National Adult Reading Test, a test of knowledge of pronunciation of irregularly spelt words such as *quay*) is frequently used as a gauge of pre-illness intelligence (see e.g. Starr and Lonie, 2007).

Visuo-spatial skills

Declines in visuo-spatial skills have been found in patients with very mild AD (Quental, Brucki and Bueno, 2009), even when the memory demands of a task are minimised (Bucks and Willison, 1997; Kaskie and Storandt, 1995). It is argued that visuo-spatial tests may be particularly effective in detecting dementia in its earliest stages (Maki, Yoshida and Yamaguchi, 2010). Armstrong and Cloud (1998) attribute the decline to the reduced efficiency of components of the working memory system. Supporting this, later research by Bisiacchi et al. (2008) found that the key distinction between non-dementing controls and AD patients on visuo-spatial tasks was in use of central executive functions.

A key example of visuo-spatial skills is drawing. Patients with AD often display a phenomenon known as **closing-in**. Some tests of drawing give the participant a piece of paper on which is printed a figure, which the participant is requested to copy on the blank section of the same piece of paper. Non-dementing people will tend simply to draw a copy on the blank section, keeping it distinct from the target figure. However, participants with AD and VaD have a tendency to draw on or near the target (Chin et al., 2005). The phenomenon seems to be an attempt to compensate for a particularly pronounced visuo-spatial dysfunction, since AD patients with relatively preserved visuo-spatial skills are less likely to display closing-in (Serra et al., 2009).

A commonly used visuo-spatial measure is the **clock drawing test (CDT)**, in which the participant must copy an analogue clock face.[17] Nair et al. (2010) reported very high interrater reliability and sensitivity for identifying very mild cases of AD when the CDT was scored by experienced dementia specialists. Again, AD patients score significantly less well on the CDT than people with MCI (Persey and Schmitter-Edgecombe, 2011) and a relatively poor performance on the test in a non-

---

17 The test is more sensitive if the participant is required to produce a time setting on the drawn clock (Berger et al., 2008).

dementing older adult is predictive of the later development of dementia (Babins *et al.*, 2008; Paganini-Hill and Clark, 2007).[18]

It should be noted that there is nothing particularly 'special' about clock drawing *per se* and that visuo-spatial skills are often poor in dementia in general and AD in particular (see Lezak, 1995). Deficits have also been found in skills as diverse as copying simple displays of crosses (Grossi and Orsini, 1978) and iconic memory (Coyne, Liss and Geckler, 1984; Moscovitch, 1982; Schlotterer *et al.*, 1984). Nor should it be supposed that problems are only at a relatively complex level of processing. For example, Neargarder *et al.* (2003) demonstrated that AD patients show a significant decline in a process as 'basic' as the contrast sensitivity function (see also Cronin-Golomb *et al.*, 2007). Again, Pache *et al.* (2003) found that AD patients had significantly lower scores on measures of colour vision tests than did age-matched controls. Interestingly, the level of deficit was independent of degree of dementing decline.

Olfaction

Olfactory functions (i.e. smell) worsen in AD. For example, Nordin and Murphy (1996) found that AD patients had a higher odour threshold (i.e. the smell had to be more powerful before it was detected) and poorer memory for smells. In a review of the literature, Thompson, Knee and Golden (1998) conclude that olfactory problems are effective in distinguishing between AD patients and non-dementing older adults, and may also be effective in distinguishing AD from some other forms of dementia (e.g. Huntington's disease: see Murphy, 1999). A link between the brain's olfactory structure and expression of ApoE has been identified, and this might ultimately demonstrate an important causal link (see Finkel *et al.*, 2011).

The effect on caregivers

All forms of illness can have negative effects not just on patients but also on those family members and friends who look after them. However, the effect may be particularly strong on caregivers for demented patients, because the nature of the illness means that the patient cannot give adequate feedback. It takes little imagination to envisage the unique stress induced by looking after a spouse or a parent who needs constant attention and yet who will never get better and cannot even recognise the caregiver. Levesque, Ducharme and Lachance (1999) demonstrated in a large-scale study of caregivers that the stresses experienced by people looking after demented patients are significantly greater than in caring for patients with other illnesses.

---

18   It should be noted that, although most work on the CDT has been directed at AD, patients with other dementia subtypes can also perform badly at the task. For example, The CDT also appears to be similarly badly performed by people with dementia with Lewy bodies (Pernecky, Drzezga, Boecker *et al.*, 2010).

Because dementia is incurable and the effects on the caregivers so profound, it is not unreasonable to argue that the success of any treatment of demented patients should include a measure of how the lives of caregivers have been affected (see Brodaty, 2007).

The level of caregiver burden is determined by a large range of factors. The following is an illustrative rather than exhaustive list:

- The burden is generally higher with younger than older demented patients (Freyne *et al.*, 1999).

- VaD patients present greater problems than AD patients in the early stages of the illnesses, with a reversal in the later stages (Vetter *et al.*, 1999).

- The more demands the symptoms of the patient place on the carer, the greater the burden (Tun, Murman and Colenda, 2008).

- Similarly, the more daily activities the person with dementia can do for themselves, the lower the caregiver burden (Razani *et al.*, 2007).

- Or, put yet another way, the greater the dependence of the person with dementia on the caregiver, the greater the caregiver burden (Gallagher *et al.*, 2011).

- The higher the satisfaction with the premorbid relationship with the person with dementia, the lower the perceived burden of caring for them (Steadman, Tremont and Davis, 2007).

In addition, caregivers living in countries such as the UK must endure health and welfare systems that will often happily bleed them white before paying out for any treatment themselves. The simple truth is that the main reason for caregiver burden is that, unless a caregiver is very rich, he or she cannot afford to pay for others to share the load. Japan has instituted compulsory insurance to cover the cost of long-term care of older adults and early signs are optimistic (Arai and Zarit, 2011). However, larger scale assessment still has to be done, and it is doubtful whether all countries will react with equal enthusiasm to what is, after all, yet another tax.

Not surprisingly, there is a large body of evidence that caring for a demented relative usually results in significantly higher levels of depression, stress and other related health problems (e.g. Coppel *et al.*, 1985; Kennedy, Kiecolt-Glaser and Glaser, 1988; Morrisey *et al.*, 1990; Valimaki *et al.*, 2009). This tends to worsen the more severe the patient's problem behaviours become (Garcia-Alberca, Lara and Luis Berthier, 2011; Hooker *et al.*, 2002; Neundorfer *et al.*, 2001; Schulz *et al.*, 2008). Suicide risk is also higher (Fry, 1986), and murder of the patient followed by the caregiver committing suicide is not unknown (Bourget, Gagne and Whitehurst, 2010). It should also be noted that, because of the immense pressure the caregiver (either family or professional) is placed under, elder abuse is not uncommon (e.g.

Buzgova and Ivanova, 2009; Lowenstein, 2009). Note that this does not necessarily imply violence, but may include nonetheless undesirable behaviours such as neglect (see Pritchard, 1995).

A person-centred approach

It is entirely right and proper that we should be concerned about dementia. It is a nasty illness with horrible consequences for both patient and loved ones. Even if one is not moved by that thought, then the huge financial bill that the illness presents should be enough to attract the attention of even the flintiest of hearts. However, we can overplay the arguments to the disadvantage of the very people we are trying to help. The following extract from a paper by George (2010) very eloquently expresses this:

> The everyday language we use to describe dementia shapes our perceptions of brain ageing and even contributes to what has been called the 'social death' of those most severely affected. Guided by the language of warfare, we have come to view people with dementia as 'victims' who are ravaged by a singular marauding disease. Alzheimer's disease is personified as a 'mind-robber' that 'attacks' or 'strikes' the brains of individuals, leaving plaques and tangles in its wake. One can appreciate how such primal metaphors have been useful in piquing the interest of those who control the public coffers, as well as comforting to those observing inexplicable changes in a loved one. However, [...] if such metaphors guide feelings of enmity and fear towards those natural processes, then the war metaphors so prevalent in our culture could be said to demonize our own human susceptibility to ageing processes while personifying those processes as something external of us. (p.586)

It can also be argued that, by presenting dementia as something that changes a patient's mental state, we are losing sight of the fact that the person with dementia is still trying to make sense of the world and to enjoy living in it. Kitwood (1993, 1997) argued that the person with dementia is more than just a patient with a disease – he or she is a rich mixture of many influences. This led him to create the following equation:

$$D = P + B + H + NI + SP$$

where D is the demented patient as they present themselves. This presentation is made up principally of their personality (P), their life experiences up to that point, or biography (B), their physical health (H), their level of neurological impairment from the dementia (NI) and social psychology (SP). These phrases are reasonably self-explanatory except for the last one. 'Social psychology' means what is often termed **malignant social psychology**, where the surroundings the people with dementia finds themselves in are intimidating and strip the person of a sense of personal identity. Anyone who has ever visited a badly run residential home will know instantly what this means. But it is not just the obviously badly run institutions that are at fault. Bullying and sadistic staff are mercifully rare, but just as damaging can be care homes that, whilst consciously doing their best for the residents, strip away dignity and independence by doing everything for the residents, not allowing them any leeway in their behaviours so that things are kept neat and tidy.

The central message of Kitwood's work is that dementia care should be person-centred. A measure of this is **dementia care mapping**, which involves analysing patients with dementia to see how they react to not only their own treatment but also the general activities on the ward.[19] The observations are then fed back in an attempt to amend behaviours to create a better environment. Some behaviours can appear surprisingly trivial. For example, care practitioners are often unaware that things they take for granted, such as chatting to each other as they enter a room or ward, and not greeting or involving patients, can be isolating and upsetting. Dementia care mapping and a person-centred approach to care of people with dementia has a lot of supporters (see Baldwin and Capstick, 2007; Kelly, 2010). However, there have been criticisms of the scoring rationale in the dementia care mapping procedure (Douglass *et al.*, 2010) and validation (Edvardsson and Innes, 2010). There have also been debates about whether Kitwood's concept of 'personhood' is entirely valid (see Dewing, 2008). However, as a practical tool, Kitwood's model has proven very effective in most instances (see Ballard and Aarsland, 2009).

Dementia – a summary

Dementia is a progressive loss of memory, intellectual and linguistic skills, usually accompanied by radical changes in personality and sometimes in motor skills. Symptoms vary markedly between patients, but generally the different dementias are distinguishable by their patterns of development. Several illnesses can be confused with dementia because of a superficial similarity of symptoms, but these can usually be easily identified. At a physical level, dementias often differ in patterns and type of atrophy, but, as has been seen, the correlation between damage and psychological symptoms is far from watertight. Almost all intellectual functions decline in dementia. Although there are some interesting qualitative differences in functioning, it should be noted that these are usually only found in patients in the very early stages of the illness – as the disease progresses, patients usually lack sufficient psychological skills to comprehend or perform the tasks presented to them. It must also be remembered that in dementia, like many other illnesses, it is not only the patient who suffers, and that the disease can be a great source of stress and burden to caregivers.

---

19   More precisely, pairs of observers code patient behaviour every five minutes for six hours, making note of level of well-being and documenting any events that occur in the patients' vicinity.

In closing this section, it is worth noting that the severity and awfulness of dementia's symptoms can lead to an exaggerated view of its prevalence and to views that 'all is lost' if a person develops the disease. It is very important to stress that most people who develop dementia will only experience the early stages of it before they die. And a person who develops dementia is still a person, with rights to dignity, self-worth and enjoyment.

Learning disabilities

Research on learning disabilities in later life[20] is relatively scarce (Holland, 2000) and responsibility for service provision for older adults with learning disabilities is (if you will pardon the phrase) something of a grey area (Benbow, Kingston, Bhaumik *et al.*, 2011). Some specific conditions are already reasonably well documented (e.g. there is a considerable literature on cognitive skills in people with Down syndrome in later life, because of the potential relevance to Alzheimer's disease; for example, McCallion and McCarron, 2004) but others are not. For example, Stuart-Hamilton and Morgan (2011) found that in the previous decade there had been more than 20,000 papers written on autism spectrum disorder; of these, under ten had looked at older people.

Where studies have been conducted, a key finding is that older people with learning difficulties have significantly higher levels of anxiety and depression than the general population (e.g. Cooper, 1997a; Patel, Goldberg and Moss, 1993), a conclusion echoed in subsequent studies (e.g. Smiley, 2005). A note of caution is sounded by Perez-Achiaga, Nelson and Hassiotis (2009). They conducted a review of studies of depression in older adults with learning disabilities, and found that some studies had used diagnostic tools that were fit for purpose,[21] while others were less reliable. This creates a potential problem – if a test is not properly standardised (and thus norms are unknown), there is a danger that a condition will be either under- or over-diagnosed.

An especially worrying point is that many of those identified as having depression were not at the time of testing being treated for it. Patel *et al.* (1993) noted that caregivers had often noted symptoms of depression but had not realised their significance. Within the mainstream older population, depression is known to lower intellectual functioning. In extreme cases this can lead to pseudodementia (Kiloh, 1961), as noted earlier in the chapter. In the case of people with learning disabilities, the effect could be very profound (of interest in this context is a 2004

---

20 This section is on learning disabilities in older people. For the important topic of older parents of adult children with learning disability, see Davys and Haigh (2008).

21 For the record, the two psychometric scales they found best suited were the Reiss Screen for Maladaptive Behaviors (RSMB) (Reiss, 1988), and the Psychiatric Assessment Schedule for Adults with Developmental Disabilities (PAS-ADD) (Moss *et al.*, 1993).

case study by Pollard and Prendergast of a child with autism who presented with pseudodementia). Tsiouris and Patti (1997) conducted a study of pseudodementia in older people with Down syndrome. The paper in question addressed the efficacy of selective serotonin reuptake inhibitors (SSRIs) on depression in people with Down syndrome. The paper noted that, in 4 of 37 cases studied, the individuals in question had pseudodementia (response to the SSRIs differentiated them from the ten people in the sample who had dementia).

In addition to pseudodementia, people with learning disabilities might contract 'true' dementia (Kerr, 2007). It is known that people with Down syndrome have a greatly elevated risk of developing dementia (McCallion and McCarron, 2004). Strydom *et al.* (2009) argued that, in adults over 60 with learning disability but *without* Down syndrome, dementia was between two and three times more prevalent than in the general population. An earlier study by Cooper (1997b) found a four times higher incidence in her sample. Whether all these people have developed 'true' dementia might be questioned. It is possible that some of them have experienced standard senescent decline, but because they already had a low level of cognitive skills this has made them *functionally* resemble patients with dementia. Studies of neuroimaging in older adults with learning difficulties and dementia have so far been somewhat inconclusive (see Gangadharan and Bhaumik, 2006). Whether older people with learning disabilities develop 'true' dementia at a higher rate, or simply come to functionally resemble people with dementia, is for the moment a moot point. However, it has been observed that the behavioural changes in people with learning disabilities diagnosed with dementia are similar to those in people without a learning disability (Duggan, Lewis and Morgan, 1996).

It should also be noted that diagnosis of dementia in people with learning disabilities is difficult. Because a person with learning disabilities is already performing at a low level on cognitive tasks, discriminating between this and a demented state can be problematic (Bell, Turnbull and Kidd, 2009; Nagdee and O'Brien, 2009; Torr, 2009). Although there are measures available to assess dementing change in people with learning disabilities (see Kirk, Hick and Laraway, 2006), many are not necessarily appropriate (see Perkins and Small, 2006) and typically measure functional change. Added to this is the problem that cognitive changes in people with learning disabilities are often discounted or overlooked (Hassiotis *et al.*, 2003).

It should be noted that not everyone with learning disabilities is going to develop depression or dementia. When no problems of great magnitude appear, the evidence points to neurotypical and learning disabled older people experiencing very similar patterns of ageing (Oliver, Adams and Kaisy, 2008).

Depression

Depression[22] is a condition that almost all people experience in a relatively mild form many times in their lives. In most cases, the feeling of melancholy is in reaction to a specific event, disperses in a few days, and would not typically be considered a mental illness. Depression meriting clinical attention is long-lasting, and severe enough to interfere with normal functioning. It is important to stress that clinical depression is not solely 'feeling down' – the patient is in effect incapacitated by the condition. In addition to a depressed mood, he or she is typically lacking in both mental and physical energy to an extreme degree, has irrational feelings of worthlessness and/or guilt, and may have preoccupations with dying and suicide (generally, older patients have a greater preponderance of physical symptoms; Caine et al., 1994). Depression of this magnitude is far less common in later life than in any other age group (Luijendijk et al., 2008). However, there are exceptions – people in institutionalised care,[23] people with dementia and caregivers of people with dementia all have a very elevated risk of developing depression (Woods, 2011). Also, older adults might be less likely to report symptoms of depression (Bryant, 2010). In addition, isolated *symptoms* of depression are far more frequent (Kasl-Godley, Gatz and Fiske, 1998; Smyer and Qualls, 1999; see also Teachman, 2006). The latter finding is probably due to older people being exposed to a higher proportion of depressing events, such as bereavement, painful illness, and so on. It is also worth noting that, although some of the key features of depression experienced by sufferers are reasonably similar across the lifespan (Nolen-Hoeksema and Ahrens, 2002), older depressed people carry the unique risk of developing pseudodementia (see earlier; estimates of the prevalence of pseudodementia vary wildly between studies; however, Kasl-Godley, Gatz and Fiske's estimate of c.11% is a plausible average). This can hamper making an accurate diagnosis (see also Lezak, 1995).

Causes of depression in later life are often attributed (unsurprisingly) to stressful and negative events. For example, bereavement is known to cause depressive symptoms (see Chapter 8), though these in most instances are relatively short-lasting. Sleep disturbance is a known factor in depression, independent of physical illness (Cho et al., 2008). Again, illness and medical treatment side effects can cause or exacerbate depression in some patients (see Sadavoy et al., 1995). Osborn et al. (2003) argued that having two or more physical illnesses increases the risk of developing depression. Penninx et al. (1996) reported that depressive symptoms increase with the number of illnesses from which the patient suffers. In addition, some diseases seem to be more conducive to depression than others: perhaps unsurprisingly, conditions that create chronic pain, such as arthritis, were found to be more likely to be associated

---

22 For the related topic of suicide, see Chapter 8.

23 Contrary to the popular myth that it is the institution that makes people depressed, the available evidence is that most depressed people are depressed *before* they enter a care home or similar (Woods, 2011). This does not mean that institutionalised care necessarily always helps matters, however.

with depression than were serious but less painful conditions such as diabetes.[24] Beekman et al. (1997) argue that an even stronger predictor of depression is level of physical health as opposed to disease; in a similar vein, Palinkas, Wingard and Barrett-Connor (1996) found depression to be significantly greater in obese older people. However, it should be noted that the depression–illness relationship works both ways. For example, a 12-year longitudinal study by Karakus and Patton (2011) demonstrated that, amongst 10–62-year-olds, depression at the start of the study predicted a significantly higher level of illness.

Numerous other factors have been linked with depression. The following list is illustrative of their variety:

• Perceived level of social support (Taylor and Lynch, 2004).

• Financial problems (West, Reed and Gildengorin, 1998).

• Genetic inheritance (Carmelli et al., 2000).

• Perceived level of informal care (Wolff and Agree, 2004).

• Apparent failure or stalling of recovery after an injury (Scaf-Klomp et al., 2003).

• Low level or lack of religious faith (see Braam et al., 1997).

• Increased dependency on others (Anstey et al., 2007).

This variety of causes illustrates that, even allowing for confounding variables, depression can strike for many reasons. It is also important to note that depression can be caused by single or multiple factors. Harris et al. (2003) found that level of disability, health, socio-economic status, feeling of control and social support all were separate predictors of depression. As evidence for more complex effects, Fukukawa et al. (2004) demonstrated that the quality of familial relations could act as a buffer between health problems and depressive symptoms.

There is little age difference in responsivity to treatment, with the majority of both younger and older depressed patients recovering (Kasl-Godley et al., 1998; see also Andreescu et al., 2008), though recurrence of symptoms is higher in late-onset depression (Woods, 2011). Increased exercise also appears to be beneficial to older depressed people (Penninx et al., 2002).

Anxiety

The term 'anxiety', rather like 'depression', is something that most people can understand from their own experience. Practically everyone has at some time felt anxious about a situation they have found themselves in. The level of anxiety

---

24 Type II diabetes does not increase the risk of depression once confounding variables are accounted for (Brown et al., 2006).

experienced by a person seeking clinical treatment is far greater than this, and is often identified by the term **anxiety disorder**. This refers to a long-lasting state of anxiety characterised by symptoms such as extreme restlessness, insomnia and fatigue, producing distress and impairment of function. It can manifest itself in many forms, including **phobias** (an irrational or inappropriately high fear of an item or event, such as open spaces, spiders, and so on), **generalised anxiety** (according to Wetherell, Le Roux and Gatz, 2003, characterised in older adults by a perpetual or frequent feeling of uncontrollable anxiety, sleep disturbance, and muscle rigidity; see also Chou, 2009), **obsessive-compulsive disorder** (a condition in which to relieve anxiety feelings the patient is compelled to repeat the same act, e.g. repeatedly washing the hands to remove anxiety-invoking dirt, and so on; see Gupta, Austin and Black's 1997 case study of a 93-year-old patient), and **panic disorder** (characterised by repeated **panic attacks** – sudden attacks of overwhelming apprehension, shortness of breath, feeling of loss of control, and so on).

Anxiety is relatively rare in older adults in comparison with the younger population (Smyer and Qualls, 1999), but this does not mean it is not a cause for concern, since within any one age group it is one of the most common mental illnesses (Scogin, 1998), and is often found in tandem with depression (e.g. Flint and Rifat, 1997; though note anxiety symptoms are generally more stable than depression [see Wetherell, Gatz and Pedersen, 2001] and dementia [see Scogin, 1998]). It is also possible that older adults under-report symptoms of anxiety (Bryant, 2010).

Researchers are generally agreed that about 10 per cent of older adults report some form of anxiety disorder, the majority of these being a phobia (Lindesay *et al.*, 1989; Cohen *et al.*, 2006; Woods, 1999). Of the phobias, a commonly reported one is **agoraphobia** (fear of open spaces), which tends to be conflated with a more specific fear of 'leaving the house'. Other commonly reported sources of concern include falling, dying and social situations (see Woods, 1999). These can undoubtedly be sources of anxiety, but one cannot help feeling that calling them 'phobias' may be perhaps a little harsh, since they are palpably more rational than more stereotypical phobias. For example, an often-cited paradox is that older people are the least likely victims of crime but are the age group that most fear crime. Therefore, does this mean that older people are being illogical in fearing crime or in not going out for fear of being mugged? Statistically, the answer to this simplistic interpretation must be 'yes'. However, as Woods (1999) and others have observed, this statistic applies to crimes overall, and for certain types of misdemeanour older people are not much less at risk. The most plausible explanation is that a phobia may arise because a heightened level of anxiety 'fixes' onto a tangible and rational topic of concern.

Perversely enough, a little anxiety can be advantageous under certain circumstances. Bierman *et al.* (2008) found an inverted U relationship between anxiety and cognitive performance in older people. In other words, participants with relatively mild levels of anxiety did better (and within this group the higher the anxiety, the better the cognitive test score) but those with relatively high levels did worse (and within *this* group the higher the anxiety, the worse the cognitive test score).

Substance abuse

The term 'substance abuse' refers to the use of either illegal substances or licit substances with an addictive quality (such as alcohol) in excessive quantities to the point where everyday functioning is severely affected. The stereotype of older people militates against an image of them as addicts, but health authorities are becoming increasingly concerned at the prospect of a significant proportion of older adults suffering from one or more addictive behaviours (Blow and Oslin, 2003; Stewart and Oslin, 2001). Often in the past health care providers were arguably under-trained to recognise and deal with these problems (see Finlayson, 1995; Schonfeld *et al.*, 1993).

The idea of 'addiction' immediately brings to mind alcohol and drug abuse, but it can also include gambling. In the USA in particular, casinos are widespread and offer not only gambling but a social experience, with organised visits (often sponsored or encouraged by the casinos; see McNeilly and Burke, 2001) by seniors groups a common feature. This means that gambling presents both an attractive and an unattractive face. On the negative side, McNeilly and Burke (2002) report case studies of older adults who had developed gambling problems. A slightly more recent study found that circa 3 per cent of older American adults are gambling at a level probably meriting treatment (Wiebe and Cox, 2005). Also, the more available gambling is, the greater the risk that an older person will develop a gambling habit that places them at least in the at-risk (of developing an addiction) category (Preston, Shapiro and Keene, 2007).[25] However, on the positive side, researchers have reported that, for some older individuals, participating in gambling (visits to casinos, etc.) is a key social activity with no notably negative effects (e.g. Hope and Havir, 2002; Vander Bilt *et al.*, 2004). Stitt, Giacopassi and Nichols (2003) also concur that gambling appears on the whole to have little negative effect on older people in general. However, it is easy to overlook that the social side of gambling, like other addictive behaviours such as alcohol consumption, can mask a serious problem. A study by Southwell, Boreham and Laffan (2008) of electronic gaming machine use in licensed gambling venues in Queensland, Australia, found that older people used the clubs as a social meeting place. Many had no partner and had physical disabilities. However, 27 per cent of those interviewed said that they had drawn on savings to fund their gambling, and the group as a whole had a low annual income. It does not help matters that older adults with mild cognitive impairment are very poor at making risk judgements in gambling tasks (Zamarian, Weiss and Delazer, 2011).

---

25 Preston *et al.* (2007) studied a group of people who had retired to Las Vegas – not perhaps the wisest of moves if one wishes to avoid gambling.

Even someone with very egalitarian views of ageing would find it hard to imagine older people using psychoactive drugs, but in fact they are heavy consumers of (legitimately prescribed) hypnotic (i.e. sleep inducing) and sedative drugs. Simoni-Wastila and Yang (2006) estimated that 1 in 4 older Americans take drugs that could (at least in theory) be abused and that about 11 per cent actually do so. Misuse (accidental or deliberate) of these drugs is one of the most common causes of admission to the casualty department/emergency room of a US hospital (Midlov, Eriksson and Kragh, 2009). In many instances, the reason for this is that the ageing body cannot adequately metabolise the drug in question even when on the dosage schedule prescribed by the doctor, leading to serious health problems, such as delirium (Midlov *et al.*, 2009). However, an appreciable proportion of older adults are taking prescription sedatives and similar, and have become dependent on them (e.g. Gomberg and Zucker, 1998; Midlov *et al.*, 2009). The problem is exacerbated by the fact that patients may be unaware of the risks associated with many psychoactive drugs, reasoning that, if a medical professional has prescribed them, then 'they must be all right', and thus, deterioration in, for example, alertness and cognitive abilities is ignored.

Ironically, in many instances the drugs should probably never have been prescribed in the first place. For example, a study by Avorn *et al.* (1992) demonstrated that the proportion of residential older adults on psychotropic drugs could be drastically reduced without any effect on behaviour or psychological symptoms. McGrath and Jackson (1996) found that 88 per cent of older residents with behavioural problems were being inappropriately prescribed **neuroleptic drugs** (in effect, major tranquillisers). This is of concern not only because use of a 'chemical cosh' is a morally dubious method of controlling undesirable behaviour but also because neuroleptic drugs may lower cognitive functioning (Brown, Chobor and Zinn, 1993) or, in the case of patients with dementia, accelerate the rate of decline (McShane *et al.*, 1997). Although the precise rate of over-prescribing of such drugs can be questioned and may not be applicable across all settings, nonetheless *any* mis-prescribing of this type is a cause for concern. Alas, more recent studies (Fahey *et al.*, 2003; Gallagher, Barry and O'Mahony, 2007) demonstrate that, in the UK as well as the rest of Europe and the USA, poor prescribing is still taking place for older adults in both residential and community settings.

However, drug use in older adults is not simply confined to misuse of legal drugs, but involves use of illicit drugs as well. Whilst absolute numbers are not on a par with young adults, nonetheless older drug addicts can be found (see Rosenberg, 1997). It might be intuitively assumed that older addicts form a rump of younger adults who through some medical miracle have survived into old age. Certainly there are such people, and the available evidence suggests that those who have used drugs throughout their lives will not give up their habit with any ease. The concept that older people grow out of drug habits is very wide of the mark (Chait, Fahmy and Caceres, 2010). For example, Levy and Anderson (2005) found that the older drug users they studied (aged 50–68 years) would only give up use of illicit injection drugs for two things – serious illness or death. Given that long-term drug abuse is associated with a hugely increased risk of early death at worst, and serious physical and mental health problems at best (Chait et al., 2010; Hser et al., 2001), this is an eventuality likely to happen sooner than is desirable. In addition, such behaviour is likely to lead to imprisonment, either for drug use or for crimes committed to pay for the habit. Arndt, Turvey and Flaum (2002), in a study of US prison inmates, found that 71 per cent of older (defined here as 55 years and over) prisoners had a substance abuse problem (drugs and/or alcohol) and a third had never received any treatment at all for it. Those older drug users who avoid prison may nonetheless find themselves marginalised by the drug-using community, which is predominantly composed of much younger adults (Anderson and Levy, 2003). This problem is likely to get worse. The ageing 'baby boomer' generation will bring with it a higher amount of drug abuse, not only because of an increase in absolute numbers but also because, amongst drug users of that cohort, abuse has not abated as has been the case with earlier generations (Johnson and Sung, 2009). Gfroerer et al. (2003) estimated that, in the USA alone, the number of older adults requiring treatment for substance abuse will rise from the 2001 figure of 1.7 million to 4.4 million by 2020. Using more recent data, Han, Gfroerer, Colliver and Penne (2009) raised the projected figure to 5.7 million.[26] The attendant health issues (including a raised danger of contracting HIV/AIDS) present health care services with a new range of problems for the future (see Topolski et al., 2002). However, a recent study by Kerfoot, Petrakis and Rosenheck (2011) found that treatment for substance abuse declined with age, though the authors acknowledged that the condition could be under-diagnosed in older adults.

It is also worth noting that not all drug habits start in youth. For example, a study by Lofwall et al. (2005) found that the older drug users in their study (a group of 41 adults aged 50–66 years) had begun using opioid drugs later in life. But this is probably not a case of middle-aged adults suddenly succumbing after a lifetime of drug-free living. Lofwall et al. found that the participants had a prior history of other forms of substance abuse and psychiatric problems. Roe et al. (2010) reported similar findings, noting that early deaths of friends and family members (leading to isolation) were contributory factors in some cases. Roe et al. also noted that there was no single gateway drug that seemed to have led older adults into abuse. Research by Rosen (2004) explains the likely course of events. His study found that amongst older (aged over 50) methadone users there was a willingness to try other illicit drugs if they were available within their social network. Accordingly, one addictive behaviour can lead to another. There is also a racial difference in some cultures. Vogt Yuan (2011) reports that in young adulthood white Americans are more likely to take drugs than black Americans. However, in later adulthood, black Americans catch

---

26   Based on an annual average of 2.8 million illicit drug users aged 50+ in 2002–06.

up in their usage. This is explained as being due to white Americans getting more opportunities to make the transition into more responsible high-status social roles. Black Americans, being probabilistically less likely to be afforded this opportunity, are more likely to display behaviour that deviates from social norms.

Another common form of substance abuse is excessive alcohol consumption. Generally, it is assumed that alcohol consumption declines in later life. In part this may be explained by the macabre argument that heavier drinkers are likely to die before they reach old age, either through the effects of alcohol or because they have tended to lead unhealthier lives (see Fillmore et al., 1998; Leino et al., 1998), thereby accounting for at least some of these statistics. Gilhooly (2005) has further argued that much of our knowledge of changes in drinking across the lifespan are based on cross-sectional studies, and it is possible that a cohort effect accounts for the observed 'decline' in drinking – quite simply, older cohorts have always drunk less and thus it coincidentally appears that as people get older they consume less alcohol. A careful analysis of evidence across three countries (the UK, the USA and the Netherlands) indicated that drinking does seem to decline as people get older, but there are also cohort effects. As Gilhooly notes, this is potentially a serious problem because the 'baby boomer' generation, who have been relatively heavy drinkers, may lack the prudence to lower their alcohol levels as much as is medically desirable, thereby creating problems, not least of which is the added burden on health care services.

However, regardless of the rate of change, it is estimated that circa 5 per cent of older American adults living independently have an alcohol problem (Emlet, Hawks and Callahan, 2001; Stoddard and Thompson, 1996). Hajat et al. (2004) report similar data for UK older adults (c.5% of men[27] and c.2.5% of older women). Stoddard and Thompson found that over-drinking appears to be prompted by feelings of loneliness, underpinned by numerous factors encompassing (perhaps not surprisingly) negative life events, health problems, and similar. In Hajat et al.'s UK study, however, the over-drinkers were generally people who were financially secure (i.e. could afford to buy alcohol) and tended to have more active social lives.[28] St John, Montgomery and Tyas (2009) found that alcohol misuse was correlated with depressive symptoms and poor functional status (i.e. problems with performing everyday activities).

DeHart and Hoffmann (1995) and O'Connell et al. (2003) note the problems in identifying alcohol problems in older adults. Many of the current diagnostic measures are designed for younger adults, since in general the research literature has

---

27   The average older man's frequency of alcohol consumption in the UK is almost on a par with younger adults' (Hallgren, Hogberg and Andreasson, 2010).

28   Before too much is made of this comparison, it is perhaps worth noting that like may not be being compared with like (and different methods of measuring alcohol consumption may not tally with each other, especially in cases of over-drinking; see Wilcox and King, 2000). For further discussion of national differences in alcohol use, see Blay et al. (2009); Castro-Costa et al. (2008); Du, Scheidt-Nave and Kopf (2008); Haarni and Hautamaki (2010); Popova et al. (2007).

assumed that over-drinking is largely a younger person's problem – one has only to consider the current preoccupation of health authorities with binge drinking in teenagers and 20-somethings to appreciate this. O'Connell *et al.* argue that current screening methods may under-estimate the level of the problem in older people. DeHart and Hoffmann also note that alcohol abuse may be linked with a myriad of health problems in older adults (see Stoddard and Thompson's findings earlier), and this also makes a simple identification of likely precursors of increased drinking problematic. Similarly, measuring the effects on health of cutting down alcohol consumption in older problem drinkers is made difficult by confounding variables (see Sinforiani, Zucchella, Pasotti *et al.*, 2011).

In general, studies find that older men are more prone to alcohol abuse than women (e.g. Graham *et al.*, 1996; Hajat *et al.*, 2004; Hallgren, Hogberg and Andreasson, 2010). Emlet *et al.* (2001) found that men were three times more likely to drink than women. Note however that precise figures can vary between studies (e.g. Hajat *et al.* found that men were 'only' twice as likely), depending upon the particular culture tested and measurement method used, and may also to some extent be dependent on cohort effects.

Regardless of what percentage of the population have a problem with alcohol, the health risks for alcoholics and heavy drinkers are greater (O'Connell *et al.*, 2003; Weyerer *et al.*, 2009). However, there is a danger that a 'killjoy' attitude can be extrapolated from this, implying that *all* alcohol consumption must have a negative effect in older people. In fact, when drinking variables are controlled for, older adults have fewer behavioural problems than younger drinkers (Livingston and Room, 2009). In many instances, the association between alcohol consumption and illness and injury in later life is not clear-cut (Reid *et al.*, 2002). Indeed, it appears that alcohol consumption can be beneficial for health. McCaul *et al.* (2010) conducted a ten-year longitudinal study and found that moderate daily alcohol intake (up to 4 units/day for men, 2 for women) significantly lowered the mortality risk compared with people who did not drink every week. However, it should be noted that those individuals who regularly drank, but abstained from alcohol for one or two days a week, had even better mortality rates. This raises the possibility that it is having a relaxed happy lifestyle that matters rather than consuming alcohol *per se*. There is some evidence that, for people in their fifties, alcohol consumption is associated with a slower decline in memory for the men and a significant worsening of psychomotor skills in the women (Richards, Hardy and Wadsworth, 2005). However, later research has claimed that moderate alcohol consumption does not protect from cognitive decline in later life (Cooper *et al.*, 2009).

Before leaving this section, it is perhaps worth inserting a reality check. Although substance abuse problems are a serious matter and are undoubtedly growing, they still affect only a small minority of older adults. This should not lessen our level of concern for these people, but it is also worth noting that, amongst healthy older adults, substance abuse is at its lowest for any adult age group (Satre *et al.*, 2004).

Personality disorder

Whilst it has been seen in Chapter 5 that there are a wide variety of personality types that can legitimately be seen as of equal value, there are nonetheless some patterns of behaviour that are sufficiently extreme and at odds with societal norms to cause distress to the patient and/or those whom he or she comes into contact with. It is important to note that these personalities go beyond the bounds of what might be considered 'eccentric' but nonetheless tolerable behaviour. The incidence of personality disorder is believed to be low in later life, but there is a danger that clinicians are willing to overlook patterns of behaviour that would be considered unusual in a younger person because of different expectations about how older adults 'should' behave. Certainly there is a lower tendency for older adults to be diagnosed as having a personality disorder (Rayburn and Stonecypher, 1996). Amongst the types of personality disorder most commonly described in the literature from the UK and USA (see Smyer and Qualls, 1999) are the *avoidant* (low self-image and avoidant of company) and *dependent* (over-willingness to let others decide everything). Since these concur with the stereotype of the retiring older person, it is conceivable that they could be falsely identified as 'normal' behaviour. Again, Sadavoy (1996) argues that personality disorders could be masked by other behaviours associated with other mental or even physical illnesses. Because of considerations such as these, the true level of personality disorder may be higher than has been supposed (see reviews by Abrams and Horowitz, 1996; Oltmanns and Balsis, 2011). However, the level is felt to be particularly high in patients with depression (see Abrams *et al.*, 1998), and personality disorder is significantly correlated with acts of self-harm in older people (Ritchie *et al.*, 2011). Note that there are possible cultural differences in the relative frequency of these disorders. For example, some Croatian researchers reported the highest prevalence in their country was for sadistic and antisocial disorders in men, and self-defeating, borderline and schizotypal disorders in women (Mandic and Barkic, 1996).

Schizophrenia

The final illness to be considered in this chapter is **schizophrenia**. The term means 'cloven mind' in the sense of a broken or fragmented self, rather than the popular misconception of a 'split personality'. In essence, it is a profound disorder of thought, perception and language in the absence of intellectual disability, characterised by a severe distortion of perception of reality and concomitant changes in emotions and behaviour. There are various forms of the illness, each with a distinct set of symptoms. The most common of these symptoms include irrational beliefs about the way the world functions, often with a central theme that the patient is being persecuted. There may also be hallucinations (such as 'voices in the head'). Language can often be best described as 'surreal', with unusual expressions and ideas, and invented words (see Stuart-Hamilton, 1999a).

Most commonly, schizophrenia first appears in early adulthood (**early onset schizophrenia**, or **EOS**), but about a quarter of cases arise in middle age or later (**late onset schizophrenia**, or **LOS**),[29] and some studies have estimated that about a tenth of schizophrenic patients first show symptoms in their sixties or older (see e.g. Bartels and Mueser, 1999; Karon and VandenBos, 1998). Thus, older schizophrenic patients can be divided into EOS and LOS groups, depending upon the length of time they have had the illness. It would be misleading to create the impression that LOS suddenly appears without warning. Studies often report that LOS patients have led fairly reclusive, undemanding lives, with few social contacts. They have typically been protected either consciously or tacitly by parents or friends, and it is often the death or incapacitation of the latter that precipitates the onset of the illness (see Quin et al., 2009). In other words, LOS may have been an illness waiting to happen.

Straightforward comparisons of these groups are not always easy, however. For example, because EOS patients have received radically different treatments for their illness than LOS patients, there may be a strong cohort effect. Again, the age at which patients are first introduced to antipsychotic drugs appears to have an effect, with older patients reporting significantly more adverse reactions (though these can be ameliorated; see Bartels and Mueser, 1999). There would appear to be little difference in the symptoms found in EOS and LOS (Lacro, Harris and Jeste, 1995; Reicher-Roessler et al., 1997; Sponheim et al., 2010), although some EOS–LOS differences have been identified in such measures as EEG patterns in response to auditory stimuli (Olichney et al., 1998). It has also been noted that a disproportionate number of schizophrenic patients develop dementia or at least dementing symptoms (see Arnold and Trojanowski, 1996). However, after some early histological studies supporting a link, more recent work has failed to find DAT-like atrophy in the brains of older schizophrenic patients (Arnold et al., 1998; Purohit et al., 1998). Notwithstanding these comments, the prognosis for treating patients with either form of the illness is reasonably optimistic (Karon and VandenBos, 1998), though there might be fewer resources available for treating LOS patients (Mitford et al., 2010).

Overview

It should be recalled that mental illness in older adults is often lower than for the population as a whole. The problems faced by older patients can of course be grave, but, in many instances, evidence points to these not being appreciably worse in themselves than those faced by younger patients with the same illnesses. Of course, contracting a mental illness in later life does not absolve the patient from becoming ill with common age-related physical complaints such as arthritis or hearing impairment, and of course it may be anticipated that these will exacerbate the problem.

---

29 Some researchers reserve the label of LOS for cases beginning between 40 and 59 years, with cases older than this being labeled very late onset schizophrenia-like psychosis.

Suggested further reading

Woods (1999, 2011) provides an excellent introduction to this area. So do Smyer and Qualls (1999) and Nordhus *et al.* (1998). Lezak's *Neuropsychological Assessment* (Lezak, 1995) is a vast and comprehensive review of its subject. *Dementia UK* (Alzheimer's Society, 2007) is a good general guide to the prevalence of the dementias and their financial and care costs in the UK. A good general introduction to dementia for the layperson is Graham and Warner (2009). A very useful guide to MCI and CIND is provided by Chertkow, Massoud and Nasreddine (2009). There is a good guide to developmental disability and ageing by O'Brien and Rosenbloom (2009). Tallis and Fillit (2003) is an embarrassment of riches on all matters connected with mental illness in later life as well as physical health. However, some chapters are perhaps a little 'technical' for some readers. More accessible perhaps is Manthorpe and Iliffe's (2005) book on depression in later life, which also takes a more applied approach that some readers may find useful. Leentjens and van der Mast (2005) provide a useful overview of studies of delirium. Stuart-Hamilton (1999a) provides an overview of mental illnesses, their classification and treatment.

CHAPTER 7

Problems in Measuring the Psychological Status of Older People

Introduction

This book attempts to introduce the psychology of ageing from what might be reasonably described as a consensus mainstream viewpoint. But there are other ways of looking at the subject. For example, approaching the topic from a completely different angle and set of research traditions, Calasanti (2004) makes a case for feminist gerontology. For those readers with a degree-level background in psychology, Dixon, Backman and Nilsson's (2004) volume exploring potential new directions in cognitive ageing research will be of great interest. Also, the upsurge of interest in relating brain scans to psychological functioning (see Chapter 2) is likely to result in an explosion of interest in gerontological neuropsychology and molecular psychology[1] and psychiatry (see Licinio, 2009).

However, for the moment, the topics covered in this book arguably constitute the majority research activity in the psychology of ageing. The research that has taken place is not immune to criticism, as has been seen. But the criticisms offered in earlier chapters have largely concerned specific theories and models rather than the subject as a whole. What has not been addressed so far in any detail are criticisms of some of the general assumptions and methodologies that span multiple topics within the psychology of ageing. In this chapter, we shall consider some of these broader considerations. This is not intended to be an exhaustive commentary, but simply to stimulate the reader, who, having acquired the basic facts, must now begin to look at the subject critically for themselves.

---

1   An older subject than most people realise. The first general guide to the subject this author could find is Franklin (1987).

Confounding variables and the search for 'pure' ageing

Research on ageing is predicated on the assumption that we can measure something called 'pure' ageing. It is essentially the belief that, after cohort effects have been accounted for, any age difference left 'must' be due to ageing alone. Researchers rarely state this explicitly, but it is at least tacit in most arguments. In Chapter 2 it was noted that, to a certain extent, age differences on fluid and crystallised intelligence tests depend upon the test methods used. Fluid intelligence test performance, for example, is partly governed by the speed at which a person can write down their answers. Older people, because of arthritis, rheumatism and similar conditions, generally write less quickly, and this can affect how many answers they can produce in a paper-and-pencil test against the clock. In short, test artifacts may be under-estimating the true mental state of an older person. Conversely, the absence of age differences in crystallised tests may be due to the reverse reason – namely, that tests are generally untimed and that, were time limits imposed, an age difference would display itself.

Writing speed and issues about whether a test should be timed or not are far from the only issues shaping age differences. Simply reading from a pile of journal abstracts to hand on the author's desk,[2] the following potential confounding variables may be identified: level of education (Anstey, Stankov and Lord, 1993; Christensen, Hendersen et al., 1997; Christensen, Korten et al., 1997; Compton, Bachman and Logan, 1997; Jones and Gallo, 2002), genetic inheritance (Deary et al., 2004a; McGue and Christensen, 2001), general health (Horn, 1982; Riegel and Riegel, 1972), level of exercise (Powell, 1974), level of motivation (Bauer, 1966), degree to which skills are practised (Charness, 1979, 1981; Milne, 1956; Plemons et al., 1978), sensory functioning (Lindenberger and Baltes, 1994), quality of social networks (Holtzman et al., 2004) and socio-economic status (Rundinger and Lantermann, 1980). This list is just the tip of the iceberg: a very long list of possible confounding variables can be devised by a person with the time and will to do it. Note that it is not necessarily the case that all these items are of equal importance, but the sheer magnitude of the list makes it likely that a significant proportion of the difference between older and younger adults may be due to cohort effects rather than 'pure' ageing.

Salthouse (1991b), in a meta-analysis of the ageing literature, found that removing health or education level lessened, but did not remove, age differences. However, with the greatest respect to Salthouse, who is a scrupulous researcher, these are just two variables from a potential list of hundreds. What if, instead of two variables, a larger number were chosen? In theory, we could decide to measure what is left of an age difference after 5, 10, 20 or 100 confounding variables are accounted for. There is no 'law' to stop researchers doing this. We could, for example,

---

2   This sentence was from an earlier edition and describes what was on my desk in 2005; a similar collection today would have more up-to-date publications (contrary to what my family and colleagues think, I do occasionally tidy my desk) but the point would be exactly the same.

continue to add in more confounding variables until an age difference completely disappeared. Statistically speaking, this would be a dubious practice, but the point is that we really have no clear grounds for knowing what constitutes a valid cohort effect that should be accounted for, and what constitutes an invalid one. Consider the following example.

Suppose that it is decided to control for effects of cardiovascular disease, since it is plausible that people with heart and circulation problems may perform less well on intellectual tasks. Thus, patients with these conditions are excluded from the experiment. However, why stick at cardiovascular problems? Why not also exclude people with arthritis, or rheumatism, or cancer? All these conditions could plausibly influence intellectual performance. Taking this policy to extremes, one would finish with a sample consisting solely of 'A1' fit older adults. This may satisfy the criteria to exclude any illness-based cohort effects, but it would be hopelessly unrepresentative of the older population (see Stuart-Hamilton, 1995). And this is solely considering health. What if we now also decide to balance older and younger adults on education levels? Older adults generally received fewer years' education. Therefore, this should be controlled for. However, how do we now control for differences in the type of education received? Older adults tended to receive rather more rigid forms of teaching with greater emphasis on rote learning, and many older adults (in the UK at least) received greater training in practical skills, such as needlework and woodwork, than younger people. How is this controlled for?

Clearly it is impossible to control for all possible confounding variables. Inevitably, some will have to be left in the analysis, and they will inevitably contaminate the data to a greater or lesser extent. As can be seen by a perusal of gerontology journals, many researchers do not even bother to start correcting for possible cohort effects; others only control for one or two. This might not matter if all researchers drew their volunteers from the same group of people, since in that case comparisons between experiments would be based upon a common ground. However, the people upon whom the tests are conducted vary enormously. To take an example of this, the author chose a single edition of a psychology of ageing journal[3] and recorded the way in which volunteers were recruited for studies of non-dementing ageing. Two of the papers gave insufficient details, but the remainder listed the following: newspaper advertisements in New York; newspaper adverts in Canada, plus 'various community organisations'; advertisements in the media; advertisement in senior centres and senior apartment complexes; members of an older volunteer pool maintained by the university in question; people originally recruited in a 1960s national survey; local volunteer groups; a sample of those aged over 70 on the electoral roll in part of Australia; and healthy community resident volunteers. The level of screening for other conditions (particularly health, which was often left to self-report) was

3   If memory serves correctly, this was a publication from 2000. I have repeated this exercise with randomly chosen publications on several occasions in student seminars, with very similar results.

extremely variable, from a rigorous exclusion of anyone not 'A1' fit to no real barriers to participation. It takes little contemplation to realise that the list of participants in these studies could potentially be enormously different. Some studies will have physically healthier participants than others, some will have people from higher socio-economic groupings, and so forth.

It might be argued that this argument is unnecessarily pedantic. However, as has been demonstrated throughout the previous chapters, variability increases considerably in later life, and any practices that are enhancing this variability and blocking sensible direct comparisons between studies are doing little to clear the picture. Added to this is the further problem that, when younger adults are included for comparison purposes, studies nearly always use students recruited from undergraduate participation pools. Given that older people are almost certainly being recruited from a much broader intellectual base (i.e. the undergraduates are almost bound to be smarter on average, since not all the older participants will have studied for a degree), and will have different motivations for participating (e.g. the desire to participate in research as opposed to doing a boring task in order to get a degree), any comparisons between older and younger adults are coloured right from the start.

Given such criticisms, it is readily apparent that any experiment on older adults is bound to contain at least some cohort effects. However, something might be done to control the most striking of these. This would involve establishing a benchmark measure of controls that all researchers would agree to abide by (similar controls exist in other sciences to great effect). This would consist of controlling for at least the most often-cited variables (education, general health, etc.), recruiting participants in a set manner (i.e. everyone agrees to recruit in the same way), and pragmatically accepting that inevitably some confounding variables will be left, so that some 'noise' will remain in the data. Regrettably, there is no 'industry standard' set of such variables that all researchers are expected to use (see Stuart-Hamilton, 1995). Thus, different researchers are left free to have different policies, as has been seen, and this makes judgements about the true size of age differences very difficult to determine (Stuart-Hamilton, 1995, 1999b).

This argument is predicated on the assumption that a measure of 'pure' ageing is submerged beneath the cohort effects, and, furthermore, that this measure is useful. However, this in turn is debatable, and the following counter-argument might be proposed. A measure of 'pure' ageing is often tacitly assumed, but rarely explicitly explored. However, since cohort effects are removed by researchers in order to get a 'more accurate' view of ageing, it may be assumed that 'pure ageing' is a measure of ageing that is free of the influences of upbringing. In short, this is the nature–nurture debate, so beloved of individual differences researchers, being played out on a new field: pure ageing is nature, cohort effects are nurture (Stuart-Hamilton, 1999a). However, it is difficult if not impossible to see how intellectual development could occur if it were totally free of influences of upbringing and social interaction: *in extremis*, it is like arguing that only a person raised in an isolation tank can experience pure ageing. Most intellectual skills shown in later life occur *because* of these, not *in spite* of them (see Pratt and Norris, 1994). Cohort effects may thus be more than just inconveniences that distort the 'true' results – they could be part and parcel of an older person's intellect to the extent that they cannot be removed without denying part of that person's intellectual status. It may thus be argued that each age cohort is inevitably different, and, if part of the difference is due to differences in upbringing, then so be it. This also throws into question the attempts to control confounding variable noise in longitudinal studies of change (see Chapter 2). In the attempt to remove practice effects, drop-out effects and similar, there is a danger that ageing features unique to each cohort might also be removed in the process. As stated in Chapter 2, the fact that finding an ageing effect is now seemingly as much reliant on the specific statistical technique used as on the data itself, we might be wise to be healthily sceptical about some of the claims being made.

Taking all these arguments into account, we are thus left with only one certain statement: older people tend to be worse at intelligence tests. However, the degree to which this is a reflection of 'pure' ageing is left open for debate – as is what we mean by 'pure' ageing.

The relevance of findings to everyday life

A further problem for ageing research is that it is often at odds with everyday life. Throughout this book, psychological tests (and intelligence tests in particular) have been presented as if they were 'pure' measures of intellectual skills. If this is so, then one would logically expect psychological tests to correlate well with abilities in everyday skills. For example, intelligence test scores should be excellent predictors of scholastic ability, job status, ability at chosen job, and so on. However, this is not the case. An old psychological chestnut is that the best correlation ever found between IQ and a real-life measure was 0.7. The real-life measure was the number of real (as opposed to false) teeth possessed by the participants. Usually, IQ tests are poor predictors of real-life performance – correlations are usually of the order of 0.2–0.3: in other words, about 10 per cent at best of the variance on the real-life measure is predicted by IQ. This is not to say that intelligence tests are useless. Even their detractors acknowledge that they are good at identifying extremes of ability. Thus, IQ tests can identify the exceptionally intellectually gifted and deprived (though it can also be argued that one really does not need an IQ test to do this). What intelligence tests cannot do with any real accuracy is identify performance of people between the extremes (i.e. the majority). This raises an uncomfortable question for psychogerontology: if intelligence tests are not an accurate reflection of everyday skills, then of what value is the bulk of work on ageing intellectual changes?

Salthouse (see Chapter 2) provides one answer to this question: namely that, although intelligence is a poor predictor of absolute ability, it is vital as a control process. This may be so, but one might wonder why psychologists have indulged in so much research on measures that have at best only a minor relevance to everyday life. An uncharitable view might be that, although IQ tests are poor predictors, they are still the best measure available and thus they continue to be used, until, to quote the song, 'the real thing comes along'. By this reckoning, the psychology of ageing is very well versed in what happens to 10 per cent of older people's intelligence, but, like the iceberg, 90 per cent of it remains hidden. This is too severe a judgement, however. At a *general* level, IQ tests are probably perfectly adequate indicators of intellectual change. Throughout this book, it can be seen that changes in specific memory, linguistic and intellectual skills are correlated with a decline in intelligence test performance. Admittedly, the correlations have often been small, but nonetheless they are statistically significant and have fallen in the expected direction. For example, there have been no instances where overall the older people have got higher fluid intelligence scores than younger participants, or where memory has improved the lower the intelligence test score of the participant. IQ tests are quite adequate – indeed they are remarkably consistent – at predicting *trends*.

It would be unfair to blame psychogerontology for this failure to find the IQ test of more than general descriptive use. The problem is one that has beset **psychometrics** (the study of psychological differences) since its inception. What is at stake is convenience. In an ideal psychometric world, participants could take a single IQ test, and this score would perfectly predict their ability on any intellectual task they could ever encounter. A single test score would thus tell one all one needed to know about a person's intellectual abilities. Unfortunately for psychometricians, this test does not exist, and it is virtually impossible that one could ever be devised. The reason for this is that psychological research has shown that intellectual skills are not determined by a single factor, but rather by several intellectual skills, each of which is at least partly autonomous of the others. The general intelligence test is really only an expression of the aggregate of performance on all these sub-skills, and hence can only hope to give an overall impression of an individual's abilities.

The situation is akin to predicting the performance of a football team. A team consists of different players with different specialist abilities. A league table gives an overall gauge of how good a particular team is, by showing its position relative to other teams. However, league position tells one little about the abilities of individual players in the team. Of course, good teams will tend to have better players than bad teams, but this is not an inevitable rule. For example, a particular side might have the best forward in the history of the game, but the side may be languishing at the bottom of the league table because the rest of the team is poor. In a similar manner, the overall score on an IQ test can give an indication of the overall intellectual performance of an individual, but it cannot accurately predict how well a person will perform a specific task. Nor can it be said that measures of sub-skills are necessarily more informative. There is a double bind in psychometrics, which is as follows. General intelligence measures are poor predictors of everyday skills. Measures of sub-skills give better predictions, because they assess abilities that are more akin to those used in 'real life'. However, there is a danger that the tests of sub-skills may be so like real-life problems that one might as well cut out the middle man and use the real-life ability as a measure. Thus, at one extreme a measure fails because it is too general, whilst at the other it flounders because it is too specific.

A further criticism of lack of realism comes from the observation made in Chapter 2 that the difference between younger and older adults on many intelligence tests amounts to nearly two standard deviations. Readers with a background in education research will recognise this as a very meaningful figure, since, in the case of children, performing at two standard deviations below average would mark a child down as potentially in need of remedial (or 'special') education. If the way older people perform on intelligence tests is genuinely indicative of the way they behave in everyday life, then a large proportion of older adults should be on a par or worse than younger adults or children unfortunate enough to fall within the 'special needs' bracket. Clearly this is not the case. However, the (on paper) similarities between older adults and learning disabled children do not excite comment in the mainstream literature. In part this is because the measures simply do not equate with everyday experience. Older adults in 'real life' palpably do not behave like children with learning disabilities, because, even if some laboratory test performances are in decline, other cognitive skills are not as badly affected by ageing, and, in addition, presumably compensatory strategies also play a role. However, it is nonetheless curious that psychology of ageing research pays such little attention to developmental psychology in general.

Consider the following argument. If we were to invent the psychology of ageing today, whom would we ask from amongst existing psychologists to do the research? The answer would surely be the developmental psychologists. They are, after all, the researchers with greatest expertise in examining development and change across time. Surely the last thing anyone would do is give the task to cognitive psychologists, who are generally interested in the workings of mental models, and to whom change within the individual is typically a confounding variable to be partialled out of the analysis. And yet, perversely enough, the psychology of ageing seems to have largely arisen from the research interests of cognitive psychologists and a handful of psychometricians. An admirable and well-written book, *A History of Geropsychology in Autobiography* (Birren and Schroots, 2000) provides information on the careers of the first generation of psychogerontologists who became active in the 1940s through to the 1960s. Almost all came from a background in cognition or individual differences. Thus, instead of coming from an area of psychology accustomed to dealing with change over time, researchers were drawn from radically different research areas and in the main appeared to want to study how ageing had a negative effect on the working of the nice neat models of mental processes they had created from studies of young adults. Thus, ageing was regarded not as a developmental process, but as a state of decay in a relatively narrow range of behaviours. It was only a short step from this to regarding young adulthood as the peak of performance and older adulthood therefore representing a fall from grace (Stuart-Hamilton, 2010).

Now at this point a critic could say that viewing ageing in negative terms was nothing new. Butler (1969) coined the term *ageism* but he was describing a prejudice that has existed in one form or another since at least the start of written records. Finding formal scientific methods for describing ageing in terms of decline would therefore be nothing more than an academic's way of expressing a very ancient prejudice. However, that is not what was ever intended by psychogerontological research. Researchers are rightly concerned about any reports on racial differences that imply a 'genuine' difference between races. However, even the largest differences between racial groups ever reported pale into insignificance next to the findings of many studies of ageing. Report after report catalogues declines that should mark down an average older person as barely capable of functioning without remedial help, and yet scarcely a comment on the practical implications of what has been found is made. It is as if psychogerontologists find age-related declines, but do not want them to matter.

This is of course a rather exaggerated argument; at the very least, declines in skills may be compensated for by other strategies, or the skills may be ones that older people do not use very much in everyday life. However, if that is the case, then why study skills that may be important to younger adults but which have little relevance to older people? In part the answer is that it is important to map out mental changes using these measures because they give a good indication of the extent to which some skills alter or decline. One cannot judge if an older person is compensating unless it is known what he or she is compensating for. However, it is also arguable that many intellectual skills are studied because of tacit assumptions made by academics about ideal ageing and ideal intellectual life. Academics have a tendency to judge events by their own standards, and to expect others to do the same. Thus, we are sporadically treated to polemics from commentators arguing that people lack the skills taught by their discipline. Thus, representatives of the arts argue that people are insensitive to aesthetics in a mechanistic world, whilst scientists counter-argue that too much time is spent on teaching 'easy' artistic subjects, and, as a result, the general public is typically illogical and lacks the necessary knowledge about scientific matters to make informed decisions. It is neither necessary nor timely to enter further into this debate here. However, the general issue makes it apparent that academics have an established interest in the types of learning and knowledge people should acquire, and this inevitably contains a value judgement that some forms of knowledge are better than others.

Which leads back to the psychology of ageing. The measures of intellectual skills which psychogerontologists use are typically not developed just for studying older people. Generally, they have already been devised for testing younger adults and then are simply given to older people to see how they perform relative to this younger age group. In other words, intellectual ageing is being set up as a measure of how far older people have fallen from the ideal standard set by younger adults. This is to say that 'successful ageing' in most psychogerontologists' eyes is the degree to which an older adult maintains the same level of performance he or she had in younger days (Stuart-Hamilton, 1999b). Thus, it is assumed that older people should not develop as much as remain in a kind of mental stasis once they hit their intellectual peak in the late teens or early twenties. Although some commentators note that older adults may attain greater depths of wisdom or become more adept at integrating pragmatic considerations with pure logic, matters are still largely couched in terms of the degree to which decay from a youthful ideal is either accelerated or diminished.

However, this begs a rather obvious, if contentious, question. Why should later life be seen negatively if someone does not analyse things as analytically or know as much as they would in a youthful ideal? Such things matter to academics, but not everyone would consider it a disaster if one day their verbal skills had declined from a previous level and they could no longer spell *charisma* or *liaison*, or remember what *manumit* means. The pursuit of high intellectual ideals is very important to some people, academics included, but they are not necessary nor desirable for everyone. The days of most older people are not filled with reading books favourably reviewed in one of the more highbrow newspapers, watching subtitled films or doing *The Times* crossword. To assume that a high intellect, or rather a particular set of intellectual skills, is a necessary part of life, is both patronising and divisive. Indeed, the goal of an intellectually powered old age bears little resemblance to anyone's ideal beyond that of university lecturers contemplating what they will do in retirement. To assume that this should be set as the goal by which all older people must be judged is foolhardy, to say the least. We have seen that psychogerontology has structured views of ageing in terms of how the older mind differs from the younger. It is assumed that both age groups perform tasks using the same set of mental skills. To take an analogy, the older and younger people are akin to two soccer teams made to compete against each other. However, what if one of the teams has given up soccer and gone off to play bowls instead? In other words, psychogerontology's view of intellectual change is predicated on the view that older adults are still using the same set of intellectual skills that younger adults use. However, the evidence for this, as has been seen, is far from compelling.

This has been demonstrated in Chapter 2 by the studies of older adults' performance on traditional measures of child development, such as Piaget's experiments. Put simply, older adults often appear to have chosen to adopt 'primitive' methods of thought in preference to more complex 'academic' problem solving. Further evidence for this is provided by Klaczynski and Robinson (2000), who found that older adults on the whole shifted towards using heuristics rather than first principles analysis to solve some types of problems. Again, Allaire and Marsiske (2002) found that problems based on everyday situations predicted older adults' everyday functioning significantly better than traditional psychometric measures.

If older adults are rejecting the skills many researchers think older adults 'should' be using, and this may in part be linked to choice of lifestyle or motivation, then it is difficult to continue comparing older and younger adults by the same rigid criteria. However, this still leaves the necessity of explaining how the shift in mental styles occurs. The following is one possible explanation.[4] We begin with the premise that development consists of the accumulation of knowledge and problem-solving strategies, determined by both genetic inheritance and the environment in which one lives (none of this should be contentious). The knowledge and problem-solving strategies can (with tongue only slightly in cheek) be described as 'idea species'. Whether an idea species thrives depends upon the conditions in which it finds itself. Species will only be acquired if the person can integrate them into an existing mental framework, and they will only be maintained if effectively stored and rehearsed. Thus, acquisition of skills in childhood and their loss in later life are governed by the same basic mechanism. Existing psychogerontological models map cross-sections of processes at one point in time – they add a depth to the model whilst developmental studies add breadth. Much of this has been voiced in one way or another before. The key difference is that in the past it has been tacitly assumed that development and ageing are essentially directed towards specific goals. Arguably this ultimately replays the homunculus problem that plagued computer modelling studies for years. The difference here is that the whole process is essentially blind – the individual has no truly conscious awareness of these processes, and whether a mental process is gained or lost is ultimately down to probabilistic odds. We can stack the odds in particular directions through planning, but essentially the process is removed from the concerns of current studies, which tacitly assume a single desirable path of development. Note that this theory does not negate either the disuse or general slowing theories – both provide possible mechanisms to drive changes. For example, Singer *et al.* (2003a), finding that skills in extreme old age show greater reliance on fluid-based skills (thus fuelling the argument for general slowing), may in turn account for older adults embracing relatively primitive heuristics in response to failing skills in other cognitive domains.

Unwitting ageism

This argument creates a case for arguing that ageing is essentially what a person makes it, and that defining it in simple terms of being worse or better at tests is rather missing the point. Many researchers, even if they disagree with the model presented, would probably concur with this conclusion. However, it is still very easy to create an artificial barrier between age groups, even armed with an egalitarian philosophy. Simone de Beauvoir divided her classic study *Old Age* (de Beauvoir, 1970) into two main sections: one was the view from without, and the other the view within later life. Most research on ageing is conducted by younger adults. The perennial problem is that this heightens the risk of **ageism** (an irrational prejudice against older adults

---

4   A similar model was developed utterly independently by Hendry and Kloep (2002).

and/or ageing). Deliberate ageism is a vile condition and unusually stupid, even by the low standards of other prejudices. A racist may be a vile piece of pond slime, a male chauvinist may sully the name of as noble a creature as the pig, but both can attack their objects of hate in the sound knowledge that they will never change race or sex. Ageists, on the other hand, have a high chance of turning into that which they hate – namely, that they will themselves grow old. Thankfully, few ageist people take careers in caring for, or researching into, older adults. Even so, gerontology is not free of all ageist philosophies.

It is *not* ageist to say that older adults are more prone to physical ailments than younger people, that they are more likely to get dementia, or that they are generally less able at intelligence tests. It is likewise not sexist to say that on average women are shorter than men, cannot lift weights as heavy, or run as quickly. However, if these measures are taken as value judgements rather than simple statements of *average* difference on measures of dubious importance, then this paves the way towards viewing one group as intrinsically inferior to another. This can be done for the most egalitarian of motives. For example, it might begin with a laudable general declaration that older adults need greater care because, on average, they have greater needs. It is a short step from this to regarding older people as automatically being weaker and less adept on a wide range of measures. A person holding these views can still be doing so for the very best of reasons, but a stigma is being created. For example, consider the following statement in an instructional video for nurses concerning sexual abuse of patients. The presenter reports that there have been cases of older patients being sexually abused, demonstrating that 'even the elderly are not immune from attack'. At one level this of course raises a very proper level of concern: sexual abuse is a very serious matter. However, the phrase 'even the elderly' carries a striking value judgement that older people are enfeebled and sexually unattractive: a strong piece of stereotyping that has arisen from what was undoubtedly a genuine and laudable concern.

However, even if ageism has never been intended, there is a grave danger that by concentrating research on age-related decline, too great an emphasis is placed on the questions of why and how change happens. Whilst rigorous scientific enquiry is to be encouraged, there is a grave danger that we pursue research for its own sake, forgetting why the research question was asked in the first place. Elsewhere (e.g. Stuart-Hamilton, 2010) I have likened the process to Winnie-the-Pooh tracking a dangerous beast called a *woozle* through the snow. Of course the beast does not exist – the foolish bear has been tracking his own footprints, but the more times he traces his own prints round the same circular path, the more beasts he thinks lie ahead of him. There is no implication intended that researchers in the psychology of ageing look or think like fictional bears, but surely even the most enthusiastic fans of geropsychology must wonder what new light can be shed on the subject by yet another research paper on old favourites such as general slowing, caregiver stress *et al*.

CHAPTER 8

Death, Dying and Bereavement

Introduction

As noted in Chapter 1, until the nineteenth century, death was usually something that happened *before* old age was reached. Even today, older adults by no means have a monopoly on death. In Chapter 1 it was stated that about 70 per cent of today's Western population can expect to live past 65, and 30–40 per cent past 80. This can sound very agreeable, until one realises that this means that about 30 per cent of people die before they reach old age, and this figure is of course higher in developing countries. Nor are causes of death particularly age-specific. For example, in 2010, 16 per cent of male deaths from circulatory system diseases were in men aged under 65. Conversely, 14 per cent of male deaths from HIV were in men aged over 65 (Office for National Statistics, 2011). But nonetheless, old age is, inevitably and obviously, the time most associated with death, if for no other reason than the prosaic fact that there is no further 'age' after old age. One of the most poignant aspects of death is that it happens no matter how healthy and virtuous a life one leads. As the notice placed in one of David Hockney's artworks states, 'Death awaits you even if you do not smoke' (Malvern, 2011).

The study of the psychological factors involved in death, dying and bereavement is thus not automatically considered part of the study of the psychology of ageing. It probabilistically applies most to older adults, but it is not *exclusively* associated with ageing. Nonetheless, old age brings with it many chronic and debilitating illnesses and conditions, some of which (e.g. cancer, cardiovascular and pulmonary problems) are likely in the long run to prove fatal. Thus, although death is not the sole preserve of old age, it is the time when it is perhaps most obvious and most in the minds of people.

Death awareness

Psychoanalysis has often argued that our awareness that we are mortal is a key factor shaping our personality and behaviour (e.g. Akhtar, 2011). The obvious counterargument that people are often unaware of ever thinking about death that deeply is met with the ubiquitous psychoanalytic response that the reactions are often subconscious, and thus beyond our awareness. This is, like so much of psychoanalysis, untestable. However, it is certainly true that in Western society discussion of death is highly restricted, with an unusually high number of euphemisms (e.g. 'passed over', 'gone', 'in a higher place', etc.) and a general emphasis on restrained behaviour during mourning (Hoyer and Roodin, 2003). But this 'repression of death' argument can be taken too far. It is generally only death close to home that is treated in euphemistic and hushed terms. For instance, whilst pictures of dead British people are generally not shown on UK television, there is no such restriction when the bodies are in, for example, the developing world. The same applies for many other Western countries. Nor is denial of death universally absent. Researchers have argued that, in groups with strong spiritual belief systems, death and dying are, and should be, embraced as adding to, not subtracting from, our understanding of life (e.g. Green, 2002; Moller, 1987; Sheikh and Sheikh, 2007). Furthermore, sociologists have argued that, although there might be relatively superficial trappings of avoiding talking about the subject, in reality, Western societies are not in denial about death (Kellehear, 1984).

For most individuals, the first conscious harbingers of their own mortality occur in middle age. People will probably have encountered the death of relatives or loved ones before this time. For example, the average age for first encountering the death of a non-stranger in the USA is circa eight years (Dickinson, 1992). However, arguably it is in middle age when deaths become meaningful in respect of thoughts of one's own mortality. This is the time at which most middle-aged people's parents are likely to die, and the first of their friends is likely to develop a life-threatening or even fatal illness such as cancer (Coleman and O'Hanlon, 2004). People thus develop what might be termed **death awareness** – not simply understanding what death and dying are as abstract concepts, but becoming aware in practical and emotional terms of what it means to them both in terms of their own mortality and also as a bereaved friend or relative. This is separate from the experience of actually dying, but it arguably is an important precursor that will shape how the final weeks or months of life are experienced.

For the reasons already discussed, people generally have a greater awareness of death and dying the older they get (Woodruff-Pak, 1988). And with greater awareness comes a lowered fear (Bengtson, Cuellar and Ragan, 1977; Woodruff-Pak, 1988), so it is young adult and middle-aged people who tend to have significantly greater expressed fears of death than older adults. This is unlikely to be due to differences in level of wealth and possessions, since evidence suggests that attitudes to death vary little between socio-economic groups (Bengtson *et al.*, 1977). A key difference between older and younger adults' attitudes seems to be in the level of concern about the process of dying itself, which is a greater preoccupation in younger adults (de Vries, Bluck and Birren, 1993). Older people are in general more concerned about the circumstances of their death (who will find their body and similar) than dying (Woodruff-Pak, 1988). In addition, older people are more likely to feel anxious about death if they believe that they lack control over their own lives (Baum, 1984).

Various models, examining in greater detail how death and dying are perceived, have been produced. Some of the most influential are the final stages of various models of personality change across the lifespan (e.g. Erikson's), and these have been discussed in Chapter 5. These generally argue that the end of life should be a time when all conflicts have been resolved and a state of transcendence has been reached. Typical in many respects of this approach is Tornstam's theory of **gerotranscendence**: 'Simply put, gerotranscendence is a shift in meta-perspective, from a materialistic and pragmatic view of the world to a more cosmic and transcendent one' (Tornstam, 1997, p.17).

The theory thus argues that much of later life is a shift in attitude from the here and now to the transcendental. Some older adults can attain at least some of this enlightenment for themselves, given the time to sit and contemplate, whilst others must be directed. It is easy to take phrases like the one just quoted out of context and see them and the model as pseudo-religious,[1] and indeed Tornstam's model is in part based on Zen Buddhism, which sees later life as a time to withdraw from worldly things to concentrate on attaining a transcendent awareness, divorced from superficial issues such as space and time. However, Tornstam is a respected sociologist and the model is a serious attempt to present a model of later life and dying that removes much of the negativity from both. Thus, dying is seen in the context of being part of a larger process of the constant flux that is human progress. Death when centred solely on the individual is almost inevitably petrifying. When seen as part of a bigger picture, it becomes less so, and indeed can be seen as a necessary part of our continued existence.

The work of Tornstam, like that of Erikson and others, is arguably an attempt to install at least the basic framework of a model of death awareness. The at times quasi-religious tone of the work might make uneasy reading for some, but the arguments made by definition have to be prescriptive as well as descriptive, and, in dealing with the end of life and considering issues wider than the needs of the self, what other tone is feasible? However, it is perhaps not surprising that the level of a person's spiritual/religious belief influences the degree to which they are willing to adopt gerotranscendence (Ahmadi, 2001). Research indicates that gerotranscendence is more positively correlated with a perceived understanding of the meaning of life and existence the *less* the older person is involved in formal religion (Braam *et al.*, 2006).[2] In other words, if a person does not have an existing spiritual belief that diminishes fear of death and dying, then gerotranscendence might act as a substitute. This accords with a body of research that demonstrates that thinking about the world

---

1   Try imagining the quotation said in the voice of Obi Wan Kenobi, and you will see what I mean.
2   In Western societies; however, lower religiosity was associated with *higher* death anxiety in a study of Hong Kong Chinese students (Hui, Bond and Ng, 2007).

soon to be departed in broader, more spiritual terms can be effective. For example, Wadensten (2010) conducted an intervention study in an older people's residential home, based on gerotranscendence principles, and found some signs of improvement in self-awareness and also in the social life of the institution. Indeed, in general, gerotranscendence does seem to bring about improvements when older adults and carers are encouraged to use it (see Tornstam, 1999).

However, the model does have its limits. For example, many of the intervention studies appear to lack control treatments. Therefore, we have no means of knowing if other interventions would have been equally, or more, effective. Second, one person's sign of enlightenment is another person's sign of staring vacantly into space. Tornstam and Tornqvist (2000) took a set of behaviours that they said were aspects of gerotranscendence and asked nursing home staff if they had noticed such behaviours in their residents. What Tornstam and Tornqvist labeled as evidence of discovering the transcendence of time was often taken by staff as symptomatic of either: (1) dementia or (2) an unwanted product of too much inactivity. These alternative explanations might, as the authors argue, be the result of a lack of enlightenment by the nursing staff, but they could also be a robust pragmatic response based on experience and verifiable observable measures.

Whether the gerotranscendence model is valid or not, there is a clear need for some firm guidance in the study of death awareness. As was noted in Chapter 1, old age as the experience of the majority of the population is less than a century old. Within the same time period we have come to accept more or less uncritically that old age is synonymous with retirement. This is now so ingrained that we take retirement in later life practically as an innate right, one that is 'natural' and planned for the best. But the simple truth is that we have no thoroughly worked-out plan for later life, there is nothing 'natural' to it, and by extension there is no carefully worked logic justifying how we spend the final phase of our lives. What we have has more or less happened as a result of historical accident, no more and no less. As Baltes (1997, p.367) forcefully argues, '…neither biological nor cultural evolution has had sufficient opportunity to evolve a full and optimizing scaffolding for the later phases of life.'

Wong and Tomer (2011) argue that currently we have barely begun to acknowledge the need to study death acceptance. Too little is known about how it develops in the individual, and the roles of individual differences and culture are poorly understood. Without this information, it is impossible to tailor an optimal approach for the individual person. Scalmati and Kennedy (2009) state that psychotherapy addressing end of life care is similarly underdeveloped. The authors also note that any model that is developed must have an unusual degree of flexibility, since the needs of individuals and their loved ones often vary enormously. There is thus a need for greater understanding of death awareness, but as yet we arguably do not have a particularly satisfactory set of models to choose from. What then, of models of the process of dying itself? As we shall see, the research literature has been dominated by one theory.

Kübler-Ross's five stages of dying model

People very rarely experience sudden death. Almost always individuals know that they are dying and have time to respond to this knowledge. This obviously is a fraught time, and various psychological and psychiatric texts on the subject were written by early researchers (e.g. Eissler, 1955). However, it is the work of Elisabeth Kübler-Ross (e.g. Kübler-Ross, 1969) and her five stages of dying model[3] that first became widely adopted. Kübler-Ross was a psychiatrist and, in working with terminally ill patients, she observed what she believed were consistent patterns of behaviour. From this she created her model, which argues that, after receiving the news that death is inevitable, the individual goes through five stages of response.

1. **Denial** – quite simply, a refusal to accept the news. Typically, this is followed by one of two responses. For a few, a 'head in the sand' mentality sets in, with a blank refusal to accept the inevitable being maintained. For others, it evolves into an increased awareness of all that is being left behind. An often-reported phenomenon is that people suddenly become aware of the beauty in even the simplest and most mundane things.

2. **Anger** – a range of responses are possible at this stage; individuals become angry with themselves and/or with others. The key feature is the anger and rage that this is happening. Clearly this can affect the ease with which such people can be cared for by others and the degree to which they are receptive to advice.

3. **Bargaining** – the individual now seeks to bargain to get an extension of life. This can take several forms, but for those with religious beliefs it often takes the form of pleading with their deity to be allowed a longer life in exchange for better behaviour, giving up their possessions, and similar.

4. **Depression** – this stage has been described, not without reason, as grieving for the self. The individual gains a feeling of hopelessness and helplessness that death cannot be prevented, and therefore a profound feeling of melancholy and a disinterest in others is created. Often the prospect of doing anything is met with a response of 'what's the point?' or similar.

5. **Acceptance** – individuals now resign themselves to accept the situation and plan and behave as best they can in the circumstances.

Some readers who have experienced traumatic events might find that these stages echo their own responses, and indeed Kübler-Ross later argued that the cycle might be triggered not just by death but by serious events such as divorce and similar (see Kübler-Ross, 2005). The model's general idea is easy to understand and intuitive, and

---

3   Note that the term 'stages of grief' is also in common use. For the sake of uniformity the 'dying' form of the phrase will be used throughout.

it has been widely disseminated, particularly in the USA.[4] Furthermore, there is little dispute that dying people can show behaviours characteristic of the five stages. For example, up to the point of near death, a significant proportion of dying people are in denial that they are dying. In one study, it was found that approximately a quarter of a sample of dying people flatly denied that they were near death (Kastenbaum, 1985).

However, the apparent simplicity of the model is arguably a weakness, since a 'strong' interpretation of the model states that dying individuals 'must' pass through the five stages – in other words, not that dying people can be found who display denial, anger, bargaining, depression or acceptance (that is not really disputed) but that dying people will pass through each of these in an inevitable stage-like progress. Thus, if you find a dying person in the denial stage, they will then inevitably go through the next four stages. Similarly, someone in the bargaining stage will inevitably go into the depression and then the acceptance stage. However, a survey of the literature shows that researchers have almost inevitably failed to find this stage-like progression (Neimeyer, 2001). Thus, the strong interpretation can be rejected.

In fact, in some of her writings, Kübler-Ross stressed that the stages were only guidelines; she said they do not last for the same length of time in all individuals and, indeed, people might go through the cycle several times, or show evidence of being in more than one stage simultaneously. What Kübler-Ross thus really seems to be saying is that dying people might show a number of behaviours, and these *sometimes* (but not inevitably) come in a sequence. This gets Kübler-Ross off the hook when she is criticised that her stage model is too invariant, but the escape carries a price. If there is no reliable sequence to these stages, then has Kübler-Ross really done anything more than make a set of observations that dying people can show symptoms of denial, anger, bargaining, depression or acceptance? This is not really new, and many other researchers have made similar observations, as indeed have playwrights, poets and novelists over millennia. Add to this the fact that there is no evidence that Kübler-Ross employed a systematic and consistent approach to collecting her data. Her arguments were based on her clinical notes, but these did not use a consistent system. It is thus easy to see why a considerable body of researchers and clinicians are doubtful about her model and arguments (Newman, 2004),[5] and have been in many cases extremely critical (e.g. Konigsberg, 2011).

---

4   Arguably one of the best indicators of popular awareness is when something is parodied in mainstream culture, since it is only possible if the writers know the audience has shared knowledge. Witness thus the numerous comedic treatments of the stages (typically, with a character going through the five stages in improbably high speed) that have been used on TV shows, comics, books and similar. On a slightly more rarified note, it is worth watching the movie *Groundhog Day* – observe how the central character, apparently doomed to relive the same day *ad nauseum*, goes through the five stages before finally becoming a better person.

5   Her belief in the occult did not help matters either (see Appendix IV).

However, for all the criticisms directed at Kübler-Ross's work, it had an undeniable effect in kick-starting the academic and clinical study of death, dying and bereavement (Edgley, 2003). This has not always been seen as a good thing. Kübler-Ross's emphasis on a 'good death' appears on the surface to be in and of itself desirable. However, taken too far, it falls foul of what Lofland (1978) disparagingly referred to as the **happy death** mentality – namely, the belief that complaint, despair and other negative emotions found in many dying people can be resolved through discussion and negotiation, and the whole process *controlled*. If a patient does not conform to the standard Kübler-Ross pattern of change, and thus 'fails' to end their days in a state of calm philosophical resignation, they are in effect refusing to be controlled and the patient is labeled as unco-operative. Edgley (2003) argues that, in sociological terms, this can be seen in terms of deviance, with the patient in effect refusing to conform to the norm expected of them by health care professionals (see also Zimmerman, 2004). Alternatively, a dying patient might be denied their wish to express frustrations and sadness because they are being coerced into being more cheerful and philosophical in their behaviour. Is it fair that a person should die without being able to air a long-held worry or grievance and 'get it off their chest'?

These criticisms can be questioned on pragmatic grounds – an assumption is being made that a high proportion of health care professionals slavishly follow Kübler-Ross's writings to the point of exercising suppressive control if the dying patient dares to step out of line. This seems improbable, not least because there is often a considerable gulf between health care units' official end of life care policies and their implementation in practice (Goodridge, 2010). But equally, a line has to be drawn between carers wanting a dying person to be content and their suppressing a dying person's wishes in order that the person *appears* to be content.

The rejection of Kübler-Ross's work can leave a feeling of despair that nothing seems to be satisfactory in this field of research. However, there are other, more pragmatic approaches that may be taken to the study of dying. One way is to argue that what matters first and foremost is not any overarching grand spiritual philosophy, but the pragmatic consideration that a person dies with as little suffering and as much dignity as possible. This is the cornerstone of palliative care.

Palliative care

In a nutshell, palliative care is any treatment designed to lessen discomfort rather than cure or lessen the underlying cause of the illness. Thus, taking a painkiller for toothache is an example of palliative care – it lessens the pain, but does nothing to treat the cause of the toothache. In the cases of many fatal and incurable illnesses, palliative care can be the only medical option – after treatment has failed, all a responsible carer can do is to ensure that the patient suffers as little as possible. This sounds relatively straightforward, but it is, as we shall see, laden with problems. This is why the World Health Organization and other authors define palliative care at rather greater length. For example:

Palliative care:

- provides relief from pain and other distressing symptoms
- affirms life and regards dying as a normal process
- intends neither to hasten or postpone death
- integrates the psychological and spiritual aspects of patient care
- offers a support system to help patients live as actively as possible until death
- offers a support system to help the family cope during the patient's illness and in their own bereavement
- uses a team approach to address the needs of patients and their families, including bereavement counselling, if indicated
- will enhance quality of life, and may also positively influence the course of illness
- is applicable early in the course of illness, in conjunction with other therapies that are intended to prolong life, such as chemotherapy or radiation therapy, and includes those investigations needed to better understand and manage distressing clinical complications.

(World Health Organization, 2011)

Why does palliative care require such a lengthy definition, and why does it stress so many aspects of the person's life and family, and not just the person's health? The answer in part is due to a shift in medical opinion. From the late nineteenth century to the early 1960s, medicine was more heavily focused on curing the disease than on relieving the suffering of the patient; thus, finding the cause of the illness rather than treating the symptoms became the order of the day. This is not an intellectual atmosphere conducive to palliative care. Gradually, however, attitudes changed, spearheaded by the work of Dame Cecily Saunders in the UK, leading to the widespread adoption of the hospice movement (see Welsh, Fallon and Keeley, 2003).

The key issue in palliative care is arguably **quality of life (QOL)**. This is a rather nebulous concept, not least because authors' definitions vary widely (Bowling, 2007). However, in essence, it is the measure of how comfortable and satisfied a person feels about their health and general situation. QOL was devised to measure an important, but often overlooked aspect of patient care: namely, the trade-off between treatment effectiveness and patient comfort. This is best explained by an example. Suppose that there are two treatments for the same disease. Treatment *A* is very effective at curing the patient, but has horribly unpleasant side effects. Treatment *B* is less effective, but has no side effects. Which treatment should be given to the patient? Treatment *A* is the correct choice in terms of likelihood of removing the disease, but the side effects mean that the patient's QOL is significantly lowered. Treatment *B*, although less likely to cure the patient, does not impinge on QOL. Most people, presented with this problem, argue that treatment *B* should be tried first since, if it works, the patient has the better experience, and *A* should only be used if *B* fails. However, what if the disease is life threatening and/or there is no time to try both treatment *A* and treatment *B*? Should a clinician place patient comfort over certainty of curing the disease?

A similar problem faces clinicians deciding whether to offer solely palliative care to patients in a terminal state. It is possible to pursue aggressive treatments (i.e. continue to try to defeat the disease as the primary objective with pain relief and patient comfort as secondary considerations) to the very end of life. But aggressive treatments often have unpleasant side effects and from experience of hundreds of similar cases the clinician might know that the chances of success for an individual patient with a particular set of symptoms are extraordinarily slim or non-existent (see Mallery and Moorhouse, 2011). The patient is likely to be in discomfort and is clutching at straws in supposing that they will survive. In other words, their QOL is low. The alternative is to accept that the patient's condition will worsen to its inevitable fatal conclusion and to offer palliative care, thereby significantly increasing the patient's QOL. But: humane as palliative care sounds, there is always a nagging doubt that it is 'giving in' and, unsurprisingly, some patients want to pursue aggressive treatment for as long as possible (Johnson, Kuchibhatia and Tulsky, 2008).

A further reason for the lengthy list of caveats in the World Health Organization definition is to stress that palliative care is not euthanasia by another name.[6] Palliative care can sometimes shorten life: opioid painkillers, often the only viable analgesia available, have a side effect of suppressing breathing. There is thus a fine line between numbing sensations of pain and unduly restricting breathing, and similarly with other related conditions such as excessive restlessness (see Welsh *et al.*, 2003). However, if the alternative is unendurable pain, then which is better is arguably a matter for individual decisions. Perversely, another problem with palliative care is the exact opposite – namely, instead of hastening death, it can delay its arrival. Advances in medical science mean that dying patients can now be kept alive far longer than was once possible. But does this prolonging of life really benefit anyone? Unless pain control is extremely well managed, this can be a time of great suffering, and even if pain *is* controlled, a person is still incapacitated and might feel overly reliant

---

6   It is worth noting that, in countries where euthanasia is legal, a request for it is not automatically granted. For example, one study found that almost 75 per cent of requests were turned down (Onwuteaka-Philipsen *et al.*, 2010), though in circa half these cases this was because the patient died before a decision could be reached.

on others (Meier, Isaacs and Hughes, 2010). To this can be added the huge increase in financial costs if the illness is protracted with not the remotest hope of recovery. This is a burden to the tax payer in countries with state-funded health services and to the individual in countries with private health care.

However, once again there is a nagging feeling of doubt about this. We shall illustrate this with a specific example. In the UK, palliative care in many instances is being formalised into the **Liverpool Care Pathway (LCP)** (Ellershaw and Wilkinson, 2003; see also Partington, 2006) named after the UK city where the procedure was first implemented. In the terminal stages of life, the LCP often advocates, alongside pain relief, discontinuing antibiotics, intravenous fluids, etc. (Preston, 2007). The LCP does appear to be effective by some criteria. For example, bereaved relatives of patients who had died under the LCP system were slightly but significantly less distressed circa four months after the death (Veerbeek, van der Heide et al., 2008). In addition, LCP has been shown to reduce **symptom burden** (in essence, the degree to which symptoms have a negative effect on QOL), and lead to more comprehensive documentation of care (Veerbeek, van Zuylen et al., 2008). However, this is an emotive subject and the LCP has elicited emotive reactions. The following is from a letter signed by a number of eminent academics and clinicians expressing concern about the LCP:

> The Government is rolling out a new treatment pattern of palliative care into hospitals, nursing and residential homes. It is based on experience in a Liverpool hospice. If you tick all the right boxes in the Liverpool Care Pathway, the inevitable outcome of the consequent treatment is death.
>
> As a result, a nationwide wave of discontent is building up, as family and friends witness the denial of fluids and food to patients. Syringe drivers are being used to give continuous terminal sedation, without regard to the fact that the diagnosis could be wrong.
>
> It is disturbing that in the year 2007–2008, 16.5 per cent of deaths came about after terminal sedation. Experienced doctors know that sometimes, when all but essential drugs are stopped, 'dying' patients get better.[7] (Millard et al., 2009)

It is not surprising that the newspaper that published the letter did an accompanying article entitled 'Sentenced to death on the NHS' (Devlin, 2009), and presented the image that the UK National Health Service (NHS) was encouraging clinicians to give up on elderly dying patients and put them on continuous sedation until they passed away. These are serious allegations. It is one thing to want to relieve suffering. It is quite another to hasten death if some individuals might recover when given a different treatment. However, before the LCP is blamed for hastening the deaths

---

7   How much longer these patients live, and what their quality of life is like, are not mentioned, nor could I find studies that examined this.

of every older adult in the UK, it should be remembered that, even in hospitals where it is implemented, the LCP is not used on every patient automatically and the psychological and spiritual needs of the patient and the family are given prime consideration (Preston, 2007). Second, as of 2010, the LCP or similar systems are not by any means in the majority – it is estimated that they are used in just under a quarter of health care settings (Hughes *et al.*, 2010).[8] It is thus hard to attribute all the 16.5 per cent of deaths due to terminal sedation to the LCP. It is far easier to see the rise in deaths whilst under sedation as being the product of changing demographics and, in particular, the changing nature of what people die from and the treatments available (see Chapter 1).

This is not the end of the problems for palliative care, however. Palliative care, in order to be effective, has to be tailored to the individual needs of the patient. This is of no use, however, unless the wishes are carried out. A study of general practitioners (GPs) in the Netherlands found that almost half the GPs were unaware of where their patients wanted to die (i.e. hospice, home, hospital, etc.). Patients with higher incomes and/or who had links with a palliative care programme were more likely to have GPs who knew their chosen place of dying (Abarshi *et al.*, 2009). Furthermore, the fact that palliative care has to be tailor-made to be truly effective makes extrapolation from studies difficult, because what might work well for the patients in one study, based in a small number of hospitals or even a single ward, might not work elsewhere.

These problems are compounded when cross-cultural issues arise. For example, although excellent studies outlining areas of strengths and weaknesses have been performed in individual hospitals (e.g. Woo *et al.*, 2011), these might not automatically be applicable if, for example, the study is in mainland China and the reader is looking for advice on how to apply the findings to care in a hospital in rural Wales. Added to this is the consideration that different causes of death could also affect what will be the optimal response. But this does not mean that within a specific condition a 'one size fits all' policy will work either. For example, a study of changes in QOL in renal cancer patients demonstrated that a variety of responses were needed, depending upon the individual circumstances (Bird and Hayter, 2009). Furthermore, although health authorities often trumpet the need for QOL in their literature, there is often a considerable distance between theory and practice, with quality of *care* often failing to match QOL needs (Vaarama, Pieper and Sixsmith, 2008). Problems also arise from the fact that for obvious ethical reasons it is extremely difficult to get measurements on QOL and similar during a person's last few days of life. For example, they are either too ill or (perfectly reasonably) want to spend their last hours with loved ones and not with a social scientist touting a clipboard. Thus, many studies rely on estimates made by relatives after (often many months after) the death (see Lawton, 2001).

---

8   There is considerable variability between health care units in many aspects of palliative/terminal care (see e.g. Galanos *et al.*, 2010).

Death

The concept of what constitutes 'death' has varied across time and today varies across cultures. Many cultures, both past and present, have argued that deep unconsciousness constitutes death. For example, the inhabitants of Vanatinai (in Papua New Guinea) believe that being unconscious is being dead, and thus some inhabitants have come 'back to life' on multiple occasions (Lepowsky, 1985). In the past, many tales of people rising from the dead might simply be instances of someone awaking from a coma – they came back from the dead by the criteria of the time, but not by modern medical standards.

In industrialised societies, movies, plays and books all can leave one with the impression that currently death is indicated by the cessation of heart beat and breathing – thus, the absence of a pulse or no fogging of a hand mirror placed before the mouth indicates a person is dead. Indeed, such a definition would have satisfied most medical authorities until the twentieth century. However, there are reasons for rejecting this definition. The first is that this is an unreliable diagnostic method. A very faint pulse or extremely shallow breathing can be difficult to detect, with the result that a supposedly 'dead' person can still be alive. A particularly macabre upshot of this is that a person in this state could in theory be buried alive, and people in the nineteenth century in particular were obsessed with this, following several well-publicised cases where scratch marks and similar were found on the *interior* of coffins.[9] Hence, the funeral trade for a time offered coffins with an internal bell pull – if the 'deceased' awoke and found themselves buried, a quick pull on the chain should (it was hoped) attract help. It is difficult to find instances of an actual live burial that cannot be explained by other more prosaic means. However, the *fear* of being buried alive was very real. One illustrative example will suffice:[10]

> Some days since a corpse was brought from Charterhouse Square, and buried in Islington Churchyard, and a stone erected at the place with this inscription:
>
> IN MEMORY OF
> MRS ELIZABETH EMMA THOMAS
> Who died 28th October, 1808
> AGED 27 YEARS
> She had no fault, save what trav'llers give the moon,
> The light was bright, but died, alas! too soon
>
> Mr Hodson, the Coroner, received a letter, intimating very strong suspicions that the deceased had not died naturally, in consequence of which he applied to the parish officers, who ordered the grave to be opened, which was done and the body removed to the vault under the church, for the inspection of the jury, which sat upon it, when the following appeared in evidence. The lady died on

9   Which could in fact often have been due to other causes, such as rats.
10   For ease of reading I have modernised the spelling and punctuation. The italics are original.

Friday week, was buried on Saturday, and the gentleman with whom she lived left town on Sunday, and embarked at Portsmouth on Monday for Spain. On examining the body, *a silver pin, about nine inches long, was found sticking in the heart*, through the left side of the body. A medical gentleman who had attended the deceased, declared that the pin was *inserted* at the request of the gentleman, to prevent the possibility of her being buried alive. The jury brought in a verdict of *died by the visitation of God*. The corpse still lies unburied in the vault. (*The Morning Post*, London, Monday, 7 November, 1808)[11]

A second reason for rejecting the cardio-pulmonary diagnosis is that with modern medical equipment a person can often be resuscitated by means of electric shock and similar. This is often termed **clinical death.** At this point, although the heart is not pumping and the lungs are not breathing, the cells in the body are to all intent and purposes alive, and *if* the heart can be restarted within circa three minutes, then life can continue. Thus, the pulse stopping is, in a fully equipped hospital with a resuscitation team on hand, not enough to signal inevitable death. Hence, clinicians began to argue that a more satisfactory definition of death is **brain death** – in other words, when measures such as an EEG record no brain activity. The argument is in many respects compelling – absence of brain activity indicates that there is no mental activity, and even if a person is revived it is highly probable that he or she will lack higher intellectual processes and indeed might have poor control over almost all bodily functions. Therefore, many authorities now lean towards absence of brain activity as the cardinal diagnostic symptom.

But this approach is not without its disadvantages. First, because in many instances the body can be kept alive by artificial respirators taking over the functions that the brain once performed. Thus, the body's cells can stay alive by artificial means even after the brain has ceased to function. Second, because measures of 'brain death' might be inaccurate – there are recorded instances of patients who were supposedly brain dead being taken off respirators and continuing to live, albeit in a vegetative state (Oboler, 1986). Arguably, 'complete' death (often called **biological death** or **somatic death**) only occurs when not only the heart, lungs and brain cease to function, but the cells within the rest of the body cease their activity for want of oxygen and nutrition.

A person who is clinically dead and then can be revived and can live without artificial assistance is arguably truly alive. But what of a person who is clinically or brain dead and whose body is *solely* alive because of artificial means, such as a respirator? It can be argued that if there had been no intervention, the person would be biologically dead. He or she is only 'alive' because of intervention. Furthermore, the person is almost certainly deeply unconscious and incapable of higher cognitive processes – it is not that they are capable of appreciating their status as a 'living'

---

11 Retrieved from the nineteenth century British Library Newspapers online archive, 10 September 2011.

person (Oboler, 1986). However, it has also been argued that measures of brain death are inaccurate, and that, in any case, why should the brain be considered to be the primary bodily system that in essence represents the whole body (Shewmon, 1998)? Added to this, it can be argued that the definition of brain death is a useful one for keeping a dead person alive for sufficient time for their organs to be extracted for donation to living patients in need of transplants. Whilst this is useful for the recipients, it has been argued that it is potentially unfair to the patient, who is in effect being killed by the organ extraction (Potts, 2002).

This issue might initially appear solely to be a matter for medical ethics, but it has psychological consequences for the family of the dying person. At what point and by whom should the decision be made to end this artificial support and allow biological death to occur? The issue is one that is obviously emotive. A prime case in point is the **Terri Schiavo case**. Mrs Schiavo suffered massive brain damage following a heart attack in 1990, and was reduced to a persistent vegetative state. After several years of therapeutic intervention, it was concluded that this was an irreversible state; Mrs Schiavo was being kept alive entirely by artificial means, namely a feeding tube. Her husband then requested that doctors remove the tube and allow her to die. Her parents objected, and took the case to court. A series of legal cases followed, with the result that the tube was removed, and then, following rapid legal injunctions, the tube was restored pending the next court case. Eventually, in 2005, the tube was removed permanently and Mrs Schiavo died about two weeks later (*Daily Telegraph*, 2005). Other, less publicised cases further demonstrate the complexity of the situation. For example, a Robert Wendland was left in a severely brain-damaged state following a traffic accident. His wife and the clinicians treating him wanted artificial support to be terminated. However, Mr Wendland's mother objected, and a court case ensued. In this instance, Mr Wendland's wife said that on several occasions prior to the accident Mr Wendland had expressed a wish to have treatment terminated if he were ever to be severely brain damaged. However, in this instance the judge in the case ruled that the evidence, although strong, was not compelling, and thus ordered that life support be continued[12] (Eisenberg and Kelso, 2002).

Both the Schiavo and the Wendland cases took place in the USA, and it is clear that even within the same culture there is no single consensus of opinion. Furthermore, the causes of conflicts between family members over the most appropriate treatment of a dying patient are multifaceted and the outcome of the conflict hard to predict (Kramer *et al.*, 2010). The problem only gets more complicated when different cultures are brought into consideration. In an extremely clear review of the problem, Klessig (1992) elicited the views of people from African American, Chinese, Jewish, Iranian, Filipino, Mexican American and Korean ethnicities on a series of vignettes

---

12 Mr Wendland in effect resolved the case himself by dying of pneumonia just before the formal verdict was delivered.

concerning dying patients where two decisions had to be made: first, whether to start life support, and, second, whether to terminate life support when it was clear there was no hope of recovery. The white American controls and the Jewish participants were almost always against initiating life support and in favour of terminating it. Largely the reverse applied to many of the other groups (notably the Filipino, Iranian and Korean), with the others being more equivocal. Klessig argues that the reason for these differences might in part be religious (e.g. some religions state clearly whether life should be preserved and/or whether suffering should be allowed in the face of certain death). However, it can also be cultural (e.g. Klessig observed that Christians and Muslims in the Iranian group, for example, gave very similar responses). It is also easy to overlook that within a specific cultural group there will be considerable individual differences. For example, within an apparently homogenous set of people, level of spirituality will vary drastically, and this needs to be considered if nursing care of a dying patient is to be effective (Nixon and Narayanasamy, 2010).

There are further complicating factors as well, many surrounding care practices. There is some evidence, for example, that doctors are less willing to involve older patients (if they are capable of speaking) in end of life discussions than they are with younger patients (Chambaere et al., 2011). Also, older patients are less likely to receive sedation as part of palliative care. Alonso-Babarro et al. (2010) found that patients dying at home who received palliative sedation[13] were on average 58 ± 17 years old, compared with an average of 69 ± 15 years old for the non-sedated. This appears to be due not to ageist practice, but because the younger dying patients were more likely to display delirium and other physically restless symptoms. The quality of communication offered by hospital staff, particularly nurses, can be crucial in affecting the emotional response and its after-effects amongst relatives of the patient (Efstathiou and Clifford, 2011). The fact that some health care professionals (e.g. consultants) see the patient for only a limited time rather than (as with nurses) for longer periods can also add to this dynamic (Fine, 2010). Again, different health care units have different practices concerning palliative care and what is withdrawn and when (e.g. Schildmann et al., 2011).

Bereavement and cultural differences

Kübler-Ross's five stages model was applied to the grieving process, but it is now recognised to be as inaccurate here as it is in describing adjustment to dying. In other words, some behaviours such as denial and anger might well show themselves, but there is no strict sequence and not all people show all behaviours (Hoyer and Roodin, 2003). This, however, has not stopped a very large number of websites and similar giving firm advice on the stages of grieving that a bereaved person can expect to go through. Although such advice might help some people, it might

---

13 Palliative sedation appears to have little effect on remaining life expectancy (Claessens et al., 2011).

make others feel guilty or anxious that they have shown insufficient grief because they have 'failed' to show similar patterns of behaviour. The blunt truth is that grief and bereavement,[14] just like dying, form an intensely individual experience (e.g. Konigsberg, 2011). This has been demonstrated since the earliest modern work on grief, Lindeman's (1944) systematic study of grief in family members who had lost a loved one in a large fire at a Boston nightclub.

Nonetheless, some behaviours are *common* (though not universal): a state of disbelief (e.g. feeling that the death is impossible); severe distress; the bereaved person hallucinating that they can hear the dead person talking or feel them touching them; symptoms of anxiety and depression; feelings of guilt that the bereaved have survived, etc. (Hoyer and Roodin, 2003; Konigsberg, 2011). Furthermore, the level of grief experienced during bereavement is related to the level of grief experienced prior to the death of the patient (at least in the case of patients with dementia; see Givens *et al.*, 2011). A lot of the symptoms of grief are very akin to clinical depression, and there is a danger that a period of bereavement, which might eventually resolve itself healthily, will be misdiagnosed as depression, leading to unnecessary treatment (Flaskerud, 2011). It is important to stress that bereavement is a time when atypical symptoms that would normally require treatment are regarded as the norm, and indeed in many cultures are sanctioned. It is thus expected that a bereaved person will be atypically depressed and show other behaviours that in a non-bereaved person would be treated as symptomatic of illness.

Simultaneously, it is expected that bereaved people will *not* engage in other activities such as participating in overly cheerful events or remarrying. In an age when individuals often consider themselves unshockable, remarrying within a couple of months of the death of a partner would still be scandalous. This is so ingrained that we might almost consider it instinctive. However, it is a cultural artifact. When Hamlet rages about his widowed mother remarrying so soon after the death of her first husband ('The funeral baked meats did coldly furnish forth the marriage table,' etc. *Hamlet*, Act I, Scene ii, 180–1) to modern audiences, Hamlet's anger seems entirely reasonable. But to Shakespeare's contemporary audience his reaction would probably have seemed the opposite. Women often remarried within a few months of being widowed, since without the protective status of being a wife their lives were extremely restricted (see McDermott and Berk, 2010). Expectations of appropriate behaviour during bereavement are to a great degree cultural.

There is no short easily assimilated description of the range of cultural differences in bereavement, with one researcher aptly describing the field as 'an infinite variety in people's responses to death, in how they mourn, and in the nature of their internalization of the lost object' (Hagman, 1995, p.909). Wherever one looks, there appear to be cultural differences. For example:

---

14 This section is about grief and bereavement for *any* loved person or close friend. Reactions specific to a life partner are given later in the widowhood section.

- Consider the issue of cultural differences in the behaviour of the dying patient and their family. Trill and Holland (1993) identified ten key factors, including differences in family function, gender roles, linguistic competence, attitudes towards illness and health practices, and so forth. And each of these topics in turn can be broken down into a myriad of sub-groups.

- Attempts to adapt a scale of measurement of bereavement grief for the majority population in the USA for use in the minority Latino population results in a different factor structure (Wilson, 2006). The same Latino population also shows significantly higher levels of grief (Grabowski and Frantz, 1993).

- In a comparison of six European countries, Janssen et al. (2006) found that there were wide differences in when palliative care drugs (which can hasten the end of life through side effects) were administered. This led to national differences in the shortening of the patient's life of almost two weeks when the most extreme cases are taken (see also Miccinesi et al., 2005).

- In a sample of bereaved people in the People's Republic of China, the strength of feeling of a continuing bond with the deceased at 4 months post-death led to better adjustment after 18 months of bereavement. In contrast, a stronger feeling of continuing bond led to *worse* adjustment after 18 months in a similar sample of people living in the USA (Lalande and Bonanno, 2006).

- Although many Western people have a preference for dying at home, the reverse is true in Chinese communities, because of traditional beliefs about ghosts inhabiting the place they died. Even if this is a superstition and recognised as such by many Chinese people, it nonetheless can have an effect on property prices[15] (Koenig and Gates-Williams, 1995).

- Social networks had a direct influence on some features of bereavement in Germany and Japan, were mediated by gender and age in France, and had no effect in the USA (Antonucci et al., 2001).

- African Americans have less positive belief about hospice care, are more in favour of aggressive treatment at the end of life, and are less likely to have completed an advance directive (Johnson et al., 2008).

Indeed, practically every researcher on bereavement notes the cultural differences (e.g. Berzoff, 2003; Eisenbruch, 1984; Szabo, 2010). Furthermore, cross-cultural research points to the fact that a Western view of the topic is not automatically correct and might indeed provide a too narrow approach. However, it is nonetheless possible to overplay the cultural differences argument. First because, although it is

---

15 This is categorically *not* intended as a racist comment. There are similar examples in Western culture: for example, when was the last time you saw a seat row 13 in a passenger aircraft run by a European or American airline?

correct that clinicians and researchers should be sensitive to cultural practices, even within a single cultural group not everyone acts the same or has the same beliefs:

> Considering culture as a predictive variable is inherently limited – that is, simply plugging race or ethnicity into a multiple-regression analysis or, in a clinical context, assuming someone's name, appearance of national origin is a predictive factor. The image that comes to mind is of a young medical resident, recently returned from a lecture on cultural sensitivity in health care, who pulls his or her index card from a pocket when dealing with [an elderly Chinese man] and, assuming that there is no need to discuss his care directly with him – because Chinese culture is family-oriented – concludes that the resident's only responsibility is to follow the son's wishes. (Koenig and Gates-Williams, 1995)

Furthermore, some studies have found far greater similarities than differences (e.g. Bonanno, 1999; Cleiren *et al.*, 1996). Again, although cultures differ in some of their concepts of death and bereavement, they share others in common (Long, 2003). Many other differences are of the manner of *expression*, with the underlying feeling being identical. Thus, for example, different cultures adopt black, white or red clothing as a sign of mourning. But in all cases it is the same basic motivation – namely, to wear a special kind of dress to signify a specific state. This has led some researchers to argue that although there are a myriad of ways to *express* bereavement, all are based on a set of universal beliefs and attitudes (Parkes, 2000).

Across all cultures, grieving does in most cases resolve itself. However, in a small proportion of instances, it does not, and the bereaved person continues to have adverse reactions that persist after the end of what is considered a culturally appropriate period of mourning. Clinicians have typically categorised such cases as depression or similar, but recently there has been an attempt to identify a new condition, known as **prolonged grief disorder (PGD)** (Prigerson *et al.*, 2009). The cardinal symptoms are an atypically prolonged yearning to be reunited with a deceased loved one, combined with frequent and/or disabling symptoms of bereavement. In addition, the symptoms must have been present for six months or longer. Prigerson *et al.* argue that PGD is associated with a range of risk factors, including parental abuse, poor preparation for death and a history of childhood separation anxiety. PGD can occur at any age, but probabilistically it is more likely to affect older adults, who are similarly more likely to suffer **bereavement overload**. This is a condition of being unable to cope with the grieving process, resulting from experience of a succession of bereavements in too short a space of time. Since older adults are in statistical terms more likely to die within a particular time period than younger adults, it follows that older people are probabilistically more likely to experience multiple bereavements of same-age friends and family.[16]

---

16 The phenomenon is also observed in other groups – for example, gay men coping with loss of friends during the first wave of the AIDS epidemic (Elia, 1997).

Widowhood

Widowhood refers to the period of life following loss of one's life partner. The term refers equally to men and women, but in practice the experience of widowhood is far more that of women than men, because of the differing life expectancies of the two sexes (see Chapter 1; though for a view on the male experience of widowhood, see van den Hoonaard, 2010). Widowhood is known to be a key factor in lowering both mental and physical health in many individuals (Vink et al., 2009) and increasing vulnerability (Sreerupa and Rajan, 2010). It should be noted that there is also likely to be a strong cohort effect for the current generation of older adults. In many instances, widowhood brings with it the first ever experience of living alone, since many individuals moved straight from the parental to the marital home, with no period of single independence in between.

The degree to which widowhood affects an individual is shaped by many factors, including how anticipated the death of the partner was. For example, Eisdorfer and Wilkie (1977) found that the loss was less stressful if the deceased had been ill for some time (see also Wells and Kendig, 1997). Also, it has been argued that older people tend to have a milder reaction than younger adults (Cook and Oltjenbruns, 1989), because older people are better primed to accept the death of a partner, and might have experienced a period of **anticipatory grief** (i.e. grieving for the loss of a person before they have actually died). However, Carr et al. (2001) contradict these findings. In their longitudinal study, they found that the degree to which the death was expected had no significant effect on factors such as grief or depression. A sudden death slightly increased feelings of yearning in a bereaved woman, but *lowered* it in a bereaved man. These contradictory findings may depend on the sensitivity of measures taken and also the age spread of the participants tested. It should also be noted that, even in later life, death can still be unexpected, with circa 23 per cent of respondents in one study stating that the death of a loved one was 'extremely' unexpected (Teno et al., 2004). However, as O'Neill and Morrison (2011) note, some 'unexpected' deaths might be the result of insufficient briefing of the relatives of the deceased. With greater care and sensitive briefing, much bereavement-related stress can be avoided – there is ample evidence that the less the briefing prior to death, the more severe the symptoms of grief afterwards (O'Neill and Morrison, 2011).

Again, the level of loss (and anxiety) is positively correlated with how reliant a person was on the deceased for support (Carr et al., 2000). It is also known that a belief in a good spiritual afterlife results in lower levels of hypertension amongst the bereaved (Krause et al., 2002). Bereavement is also associated with poorer health, but a longitudinal study by Williams (2004) argues that this is due to a decline in health maintaining behaviours, and that bereaved people who maintain health maintenance behaviours do not show a health decline. In the majority of cases, adjustment to loss is reported as being at least satisfactory or robust (see Bonanno, Wortman and Nesse, 2004), though there are some residual signs of grief and other negative feelings 30 months after the bereavement (Thompson *et al.*, 1991), and a sizeable proportion (20%) of widowed persons report a failure to cope adequately (Lopata, 1973). Furthermore, the number of negative aspects of personal relationships within a widow's social circle has been found to increase in the years following bereavement (Morgan, Neal and Carder, 1997). A study by van Baarsen (2002) echoes this. However, changing friends and acquaintances after bereavement can also create problems. Zettel and Rook (2004) demonstrated that, following bereavement, the greater the change in a widow's social network, the greater the damage to psychological health (see also Van Dussen and Morgan, 2009). Korinek, Zimmer and Gu (2011) found that in Chinese older adults widowhood was associated with increased probability of coresidency (i.e. moving in) with their adult children. The research concluded that this coresidency blunted some of the negative effects of both widowhood and declining health in the older person. However, moving in with adult children, or becoming increasingly reliant on adult children, is fraught with problems, and failure to maintain adequate control over 'rules' of interaction can lead to serious friction between family members (see Ngan, 2011).

Carey (1979) argued that men are better able to adjust post-bereavement than women. This may be because in traditional sex(ist) roles a married woman's status is determined by the presence of her husband, while the reverse does not apply as strongly. Also, a widowed man is likely to be financially more secure, and may have greater opportunities to find another partner. Other studies, however, have contradicted this viewpoint (Cook and Oltjenbruns, 1989), possibly because more men than women are inept at looking after themselves, and also because widowhood is primarily a woman's experience. Lee *et al.* (2001) found that men became more depressed than women following bereavement, but argued that prior to this they were less depressed, and the level of increase simply brought them on a par with the typical depressed level of older women. Factors underlying this included a greater dislike of domestic chores and a feeling of being less able to give assistance to younger relatives. Moore and Stratton (2003) argue that the reason male widowers appear more resilient is because they tend to disappear from the radar. Either they remarry with relative ease (because there are far larger numbers of widowed women than men) or they disappear from awareness because they feel excluded from aid groups, which are predominantly seen as being for women and which might deliberately exclude men.

More recent research points to a yet more complex picture. For example, Jung-Hwa *et al.* (2006) found that widowhood made the surviving partner (of either gender) more reliant on their adult children. Surviving women were more dependent on their children for legal and financial advice (possibly reflecting traditional gender roles, where the man took prime responsibility for such matters). However, this level of dependency decreased the higher the level of education the woman had received. Furthermore, the higher the level of education, the higher the level of emotional support the widow offered her children. Sobieszczyk, Knodel and Chayovan (2003), examining Thai widowers, found a similarly complex picture. Widowed women often had lower levels of literacy and income. However, widowed men had a worse survival rate and were less likely to get financial assistance from their children (and thus had a higher probability of being in debt). But there is a problem with many of these studies in that they are cross-sectional. Bennett (2005) conducted an eight-year longitudinal study and found that many of the deleterious effects of being widowed disappeared when viewed from a longitudinal perspective.[17] Furthermore, a gender difference was not found.

It thus appears that the experience of widowhood is dictated by a multitude of factors, and, as with many aspects of ageing research, it is difficult to make comfortable generalisations about the effects of bereavement beyond a superficial gloss.

Suicide

So far we have considered death and dying when the person has not elected to die. However, suicide is also a cause of death probabilistically associated with later life. In general, suicide rates increase with age (Cukrowicz et al., 2011; Shah, 2011b). This is not true for every single country: there are indications that the rate has recently fallen in some countries, including the UK, possibly because of greater prescribing of a new generation of more effective anti-depressant drugs (Shah and Buckley, 2011).[18] However, others, notably many countries in the former Soviet Bloc, have higher suicide rates than the world average (Shah, 2011b). It is often supposed that suicide is a younger person's death. This is due to a misreading of the statistics. In absolute terms, the *number* (rather than percentage) of teenage and young adult suicides is smaller than the number of older adult suicides. But because younger people die in far smaller numbers than older people, suicide forms a much higher *proportion* of the total deaths within the young adult age group.

Suicide attempts by older people are more likely to 'succeed' than younger adults' efforts (Conwell, 1997), where there is over a 50 per cent 'failure' rate (Cook and Oltjenbruns, 1989). In part this is because of differences in the physical robustness of the age groups, but also because of methods chosen. Older adults are more likely to select a method that practically guarantees death, such as shooting, drowning and asphyxiation (see Adamek and Kaplan, 1996a, b; Shah and Buckley, 2011) whereas younger adults are more likely to choose less certain methods, such as taking an overdose in a place where they are likely to be found by friends or relatives before the drugs can take effect (see Woods, 1999). This difference also applies on a relative scale within the older age group, with the oldest old electing more 'definite' methods than younger older adults (Erlangsen, Bille-Brahe and Jeune, 2003).

---

17   In essence, only age and being *recently* widowed had an effect on expressed levels of morale.
18   In Eire, suicide rates in women have stabilised, but declined in recent years in men (Corcoran *et al.*, 2010).

In part the method chosen may be a reflection of the reason for the suicide attempt. Older adults are often attempting suicide to *escape* from a life of pain and suffering. Younger adults may want to *change* their situation and the suicide attempt is a response to this (see Fremouw, Perezel and Ellis, 1990). However, it will not suffice to say that suicides amongst older people are purely a response to suffering, since there is also a notable racial and sexual difference in suicide rates (though note there are no gender or racial differences in *attitudes* to suicide; Parker, Cantrell and Demi, 1997) – namely, older women and older black men do not show an increase in suicide in later life (in fact, if anything, there is a decline). The increase in suicide rate is principally due to older white men. The most parsimonious explanation of this phenomenon is that white men are more accustomed to power and a high standard of living, and a loss of or a decline in these is too much for some individuals to cope with (e.g. Miller, 1979). This is suggested in the findings of a longitudinal study by Barefoot *et al.* (2001). They found that from the age of 60–80 men show an increase in depressive symptoms whilst women do not (though note that Fiske, Gatz and Pedersen, 2003 did not find such a pronounced gender difference). Again, Leenaars and Lester (1998) found that, in Canada, suicides amongst older people were higher in provinces where there was general affluence, but a higher percentage of older people were on low incomes.

However, this is not a full explanation. Other factors have also been identified, such as:

- medical problems and relationship loss (Florio *et al.*, 1997)

- feeling of being let down by medical care practitioners and the health service in general (Kjølseth, Ekeberg and Steihaug, 2010)

- (for the oldest old) bereavement within the past year (Erlangsen *et al.*, 2004)

- depression (see Johnston and Walker, 1996; McLaren *et al.*, 2007)

- low extraversion and high neuroticism scores (Duberstein *et al.*, 2000)

- perceived level of burden to others (Jahn *et al.*, 2011)

- poorer coping strategies (Marty, Segal and Coolidge, 2010)

- low level of social inclusion (Yur'yev *et al.*, 2010)

- (in older men) birthdays (Williams *et al.*, 2011)

- humidity (Salib, 1997; though see Godber, 1998 for a critique).

This plethora of possible causes (and it is far from an exhaustive list) can create the impression that nothing can be done to predict older adult suicide, because there are too many variables. However, the variables listed here are not all necessarily of equal importance and some could be totally or to a very large extent accounted for by other variables in the list. In other words, in statistical terms, there is a lot of covariance.

At a broad level, Shah (2011c) has developed a formula that creates a broad prediction of national suicide rates – namely:

$$Y = A + BX + CX2$$

Y is suicide rate, X socio-economic status, and A, B and C are constants. Shah claims that the equation accurately maps suicide rates as they fluctuate with changes in socio-economic conditions. However, on the basis of individual behaviour, we currently lack a model that will adequately explain *individual* suicides amongst older adults. This is not helped by a conspicuous absence of detailed prevention strategies amongst social workers and similar groups (Manthorpe and Iliffe, 2011).

Conclusions

The field of death, dying and bereavement is one that is inherently imbued with emotionally loaded issues. It is therefore an area that cries out for clear-sighted research with well-established frameworks of enquiry that allow for logical analysis when reasoning might be most clouded by emotion. Alas, that is rarely what has happened in practice. Key models have been shown to be based on poor data collection and to be inaccurate in their conclusions. Much of the remaining research, although sound in its own terms, has served to uncover confounding variables and give reason for strong ethical questions to be raised about the appropriateness of many of the decisions that have to be made in a person's last few days. What is clear, however, is the need for individuals to make a clear statement of how they wish to be treated should they become incapable of higher cognitive thought and be reliant on life support. For example, Bagheri (2007) argues that people should be allowed to choose whether cessation of cardio-respiratory function *or* loss of brain function constitutes death. This concords with the finding that the majority of older people indicate that they wish to make their own decision about how they should be treated at the end of life (Moorman, 2011). However, few stop to think that by the time this is reached they might be incapable of expressing their needs. In a study of 3746 case histories of older dying (American) patients, Silveira, Kim and Langa (2010) found that 42.5 per cent required decision-making processes in their final days, and, of these, 70.3 per cent had lost decision-making capacity. Thus, almost a third of dying patients are incapable of making vital decisions concerning their final few days of life. Silveira *et al.* demonstrate that, when older adults did leave prior instructions, their treatment was often radically different from the treatment given to patients who had left no prior instructions. Thus, it is highly probable that, although medical and nursing staff worked in what they sincerely believed was the best manner possible, their actions were in contradiction of what the patient would have chosen had he or she been able to. In all the studies cited in this chapter that address the issue, only a minority (and often a tiny minority) of participants left clear written and signed statements indicating how they wished to be treated in the event of being in need of life support and similar. Confusion over end of life wishes are upsetting for all concerned, and when things end up in court often only the lawyers benefit.

Suggested further reading

Szabo (2010) provides a large (over 2000) list of references to works on death and dying. There is an excellent summary of the LCP by Preston (2007). Klessig (1992) provides a very useful introduction to the minefield surrounding cultural differences concerning death and the termination of life support (see also Bullock, 2011). For a more recent study of the (US) legal problems surrounding termination of life support, see Brutoco (2010).

CHAPTER 9

What is the Future of Ageing?

Introduction

In this final brief chapter, the ways in which older adults will react to and behave within a future, more technologically driven society will be considered. This will be done by bringing to bear arguments and information described in earlier chapters.

What will constitute being 'old'?

At the current time, judgements about what makes a person 'old' are based on several criteria, including appearance, attitudes and amount of leisure time. However, a variety of developments is likely to change all of these in the future. Appearance may well be the most fundamental factor to be affected. Already, plastic surgery and hormone replacement therapy can remove a decade or more from a person's appearance. These are of course largely cosmetic changes. There is little reason to doubt that techniques in this field will improve and possibly become more affordable, so that a wider range of people can make use of them. This is aside from the possibility that advance in medical services may find further ways of retarding the ageing process. It is already well established that some animals can live much longer by simple manipulations of their environment and diet. The leap from this to humans is not a simple one, but at some point the change will almost certainly come, and the over-sixties will no longer look 'old' in the stereotypical meaning of the term. However, will this necessarily change matters? Might it not be the case that people will look for different indicators of age, so that, instead of looking for wrinkles or greying hair, attention shifts to, for example, the brightness of the eye? It can be demonstrated that cultures differ in their perception of key physical attributes in other respects, such as erogenous zones. Heterosexual males of different cultures might be most attracted by breasts, buttocks, legs or the nape of the neck. Why should the prime indicator of age not similarly shift across cultures separated by time?

Alternatively, ageing retardation may be very successful, so that no one can tell how old an adult is. This raises a series of possible dilemmas. Will some individuals deliberately select to grow older 'naturally' and choose to make themselves outcasts?

Perhaps anti-ageing treatments may be very expensive, so that only particular social castes can afford them. Again, perhaps a new neurosis will arise, afflicting people who feel 'trapped' in a body that is the wrong age for their thoughts and attitudes. Perhaps treatments might delay the onset of signs of ageing, but nonetheless it will eventually arrive (i.e. at the point when the treatment 'fails'), albeit at a later age. Might this physical change (which the individual has taken deliberate steps to avoid) be more traumatic than for a person who has aged naturally and passively allowed his or her body to undergo the ageing process? Before voting too hastily in favour of anti-ageing treatments, it would be wise to consider the potentially serious psychological consequences. It should also be noted that, whatever the outcome, images of ageing are still likely to be predicated on the assumption that the process is synonymous with physical decline. Warren (1998), in an interesting review of the history of identifying markers of ageing, identifies this as the prime marker of the ageing process in the future.

Attitudes are supposedly a good indicator of age. The popular conception of the older person is that he or she is conservative and cantankerous – a thoroughly erroneous view, as was noted in Chapter 5. However, there is a further reason for doubting this assumption. There has been a radical sociological shift in the past 50 years towards a far more liberal and permissive society, which has allowed young adults to express and celebrate being young, rather than attempting to become carbon copies of their parents' generation as quickly as possible. The first rock 'n' roll generation is past retirement age, and the flower power generation is more or less in its sixties. The full ramifications of this are complex and more properly dealt with by a sociological text, but an important psychological prediction emerges from this – namely, that older people of the future are unlikely to fit into the niches that have been established by societal expectations with quite the same willingness as previous cohorts. They have seen that conventions can be flouted and that protest can work. Accordingly, if younger generations do not change societal mores to better cater for older people, then older people are more likely to do it themselves.

A final consideration concerns leisure time. Perversely, in industrial societies where leisure is treasured, an excess of it is usually greeted with distaste, since it often indicates unemployment or retirement. However, the increased automation of work (particularly computerisation) may well change this attitude. Shorter working weeks, and an increase in flexihours and home offices may lead to more people of working age spending a greater proportion of time in their homes than in traditional workplaces. This means that retired and older people may no longer be marked out simply because they are not 'at work'. At the time of writing, many industrialised countries are concerned about altering the retirement age, but in essence this is tinkering with details. Fundamental issues about leisure are not really affected by this.

Older people and the technological society

It is a cliché to note the immense changes in lifestyles of people in industrialised nations that have resulted from the technological and scientific advances of the past hundred or so years. It is tempting to imagine that older people will be swept up in this tidal wave of changes, and this raises the issue of how well they will cope.

Intuitively, one might suppose that the greatest impact will be in improved medical care, and that people will live longer because of this. However, as was noted in Chapter 1, this is not necessarily so. The increase in the average life expectancy has primarily resulted from fewer people dying in infancy rather than a lengthening life expectancy *per se*. Indeed, the older the age group considered, the less the increase in life that modern medicine can provide. Many of the illnesses that afflict older adults, such as cancers and cardiovascular complaints, are as incurable now as they were in 1900 (though modern palliative care can certainly alleviate the suffering more efficiently and may be able to prolong life expectancy slightly further). Again, if a cure for a disease is found, this need not prolong life by a significant degree. Finding a cure for one form of cancer, for example, does not cure all the other varieties. Furthermore, curing an older person of one illness does not necessarily improve his or her life expectancy to a significant degree. As has already been noted, older adults (particularly those aged over 75) may have several physical processes on the verge of collapse. Preventing a disease striking one of these down does not make the others any less immune to degradation. In short, curing a fatal heart disease may simply make a failing liver the cause of death instead (please note this is *not* an argument in favour of denying older adults medical care because it is a 'lost cause'; although it may apply to a proportion of older adults, it is not a universal truth).

Because of these considerations, it is unlikely that people aged 70 or over are likely to display an appreciable rise in life expectancy in the future. This is simply because, although cures for individual illnesses may be found, methods of overcoming widespread ageing decline will have to be discovered before much benefit can be reaped. This raises a further, more controversial issue – will there be the impetus to pursue this? The financial burden imposed by the greying population was noted in Chapter 1. Any appreciable lengthening of the lifespan will simply compound this problem. There is also a moral issue – if a method is found to prolong life, it carries with it the question of whether the quality of life makes the effort worthwhile. In addition, the procedure may be hazardous – current medical thinking assumes that, for example, lengthening telomeres may also increase the risk of contracting cancer (see Concar, 1996, and Chapter 1). What if a person considers the prospect of an artificially longer life and decides, for whatever reason, that he or she does not want it. Will this refusal be counted as voluntary euthanasia? Again, what if the treatment is expensive and thus only within the reach of the very wealthy. Should they be allowed to enjoy extra life just because they have more money? Mercifully, such questions can for the foreseeable future remain the preserve of science fiction writers (e.g. John Wyndham's excellent *Trouble With Lichen*, 1960), because the imminent advent of truly effective life-prolonging drugs seems unlikely.

Another major impact of technological change is the automation of tasks. It is a commonplace of science fiction to envisage a time when manual tasks have become the preserve of machines, and the marked decline in manual labour as a proportion of the workforce is testament to this. However, the advent of word processors, copiers, and so forth has also seen a decline in 'white collar' occupations (copy typists, to give one example). These changes are not likely to be limited to relative routine occupations. The use of 'expert systems', which seek to emulate the diagnostic abilities of a specialist, is also likely to come to the fore. Large investment and banking firms already use computers to monitor changes in stock market prices, and can automatically initiate the buying and selling of shares. In the future, it may be possible to consult a computerised doctor, which will perform the same role as a general practitioner by analysing the patient's responses to a series of questions, using algorithms based on the diagnostic processes of a real doctor. The impact of automation is almost certain to affect the lives of future cohorts of older people. One of the most basic issues (and one already touched upon) concerns shifts in working practices. There will undoubtedly be changes in the socio-economic backgrounds of retired persons. As noted in Chapter 5, social class and occupation type are predictive of attitudes towards later life, and, accordingly, there may be a shift in the pattern of behaviour and lifestyle in the older population as a whole.

However, any consideration of future trends based on technological innovation is inevitably highly speculative, and a perusal of future predictions in 1960s textbooks provides a suitable warning. In the 1960s, there were authoritative predictions that by the 1990s everyone would have died from pollution, nuclear war, famine and/or overpopulation. Alternatively, everyone would be living a life of luxury, with every whim catered for by robots. It is highly probable that the predictions made here will be similarly ludicrous. Humanity has a strange habit of finding more work when old employment opportunities are replaced by automation.

Of greater interest to the psychologist are the likely direct effects of technology on older people. The effects of this can be somewhat anticipated from the impact of previous technological innovations. The by now almost ubiquitous telephone, television and radio allow older people access to an outside world that would have been unthinkable for all but the very wealthy 50 years ago. In shaping leisure activities, the impact of television on modern life is difficult to under-estimate. Besides being entertaining, television enables older people to see places, plays, concerts and other cultural events that they perhaps are no longer physically or financially robust enough to attend in person. Often older people (especially those living alone) report using the television or radio as a comforting background noise without especially attending to the programme. However, there are disadvantages as well. The programmes on television and radio are primarily geared to the needs and demands of younger adults. Programmes may be either presented in a manner too lurid for an older person's tastes, or possibly even the basic content may be unappealing (e.g. 'youth'-orientated programmes). The advent of 'niche television' afforded by the multi-channel delights of satellite and cable television has not yielded much which could be said to be of especial interest to older adults. Certainly there is no channel dedicated to older people (though there are tens of channels specifically for children and a certain kind of lobotomised young adult male), and few programmes of special interest, other than an occasional worthy (and usually rather dull) magazine programme by a community television unit filling up the off-peak hours. The majority of programming is aimed solidly at younger audiences. However, older people are generally the heaviest consumers of television programmes, a finding echoed across different countries (e.g. Dubois, 1997; Grajczyk and Zoellner, 1998). Perhaps (as was suggested in the first edition of this book more than nine years ago) there will eventually be an outlet for smaller, community-led television stations that will allow airtime for a significant proportion of programmes by and for older viewers, but as yet there is no real evidence of this outside a few pockets of activity in the USA, where it appears to have met with some success (Burns, 1988). Printed outlets for older adults, such as magazines, have met with greater success, and several specialist publications are commercially successful. However, these can be seen as appealing to a particular niche within the older community, such as the affluent middle classes interested in expensive holidays and investment advice (see Featherstone and Wernicke, 1997). For a variety of demographic and socio-economic reasons, a publication with wider appeal is unlikely to be a viable commercial proposition.

There may be similar demographic limits to the degree older adults use the Internet. The medium should hold especial benefits to many older people. For example, there is a vast range of information available, there are opportunities to join discussion groups, there is not the feeling of being 'rushed', which there may be in an oral discussion, and all without needing to leave the safety and comfort of one's house. In the previous edition of this book, it was noted that:

> 'Net use was far commoner in the USA than in the rest of the world, but the difference between countries is shrinking year by year as computers and phone links become increasingly affordable. However, even in the USA, older adults are the age group least likely to use a computer. (Cutler, Hendricks and Guyer, 2003, p.271)

In part, older people may be deterred from using a computer through feelings of lack of control, dehumanisation (Czaja and Sharit, 1998) and anxiety, though this may be unrelated to real computing ability (Laguna and Babcock, 1997). The degree to which people succeed during their initial training also plays a key role in determining future participation in computing (Kelley *et al.*, 1999). Others may perceive that there is little of interest to them. Lurid media reports of prosecutions of individuals possessing child pornography downloaded from the 'Net does little to enhance the image that surfing the web is a suitable activity for a respectable older person.

When older adults do use the 'Net, then in the USA at least, they are most likely to use it for emails (Hilt and Lipschultz, 2004). Whilst this serves a clearly useful social function, potentially the 'Net could be especially useful for older adults in such areas as health education and perhaps this should be promoted more strongly to older people. Older adults are also more likely to find use of the Internet a positive experience (Chen and Persson, 2002). Other studies have likewise found that, once older adults take to computers, they have an empowering or at least enjoyable experience. However, resistance to starting use and/or drop-out from training may be high (Namazi and McClintic, 2003). In addition, Priest, Nayak and Stuart-Hamilton (2006) demonstrated that the biggest barrier to web use was typically poor web design rather than intelligence or prior experience of the older user. This indicates that many of the blocks to effective web use may be illusory and the products of poor design rather than an intrinsic age-related deficit. More recent studies indicate that although computer use in older adults is the fastest growing segment of the market, older users might still find computers especially difficult (Wagner, Hassanein and Head, 2010).

Other technological changes might also bring mixed blessings, in part because, although they should in theory be a boon to older adults, lack of relevant prior experience may militate against their successful use (see Charness and Schaie, 2003). Modern household appliances take much of the strain out of cooking and general housework. These items are financially available to most if not all older people, and undoubtedly are immensely advantageous. For example, refrigeration and better methods of preserving food reduce the risk of food poisoning when an older person's senses become blunted to the point where they cannot detect something that has 'gone off'. Furthermore, the long-promised arrival of 'smart' fridges (which will read bar codes on pre-wrapped foods and warn when something is unsafe to eat) will further enhance this. Simultaneously, labour-saving devices and safety checks may encourage some older adults to avoid exercise and become too complacent. Thus, their health may decline through lack of physical activity, and a misplaced optimism in food safety may lead to poisoning.

Other technological changes may still be prone to misuse. For example, use of microchip-controlled medicine dispensers have been mooted (see Kapur, 1995). The time at which some drugs are taken is vital for their efficacy, and, because some older people are forgetful, the automated dispenser emits a beep when it is time for the patient to take the next dose. There is of course one minor snag with this device, which is that it relies upon a forgetful person remembering to keep the dispenser within earshot and to remember what to do when the device goes beep. This is a problem that pervades most of the gadgetry designed to help mentally disadvantaged people – they have to remember to use it. Aides-memoire, be they beeping pillboxes, palm-held computers or electronic diaries, clearly fall foul of this problem. The difficulties created by a declining memory show the magnitude of the problem facing designers. Other technological innovations do not face these problems, and seem at first sight to be quite benevolent, such as the expert systems described earlier. However, expert systems require a computer, and where will the computer be located? We have already noted that computer use may be limited amongst older adults. If an older person has had to make the effort to travel to somewhere where there is a computer (e.g. the doctor's surgery in the case of a medical expert system), then they will surely want to see a real person as a reward for their efforts. Assuming there is a computer and a doctor programme in the house, there are still problems. An expert system only works as well as the information it is fed. What if people choose to lie or gloss over some symptoms? A human doctor, by observing voice tone and body language, should be better at detecting subterfuge than a computer, unless both hardware and software improve considerably beyond their present limits. In short, the system is open to serious, and potentially fatal, abuse.

A further consideration is that new technology is largely designed for younger adults. Miniaturised electronic gadgets are no doubt a tribute to the designer's art, but they are often too small for an older person to see or handle efficiently. In Chapter 1, it was noted that the ageing perceptual system loses its ability to process fine detail in any sensory modality, and it thus appears that many pieces of modern technology are designed to handicap the older person. The Centre for Applied Gerontology at Birmingham University in the UK has a notable slogan – 'design for the young and you exclude the old; design for the old and you include the young'. It is not being argued that every item should be designed to be age-impartial, but it is hard to see why manufacturers seem to want to exclude at least 20 per cent of their potential market by making things difficult. It should also be noted (and this is not intended to be an ageist statement) that, in designing with older people in mind, it is also aiding many younger adults with physical problems, such as people with poor vision or limited dexterity. On the reverse side of this argument, there is a danger that in making such pronouncements one is presenting a view of older people being disadvantaged to a greater extent than they are. For example, several publications and websites give advice on designing computer interfaces that as first priority stress the need for adequate wheelchair access, simple instructions and very large print. Of course these are necessary pieces of advice (for a small proportion of older adults), but at times one might wish that they were given a little less prominence.

Accordingly, technological advances are a mixed blessing to older people. While they promise great hope, many of the details of their operation have not been sufficiently thought through. Machines that are designed to help save labour may be impossible to operate or create more harm than good. Medical advances will cure some illnesses but still leave older adults vulnerable to others. A medical breakthrough that could delay the ageing process invites people to extend the time in which they can suffer as well as enjoy life. To imagine that older people will automatically be made happier by such advances is foolishly optimistic.

Conclusion

A view of the future almost inevitably stems from a criticism of the present, and many of the predictions and arguments raised in this and the previous chapter are fuelled by the current problems with gerontological research and with the lot of older people in industrialised societies. However, it would be unfair to conclude from this that something is rotten in the state of psychogerontology. The area shows a healthy growth and an agreeably wide range of interests. The predictions presented in these final two chapters can be divided into two sorts – those which ought to come true and those which might. In the former camp fall those born of criticisms of existing research methods. Researchers *must* stop treating older people as if they are a race apart. Not only is it unscientific, but it is also patronising and divisive. On a milder note, although some moves have been made in this direction, the ageing mind needs to be seen more as an interactive process and less as a set of single systems. The approach of isolating a single aspect of ageing and analysing it in great detail is analogous to the old chestnut about three blind men examining an elephant – depending upon which part of the animal they felt, the men identified the animal as being like a snake, a tree or a bird (there are other, often ruder versions of the same tale, in case this one is unfamiliar to the reader). Inevitably, changing to a multifactorial model leads to problems and a single figure result is never likely to suffice. However, as the inestimable Mr Wilde wrote, the truth is never pure and rarely simple. The second set of predictions concerns possible future changes in technology and attitudes, and how these might affect older people. It is improbable that many of the changes described will be readily apparent for several years at least. It is always tempting to think that technology will inevitably shape lives. A possibility rarely considered is that people will simply ignore it. Older people may resist new inventions, not because of inbuilt conservatism (which in any case Chapter 5 demonstrated to be an ageist conceit), but because they cannot see the worth of adopting new practices which are likely to be of only limited use. Perhaps in many ways this is the most optimistic vision one could have of future generations of pensioners – older adults standing up for what *they* want, rather than what younger adults are foisting on them 'for their own good'.

If there is a message to be taken from this book it is this:

Whether an older person is mentally advantaged or disadvantaged, content with life or suicidal, healthy or housebound, principally or solely depends upon their genetic inheritance and how he or she behaved earlier in life. A content later life is a reward, not an automatic right. It can only be reached by approaching the prospect of ageing with a clear and open mind. Some changes, such as those to the intellect, can only be partially controlled, but even though there may be some decline this should never, with the exception of dementia, be sufficient to mar a productive and happy later life. For those unmoved by this argument, and who still insist on stereotyping older people as an homogenous, inferior group, there remains a final thought. All older people are survivors: this is an accolade that not all their younger detractors will live long enough to proclaim for themselves. This is the one fact that describes every older person.

Basic Anatomy of the Nervous System

The neuron

The basic building block of the nervous system is the **neuron** (or, less accurately, the 'nerve cell'). Neurons vary enormously in shape and size, but all have the basic function of receiving signals from other neurons or specialised sensory receptors (for touch, pain, heat, etc.), and passing signals on to other neurons or sense organs. These signals are transmitted along thread-like projections, called **axons**. Neurons connect with each other at junctions called **synapses**, where signals are transferred from one neuron to another. When a neuron is activated, an electrical pulse passes down its length until it reaches a synapse, where two neurons meet with only a microscopic gap separating them. The activated neuron 'spits' a chemical across the gap onto the receiving neuron, causing one of four things:

1. It was dormant, and it is activated into sending a signal.

2. It was already sending a signal, but the new input causes it to fire with greater vigour.

3. It was already active, but the new input makes it either stop firing, or fire with less vigour.

4. It was dormant, and the new input prevents other neurons exciting it into firing.

In cases 1 and 2, the effect is said to be **excitatory** and in cases 3 and 4 the effect is said to be **inhibitory**. Therefore, neurons can either spur each other on, or they can suppress activity. The chemical transmitters employed to do this (i.e. the chemicals 'spat' at synapses) are called **neurotransmitters**. On some occasions, it is convenient to classify neurons according to the type of transmitter they use. For example, there is the **cholinergic system**, which uses the transmitter **acetylcholine**. About 90 per cent of the neurons in the brain are cholinergic. The other principal use of the cholinergic system is in the control of skeletal muscle. Conversely, the **noradrenergic system** (using **noradrenaline**) is primarily employed in the control of smooth muscle. Many neurons are covered with a layer of fatty substance called

myelin, which acts rather like the insulation around electrical wires as it stops the signal from escaping and also helps to increase the speed at which the signal is sent.

Anatomy of the nervous system

The simplest division of the nervous system is into the **central nervous system (CNS)** and the **peripheral nervous system (PNS)**. The CNS consists of the brain and the spinal cord, the PNS of the neurons connecting the CNS to the rest of the body. The nervous system consists of at least 10^{10} neurons, most of which are in the brain. The 'textbook definition' of the fundamental difference between the neurons of the CNS and the PNS is that the former cannot be replaced if they die, whilst the latter can (though as noted earlier, see Brewer, 1999).

PNS anatomy

The PNS can be divided into subsections, according to function. **Afferent** neurons carry information into the CNS, and are said to be 'somatic' if they carry information from the joints or skin of skeletal muscle and 'visceral' if they carry information from the **viscera** (intestines). **Efferent** neurons carry commands from the CNS to the body, and are said to be 'motor' if they send signals to the skeletal muscle and **autonomic** if they send signals to glands, smooth muscle, cardiac muscle, etc. (i.e. bodily functions over which there is little conscious control).

CNS anatomy

The **spinal cord**'s principal function is to channel information between the PNS and the brain. However, it is capable of some simple processing. By means of a mechanism called the **reflex arc** (a simple connection between afferent and efferent neurons), it can make the body respond to some forms of stimulation. Many reflexes (such as the well-known knee-jerk reflex) are produced in this manner.

The spinal cord projects into the brain, or, more accurately, the section of the brain called the **brainstem**. Many lay persons think of the brain as being a homogeneous mass of 'grey matter', but in fact the brain is a collection of distinct though interconnecting structures. For anatomical and functional reasons, the brain is often divided into four principal divisions. The first is the brainstem. Located behind this at the base of the skull is the **cerebellum**. Located above the brainstem is the **diencephalon**, or **interbrain**. Seated above and overlapping the other three segments is the **cerebral cortex** (often simply called the 'cortex'), the wrinkled 'top' of the brain. Generally, the further a structure is away from the spinal cord, the more sophisticated its functions.

The brainstem is chiefly concerned with the maintenance of 'life support' mechanisms, such as control of blood pressure, digestion, respiration, and so forth.

It also receives inputs from the senses and channels them through to other systems in the brain.

The cerebellum receives somatic input, and information from the semicircular canals (the balance sensors located in the inner ear). Given this information, it is not surprising to learn that the cerebellum is responsible for co-ordinating movement.

The diencephalon is a collection of several components. Among the more important of these are the following. The **thalamus** co-ordinates and channels sensory information and the execution of motor movements. Damage to this region gives rise to Parkinsonism (see Chapter 6). The **hypothalamus** might be loosely said to control bodily needs such as hunger and satiety, sexual drive, anger, and so forth. The **hippocampus** is, in evolutionary terms, amongst the oldest sections of the brain. It is involved in emotional control, but of principal interest to psychologists is its role in memory. Some unfortunate individuals who have had this area of the brain destroyed (by disease or accident) cannot retain any new information in their memories for more than about two minutes. Therefore, the hippocampus is in some manner involved in retaining information in a long-term memory store.

The cortex is responsible for the execution of most higher intellectual functions. It is divided into two **hemispheres**. The divide runs vertically from front to back, along the centre of the head. The hemispheres are linked by several pathways, of which the most important is the **corpus callosum**. For most individuals, the right hemisphere is principally responsible for visuo-spatial skills, the left for verbal skills. The cortex can also be divided into lobes, based upon the psychological functions that each of them controls. The **frontal lobes** extend from the front of the skull back to the temples. They are mainly involved in the control and planning of actions, such as producing sequences of movements, getting words and letters in the right order in speech and spelling, and producing socially appropriate behaviour. The frontal lobes are also involved in memory, principally in identifying which events in memory occurred in the recent and which in the distant past. The **temporal lobes** are situated in the positions of the right and left temples. One of their principal tasks is in interpreting information, and in particular the left temporal lobe is vital in comprehending speech and print. The temporal lobes are also strongly involved in memory, particularly the long-term retention of information. Because of the specialisation of the left and right hemispheres, the left temporal lobe tends to store verbal memories and the right temporal lobe tends to store spatial information. The **occipital lobes** are at the rear of the brain. They are involved in reading, but their principal function is vision. Virtually all processing of visual information takes place in the occipital lobes. The **parietal lobes** are located at the 'top' of the brain, surrounded by the other three lobes (they lie roughly in the position of an Alice band or the headband of a pair of headphones). In part they are responsible for maintaining awareness of the body's state and location. Their principal intellectual role might be said to be symbol interpretation, and they are involved in object recognition and reading.

Fluid and Crystallised Intelligence

When psychologists began to consider the issue in the early years of this century, it was generally felt that 'intelligence' was a unitary skill. In other words, no matter what type of intellectual task was set, be it verbal, numerical or visuo-spatial (i.e. shapes and figures), the same basic ability dictated a person's performance. This was christened g (for 'general intelligence') by one of the founding fathers of intelligence testing, Charles Spearman. The term 'g' or 'Spearman's g' is still in use, although it is now generally employed more loosely to describe overall ability or score on a battery of intellectual tests that have assessed a variety of intellectual skills. Most researchers now reject the more rigid definition of g, arguing that 'intelligence' is composed of several interrelated skills. What these are is still open to debate (see Deary, 2001; Eysenck and Kamin, 1981; Kail and Pelligrino, 1985; Rebok, 1987). However, perhaps the most widely accepted theory has been the **hierarchical approach** (Cattell, 1971). This argues that all intellectual skills make use of a general intellectual ability, but they also call upon more specialised skills, depending upon the needs of the task at hand. Cattell (1971) and Horn (1978) identified two of these specialised skills, and called them **crystallised intelligence** and **fluid intelligence**.

Crystallised intelligence measures the amount of knowledge a person has acquired during his or her lifetime. Usually it is measured by simple direct questions, such as asking the person to define obscure words (e.g. 'What is the meaning of *manumit?*'), or to answer 'general knowledge' questions (e.g. 'What is or are the *Apocrypha?*'). The questions can also ask a person to solve problems based on his or her existing knowledge. They can be practical (e.g. 'What do you do if you cut your finger?') or moral (e.g. 'Why should we pay our taxes?'). Such questions can only be answered correctly if one already has the necessary information in one's head and can retrieve it. One cannot create definitions of words or knowledge of sticking plasters, antiseptics, taxation structures or fiscal policy on the spur of the moment. Fluid intelligence tests, on the other hand, draw on acquired knowledge as little as possible, and measure what might be defined as the ability to solve problems for which there are no solutions derivable from formal education or cultural practices. In other words, it is the ability of the person to solve novel problems. The most commonly used method is to ask a person to identify a rule governing a group of items (verbal, numerical or visuo-spatial) and then provide the next one in the series:

A C F J ?

or to spot the odd one out:

245 605 264 722

Typically, fluid intelligence tests have a time limit imposed on them so that to be proficient a person must not only be accurate but fast as well.

There is also the measure of overall intelligence called (not surprisingly) g, which, according to Horn and Cattell's framework, is the aggregate of fluid and crystallised intelligence scores.

Basic Psycholinguistic Concepts

It is perhaps easiest to introduce the area through an examination of the psychological processes involved in reading (which in any case is the linguistic skill perhaps most often studied by psychologists and educational gerontologists). Introspectively, reading is perceived as being a fairly automatic and instantaneous process (e.g. try not reading *don't read this*) but in fact it involves the co-ordination of a variety of different skills, from the very basic to the very complex. On *a priori* grounds, normal reading must involve at the very least the following processes. First, there must be a mental mechanism for identifying individual letters, to distinguish them from, say, random splodges of ink, or items from a foreign alphabet. Furthermore, there must be a method of identifying whether sequences of letters form real words or whether they are merely nonsense strings (e.g. *aslkdhf*), and also of judging how to pronounce the word (i.e. of converting the printed into a spoken representation). Following from these stages must be a skill of judging if sequences of words form meaningful phrases. These have to be judged for both their **syntactic** and **semantic** acceptability. For example, the phrase:

goldfish make suitable pets

is sensible, if banal. The phrase:

hypotheses make suitable pets

is more interesting, but is obviously nonsense, and is said to be semantically unacceptable (loosely, semantics is the expression of meaning). However, the phrase's syntax (loosely, its grammar) is acceptable. Conversely, a phrase such as:

goldfish makes suitable pets

is syntactically unacceptable (because it is grammatically incorrect), but it could be argued that it still conveys a meaning, and thus is semantically acceptable. A final stage in the reading process must involve extracting meaning from the phrases. Introspection shows that one does not remember every word of what has been read – instead, one recalls the gist of the story. Thus, readers must possess a method of extracting the key features of a piece of text.

It must not be supposed that all the processing is in one direction from the basic skill of letter recognition to the relatively complex one of meaning extraction, since the latter operations can send information back down the processing chain to speed up reading. For example, suppose one is reading a passage of text written in an appallingly untidy hand, and suppose that some letters are completely unrecognisable, represented below by 'x's:

Ix is xoubtful if anx moxe axxixtance is rexxired. Remxmbxr the xroverb: txo maxy coxks xpoil the xxxxh.

Most readers should have little difficulty in decoding this message. There are several reasons for this. First, some words like *xoutful* and *xroverb* can only be *doubtful* and *proverb*. Thus, the reader makes use of knowledge of which letter combinations make real words to work out what the indecipherable letters stand for. In other instances, semantic knowledge is used. For example, *Ix* alone could be *If, It, In* or *Is*. However, *Ix is* only makes sense if *Ix* is *It*. The final word of the passage – *xxxxh* – is unrecognisable by itself, but is easily recognised as 'broth' because it is the last word of a well-known saying. This is an example of **semantic facilitation**, where the semantic content of a passage enables one to predict the words coming up. This does not just apply to reading sloppy handwriting. For normal print, one uses one's expectations to facilitate word recognition, and it has been demonstrated that words that are logically linked to what has just been read are read faster than less predictable words. Thus, if one had been reading about animals, one would read *tiger* faster than *chair*. In formal experimental situations, the phenomenon is tested by presenting participants with a word or sentence (the 'prime') and then presenting them with a word which may or may not be semantically related to the prime. Participants are usually asked to decide if the word is a word or not, or to say the word out loud. In both instances, responses are faster if the prime is semantically related. How facilitation occurs is still hotly contested, but generally it appears that the mind in effect places mental representations of semantically related words on 'standby' so that, if they appear in print, their meaning is accessed faster.

A final consideration is the role of memory. Obviously, without long-term memory, it would be impossible to read a story and understand it, simply because one would keep forgetting the plot. Less obvious is the need for working memory (see Chapter 3, or the Glossary), but one must be able to keep in mind what has just been read, otherwise by the time one reached the end of the sentence, one would have forgotten the point of it, and this would be especially true of long convoluted sentences such as this.

Thus, reading involves the active integration of a number of perceptual, cognitive, linguistic and memory skills. It will not have escaped some readers' attention that the processes involved in the comprehension of spoken language are similar. There must be the capacity for recognising individual letters or words; for identifying they are correctly pronounced; for identifying meaning and whether phrases are syntactically acceptable; and, finally, for extracting the gist of a spoken message. Obviously, there are differences – reading is accessed visually, speech acoustically, so readers can (and do) look back at something they have not understood, whilst listeners usually have fewer opportunities to do an analogous thing, and instead have to ask a speaker to repeat something they have difficulty with. Speech and writing also have different conventions. Writing, for example, tends to be more formal and grammatically correct. Indeed, there has been a debate as to whether speech and writing share *any* processes in common (Olsen *et al.*, 1985). In Chapter 4, this was not addressed, but, given that reading and listening have functionally analogous processes, examination of the effects of ageing on the two skills will be conducted in tandem. It is not necessarily implied, however, that a change in a reading sub-skill is automatically linked to a change in the analogous listening sub-skill. It should also be noted that the effects of ageing on the skills of speech production and writing have received relatively little attention, but such experimental findings as there are will be placed at appropriate points in the commentary.

The Later Career of Elisabeth Kübler-Ross

In the 1970s, Elisabeth Kübler-Ross met Jay Barham, a self-ordained minister who claimed he could commune with the spirits of the dead. It is fascinating how many intelligent famous people have been taken in by such claims and alas Dr Kübler-Ross was no exception. The essence of Barham's claims was that he could make spirits materialise. The following extract from Kübler-Ross's obituary gives a flavour of the more publically acceptable aspect of what was (supposedly) taking place:

> Kübler-Ross alleged that guides took 'actual molecules' out of Barham to clone a human being, in which form they appeared. 'The bulk energy to create the guide who comes to visit comes from us, the group. And the more people there are in the group, the faster the materialisation happens. It is a true cloning,' she said. One spirit guide, 'Mario', appeared from the waist up and gave her a back rub for 15 minutes. (Schatzman, 2004)

The reality was probably a lot less palatable. Defecting members of the group alleged that Barham was masquerading as the spirits made flesh, aided by confederates. On occasions, in a darkened room, spirits would supposedly enter the room and engage in sexual activity with the congregation. Several women in the group, comparing notes afterwards, thought the spirit sounded an awful lot like Jay Barham, and four female members of the congregation contracted the same vaginal infection after being visited by the same entity on one night (*Time Magazine*, 1979). A persistent rumour is that at one session a doubting member of the flock flicked on the light switch to reveal the minister naked save for a turban.

There is no evidence linking Kübler-Ross to these specific activities, but, when news reached her, and prudence might have been wise, she defended Barham up to the hilt. As she is reported as saying in a popular magazine at the time, 'He has so much integrity,' she says. 'The truth does not need to be defended.' (Jackovitch, 1979). A defector from the centre was rather less charitable: 'She is so emotionally dependent on [the minister and his entourage] that she can't see' (*Time Magazine*, 1979).

Eventually Kübler-Ross dissociated herself from Barham but by then serious damage to her reputation had been done (arguably not helped by an interview with

Playboy magazine in the early 1980s where she outlined some of her more extreme occult theories). She continued to court controversy, however. In the 1980s, she was conducting research on death in AIDS victims and announced that she would adopt 20 babies with AIDS. AIDS and HIV were far less understood and far more feared in the 1980s, particularly in rural areas akin to where Kübler-Ross was then living. Her house was torched and her pets shot. Kübler-Ross's son took her to Arizona for her own safety, and it was there that she lived out the remainder of her life, dying, after a series of strokes, in 2004.

Glossary of Technical Terms

The glossary contains definitions of the technical terms printed in bold type in the main body of the text. In addition, it includes definitions of terms not mentioned in the text, but in common or relatively common use in the gerontological literature.

Italicisation of a word or term within a definition indicates that it has its own entry in the glossary.

A-68 Protein found in abnormally high concentration in patients with *dementia of the Alzheimer type* (DAT).

AAMI *age-associated memory impairment.*

acceptance of prospect of dying stage See *Kübler-Ross's stages of dying.*

accommodation (vision) The ability to focus at different distances.

acetylcholine Type of *neurotransmitter.*

acetylcholinesterase inhibitor (AChEI) A drug that stimulates the *cholinergic system.*

AChEI *acetylcholinesterase inhibitor.*

acquired dysgraphia A profound difficulty in writing (particularly spelling) resulting from brain damage.

acquired dyslexia A profound difficulty in reading resulting from brain damage.

ACS *acute confusional state.* See *delirium.*

active life expectancy The average number of years remaining in which an individual, or more generally members of an *age cohort,* can expect to lead an active life.

activity theory The counter-argument to *disengagement theory,* which argues that older people should be kept involved and active in the community.

acuity (vision) Ability to focus clearly.

acute brain disorder *delirium.*

acute brain dysfunction *delirium.*

acute confusional state (ACS) *delirium.*

acute crisis phase (of dying) See *Pattison's stages of dying.*

AD *Alzheimer's disease.* See *dementia of the Alzheimer type.*

ADL *assessment of daily living.*

AD-MID A *dementia* in which the patient displays symptoms of *dementia of the Alzheimer type* and *multi-infarct dementia* simultaneously.

aetiology The origin and causes (particularly of disease).

affect Emotion.

afferent (neurons) Carrying signals from the *peripheral* nervous system to the *central nervous system.*

age × complexity effect The phenomenon that the difference between older and young adults gets disproportionately larger the more complex the task set. See *age × treatment interaction*.

age × process interaction *age × treatment interaction*.

age × treatment interaction The phenomenon that some psychological skills decline more than others in later life (see *differential preservation* and *preserved differentiation*). Thus: if skill 1 requires mental process *X* and skill 2 process *Y*, but skill 1 declines disproportionately more than skill 2 in later life, then process *X* must be more affected by ageing than is process *Y*. This is not the same as the *age × complexity effect*, which argues that changing the complexity of items which the same skill has to process has a disproportionate effect on older participants.

age-appropriate behaviour *social age*.

age-as-leveller The argument that later life diminishes the perceived differences between socio-economic/ethnic groups.

age-associated memory impairment (AAMI) Pronounced memory decline in later life, which is associated with ageing, rather than *dementia* or similar.

age bias *age discrimination*.

AGECAT A computerised package for assessing the mental state of older patients.

age cohort A group of people born and raised in the same period of time/history.

age discrimination Unfair bias against a person because of his or her age.

age-equivalent scale Test scores expressed in terms of the proportion of an age group who typically possess them. Thus, whether a person is advanced or less able for their age can be assessed.

age grading The societal pressures which determine what is considered appropriate for different *social ages*.

ageing Process of change occurring with the passage of time. Usually restricted to changes (often perceived as negative) which occur after

adolescence. See *anatomical age, biological age, carpal age, chronological age, distal ageing effects, physiological age, primary ageing, probabilistic ageing, proximal ageing effects, secondary ageing, social age* and *universal ageing*.

ageing/aging Either spelling is acceptable. However, citizens of the USA tend to use 'aging' and UK inhabitants 'ageing'.

ageism *age discrimination* (usually refers to discrimination against older people).

age norm The mean score on a test for a given age group, and hence a gauge of what is typical for that age group.

age-normative effect A factor which influences the majority of people at the same point in their lives.

agerasia Compare with *Hutchinson-Gilford syndrome*.

age scale *age-equivalent scale*.

age set *age cohort*.

age-specific mortality rate Proportion of people in an age group likely to die before they get too old to be in the said group.

age stratification Dividing the lifespan into a series of *social ages*.

aging See *ageing* and *ageing/aging*.

Aging Semantic Differential (ASD) Method of measuring attitudes to ageing by asking people to judge older adults in terms of pairs of adjectives, deciding in each case which adjective is preferred. Three traits were identified in the original study – competence, autonomy and acceptability. Subsequent researchers have sometimes failed to find these and other researchers argue for a modified four-factor model.

agitation Term covering a set of symptoms indicative of restlessness and dissatisfaction, including acts of physical aggression, grabbing, complaining, shouting, verbal abuse, etc. Often used to describe a range of problematic behaviours found in institutionalised older adults, particularly those who are intellectually compromised or suffering from *dementia*.

agoraphobia Fear of open spaces.

AIDS dementia Form of *dementia* found in some patients in the terminal stages of acquired immune deficiency syndrome (AIDS).

alcoholic dementia (1) Old (and misleading) synonym for *Korsakoff's syndrome*. (2) A *dementia* resulting from long-term alcohol abuse, and similar to *Korsakoff's syndrome* although with a different neuroanatomical pattern of decay (this distinction is controversial and not universally accepted).

ALE Average *life expectancy*.

alexia A complete failure to read or to recognise words or letters (in *dyslexia* there is a partial ability). Only usually seen in brain-damaged individuals.

allocation policy Model of reading that argues that older people compensate for declines in some reading sub-skills by placing greater reliance on other sub-skills and abilities.

alpha waves A pattern of electrical activity detected by *EEG* (see *electroencephalograph*) with a frequency between 8 and 12 Hz.

aluminium theory of dementia of the Alzheimer type Brain cells of Alzheimer patients show unusually large concentrations of aluminium, leading to the theory that the principal cause of *dementia of the Alzheimer type* is the 'poisoning' of the brain with aluminium contamination. However, recent work suggests that this may be an artefact of the manner in which the cells are analysed.

alumni education US term for education schemes for former students (alumni) of an institution of higher education. The courses are typically intended for intellectual enrichment, rather than for specific postgraduate qualifications such as a Master's or PhD degree.

Alzheimer's disease (AD) *dementia of the Alzheimer type*.

Alzheimer-type dementia *dementia of the Alzheimer type*.

ambiguous loss Phenomenon usually encountered in severely *demented* patients, that the afflicted individual exists only physically – there is no sign of a sentient being occupying the body.

amenity migration Moving from one country or area of the country to another because it offers better amenities/lifestyle, etc. The term is often used to describe retired people moving to a 'nice place in the country'.

amnesia A failure of memory. Usually arises as a result of *stroke*, head injury, illness (e.g. *dementia*) or poisoning (e.g. chronic alcoholism).

amyloid precursor protein (APP) A gene located on chromosome 21 associated with some forms of early onset *dementia of the Alzheimer type*.

anaphoric reference Referring to a previously named person, persons, thing or things by the appropriate noun (e.g. mentioning 'the man' and then in the next sentence citing the same character as 'he').

anatomical age *Biological age*, measured through relatively gross state of body (e.g. bone structure, body build, etc.) rather than through *physiological age*. See *carpal age*.

anger at prospect of dying stage See *Kübler-Ross's stages of dying*.

anniversary reaction Negative feelings engendered by it being the anniversary (or general time of year) of an event distressing to a person (e.g. death of a close friend or relative).

Anomalous Sentences Repetition Test (ASRT) Test designed to identify patients in early stages of *dementia* from those with *pseudodementia*. Participants are required to repeat sentences spoken by the tester.

anomia A failure to name objects.

antagonistic pleiotropy theory The theory that many of the deleterious changes found in later life are the products of genes that in earlier life conferred advantages.

antediluvian ageing myth Myth that at some distant time ('antediluvian' means 'before the flood') a (usually virtuous and pious) race of people existed, who had incredibly long lifespans. Also known as *hyperborean ageing myth*.

anticholinergic Anything which blocks the action of the cholinergic system. This can lead to severe memory loss, and this information is one of the cornerstones of the *cholinergic hypothesis*.

anticipatory grief Grieving for the expected loss of a person before they have actually died. Thus, more generally, preparing for the death of a loved one.

anxiety disorder A long-lasting state of anxiety characterised by symptoms such as extreme restlessness, insomnia and fatigue, producing distress and impairment of function. It can manifest itself in many forms, including *phobias* (an irrational or inappropriately high fear of an item or event, such as open spaces, spiders, etc); *generalised anxiety* (a perpetual feeling of anxiety, often accompanied by physical symptoms such as sweating, being aware of a pounding pulse, etc.); *obsessive-compulsive disorder* (a condition in which to relieve anxiety feelings; the patient is compelled to repeat the same act – e.g. repeatedly washing the hands to remove anxiety-invoking dirt, etc.); and *panic disorder* (characterised by repeated *panic attacks* – sudden attacks of overwhelming apprehension, shortness of breath, feeling of loss of control, etc.).

apathetic (personality) See *passive-dependent personality*.

aphasia A failure of language. See *Broca's aphasia* and *Wernicke's aphasia*.

Aphasia Screening Test Sub-test of the *Halsted-Reitan Neuropsychological Battery*, used to assess for signs of *aphasia*.

apnoea Temporary suspension of breathing, usually in sleep. Commoner in infants and older people. Several possible causes.

ApoE *Apolipoprotein E.*

Apolipoprotein E (ApoE) A gene found on chromosome 19 believed to be linked to *dementia of the Alzheimer type* (and also *vascular dementia*). The gene comes in several forms, the commonest being e2, e3 and e4. It is e4 that is believed to be associated with a higher possibility of developing late-onset DAT. Interestingly, the e2 variant seems to carry a lower risk of developing DAT.

apoptosis Programmed cell death.

APP *amyloid precursor protein.*

apportioned grandmother See *Robertson's taxonomy of grandmothers*.

apraxia An inability to perform skilled movements.

ARHL Age-related hearing loss (i.e. any hearing loss that is attributable to or occurs with ageing).

armoured approach personality *defensiveness personality.*

armoured-defensive personality *Personality type* found in Neugarten *et al.*'s (1961, 1968) studies. Possessors of this type were either *holding on* (maintaining a high level of activity to 'defeat' ageing); or *constricted* (dwelling on what they had lost through ageing).

articulatory loop Previous term for the *phonological loop*.

ASD *Aging Semantic Differential.*

ASRT *Anomalous Sentences Repetition Test.*

assembled cognition An intellectual skill that, whilst reliant upon 'pure' intelligence, also draws in other, often learnt skills and/or cultural practices.

assessment of daily living (ADL) Any method of measuring daily activities, usually with the purpose of identifying memory slips, ability to cope independently, etc.

attention The ability to concentrate on a target item(s) despite distracting stimuli. See *divided attention, selective attention* and *sustained attention*.

autobiographical memory Memory for events peculiar to one's own life, as opposed to past events which everyone has experienced (i.e. events which have been 'in the news' such as general elections, train crashes). See *flashbulb memory* and *observer memory*.

autoimmune theory of ageing Theory that the ageing body's autoimmune system falters and begins to attack the body's own cells as if they were infections. See *disposable soma theory of ageing, Hayflick phenomenon* and *somatic mutation theory of ageing*.

autonoetic consciousness Having self-awareness. In particular, being able to mentally 'travel' back through one's memories.

autonomic (neuron) Carrying signals from the *central nervous system* to bodily systems over which there is little conscious control (e.g. glands, smooth and cardiac muscle).

awareness of dying The degree to which a person is aware he or she has a fatal illness.

axons Thread-like projections from a *neuron* that transmit neural impulses.

baby boom Strictly speaking, any period of time in which there has been a notable increase in the birth rate (generally, following the end of a war and the return home of troops after a long absence). However, the term usually refers to the *age cohort* of people born between the mid-1940s and 1960s, when there was an appreciable increase in the birth rate in the USA and other westernised nations.

baby boomer Person born during the *baby boom* period.

backward masking A method used in *iconic memory* experiments. A *to-be-remembered* item is presented for a brief period of time on a display screen, and is immediately supplanted by a different image (a 'mask') which has the potential (depending upon its appearance, intensity, etc.) to destroy the memory of the to-be-remembered item. This process of disrupting the *memory trace* is called backward masking.

backward span A *short-term memory* task in which a list of items is presented to the participant, who must repeat them back in reverse order of presentation – a more sadistic form of the *ordered recall* task.

Baltes's theory of lifespan development A rich and complex theory, devised by psychologist P. Baltes. Argues that development is determined by three factors – purely environmental, purely biological, and mixtures of biological and environmental. These influences express themselves through three strands of development: (1) *normative age-graded development* is the basic developmental pattern one would expect to find in any normal individual (e.g. in terms of *biological ageing*, the onset of puberty, in terms of *social ageing*, the effects of retirement on behaviour and attitudes); (2) *normative history-graded development* charts the effects of historical events which would normally be experienced by the whole of the *age cohort* (e.g. experience of food rationing would be normal for most English people born before 1940, but would be unusual for people in their twenties); (3) 'non-normative life development' measures the effects of major events unique to an individual's life.

bargaining at prospect of dying stage See *Kübler-Ross's stages of dying*.

BASE *Berlin Ageing Study*.

BDI *Beck Depression Inventory*.

BDS *Blessed Dementia Scale*.

Beck Depression Inventory (BDI) A multiple choice questionnaire, where the participant is required to indicate which of a choice of responses best describes him or herself in relation to a range of potentially depressive attributes.

behavioural variant frontotemporal dementia (bvFTD) *Pick's disease*.

Behaviour Rating Scale (BRS) See *Clifton Assessment Procedure for the Elderly*.

benign senescent forgetfulness *age-associated memory impairment*.

bereavement overload Inability to cope with the grieving process due to experiencing multiple bereavements in a short time period.

Berlin Ageing Study (BASE) *Longitudinal* study of older inhabitants in Berlin, commenced in the early 1990s, examining ageing change from many perspectives, including psychological and health changes.

best practice life expectancy The highest *life expectancy* found in any country in the world at a particular point in historical time.

beta waves A pattern of electrical activity detected by *EEG* with a frequency above 12 Hz.

Big Five (personality) Model of *personality* which identifies five basic personality traits: conscientiousness (how reliable a person is), agreeableness (how compliant with others' wishes), openness (how willing to cope with the unfamiliar), *extraversion* and *neuroticism*.

Binswanger's disease Form of *vascular dementia*.

biographical approach The analysis of the lives of pre-eminent members of professions, etc., to see if there are any common factors to explain their greatness. Has been widely used in *creativity* research.

biological age The body's state of physical development/degeneration. This is gauged against the state of an average person of the same *chronological age*. See *anatomical age, physiological age*.

biological death Irreversible death of all cells within the body.

bipolar disorder Mental illness characterised by alternate episodes of extreme and unrealistic elation and hyperactivity (mania) and depression. Better known by its older name of *manic depression*.

birth cohort A group of people born in the same period of time. See *cohort*.

Blessed Dementia Scale (BDS) A measure of intellectual impairment and functioning, usually employed in the assessment of *demented* patients. The test requires the patient to answer some simple memory questions (e.g. 'What is your name?', 'Who is the current prime minister?') and to perform some simple intellectual tasks (e.g. 'Count backwards in

steps of three'). Details of how capable the patient is of looking after him- or herself are collected from a *caregiver*. The test provides a useful 'ready reckoner' of how intellectually impaired a patient is, and how much professional nursing care and assistance is required. The Blessed Dementia Scale (named after its author, Dr Blessed) is a British test. The American equivalent is the *Mental Status Questionnaire* which has a similar format.

blood–brain barrier A physiological mechanism which prevents potentially damaging chemicals in the bloodstream from entering the brain.

body transcendence versus body preoccupation In Peck's theory, realising that in later life, bodily fitness and health can no longer be a prime cause of self esteem.

BOLD-fMRI (Blood-Oxygen-Level-Dependent fMRI) Commonly-used *fMRI* technique.

bovine spongiform encephalopathy (BSE) Degenerative disease of the nervous system in cattle, colloquially known as *mad cow disease*. The cause is unknown – the most popular theory is that it is due to cattle eating infected feed, possibly accidentally contaminated with remains of humans who died from a form of *dementia*.

bradykinesia Very slow movement; a common feature of *Parkinsonism*.

bradylexia Very slow (but not necessarily inaccurate) reading.

brain death Cessation of brain activity.

brainstem Section of the brain which is the meeting place between the *spinal cord* and the brain. Besides acting as a relay station between the spinal cord and other areas of the brain, the brain stem controls many life support mechanisms (e.g. blood pressure, respiration).

brick test Semi-serious term for a *creativity* test in which the participant must think of novel uses for an everyday object (often a house brick, hence the name).

Brinley plot Plot of older adults' response times versus younger adults' response times on the same set of tasks. For both age groups, times get slower the more complex the task, but the plot of the older versus the younger times is linear (i.e. it appears as a straight line on a graph). This supports the *general slowing hypothesis*.

Broca's aphasia A specific problem with producing speech, resulting from brain damage.

Brown-Peterson task Named after its inventors, the task presents participants with a list of *to-be-remembered* items, then gives them a distracting task (usually counting backwards in units of 2 or 3), before asking participants to recall the *to-be-remembered* items.

BRS *Behaviour Rating Scale*. See *Clifton Assessment Procedure for the Elderly*.

BSE *bovine spongiform encephalopathy*.

bulimia The uncontrollable urge to overeat.

bvFTD *behavioural variant frontotemporal dementia*.

CAD *cortical atherosclerotic dementia*.

CAMDEX Cambridge Mental Disorders of the Elderly Examination – a *test battery* of measures for assessing older people for *dementia* and other aspects of mental health and psychological well-being.

CANTAB Cambridge Automated Neuro-psychological Test Battery. A *test battery* of measures assessing neuropsychological functioning and thus assessing for signs of brain damage.

CAPE *Clifton Assessment Procedure for the Elderly*.

caregiver A person who looks after a patient or child. In the context of this book, the term usually refers to the relative of an older patient who is principally responsible for the latter's welfare.

Caregiver Strain Index (CSI) Measure of stress and strain in *caregivers* (usually caregivers of older patients).

caretaker (1) *Caregiver*. (2) For the benefit of American readers, 'caretaker' is commonly used in British English to denote a janitor, particularly of a school.

carpal age *Chronological age* calculated through the state of the wrist (carpal) bones.

CAS *Cognitive Assessment Scale*. See *Clifton Assessment Procedure for the Elderly*.

cascade model of ageing Model of ageing which argues that changes begin in a relatively slight fashion, and then gather momentum and accelerate in severity.

cataracts A progressive opaqueness of the lens, ultimately causing blindness.

catastrophe theory *error catastrophe theory*.

CBS *chronic brain syndrome*.

CDR *Clinical Dementia Rating*.

CDT *clock drawing test*.

cellular garbage theory Model of ageing which argues that the decline of the older body is attributable to the accumulation of 'waste products' from the cells' metabolic processes.

central executive The section of the *working memory* model which controls and oversees the specialist *slave systems*. The central executive is itself a memory store (though of limited capacity).

central nervous system (CNS) The collective term for *neurons* forming the brain and the *spinal cord*.

cerebellum Area of the brain primarily responsible for balance and co-ordinating movement.

cerebral cortex Usually known by its abbreviated name of *cortex*. The cerebral cortex is the characteristic wrinkled surface of the brain. It is divided into two linked *hemispheres* and can be divided into four regions or lobes which display different functions. The cerebral cortex is responsible for the majority of higher intellectual functioning.

cerebral haemorrhage Bleeding in the brain.

cerebrospinal fluid Fluid which cushions and in part supplies the brain with nutrients.

CFQ *Cognitive Failures Questionnaire*.

changing environment effect *cohort effect.*

Charles Bonnet syndrome Visual hallucinations in the absence of other symptoms of mental illness. Exact causes are as yet unknown, but probabilistically related to older adults with visual impairment.

childhood amnesia Phenomenon that *autobiographical memories* of early childhood are scarce or non-existent.

choice reaction time (CRT) The time taken for a participant to make the correct response when there is more than one stimulus, and each stimulus requires a different response. Compare with *simple reaction time.*

cholinergic hypothesis Theory that much of the memory loss in *dementia of the Alzheimer type* can be attributed to depletion of the *cholinergic system.* See *ganglioside, ondansetron,* and *tacrine.*

cholinergic system Shorthand for the network of *neurons* which use the chemical *acetylcholine* as their *neurotransmitter.* About 90 per cent of neurons in the brain are cholinergic.

chronic brain syndrome (CBS) Long-term degeneration of brain tissue, resulting in severe impairment of *personality* and/or intellectual functioning.

chronic living–dying phase (of dying) See *Pattison's stages of dying.*

chronological age The length of time a person has been alive.

chunking A *mnemonic* strategy for making long lists of items easier to remember. Items are grouped ('chunked') into sub-groups of 3 or 4 instead of being treated as a continuous list. Thus, the sequence 1789675401 might be 'chunked' into 178 967 5401.

CI *cognitive impairment.*

CIND *cognitive impairment, not dementia.*

circumlocution Talking around the topic in question because the appropriate word cannot be recalled (found to spectacular effect in some *demented* patients).

CJD *Creutzfeldt-Jakob Disease.*

classic ageing curve (Erroneous) belief of some early researchers that intelligence peaked in early adulthood and then gently declined across the rest of the lifespan.

classic ageing decline Pattern of relative preservation of *crystallised intelligence*-based skills and decline of *fluid intelligence*-based skills in older people.

Clifton Assessment Procedure for the Elderly (CAPE) *Test battery* consisting of two 'sub-batteries' – the *Cognitive Assessment Scale (CAS)* and the *Behaviour Rating Scale (BRS),* measuring intellectual skills and *personality* respectively, in older participants (particularly hospital patients and institutionalised older people).

clinical death Cessation of heart beat and breathing that will lead to *brain death* unless resuscitation occurs within 3–4 minutes.

Clinical Dementia Rating (CDR) A 'checklist' for assessing the level of functioning a patient suspected of *dementia* is capable of on various tasks. From this his or her level of impairment, and hence the severity of the dementia, can be calculated.

clock drawing test (CDT) Measure of *visuo-spatial* skills in which the participant is required to copy an analogue clock face.

closing-in The tendency by some patients with *dementia* to draw near or on the target they are supposed to be copying.

CNS *central nervous system.*

cognition The study of thought processes (including memory and problem solving).

cognitive Pertaining to *cognition.*

Cognitive Assessment Scale (CAS) See *Clifton Assessment Procedure for the Elderly.*

Cognitive Failures Questionnaire (CFQ) A test which asks participants to report instances of memory failure in recent everyday life (e.g. forgetting to buy items when shopping).

cognitive impairment (CI) An appreciable impairment of *cognitive* abilities sufficient to interfere with the norms of independent living. Often used as a general term for the declining intellectual skills in patients suffering from *dementia, delirium* and other illnesses with similar effects.

cognitive impairment, not dementia (CIND) Cognitive impairment in older people that cannot be attributed to *dementia.*

cognitive reserve An hypothesized 'buffer' that enables people with higher levels of intelligence and/or education to experience greater loss before there is a measurable effect on their intellectual performance on tasks.

cohort A group of people with a shared characteristic. Usually describes a group of people raised in the same environment and/or period of time, and thus is often used as a synonym for *age cohort.*

cohort effect A difference between age groups which is better attributed to differences in the ways they were raised and educated rather than to their ages *per se.*

cohort sequential design *overlapping longitudinal study.*

compensation General and often ill-defined theory that older people can compensate for failings in one (usually *fluid intelligence*-based) skill by increasing their reliance on another (usually *crystallised intelligence*-based). See *molar equivalence (ME).*

Compensation-Related Utilization of Neural Circuits Hypothesis (CRUNCH) Model of ageing neural processing that argues that neural representation is *more* distinctive in older adults when task demands are low, and *less* distinctive when task demands are high.

complexity effect *age × complexity effect.*

component efficiency hypothesis Hypothesis that the decline in a skill is due to a decline in one or more of the 'basic' sub-skills governing it.

compression of morbidity theory Theory that *healthy life expectancy* has increased or can increase because: (1) with the advent of inoculation programmes, better treatments, etc., people are on average older before they contract a disease or condition that medical science cannot cure and (2) the time spent suffering from a terminal disease has decreased relative to earlier generations.

computed tomography (CT scan) A method of electronically scanning the body (in the context of this book, the brain) and taking the equivalent of X-rays of narrow slices of tissue.

conceptual organisation The ability to treat items at an abstract level in order to uncover basic rules and principles and group items accordingly.

concurrent processing Holding items in *working memory* while performing a potentially distracting task at the same time (a common everyday experience is remembering a telephone number while dialling). By changing the nature and/or level of difficulty of the distracting task, the degree of memory loss can be affected. A technique frequently used to test how well participants can retain information in memory. In the working memory model, concurrent processing is held to be controlled by the *central executive.*

confabulating Condition in which the patient makes up stories or other implausible explanations to cover up gaps in his or her memory or other skills. Generally, the term is reserved for situations in which there is no conscious attempt to deceive.

confounding variable A variable which may distort the finding of primary interest. In psychology of ageing, this nearly always means the *cohort effect.*

constraint seeking strategy In solving a problem (e.g. in a '20 questions' game), seeking answers which progressively reduce the set size of all possible answers.

constricted (personality) See *armoured-defensive personality.*

constructiveness *Personality* type discovered by Reichard *et al.* (1962). Older people possessing it had come to terms with their lives, and were prepared to help others.

contextual perspective The belief that ageing effects are in a large part attributable to social and environmental effects rather than to a biological process.

continuity theory of retirement Theory that, in retirement, people maintain their sense of identity and thus retirement is not stressful.

contrast sensitivity function (CSF) A measure of the changing ability to focus clearly on a fine pattern of dark and light parallel lines when the relative darkness and lightness and thickness of the lines is altered.

corpus callosum The principal link between the left and right *hemispheres* of the brain.

correlation A statistical term which, technically speaking, means how much of the variance in one variable can be predicted by variance in another. In layperson's terms, a correlation describes the strength of the relationship between two variables, and the extent to which a change in one is met by a change in the other. Correlations are represented by the symbol *r*. Correlations can be positive (i.e., as one variable increases, so does the other) or negative (i.e., as one variable increases, the other decreases). Correlations also vary in strength – a value of 0 means that no relationship exists between the variables, a value of 1 indicates perfect positive correlation (i.e., for every increase in one variable, there is exactly the same increase in the other) and a value of -1 indicates perfect negative correlation (i.e., every rise in one variable is met with exactly the same fall in the other). In 'real life', correlations fall somewhere between these extremes. The closer the figure is to 1 or -1, the stronger the correlation (typically, a value of 0.3 or better is taken to be a good indicator). 'Correlation' is not synonymous with 'causation'. There is no method of deciding whether one variable is causing the other to alter. It should also be considered if both might not be governed by a third party (see *partial correlation*). A correlation can only show that two variables are associated with each other. For the mathematically minded: the percentage of the variance in one variable which the other predicts can be easily calculated by squaring *r* and multiplying the result by 100 (e.g. variables *A* and *B* correlate at 0.6; *A* predicts 36% of *B*'s variance).

Corsi Blocks Test A test of *visuo-spatial memory*. Participants are shown an array of blocks positioned on a table. The experimenter taps on some of these blocks in a sequence which the participant is asked to copy. The experimenter gradually increases the length of sequence until the subject's *memory span* is discovered.

cortex See *cerebral cortex*.

cortical Pertaining to the *cerebral cortex*.

cortical atherosclerotic dementia (CAD) *Vascular* dementia whose primary damage occurs in the *cortex*.

cortical dementias *Dementias* whose principal focus of damage is in the *cerebral cortex*.

creativity The ability to produce novel and appropriate ideas and solutions.

Creutzfeldt-Jakob Disease (CJD) A very rare *dementia,* contracted through contact with diseased nervous tissue. In addition to archetypal *demented* symptoms, there are severe disturbances of gait and movement. A new variant (*nvCJD*) has appeared in recent years, and has been plausibly (though not conclusively) linked to consuming beef or other products infected with *bovine spongiform encephalopathy*.

critical loss Pertaining to the *terminal drop model*, the theory that a decline in some intellectual abilities can be endured, but that a fall in others constitutes a 'critical loss' which heralds death.

cross-linking theory of ageing Theory that the physical decline of the older body can be attributed to a loss of elasticity of tissues (skin, muscle, etc.).

cross-sectional research/samples/study An experimental method where age differences are measured by testing different age groups in the same test period. Contrast with *longitudinal research/samples/study*, and see *overlapping longitudinal study*.

CRT *choice reaction time*.

CRUNCH *Compensation-Related Utilization of Neural Circuits Hypothesis*.

crystallised intelligence The amount of factual (as opposed to autobiographical) knowledge a person has acquired during a lifetime – this roughly corresponds to the lay term 'general knowledge'.

CSI *Caregiver Strain Index.*

CT/CT scan See *computed tomography.*

cued recall Experimental technique for assessing memory in which the participant is given information about the item he or she is supposed to recall (i.e. he or she is given a 'hint', such as the first letter of a *to-be-remembered* word).

culture fair Accessible equally by people of all backgrounds.

CV Cardiovascular (i.e., pertaining to the heart and blood vessels).

cytologic theory Theory of ageing that bodily decline can be attributed to 'poisoning' by toxins (including the waste products of metabolic processes). Compare with *wear and tear theory.*

DAT *dementia of the Alzheimer type.*

death awareness Awareness of the experience and practicalities of death and dying.

death preparation Preparing for the psychological and practical impact of the death of oneself or of a loved one. Usually helps to lessen the negative effects of the event. To some extent, 'passive' death preparation increases with age, as the probability of dying increases.

dedifferentiation The process of becoming more similar after a period of being more dissimilar. The term is especially applied to the theory that older adults' intellectual sub-skills become more related in later life.

defensiveness personality *Personality* type discovered by Reichard *et al.* (1962). Older people possessing it had a strong urge to carry on working to 'prove' they were still young.

deficit attenuation hypothesis Theory that older people's decision-making strategies adjust to cope with declining cognitive skills.

delirium A major disturbance (usually temporary) in intellect and perception resulting from a general deleterious change in the central nervous system's metabolism (e.g. through fever, intoxication, drug overdose). Can be confused with *dementia*, but its very rapid onset is in itself a sufficiently distinguishing feature. Occurs in three basic forms: *hyperactive delirium* is characterised by an agitated level of behaviour; *hypoactive delirium* by an unusually subdued level of behaviour; and *mixed delirium* by a mixture of hyperactive and hypoactive symptoms. Delirium may also occur without any 'obvious' behavioural symptoms.

Delirium Rating Scale (DRS) A test assessing the likelihood that a patient's symptoms indicate *delirium* (*acute confusional state*) rather than an illness with which it can be easily confused (e.g. *dementia*).

delta waves A pattern of electrical activity detected by *EEG* with a frequency between 0 and 4 Hz.

demented Describing the state associated with *dementia.*

demented dyslexia A condition found in some *demented* patients, where they can read aloud perfectly normally, and yet have no understanding of what they are reading.

dementia A global deterioration of intellectual function, resulting from atrophy of the *central nervous system*. The illness takes many forms: the commonest are *dementia of the Alzheimer type* and *multi-infarct dementia*. In some (older) textbooks, 'dementia' refers purely to those cases arising in pre-*senile* patients and *senile dementia* to cases in senile patients. This distinction is now largely disregarded.

dementia care mapping Method of analysing demented patients' reactions to their ward/care home environment. Pairs of observers code patient behaviour every 5 minutes for 6 hours, making note of level of well-being, and documenting any events that occur in the patients' vicinity. Findings and recommendations on how to ameliorate problems are fed back to the care staff.

dementia of the Alzheimer type (DAT)
Form of *dementia* whose symptoms have a characteristic pattern, first described by Alois Alzheimer in the 1900s.

dementia praecox Outmoded term (invented by Emil Kraeplin 1883) for the illness now known as *schizophrenia*. The term means 'pre-senile dementia', but should not be confused with the condition now graced with that name.

dementia pugilistica *pugilistic dementia*.

dementia syndrome of depression (DSD) *pseudodementia*.

dementia with Lewy bodies (DLB)
Dementia caused by presence of *Lewy bodies* in basal ganglia and elsewhere in the brain. Onset of DLB is relatively rapid and hallucinations are a common (but not universal) symptom. Movement problems similar to *Parkinson's disease* might be present. Cognitive skills can be impaired, but memory impairment is rarely a notable early symptom. Level of alertness can fluctuate across the same day or between days.

demographic time bomb The major financial and administrative burden created by the increase in the proportion of older adults in the population. Called a 'time bomb' because its future effects were known a long time ago, but the problem was not dealt with there and then.

denial of dying stage See *Kübler-Ross's stages of dying*.

dental age Calculation of *chronological age* from the state of the subject's teeth. Useful for dead humans and live horses.

dependency ratio The ratio of working to non-working members of the population. The phrase sometimes more specifically denotes the ratio of pensioners to working adults.

dependent personality *Personality* type discovered by Reichard *et al.* (1962). Older people possessing it had some life satisfaction, but relied on others to help them.

depression at prospect of dying stage See *Kübler-Ross's stages of dying*.

depression-related cognitive dysfunction *pseudodementia*.

depression with cognitive impairment *pseudodementia*.

depressive pseudodementia *pseudodementia*.

destination memory Remembering who has already told or been told the same information.

deterioration quotient (DQ) Measure of rate of intellectual decline associated with ageing. Sections of the *Wechsler Adult Intelligence Scale (WAIS)* (or indeed many other intelligence *test batteries*) can be divided into those measuring *crystallised intelligence* (held to be unaffected by ageing), and those measuring *fluid intelligence* (held to decline with ageing). These can also be referred to as *hold tests* and *don't hold tests* respectively. The DQ is calculated as $\{[(\text{score on hold tests}) - (\text{score on don't hold tests})]/(\text{score on hold tests})\} \times 100$. A phenomenon of the WAIS is that hold and don't hold scores are equal in early adulthood. Hence the bigger the gap in an older person's hold and don't hold test scores, the greater the deterioration. The DQ expresses this change as a percentage. See *efficiency quotient*.

Dewey's paradox of ageing John Dewey, philosopher, argued that 'we are…in the unpleasant and illogical condition of extolling maturity and depreciating age' (Dewey, 1939, p.iv).

diabetic retinopathy Disorder of vision resulting from diabetes-created damage to the retina's blood vessels.

Diagnostic and Statistical Manual of Mental Disorders (DSM) Usually known by its abbreviation, followed by the suffix of the edition in question. At the time of writing, the current edition is the fourth (*DSM IV*). The DSM is the American Psychiatric Association's (1994) classification of all mental illnesses and disabilities. It is a hugely influential publication, not only in the USA, but also worldwide. The DSM lists the major symptoms which characterise and distinguish between different mental illnesses and disabilities. It also takes note of life events and physical illnesses which may exacerbate or ameliorate the condition a patient is suffering from.

dichotic listening task A measure of divided attention. Participants hear (via stereo headphones) different messages in either ear, and must then report what they have heard in either ear.

diencephalon Also called the *interbrain*. A collective term for a number of key segments of the brain 'sandwiched' between the *brain stem, cerebellum and cortex*. More important areas include the *thalamus, hypothalamus* and *hippocampus*.

differential preservation The theory that some intellectual skills may be preserved better than others in ageing. See *preserved differentiation* and *age × treatment interaction*.

digit span *Memory span* for numbers.

digit-symbol test A member of the *Wechsler Adult Intelligence Test* battery, which assesses the ability to learn an arbitrary matching of abstract symbols and numbers.

Diogenese syndrome A condition of extreme self-neglect found in some patients with *dementia*, characterised by a very pronounced lack of personal hygiene, lack of awareness of the filthy and untidy state of their surroundings, etc.

disease cohort A group of people suffering from the same disease. See *cohort, patient cohort*.

disengaged (personality) See *integrated personality*.

disengagement theory The theory that older people seek to lose much of their contact with the outside world, in preparation for death. See *activity theory*.

disorganised personalities *Personality* type found in Neugarten *et al.*'s (1961, 1968) studies. Possessors of this type were not capable of normal functional behaviour.

disposable soma theory of ageing The theory that the body 'sacrifices' replacing all somatic (non-reproduction) cells lost through natural 'wear and tear' to concentrate on reproductive fitness. This, it is argued, is the evolutionary force which 'causes' ageing. See

autoimmune theory of ageing, free radical theory of ageing, Hayflick phenomenon and *somatic mutation theory of ageing*.

dispositional optimism A tendency to expect a higher proportion of positive than negative outcomes.

distal ageing effects Ageing changes attributable to relatively distant events (e.g. poor self-image in later life because of childhood bullying) or events which are only felt through several intermediaries. See *proximal ageing effects*.

distracters Items which are included along with *targets* and which the participant may erroneously choose.

disuse theories (of ageing) Theories which argue that intellectual skills worsen in later life because they are not practised frequently enough.

divergent thinking Usually associated with *creativity*. The ability to create ideas and solutions stemming from a simple proposition or problem.

divided attention The ability to attend to and process information from more than one source simultaneously.

DLB *dementia with Lewy bodies*.

don't hold tests See *deterioration quotient (DQ)*.

dopamine Type of *neurotransmitter*.

double ABCX model An attempt to account for the stress induced in a family by a major crisis befalling one of its older members. The letters refer to variables expressing the seriousness of the crisis, the amount of available help, etc.

double jeopardy Term denoting the problem faced by older members of an ethnic minority who face not only *ageism* but racism as well.

drop-out effect Phenomenon that in a *longitudinal study*, participants who perceive themselves as performing badly tend to withdraw from further participation, leaving a rump of 'better preserved' volunteers, thereby artificially minimising the measurements of ageing change.

DRS *Delirium Rating Scale.*

DSD *dementia syndrome of depression.* See *pseudodementia.*

DSM-IV *Diagnostic and Statistical Manual of Mental Disorders,* 4th edition.

Duke Longitudinal Study 20 years' *longitudinal study* of community residents aged 50+ years in Raleigh-Durnham, North Carolina, USA.

dying trajectory (1) The speed with which a person is likely to die. (2) The emotional and intellectual states associated with dying.

dynamic equilibrium theory Theory that as *life expectancy* has increased, the time spent experiencing mild disability has increased, but the time spent experiencing severe disability has decreased.

dysarthria Disorder of muscular control of speech (and often of skills associated with the same muscles, such as eating and drinking).

dyscalculia A profound problem with arithmetic skills. Can be developmental or acquired as the result of brain damage in adulthood.

dyslexia A profound reading problem (though note there is evidence of some reading ability). The syndrome can be inherited (developmental dyslexia) or can be acquired through brain damage (acquired dyslexia).

dyslogia Poor spoken articulation.

dysphasia A profound spelling problem.

dysphonia Disorder of voice production.

E *extraversion–introversion.*

early onset dementia (EOD) *Dementia* whose first symptoms appear before the patient is 60 years old.

early onset schizophrenia (EOS) *Schizophrenia* which first manifests itself before middle age.

echolalia Abnormal repetition of what has just been said.

ecogenic An event not tied to a particular historical epoch. See *epogenic.*

ecological validity The degree to which a study's findings bear any relevance to everyday life.

educational gerontology Broadly speaking, the study of education in later life. Chiefly concerned with the benefits and practicalities of education for older people and the real or illusory barriers to learning they may experience.

EEG See *electroencephalograph.*

efferent (neurons) Carrying signals from the *central nervous system* to the *peripheral nervous system.*

efficiency quotient (EQ) Measure of an older person's intellectual abilities relative to those of younger adults (who are assumed to be at their peak). Basically, it is the IQ which the younger adult would be recorded as possessing if he or she had the same *raw score* as the older person. For example, an older man has a raw test score of 95, which is good for his age group, and gives him an IQ of 130. A score of 95 would be poor for a younger adult, and would give him/her an IQ of, for example, 70. The older person's EQ is therefore classed as 70. By comparing EQ with IQ, a measure of age-related decline can thus be calculated. However, a more useful single measure is probably the *deterioration quotient.*

ego In Freudian theory, a person's rational self. See also *id* and *superego.*

ego differentiation versus work-role preoccupation In Peck's theory, coming to terms with retirement, and realising that status is no longer conferred by one's employment.

ego integration See *integrity versus despair.*

ego transcendence versus ego preoccupation In Peck's theory, coming to terms with the fact that one is inevitably going to die.

elder abuse Abuse of older people, particularly those who are mentally enfeebled. The abuse can be physical, but also psychological and/or financial (e.g. extorting money).

eldering Ageing in terms of *social age.*

elderspeak The use of patronising 'baby talk' when talking to older adults.

electroencephalograph Often (understandably) shortened to *EEG,* this is a device which measures the pattern of electrical activity on the scalp and by extrapolation of the *cerebral cortex* underneath. The rate of activity and where on the scalp it occurs can give some insight into how active and healthy an individual's brain is.

embolism Caused by a blood clot becoming detached and being sent around the blood vessels until it becomes 'stuck', causing a blockage.

encoding The process of creating a *memory trace.*

encopresis Faecal incontinence. See *enuresis.*

enuresis Urinary incontinence. See *encopresis.*

EOD *early onset dementia.*

EOS *early onset schizophrenia.*

episodic memory Memory for personal experiences.

epogenic An event unique to a particular historical epoch. See *ecogenic.*

EPQ *Eysenck's Personality Questionnaire.*

EQ *efficiency quotient.*

ERP *event related potential.*

error catastrophe theory Model of ageing which attributes bodily decline in later life to faulty replication of proteins.

ethnogerontology Study of ageing in different ethnic/cultural groups.

etiology See *aetiology.*

event-based task In *prospective memory* experiments, a task which requires a response which is prompted by an event or other 'sign'.

event related potential (ERP) A measure of electrical activity within the brain assessed by recording electrodes placed on the scalp. Although in some respects relatively crude compared with many more modern scanning methods, the ERP can still give valuable information about general levels of activity in the brain and how these change qualitatively and quantitatively depending upon the mental task being undertaken.

excitatory (neurons) An excitatory *neuron* either (1) causes (almost invariably in combination with other excitatory neurons) another neuron to become active, and/or (2) makes a neuron already active send signals at a faster rate.

executive functioning Mental processes involved in the control and/or sequencing of behaviours or other thought processes.

expansion of morbidity theory Theory that *life expectancy* has increased because modern medical treatments can extend the lives of those suffering from diseases that would in earlier generations have been fatal at an earlier age. This usually carries the implication that suffering in later life is increasing.

explicit attitude An attitude of a person who has had time to prepare an expression of an attitude that is fully planned in its expression.

explicit memory Memory which is consciously retrieved/searched for. Contrast with *implicit memory,* which is the recall of items or the use of memorised information which the person is unaware of recalling or even possessing.

external cue See *internal cue.*

extraversion–introversion (E) A *personality trait* from *Eysenck's personality model,* measuring the degree to which a person is outgoing and self-confident (extraversion) or shy and retiring (*introversion*).

Eysenck's personality model A model of *personality* which argues that personality is composed of a mix of three personality traits – *extraversion–introversion, neuroticism* and *psychoticism.*

Eysenck's Personality Questionnaire (EPQ) A test assessing the degree to which a person possesses the *personality traits* of *Eysenck's personality model.*

FAD *familial Alzheimer's disease.*

familial Alzheimer's disease (FAD)
Relatively rare form of *dementia of the Alzheimer type* which invariably has its onset before old age, and where the patient has close older relatives who also had the condition. Children of a FAD patient usually have a 50 per cent chance of contracting the disease themselves. See *sporadic Alzheimer's disease.*

Famous Names Test (FNT) A measure of *remote memory*. Participants are presented with a list of names of people famous for brief periods of time since the 1920s and are asked to identify those names which they can remember. Included in the list are some fictitious names, designed to prevent participants from simply replying 'yes' to every item.

FAST model Model by Reisberg *et al.* (1989) which describes seven stages of progressively worsening intellectual deterioration found in patients suffering from *dementia of the Alzheimer type.*

feeling of knowing (FOK) A person's understanding of his or her own level of knowledge (i.e. how good he or she feels his or her knowledge is).

five stages of dying model Elisabeth Kübler-Ross's model of how people respond to news that they are dying, arguing that they go through five distinct phases: denial, anger, bargaining, depression and acceptance.

flashbulb memory An *autobiographical memory* of a key event in one's life which is perceived as being unusually vivid (like a photograph taken with a flashbulb). There is a debate over whether such events are qualitatively different from others, or whether they simply subjectively appear to be more vivid.

fluid intelligence The ability to solve problems for which there are no solutions derivable from formal training or cultural practices. There is usually an added assumption that to have a high level of fluid intelligence, a person must be able to solve the problems quickly.

Flynn effect The phenomenon that IQ test scores have increased with each generation of the population in the twentieth century

(Flynn, 1987). The reasons are not completely understood – in part it may reflect an increase in ability to think in abstract terms as a result of changes in education and lifestyle, but the effect is certainly not applicable to all types of intellectual performance, and a full explanation of the phenomenon has proved elusive.

fMRI *Functional magnetic resonance imaging.* A scanning technique that assesses structure and activity within the body simultaneously.

FNT *Famous Names Test.*

focused (personality) See *integrated personality.*

FOK *feeling of knowing.*

formal operations In Piaget's theory of cognitive development, the period from the age of 11 years+ when the child begins to think in genuinely abstract terms.

fountain of youth The belief in a foodstuff that can keep a person perpetually young.

fourth age Period of later life (usually during terminal illness, *dementia,* etc.) when a person is dependent on others for basic welfare provision. See *third age.*

Fraboni Scale of Ageism (FSA) Scale devised by Fraboni *et al.* (1990) measuring attitudes to ageing, and yielding three measures: antilocution (speaking negatively about older adults), avoidance (avoiding contact with older people), and discrimination (feeling that older adults are inferior). The FSA consists of a set of 29 statements – for each one the respondent indicates his or her strength of agreement/disagreement.

free radical theory of ageing Free radicals are ions (charged atomic particles) produced in chemical reactions in the body. The theory argues that free radicals damage cells and their chromosomes, thereby causing physical decline. Some theorists argue that consuming extra daily quantities of vitamin C will offset these effects. See *autoimmune theory of ageing, disposable soma theory of ageing, Hayflick phenomenon* and *somatic mutation theory of ageing.*

free recall A memory task in which items can be recalled in any order (i.e. the order in which they were originally presented does not have to be reproduced). Compare with *ordered recall*.

frontal lobe dementia *Dementia* whose origin and primary focus is the *frontal lobes*. The principal form is *Pick's disease*.

frontal lobes The front section of the *cerebral cortex* extending back to the temples. Primarily involved in planning and controlling actions and thoughts (e.g. by getting words in the correct order whilst speaking, producing socially appropriate behaviour).

fronto-temporal dementia *Dementia* originating in the *frontal lobes* and/or the *temporal lobes*. In practice, the term is used interchangeably with *frontal lobe dementia*.

FSA *Fraboni Scale of Ageism*.

functional age The average age at which a particular set of abilities are found (i.e. it measures how well an individual performs relative to his or her age group).

g General intellectual capacity; the general intellectual ability felt by many researchers to underpin all intellectual skills to a greater or lesser extent (though researchers differ considerably over the extent to which g exerts an influence and the degree to which it is genetically determined).

ganglioside Drug whose effects included the enhanced release of *acetylcholine* (see *cholinergic hypothesis*). Has been cited as a possible treatment for patients suffering from *dementia*. See *ondansetron* and *tacrine*.

garden path sentence A sentence that appears to be saying one thing until at a certain point it becomes obvious that another meaning is intended (e.g. *While John brushed the dog scratched for fleas*).

Gc/gc Symbol for *crystallised intelligence*.

GDS *Geriatric Depression Scale*.

general ageing effect An effect which is known to be related to ageing, but whose precise nature is unknown. The effect is most commonly found in studies of correlation, where a significant part of the variance

is attributable to *chronological age*. Since chronological age is essentially an arbitrary measure (how many times the Earth has been around the sun since you were born) and in and of itself is meaningless, there must be as yet unknown or unidentified processes that are associated with chronological age that account for the effect.

general intelligence General intellectual ability seen as a compendium measure of all types of intellectual skill (verbal, mathematical, etc.).

generalised anxiety See *anxiety disorder*.

general slowing hypothesis Theory that age changes in intellectual tasks are attributable to a general slowing of neural transmission speeds. Generally used more specifically to denote the argument that performance on all tasks, regardless of complexity, is affected by a constant (as opposed to a disproportionately increasing deficit the more complex the task), as witnessed by *Brinley plots*.

generationally biased stimuli Stimuli (or other test materials) which will only be recognised by, or be most familiar to, a particular *age cohort*.

Geriatric Depression Scale (GDS) A 'yes–no' questionnaire measuring the level of depression in the respondent. The questions are geared to match the symptoms and lifestyles typically found in depressed older people.

Geriatric Mental State (GMS) A standardised interview package for assessing the mental status of older patients.

geriatrics Medical treatment and study of older people. See *gerontology*.

geronting Ageing in terms of *psychological ageing*.

gerontologists Practitioners of *gerontology*.

gerontology The study of ageing and later life. The term is often restricted to psychological, sociological and more generally the social-scientific aspects of ageing.

gerontopsychology *psychogerontology*.

geropsychology *psychogerontology.*

gerotranscendence Attaining spiritual fulfillment in later life by transcending the physical needs of the here and now.

Gf/gf Symbol for *fluid intelligence.*

Gibson Spiral Maze A test of *psychomotor* skill, in which the participant is required to trace a pencil line around a spiral shaped path as quickly and accurately as possible.

glaucoma An excess accumulation of fluid in the eyeball, increasing pressure on retinal cells, leading to their (permanent) destruction.

GMS *Geriatric Mental State.*

golden age myth The myth that, in historical times, multigenerational families living under the same roof were the norm.

Gorham Proverb Interpretation Test Measure of intelligence through ability to interpret proverbs. See *proverb interpretation.*

graceful degradation The phenomenon that the considerable cell loss which typically accompanies ageing is reflected in a gentle loss of memories and level of skill (rather than a wholesale and absolute loss).

granny dumping Slang term for the process whereby caregivers (usually adult children) who cannot cope with an older relative abandon him or her to the local authorities (sometimes literally leaving him or her on the doorstep of the local hospital/social services office).

granulovacuolar degenerations Malformed dead neurons which under a microscope look like dense granules.

grey matter The cell bodies, synapses, etc., of nerve cells of the *central nervous system,* responsible for neural processing. Contrast with *white matter,* which is principally composed of the parts of the cells responsible for transmitting the information.

greying population A population in which there is an appreciable increase in the proportion of older adults within it.

Hachinski Ischaemic Score (IS) A diagnostic technique identifying *vascular dementias.* Patients are scored on the number of symptoms they display, with strongly indicative symptoms being weighted.

haemorrhage Rupture of a blood vessel wall.

HALE *healthy life expectancy.*

Halsted-Reitan Neuropsychological Battery (HRNB) A battery of neuropsychological tests, assessing abstract reasoning and linguistic, sensory, *visuo-spatial* and *motor skills.*

happy death Disparaging term devised by Lofland (1978) to describe models of death that stress how everything 'must' be peaceful, thereby denying a role for protest and other negative emotional expressions.

HAROLD *hemispheric asymmetry reduction in older adults.*

Harvard Alumni Study A study of the relationship between disease risk and level of exercise, diet, lifestyle, etc. in over 11,000 Harvard alumni (mean age late fifties).

Hayflick limit See *Hayflick phenomenon.*

Hayflick phenomenon Named after its discoverer, L. Hayflick. Living cells taken from a body can be reared in a laboratory and will reduplicate a limited number of times (the *Hayflick limit*). The older the animal from which the cells are taken, the lower this number is. This implies that the upper limit of life expectancy may be due to the simple fact that the body's cells only reduplicate a limited number of times (which in turn may be affected *inter alia* by the length of the *telomeres*).

health literacy The ability to access and constructively use health care information.

health transition A radical change in the general health of a group. In the context of ageing, the term is often used to denote the radical changes in the pattern of health and social care brought about by the decline in infectious diseases and the rise in the proportion of older adults in the populations of developed countries.

healthy life expectancy (HALE) The amount of remaining *life expectancy* that can be expected to be lived free of poor health.

hearing impairment (HI) Loss of auditory sensitivity sufficient to cause disability. Often measured in terms of the minimum volume (measured in decibels, or dB) which can be reliably heard (the higher the figure the worse the impairment). For example, a hearing loss of 90 dB means that the quietest sound which a person can hear is over 90 dB (i.e. about the same noise level as heavy traffic). See *profound hearing impairment*.

hemispheres (cortex) The *cerebral cortex* is divided into two equally sized halves, or hemispheres, along a vertical axis running from the front to the back of the head. In most individuals, the left hemisphere tends to specialise in linguistic and the right in *visuo-spatial* skills. The hemispheres are linked by several pathways, of which the most important is the *corpus callosum*.

hemispheric asymmetry reduction in older adults (HAROLD) Model of brain functioning that argues that activity in the brain's hemispheres becomes more equal in later life.

HI *hearing impairment.*

hierarchical approach (intelligence) The theory that intelligence comprises a general intellectual ability (*g*) and a range of more specialised skills.

hippocampus Area of the brain particularly concerned with memory and the transfer of information from short- to long-term memory. Damage to this area can result in a particularly debilitating amnesia, characterised by failure to retain any new information.

holding on See *armoured defensive personality.*

hold tests See *deterioration quotient (DQ).*

hostility An irrational level of antagonism towards others for real (or imagined) acts that have acted adversely on a person.

Huntingdon's disease Genetic disorder resulting in neural decay. Early symptoms include disturbances of movement and jerking movements. There is also a severe decline in cognitive abilities.

Hutchinson-Gilford syndrome Extremely rare disease with onset in infancy characterised by accelerated physical (though not mental) ageing. Patients have a characteristic 'bird-like' appearance of large hooked nose and bulging eyes. Death is typically in the early teens.

hyperactive delirium See *delirium.*

hyperactivity An inappropriately high level of activity, which either cannot be controlled, or can be, but only with difficulty. Characteristic of some patients with *dementia*, who may pace up and down or begin *wandering*.

hyperborean ageing myth Myth that there is a distant land where people have incredibly long lifespans. Also known as *antediluvian ageing myth.*

hyperlexia Reading accurately but with no or little comprehension of what is being read. See *demented dyslexia.*

hypermetamorphosis The compulsive urge to touch everything.

hyperorality The urge to put everything seen into the mouth.

hypoactive delirium See *delirium.*

hypokinesia Difficulty in imitating a movement.

hypothalamus *Subcortical* section of the brain, whose primary task is to assist in the control of bodily drives (e.g. hunger and satiety, anger, sex).

hypothesis scanning Asking specific questions to seek verification of a specific hypothesis.

iatrogenic illness Describes any complaint induced by medical treatment (e.g. drug side-effects).

iconic memory Memory for items which appear for a fraction of a second and disappear before there is time for them to be fully processed and recognised.

id The basic appetitive urge that Freud argued underpinned human behaviour. See *ego* and *superego*.

illusions Distorted perceptions.

immune system theory of ageing *autoimmune theory of ageing.*

implicit attitude The immediate attitude of a person before conscious control has imposed any restrictions on or amendments to it.

implicit memory See *explicit memory.*

individualised grandmother See *Robertson's taxonomy of grandmothers.*

infarct (1) The cell death caused by damage to the blood vessels supplying the cells in question. (2) The whole process of blood vessel damage and resulting cell death (though strictly speaking this is *infarction*).

infarction The creation of an *infarct.*

inhibition deficit Generally, a failure to inhibit: can refer to an age-related problem of failing adequately to inhibit unnecessary pieces of information or actions. For example, in trying to remember a list of words, failing to 'block out' items from a now-redundant list learnt earlier.

inhibition theory A theory of cognitive ageing which argues that older people become less proficient at inhibiting extraneous information and concentrating on the task at hand.

inhibitory (neurons) An inhibitory neuron (almost invariably in combination with many other inhibitory neurons) either slows or prevents the activation of another neuron.

inhibitory deficit hypothesis The argument that memory failure can in some circumstances be attributed to an inability to distinguish between memories for to-be-remembered (TBR) items and items that are irrelevant (e.g. that were items from earlier lists). More specifically, the term usually describes a failure to suppress the irrelevant memories.

inhibitory functioning Inhibiting (i.e. preventing) alternative course of action so that only the correct action is executed. The phrase is often applied to one of the principal functions of the frontal lobes.

initial letter priming Providing participants with the initial letters of words which the participants are trying to recall.

institutionalised behaviour Nebulous term for deleterious changes in some individuals, resulting from a (usually lengthy) spell in an institution (e.g. hospital, retirement home). Such afflicted individuals tend to have poor social skills, lack of 'individuality', lowered intelligence test scores, and so forth.

integrated personality *Personality* type found in Neugarten *et al.*'s (1961, 1968) studies. Possessors of this type were of three kinds: *reorganisers* (finding new things to do as old ones became impractical), *focused* (activities were restricted in scope, but were rewarding) or *disengaged* (deliberately avoiding responsibilities).

integrity versus despair In Erikson's theory, a conflict which has to be resolved in later life – whether to come to terms with one's past (*ego integration*) or to feel that past events cannot be amended.

intellectual realism Term (first used by Luquet, 1927) describing drawings or pictures in which the 'true' state of the object is represented rather than what can be seen ('perceptual realism').

intelligence quotient (IQ) Often (erroneously) used as an exact synonym of 'intelligence'. IQ denotes a person's intellectual skills relative to his or her *age cohort* (traditionally, a score of 100 denotes average, and scores less than 70 or greater than 130 fairly exceptional). Thus, the same number of questions answered correctly (the *raw score*) means different things to different age groups. For instance, an older person with a raw score of, for example, 40 is probably more gifted than a younger adult with a raw score of 40 on the same test. Hence, the older adult's IQ is higher than the younger adult's. IQ tends to stay reasonably constant throughout life (i.e. a person remains in the same position relative to his or her age peers)

– it is the raw score which declines in later adulthood.

interbrain See *diencephalon*.

internal cue A mental prompt ro something that is produced within the mind without an external reminder such as an alarm. Compare with an *external cue*, which is a physical prompt to do something (e.g. an alarm clock, a note in a diary).

introversion See *extraversion–introversion*.

intrusions When referring to linguistic errors, an inappropriate segment of language (e.g. a repetition of an earlier phrase in an inappropriate place in the current statement).

involuntary memory See *voluntary memory*.

IQ *intelligence quotient*.

irregular spelling A word whose pronunciation disobeys the normal rules of spelling-to-sound correspondence. Irregular words abound in English (e.g. 'quay', 'misled').

IS *Hachinski Ischaemic Score*.

KDCT *Kendrick Digit Copying Test*.

Kendrick Battery for the Detection of Dementia in the Elderly Early version of the *Kendrick Cognitive Tests for the Elderly*.

Kendrick Cognitive Tests for the Elderly A *test battery* for identifying *dementia* in participants aged 55 years and over. Consists of two tests. The *Kendrick Object Learning Test (KOLT)* is a memory test for arrays of pictures and the *Kendrick Digit Copying Test (KDCT)* measures the speed at which the participant copies a set of numbers.

Kendrick Digit Copying Test (KDCT) See *Kendrick Cognitive Tests for the Elderly*.

Kendrick Object Learning Test (KOLT) See *Kendrick Cognitive Tests for the Elderly*.

Kluver-Bucy syndrome A collection of abnormal behaviours, including *hyperorality, bulimia, visual agnosia, hypermetamorphosis* and loss of *affect*.

KOLT *Kendrick Object Learning Test*.

Korsakoff's syndrome (KS) Severe amnesia (particularly for new information) resulting from brain damage caused by long-term alcohol abuse coupled with vitamin deficiency through poor diet. Damage is particularly centred in the *hippocampus*.

Kübler-Ross's stages of dying Psychological stages exhibited by dying people, according to the work of E. Kübler-Ross (e.g. 1969). Consist of *denial of dying stage*, followed by *anger*. *Bargaining* follows (pleas to the deity, fate, etc.), followed by *depression* and finally, *acceptance*. See *Pattison's stages of dying*.

Kuru Type of *prion disease* found in New Guinea. Probably orginated in burial practices that included eating brain tissue.

lacunar deficits The phenomenon sometimes encountered in brain-damaged patients, where some intellectual functions are almost completely destroyed, whilst others remain relatively intact.

lacunar strokes Form of *subcortical arteriosclerotic dementia*.

late adult transition The period surrounding retirement.

late life psychosis Any psychosis (any mental illness characterised by a severe loss of contact with reality in the absence of *dementia* or *delirium*; principally the term describes *schizophrenia*) which manifests itself in later life. The condition can appear in tandem with dementing symptoms, but need not do so.

late onset dementia (LOD) *Dementia* whose first symptoms appear after the patient is 60 years old.

late onset schizophrenia (LOS) *Schizophrenia* which first manifests itself in middle age or later.

late paraphrenia Mental disorder of later life, characterised by symptoms of feelings of persecution and elaborate fantasies of the same. Commoner in women. Can have a variety of causes, including cardiovascular problems and previous episodes of mental illness.

LBD *Lewy body dementia*.

LCP *Liverpool Care Pathway.*

letter strings Groups of letters which may or may not form real words.

Lewy body A form of brain cell damage found in some patients with *dementia*; the damage comprises a dense round body surrounded by looser filaments.

Lewy body dementia (LBD) *dementia with Lewy bodies.*

Lewy body disease A proposed (though not yet universally accepted) category of *dementia* attributable to the presence of *Lewy bodies.*

lexical decision task Participants are shown *letter strings* and must decide as quickly as possible if they form words.

lifecourse perspective A view of lifespan development that examines the influences of early life (including environmental and historical factors as well as medical and psychological) in shaping the older person.

life crisis A set of profoundly negative feelings created by the transition from one *social age* to another.

life expectancy How much longer a person can expect to live. Typically describes the average remaining life for a particular *age cohort*, and is often formally defined as the age at which half the cohort will be predicted to have died. Contrast with *lifespan.*

lifespan The maximum age which a member of a species can expect to live. Contrast with *life expectancy.*

Liverpool Care Pathway (LCP) Set procedure of palliative care currently used in many UK health care settings for use with terminally ill patients.

living will Usually signed and witnessed declaration that in the event of becoming so ill as to be placed on a 'life support' system, that such apparatus be switched off if there is no prospect of a satisfactory recovery.

LOD *late onset dementia.*

longevity fan A graph showing the increasingly differing predictions of *life expectancy* as different models extrapolate data further into the future.

longitudinal research/samples/study Experimental method in which the same participants are tested at different ages. Compare with *cross-sectional research/samples/study*. See *overlapping longitudinal study* and *sequential research design.*

long-term memory (LTM) Memory for events of more than a few minutes ago. Long-term memory is often sub-classified according to the nature of what is being remembered; see *autobiographical, episodic, prospective, remote* and *semantic memory.*

LOS *late onset schizophrenia.*

loudness recruitment Problem found in some forms of hearing impairment in which sounds in certain frequency bands are (mis) perceived as being louder than normal, sometimes to the point of being painful.

LTM *long-term memory.*

macular degeneration Degeneration and ultimately loss of the eye's 'yellow spot' or macula, which is responsible for the highest resolution of focus in the eye.

mad cow disease Colloquial term for *bovine spongiform encephalopathy.*

magnetic resonance imaging (MRI scan) Method of obtaining cross-sectional or three-dimensional images of body parts (including the brain). Essentially works by detecting the resonance of cell molecules in a magnetic field and extrapolating an image from these.

malignant social psychology An environment in which an older person is made to feel devalued and intimidated (whether intentionally or not).

manic depression *bipolar disorder.*

matching (participants) Process of ensuring that groups of participants have equivalent scores on certain essential measures, thereby ensuring that any group differences found on other tests are not due to differences on the measures which have been matched. For example, if groups of older and younger adults have been chosen for identical scores on intelligence tests, and an age group difference is then found on Test X, then this difference cannot be due to differences in intelligence, but must be due to something else (e.g. age).

MCI *mild cognitive impairment.*

ME *molar equivalence.*

mechanistic intelligence Term devised by Baltes to describe the current state of a person's intellectual abilities. This is contrasted with *pragmatic intelligence*, which is the knowledge a person has accumulated in the past.

ME-MD strategy See *molar equivalence.*

memory span The longest list of items which a participant can reliably remember. Researchers vary in their interpretation of 'reliably' (e.g. some hold that span is the longest list length consistently remembered, others that it is the length remembered on 50 per cent of occasions).

memory trace The storage of memory.

mental capacity The limit on how much information a mind can process at any one time, and/or how quickly it can process information.

Mental Status Questionnaire (MSQ) Devised by Kahn *et al.* (1960), a simple gauge of a (usually demented) patient's intellectual status and degree of functional independence. See *Blessed Dementia Scale.*

metaknowledge A person's understanding of the quantity and accuracy of what he or she knows.

metamemory A person's knowledge about their own memory abilities.

method of loci A technique for improving memory. Participants imagine a familiar scene and juxtapose images of *to-be-remembered* items onto it. By taking a 'mental walk' through the scene, participants should be able to remember the items.

MID *multi-infarct dementia.*

mild cognitive impairment (MCI) A *cognitive* decline that is greater than expected in typical ageing but nonetheless does not have the same severity of symptoms as *dementia.* Some patients with MCI subsequently develop dementia, but this is not an inevitable progression.

Mill Hill Vocabulary Test A measure of vocabulary – the test requires participants to provide definitions of words, whose obscurity increases as the test progresses (there is no time limit).

Mini Mental State Examination (MMSE) A quickly-administered assessment of the general intellectual state of a patient. Questions include measures of orientation for time and place, basic tests of *short-term memory*, and ability to name common objects.

Minnesota Multiphasic Personality Inventory (MMPI) *Personality* test, yielding scores on ten scales, which are indices of (principally abnormal) personality traits.

mixed delirium See *delirium.*

mixed dementia A *dementia* comprised of two different dementia subtypes, typically *Alzheimer's disease* and *vascular dementia.*

MMPI *Minnesota Multiphasic Personality Inventory.*

MMSE *Mini Mental State Examination.*

mnemonic (1) Memory aid. (2) More generally, pertaining to memory and its workings.

molar equivalence (ME) A *molar skill* is one which can be broken down into a number of sub-skills (*molecular decomposition*). If a molar skill is performed equally well by groups of differing ages, then 'molar equivalence' is said to have occurred. However, if a skill is performed equally well but some of the sub-skills are performed better by some groups than others, then an *ME-MD strategy* (or *compensation*) has occurred.

molar skill See *molar equivalence.*

molecular decomposition See *molar equivalence.*

morphological processing The processing of word structure.

morphology Strictly speaking, the science of form. More generally, an awareness and knowledge of word meanings and word structure.

motor (neurons) Carrying signals from the *central nervous system* to skeletal muscle.

motor skills Ability to control bodily movements. 'Fine motor skills' describes control of relatively delicate movements, such as manual dexterity.

MPVA *multi-voxal pattern analysis.*

MRI scan *magnetic resonance imaging.*

MSQ *Mental Status Questionnaire.*

multi-infarct dementia (MID) Form of *dementia* characterised by the brain suffering a large number of *infarcts*. Patients typically suffer a steplike rather than progressive decline.

multiple regression Statistical technique for predicting the value of a variable given the value of several others. The technique can also be used to see which variable of several is the best predictor of another variable and whether once the best predictor's performance has been taken into account, the remaining variables can add any further predictive value to the equation.

multi-voxal pattern analysis (MPVA) Technique in neural imaging that identifies patterns of activity in *fMRI* scans that predict the task conditions being undertaken at that time.

mutation accumulation theory The theory that many of the deleterious changes found in later life have evolved because it is a period of life after breeding has taken place and in any case few animals reach this stage 'in the wild'. Thus, there is no or little evolutionary pressure preventing ageing.

myelin Fatty insulating layer found around many *neurons*. Acts in a manner akin to the insulating plastic around electrical wires.

N *neuroticism.*

naming latency The speed with which a new word can be read aloud.

NART *National Adult Reading Test.*

National Adult Reading Test (NART) A list of words, most with *irregular spellings*, which participants must read out loud (i.e. pronounce).

need for cognition A measure of the drive to pursue intellectually demanding tasks.

negative correlation A value of *r* falling below 0 and greater than -1. In other words, a relationship in which as one variable increases in value, the other declines (e.g. number of sweets eaten and desire to eat more). See *correlation*.

negative priming Creating the conditions so that performance on a subsequent task is marred. This generally involves swapping which items are used as targets and distractors, but other methods are possible.

nerve See *neuron*.

neural noise Concept that neural signals lose some of their fidelity because of interfering signals from neighbouring neurons (loosely, akin to poor radio reception because of interference from other stations). This is assumed to increase in later life, making mental processing less efficient and hence lowering intellectual ability.

neural specificity The opposite of *dedifferentiation*.

neuritic plaque *senile plaque.*

neurofibrillary tangles (NFT) Clumps of dead brain neurons which (under a microscope and with some artistic licence) look like knotted string. Common feature of the brains of patients with *dementia of the Alzheimer type*.

neuroleptic drug Drug primarily designed to lessen the disturbed behaviours seen in many forms of psychosis, but because of its calming effects is sometimes (and often inappropriately) used as a tranquilliser for patients presenting 'awkward' behaviours.

neuron/neurone An individual 'nerve' or 'nerve cell' (strictly speaking, a *nerve* is a collection of neurons forming a common path for sending messages in the *peripheral nervous system;* a similar structure in the *central nervous system* is called a *tract*).

neuroticism As used in this book a *personality trait* from *Eysenck's personality model*. Generally, neuroticism measures how anxious and emotionally unstable a person is.

neurotransmitters Chemicals transmitted between neurons at *synapses,* and hence the means by which neurons communicate with each other.

new learning deficit Relative difficulty in learning new information, in comparison with older information and/or another group of people. Used by some commentators to describe the relative weakness of older people in learning a new piece of information and/ or task.

NFT *neurofibrillary tangle.*

NINCDS-ADRDA criteria A set of criteria for evaluating the probability that a patient is suffering from *dementia of the Alzheimer type*. The initials refer to the organisations who jointly devised the scheme. It provides a diagnosis of 'probable', 'possible' or 'definite'.

nocturnal delirium *sundown syndrome.*

noise in nervous system *neural noise.*

non-normative life development Aspects of a person's life unique to them (i.e. as opposed to experiences held in common with others alive at the same time, such as major news events, etc.).

noradrenaline A *neurotransmitter.*

noradrenergic system Network of neurons using *noradrenaline* as their *neurotransmitter*. Primarily used in the control of smooth muscle.

normal distribution A distribution of scores/ measurements which has a characteristic bell-shaped curve with a peak above the horizontal axis, and which is symmetrical about its vertical midpoint. The peak of the curve represents the mean (i.e. average), median (the score which is bigger than 50 per cent of the values represented by the curve) and the mode (the commonest score). Because the distribution is found for many types of measurement, it is termed 'normal' and many types of statistical test are predicated on the assumption that data are drawn from normally distributed populations.

normal pressure hydrocephalus Caused by a failure of *cerebrospinal fluid* to drain away, leading to a destructive pressure on brain tissue. The complaint can lead to *dementia.*

normative age-graded development See *Baltes's theory of lifespan development.*

normative history-graded development See *Baltes's theory of lifespan development.*

nun study A longitudinal study of a group of American nuns who have agreed to be tested on a battery of psychological and medical tests each year, and have agreed that on death their brains will be made available for autopsy.

nvCJD See *Creutzfeldt-Jakob Disease.*

Object Memory Evaluation (OME) Measure of memory for objects at different gaps of time and employing learning trials.

observer memory The phenomenon that one's distant *autobiographical memories* are usually recalled as if one were a bystander.

obsessive-compulsive disorder See *anxiety disorder.*

obsolescence effect Theory that some age-related deterioration may be because older people's memories may no longer be attuned to the contemporary world (i.e. are obsolete rather than lost).

occipital lobes Regions of the *cerebral cortex* roughly in the region of the back of the head. Their principal function is in vision.

old age dependency ratio The number of people aged 60 and over divided by the number aged 20–64. This gives an indication of the proportion of people drawing pensions and other welfare and health benefits to those in employment who will be the principal financial supporters of this through taxation.

old elderly Most commonly defined as those people aged over 75 years (though note commentators differ over the precise figure). See *young elderly*.

OME *Object Memory Evaluation*.

ondansetron Drug whose effects include the enhanced release of acetylcholine (see *cholinergic hypothesis*) and thus a potentially beneficial treatment of some forms of *dementia*. See *ganglioside* and *tacrine*.

ordered recall A memory task in which items have to be recalled in exactly the order in which they were originally presented. Compare with *free recall*.

overlapping longitudinal study Type of *longitudinal study* in which several *age cohorts* are tested at regular intervals on the same body of tests. Cross-cohort comparisons can be made at each test session (as in a *cross-sectional study*); ageing change within the same individuals can be measured (as in a longitudinal study), and by comparing performance of different cohorts as they reach the same age at different calendrical times, it is possible to assess the strength of *cohort effects*.

P *psychoticism*.

paired associate learning Remembering which item was previously presented with which (e.g. the participant sees the words 'cat' and 'briefcase' presented together, and later when shown 'cat' must recall 'briefcase').

panic attack See *anxiety disorder*.

panic disorder See *anxiety disorder*.

paradox of well-being The phenomenon that, in spite of greater material hardship and emotional problems, some groups (such as older people) nonetheless report high levels of well-being.

parietal lobes The region of the *cerebral cortex* which occupies an area contiguous with an Alice band (or headphones strap) across the head. Their role is hard to define concisely, but they can be said to be involved in maintaining an awareness of the body's state and location, and in interpreting symbols.

Parkinsonian dementia *Dementia* in which *Parkinsonism* is present.

Parkinsonism Set of symptoms, including a shuffling gait and trembling hands, *bradykinesia* and *hypokinesia*, found in *Parkinson's disease* and also in several other brain disorders, including some of the *dementias*.

Parkinson's disease (PD) Illness caused by a decline in the substantia nigra (an area of the brain responsible for producing *dopamine*). Characteristic symptoms are known collectively as *Parkinsonism*.

partial correlation A statistical technique for assessing how much of the *correlation* between two variables is due to the coincidental effect of a third variable (the removal of whose influence is known as *partialling out*).

partialling out See *partial correlation*.

passive-dependent personality *Personality* type identified by Neugarten *et al*.'s (1961, 1968) studies. Possessors of this type rely on others to help them (*succourant seeking*) or withdraw from human interaction as much as possible (*apathetic*).

passive euthanasia Allowing someone to die by not administering life-saving or life-prolonging treatment.

patient cohort Group of patients with not only an illness in common but also a set of attitudes (e.g. feeling 'unhealthy'). Compare with *disease cohort*.

patient-years A figure used in calculating the incidence rate for a disease. The basic expression is typically x cases per y patient-years. Thus, if you have a sample of y people, then x of them are likely to develop the illness in the next year. For example, if a disease has an incidence of 100 cases per 1000 patient-years, then out of 1000 people 100 can expect to develop the illness in the next year.

Pattison's stages of dying Psychological stages which a dying patient passes through according to E.M. Pattison (1977). (1) *Acute crisis phase* – great anxiety upon realising that death is imminent. (2) *Chronic living-dying phase* – a period of mourning for what is being lost.

(3) *Terminal phase* – an inward withdrawal and resignation/acceptance. See *Kübler-Ross's stages of dying.*

PD *Parkinson's disease.*

PDD *primary degenerative disorder.* See *dementia of the Alzheimer type.*

peg board task Several variants of this task, but all have the central feature of requiring the participant to put pegs into holes as quickly as possible.

percentile Measure of the percentage of a sample or population with a score higher or lower than the score in question.

peripheral nervous system (PNS) *Neurons* connecting the *central nervous system* to the rest of the body.

perseverations Inappropriate repetition (e.g. repeating the same phrase or keeping at a particular problem-solving strategy after it has been demonstrated to be inappropriate).

personality 'The individual characteristics and ways of behaving that, in their organisation or patterning, account for an individual's unique adjustments, to his or her total environment' (Hilgard *et al.*, 1979, p.541).

personality trait An enduring characteristic of *personality* which is hypothesised to underpin all or most behaviour.

personality type *Personality* defined as membership of exclusive categories. (i.e. people are classified as having a particular type of personality from a set of alternatives, rather than everyone being classified on the same continuum as in a *personality trait.*

PET scan See *positron emission tomography.*

PGD *prolonged grief disorder.*

PHI *profound hearing impairment.*

phobia See *anxiety disorder.*

phoneme The smallest unit of speech whose substitution or removal from a word causes a change in the word's sound. More loosely, the basic sounds which make up words (and even more loosely, the verbal equivalent of letters).

phonological Pertaining to *phonemes.*

phonological loop *Slave system* in the *working memory model* responsible for the temporary storage of any information capable of being stored *phonologically.*

phonology Strictly speaking, the study of phonetics. Sometimes used to denote a person's awareness and understanding of phonological structure.

physiological age *Biological age* expressed through the state of the body's physiological processes, such as metabolic rate. See *anatomical age.*

Piagetian conservation tasks A series of tests (named after their inventor, Piaget) intended to demonstrate the illogicality of children's thought processes.

Piaget's 'kidnapping' Anecdote by Piaget (the famous developmental psychologist) illustrating the fallibility of *autobiographical memory.* Piaget had a distinct memory of a kidnap attempt on himself when aged two years, which his nurse successfully repulsed. Years later, he discovered that the nurse had invented the whole episode, and therefore his memory was an elaboration of her story rather than the recall of a real event.

Pick's bodies Damaged neurons, found in *Pick's disease* patients, and possessing a characteristic swollen appearance.

Pick's disease A form of *dementia* characterised by a progressive deterioration of the frontal lobes and other subcortical areas of the brain. Psychologically, there are often disturbances in *personality* before intellect or memory.

plasticity The degree to which neurological connections can change.

PMA *Primary Mental Abilities Test.*

PNS *peripheral nervous system.*

positive correlation A value of *r* greater than 0 and less than 1. In other words, a relationship where as one variable increases, so does another. See *correlation.*

positron emission tomography (PET) An electronic scanning method which measures how a section of the body (in the context of this book, typically the brain) metabolises a (mildly radioactive) tracer injected into the blood. This gives an indication of the relative level of activity, and by implication, health, of the area of the body being surveyed.

post-developmental A phrase used by some *gerontologists* to denote that changes in later life are often detrimental rather than developmental and/or beneficial.

postformal thought Theory that in adulthood, people develop the ability to combine subjective and objective criteria in resolving a problem. The term refers to the concept that it develops after *formal operations*.

potential lifespan *lifespan*.

practice effect The phenomenon that the more times a person takes part in psychological tests, the better their performance on them. This can apply even when the tests are not particularly similar (i.e. it is not simply the case that the person is remembering the correct answers from a previous test session). It is probably attributable to becoming increasingly familiar with the general methods used, being less tense, etc.

pragmatic intelligence See *mechanistic intelligence*.

pragmatics The understanding of the intent of an utterance rather than its literal interpretation. More generally, the ability to grasp the most satisfactory solution rather than the one which is necessarily logically correct.

pre-morbid IQ The *IQ* level (usually estimated) of a person before the onset of an illness (usually one which has affected the intellect, such as *dementia*).

presby- Prefix denoting old or ageing.

presbyacusis *presbycusis*.

presbycusis Hearing loss which worsens with ageing, typically characterised by loss of ability to hear high frequency sounds.

presbyo- *presby-*.

presbyopia Inability to focus on near objects.

pre-senile dementia *Dementia* where onset is before the patient's sixtieth birthday.

presenilin-1 Gene located on chromosome 14 associated with a variant of early onset *dementia of the Alzheimer type*.

presenilin-2 Gene located on chromosome 1 associated with a variant of early onset *dementia of the Alzheimer type*.

preserved differentiation Theory that some skills are better preserved than others in later life because they have always been better. The argument is implausible for the general population, but may be feasible for specific samples of the population with very specialised skills (e.g. professional musicians).

primary ageing Age changes which all older people can expect to experience to some degree (e.g. skin wrinkling). See *secondary ageing* and *universal ageing*.

primary degenerative dementia (PDD) *dementia of the Alzheimer type*.

primary memory *short-term memory*.

Primary Mental Abilities (PMA) Test An intelligence *test battery* devised by Thurstone.

primary vascular dementia *multi-infarct dementia*.

priming In memory experiments, providing hints about features of the items a participant is trying to recall.

prion disease Group term for a range of degenerative brain disorders, such as *bovine spongiform encephalopathy* and *Creutzfeldt-Jakob Disease*, which some commentators believe are due to an abnormal protein metabolism. 'Prion' is an abbreviation of 'proteinaceous infectious particle'.

probabilistic ageing Aspects of ageing likely to affect most (but not necessarily all) older people (e.g. cardiovascular problems). Similar to *secondary ageing*. See *universal ageing*.

processing resources theory of ageing Any theory which argues that changes in ageing intellectual skills are attributable to a lowered capacity for mental calculations (e.g. of *working memory*), lowered speed of processing, etc.

prodromal Early stage.

profound hearing impairment (PHI) *Hearing impairment* of > 90 dB.

progeria Disease characterised by the symptoms of abnormally rapid ageing (patients typically die in their teens).

programmed cell death A method by which cells can keep control of total cell growth by in effect destroying themselves. The phenomenon is well documented in non-ageing aspects of cell activity. Some theories of ageing argue that programmed cell death may be the root cause of ageing. For example, the *Hayflick limit* is marked by the onset of programmed cell death.

programmed senescence Belief that the body is genetically programmed to age, usually with the implication that this is the result of evolutionary pressure. See *programmed theory of ageing*.

programmed theory of ageing Theory that cells may be predestined to die because of inbuilt faults in the replication system (see e.g. *Hayflick limit*). Not to be confused with *programmed senescence*, which more often denotes that these problems are the result of evolutionary pressure.

progressive (illness) Description of an illness in which the symptoms appear and then get worse over time.

progressive supranuclear palsy (PSP) Illness characterised by disturbances of motor function and mild to moderate *dementia*.

prolonged grief disorder (PGD) Atypically prolonged (>6 months) grieving characterised by constant yearning to be reunited with a deceased person coupled with frequent and/or disabling symptoms of loss.

prospective memory The ability to remember to do something in the future.

proverb interpretation Measure of the understanding of the meaning of proverbs (e.g. *Gorham Proverb Interpretation Test*). Patients in the early stages of *dementia* may give very literal interpretations of proverbs meant to be taken at symbolic value (e.g. 'a rolling stone gathers no moss').

proximal ageing effects Ageing changes directly attributable to changes in another process (e.g. a *stroke*). Compare with *distal ageing effects*.

PSEN1 *presenilin-1*.

PSEN2 *presenilin-2*.

pseudodementia Severe lowering of *cognitive* abilities to *dementia*-like levels caused by severe depression in some older patients.

PSP *progressive supranuclear palsy*.

psychogenic mortality Psychological factors leading to physical symptoms which in turn cause death.

psychogerontology The study of the psychology of ageing.

psychological age A person's psychological state compared to that of an average person of the same *chronological age*.

psychometrics Strictly speaking, the measurement of psychological traits and skills, but more generally, the study of psychological differences.

psychomotor skill A physical skill in which there is a strong component of intellectual prowess or vice versa.

psychotherapy Any treatment regime based on an integrated theory of mind.

psychoticism A personality trait in *Eysenck's personality model* measuring the degree of emotional 'coldness' a person possesses.

pugilistic dementia *Dementia* induced by repeated blows to the head, often over some period of time (has been observed in some older boxers, hence the name).

pursuit rotor task A task in which the participant must tap (or in some versions trace) a visual target as it moves, typically in a circular motion. Performance is typically measured by time on target (i.e. the amount of time the participant manages to keep in contact with the target). In itself the pursuit rotor task can measure motor skills, but it is often used as a distracter or secondary task alongside another *cognitive* measure.

pyramidal society Society in which there are far more younger than older people (the population can be envisaged as successively smaller age groups stacked one on top of another, forming a pyramid). This contrasts with a *rectangular society*, in which there are roughly equal numbers of people in each age group (and hence the layers stacked on each other look more like a rectangle than a pyramid).

QOL *quality of life.*

QoL Means the same as *QOL*, only harder to type.

quality of life (QOL) The degree of happiness/satisfaction a person derives from their lifestyle. In psychology, the scale is often a scale or similar measure in which the participant indicates how content they are. The same term is used by researchers in other fields (e.g. economics) to measure degree of satisfaction felt by individuals or population groups (e.g. through provision of health and welfare resources, social amenities, etc.).

quality ratio In studies of creativity, the ratio of good to indifferent or poor works produced by a person within a particular time period.

r Symbol for *correlation.*

RAGS *Relatives' Assessment of Global Symptomatology.*

RALS Rochester Adult Longitudinal Study.

Ranschburg effect The phenomenon that lists of *to-be-remembered* items are less well remembered if some of the items are repeated within the list.

Ratcliff diffusion model A model of decision-making devised by Ratcliff (1978) that assumes in making a decision involving two choices (e.g. accept versus reject), evidence accumulates in favour of both until one reaches a threshold and is accepted over the other (e.g. a person decides to accept rather than reject, or vice versa). Speed of accumulation of evidence, the level of the threshold and the discriminability between the two alternatives can all vary (e.g. through practice, the general efficiency of mental processing, the degree of

conservatism exhibited in setting thresholds, etc.). The situation is analogous to two rival cattle drovers trying to persuade a cow to pass through their respective gates. The proximity of the gate to the starting point (analogous to the threshold), the degree to which the cow can tell the drovers apart (akin to the discriminability of the two choices), and the speed and strength of the drover's cajoling (akin to the speed of accumulation of evidence) can all vary. The model (rather more complex and elegant than this description makes it sound) has been widely used in studies such as memory and reaction time tasks, in part because of its high level of correspondence with the empirical evidence, but also because it allows for different components of a response to a stimulus to be statistically separated and examined.

Raven's Progressive Matrices A test of *fluid intelligence*, in which participants are given a series of problems (against the clock) which have a common theme of a logically governed sequence from which one member is missing (the participant must find the missing member from a set of choices).

raw score The actual score on a test, as opposed to an adjusted or weighted figure, such as the *intelligence quotient.*

reaction time (RT) Time taken for a person to respond to the appearance of a stimulus. See *choice reaction time* and *simple reaction time.*

recall The ability to remember items in memory without any prompting. See *ordered recall* and *free recall.*

recognition The ability to identify which items have been previously encountered when given a list of alternatives to choose from.

rectangular society See *pyramidal society.*

rectangular survival curve Hypothesised graph of percentage of *survivors* in an *age cohort* in a future of very effective medical care. By this reckoning, very few people will die until their *lifespan* is reached, when most will die within a few years of each other. A graph of the percentage of the age cohort alive at different ages (with percentage of the vertical axis and age on the horizontal) would thus look rectangular.

re-engagement theory *activity theory.*

reflex arc A simple connection between *afferent* and *efferent neurons* in the *spinal cord*. The mechanism is responsible for several reflexes (e.g. the famous knee-jerk reflex).

regression Statistical technique predicting the value of one variable from the value of another. See *multiple regression.*

regression hypothesis Theory that older people's linguistic skills revert to the qualitative state of a child's.

rehearsal (memory) The process of repeating *to-be-remembered* items 'in the head' in an effort to remember them better.

reintegration *dedifferentiation.*

Relatives' Assessment of Global Symptomatology (RAGS) Questionnaire measure of symptoms of the patient observed by his or her *caregivers.*

reminiscence bump *reminiscence peak.*

reminiscence peak Phenomenon that the bulk of *autobiographical memories* stem from when people were 10–30 years old.

remote grandmother See *Robertson's taxonomy of grandmothers.*

remote memory Memory for non-autobiographical events which have occurred during a person's lifetime. A frequent proviso is that these events must exclude famous incidents which have been aired in the media so often that they are part of general knowledge.

reorganisers See *integrated personality.*

replicative senescence The theory that cells are in effect doomed to replicate themselves a limited number of times before dying.

retrieval-induced forgetting In essence, the phenomenon that retrieving one item from a set of TBR items can interfere with retrieving other TBR items because of inhibition. The effect is strongest when a participant is asked to remember items from two or more semantic categories – retrieval of an item will lessen the probability of accurately recalling other items from the same category more than recalling from another category. Suppose someone is asked to remember a set of animal names and colour names (e.g. gorilla, rabbit, dog, parrot, cat, red, blue, green, purple, white, pink). Being prompted to recall one of the animal names (e.g. 'Animal beginning with g') will impair recall of the other animal names more than it will affect recall of any of the colour names (e.g. 'white' will be recalled more than 'parrot' will).

reversible dementia An illness which produces symptoms of *dementia*, but which can be cured and in the process reverse or at least lessen the dementing symptoms.

reversible dementia of depression *pseudodementia.*

Ribot's hypothesis Theory that in damaged or decaying mental systems, memories for recent events are worse than memories for remote events.

Rivermead Behavioural Memory Test Set of memory tasks analogous to everyday situations where memory is required (e.g. face recognition, remembering a route).

Robertson's taxonomy of grandmothers J.F. Robertson (1977) categorised grandmothers into four types: (1) *apportioned grandmother* – has both a social and a personal set of expectations for her grandchildren; (2) *symbolic grandmother* – has a social set of expectations; (3) *individualised grandmother* – has a set of personal expectations; (4) *remote grandmother* – relatively detached from the whole idea of being a grandmother.

Rochester Adult Longitudinal Study (RALS) Longitudinal study of alumni from Rochester University, USA, based on Erikson's model of *lifespan* development.

rocking chair personality See *dependent personality.*

role theory Theory that across the *lifespan* people adopt various society-approved 'roles' befitting their *chronological age.*

Roseto effect The effect on health of changing a lifestyle. Named after an Italian-American community in Roseto, Pennsylvania, whose susceptibility to heart disease increased as it became more 'Americanised'.

RT *reaction time.*

SAD *subcortical arteriosclerotic dementia.*

SATSA *Swedish Adoption/Twin Study on Aging.*

scaffolding theory of aging and cognition (STAC) Model of neuropsychological ageing that argues that declines in neural functioning can at least be partly offset by greater reliance on the workings of the prefrontal *cortex.*

schema Collection of memories about an event or item which enable one to plan responses and to interpret information surrounding the said event or item.

schizophrenia A profound disorder of thought, perception and language in the absence of mental retardation, characterised by a severe distortion of perception of reality and concomitant changes in emotions and behaviour. There are various forms of the illness, each with a distinct set of symptoms. The commonest of these symptoms include irrational beliefs about the way the world functions, often with a central theme that the patient is being persecuted. There may also be hallucinations (such as 'voices in the head'). Language can often be best described as 'surreal', with unusual expressions and ideas and invented words.

SDAT *senile dementia of the Alzheimer type.*

Seattle Longitudinal Aging Study *Longitudinal study* of psychological ageing, run by K.W. Schaie and colleagues. The first participants were tested in 1956 and have been retested (along with new cohorts of participants) at regular intervals ever since.

secondary ageing Age changes associated with, but not necessarily an inevitable consequence of, ageing (e.g. arthritis). See *primary ageing* and *probabilistic ageing.*

selective attention The ability to attend to one stimulus set against distracting stimuli.

self-hatred personality *Personality* type identified by Reichard *et al.* (1962)

characterised by unrealistic self-blame for misfortune

self-regulated language processing (SRLP) Model of reading that argues that the emphasis placed on different reading sub-skills can be altered based upon specific circumstances.

semantic Pertaining to meaning.

semantic deficit hypothesis Model of ageing which argues that age-related deficits in intellectual functioning are attributable to a failure adequately to process incoming items (e.g. items to be memorised) for the information they contain.

semantic dementia *Dementia* resulting from atrophy beginning in the *temporal lobes.* Atrophy in the left temporal lobe causes language skills to deteriorate, whilst atrophy in the right temporal lobe causes loss of facial recognition and the ability to recognise emotions. Atrophy on one side of the brain eventually leads to atrophy on the other side. Symptoms then develop akin to *Pick's disease.*

semantic facilitation Phenomenon that items are identified faster if preceded by items related in meaning (e.g. 'bread' is identified faster if the participant has just seen 'butter' as opposed to 'car').

semantic memory Memory for facts. Compare with *episodic memory.*

semantic priming *semantic facilitation.*

senescence Later life, with the implication of ageing free from *dementia* and other impairments of psychological functioning.

senescing Ageing in terms of *biological age.*

senile Medical term for 'old'; *never* to be used as a synonym for later life.

senile dementia See *dementia.*

senile dementia of the Alzheimer type (SDAT) Typically means the same as *dementia of the Alzheimer type,* but in some older texts it might refer specifically to cases of people aged over 60.

senile plaque (SP) Amorphous clumps of dead *neurons* found in high concentrations in the brains of some patients with *dementia.*

sentential grouping A (typically inefficient) method of classifying objects on the grounds that they can be included in the same sentence or story.

sequential research design *Longitudinal study* in which different *age cohorts* are tested at intervals over several years. In addition, age cross-sections of the population are tested in tandem with the longitudinal test panel, to gain an insight into possible *cohort effects*.

SETOF *speed-error-tradeoff function.*

short-term memory (STM) Temporary memory for events which have occurred in the past few seconds/minutes. Has a limited capacity (typically between five and nine items, depending upon the task and the individual), is easily disrupted and items are quickly forgotten unless a conscious effort is made to remember them. See *long-term memory* and *working memory.*

silent stroke *Stroke* which produces no symptoms, and is only discovered by either a brain scan or at autopsy. The term is sometimes used to describe a stroke which is unnoticed at the time of occurrence, but which subsequently causes a significant alteration in behaviour or functioning.

simple reaction time (SRT) Time taken to respond when there is only one choice of response to the stimulus. See *choice reaction time.*

single infarct dementia *Dementia* resulting from a single *infarct.*

slave systems Term derived from computing to denote systems (usually capable of one type of operation only) which cannot operate unless under the command of a master controller.

smoking gun symptom A symptom that unambiguously identifies the presence of a specific disease.

SOA *stimulus onset asynchrony.*

SOC model A model of development originally devised by Paul and Margaret Baltes that argues that we develop in adult life through the selection of skills we wish to develop, and the optimisation of these skills through practice and study, and we compensate against loss of these skills in later life.

social age A set of behaviours and attitudes considered to be socially appropriate for the *chronological age* of the individual.

social clock Hypothesised mechanism which an individual 'consults' to determine the most appropriate behaviour for his or her *social age.*

somatic (peripheral nervous system) Information from joints, skin and skeletal muscle transmitted to the *central nervous system.*

somatic death *biological death.*

somatic mutation theory of ageing Theory that as cells are lost through natural 'wear and tear' they are replaced by imperfect copies because of genetic errors, and thus are less likely to function efficiently. See *autoimmune theory of ageing, disposable soma theory of ageing, free radical theory of ageing* and *Hayflick phenomenon.*

source memory Memory for the circumstances under which an item was learnt as opposed to memory for the item itself.

SP *senile plaque.*

span Abbreviation of *memory span.*

speed-error-tradeoff function (SETOF) Measure of the degree to which an individual is prepared to trade speed at performing a task (i.e. slow down) in order to reduce the number of errors made. A measure often used in *reaction time* experiments.

speed hypothesis *general slowing hypothesis.*

spinal cord The principal meeting point between *peripheral* and *central nervous system* neurons.

sporadic Alzheimer's disease Form of *dementia of the Alzheimer type* in which the patient developing the disease has no 'obvious' genetic predisposition to develop the illness, such as a parent who contracted the same disease at an early age. The term is slightly misleading since there may in fact be a genetic cause (hence why it is avoided in the main body of the book). It is used to distinguish the condition from *familial Alzheimer's disease.*

SRLP *self-regulated language processing.*

SRT *simple reaction time.*

STAC *scaffolding theory of ageing and cognition.*

standard deviation Statistical measure used, *inter alia*, to indicate the range of scores in a sample. A useful rule is that for a *normal distribution* the range of scores between the mean minus 2 standard deviations and the mean plus 1.96 standard deviations accounts for 95 per cent of the sample's scores.

statistical theory of ageing The theory that ageing occurs because of random cumulative damage and loss. Most such events are relatively minor in themselves but it is their combined impact that is of importance.

stimulus onset asynchrony (SOA) In a *backward masking* experiment, the difference between the length of time the *to-be-remembered* item has to be presented alone and the length of time it has to be presented when it is followed by a mask for it to be correctly recognised.

STM *short-term memory.*

stroke Damage to brain tissue caused by the cessation of its blood supply. The psychological effect of the stroke depends upon the location of the injury.

Stroop task Measure of *selective attention*, in which the participant must identify one feature of a stimulus whilst ignoring other features. The original and most commonly used version requires participants to name the colour of a word. When the word is itself the name of another colour (e.g. 'RED' printed in blue, with the participant expected to respond 'blue'), this becomes extremely difficult, largely because reading is a practically automatic process and the name of the word interferes with producing the required response.

subcortical Pertaining to the areas of the brain other than the *cerebral cortex*.

subcortical arteriosclerotic dementia (SAD) *Vascular dementia* whose primary damage occurs in regions of the brain other than the *cortex*.

subcortical dementia *Dementia* whose principal focus of damage is not in the *cerebral cortex*.

subdural haematoma Blood clot in the brain. See *cerebral haemorrhage*.

subitization The ability to count the number of items in an array 'at once' without counting the individual items. Most people can count between two and four items in this manner, though larger numbers are possible.

successful ageing Rather nebulous term describing (1) older people whose lifestyles are successful, or at least trouble-free, and/or (2) more specifically, the retention of youthful levels of performance of the skill in question.

succourant-seeking See *passive-dependent personality*.

Sullivan method Method of calculating the proportion of remaining *life expectancy* that can be expected to be free of significant disability.

sundown syndrome The phenomenon observed in some patients with *dementia*, who get up during the night and wander about, without regard for the propriety of the time or place. See *wandering*. The term may also refer to increased confusion, aggressive or erratic behaviour at the close of day.

superego In Freudian theory, a person's set of (often over-harsh) moral dictums. See *ego* and *id*.

supraspan learning Learning lists of items whose number exceeds one's *memory span*.

survival curve Graph plotting the numbers of people within an *age cohort* still living at different ages.

survivors Members of an *age cohort* who have lived past a particular age.

sustained attention The ability to concentrate on a set task without being distracted.

Swedish Adoption/Twin Study on Ageing (SATSA) *Longitudinal study*, commenced in 1979, of Swedish identical and non-identical twins reared apart or together.

symbolic grandmother See *Robertson's taxonomy of grandmothers.*

symptom burden The degree to which symptoms of an illness impinge negatively on a person's life.

synapse The junction between two *neurons*, in the form of a microscopic gap across which *neurotransmitters* can be sent.

syntactical Pertaining to grammar.

syntax Grammar.

tacrine Drug whose effects include the enhanced release of *acetylcholine* (see *cholinergic hypothesis*), and thus a possible treatment for some forms of *dementia.*

talking book Cassette or other audio recording of a person reading a book. Most talking books are readings of edited versions of the originals to keep the size of the package down to one or two cassettes, discs, etc.

target (1) In *recognition* tasks, the item which has been previously encountered and which must be distinguished from any *distracters* present. (2) In *attention* tasks, the item to be located from amongst the distracters.

tau A type of protein, damage to which causes *neurofibrillary tangles.*

TBR *to-be-remembered.*

telomerase Enzyme responsible for maintaining the length of *telomeres* in some specific cell types (principally, egg and sperm cells). Telomerase is not used in all cells, probably because there would be a too-high risk of cancerous cell production.

telomere Section of DNA felt to be involved in ageing. When a cell duplicates itself, the length of the telomere is shortened; after several duplications, it reaches its shortest length and cell duplication can no longer take place.

temporal gradient In studies of memory, the finding that events from one time period are better remembered than those from another. The phrase can mean that recent events are remembered better, or that distant events are remembered better, depending upon the

specific circumstances. Researchers often forget this salient point and assume it only means the direction they are thinking of, so *extreme caution* is advised in interpreting the phrase.

temporal lobes Section of the *cerebral cortex* occupying (roughly speaking) the areas of the right and left temples. Chief function is in interpretation of information; in most people, the left temporal lobe is essential in language comprehension and production. Also strongly involved in the storage of memory.

temporal variant frontotemporal dementia (tvFTD) *semantic dementia.*

terminal drop model The theory that in older individuals, there is a sudden and marked decline in intellectual skills a few months/years before their death.

terminal phase (of dying) See *Pattison's stages of dying.*

Terri Schiavo case A legal case that illustrated the dilemma of deciding when terminating life support is in the patient's best interests; the husband of a woman on life support wanted the support terminated; other family members took different views leading to years of court battles.

tertiary ageing A rapid deterioration during the process of dying.

tertiary memory *remote memory.*

test battery A group of tests designed to assess the same skill (e.g. intelligence).

test wise The condition of becoming attuned to the general design of psychological tests (particularly intelligence tests) and improving in performance as a result. The phenomenon usually arises from using the same panel of volunteers too often, thereby artificially elevating their apparent skills. The problem is of particular concern in *longitudinal studies.*

thalamus Area of brain co-ordinating and channelling information and executing motor movements. Damage to this area is heavily involved in *Parkinsonism.*

thanatology The study of death and dying.

theta waves A pattern of electrical activity detected by *EEG* with a frequency between 4 and 8 Hz.

third age Active and independent later life. Contrast with *fourth age.*

threshold age The *chronological age* which (arbitrarily) denotes the division between one age group and another.

threshold model of dementia The theory that individuals have a genetically fixed predisposition to develop *dementia*, but whether they actually do depends upon a trigger in the environment. In people with a low predisposition, a large environmental input is required, and vice versa.

thrombosis Blood vessel blocked due to clotting.

TIE *typical intellectual engagement.*

time-based task In *prospective memory* experiments, a task requiring a response which must be self-initiated at the appropriate time.

time-lag comparison Comparing different *age cohorts* at the same age in a *longitudinal study.*

time-lag effect *cohort effect.*

time-sequential design An 'extended' *cross-sectional study* design now generally no longer practised. Two or more groups are compared at one time period, and then several years later, different participants are tested, who are the same ages as the participants were in the original study.

tinnitus A hearing complaint characterised by a (usually permanent) irritating noise (often akin to a 'ringing in the ears', and sometimes painful) which interferes with normal hearing.

tip of the tongue (TOT) Phenomenon of recalling features of an item (e.g. what it sounds like, number of syllables, and so forth) but not its identity. Often induced in experiments by providing people with the definition of a word and asking them to name it.

Tithonus error *Tithonus myth.*

Tithonus myth The (erroneous) belief that medical science and gerontology want to prolong life no matter what the cost in suffering.

to-be-remembered (TBR) Items in a memory task which the participant is asked to remember.

TOT *tip of the tongue.*

tract See *neuron.*

Trail Making test Sub-test of the *Halsted-Reitan Neuropsychological Battery,* assessing ability to follow sequences. The participant must make a pencil trail between particular numbers (or in another version, numbers and letters) printed on a sheet of paper.

transient ischaemic attack *Stroke* where effects are usually relatively trivial, and are gone within 24 hours.

transmission deficit hypothesis Model of linguistic functioning that argues that activation of words (either in recognition or production) is underpinned by priming of possible alternatives. The speed and efficiency with which these primes are produced will greatly facilitate the speed and accuracy of recognition/production. Ageing is assumed to lower the speed and efficiency with which the priming takes place (more so for production than recognition).

triple jeopardy Term illustrating that older people facing *double jeopardy* often also face a third problem of prejudice and/or communication problems barring them from the help they need and deserve.

tvFTD *temporal variant frontotemporal dementia.*

two-factor theory of well-being In essence, the theory that positive events tend to influence the positive aspects of one's mood, and negative events the negative aspects of one's mood.

Type A personality A *personality* type prone to being competitive and 'hard edged'. Contrasts with *Type B personality,* which is prone to being (over)easy-going and relaxed.

Type B personality See *Type A personality.*

typical intellectual engagement (TIE) Measure of level of preference for intellectually demanding activities.

UFOV *useful field of view.*

Ulverscroft large print series Series of popular books in large print size intended for people with visual impairments. Traditional patrons are older users of public libraries.

universal ageing Aspects of ageing held to affect everyone who reaches later life (e.g. wrinkling skin). See *probabilistic ageing.*

useful field of view (UFOV) A measure of the size of visual field a person can accurately identify stimuli in. Typically measured by getting a participant to fixate on a symbol in the middle of a computer screen and presenting stimuli at various distances from the symbol. The further away from the symbol that items are accurately identified, the bigger the UFOV.

VaD *vascular dementia.*

vascular dementia (VaD) *Dementia* caused by damage to the blood vessels within the brain.

verbal span *Memory span* for words.

view from the bridge Title of an Arthur Miller play. Also, in Levinson's theory, the desired state in late life when older people have come to terms with their past.

viscera Intestines.

visual agnosia Inability to recognise objects by sight.

visual marking In a *visual search task*, the inhibition of old items (with the effect of speeding up the search for the target).

visual search task Test of *selective attention*. The participant must find a *target* item which is located in an array of distracter items.

visuo-spatial Pertaining to visual appearance and spatial characteristics (e.g. where items in a display are relative to each other).

visuo-spatial memory The ability to remember visual and/or spatial information.

visuo-spatial sketchpad A *slave system* of the *working memory* model: a temporary store of *visuo-spatial* information.

voluntary memory A memory that appears spontaneously or is prompted by an event in the immediate present. This is contrasted with an *involuntary memory*, which is a memory that has been requested, either specifically (e.g. 'repeat back the list of numbers you just heard') or more generally (e.g. 'give me a memory from your childhood').

WAIS *Wechsler Adult Intelligence Scale.*

wandering (dementia) Nebulous term describing any inappropriate walking behaviour. This can manifest itself as part of *hyperactivity*, but may also describe walking about apparently aimlessly or 'wandering off' on a walk for no apparently obvious reason (see also *sundown syndrome*).

wear and tear theory Theory of ageing that parts of the body gradually 'wear out' with use. Compare with *cytologic theory*.

Wechsler Adult Intelligence Scale (WAIS) Intelligence *test battery* covering all commonly assessed areas of intelligence.

Wechsler Memory Scale Memory sub-tests from the *Wechsler Adult Intelligence Scale*.

Werner's syndrome Extremely rare disease with onset in teens (though first symptoms may not become 'obvious' for some years), characterised by accelerated physical ageing, notably the skin, hair and cardiovascular system. Death is typically in the forties.

Wernicke's aphasia Specific failure to understand speech, resulting from brain damage.

Wernicke's dementia *Dementia* caused by vitamin deficiency (particularly vitamin B). Often there is an associated motor impairment.

white matter See *grey matter*.

Winston Churchill argument The argument that some individuals (such as Winston Churchill) have lifestyles that modern medical opinion insists are unhealthy and yet lead long productive lives.

Wisconsin Card Sorting Task Measure of hypothesis formation and the ability to reject or not persevere with an invalid one. Participants must discover the correct rule for matching up cards of different patterns and colours (e.g. a yellow card must always be matched with a red card). Once participants have discovered the correct rule, the experimenter changes it, and how quickly the participants stop using the old rule and search for the new one is measured, as well as how quickly they solve the new problem. Abnormally persevering with an old rule can be indicative of brain damage, particularly to the *frontal lobes*.

wisdom Somewhat nebulous concept, with several separate though related definitions, depending upon the researcher in question. Most agree in essence that it refers to an ability to judge and resolve real-life problems which require a balance of logical and pragmatic factors, tempered by experience. However, within this broad remit, individual authors have used the term loosely, ranging from a synonym of *crystallised intelligence* to psychoanalytic theories.

word completion task Task in which the participant is required to complete a word given the first letter(s).

word span *Memory span* for words.

working memory Popular and influential model of *short-term memory*, first described by Baddeley and Hitch (1974). The model argues that short-term memory is controlled by a *central executive*, which delegates memory tasks to specialist *slave systems*, principally the *phonological loop* and *visuo-spatial sketchpad*.

wrap up The slowing down in reading rate when the end of a syntactically meaningful phrase is reached.

Yngve depth An analytic technique which gives a 'score' for the syntactic complexity of a sentence or phrase.

young elderly The commonest definition is the age group between 60 and 75 years (though lower and higher boundaries are not unknown). See *old elderly*.

young–old plot Plotting a graph of the performances of younger adults against older adults on the same task. Best known example is the *Brinley plot*.

zeitgeist Spirit of the (historical) age.

References

Aartsen, M.J., Smiths, C.H.M., van Tilburg, T., Knopscheer, K. and Deeg, D. (2002) Activity in older adults: Cause or consequence of cognitive functioning? *The Journals of Gerontology Series B: Psychological Sciences and Social Sciences, 57*, 153–62.

Abada, S., Baum, S. and Titone, D. (2008) The effects of contextual strength on phonetic identification in younger and older listeners. *Experimental Aging Research, 34*, 232–50.

Abarshi, E., Onwuteaka-Philipsen, B., Donker, G., Enchteld, M. *et al.* (2009) General practitioner awareness of preferred place of death and correlates of dying in a preferred place: A nationwide mortality follow-back study in the Netherlands. *Journal of Pain and Symptom Management, 38*, 568–77.

Abas, M., Punpuing, S., Jirapramukpitak, T., Guest, P. and Tangchoniatip, K. (2009) Rural-urban migration and depression in ageing family members left behind. *British Journal of Psychiatry, 195*, 54–60.

Abel, T. and Werner, M. (2003) HIV risk behaviour of older persons. *European Journal of Public Health, 13*, 350–2.

Aboderin, I. (2004) Decline in material family support for older people in urban Ghana, Africa: Understanding processes and causes of change. *The Journals of Gerontology Series B: Psychological Sciences and Social Sciences, 59*, 128–37.

Abrams, L., Farrell, M. and Margolin, S. (2010) Older adults' detection of misspellings during reading. *Journals of Gerontology: Series B: Psychological Sciences and Social Sciences, 65*, 680–3.

Abrams, L., Trunk, D. and Merrill, L. (2007) Why a superman cannot help a tsunami: Activation of grammatical class influences resolution of young and older adults' tip of the tongue states. *Psychology and Aging, 22*, 835–45.

Abrams, R.C. and Horowitz, S.V. (1996) Personality disorders after age 50: A meta-analysis. *Journal of Personality Disorders, 10*, 271–81.

Abrams, R.C., Spielman, L.A., Alexopoulos, G.S. and Klausner, E. (1998) Personality disorder symptoms and functioning in elderly depressed patients. *American Journal of Geriatric Psychiatry, 6*, 24–30.

Ackerman, P., Kanfer, R. and Calderwood, C. (2010) Use it or lose it? Wii brain exercise practice and reading for domain knowledge. *Psychology and Aging, 25*, 753–66.

Adamek, M.E. and Kaplan, M.S. (1996a) The growing use of firearms by suicidal older women, 1979–1992: A research note. *Suicide and Life-Threatening Behavior, 26*, 71–8.

Adamek, M.E. and Kaplan, M.S. (1996b) Firearm suicide among older men. *Psychiatric Services, 47*, 304–6.

Adams, C. (1991) Qualitative age differences in memory for text: A life-span developmental perspective. *Psychology and Aging, 6*, 323–36.

Adams, C., Smith, M.C., Pasupathi, M. and Vitolo, L. (2002) Social context effects on story recall in older and younger women: Does the listener make a difference? *The Journals of Gerontology Series B: Psychological Sciences and Social Sciences, 57*, 28–40.

Adams-Price, C. (1992) Eyewitness memory and aging: Predictors of accuracy in recall and person recognition. *Psychology and Aging, 7,* 602–8.

Addis, D.R., Leclerc, C.M., Muscatell, K. and Kensinger, E.A. (2010) There are age-related changes in neural connectivity during the encoding of positive, but not negative information. *Cortex, 46,* 425–33.

Adkins, G., Martin, P. and Poon, L. (1996) Personality traits and states as predictors of subjective well-being in centenarians, octogenarians and sexagenarians. *Psychology and Aging, 11,* 408–16.

Adrian, J., Postal, V., Moessinger, M., Rascle, N. and Charles, A. (2011) Personality traits and executive functions related to on-road driving performance among older drivers. *Accident Analysis and Prevention, 43,* 1652–9.

Ahmadi, L. (2001) Gerotranscendence and different cultural settings. *Ageing and Society, 21,* 395–415.

Aihie Sayer, A. and Cooper, C. (1997) Undernutrition and aging. *Gerontology, 43,* 203–5.

Aiken, L.R. (1989) *Later Life.* Hillsdale, NJ: Lawrence Erlbaum Associates.

Aitchison, J. (2007) *The Articulate Mammal: An Introduction to Psycholinguistics.* London: Routledge.

Aizpurua, A., Garcia-Bajos, E. and Migueles, M. (2009) Memory for actions of an event: Older and younger adults compared. *Journal of General Psychology, 136,* 428–41.

Akhtar, S. (2011) *Matters of Life and Death: Psychoanalytic Reflections.* London: Karnac Books.

Akiyama, H., Antonucci, T., Takahashi, K. and Langfahl, E.S. (2003) Negative interactions in close relationships across the life span. *The Journals of Gerontology Series B: Psychological Sciences and Social Sciences, 58,* 70–9.

Alain, C. and Woods, D. (1999) Age-related changes in processing auditory stimuli during visual attention: Evidence for deficits in inhibitory control and sensory memory. *Psychology and Aging, 14,* 507–19.

Albert, M.S. (1988) Cognitive function. In M.S. Albert and M.B. Moss (eds) *Geriatric Neuropsychology.* New York: Guilford.

Albert, M.S. and Heaton, R.K. (1988) Intelligence testing. In M.S. Albert and M.B. Moss (eds) *Geriatric Neuropsychology.* New York: Guilford Press.

Albert, M.S., Duffy, F.H. and Naeser, M.A. (1987) Nonlinear changes in cognition and their non-psychological correlation. *Canadian Journal of Psychology, 41,* 141–57.

Allaire, J.C. and Marsiske, M. (2002) Well- and ill-defined measures of everyday cognition: Relationship to older adults' intellectual ability and functional status. *Psychology and Aging, 17,* 101–15.

Allemand, M., Zimprich, D. and Hendriks, A. (2008) Age differences in five personality domains across the life span. *Developmental Psychology, 44,* 758–70.

Allemand, M., Zimprich, D. and Martin, M. (2008) Long-term correlated change in personality traits in old age. *Psychology and Aging, 23,* 545–57.

Allen, P.A., Hall, R.J., Druley, J.A., Smith, A.F., Sanders, R.E. and Murphy, M.D. (2001) How shared are age-related influences on cognitive and noncognitive variables? *Psychology and Aging, 16,* 532–49.

Allen, P.A., Madden, D.J., Weber, T.A. and Groth, K.E. (1993) Influence of age and processing stage on visual word recognition. *Psychology and Aging, 8,* 274–82.

Allen, P.A., Murphy, M.D., Kaufman, M., Groth, K.E. and Begovic, A. (2004) Age differences in central (semantic) and peripheral processing: The importance of considering both response times and errors. *The Journals of Gerontology Series B: Psychological Sciences and Social Sciences, 59,* 210–9.

Allen, P.A., Sliwinski, M., Bowie, T. and Madden, D.J. (2002) Differential age effects in semantic and episodic memory. *The Journals of Gerontology Series B: Psychological Sciences and Social Sciences, 57,* 173–86.

Allen-Burge, R. and Storandt, M. (2000) Age equivalence in feeling-of-knowing experiences. *The Journals of Gerontology Series B: Psychological Sciences and Social Sciences, 55*, 214–23.

Alonso-Babarro, A., Varela-Cerdeira, M., Torres-Vigil, I., Rodrigo-Barrientos, R. and Bruera, E. (2010) At-home palliative sedation for end-of-life cancer patients. *Palliative Medicine, 24*, 486–92.

Alpaugh, P.K. and Birren, J.R. (1977) Variables affecting creative contributions across the adult life span. *Human Development, 20*, 240–8.

Alsenany, S. (2009) Student nurses' attitudes and knowledge towards the care of older people in Saudi Arabia. *Generations Review, 19*, 1–9.

Altgassen, M., Kliegel, M., Brandimonte, M. and Filippello, P. (2010) Are older adults more social than younger adults? Social importance increases older adults' prospective memory performance. *Aging, Neuropsychology and Cognition, 17*, 312–28.

Alwin, D.F. and McCammon, R.J. (2001) Aging, cohorts and verbal ability. *The Journals of Gerontology Series B: Psychological Sciences and Social Sciences, 56*, 151–61.

Alzheimer's Society (2007) *Dementia UK*. London: Alzheimer's Society.

American Psychiatric Association (1994) *Diagnostic and Statistical Manual of Mental Disorders*. 4th edition. Washington, DC: American Psychiatric Association.

Anderson, T.L. and Levy, J.A. (2003) Marginality among older injectors in today's illicit drug culture: Assessing the impact of ageing. *Addiction, 98*, 761–70.

Andreescu, C., Mulsant, B., Houck, P., Whyte, E. *et al.* (2008) Empirically derived decision trees for the treatment of late-life depression. *American Journal of Psychiatry, 165*, 855–62.

Angel, L., Fay, S., Bouazzaoui, B., Baudouin, A. and Isingrini, M. (2010) Protective role of educational level on episodic memory aging: An event-related potential study. *Brain and Cognition, 74*, 312–23.

Anstey, K., Stankov, L. and Lord, S. (1993) Primary aging, secondary aging and intelligence. *Psychology and Aging, 8*, 562–70.

Anstey, K., von Sanden, C., Sargent-Cox, K. and Luszcz, M. (2007) Prevalence and risk factors for depression in a longitudinal, population-based study including individuals in the community and residential care. *American Journal of Geriatric Psychiatry, 15*, 497–505.

Anstey, K.J., Dain, S., Andrews, S. and Drobny, J. (2002) Visual abilities in older adults explain age-differences in Stroop and fluid intelligence but not face recognition: Implications for the vision-cognition connection. *Aging, Neuropsychology and Cognition, 9*, 253–65.

Anstey, K.J., Hofer, S.M. and Luszcz, M.A. (2003) A latent growth curve analysis of late-life sensory and cognitive function over 8 years: Evidence for specific and common factors underlying change. *Psychology and Aging, 18*, 714–26.

Anstey, K.J., Luszcz, M.A. and Sanchez, L. (2001) A reevaluation of the common factor theory of shared variance among age. *The Journals of Gerontology Series B: Psychological Sciences and Social Sciences, 56*, 3–11.

Antonucci, T.C., Lansford, J.E., Schaberg, L., Smith, J. *et al.* (2001) Widowhood and illness: A comparison of social network characteristics in France, Germany, Japan and the United States. *Psychology and Aging, 16*, 655–65.

Appell, J., Kertesz, A. and Fisman, M. (1982) A study of language functioning in Alzheimer patients. *Brain and Language, 17*, 73–91.

Arai, Y. and Zarit, S. (2011) Exploring strategies to alleviate caregiver burden: Effects of the national long-term care insurance scheme in Japan. *Psychogeriatrics, 11*, 183–9.

Arbuckle, T.Y., Nohara-LeClair, M. and Pushkar, D. (2000) Effect of off-target verbosity on communication efficiency in a referential communication task. *Psychology and Aging, 15*, 65–77.

Ardelt, M. (1997) Wisdom and life satisfaction in old age. *The Journals of Gerontology Series B: Psychological Sciences and Social Sciences, 52*, 15–27.

Ardelt, M. (1998) Social crisis and individual growth: The long-term effects of the Great Depression. *Journal of Aging Studies, 12*, 291–314.

Ardelt, M. (2008) Wisdom, religiosity, purpose in life, and death attitudes of aging adults. In A. Tomer, G.T. Eliason and P. Wong, P. *Existential and Spiritual Issues in Death Attitudes.* Mahwah: Lawrence Erlbaum Associates.

Ardelt, M. (2010) Are older adults wiser than college students? A comparison of two age cohorts. *Journal of Adult Development, 17*, 193–207.

Ardelt, M. and Jacobs, S. (2009) Wisdom, integrity, and life satisfaction in very old age. In M. Smith and N. DeFrates-Densch (eds) *Handbook of Research on Adult Learning and Human Development.* New York: Routledge.

Arenberg, D. (1982) Changes with age in problem solving. In F.M. Craik and A.S. Trehub (eds) *Aging and Cognitive Processes.* New York: Plenum.

Arias-Castillo, L., Ceballos-Osorio, J., Ochoa, J. and Reyes-Ortiz, C. (2009) Correlates of sexuality in men and women aged 52–90 years attending a university medical health service in Colombia. *Journal of Sexual Medicine, 6*, 3008–18.

Aries, M., Le Bastard, N., Debruyne, H., Van Buggenhout, M. *et al.* (2010) Relation between frontal lobe symptoms and dementia severity within and across diagnostic dementia categories. *International Journal of Geriatric Psychiatry, 25*, 1186–95.

Armstrong, C.L. and Cloud, B. (1998) The emergence of spatial rotation deficits in dementia and normal aging. *Neuropsychology, 12*, 208–17.

Arndt, S., Turvey, C.L. and Flaum, M. (2002) Older offenders, substance abuse and treatment. *The American Journal of Geriatric Psychiatry, 10*, 733–40.

Arnold, S.E. and Trojanowski, J.Q. (1996) Cognitive impairment in elderly schizophrenia: A dementia (still) lacking distinctive histopathology. *Schizophrenia Bulletin, 22*, 5–9.

Arnold, S.E., Trojanowski, J.Q., Gur, R.E., Blackwell, P., Han, L. and Choi, C. (1998) Absence of neurodegeneration and neural injury in the cerebral cortex in a sample of elderly patients with schizophrenia. *Archives of General Psychiatry, 55*, 225–32.

Aslan, A., Baumi, K. and Pastotter, B. (2007) No inhibitory deficit in older adults' episodic memory. *Psychological Science, 18*, 72–8.

Atchley, R. (1989) A continuity theory of normal aging. *Gerontologist, 29*, 183–90.

Athaide, H.V., Campos, M. and Costa, C. (2009) Study of ocular aberrations with age. *Aruquivas Braslia Oftalmologica, 72*, 617–21.

August, K. and Sorkin, D. (2011) Racial/ethnic disparities in exercise and dietary behaviors of middle-aged and older adults. *Journal of General Internal Medicine, 26*, 245–50.

Austad, S.N. (2006) Why women live longer than men: Sex differences in longevity. *Gender Medicine, 3*, 79–92.

Avorn, J., Soumerai, S.B., Everitt, D.E. and Ross-Degna, D. (1992) A randomized trial of a program to reduce the use of psychoactive drugs in nursing homes. *New England Journal of Medicine, 327*, 168–73.

Ayalon, L. and King-Kallimanis, B. (2010) Trading years for perfect health: Results from the health and retirement study *Journal of Aging and Health, 22*, 1184–97.

Babins, L., Slater, M., Whitehead, V. and Chertkow, H. (2008) Can an 18-point clock-drawing scoring system predict dementia in elderly individuals with mild cognitive impairment? *Journal of Clinical and Experimental Neuropsychology, 30*, 1–14.

Bäckman, L. and MacDonald, S. (2006) Death and cognition: Viewing a 1962 concept through 2006 spectacles. *European Psychologist, 11*, 161–3.

Bäckman, L. and Nyberg, L. (2010) Dopamine, cognition, and human aging: New evidence and ideas. In L. Bäckman and L. Nyberg (eds) *Memory, aging and the brain: A Festschrift in honour of Lars-Goran Nilsson.* New York: Psychology Press.

Bäckman, L., Laukka, E.J., Wahlin, A., Small, B.J. and Fratiglioni, L. (2002) Influences of preclinical dementia and impending death on the magnitude of age-related cognitive deficits. *Psychology and Aging, 17*, 435–42.

Baddeley, A. (2010) Long term and working memory: How do they interact? In L. Bäckman, L. and L. Nyberg, L. (eds) *Memory, Aging and the Brain: A Festschrift in honour of Lars-Goran Nilsson.* New York: Psychology Press.

Baddeley, A.D. (1983) *Your Memory: A User's Guide.* London: Penguin.

Baddeley, A.D. (1986) *Working Memory.* Oxford: Oxford Scientific Publications.

Baddeley, A.D. (1995) *Memory.* 2nd edition. London: Lawrence Erlbaum.

Baddeley, A., Eysenck, M. and Anderson, M. (2009) *Memory.* New York: Psychology Press.

Baddeley, A.D., Bressi, S., Della Sala, S., Logie, R. and Spinnler, H. (1991) The decline of working memory in Alzheimer's disease: A longitudinal study. *Brain, 114*, 2521–42.

Baddeley, A.D. and Hitch, G. (1974) Working memory. In G.H. Bower (ed.) *Attention and Performance VI.* New York: Academic Press.

Bagheri, A. (2007) Individual choice in the definition of death. *Journal of Medical Ethics, 33*, 146–9.

Bailey, H., Dunlosky, J. and Hertzog, C. (2009) Does differential strategy use account for age-related deficits in working memory performance? *Psychology and Aging, 24*, 82–92.

Bailey, P., Henry, J., Rendell, P., Phillips, L. and Kliegel, M. (2010) Dismantling the 'age-prospective memory paradox': The classic laboratory paradigm simulated in a naturalistic setting. *Quarterly Journal of Experimental Psychology, 63*, 646–52.

Bailey, S. and Letiecq, B. (2009) Family coping and adaptation among grandparents rearing grandchildren. *Journal of Intergenerational Relationships, 7*, 144–58.

Bailis, D.S. and Chipperfield, J.G. (2002) Compensating for losses in perceived personal control over health: A role for collective self-esteem in healthy aging. *The Journals of Gerontology Series B: Psychological Sciences and Social Sciences, 57*, 531–9.

Baker, D., Gazmararian, J., Sudano, J. and Patterson, M. (2000) The association between age and health literacy among elderly persons. *The Journals of Gerontology Series B: Psychological Sciences and Social Sciences, 55*, 368–74.

Bakos, D., Denburg, N., Fonseca, R. and de Mattos Pimenta Parente, M. (2010) A cultural study on decision making: Performance differences on the Iowa Gambling Task between selected groups of Brazilians and Americans. *Psychology and Neuroscience, 3*, 101–7.

Baldwin, C. and Capstick, A. (eds) (2007) *Tom Kitwood on Dementia: A Reader and Critical Commentary.* Maidenhead: McGraw Hill/Open University Press.

Balinsky, B. (1941) An analysis of the mental factors of various age groups from nine to sixty. *Genetic Psychology Monographs, 23*, 191–234.

Ball, K., Berch, D.B., Helmers, K.F., Jobe, J.B. *et al.* (2002) Effects of cognitive training interventions with older adults: A randomized controlled trial. *Journal of the American Medical Association, 288*, 2271–81.

Ball, K., Owsley, C., Sloane, M.E., Roenker, D.L. and Bruni, J.R. (1993) Visual attention problems as a predictor of vehicle crashes among older drivers. *Investigative Ophthalmology and Visual Science, 34*, 3110–23.

Ballard, C. and Aarsland, D. (2009) Person-centred care and care mapping in dementia. *The Lancet Neurology, 8*, 302–3.

Baltes, M. (1996) *The Many Faces of Dependency in Old Age.* New York: Cambridge University Press.

Baltes, M. and Wahl, H.W. (1996) Patterns of communication in old age: The dependence-support and independence-ignore script. *Health Communication, 8*, 217–31.

Baltes, P. (1997) On the incomplete architecture of human ontogeny: Selection, optimization and compensation as foundation of developmental theory. *American Psychologist, 52*, 366–80.

Baltes, P.B. and Baltes, M.M. (1990). Psychological perspectives on successful aging: The model of selective optimization with compensation. In P.B. Baltes and M.M. Baltes (eds) *Successful Aging: Perspectives from the Behavioral Sciences.* Cambridge: Cambridge University Press.

Baltes, P.B. and Lindenberger, U. (1997) Emergence of a powerful connection between sensory and cognitive functions across the adult life span: A new window to the study of cognitive aging? *Psychology and Aging, 12,* 12–21.

Baltes, P.B. and Mayer, K.U. (1999) The Berlin Aging Study: Aging from 70 to 100. Cambridge: Cambridge University Press.

Baltes, P.B. and Smith, J. (1990) Toward a psychology of wisdom and its ontogenesis. In R.J. Sternberg (ed.) *Wisdom: Its nature, origins and development.* Cambridge: Cambridge University Press, 87–120.

Baltes, P.B. and Staudinger, U.M. (2000) Wisdom: A metaheuristic (pragmatic) to orchestrate mind and virtue toward excellence. *American Psychologist, 55,* 122–36.

Band, G.P.H., Ridderinkhof, K.R. and Segalowitz, S. (2002) Explaining neurocognitive aging: Is one factor enough? *Brain and Cognition, 49,* 259–67.

Bann, C., Bayen, U., McCormack, L. and Uhrig, J. (2006) Effects of reading habits, reading comprehension, and memory beliefs on older adults' knowledge about Medicare. *Journal of Applied Gerontology, 25,* 49–64.

Banning, M. (2007) Medication review for the older person. *Reviews in Clinical Gerontology, 17,* 25–32.

Barefoot, J.C. (1992) Developments in the measurement of hostility. In H. Friedman (ed.) *Hostility, Coping and Health.* Washington DC: American Psychological Association, 13–31.

Barefoot, J.C. Beckham, J.C., Haney, T.L., Siegler, I.C. and Lipkus, I.M. (1993) Age differences in hostility among middle-aged and older adults. *Psychology and Aging, 8,* 3–9.

Barefoot, J.C., Mortensen, E.L., Helms, M.J., Avlund, K. and Schroll, M. (2001) A longitudinal study of gender differences in depressive symptoms from age 50 to 80. *Psychology and Aging, 16,* 342–5.

Barnes, L.L., Mendes de Leon, C.F., Bienias, J.L. and Evans, D.A. (2004) A longitudinal study of black white differences in social resources. *The Journals of Gerontology Series B: Psychological Sciences and Social Sciences 59,* 146–53.

Barnes, L.L, Mendes de Leon, C.F., Bienias, J.L, Wilson, R.S. *et al.* (2009) Hostility and change in cognitive function over time in older blacks and whites. *Psychosomatic Medicine, 71,* 652–8.

Baron, A. and Banaji, M. (2006). The development of implicit attitudes: Evidence of race evaluations from ages 6 to 10 and adulthood. *Psychological Science,* 17, 1, 53–58

Bartels, S.J. and Mueser, K.T. (1999) Severe mental illness in older adults: Schizophrenia and other late-life psychoses. In M.A. Smyer and S.H. Qualls (eds) *Aging and Mental Health.* Oxford: Blackwells, 182–207.

Bartlett, F.C. (1932) *Remembering.* Cambridge: Cambridge University Press.

Barton, E.M., Plemons, J.K., Willis, S.L. and Baltes, P.B. (1975) Recent findings on adult and gerontological intelligence: Changing a stereotype of decline. *American Behavioral Scientist, 19,* 224–36.

Bashore, T.R., Ridderinkhof, K.R. and van der Molen, M.W. (1997) The decline of cognitive processing speed in old age. *Current Directions in Psychological Science, 6,* 163–9.

Basso, M.R., Schefft, B.K. and Hamsher, K. (2005) Aging and remote memory declines: Preliminary findings. *Aging Neuropsychology and Cognition, 12,* 175–86.

Bauer, B. (1966) Results and problems of intelligence testing of aging subjects. [English translation] *Probleme und Ergebnisse der Psychologie, 16,* 21–39.

Bauer, M., McAuliffe, L. and Nay, R. (2007) Sexuality, health care and the older person: An overview of the literature. *International Journal of Older People Nursing, 2,* 63–8.

Baum, S. (1984) Age denial: Death denial in the elderly. *Death Education, 8,* 419–23.

Baum, S.R. (1993) Processing of center-embedded and right-branching relative clause sentences by normal elderly individuals. *Applied Psycholinguistics, 14,* 75–88.

Bayles, K.A. and Tomoeda, C.K. (1983) Confrontation naming impairment in dementia. *Brain and Language, 19,* 98–114.

Bayley, N. (1968) Behavioral correlates of mental growth: Birth to thirty-six years. *American Psychologist, 23,* 1–17.

Beardsall, L. (1998) Development of the Cambridge Contextual Reading Test for improving the estimation of premorbid verbal intelligence in older persons with dementia. *British Journal of Clinical Psychology, 37,* 229–40.

Becker, G., Beyene, Y., Newsom, E. and Mayen, N. (2003) Creating continuity through mutual assistance: Intergenerational reciprocity in four ethnic groups. *The Journals of Gerontology Series B: Psychological Sciences and Social Sciences, 58,* 151–9.

Becker, J.T., Boller, F., Saxton, J. and McConigle-Gibson, K.L. (1987) Normal rates of forgetting of verbal and non-verbal material in Alzheimer's Disease. *Cortex, 23,* 59–72.

Beckman, A., Parker, M. and Thorslund, M. (2005) Can elderly people take their medicine? *Patient Education and Counselling, 59,* 186–91.

Beekman, A.T.F., Penninx, B.W., Deeg, D.J., Ormel, J., Braam, A.W. and van Tilburg, W. (1997) Depression and physical health in later life: Results from the Longitudinal Aging Study Amsterdam (LASA). *Journal of Affective Disorders, 46,* 219–31.

Beers, M.H. and Berkow, R. (eds) (2000) *The Merck Manual of Geriatrics.* 3rd edition. Whitehouse Station, NJ: Merck and Co.

Beier, M.E. and Ackerman, P.L. (2001) Current-events knowledge in adults: An investigation of age, intelligence and nonability determinants. *Psychology and Aging, 16,* 615–28.

Bekris, L., Galloway, N., Millard, S., Lockhart, D. *et al.* (2011) Amyloid precursor protein (APP) processing genes and cerebrospinal fluid APP cleavage product levels in Alzheimer's disease. *Neurobiology of Aging, 32,* 13–23.

Bell, D., Turnbull, A. and Kidd, W. (2009) Differential diagnosis of dementia in the field of learning disabilities: A case study. *British Journal of Learning Disabilites, 37,* 56–65.

Bell, L.J. (1980) *The Large Print Book and Its User.* London: Library Association.

Belmont, J.M., Freeseman, L.J. and Mitchell, D.W. (1988) Memory and problem solving: The cases of young and elderly adults. In M.M. Gruneberg, P.E. Morris and R.N. Sykes (eds) *Practical Aspects of Memory, Current Research and Issues, Volume 2.* Chichester: Wiley.

Benbow, S., Kingston, P., Bhaumik, S., Black, S. *et al.* (2011) The interface between learning disability and old age psychiatry: Two specialities travelling alone or travelling together? *Mental Health Review Journal, 16,* 25–35.

Ben-David, B. and Schneider, B. (2010) A sensory origin for color-word Stroop effects in aging: Simulating age-related changes in color-vision mimics age-related changes in Stroop. *Aging, Neuropsychology and Cognition, 17,* 730–46.

Benedetti, F., Vighetti, S., Ricco, C., Lagna, E. *et al.* (1999) Pain threshold and tolerance in Alzheimer's disease. *Pain, 80,* 377–82.

Bengston, U.L. and Kuypers, J. (1986) The family support cycle: Psychosocial issues in the aging family. In J.M.A. Munnichs, P. Mussen and E. Olbrich (eds) *Life Span and Change in a Gerontological Perspective.* New York: Academic Press.

Bengston, U.L. and Treas, J. (1980) The changing family context of mental health and aging. In J.E. Birren and B. Sloane (eds) *Handbook of Mental Health and Aging.* New Jersey: Prentice Hall.

Bengtson, V., Cuellar, J. and Ragan, P. (1977) Stratum contrasts and similarities in attitudes toward death. *Journal of Gerontology, 32,* 76–88.

Bennett, D.J. and McEvoy, C.L. (1999) Mediated priming in younger and older adults. *Experimental Aging Research, 25,* 141–59.

Bennett, K. (2005) Psychological wellbeing in later life: the longitudinal effects of marriage, widowhood and marital status change. *International Journal of Geriatric Psychiatry, 20,* 280–4.

Bennett, K.M. (2002) Low level social engagement as a precursor of mortality among people in later life. *Age and Ageing, 31,* 165–8.

Bent, N., Rabbitt, P. and Metcalfe (2000) Diabetes mellitus and the rate of cognitive ageing. *British Journal of Clinical Psychology, 39*, 349–63.

Berg, C.A. and Sternberg, R.J. (1992) Adults' conceptions of intelligence across the adult life span. *Psychology and Aging, 7*, 221–31.

Berg, L. (1988) Mild senile dementia of the Alzheimer type: Diagnostic criteria and natural history. *Mount Sinai Journal of Medicine, 55*, 87–96.

Bergeman, C.S. (1997) *Aging: Genetic and Environmental Influences*. Thousand Oaks: Sage.

Berger, G., Frolich, L., Weber, B. and Pantel, J. (2008) Diagnostic accuracy of the clock drawing test: The relevance of 'time setting' in screening for dementia. *Journal of Geriatric Psychiatry and Neurology, 21*, 250–60.

Bergfield, K.L., Hanson, K., Chen, K., Teipei, S. *et al.* (2010) Age-related networks of regional covariance in MRI grey matter: Reproducible multivariate patterns in health aging. *Neuroimage, 49*, 1750–9.

Bergman, M., Blumenfeld, V.G., Casardo, D., Dash, B., Levett, H. and Margulies, M.K. (1976) Age-related decrement in hearing for speech: Sampling and longitudinal studies. *Journal of Gerontology, 31*, 533–8.

Berkowitz, B. (1964) Changes in intellect with age: IV. Changes in achievement and survival. *Newsletter for Research in Psychology, 6*, 18–20.

Berlingeri, M., Bottini, G., Basilico, S., Silani, G. *et al.* (2008) Anatomy of the episodic buffer: A voxel-based morphometry study in patients with dementia. *Behavioural Neurology, 18*, 29–34.

Bernaducci, M.P. and Owens, N.J. (1996) Is there a fountain of youth? A review of current life extension strategies. *Pharmacotherapy, 16*, 183–200.

Berntsen, D. and Rubin, D.C. (2002) Emotionally charged autobiographical memories across the life span: The recall of happy, sad, traumatic and involuntary memories. *Psychology and Aging, 17*, 636–52.

Bertram, L. and Tanzi, R.E. (2004) The current state of Alzheimer's disease genetics. What do we tell the patients? *Pharmacological Research, 50*, 385–96.

Berzoff, J. (2003) Psychodynamic theories in Grief and Bereavement. *Smith College Studies in Social Work, 73*, 273–98.

Beukelaar, L.J. and Kroonenberg, P.M. (1986) Changes over time in the relationship between hand preference and writing hand among left-handers. *Neuropsychologia, 24*, 301–3.

Bherer, L. and Belleville, S. (2004) Age-related differences in response preparation: The role of time uncertainty. *The Journals of Gerontology Series B: Psychological Sciences and Social Sciences, 59*, 66–74.

Bidewell, J. and Chang, E. (2011) Managing dementia agitation in residential aged care. *Dementia, 10*, 299–315.

Bielefeld, E.C., Tanaka, C., Chen, G.D. and Henderson, D. (2010) Age-related hearing loss: Is it a preventable condition? *Hearing Research, 264*, 98–107.

Bierman, E. Comijs, H., Rijmen, F., Jonker, C. and Beekan, A. (2008) Anxiety symptoms and cognitive performance in later life: Results from the longitudinal aging study Amsterdam. *Aging and Mental Health, 12*, 517–23.

Bird, J. and Hayter, M. (2009) A review of the literature on the impact of renal cancer therapy on quality of life. *Journal of Clincal Nursing, 18*, 2783–800.

Birren, J.E., Butler, R.N., Greenhouse, S.W., Solokoff, L. and Yarrow, M.R. (1963) *Human Aging*. Washington Public Health Service Publication No. 986.

Birren, J.E. and Fisher, L.M. (1995) Aging and speed of behavior: Possible consequences for psychological functioning. *Annual Review of Psychology, 46*, 329–53.

Birren, J.E. and Schroots, J.J.F. (eds) (2000) *A History of Geropsychology in Autobiography*. Washington: American Psychological Association.

Bischmann, D.A. and Witte, K. (1996) Food identification, taste complaints and depression in younger and older adults. *Experimental Aging Research, 22*, 23–32.

Bisiacchi, P., Borella, E., Bergamaschi, S., Carretti, B. and Mondini, S. (2008) Interplay between memory and executive functions in normal and pathological aging. *Journal of Clinical and Experimental Neuropsychology, 30*, 723–33.

Black, H.K. and Rubinstein, R.L. (2004) Themes of suffering in later life. *The Journals of Gerontology Series B: Psychological Sciences and Social Sciences, 59*, 17–24.

Blackburn, J.A. and Papalia, D.E. (1992) The study of adult cognition from a Piagetian perspective. In R.J. Sternberg and C. Berg (eds) *Intellectual Development.* Cambridge: Cambridge University Press.

Blake, S. (2009) Subnational patterns of population ageing. *Population Trends, 136*, 43–63.

Blanchard-Fields, F., Chen, Y., Horhota, M. and Wang, M. (2007) Cultural differences in the relationship between aging and the correspondence bias. *Journal of Gerontology B: Psychological Sciences and Social Sciences, 62*, 362–5.

Blay, S., Fillenbaum, G., Andreoli, S. and Gastal, F. (2009) Correlates of lifetime alcohol misuse among older community residents in Brazil. *International Psychogeriatrics, 21*, 384–91.

Blelak, A.A.M., Hultsch, D.F., Strauss, E., MacDonald, S.W.S. and Hunter, M.A. (2010) Intraindividual variability is related to cognitive change in older adults: Evidence for within-person coupling. *Psychology and Aging, 25*, 575–86.

Blessed, G., Tomlinson, B.E. and Roth, M. (1968) The association between quantitative measures of dementia and senile changes in the cerebral grey matter of elderly subjects. *British Journal of Psychiatry, 114*, 797–811.

Blow, F.C. and Oslin, D.W. (2003) Late-life addictions. *Geriatric Psychiatry, 22*, 111–43.

Blum, J.E., Clark, E.T. and Jarvik, L.F. (1973) The NYS Psychiatric Institute Study of aging twins. In L.F. Jarvik, C. Eisdorfer and J.E. Blum (eds) *Intellectual Functioning in Adults.* New York: Springer.

Boekamp, J.R., Strauss, M.E. and Adams, N. (1995) Estimating premorbid intelligence in African-American and White elderly veterans using the American version of the National Adult Reading Test. *Journal of Clinical and Experimental Neuropsychology, 17*, 645–53.

Boeras, D., Granic, A., Padmanabhan, J., Crespo, N. *et al.* (2008) Alzheimer's presenilin 1 causes chromosome missegragation and aneuploidy. *Neurobiology of Aging, 29*, 319–28.

Boggatz, T., Farid, T., Mohammedin, A., Dijkstra, A. *et al.* (2009) Psychometric properties of the Extended Care Dependency Scale for older persons in Egypt. *Journal of Clinical Nursing, 18*, 3280–9.

Boggatz, T., Farid, T., Mohammedin, A., Dijkstra, A. *et al.* (2010) Socio-demographic factors related to functional limitations and care dependency among older Egyptians. *Journal of Advanced Nursing, 66*, 1047–58.

Bohensky, M., Charlton, J., Odell, M. and Keeffe, J. (2008) Implications of vision testing for older driver licensing. *Traffic Injury Prevention, 9*, 304–13.

Bohnen, N.I., Kaufer, D.I., Hendrickson, R., Ivanco, L.S. *et al.* (2005) Cognitive correlates of alterations in acetylcholinesterase in Alzheimer's disease. *Neuroscience Letters, 380*, 127–32.

Bohr, V.A. and Anson, R.M. (1995) DNA damage, mutation and fine structure DNA repair in aging. *Mutation Research, 338*, 25–34.

Boland, R.J., Diaz, S., Lamdan, R.M., Ramchandani, D. and McCartney, J.R. (1996) Overdiagnosis of depression in the general hospital. *General Hospital Psychiatry, 18*, 28–35.

Bonanno, G. (1999) Emotional dissociation, self-deception, and adaptation to loss. In C. Figley (ed.) *Traumatology of Grieving: Conceptual, Theoretical, and Treatment Foundations.* Philadelphia: Brunner-Mazel, 89–105.

Bongaarts, J. and Zimmer, Z. (2002) Living arrangements of older adults in the developing world: An analysis of demographic and health survey household surveys. *The Journals of Gerontology Series B: Psychological Sciences and Social Sciences, 57,* 45–57.

Bonilha, L., Eckert, M.A., Fridriksson, J., Hirth V.A. *et al.* (2009) Age-related relative volume preservation of the dominant hand cortical region. *Brain Research, 13,* 14–9.

Bonini, M. and Mansur, L. (2009) Comprehension and storage of sequentially presented radio news items by healthy elderly. *Dementia and Neuropsychologia, 3,* 118–23.

Bonanno, G. A., Wortman, C. B. and Nesse, R.M. (2004) Prospective patterns of resilience and maladjustment during widowhood. *Psychology and Aging, 19,* 260–271.

Bookwala, J., Harralson, T.L. and Parmelee, P.A. (2003) Effects of pain on functioning and well-being in older adults with osteoarthritis of the knee. *Psychology and Aging, 18,* 844–50.

Bopp, K.L. and Verhaeghen, P. (2005) Aging and verbal memory span: A meta-analysis. *The Journals of Gerontology Series B: Psychological Sciences and Social Sciences, 60,* 223–33.

Bosma, H., van Boxtel, M.P.J., Ponds, R.W.H.M., Houx, P.J.H. and Jolles, J. (2003) Education and age-related cognitive decline: The contribution of mental workload. *Educational Gerontology, 29,* 165–73.

Bosman, E.A. (1993) Age-related differences in the motoric aspects of transcription typing skill. *Psychology and Aging, 8,* 87–102.

Botwinick, J. (1967) *Cognitive Processes in Maturity and Old Age.* New York: Springer.

Botwinick, J. (1973) *Aging and Behavior.* New York: Springer.

Botwinick, J. (1977) Intellectual abilities. In J.E. Birren and K.W. Schaie (eds) *Handbook of the Psychology of Aging.* New York: Van Nostrand Reinhold.

Botwinick, J. and Storandt, M. (1974) Vocabulary ability in later life. *Journal of Genetic Psychology, 125,* 303–8.

Botwinick, J., West, R. and Storandt, M. (1978) Predicting death from behavioral performance. *Journal of Gerontology, 33,* 755–62.

Bouazzaoui, B., Isingrini, M., Fay, S., Angel, L. *et al.* (2010) Aging and self-reported internal and external memory strategy uses: The role of executive functioning. *Acta Psychologia, 135,* 59–66.

Bouchard Ryan, E., Anas A.P., Beamer, M. and Bajorek, S. (2003) Coping with age-related vision loss in everyday reading activities. *Educational Gerontology, 29,* 37–54.

Bouma, H., Legein, C.P., Melotte, H.E. and Zabel, L. (1982) Is large print easy to read? Oral reading rate and word recognition of elderly subjects. *IPO Annual Progress Report, 17,* 84–90.

Bouras, C., Riederer, B.M., Kovari, E., Hof, P.R. and Giannakopoulos, P. (2005) Humoral immunity in brain aging and Alzheimer's disease. *Brain Research, 48,* 477–87.

Bourget, D., Gagne, P. and Whitehurst, L. (2010) Domestic homicide and homicide-suicide: The older offender. *Journal of the American Academy of Psychiatry and the Law, 38,* 305–11.

Bowles, N.L. and Poon, L.W. (1981) The effect of age on speed of lexical access. *Experimental Aging Research, 7,* 417–25.

Bowles, N.L. and Poon, L.W. (1985) Aging and retrieval of words in semantic memory. *Journal of Gerontology, 40,* 71–7.

Bowles, R.P. and Salthouse, T.A. (2003) Assessing the age-related effects of proactive interference on working memory tasks using the Rasch model. *Psychology and Aging, 18,* 608–15.

Bowling, A. (2007) Quality of life in older age: What people say. In H. Mollenkopf and A. Walker (eds) *Quality of Life in Old Age: International and Multi-Disciplinary Perspectives.* New York: Springer.

Bowling, A., Farquhar, M. and Grundy, E. (1996) Associations with changes in life satisfaction among three samples of elderly people living at home. *International Journal of Geriatric Psychiatry, 11,* 1077–87.

Bowling, A. and Stenner, P. (2011) Which measure of quality of life performs best in older age? A comparison of the OPQOL, CASP-19 and WHOQOL-OLD. *Journal of Epidemiology and Community Health, 65*, 273–80.

Boxer, A. and Miller, B. (2005) Clinical features of frontotemporal dementia. *Alzheimer's Disease and Associated Disorders, 19*, 3–6.

Boyd, C.M., Landefeld, C.S., Counsell, S.R., Palmer, R.M. *et al.* (2008) Recovery of activities of daily living in older adults after hospitalization for acute medical illness. *Journal of the American Geriatrics Society, 56*, 2171–79.

Braam, A.W., Beekman, A.T.F., van Tilburg, T.G., Deeg, D.J.H. and van Tilburg, W. (1997) Religious involvement and depression in older Dutch citizens. *Social Psychiatry and Psychiatric Epidemiology, 32*, 284–91.

Braam, A.W., Bramsen, I., van Tilburg, T.G., van der Ploeg, H. and Deeg, D. (2006) Cosmic transcendence and framework of meaning in life: Patterns among older adults in The Netherlands. *The Journals of Gerontology Series B: Psychological Sciences and Social Sciences, 61*, 121–8.

Brady, E.M. and Sky, H.Z. (2003) Journal writing among older learners. *Educational Gerontology, 29*, 151–63.

Brandt, J., Bakker, A. and Maroof, D. (2010) Auditory confrontation naming in Alzheimer's disease. *Clinical Neuropsychologist, 24*, 1326–38.

Braskie, M., Klunder, A., Hayashi, K., Protas, H. *et al.* (2010) Plaque and tangle imaging and cognition in normal aging and Alzheimer's disease. *Neurobiology of Aging, 31*, 1669–78.

Brattberg, G., Parker, M.G. and Thorslund, M. (1996) The prevalence of pain among the oldest old in Sweden. *Pain, 67*, 29–34.

Brayne, C. and Beardsall, L. (1990) Estimation of verbal intelligence in an elderly community: An epidemiological study using NART. *British Journal of Clinical Psychology, 29*, 217–24.

Brébion, G., Smith, M.J. and Ehrlich, M.F. (1997) Working memory and aging: Deficit or strategy differences. *Aging, Neuropsychology and Cognition, 4*, 58–73.

Brewer, G.J. (1999) Regeneration and proliferation of embryonic and adult hippocampal neurons. *Experimental Neurology, 159*, 237–47.

Brickell, K., Leverenz, J., Steinbart, E., Rumbaugh, M. and Schallenberg, G. (2007) Clinicopathological concordance and discordance in three monozygotic twin pairs with familial Alzheimer's disease. *Journal of Neurology, Neurosurgery and Psychiatry, 78*, 1050–55.

Brimacombe, C., Quinton, N., Nance, N. and Garrioch, L. (1997) Is age irrelevant? Perceptions of young and old eyewitnesses. *Law and Human Behavior, 21*, 619–34.

Brinley, J.F. (1965) Cognitive sets, speed and accuracy in the elderly. In A.T. Welford and J.E. Birren (eds) *Behavior, Aging and the Nervous System.* New York: Springer-Verlag.

Brodaty, H. (2007) Meaning and measurement of caregiver outcomes. *International Psychogeriatrics, 19*, 363–81.

Brody, J.A. (1988) Changing health needs of the ageing population. *Research and the Ageing Population.* Ciba Foundation Symposium 134. Chichester: Wiley.

Bromley, D.B. (1958) Some effects of age on short-term learning and memory. *Journal of Gerontology, 13*, 398–406.

Bromley, D.B. (1988) *Human Ageing. An Introduction to Gerontology.* 3rd edition. Harmondsworth: Penguin.

Bromley, D.B. (1991) Aspects of written language production over adult life. *Psychology and Aging, 6*, 296–308.

Brommelhoff, J., Gatz, M., Johansson, B., McArdle, J. *et al.* (2009) Depression as a risk factor of prodromal feature for dementia? Findings in a population-based sample of Swedish twins. *Psychology and Aging, 24*, 373–84.

Brown, J.W., Chobor, A. and Zinn, F. (1993) Dementia testing in the elderly. *Journal of Nervous and Mental Disorders, 181*, 695–8.

Brown, L., Majumdar, S., Newman, S. and Johnson, J. (2006) Type 2 diabetes does not increase risk of depression. *Canadian Medical Association Journal, 175*, 42–6.

Brown, R. (2010) Broadening the search for safe treatments in dementia agitation: A possible role for low-dose opioids? *International Journal of Geriatric Psychiatry, 25*, 1085–6.

Brown, R. and McNeill, D. (1966) The 'tip-of-the-tongue' phenomenon. *Journal of Verbal Learning and Verbal Behavior, 5*, 325–37.

Brown, S. and Kawamura, S. (2010) Relationship quality among cohabitors and marrieds in older adulthood. *Social Science Research, 39*, 777–86.

Brown, S.L., Roebuck Bulanda, J. and Lee, G.R. (2005) The significance of nonmarital cohabitation: Marital status and mental health benefits among middle-aged and older adults. *The Journals of Gerontology Series B: Psychological Sciences and Social Sciences, 60*, 21–9.

Bruandet, A., Richard, F., Bombois, S., Maurage, C. *et al.* (2008) Cognitive decline and survival in Alzheimer's disease according to education level. *Dementia and Geriatric Cognitive Disorders, 25*, 74–80.

Brutoco, S. (2010) The Barber decision: A questionable approach to termination of life-support systems for the patient in a persistent vegetative state. *Golden Gate University Law Review, 15*. Available at: http://digitalcommons.law.ggu.edu/ggulrev/vol15/iss2/4, accessed on 21 January, 2012.

Bryan, J. and Luszcz, M.A. (1996) Speed of information processing as a mediator between age and free-recall performance. *Psychology and Aging, 11*, 3–9.

Bryant, C. (2010) Anxiety and depression in old age: Challenges in recognition and diagnosis. *International Psychogeriatrics, 22*, 511–13.

Bucks, R., Scott, M.I., Pearsall, T. and Ashworth, D.L. (1996) The short NART: Utility in a memory disorders clinic. *British Journal of Clinical Psychology, 35*, 133–141.

Bucks, R.S. and Willison, J.R. (1997) Development and validation of the Location Learning Test (LLT): A test of visuo-spatial learning designed for use with older adults and in dementia. *Clinical Neuropsychologist, 11*, 273–86.

Bullock, K. (2011) The influence of culture on end-of-life decision making. *Journal of Social Work in End-of-Life and Palliative Care, 7*, 83–98.

Bunce, D., Kivipelto, M. and Wahlin, A. (2005) Apolipoprotein E, B vitamins and cognitive function in older adults. *The Journals of Gerontology Series B: Psychological Sciences and Social Sciences, 60*, 41–8.

Bunce, D.J., Barrowclough, A. and Morris, I. (1996) The moderating influence of physical fitness on age gradients in vigilance and serial choice responding tasks. *Psychology and Aging, 11*, 671–82.

Burgmans, S., van Boxtel, M.P., Vuurman, E.F., Smeets, F. *et al.* (2009) The prevalence of cortical gray matter atrophy may be overestimated in the healthy aging brain. *Neuropsychology, 23*, 541–50.

Burke, D.M., Mackay, D.G. and James, L.E. (2000) Theoretical approaches to language and aging. In T.J. Perfect and E.A. Maylor (eds) *Models of Cognitive Aging.* Oxford: Oxford University Press, 204–237.

Burke, D.M., White, H. and Diaz, D.L. (1987) Semantic priming in young and old adults: Evidence for age constancy in automatic and attentional processes. *Journal of Experimental Psychology: Human Perception and Performance, 13*, 79–88.

Burke, D.M., Worthley, J. and Martin, J. (1988) I'll never forget what's-her-name: Aging and tip of the tongue experiences in everyday life. In M.M. Gruneberg, P.E. Morris and R.N. Sykes (eds) *Practical Aspects of Memory: Current Research and Issues.* Chichester: Wiley.

Burns, A. (1995) Cause of death in dementia. In E. Murphy and G. Alexopoulos (ed.) *Geriatric Psychiatry: Key Research Topics for Clinicians.* Chichester: Wiley, 95–101.

Burns, A. (2006) *Severe Dementia.* New York: John Wiley and Sons.

Burns, A., Allen, H., Tomenson, B., Duignan, D. and Byrne, J. (2009) Bright light therapy for agitation in dementia: A randomized controlled trial. *International Psychogeriatrics, 21*, 711–21.

Burns, R. (1988) A two-way TV system operated by senior citizens. *American Behavioral Scientist, 31*, 576–87.

Burnside, I.M., Ebersole, P. and Monea, H.E. (eds) (1979) *Psychosocial Caring Throughout the Lifespan*. New York: McGraw Hill.

Butler, K. and Zacks, R.T. (2006) Age deficits in the control of prepotent responses: Evidence for an inhibitory decline. *Psychology and Aging, 21*, 638–43.

Butler, R.N. (1967) *Creativity in Old Age*. New York: Plenum.

Butler, R.N. (1969) Ageism: Another form of bigotry. *The Gerontologist, 9*, 243–6.

Buzgova, R. and Ivanova, K. (2009) Elder abuse and mistreatment in residential settings. *Nursing Ethics, 16*, 110–26.

Byrd, M. (1985) Age differences in the ability to recall and summarise textual information. *Experimental Aging Research, 11*, 87–91.

Byrne, M.D. (1998) Taking a computational approach to aging: The SPAN theory of working memory. *Psychology of Aging, 13*, 309–22.

Cabeza, R. (2001) Cognitive neuroscience of aging: Contributions of functional neuroimaging. *Scandanavian Journal of Psychology, 42*, 277-86.

Cabeza, R. (2002) Hemispheric asymmetry reduction in old adults: The HAROLD model. *Psychology and Aging, 17*, 85–100.

Caine, E.D., Lyness, J.M., King, D.A. and Connors, B.A. (1994) Clinical and etiological heterogeneity of mood disorders in elderly patients. In L.S. Schneider, C.F. Reynolds, B.D. Lebowitz and A.J. Friedhoff (eds) *Diagnosis and Treatment of Depression in Late Life*. Washington: American Psychological Association, 23–53.

Calasanti, T. (2004) Feminist gerontology and old men. *The Journals of Gerontology Series B: Psychological Sciences and Social Sciences, 59*, 305–14.

Calvaresi, E. and Bryan, J. (2001) B vitamins, cognition and aging. *The Journals of Gerontology Series B: Psychological Sciences and Social Sciences, 56*, 327–39.

Calvo, E., Haverstick, K. and Sass, S. (2009) Gradual retirement, sense of control, and retirees' happiness. *Research on Aging, 31*, 112–35.

Camp, C.J. (1988) Utilisation of world knowledge systems. In L.W. Poon, D.G. Rubin and B.A. Wilson (eds) *Everyday Cognition in Adulthood and Later Life*. Cambridge: Cambridge University Press.

Capone, J., Della Sala, S., Spinnler, H. and Venneri, A. (2003) Upper and lower face and ideomotor apraxia in patients with Alzheimer's disease. *Behavioural Neurology, 14*, 1–8.

Cappeliez, P. and O'Rourke, N. (2002) Personality traits and existential concerns as predictors of the functions of reminiscence in older adults. *The Journals of Gerontology Series B: Psychological Sciences and Social Sciences, 57*, 116–23.

Cappell, K., Gmeindl, L. and Reuter-Lorenz, P. (2010) Age differences in prefrontal recruitment during verbal working memory maintenance depend on memory load. *Cortex, 46*, 462–73.

Carey, R.G. (1979) Weathering widowhood: Problems and adjustment of the widowed during the first year. *Omega, 10*, 263–74.

Carlson, L.E., Sherwin, B.B. and Chertkow, H.M. (2000) Relationships between mood and estradiol (E2) levels in Alzheimer's disease (AD) patients. *The Journals of Gerontology Series B: Psychological Sciences and Social Sciences, 55*, 47–53.

Carmelli, D., Swan, G.E., Kelly-Hayes, M., Wolf, P.A., Reed, T. and Miller, B. (2000) Longitudinal changes in the contribution of genetic and environmental influences to symptoms of depression in older male twins. *Psychology and Aging, 15*, 505–10.

Carp, J., Gmeindl, L. and Reuter-Lorenz, P. (2010) Age differences in the neural representation of working memory revealed by multi-voxel pattern analysis. *Frontiers in Human Neuroscience, 4*, 217–30.

Carp, J., Park, J., Polk, T.A. and Park, D.C. (2010) Age differences in neural distinctiveness revealed by multi-voxel pattern analysis. *Neuroimage, 50,* 56–71.

Carr, D., House, J.S., Kessler, R.C., Nesse, R.M., Sonnega, J. and Wortman, C. (2000) Marital quality and psychological adjustment to widowhood among older adults: a longitudinal analysis. *The Journals of Gerontology Series B: Psychological Sciences and Social Sciences, 55,* 197–207.

Carr, D., House, J.S., Wortman, C., Nesse, R. and Kessler, R.C. (2001) Psychological adjustment to sudden and anticipated spousal loss among older widowed persons. *The Journals of Gerontology Series B: Psychological Sciences and Social Sciences, 56,* 237–48.

Carreon, D. and Noymer, A. (2011) Health-related quality of life in older adults: Testing the double jeopardy hypothesis. *Journal of Aging Studies, 25,* 371–9.

Carretti, B., Borella, E. and De Beni, R. (2007) Does strategic memory training improve the working memory performance of younger and older adults? *Experimental Psychology, 54,* 311–20.

Carriere, J.S., Cheyne, J., Solman, G. and Smilek, D. (2010) Age trends for failures of sustained attention. *Psychology and Aging, 25,* 569–74.

Carswell, L.M., Graves, R.E., Snow, W.G. and Tierney, M.C. (1997) Postdicting verbal IQ of elderly individuals. *Journal of Clinical and Experimental Neuropsychology, 19,* 914–921.

Carter, J.H. (1982) The effects of aging on selected visual functions: Color vision, glare sensitivity, field of vision and accommodation. In R. Sekuler, D. Kline and K. Dismukes (eds) *Aging and Human Visual Function.* New York: Alan R. Liss, 121–30.

Caserta, M.T., Bannon, Y., Fernandez, F., Giunta, B., Schoenberg, M.R. and Tan, J. (2009) Normal brain aging clinical, immunological, neuropsychological, and neuroimaging features. *International Review of Neurobiology, 84,* 1–19.

Caspi, A. and Elder, G.H. (1986) Life satisfaction in old age: Linking social psychology and history. *Journal of Psychology and Aging, 1,* 18–26.

Caspi, A., Roberts, B.W. and Shiner, R.L. (2005) Personality development: Stability and change. *Annual Review of Psychology, 56,* 453–84.

Castel, A. (2005) Memory for grocery prices in younger and older adults: The role of schematic support. *Psychology and Aging, 20,* 718–21.

Castelo-Branco, C., Palacios, S., Ferrer-Barriendos, J. and Alberich, X. (2010) Do patients lie? An open interview vs. a blind questionnaire on sexuality. *Journal of Sexual Medicine, 7,* 873–80.

Castro-Costa, E., Ferri, C., Lima-Costa, M., Zaleski, M. *et al.* (2008) Alcohol consumption in late-life – the first Brazilian National Alcohol Survey (BNAS). *Addictive Behaviors, 33,* 1598–601.

Cattell, R.B. (1971) *Abilities: Their Structure, Growth and Action.* Boston, MA: Houghton Mifflin.

Catterall, M. and Maclaran, P. (2001) Body talk: Questioning the assumptions in cognitive age. *Psychology and Marketing, 18,* 10, 1117–33.

Cavallini, E., Pagnin, A. and Vecchi, T. (2003) Aging and everyday memory: The beneficial effect of memory training. *Archives of Gerontology and Geriatrics, 37,* 241–57.

Caza, N. and Belleville, S. (2008) Reduced short-term memory capacity in Alzheimer's disease: The role of phonological, lexical, and semantic processing. *Memory, 16,* 341–50.

Centers for Disease Control and Prevention (2007) Preventing injuries in America: Public health action. Available at www.cdc.gov/injury/wisqars.

Cerella, J. (1985) Information processing rate in the elderly. *Psychological Bulletin, 98,* 67–83.

Cerella, J. (1990) Aging and information-processing rate. In J.E. Birren and K.W. Schaie (eds) *Handbook of the Psychology of Aging.* 3rd edition. San Diego, CA: Academic Press.

Cerella, J. and Fozard, J.L. (1984) Lexical access and age. *Developmental Psychology, 20,* 235–43.

Cervera, T., Soier, M., Dasi, C. and Ruiz, J. (2009) Speech recognition and working memory capacity in young-elderly listeners: Effects of hearing sensitivity. *Canadian Journal of Experimental Psychology, 63,* 216–26.

Chait, R., Fahmy, S. and Caceres, J. (2010) Cocaine abuse in older adults: An underscreened cohort. *Journal of the American Geriatrics Society, 58,* 391–2.

Chambaere, K., Bilsen, J., Cohen, J., Onwuteaka-Philipsen, B. *et al.* (2011) Trends in medical end-of-life decision making in Flanders, Belgium 1998-2001-2007. *Medical Decision Making, 31,* 500–10.

Champley, J., Scherz, J., Apel, K. and Burda, A. (2008) A preliminary analysis of reading materials and strategies used by older adults. *Communication Disorders Quarterly, 29,* 131–40.

Chan, A.S., Salmon, D.P., Butters, N. and Johnson, S. (1995) Comparison of the semantic networks in patients with dementia and amnesia. *Neuropsychology, 9,* 177–86.

Chandler, M.J. and Holliday, S. (1990) Wisdom in a post apocalyptic age. In R.J. Sternberg (ed.) *Wisdom: Its Nature, Origins and Development.* Cambridge: Cambridge University Press, 121–41.

Chao, L.L. and Knight, R.T. (1997) Prefrontal deficits in attention and inhibitory control with aging. *Cerebral Cortex, 7,* 63–9.

Chao, T.K. and Chen, T.H. (2009) Predictive model for progression of hearing loss: Meta-analysis of multi-state outcome. *Journal of Evaluative Clinical Practice, 15,* 32–40.

Chapman, B., Duberstein, P., Sorensen, S., Lyness, J. and Emery, L. (2006) Personality and perceived health in older adults: The five factor model in primary care. *The Journals of Gerontology Series B: Psychological Sciences and Social Sciences, 61,* 362–5.

Chapman, B., Lyness, J, and Duberstein, P. (2007) Personality and medical illness burden among older adults in primary care. *Psychosomatic Medicine, 69,* 277–82.

Chapman, B., Shah, M., Friedman, B., Drayer, R. *et al.* (2009) Personality traits predict emergency department utilization over 3 years in older patients. *American Journal of Geriatric Psychiatry, 17,* 526–35.

Chapman, S., Ulatowska, H., Franklin, L. Shobe, A. *et al.* (1997) Proverb interpretation in fluent aphasia and Alzheimer's disease: Implications beyond abstract thinking. *Aphasiology, 11,* 337–50.

Chapple, A., Swift, C. and Ziebland, S. (2011) The role of spirituality and religion for those bereaved due to a traumatic death. *Mortality, 16,* 1–19.

Charlton, R., Landau, S., Schiavone, F., Barrick, T. *et al.* (2008) A structural equation modeling investigation of age-related variance in executive function and DTI measured white matter damage. *Neurobiology of Aging, 29,* 1547–55.

Charlton, R.A., Barrick, T.R., Markus, H.S. and Morris, R.G. (2010) The relationship between episodic long-term memory and white matter integrity in normal aging. *Neuropsychologia, 48,* 114–22.

Charness, N. (1979) Components of skill in bridge. *Canadian Journal of Psychology, 133,* 1–16.

Charness, N. (1981) Aging and skilled problem solving. *Journal of Experimental Psychology: General, 110,* 21–38.

Charness, N., Kelley, C.L., Bosman, E.A. and Mottram, M. (2001) Word-processing training and retraining: Effects of adult age, experience and interface. *Psychology and Aging, 16,* 110–27.

Charness, N. and Schaie, K.W. (eds) (2003) *The Impact of Technology on Successful Aging.* New York: Springer.

Chen, S. (2008) Reading practices and profiles of older adults in Taiwan. *Educational Gerontology, 34,* 428–42.

Chen, Y. and Persson, A. (2002) Internet use among young and older adults: Relation to psychological well-being. *Educational Gerontology, 28,* 731–44.

Chertkow, H., Massoud, F., Nasreddine, Z., Belleville, S. *et al.* (2009) Diagnosis and treatment of dementia: 3. Mild cognitive impairment and cognitive impairment without dementia. *Focus, 7,* 64–78.

Chin, J., Lee, B., Seo, S., Kim, E. *et al.* (2005) The closing-in phenomenon in Alzheimer's disease and vascular dementia. *Journal of Clinical Neurology, 1,* 166–73.

Chipperfield, J.G. and Havens, B. (2001) Gender differences in the relationship between marital status transitions and life satisfaction in later life. *The Journals of Gerontology Series B: Psychological Sciences and Social Sciences, 56*, 176–86.

Chiu, H., Hsieh, Y., Mau, L. and Lee, M. (2005) Associations between socio-economic status measures and functional change among older people in Taiwan. *Ageing and Society, 25*, 377–95.

Cho, C., Gilchrist, L. and White, S. (2008) A comparison between young and old adults in their ability to rapidly sidestep during gait when attention is divided. *Gerontology, 54*, 120–7.

Cho, H., Lavretsky, H., Olmstead, R., Levin, M. and Oxman, M. (2008) Sleep disturbance and depression recurrence in community-dwelling older adults: A prospective study. *American Journal of Psychiatry, 165*, 1543–50.

Choi, N. and McDougall, G. (2009) Unmet needs and depressive symptoms among low-income older adults. *Journal of Gerontological Social Work, 52*, 567–83.

Chou, K. (2009) Age at onset of generalized anxiety disorder in older adults. *American Journal of Geriatric Psychiatry, 17*, 455–64.

Christensen, H., Henderson, A.S., Griffiths, K. and Levings, C. (1997) Does ageing inevitably lead to declines in cognitive performance? A longitudinal study of elite academics. *Personality and Individual Differences, 23*, 67–78.

Christensen, H., Korten, A.E., Jorm, A.F., Henderson, A.S. *et al.* (1997) Education and decline in cognitive performance: Compensatory but not protective. *International Journal of Geriatric Psychiatry, 12*, 323–30.

Christensen, H., Mackinnon, A.J., Korten, A.E., Jorm, A.F. *et al.* (1999) An analysis of diversity in the cognitive performance of elderly community dwellers. Individual differences in change scores as a function of age. *Psychology and Aging, 14*, 365–79.

Christianson, K., Williams, C., Zacks, R. and Ferreira, F. (2006) Younger and older adults' 'good enough' interpretations of garden-path sentences. *Discourse Processes, 42*, 205 38.

Chu, S. and Downes, J. (2000) Long live Proust: the odour-cued autobiographical memory bump. *Cognition, 75*, 41–50.

Chua, E., Schacter, D. and Sperling, R. (2009) Neural basis for recognition confidence in younger and older adults. *Psychology and Aging, 24*, 139–53.

Chung, S., Domino, M. and Stearns, S. (2009) The effect of retirement on weight. *The Journals of Gerontology Series B: Psychological Sciences and Social Sciences, 64*, 656–65.

Cicirelli, V.G. (1976) Categorization behavior in aging subjects. *Journal of Gerontology, 31*, 676–90.

Claessens, P., Menten, J., Schotsmans, P. and Broeckaert, B. (2011) Palliative sedation, not slow euthanasia: A prospective, longitudinal study of sedation in Flemish palliative care units. *Journal of Pain and Symptom Management, 41*, 14–24.

Clark, L., Gatz, M., Zheng, L., Chen, Y. *et al.* (2009) Longitudinal verbal fluency in normal aging, preclinical, and prevalent Alzheimer's disease. *American Journal of Alzheimer's Disease and Other Dementias, 24*, 461–8.

Clark, M.S. (1999) The double ABCX model of family crisis as a representation of family functioning after rehabilitation from stroke. *Psychology, Health and Medicine, 4*, 203–20.

Clarke, P. and Smith, J. (2011) Aging in a cultural context: Cross-national differences in disability and the moderating role of personal control among older adults in the United States and England. *The Journals of Gerontology Series B: Psychological Sciences and Social Sciences, 66*, 457–67.

Clarke, R., Grimley Evans, J., Schneede, J., Nexo, E. *et al.* (2004) Vitamin B12 and folate deficiency in later life. *Age and Ageing, 33*, 34–41.

Clay, O.J., Edwards, J.D., Ross, L.A., Okonkwo, O. *et al.* (2009) Visual function and cognitive speed of processing mediate age-related decline in memory span and fluid intelligence. *Journal of Aging and Health, 21*, 547–66.

Clayton, V.P. and Birren, J.E. (1980) The development of wisdom across the life span: A reexamination of an ancient topic. In P.B. Baltes and O.G. Brim (eds) *Life-Span Development and Behavior, 3*. New York: Academic Press.

Cleiren, M., Grad, O., Zavasnik, A. and Diekstra, R. (1996) Psychosocial impact of bereavement after suicide and fatal traffic accident: A comparative two-country study. *Acta Psychiatrica Scandinavica, 94*, 37–44.

Cockburn, J. and Smith, P.T. (1988) Effects of age and intelligence on everyday memory tasks. In M.M. Gruneberg, P.E. Morris and R.N. Sykes (eds) *Practical Aspects of Memory: Current Research and Issues*. Chichester: Wiley.

Coffey, C.E., Saxton, J.A., Ratcliff, G., Bryan, R.N. and Lucke, J.F. (1999) Relation of education to brain size in normal aging: Implications for the reserve hypothesis. *Neurology, 53*, 189–96.

Coghlan, A. (2011) Curtain falls on mad cow disease. *New Scientist, 209*, 6–7.

Cohen, C., Magai, C., Yaffee, R., Huangthaisong, P. and Walcott-Brown, L. (2006) The prevalence of phobia and its associated factors in a multiracial aging urban population. *American Journal of Geriatric Psychiatry, 14*, 507–14.

Cohen, D. and Dunner, D. (1980) The assessment of cognitive dysfunction in dementing illness. In J.O. Cole and J.E. Barrett (eds) *Psychopathology in the Aged*. New York: Raven.

Cohen, G. (1981) Inferential reasoning in old age. *Cognition, 9*, 59–72.

Cohen, G. (1988) Age differences in memory for texts: Production deficiency of processing limitations? In D.M. Burke and L.L. Light (eds) *Language, Memory and Aging*. New York: Cambridge University Press.

Cohen, G. (1989) *Memory in the Real World*. Hove: Lawrence Erlbaum Associates.

Cohen, G. (1996) Memory and learning in normal ageing. In R. Woods (ed.) *Handbook of the Clinical Psychology of Ageing*. Chichester: Wiley, 43–58.

Cohen, G. and Faulkner, D. (1984) Memory for text. In H. Bouma and D. Bouwhuis (eds) *Attention and Performance X: Control of Language Processes*. Hillsdale, NJ: Lawrence Erlbaum.

Cohen, G. and Faulkner, D. (1986) Memory for proper names: Age differences in retrieval. *British Journal of Developmental Psychology, 4*, 187–97.

Cohen, G. and Faulkner, D. (1988) Life span changes in autobiographical memory. In M.M. Gruneberg, P.E. Morris and R.N. Sykes (eds) *Practical Aspects of Memory, Current Research and Issues, Volume 2*. Chichester: Wiley.

Cohen, G. and Faulkner, D. (1989) The effects of aging on perceived and generated memories. In L.W. Poon, D.C. Rubin and B.A. Wilson (eds) *Everyday Cognition in Later Life*. Cambridge: Cambridge University Press.

Cohen-Mansfield, J. (2007) Temporal patterns of agitation in dementia. *American Journal of Geriatric Psychiatry, 15*, 395–405.

Cohen-Mansfield, J., Shmotkin, D., Eyal, N., Reichental, Y. and Hazan, H. (2010) A comparison of three types of autobiographical memories in old-old age: First memories, pivotal memories and traumatic memories. *Gerontology, 56*, 564–73.

Cohn, E.S. (1999) Hearing loss with aging: Presbycusis. *Clinical Geriatric Medicine, 15*, 145–61.

Cole, M.G. (2004) Delirium in elderly patients. *The American Journal of Geriatric Psychiatry, 12*, 7–22.

Coleman, P.G. and O'Hanlon, A. (2004) *Ageing and Development: Theories and Research*. London: Arnold.

Collette, F., Van der Linden, M., Bechet, S. and Salmon, E. (1999) Phonological loop and central executive functioning in Alzheimer's disease. *Neuropsychologia, 37*, 905–18.

Collinge, J., Whitfield, J., McKintosh, E., Frosh, A. *et al.* (2008) A clinical study of kuru patients with long incubation periods at the end of the epidemic in Papua New Guinea. *Philosophical Transactions of the Royal Society B: Biological Sciences, 363*, 3725–39.

Comijs, H.C., Jonker, C., van Tilburg, W. and Smit, J.H. (1999) Hostility and coping capacity as risk factors of elder mistreatment. *Social Psychiatry and Psychiatric Epidemiology, 34,* 48–52.

Compton, D.M., Bachman, L.D. and Logan, J.A. (1997) Aging and intellectual ability in young, middle-aged and older educated adults: Preliminary results from a sample of college faculty. *Psychological Reports, 81,* 79–90.

Concar, D. (1996) Death of old age. *New Scientist, 150,* 24–9.

Cong, Y.S., Wright, W.E. and Shay, J.W. (2002) Human telomerase and its regulation. *Microbiology and Molecular Biology Review, 66,* 407–25.

Connelly, S.L., Hasher, L. and Zacks, R. (1991) Age and reading: The impact of distraction. *Psychology and Aging, 6,* 533–41.

Connor, L.T., Spiro, A., Obler, L.K. and Albert, M.L. (2004) Change in object naming ability during adulthood. *The Journals of Gerontology Series B: Psychological Sciences and Social Sciences, 59,* 203–9.

Continuous Mortality Investigation (2006a) *The Graduation of the CMI 1999-2002 Mortality Experience: Final '00' Series Mortality Tables – Assured Lives.* Working Paper 21 (a).

Continuous Mortality Investigation (2006b) *The Graduation of the CMI 1999-2002 Mortality Experience: Final '00' Series Mortality Tables – Annuitants and Pensioner.* Working Paper 22 (b).

Contreras-Vidal, J.L., Teulings, H.L. and Stelmach, G.E. (1995) Micrographia in Parkinson's disease. *Neuroreport: An International Journal for the Rapid Communication of Research in Neuroscience, 6,* 2089–92.

Contreras-Vidal, J.L., Teulings, H.L. and Stelmach, G.E. (1998) Elderly subjects are impaired in spatial coordination in fine motor control. *Acta Psychologica, 100,* 25–35.

Conway, S.C. and O'Carroll, R.E. (1997) An evaluation of the Cambridge Contextual Reading Test (CCRT) in Alzheimer's disease. *British Journal of Clinical Psychology, 36,* 623–5.

Conwell, Y. (1997) Management of suicidal behavior in the elderly. *Psychiatric Clinics of North America, 20,* 667–83.

Cook, A.S. and Oltjenbruns, K.A. (1989) *Dying and Grieving.* New York: Holt, Rinehart and Winston.

Cook, E.A. (1998) Effects of reminiscence on life satisfaction of elderly female nursing home residents. *Health Care for Women International, 19,* 109–18.

Cooper, C., Bebbington, P., Meltzer, H., Jenkins, R. *et al.* (2009) Alcohol in moderation, premorbid intelligence and cognition in older adults: Results from the Psychiatric Morbidity Survey. *Journal of Neurology, Neurosurgery and Psychiatry, 80,* 1236–9.

Cooper, S. (1997a) Epidemiology of psychiatric disorders in elderly compared with younger adults with learning disabilities. *British Journal of Psychiatry, 170,* 375–80.

Cooper, S. (1997b) High prevalence of dementia among people with learning disabilities not attributable to Down's syndrome. *Psychological Medicine, 27,* 609–16.

Coppel, D.B., Burton, C., Becker, J. and Fiore, J. (1985) Relationships of cognition associated with coping reactions to depression in spousal caregivers of Alzheimer's disease patients. *Cognitive Therapy and Research, 9,* 253–66.

Corcoran, P., Reulbach, U., Perry, I. and Arensman, E. (2010) Suicide and deliberate self harm in older Irish adults. *Interntional Psychogeriatrics, 22,* 1327–36.

Cordingly, L. and Webb, C. (1997) Independence and aging. *Reviews in Clinical Gerontology, 7,* 137–46.

Corkin, S., Growden, J.H., Nissen, M.J., Huff, F.J., Freed, D.M. and Sagar, H.J. (1984) Recent advances in the neuropsychological study of Alzheimer's disease. In R.J. Wurtman, S. Corkin and J.H. Growden (eds) *Alzheimer's Disease: Advances in Basic Research and Therapies.* Cambridge, MA: Center for Science and Metabolism Trust.

Corley, J., Gow, A.J., Starr, J.M. and Deary, I.J. (2010) Is body mass index in old age related to cognitive abilities? The Lothian Birth Cohort 1936 Study. *Psychology and Aging, 25,* 867–75.

Cornelissen, F.W. and Kooijman, A.C. (2000) Does age change the distribution of visual attention? A comment on McCalley, Bouwhuis and Juola (1995). *The Journals of Gerontology Series B: Psychological Sciences and Social Sciences 55*, 187–90.

Cornman, J.C., Lynch, S.M., Goldman, N., Weinstein, M. and Lin, H.S. (2004) Stability and change in the perceived social support of older Taiwanese adults. *The Journals of Gerontology Series B: Psychological Sciences and Social Sciences 59*, 350–7.

Corrada, M., Brookmeyer, R., Paganini-Hill, A., Berlau, D. and Kawas, C. (2010) Dementia incidence continues to increase with age in the oldest old: The 90+ study. *Annals of Neurology, 67*, 114–21.

Corso, J.F. (1981) *Aging Sensory Systems and Perception*. New York: Praeger.

Corso, J.F. (1987) Sensory-perceptual processes and aging. *Annual Review of Gerontology and Geriatrics, 7*. New York: Springer.

Cosentino, S., Manly, J. and Mungas, D. (2007) Do reading tests measure the same construct in multiethnic and multilingual older persons? *Journal of the International Neuropsychological Society, 13*, 228–36.

Costa, P.T. and McCrae, R.R. (1980) Still stable after all these years: Personality as a key to some issues of adulthood and old age. In P.B. Baltes and G.G. Brim (eds) *Life-span Development and Behaviour, Volume 3*. New York: Academic Press.

Costa, P.T. and McCrae, R.R. (1982) An approach to the attribution of aging: Period and cohort effects. *Psychological Bulletin, 92*, 238–50.

Cottle, N. and Glover, R. (2007) Combating ageism: Change in student knowledge and attitudes regarding aging. *Educational Gerontology, 33*, 501–12.

Coudin, G. and Alexopoulos, T. (2010) 'Help me! I'm old!' How negative aging stereotypes create dependency among older adults. *Aging and Mental Health, 14*, 516–23.

Coupland, N., Coupland, J. and Giles, H. (1991) *Language, Society and the Elderly*. Oxford: Blackwells.

Cowart, B.J., Yokomukai, Y. and Beauchamp, G.K. (1994) Bitter taste in aging: Compound-specific decline in sensitivity. *Physiology and Behavior, 56*, 1237–41.

Cowgill, D. (1970) The demography of aging. In A.M. Hoffman (ed.) *The Daily Needs and Interests of Older People*. Springfield, IL: C.C. Thomas.

Coxon, P. and Valentine, T. (1997) The effects of the age of eyewitnesses on the accuracy and suggestibility of their testimony. *Applied Cognitive Psychology, 11*, 415–30.

Coyne, A.C., Liss, L. and Geckler, C. (1984) The relationship between cognitive status and visual information processing. *Journal of Gerontology, 39*, 711–17.

Craig, L., Hong, N. and McDonald, R. (2011) Revisiting the cholinergic hypothesis in the development of Alzheimer's disease. *Neuroscience and Biobehavioral Reviews, 35*, 1397–409.

Craik, F. and Salthouse, T.A. (eds) (2008) *The Handbook of Aging and Cognition*. 3rd edition. New York: Psychology Press.

Craik, F.I.M. (1977) Age differences in human memory. In J.E. Birren and K.W. Schaie (eds) *Handbook of the Psychology of Aging*. New York: Van Nostrand Reinhold.

Craik, F.I.M. (1986) A functional account of age differences in memory. In F. Klix and H. Hagendorf (eds) *Human Memory and Cognitive Capabilites, Mechanisms and Performance*. Amsterdam: Elsevier, 409–22.

Craik, F.I.M. (2000) Age-related changes in human memory. In D.C. Park and N. Schwarz (eds) *Cognitive Aging: A Primer*. Philadelphia: Taylor and Francis, 75–92.

Craik, F.I.M., Anderson, N.D., Kerr, S.A. and Li, K.Z.H. (1995) Memory changes in normal ageing. In A.D. Baddeley, B.A. Wilson and F.N. Watts (eds) *Handbook of Memory Disorders*. Chichester: Wiley, 211–42.

Craik, F.I.M. and Jennings, J.M. (1992) Human memory. In F.I.M. Craik and T.A. Salthouse (eds) *The Handbook of Aging and Cognition*. Hillsdale, NJ: Lawrence Erlbaum.

Craik, F.I.M. and Rabinowitz, J.C. (1984) Age differences in the acquisition and use of verbal information. In H. Bouma and D. Bouwhuis (eds) *Attention and Performance X: Control of Language Processes.* Hillsdale, NJ: Erlbaum, 471–99.

Cramer, P. (2003) Personality change in later adulthood is predicted by defense mechanism use in early adulthood. *Journal of Research in Personality, 37,* 76–104.

Crandall, R.C. (1980) *Gerontology. A Behavioral Science Approach.* Reading, MA: Addison-Wesley.

Crawford, J.R., Stewart, L.E., Garthwaite, P.H., Parker, D.M. and Bessan, J.A.O. (1988) The relationship between demographic variables and NART performance in normal subjects. *British Journal of Clinical Psychology, 27,* 181–2.

Cronin-Golomb, A., Gilmore, G., Neargarder, S., Morrison, S. and Laudate, T. (2007) Enhanced stimulus strength improves visual cognition in aging and Alzheimer's disease. *Cortex, 43,* 952–66.

Crook, T.H. and West, R.L. (1990) Name recall performance across the adult life span. *British Journal of Psychology, 81,* 335–49.

Crosson, C.W. and Robertson-Tchabo, E.A. (1983) Age and preference for complexity among manifestly creative women. *Human Development, 26,* 149–55.

Crowley, K., Mayer, P. and Stuart-Hamilton, I. (2009) Changes in reliance on reading and spelling subskills across the lifespan. *Educational Gerontology, 35,* 503–22.

Cruz-Jentoft, A.J., Franco, A., Sommer, P., Baeyens, J.P. *et al.* (2008). European silver paper on the future of health promotion and preventive actions, basic research, and clinical aspects of age-related disease. *Gerontechnology, 7,* 331–9.

Cuetos, F., Rosci, C., Laiacona, M. and Capitano, E. (2008) Different variables predict anomia in different subjects: A longitudinal study of two Alzheimer's patients. *Neuropsychologia, 46,* 249–60.

Cukrowicz, K., Cheavens, J., Van Orden, K., Regan, R. and Cook, R. (2011) Perceived burdensomeness and suicide ideation in older adults. *Psychology and Aging, 26,* 331–40.

Cullum, S., Huppert, F., McGee, M., Dening, T. *et al.* (2000). Decline across different domains of cognitive function in normal ageing: Results of a longitudinal population-based study using CAMCOG. *International Journal of Geriatric Psychiatry, 15,* 853–62.

Cumming, E. and Henry, W.E. (1961) *Growing Old.* New York: Basic Books.

Cunningham, W.R. and Brookbank, J.W. (1988) *Gerontology: The Psychology, Biology and Sociology of Ageing.* New York: Harper and Row.

Cunningham, W.R., Clayton, V. and Overton, W. (1975) Fluid and crystallised intelligence in young adulthood and old age. *Journal of Gerontology, 30,* 53–5.

Cutler, S.J., Hendricks, J. and Guyer, A. (2003) Age differences in home computer availability and use. *The Journals of Gerontology Series B: Psychological Sciences and Social Sciences, 58,* 271–80.

Czaja, S.J. and Sharit, J. (1998) Age differences in attitudes towards computers. *The Journals of Gerontology B: Psychological Sciences and Social Sciences, 53,* 329–40.

Dahlin, E., Backman, L., Neely, A. and Nyberg, L. (2009) Training of the executive component of working memory: Subcortical areas mediate transfer effects. *Restorative Neurology and Neuroscience, 27,* 405–19.

Dahlin, E., Nyberg, L., Backman, L. and Neely, A. (2008) Plasticity of executive functioning in young and old adults: Immediate training gains, transfer, and long-term maintenance. *Psychology and Aging, 23,* 720–30.

Daily Telegraph (2005) Terri Schiavo dies. *Daily Telegraph,* 31 March, 2005.

Davies, E. and Cartwright, S. (2011) Psychological and psychosocial predictors of attitudes to working past normal retirement age. *Employee Relations, 33,* 249–68.

Davies, S. and Nolan, M. (2006) 'Making it better': Self-perceived roles of family caregivers of older people living in care homes: A qualitative study. *International Journal of Nursing Studies, 43,* 281–91.

Davis, P.E. and Mumford, S.J. (1984) Cued recall and the nature of the memory disorder in dementia. *British Journal of Psychiatry, 144*, 383–6.

Davys, D. and Haigh, C. (2008) Older parents of people who have a learning disability: Perceptions of future accommodation needs. *British Journal of Learning Disabilities, 36*, 66–72.

Dawe, B., Procter, A. and Philpot, M. (1992). Concepts of mild memory impairment in the elderly and their relationship to dementia – a review. *International Journal of Geriatric Psychiatry, 7*, 473–9.

Dawkins, R. (1976) *The Selfish Gene*. Oxford: Oxford University Press.

de Beauvoir, S. (1970) *Old Age*. London: Penguin Books.

De Beni, R., Borella, E. and Carretti, B. (2007) Reading comprehesion in aging: The role of working memory and metacomprehension. *Aging, Neuropsychology and Cognition, 14*, 189–212.

De Bot, K. and Makoni, S. (2005) *Language and Aging in Multilingual Contexts*. Clevedon: Cromwell Press.

De Frias, C.M., Lovden, M., Lindenberger, U. and Nilsson, L. (2007) Revisiting the dedifferentiation hypothesis with longitudinal multi-cohort data. *Intelligence, 35*, 381–92.

De Jong Gierveld, J., Marjolein van Groenou, B., Hoogendoorn, A. and Smit, J. (2009) Quality of marriages in later life and emotional and social loneliness. *The Journals of Gerontology Series B: Psychological Sciences and Social Sciences, 64*, 497–506.

De la Torre, J. (2011) Three postulates to help identify the cause of Alzheimer's disease. *Journal of Alzheimer's Disease, 24*, 657–88.

De Leo, G., Brivio, E. and Sautter, S. (2011) Supporting autobiographical memory in patients with Alzheimer's disease using smart phones. *Applied Neuropsychology, 18*, 69–76.

de Magalhaes, J.P. (2011) The biology of ageing: A primer. In I. Stuart-Hamilton (ed.) *An Introduction to Gerontology*. Cambridge: Cambridge University Press.

de Mendonca Lima, C., Leibing, A. and Buschfort, R. (2007) Mental health resources for older persons in the Western Pacific Region of the World Health Organization. *Psychogeriatrics, 7*, 81–6.

de Vaus, D., Wells, Y., Kendig, H. and Quine, S. (2007) Does gradual retirement have better outcomes than abrupt retirement? Results from an Australian panel study. *Ageing and Society, 27*, 667–82.

de Vries, B., Bluck, S. and Birren, J. (1993) The understanding of death and dying in a life-span perspective. *The Gerontologist, 33*, 366–72.

Deary, I.J. (2001) *Intelligence: A Very Short Introduction*. Oxford: Oxford University Press.

Deary, I.J, Allerhand, M. and Der, G. (2009) Smarter in middle age, faster in old age: A cross-lagged panel analysis of reaction time and cognitive ability over 13 years in the West of Scotland Twenty-07 Study. *Psychology and Aging, 24*, 40–7.

Deary, I.J. and Der, G. (2005) Reaction time, age, and cognitive ability: Longitudinal findings from age 16 to 63 years in representative population samples. *Aging, Neuropsychology, and Cognition, 12*, 187–215.

Deary, I., Johnson, W. and Starr, J. (2010) Are processing speed tasks biomarkers of cognitive aging? *Psychology and Aging, 25*, 219–28.

Deary, I.J., Leaper, S.A., Murray, A.D., Staff, R.T. and Whalley, L.J. (2003) Cerebral white matter abnormalities and lifetime cognitive change: A 67-year follow-up of the Scottish Mental Survey of 1932. *Psychology and Aging, 18*, 140–8.

Deary, I.J., Whalley, L.J., Batty, G.D. and Starr, J.M. (2006) Physical fitness and lifetime cognitive change. *Neurology, 67*, 1195–200.

Deary, I.J., Whalley, L.J., Lemmon, H., Crawford, J.R. and Starr, J.M. (2000) The stability of individual differences in mental ability from childhood to old age: Follow-up of the 1932 Scottish Mental Survey. *Intelligence, 28*, 49–55.

Deary, I.J., Whalley, L. and Starr, J. (2009) Validating the National Adult Reading Test. In I.J. Deary, L. Whalley and J. Starr (eds) *A Lifetime of Intelligence: Follow-up Studies of the Scottish Mental Surveys of 1932 and 1947.* Washington: American Psychological Association.

Deary, I.J., Whiteman, M.C., Pattie, A., Starr, J.M. *et al.* (2004a) Apolipoprotein E gene variability and cognitive functions at age 79: A follow-up of the Scottish Mental Survey of 1932. *Psychology and Aging, 19,* 367–71.

Deary, I.J., Whiteman, M.C., Starr, J.C., Whalley, L.J. and Fox, H.C. (2004b) The impact of childhood intelligence on later life: Following up the Scottish Mental Surveys of 1932 and 1947. *Journal of Personality and Social Psychology, 86,* 130–47.

Debette, S., Belser, A. and Hoffman, U. (2010) Visceral fat is associated with lower brain volume in healthy middle-aged adults. *Annals of Neurology, 68,* 136–44.

Decker, D.L. (1980) *Social Gerontology.* Boston, MA: Little, Brown and Company.

DeDe, G., Caplan, D., Kemtes, K. and Waters, G. (2004) The relationship between age, verbal working memory and language comprehension. *Psychology and Aging, 19,* 601–16.

DeHart, S.S. and Hoffmann, N.G. (1995) Screening and diagnosis of 'alcohol abuse and dependence' in older adults. *International Journal of the Addictions, 30,* 1717–47.

Dehon, H. and Brédart, S. (2004) False memories: Young and older adults think of semantic associates at the same rate, but young adults are more successful at source monitoring. *Psychology and Aging, 19,* 191–7.

Del Duca, D. and Duque, G. (2006) A reflection on aging: A portfolio of change in attitudes toward geriatric patients during a clerkship rotation. *Educational Gerontology, 32,* 605–10.

DeLamater, J.D. and Sill, M. (2005) Sexual Desire in Later Life. *Journal of Sex Research, 42,* 138–49.

Delbaere, K., Crombez, G., Vanderstraeten, G., Willems, T. and Cambier, D. (2004) Fear-related avoidance of activities, falls and physical frailty. A prospective community-based cohort study. *Age and Aging, 33,* 368–73.

Dellenbach, M. and Zimprich, D. (2008) Typical intellectual engagement and cognition in old age. *Aging, Neuropsychology and Cognition, 15,* 208–31.

Deltsidou, A., Gesouli-Voityraki, E., Mastrogiannis, D., Mantzorou, M. and Noula, M. (2010) Nurse teachers' and student nurses' attitudes towards caring the older people in a province of Greece. *Health Science Journal, 4,* 245–57.

Dennerstein, L., Alexander. J.L. and Kotz, K. (2003) The menopause and sexual functioning: A review of the population-based studies. *Annual Review of Sex Research, 14,* 64–83.

Denney, D.R. and Denney, N.W. (1973) The use of classification for problem solving: A comparison of middle and old age. *Developmental Psychology, 9,* 275–8.

Denney, D.R. and Denney, N.W. (1974) Modelling effects on the questioning strategies of the elderly. *Developmental Psychology, 10,* 458.

Denney, N.W. (1974) Evidence for developmental changes in categorization criteria for children and adults. *Human Development, 17,* 41–53.

DePaola, S.J., Griffin, M., Young, J.R. and Neimeyer, R.A. (2003). Death anxiety and attitudes toward the elderly among older adults: The role of gender and ethnicity. *Death Studies, 27,* 335–54.

Derwinger, A., Neely, A.S. and Bäckman, L. (2005) Design your own memory strategies! Self-generated strategy training versus mnemonic training in old age: An 8-month follow-up. *Neuropsychological Rehabilitation, 15,* 37–54.

Devlin, K. (2009) Sentenced to death on the NHS. *The Telegraph,* 2 September, 2009.

Dewey, J. (1939) Introduction. In E.V. Cowdrey (ed.) *Problems of Ageing.* Baltimore, MD: Williams and Wilkins.

Dewing, J. (2008) Personhood and dementia: Revisiting Tom Kitwood's ideas. *International Journal of Older People Nursing, 3,* 3–13.

Di Rosa, M., Kofahl, C., McKee, K., Bien, B. *et al.* (2011) A typology of caregiving situations and service use in family carers of older people in six European countries: The EUROFAMCARE study. *GeroPsych: The Journal of Geontopsychology and Geriatric Psychiatry, 24*, 5–18.

Dickinson, G.E. (1992) First childhood death experiences. *Omega: Journal of Death and Dying, 25*, 169–82.

Diehl, M., Willis, S.L. and Schaie, K.W. (1995) Everyday problem solving in older adults: Observational assessment and cognitive correlates. *Psychology and Aging, 10*, 478–91.

Dijkstra, K. and Misirlisoy, M. (2009) Recognition accuracy for original and altered verbal memory reports in older adults. *Quarterly Journal of Experimental Psychology, 62*, 248–56.

Dilworth-Anderson. P., Goodwin. P.Y. and Wallace Williams, S. (2004) Can culture help explain the physical health effects of caregiving over time among African American caregivers? *The Journals of Gerontology Series B: Psychological Sciences and Social Sciences, 59*, 138–45.

Dixon, R.A., Backman, L. and Nilsson, L.G. (2004) *New Frontiers in Cognitive Ageing.* Oxford: Oxford University Press.

Dixon, R.A., Kurzman, D. and Friesen, I.C. (1993) Handwriting performance in younger and older adults: Age, familiarity and practice effects. *Psychology and Aging, 8*, 360–70.

Dodge, H., Chang, C., Kamboh, I. and Ganguli, M. (2011) Risk of Alzheimer's disease incidence attributable to vascular disease in the population. *Alzheimer's and Dementia, 7*, 356–60.

Dodson, C., Bawa, S. and Krueger, L. (2007) Aging, metamemory, and high-confidence errors: A misrecollection account. *Psychology and Aging, 22*, 122–33.

Dodson, C. and Krueger, L. (2006) I misremember it well: Why older adults are unreliable eyewitnesses. *Psychonomic Bulletin and Review, 13*, 770–5.

Doeller, C.F., King, J.A. and Burgess, N. (2008) Parallel striatal and hippocampal systems for landmarks and boundaries in spatial memory. *Proceedings of the National Academy of Sciences, U.S.A., 105*, 5915–20.

Domey, R.G., McFarland, R.A. and Chadwick, E. (1960) Dark adaptation as a function of age and time. *Journal of Gerontology, 15*, 267–79.

Dong, X., Simon, M., Wilson, R., Beck, T. *et al.* (2011) Association of personality traits with elder self-neglect in a community-dwelling population. *American Journal of Geriatric Psychiatry, 19*, 743–51.

Donix, M., Poettrich, K., Weiss, P., Werner, A. *et al.* (2010) Age-dependent differences in the neural mechanisms supporting long-term declarative memories. *Archives of Clinical Neuropsychology, 25*, 383–95.

Doty, R.L. (1990) Aging and age-related neurological disease: Olfaction. In F. Goller and J. Grafman (eds) *Handbook of Neuropsychology.* Amsterdam: Elsevier, 459–62.

Douglass, C., Keddie, A., Brooker, D. and Surr, C. (2010) Cross-cultural comparison of the perceptions and experiences of dementia care mapping 'mappers' in the United States and the United Kingdom. *Journal of Aging and Health, 22*, 567–88.

Dowd, K., Blake, D. and Cairns, A.J.G. (2010) *Facing Up to Uncertain Life Expectancy: The Longevity Fan Charts.* London: Pensions Institute. Available at www.pensions-institute.org/workingpapers/wp0703.pdf, accessed on 21 January 2012.

Drewnowski, A. and Shultz, J.M. (2001) Impact of aging on eating behaviors, food choices, nutrition and health status. *Journal of Nutrition, Health and Aging, 5*, 75–9.

Dreyfus, D., Roe, C. and Morris, J. (2010) Autobiographical memory task in assessing dementia. *Archives of Neurology, 67*, 862–6.

Druks, J., Masterson, J. Kopelman, M., Clare, L. *et al.* (2006) Is action naming better preserved (than object naming) in Alzheimer's disease and why should we ask? *Brain and Language, 98*, 332–40.

Druley, J.A., Stephens, M.A.P., Martire, L.M., Ennis, N. and Wojno, W.C. (2003) Emotional congruence in older couples coping with wives' osteoarthritis: Exacerbating effects of pain behavior. *Psychology and Aging, 18,* 406–14.

Du, Y., Scheidt-Nave, C. and Kopf, H. (2008) Use of psychotropic drugs and alcohol among non-institutionalised elderly. *Pharmacopsychiatry, 41,* 242–51.

Duberstein, P., Chapman, B., Tindle, H., Sink, K. *et al.* (2011) Personality and risk for Alzheimer's disease in adults 72 years of age and older: A 6-year follow-up. *Psychology and Aging, 26,* 351–62.

Duberstein, P.R., Conwell, Y., Seidlitz, L., Denning, D.G., Cox, C. and Caine, E.D. (2000) Personality traits and suicidal behavior and ideation in depressed inpatients 50 years of age and older. *The Journals of Gerontology Series B: Psychological Sciences and Social Sciences, 55,* 18–26.

Dubno, J.R., Dirk, D.D. and Morgan, D.E. (1984) Effects of age and mild hearing loss on speech recognition in noise. *Journal of Acoustical Society of America, 76,* 87–96.

Dubois, L. (1997) La representation du vieillissement à la télévision: Des images de negation et d'exclusion dans une logique de mise en marche. *Canadian Journal on Aging, 16,* 354–72.

Duckworth, A.L. and Seligman, M. (2005) Self-discipline outdoes IQ in predicting academic performance of adolescents. *Psychological Science, 16,* 939–44.

Duerson, M., Thomas, J., Chang, J. and Stevens, C. B. (1992) Medical students' knowledge and misconceptions about aging: Responses to Palmore's Facts on Aging quizzes. *The Gerontologist, 32,* 171–174.

Duff, K., Mold, J.W. and Gidron, Y. (2009) Cognitive functioning predicts survival in the elderly. *Journal of Clinical and Experimental Neuropsychology, 31,* 90–5.

Duggan, L., Lewis, M. and Morgan, J. (1996) Behavioural changes in people with learning disability and dementia: A descriptive study. *Journal of Intellectual Disability Research, 40,* 311–21.

Duke, J., Leventhal, H., Brownlee, S. and Leventhal, E.A. (2002) Giving up and replacing activities in response to illness. *The Journals of Gerontology Series B: Psychological Sciences and Social Sciences, 57,* 367–76.

Dulay, M. and Murphy, C. (2002) Olfactory acuity and cognitive function converge in older adulthood: Support for the common cause hypothesis. *Psychology and Aging, 17,* 392–404.

Duñabeitia, J.A., Marín, A., Avilés, A., Perea, M. and Carreiras, M. (2009) Constituent priming effects: Evidence for preserved morphological processing in healthy old readers. *European Journal of Cognitive Psychology, 21,* 283–302.

Duncan, J., Emslie, H., Williams, P., Johnson, R. and Freer, C. (1996) Intelligence and the frontal lobe: The organization of goal-directed behavior. *Cognitive Psychology, 30,* 257–303.

Dunlop, D.D., Manheim, L.M., Song, J. and Chang, R.W. (2002) Gender and ethnic/racial disparities in health care utilization among older adults. *The Journals of Gerontology Series B: Psychological Sciences and Social Sciences, 57,* 221–33.

Dunning, T. (2009) Aging, activities, and the Internet. *Activities, Adaptation and Aging, 33,* 120–1.

Dupuis, K. and Pichora-Fuller, M. (2010) Use of affective prosody by young and older adults. *Psychology and Aging, 25,* 16–29.

Dwyer, J.T. (1988) Health aspects of vegetarian diets. *American Journal of Clinical Nutrition, 48,* 712–38.

Dywan, J. and Murphy, W.E. (1996) Aging and inhibitory control in text comprehension. *Psychology and Aging, 11,* 199–206.

Earles, J.L., Kersten, A.W., Mas, B.B. and Miccio, D.M. (2004) Aging and memory for self-performed tasks: Effects of task difficulty and time pressure. *The Journals of Gerontology Series B: Psychological Sciences and Social Sciences, 59,* 285–93.

Edgley, C. (2003) Dying as deviance. An update on the relationship between terminal patients and medical settings. In C.D. Bryant *et al.* (eds) *Handbook of Death and Dying.* Vol. I: *The Presence of Death.* Thousand Oaks, CA: Sage, 448–56.

Edvardsson, D. and Innes, A. (2010) Measuring person-centered care: A critical comparative review of published tools. *The Gerontologist, 50,* 834–46.

Efstathiou, N. and Clifford, C. (2011) The critical care nurse's role in end-of-life care: Issues and challenges. *Nursing in Critical Care, 16,* 116–23.

Eggermont, J.J. and Roberts, L.E. (2004) The neuroscience of tinnitus. *Trends in Neurosciences, 27,* 676–82.

Egolf, B., Lasker, J., Wolf, S. and Potvin, L. (1992) The Roseto effect: A 50-year comparison of mortality rates. *American Journal of Public Health, 82,* 1089–92.

Eichenbaum, H. (2003) How does the hippocampus contribute to memory? *Trends in Cognitive Science, 7,* 427–9.

Einstein, G.O., Earles, J.L. and Collins, H.M. (2002) Spared inhibition for visual distraction in older adults. *The Journals of Gerontology Series B: Psychological Sciences and Social Sciences, 57,* 65–73.

Einstein, G.O., McDaniel, M.A. and Guynn, M.J. (1992) Age-related deficits in prospective memory: The influence of task complexity. *Psychology and Aging, 7,* 471–8.

Einstein, G.O., McDaniel, M.A., Smith, R. and Shaw, P. (1998) Habitual prospective memory and aging: Remembering instructions and forgetting actions. *Psychological Science, 9,* 284–88.

Eisdorfer, C., Cohen, D. and Paveza, G.J. (1992) An empirical evaluation of the Global Deterioration Scale for staging Alzheimer's disease. *American Journal of Psychiatry, 149,* 190–4.

Eisdorfer, C. and Wilkie, F. (1977) Stress, disease, aging and behavior. In J.E. Birren and K.W. Schaie (eds) *Handbook of the Psychology of Aging.* New York: Academic Press.

Eisenberg, J. and Kelso, J. (2002) The Robert Wendland case. *Western Journal of Medicine, 176,* 124.

Eisenbruch, M. (1984) Cross-cultural aspects of bereavement I: A conceptual framework for comparative analysis. *Culture, Medicine and Psychiatry, 8,* 283–309.

Eissler, K.R. (1955) *The Psychiatrist and the Dying Patient.* New York: International Universities Press.

Ekerdt, D.J., Sergeant, J.F., Dingel, M. and Bowen, M.E. (2004) Household disbandment in later life. *The Journals of Gerontology Series B: Psychological Sciences and Social Sciences, 59,* 265–73.

Ekwall, A., Sivberg, B. and Hallberg, I. (2007) Older caregivers' coping strategies and sense of coherence in relation to quality of life. *Journal of Advanced Nursing, 57,* 584–96.

Elia, N. (1997) Grief and loss in HIV/AIDS work. In M. Winiarski (ed.) *HIV Mental Health for the 21st Century.* New York: New York University Press, 67–81.

Elias, J. and Ryan, A. (2011) A review and commentary on the factors that influence expressions of sexuality by older people in care homes. *Journal of Clinical Nursing, 20,* 11–20.

Elias, M.F., Elias, J.W. and Elias, P. (1990) Biological and health influences on behavior. In J.E. Birren and K.W. Schaie (eds) *Handbook of the Psychology of Aging.* New York: Academic Press.

Elias, M.F., Elias, P.K. and Elias, J.W. (1977) *Basic Processes in Adult Developmental Psychology.* St Louis: C.V. Mosby.

Ellershaw, J. and Wilkinson, S. (eds) (2003) *Care for the Dying: A Pathway to Excellence.* Oxford: Oxford University Press.

Ellison, C., Burdette, A. and Hill, T. (2009) Blessed assurance: Religion, anxiety and tranquillity among US adults. *Social Science Research, 38,* 656–67.

Elmstahl, S., Sommer, M. and Hagberg, B. (1996) A 3-year follow-up of stroke patients: Relationships between activities of daily living and personality characteristics. *Archives of Gerontology and Geriatrics, 22,* 233–44.

Elwood, P.C., Gallacher, J.E.J., Hopkinson, C.A., Pickering, J. *et al.* (1999) Smoking, drinking and other life style factors and cognitive function in men in the Caerphilly cohort. *Journal of Epidemiology and Community Health, 53,* 9–15.

Elwood, P.C., Pickering, J., Bayer, A. and Gallacher, J.E.J. (2002) Vascular disease and cognitive function in older men in the Caerphilly cohort. *Age and Ageing, 31,* 43–8.

Elwood, P.C., Pickering, J. and Gallacher, J.E.J (2001) Cognitive function and blood rheology: Results from the Caerphilly cohort of older men. *Age and Ageing, 30,* 135–9.

Emery, C.F., Pedersen, N.L., Svartengren, M. and McClearn, G.E. (1998) Longitudinal and genetic effects in the relationship between pulmonary function and cognitive performance. *The Journals of Gerontology Series B: Psychological Sciences and Social Sciences, 53*, 311–7.

Emlet, C.A. (2004) HIV/AIDS and aging: A diverse population of vulnerable older adults. *Journal of Human Behavior in the Social Environment, 9*, 45–63.

Emlet, C.A., Hawks, H. and Callahan, J. (2001) Alcohol use and abuse in a population of community dwelling, frail older adults. *Journal of Gerontological Social Work, 35*, 21–33.

Engen, T. (1977) Taste and smell. In J.E. Birren and K.W. Schaie (eds) *Handbook of the Psychology of Aging.* New York: Academic Press.

Erikson, E.H. (1963) *Childhood and Society.* New York: Norton.

Erikson, E.H. (1982) *The Life Cycle Completed: A Review.* New York: Norton.

Erlangsen, A., Bille-Brahe, U. and Jeune, B. (2003) Differences in suicide between the old and the oldest old. *The Journals of Gerontology Series B: Psychological Sciences and Social Sciences, 58*, 314–22.

Erlangsen, A., Jeune, B., Bille-Brahe, U. and Vaupel, J.W. (2004) Loss of partner and suicide risks among oldest old: A population-based register study. *Age and Ageing, 33*, 378–83.

Erten-Lyons, D., Woltjer, R., Dodge, H., Nixon, R. *et al.* (2009) Factors associated with resistance to dementia despite high Alzheimer disease pathology. *Neurology, 72*, 354–60.

Ervin, R.B. (2008) Healthy Eating Index scores among adults, 60 years of age and over, by sociodemographic and health characteristics: United States, 1999–2002. *Advance Data, 395*, 1–16.

Eskildsen, M. and Flacker, J. (2009) A multimodal aging and dying course for first-year medical students improves knowledge and attitudes. *Journal of the American Geriatrics Society, 57*, 1492–97.

Estes, A., Rivera, V., Bryan, M., Call, P. and Dawson, G. (2010) Discrepancies between academic achievement and intellectual ability in higher-functioning school-aged children with Autism Spectrum Disorder. *Journal of Autism and Developmental Disorders, 2*, 1127–30.

Exley, C. (2007) Aluminium, tau and Alzheimer's disease. *Journal of Alzheimer's Disease, 12*, 313–5.

Eysenck, H.J. (1952) The effects of psychotherapy: An evaluation. *Journal of Consulting Psychology, 16*, 319–24.

Eysenck, H.J. (1985) The theory of intelligence and the psychophysiology of cognition. In R.J. Sternberg (ed.) *Advances in Research in Intelligence, 3.* Hillsdale, NJ: Lawrence Erlbaum.

Eysenck. H.J. (1987) Personality and ageing: An exploratory analysis. *Journal of Social Behaviour and Personality, 3*, 11–21.

Eysenck, H.J. and Eysenck, M.W. (1985) *Personality and Individual Differences: A Natural Science Approach.* New York: Plenum.

Eysenck, H.J. and Kamin, L. (1981) *The Intelligence Controversy.* New York: Wiley.

Fahey, T., Montgomery, A., Barnes, J. and Protheroe, J. (2003) Quality of care for elderly residents in nursing homes and elderly people living at home: Controlled observational study. *British Medical Journal, 326*, 580–1.

Fahlander, K., Wahlin, A., Fastbom, J., Grut, M. *et al.* (2000) The relationship between signs of cardiovascular deficiency and cognitive performance in old age. *The Journals of Gerontology Series B: Psychological Sciences and Social Sciences, 55*, 259–65.

Fargeau, M., Jaafari, N., Ragot, S., Houeto, J. *et al.* (2010) Alzheimer's disease and impairment of the self. *Consciousness and Cognition, 19*, 969–76.

Farias, S., Mungas, D., Hinton, L. and Haan, M. (2011) Demographic, neuropsychological, and functional predictors of rate of longitudinal cognitive decline in Hispanic older adults. *American Journal of Geriatric Psychiatry, 19*, 440–50.

Farkas, E. and Luiten, P.G. (2001) Cerebral microvascular pathology in aging and Alzheimer's disease. *Progress in Neurobiology, 64*, 6, 575–611.

Fay, S., Isingrini, M. and Clarys, D. (2005) Effects of depth-of-processing and ageing on word-stem and word-fragment implicit memory tasks: Test of the lexical-processing hypothesis. *European Journal of Cognitive Psychology, 17, 6,* 785–802.

Featherstone, M. and Wernicke, D. (eds) (1997) *Images of Ageing – Cultural Representations of Later Life.* London: Routledge.

Federmeier, K.D. and Kutas, M. (2005) Aging in context: Age-related changes in context use during language comprehension. *Psychophysiology, 42,* 133–41.

Femia, E.E., Zarita, S.H. and Johansson, B. (2001) The disablement process in very late life: A study of the oldest-old in Sweden. *The Journals of Gerontology Series B: Psychological Sciences and Social Sciences, 56,* 12–23.

Ferrario, C., Freeman, F., Nellett, G. and Scheel, J. (2008) Changing nursing students' attitudes about aging: An argument for the successful aging paradigm. *Educational Gerontology, 34,* 51–66.

Ferraro, F.R. and Moody, J. (1996) Consistent and inconsistent performance in young and elderly adults. *Developmental Neuropsychology, 12,* 429–41.

Ferraro, K.F. and Su, Y. (1999) Financial strain, social relations, and psychological distress among older people: A cross-cultural analysis. *The Journals of Gerontology Series B: Psychological Sciences and Social Sciences, 54B,* S3–S15.

Ferrer, E., Salthouse, T.A., Stewart, W.F. and Schwartz, B.S. (2004) Modeling age and retest processes in longitudinal studies of cognitive abilities. *Psychology and Aging, 19,* 243–59.

Ferstl, E. (2006) Text comprehension in middle aged adults: Is there anything wrong? *Aging, Neuropsychology and Cognition, 13,* 62–85.

Field, D. (1981) Retrospective reports by healthy intelligent people of personal events of their adult lives. *International Journal of Behavioral Development, 4,* 443–52.

Field, D. (1997) 'Looking back, what period of your life brought you the most satisfaction?' *International Journal of Aging and Human Development, 45,* 169–94.

Field, D. and Millsap, R.E. (1991) Personality in advanced old age: Continuity or change? *The Journals of Gerontology Series B: Psychological Sciences and Social Sciences, 46,* 299–308.

Fillmore, K.M., Golding, J.M., Graves, K.L., Kniep, S. *et al.* (1998) Alcohol consumption and mortality. III. Studies of female populations. *Addiction, 93,* 219–29.

Filoteo, J.V. and Maddox, W.T. (2004) A quantitative model-based approach to examining aging effects on information-integration category learning. *Psychology and Aging, 19,* 171–82.

Fine, R. (2010) Keeping the patient at the center of patient- and family-centered care. *Journal of Pain and Symptom Management, 40,* 621–5.

Fingerman, K.L. and Birditt, K.S. (2003) Do age differences in close and problematic family ties reflect the pool of available relatives? *The Journals of Gerontology Series B: Psychological Sciences and Social Sciences, 58,* 80–7.

Finkel, D., Pedersen, N.L. and Larsson, M. (2001) Olfactory functioning and cognitive abilities. A twin study. *The Journals of Gerontology Series B: Psychological Sciences and Social Sciences, 56,* 226–33.

Finkel, D., Reynolds, C., Larsson, M., Gatz, M. and Pedersen, N. (2011) Both odor identification and ApoE-e4 contribute to normative cognitive aging. *Psychology and Aging, 26,* 872–83.

Finkel, D., Reynolds, C.A., McArdle, J.J. and Pedersen, N.L. (2007) Age changes in processing speed as a leading indicator of cognitive aging. *Psychology and Aging, 22,* 558–68.

Finkelstein, J.A. and Schiffman, S.S. (1999) Workshop on taste and smell in the elderly: An overview. *Physiology and Behavior, 66,* 173–6.

Finlayson, R.E. (1995) Misuse of prescription drugs. *International Journal of the Addictions, 30,* 1871–901.

Fiori, K., Consedine, N. and Magai, C. (2008) The adaptive and maladaptive faces of dependency in later life: Links to physical and psychological health outcomes. *Aging* and *Mental Health, 12*, 700–12.

Fischer, H., Nyberg, L. and Bäckman, L. (2010). Age-related differences in brain regions supporting successful encoding of emotional faces. *Cortex, 46*, 490–7.

Fisher, J. (1990) The function of literacy in a nursing home context. *Educational Gerontology, 16*, 105–16.

Fisk, J.E. and Warr, P. (1996) Age and working memory: The role of perceptual speed, the central executive and the phonological loop. *Psychology and Aging, 11*, 316–23.

Fiske, A., Gatz, M. and Pedersen, N.L. (2003) Depressive symptoms and aging: The effects of illness and non-health-related events. *The Journals of Gerontology Series B: Psychological Sciences and Social Sciences, 58*, 320–8.

Fitzgibbons, P.J. and Gordon-Salant, S. (2010) Behavioral studies with aging humans: Hearing sensitivity and psychoacoustics. In S. Gordon-Salant, R.D. Frisina, A.N. Popper and R.R. Fay (2010) *The Aging Auditory System*. New York: Springer.

Fjell, A.M. and Walhovd, K.B. (2010) Structural brain changes in aging: Courses, causes and cognitive consequences. *Reviews in the Neurosciences, 21*, 187–221.

Fjell, A.M., Walhovd, K.B., Fennema-Notestine, C., McEvoy, L.K. *et al.* (2009) One-year brain atrophy evident in healthy aging. *Journal of Neuroscience, 29*, 15223–31.

Flaskerud, J. (2011) Grief and depression: Are they different? *Mental Health Nursing, 32*, 338–40.

Fleischman, D.A., Wilson, R.S., Gabrieli, J.D.E., Bienias, J.L. and Bennett, D.A. (2004) A longitudinal study of implicit and explicit memory in old persons. *Psychology and Aging, 19*, 617–25.

Flint, A.J. and Rifat, S.L. (1997) Anxious depression in elderly patients: Response to antidepressant treatment. *American Journal of Geriatric Psychiatry, 5*, 107–15.

Flint, K., Walleghen, E., Kealey, E., VonKaenel, S. *et al.* (2008) Differences in eating behaviors between nonobese, weight stable young and older adults. *Eating Behaviors, 9*, 370–5.

Flood, M. and Clark, R. (2009) Exploring knowledge and attitudes toward aging among nursing and nonnursing students. *Educational Gerontology, 35*, 587–95.

Florio, E.R., Hendryx, M.S., Jensen, J.E., Rockwood, T.H., Raschko, R. and Dyck, D.G. (1997) A comparison of suicidal and nonsuicidal elders referred to a community mental health center program. *Suicide and Life-Threatening Behavior, 27*, 182–93.

Flynn, J.R. (1987) Massive IQ gains in 14 nations: What IQ tests really measure. *Psychological Bulletin, 101*, 171–91.

Fonseca, A. (2007) Determinants of successful retirement in a Portuguese population. *Reviews in Clinical Gerontology, 17*, 219–24.

Foos, P.W. and Boone, D. (2008) Adult age differences in divergent thinking: It's just a matter of time. *Educational Gerontology, 34*, 587–94.

Foreman, M.D. and Milisen, K. (2004) Improving recognition of delirium in the elderly. *Primary Psychiatry, 11*, 46–50.

Forman-Hoffman, V., Richardson, K., Yankey, J., Hillism, S. *et al.* (2008) Retirement and weight changes among men and women in the health and retirement study. *The Journals of Gerontology Series B: Psychological Sciences and Social Sciences, 63*, 146–53.

Foster, J.K., Black, S.E., Buck, B.H. and Bronskill, M.J. (1997) Ageing and executive functions: A neuroimaging perspective. In P. Rabbitt (ed.) *Methodology of Frontal and Executive Function*. Hove: Taylor and Francis, 117–34.

Foster, L. (2011) Older people, pensions and poverty: An issue for social work? *International Social Work, 54*, 344–60.

Fozard, J.L. (1980) The time for remembering. In L.C. Poon (ed.) *Aging in the 1980s: Psychological Issues*. Washington, DC: American Psychological Association.

Fraboni, M., Saltstone, R. and Hughes, S. (1990) The Fraboni scale of ageism (FSA): An attempt at a more precise measure of ageism. *Canadian Journal on Aging, 9,* 56–66.

Francis, L.J. and Bolger, J. (1997) Personality and psychological well-being in later life. *Irish Journal of Psychology, 18,* 444–7.

Franklin, J. (1987) *Molecules of the Mind: The Brave New Science of Molecular Psychology.* New York: Atheneum Publishers.

Fraser, S., Bunce, C. and Wormald, R. (1999) Risk factors for late presentation in chronic glaucoma. *Investigative Ophthalmology and Vision Science, 40,* 2251–7.

Fraser, S.A., Li,. K., DeMont, R. and Penhune, V. (2007) Effect of balance status and age on muscle activation while walking under divided attention. *The Journals of Gerontology Series B: Psychological Sciences and Social Sciences, 62,* 171–8.

Fremouw, W.J., Perezel, W.J. and Ellis, T.E. (1990) *Suicide Risk.* Elmsfor: Pergamon.

Freund, A.M. and Baltes, P.B. (2007) Toward a theory of successful aging: Selection, optimization, and compensation. In R. Fernandez-Ballesteros (ed.) *Geropsychology: European Perspectives for an Aging World.* Ashland: Hogrefe and Huber.

Freyne, A., Kidd, N., Coen, R. and Lawlor, B.A. (1999) Burden in carers of dementia patients: Higher levels in carers of younger sufferers. *International Journal of Geriatric Psychiatry, 14,* 784–88.

Friedman, D. (2003) Cognition and aging: A highly selective overview of event-related potential (ERP) data. *Journal of Clinical and Experimental Neuropsychology, 25,* 702–20.

Fries, J.F. (2000) Compression of morbidity in the elderly. *Vaccine, 18,* 1584–9.

Fry, P.S. (1986) *Depression, Stress, and Adaptations in the Elderly.* Rockville, MD: Aspen Publications.

Fu, S., Anderson, D., Courtney, M. and McAvan, B. (2006) The relationship between country of residence, gender and the quality of life in Australian and Taiwanese midlife residents. *Social Indicators Research, 79,* 25–49.

Fukukawa, Y., Nakashima, C., Tsuboi, S., Niino, N., *et al.* (2004) The impact of health problems on depression and activities in middle-aged and older adults: Age and social interactions as moderators. *The Journals of Gerontology Series B: Psychological Sciences and Social Sciences, 59,* 19–26.

Fukunaga, A., Uematsu, H. and Sugimoto, K. (2005) Influences of aging on taste perception and oral somatic sensation. *The Journals of Gerontology Series A: Biological Sciences and Medical Sciences, 60,* 109–13.

Fung, H.H., Lai, P. and Ng, R. (2001) Age differences in social preferences among Taiwanese and mainland Chinese: The role of perceived time. *Psychology and Aging, 16,* 351–6.

Fung, H.H., Stoeber, F., Yeung, D. and Lang, F. (2008) Cultural specificity of socioemotional selectivity: Age differences in social network composition among Germans and Hong Kong Chinese. *The Journals of Gerontology Series B: Psychological Sciences and Social Sciences, 63,* 156–64.

Funkenstein, H.H. (1988) Cerebrovascular disorders. In M.S. Albert and M.B. Moss (eds) *Geriatric Neuropsychology.* New York: Guilford.

Gage, T.R. and O'Connor, K. (1994) Nutrition and the variation in level and age patterns of mortality. *Human Biology, 66,* 77–103.

Galanos, A., Neff, E., Heuberger, R. and Bales, C. (2010) What is 'optimal nourishment' for older adults at the end of life? A conversation. *Journal of Nutrition for the Elderly, 29,* 386–92.

Galdo-Alvarez, S., Lindin, M. and Diaz, F. (2009) Age-related prefrontal over-recruitment in semantic memory retrieval: Evidence from successful face naming and the tip of the tongue state. *Biological Psychology, 82,* 89–96.

Gale, T., Irvine, K., Laws, K. and Ferrissey, S. (2009) The naming profile in Alzheimer patients parallels that of elderly controls. *Journal of Clinical and Experimental Neuropsychology, 31,* 565–74.

Gallagher, D., Mhaolain, A., Crosby, L., Ryan, D. and Lacey, L. (2011) Dependence and caregiver burden in Alzheimer's disease and mild cognitive impairment. *American Journal of Alzheimer's Disease and Other Dementias, 26,* 110–4.

Gallagher, P., Barry, P. and O'Mahony, D. (2007) Inappropriate prescribing in the elderly. *Journal of Clinical Pharmacological Therapies, 32,* 113–21.

Gallagher-Thompson, D., Leary, M.C., Ossinalde, C. Romero, J.J., Wald, M. and Fernandez-Gamarra, E. (1997) Hispanic caregivers of older adults with dementia: Cultural issues in outreach and intervention. *Group, 21,* 211–32.

Gallo, W.T., Bradley, E.H., Siegel, M. and Kasla, S.V. (2000) Health effects of involuntary job loss among older workers: Findings from the health and retirement survey. *The Journals of Gerontology Series B: Psychological Sciences and Social Sciences, 55,* 131–40.

Gamboz, N., Russo, R. and Fox, E. (2002) Age differences and the identity negative priming effect: An updated meta-analysis. *Psychology and Aging, 17,* 525–30.

Gangadharan, S. and Bhaumik, S. (2006) A retrospective study of the use of neuroimaging in the assessment of dementia in adults with learning disability. *British Journal of Developmental Disabilities, 52,* 97–104.

Garcia-Alberca, J., Lara, J. and Luis Berthier, M. (2011) Anxiety and depression in caregivers are associated with patient and caregiver characteristics in Alzheimer's disease. *International Journal of Psychiatry in Medicine, 41,* 57–69.

Gardner, D. and Helmes, E. (2007) Development of the interpersonal dependency scale for older adults. *Australasian Journal on Ageing, 26,* 40–4.

Garre-Olmo, J., Batlle, D., del Mar Fernandez, M., Daniel, F. *et al.* (2010) Incidence and subtypes of early-onset dementia in a geographically defined general population. *Neurology, 75,* 1249–55.

Garrett, D.D., Grady, C.L. and Hasher, L. (2010) Everyday memory compensation: The impact of cognitive reserve, subjective memory and stress. *Psychology and Aging, 25,* 74–83.

Garrett, H.E. (1946) A developmental theory of intelligence. *American Psychologist, 1,* 372–8.

Garstka, T.A., Schmitt, M.T., Branscombe, N.R. and Hummert, M.L. (2004) How young and older adults differ in their responses to perceived age discrimination. *Psychology and Aging, 19,* 326–35.

Gatz, M., Bengston, V.L. and Blum, M.J. (1990) Caregiving families. In J.E. Birren and K.W. Schaie (eds) *Handbook of the Psychology of Aging.* New York: Van Nostrand Reinhold.

Gavrilov, L.A. and Gavrilova, N.S. (2002) Evolutionary theories of aging and longevity. *The Scientific World Journal, 2,* 339–56.

Gazzaley, A., Cooney, J., Rissman, J. and D'Esposito, M. (2005) Top-down suppression deficit underlies working memory impairment in normal aging. *Nature Neuroscience, 8,* 1298–1300.

Geal-Dor, M., Goldstein, A., Kamenir, Y. and Babkoff, H. (2006) The effect of aging on event-related potentials and behavioral responses: Comparisons of tonal, phonologic and semantic targets. *Clinical Neurophysiology, 117,* 1974–89.

George, D. (2010) Overcoming the social death of dementia through language. *The Lancet, 376,* 586–7.

Geraci, L. (2006) A test of the frontal lobe functioning hypothesis of age deficits in production priming. *Neuropsychology, 20,* 539–48.

Geraci, L. and Hamilton, M. (2009) Examining the response competition hypothesis of age effects in implicit memory. *Aging, Neuropsychology and Cognition, 16,* 683–707.

Gerstorf, D., Ram, N., Rocke, C., Lindenberger, U. and Smith, J. (2008) Decline in life satisfaction in old age: Longitudinal evidence for links to distance-to-death. *Psychology and Aging, 23,* 154–68.

Gescheider, G.A., Beiles, E.J., Checkosky, C.M., Bolanowski, S.J. and Verrillo, R.T. (1994) The effects of aging on information-processing channels in the sense of touch: II. Temporal summation in the P channel. *Somatosensory and Motor Research, 11,* 359–65.

Gfroerer, J., Penne, M., Pemberton, M. and Folsom, R. (2003) Substance abuse treatment need among older adults in 2020: The impact of the aging baby-boom cohort. *Drug and Alcohol Dependence, 69,* 127–35.

Ghiselli, E.E. (1957) The relationship between intelligence and age among superior adults. *Journal of Genetic Psychology, 90,* 131–42.

Ghisletta, P. and Lindenberger, U. (2003) Age-based structural dynamics between perceptual speed and knowledge in the Berlin aging study: Direct evidence for ability dedifferentiation in old age. *Psychology and Aging, 18,* 696–713.

Ghisletta, P. and Lindenberger, U. (2004) Static and dynamic longitudinal structural analyses of cognitive changes in old age. *Gerontology, 50,* 12–16.

Ghusn, H.F., Hyde, D., Stevens, E.S. and Hyde, M. (1996) Enhancing life satisfaction in later life: What makes a difference for nursing home residents? *Journal of Gerontological Social Work, 26,* 27–47.

Giambra, L.M. (1993) Sustained attention in older adults: Performance and processes. In J. Cerella, J. Rybash, W. Hoyer and M.L. Commones (eds) *Adult Information Processing: Limits on Loss.* San Diego, CA: Academic Press, 259–72.

Giannakopoulos, P., Gold, G., Duc, M., Michel, J. *et al.* (1999) Neuroanatomic correlates of visual agnosia in Alzheimer's disease: A clinicopathologic study. *Neurology, 52,* 71–7.

Gibson, A. (1981) A further analysis of memory loss in dementia and depression in the elderly. *British Journal of Clinical Psychology, 20,* 179–85.

Gibson, H.B. (1992) *The Emotional and Sexual Lives of Older People.* London: Chapman and Hall.

Gibson, H.B. (1997) *Love in Later Life.* London: Peter Owen.

Gibson, S.J. and Farrell, M. (2004) A review of age differences in the neurophysiology of nociception and the perceptual experience of pain. *Clinical Journal of Pain, 20,* 227–39.

Gilbert, E., Ussher, J. and Perz, J. (2010) Renegotiating sexuality and intimacy in the context of cancer: The experiences of carers. *Archives of Sexual Behavior, 39,* 998–1009.

Gilchrist, A., Cowan, N. and Naveh-Benjamin, M. (2008) Working memory capacity for spoken sentences decreases with adult ageing: Recall of fewer but not smaller chunks in older adults. *Memory, 16,* 773–87.

Giles, L.C., Glonek, G.F., Luszcz, M.A. and Andrews, G.R. (2005) Effect of social networks on 10 year survival in very old Australians: The Australian longitudinal study of aging. *Journal of Epidemiological and Community Health, 59,* 574–9.

Gilhooly, M.L.M. (2005) Reduced drinking with age: Is it normal? *Addiction Research and Theory, 13,* 267–80.

Gilleard, C.J. (1997) Education and Alzheimer's disease: A review of recent international epidemiological studies. *Aging and Mental Health, 1,* 33–46.

Gillen, M. and Kim, H. (2009) Older women and poverty transition: Consequences of income source changes from widowhood. *Journal of Applied Gerontology, 28,* 320–41.

Gilmore, G.C., Tobias, T.R. and Royer, F.L. (1985) Aging and similarity grouping in visual search. *Journal of Gerontology, 40,* 586–92.

Giovannetti, T., Hopkins, M., Crawford, J., Bettcher, B. *et al.* (2008) Syntactic comprehension deficits are associated with MRI white matter alterations in dementia. *Journal of the International Neuropsychological Society, 14,* 542–51.

Givens, J., Prigerson, H., Kiely, D., Shaffer, M. and Mitchell, S. (2011) Grief among family members of nursing home residents with advanced dementia. *Journal of Geriatric Psychiatry, 19,* 543–50.

Glass, J.G. and Jolly, G.R. (1997) Satisfaction in later life among women 60 or over. *Educational Gerontology, 23,* 297–314.

Gleibs, I., Haslam, C., Jones, J., Haslam, S. *et al.* (2011) No country for old men? The role of a 'Gentlemen's Club' in promoting social engagement and psychological well-being in residential care. *Aging and Mental Health, 15,* 456–66.

Glisky, E.L. (2007) Changes in cognitive function in human aging. In D.R. Riddle (ed.) *Brain Aging: Models, Methods and Mechanisms*. Boca Raton: CRC Press.

Gluth, S., Ebner, N. and Schmiedek, F. (2010) Attitudes toward younger and older adults: The German aging semantic differential. *International Journal of Behavioral Development, 34*, 147–58.

Godber, C. (1998) Elderly suicide and weather conditions: Is there a link? *International Journal of Geriatric Psychiatry, 13*, 66.

Godschalk, M.F., Sison, A. and Mulligan, T. (1997) Management of erectile dysfunction by the geriatrician. *Journal of the American Geriatrics Society, 45*, 1240–6.

Goffman, E. (1959). *The Presentation of Self in Everyday Life*. New York: Doubleday.

Gold, G., Giannakopoulos, P., Herrmann, F., Bouras, C. and Kovari, E. (2007) Identification of Alzheimer and vascular lesion thresholds for mixed dementia. *Brain, 130*, 2830–6.

Goldstein, J.H., Cajko, L., Oosterbroek, M., Michielsen, M., van Houten, O. and Salverda, F. (1997) Video games and the elderly. *Social Behavior and Personality, 25*, 345–52.

Gomberg, E.S.L. and Zucker, R.A. (1998) Substance use and abuse in old age. In I.H. Nordhus, G.R. VandenBos, S. Berg and P. Fromholt (eds) *Clinical Geropsychology*. Washington, DC: American Psychological Association, 189–204.

Gomez, V., Krings, F., Bangerter, A. and Grob, A. (2009) The influence of personality and life events on subjective well-being from a life span perspective. *Journal of Research in Personality, 43*, 345–54.

Goncalves, D., Guedes, J., Fonseca, A., Pinto, F. *et al.* (2011) Attitudes, knowledge, and interest: Preparing university students to work in an aging world. *International Journal of Psychogeriatrics, 23*, 315–21.

Goodman, R. (2010) Silver-haired society: What are the implications? *Social Anthropology, 18*, 210–2.

Goodridge, D. (2010) End of life care policies: Do they make a difference in practice? *Social Science and Medicine, 70*, 1166–70.

Gopie, N., Craik, F. and Hasher, L. (2010) Destination memory impairment in older people. *Psychology and Aging, 25*, 922–8.

Gordon-Salant, S., Frisina, R.D., Popper, A.N. and Fay, R.R. (2010) *The Aging Auditory System*. New York: Springer.

Gorin, S.H. and Lewis, B. (2004) The compression of morbidity: Implications for social work. *Health and Social Work, 29*, 249–55.

Gorusch, N. (1998) Time's winged chariot: Short-term psychotherapy in later life. *Psychodynamic Counselling, 4*, 191–202.

Gott, M. (2004) Are older people at risk of sexually transmitted infections? A new look at the evidence. *Reviews in Clinical Gerontology, 14*, 5–13.

Gott, M. and Hinchliff, S. (2003) How important is sex in later life? The views of older people. *Social Science and Medicine, 56*, 1617–28.

Gottfries, C.G. (1996) Neurochemistry and neurotransmitters. *International Psychogeriatrics, 8*, 225–31.

Gould, O.N. and Dixon, R.A. (1993) How we spent our vacation: Collaborative storytelling by young and old adults. *Psychology and Aging, 8*, 10–17.

Gould. S.J. (1981) *The Mismeasure of Man*. New York: Norton.

Grabowski, J. and Franz, T. (1993) Latinos and Anglos: Cultural experiences of grief intensity. *Omega: Journal of Death and Dying, 26*, 273–85.

Graf, P. and Schachter, D.L. (1985) Implicit and explicit memory for new associations in normal and amnesic subjects. *Journal of Experimental Psychology: Learning, Memory and Cognition, 11*, 501–18.

Graham, I.D. and Baker, P.M. (1989) Status, age and gender: Perceptions of old and young people. *Canadian Journal on Aging, 8*, 255–67.

Graham, K., Clarke, D., Bois, C., Carver, V. *et al.* (1996) Addictive behavior of older adults. *Addictive Behaviors, 21,* 331–48.

Graham, N. and Warner, J. (2009) *Understanding Alzheimer's Disease and Other Dementias.* London: Family Doctor Books.

Grajcyk, A. and Zoellner, O. (1998) How older people watch television: Telemetric data on the TV use in Germany in 1996. *Gerontology, 44,* 176–81.

Green, D. (2002) Death, nature and uncertain spaces: A commentary from paganism. *Omega: Journal of Death and Dying, 44,* 127–49.

Greene, J.D. and Hodges, J.R. (1996) The fractionation of remote memory: Evidence from a longitudinal study of dementia of the Alzheimer type. *Brain, 119,* 129–42.

Greene, J.D., Hodges, J.R. and Baddeley, A.D. (1995) Autobiographical memory and executive function in early dementia of the Alzheimer type. *Neuropsychologia, 33,* 1647–70.

Greenwald, A. and Banaji, M. (1995) Implicit social cognition: Attitudes, self esteem and stereotypes. *Psychological Review,* 102, 1, 4–27.

Greenwood, N.A. (1999) Androgyny and adjustment in later life: Living in a veterans' home. *Journal of Clinical Geropsychology, 5,* 127–37.

Greenwood, P.M. (2007) Functional plasticity in cognitive aging: Review and hypothesis. *Neuropsychology, 21,* 657–73.

Gregoire, J. and Van der Linden, M. (1997) Effects of age on forward and backward digit spans. *Aging, Neuropsychology and Cognition, 4,* 140–9.

Gregory, T., Nettlebeck, T. and Wilson, C. (2010) Openness to experience, intelligence, and successful ageing. *Personality and Individual Differences, 48,* 895–99.

Griffiths, C. and Fitzpatrick, J. (2001) Geographical inequalities in life expectancy in the United Kingdom, 1995–97. *Health Statistics Quarterly, 9,* 16–27.

Grossi, D. and Orsini, A. (1978) The visual crosses test in dementia: An experimental study of 110 subjects. *Acta Neurologica, 33,* 170–4.

Grossman, M., Mickanin, J., Onishi, K. and Hughes, E. (1995) An aspect of sentence processing in Alzheimer's disease. *Neurology, 45,* 85–91.

Guerreiro, M., Murphy, D. and Van Gerven, P. (2010) The role of sensory modality in age-related distraction: A critical review and a renewed view. *Psychological Bulletin, 136,* 975–1022.

Guo, X., Erber, J.T. and Szuchman, L.T. (1999) Age and forgetfulness: Can stereotypes be modified? *Educational Gerontology, 25,* 457–66.

Gupta, S., Austin, R. and Black, D.W. (1997) Ninety-three – and washing. *American Journal of Geriatric Psychiatry, 5,* 354–5.

Gurland, B. and Toner, J. (1983) Differentiating dementia from nondementing conditions. In R. Mayeux and W.G. Rosen (eds) *The Dementias.* New York: Raven.

Gurung, R.A.R., Taylor, S.E. and Seeman, T.E. (2003) Accounting for changes in social support among married older adults: Insights from the MacArthur Studies of Successful Aging. *Psychology and Aging, 18,* 487–96.

Gussaroff, E. (1998) Denial of death and sexuality in the treatment of elderly patients. *Psychoanalysis and Psychotherapy, 15,* 77–91.

Haan, N. (1972) Personality development from adolescence to adulthood in the Oakland growth and guidance studies. *Seminars in Psychiatry, 4,* 399–414.

Haarni, I. and Hautamaki L. (2010) Life experience and alcohol: 60–75-year-olds' relationship to alcohol in theme interviews. *NAT Nordisk alcohol and narkotikatidskrift, 27,* 256–8.

Haase, E.R. (1977) Diseases presenting as dementia. In C.E. Wells (ed.) *Dementia.* Philadelphia: Davis.

Hachinski, V.C., Iliff, L.D., Zilkha, E., Du Boulay, G.H. *et al.* (1975) Cerebral blood flow in dementia. *Archives of Neurology, 32,* 632–7.

Hadjistavropoulos, T., Hunter, P. and Dever Fitzgerald, T. (2009) Pain assessment and management in older adults: Conceptual issues and clinical challenges. *Canadian Psychology, 50*, 241–54.

Haegerstrom-Portnoy, G., Schneck, M.E. and Brabyn, J.A. (1999) Seeing into old age: Vision function beyond acuity. *Optometry and Vision Science, 76*, 141–58.

Hagman, G. (1995) Mourning: A review and reconsideration. *International Journal of Psychoanalysis, 76*, 909–25.

Hajat, S., Haines, A., Bulpitt, C. and Fletcher, A. (2004) Patterns and determinants of alcohol consumption in people aged 75 years and older: Results from the MRC trial of assessment and management of older people in the community. *Age and Ageing, 33*, 170–7.

Hakamies-Blomqvist, L., Henriksson, P., Falkmer, T., Lundberg, C. and Braekhus, A. (2002) Attitudes of primary care physicians toward older drivers: A Finnish–Swedish comparison. *Journal of Applied Gerontology, 21*, 58–69.

Hale, S., Rose, N.S., Myerson, J., Strube, M.J. *et al.* (2011) The structure of working memory abilities across the life span. *Psychology and Aging, 26*, 147–63.

Hall, P.A., Dubin, J.A., Crossley, M., Holmqvist, M.E. and D'Arcy, C. (2009) Does executive function explain the IQ-mortality association? Evidence from the Canadian Study on Health and Aging. *Psychosomatic Medicine, 71*, 196–204.

Hallgren, M., Hogberg, P. and Andreasson, S. (2010) Alcohol consumption and harm among elderly Europeans: Falling between the cracks. *European Journal of Public Health, 20*, 616–8.

Hamm, V.P. and Hasher, L. (1992) Age and the availability of inferences. *Psychology and Aging, 7*, 56–64.

Han, B., Gfroerer, J., Colliver, J. and Penne, M. (2009) Substance use disorder among older adults in the United States in 2020. *Addiction, 104*, 88–96.

Handel , A.E., Disanto, G. and Ramagopalan, S.V. (2010) Visceral obesity and brain volume. *Annals of Neurology, 68*, 770–1.

Hannah, M.T., Domino, G., Figueredo, A.J. and Hendrickson, R. (1996) The prediction of ego integrity in older persons. *Educational and Psychological Measurement, 56*, 930–50.

Hannon, B. and Daneman, M. (2009) Age-related changes in reading comprehension: An individual differences perspective. *Experimental Aging Research, 35*, 432–56.

Hao, Y. (2008) Productive activities and psychological well-being among older adults. *The Journals of Gerontology Series B: Psychological Sciences and Social Sciences, 63*, 564–72.

Harasty, J.A., Halliday, G.M., Kril, J.J. and Code, C. (1999) Specific temporoparietal gyral atrophy reflects the pattern of language dissolution in Alzheimer's disease. *Brain, 122*, 675–86.

Hardy, D., Chan, W., Liu, C., Cormier, J. *et al.* (2011) Racial disparities in the use of hospice services according to geographic residence and socioeconomic status in an elderly cohort with nonsmall cell lung cancer. *Cancer, 117*, 1504–15.

Harman, D. (1956) Aging: A theory based on free radical and radiation chemistry. *Journal of Gerontology, 11*, 298–300.

Harrington, D.L. and Haaland, K.Y. (1992) Skill learning in the elderly: Diminished implicit and explicit memory for a motor sequence. *Psychology and Aging, 7*, 425–35.

Harris, K., Dubno, J., Keren, N., Ahlstrom, J. and Eckert, M. (2009) Speech recognition in younger and older adults: A dependency on low-level auditory cortex. *The Journal of Neuroscience, 29*, 6078–87.

Harris, L.A. and Dollinger, S. (2001) Participation in a course on aging: Knowledge, attitudes and anxiety about aging in oneself and others. *Educational Gerontology, 27*, 657–67.

Harris, T., Cook, D.G., Victor, C., Rink, E. *et al.* (2003) Predictors of depressive symptoms in older people – a survey of two general practice populations. *Age and Ageing, 32*, 510–18.

Hartke, R., King, R., Heinemann, A. and Semik, P. (2006) Accidents in older caregivers of persons surviving stroke and their relation to caregiver stress. *Rehabilitation Psychology, 51*, 1506.

Hasegawa, S., Matsunuma, S., Omori, M. and Miyao, M. (2006) Aging effects on the visibility of graphic text on mobile phones. *Gerontechnology, 4*, 200–8.

Hasher, L. and Zacks, R.T. (1979) Automatic and effortful processes in memory. *Journal of Experimental Psychology: General, 108,* 356–88.

Hasher, L., Zacks, R.T. and May, C.P. (1999) Inhibitory control, circadian arousal, and age. In D. Gopher and A. Koriat (eds) *Attention and Performance XVII, Cognitive Regulation of Performance: Interaction of Theory and Application.* Cambridge, MA: MIT Press, 653–75.

Hassiotis, A., Strydom, A., Allen, K. and Walker, Z. (2003) A memory clinic for older people with intellectual disabilities. *Aging and Mental Health, 7,* 418–23.

Hawkins, H.L., Kramer, A.F. and Capaldi, D. (1992) Aging, exercise and attention. *Psychology and Aging, 7,* 643–53.

Hayflick, L.H. (1985) The cell biology of aging. *Clinical Geriatric Medicine, 1,* 15–27.

Hayflick, L.H. (1994) *How and Why We Age.* New York: Random House.

Hayflick, L.H. (1997) Mortality and immortality at the cellular level. A review. *Biochemistry, 62,* 1180–90.

Hayflick, L.H. (1998) How and why we age. *Experimental Gerontology, 33,* 639–53.

Hayslip, B. and Sterns, H.L. (1979) Age differences in relationships between crystallised and fluid intelligence and problem solving. *Journal of Gerontology, 34,* 404–14.

Heaphy, B., Yip, A.K.T. and Thompson, D. (2004) Ageing in a non-heterosexual context. *Ageing and Society, 24,* 881–902.

Hedden, T. (2007) Imaging cognition in the aging human brain. In D.R. Riddle (ed.) *Brain Aging: Models, Methods and Mechanisms.* Boca Raton: CRC Press.

Hedden, T. and Park, D. (2001) Aging and interference in verbal working memory. *Psychology and Aging, 16,* 666–81.

Heft, M.W. and Robinson, M.E. (2010) Age differences in orofacial sensory thresholds. *Journal of Dental Research, 89,* 1102–5.

Helmes, E. and Gee, S. (2003) Attitudes of Australian therapists towards older clients: Educational and training imperatives. *Educational Gerontology, 29,* 657–70.

Hendricks, J. (1999) Creativity over the life course – a call for a rational perspective. *International Journal of Aging and Human Development, 48,* 85–111.

Hendry, L. and Kloep, M. (2002) *Lifespan Development: Resources, Challenges and Risks.* London: Thomson Learning.

Henry, J.D., MacLeod, M.S., Phillips, L.H. and Crawford, J.R. (2004) A meta-analytic review of prospective memory and aging. *Psychology and Aging, 19,* 27–39.

Heponiemi, T., Kouvonen, A., Vanska, J., Halila, H. *et al.* (2008) Health, psychosocial factors and retirement intentions among Finnish physicians. *Occupational Medicine, 58,* 406–12.

Herbst, K.G. (1982) Social attitudes to hearing loss in the elderly. In F. Glendenning (ed.) *Acquired Hearing Loss and Elderly People.* Keele: Beth Johnson Foundation Publications.

Herrman, D.J., Rea, A. and Andrzejewski, S. (1988) The need for a new approach to memory training. In M.M. Gruneberg, P.E. Morris and R.N. Sykes (eds) *Practical Aspects of Memory: Current Research and Issues.* Chichester: Wiley.

Hertzog, C. (1991) Aging, information processing speed and intelligence. In K.W. Schaie and P. Lawton (eds), *Annual Review of Gerontology and Geriatrics, 11,* 55–79.

Hertzog, C., Dixon, R.A., Hultsch, D.F. and MacDonald, S. (2003) Latent change models of adult cognition: Are changes in processing speed and working memory associated with changes in episodic memory? *Psychology and Aging, 18,* 755–69.

Hertzog, C., Dunlosky, J. and Sinclair, S. (2010) Episodic feeling of knowing resolution derives from the quality of original encoding. *Memory and Cognition, 38,* 771–84.

Hertzog, C. and Jopp, D.S. (2010) Resilience in the face of cognitive aging: Experience, adaptation and compensation. In P.S. Fry and C.L.M. Keyes (eds) *New Frontiers in Resilient Aging: Life-strengths and Well-being in Late Life.* New York: Cambridge University Press.

Hertzog, C. and Nesselroade, J.R. (2003) Assessing psychological change in adulthood: An overview of methodological issues. *Psychology and Aging, 18,* 639–57.

Herzog, A.R., House, J.S. and Morgan, J.N. (1991) Relation of work and retirement to health and well-being in old age. *Psychology and Aging, 6,* 202–11.

Hestad, K., Ellersten, B. and Klove, H. (1998) Neuropsychological assessment in old age. In I.H. Nordhus, G.R. VandenBos, S. Berg and P. Fromholt (eds) *Clinical Geropsychology.* Washington, DC: American Psychological Association, 259–88.

Hicks, M., McDermott, L., Rouhana, N., Schmidt, M. *et al.* (2009) Nurses' body size and public confidence in ability to provide health education. *Journal of Nursing Scholarship, 40,* 349–54.

Hicks-Moore, S. and Robinson, B. (2008) Favorite music and hand massage: Two interventions to decrease agitation in residents with dementia. *Dementia, 7,* 95–108.

Hickson, J. and Housley, W. (1997) Creativity in later life. *Educational Gerontology, 23,* 539–47.

Hilgard, E.R., Atkinson, R.L. and Atkinson, R.C. (1979) *Introduction to Psychology.* 7th edition. New York: Harcourt Brace Jovanovich.

Hill-Briggs, F., Kirk, J.J. and Wegener, S. (2005) Geriatric pain and neuropsychological assessment. In S.S. Bush and T.A. Martin (eds) *Geriatric Neuropsychology: Practice Essentials.* Philadelphia: Taylor and Francis.

Hilt, M.L. and Lipschultz, J.H. (2004) Elderly Americans and the internet: E-mail, TV news, information and entertainment websites. *Educational Gerontology, 30,* 57–72.

Hirono, N., Mori, E., Ischii, K., Hirono, N. and Mori, E. (1998) Regional hypometabolism related to language disturbances in Alzheimer's disease. *Dementia and Geriatric Cognitive Disorders, 9,* 68–73.

Hofer, S., Berg, S. and Era, P. (2003) Evaluating the interdependence of aging-related changes in visual and auditory acuity, balance and cognitive functioning. *Psychology and Aging, 18,* 285–305.

Hofer, S.M., Christensen, H., Mackinnon, A.J., Korten, A.E. *et al.* (2002) Change in cognitive functioning associated with ApoE genotype in a community sample of older adults. *Psychology and Aging, 17,* 194–208.

Holahan, C.K. and Chapman. J.R. (2002) Longitudinal predictors of proactive goals and activity participation at age 80. *The Journals of Gerontology Series B: Psychological Sciences and Social Sciences, 57,* 418–25.

Holden, B.A., Fricke, T.R., Ho, S.M., Wong, R. *et al.* (2008) Global vision impairment due to uncorrected presbyopia. *Archives of Ophthalmology, 126,* 1731–9.

Holland, A. (2000) Ageing and learning disability. *British Journal of Psychiatry, 176,* 26–31.

Holland, C. and Rabbitt, P. (1989) Subjective and objective measures of vision and hearing loss in elderly drivers and pedestrians. Talk at ESRC/General Accident Insurance Company Symposium on Road Traffic Accidents. University of Reading, 5 July.

Holland, C. and Rabbitt, P. (1990) Autobiographical and text recall in the elderly. *Quarterly Journal of Experimental Psychology, 42A,* 441–70.

Holliday, R. (2007) *Aging: The Paradox of Life.* Dordrecht: Springer.

Holtz, J. (2011) *Applied Clinical Neuropsychology: An Introduction.* New York: Springer.

Holtzman, R.E., Rebok, G.W., Saczynski, J.S., Kouzis, A.C., Doyle, K.W. and Eaton, W.W. (2004) Social network characteristics and cognition in middle-aged and older adults. *The Journals of Gerontology Series B: Psychological Sciences and Social Sciences, 59,* 278–84.

Hooker, K., Bowman, S.R., Coehlo, D.P., Lima, S.R. *et al.* (2002) Behavioral change in persons with dementia: Relationships with mental and physical health of caregivers. *The Journals of Gerontology Series B: Psychological Sciences and Social Sciences, 57,* 453–60.

Hooper, F.H., Fitzgerald, J. and Papalia, D. (1971) Piagetian theory and the aging process: Extensions and speculations. *Aging and Human Development, 2,* 3–20.

Hope, J. and Havir, L. (2002) You bet they're having fun! Older Americans and casino gambling. *Journal of Aging Studies, 16,* 177–97.

Hopkins, C., Roster, C. and Wood, C. (2006) Making the transition to retirement: Appraisals, post-transition lifestyle, and changes in consumption patterns. *Journal of Consumer Marketing, 23*, 89–101.

Hoppmann, C., Gerstorf, D. and Hibbert, A. (2011) Spousal associations between functional limitation and depressive symptom trajectories: Longitudinal findings from the Study of Asset and Health Dynamics Among the Oldest (AHEAD). *Health Psychology, 30*, 153–62.

Horn, J.L. (1978) Human ability systems. In P.B. Baltes (ed.) *Life-span Development and Behavior, Volume 1.* New York: Academic Press, 211–56.

Horn, J.L. (1982) The theory of fluid and crystallised intelligence in relation to concepts of cognitive psychology and aging in adulthood. In F.I.M. Craik and S. Trehub (eds) *Aging and Cognitive Processes.* New York: Plenum.

Horn, J.L. and Cattell, R.B. (1967) Age differences in fluid and crystallised intelligence. *Acta Psychologia, 26*, 107–29.

Hosokawa, A. and Hosokawa, T. (2006) Cross-cultural study on age-group differences in the recall of the literal and interpretive meanings of narrative text. *Japanese Psychological Research, 48*, 77–90.

Hough, M.S. (2006) Incidence of word finding deficits in normal aging. *Folia Phoniatrica et Logopaedica, 59*, 10–19.

House, J.S., Kessler, R.C., Herzog, A.R., Mero, R.P., Kinney, A.M. and Breslow, M.J. (1992) Social stratification, age and health. In K.W. Schaie, D. Blazer and J. House (eds) *Aging, Health Behavior and Health Outcomes.* Hillsdale, NJ: Lawrence Erlbaum, 1–37.

Houston, D.K., Johnson, M.A., Nozza, R.J., Gunter, E.W. *et al.* (1999) Age-related hearing loss, vitamin B-12 and folate in elderly women. *American Journal of Clinical Nutrition, 69*, 564–71.

Hoyer, W.J. and Ingolfsdottir, D. (2003) Age, skill and contextual cuing in target detection. *Psychology and Aging, 18*, 210–18.

Hoyer, W.J. and Roodin, P.A. (2003) *Adult Development and Aging.* 5th edition. Boston, MA: McGraw Hill.

Hoyte, K., Brownell, H. and Wingfield, A. (2009) Components of speech prosody and their use in detection of syntactic structure by older adults. *Experimental Aging Research, 35*, 129–51.

Hser, Y.I., Huffman, V., Grella, C.E. and Anglin, M. D. (2001) A 33-year follow-up of narcotics addicts. *Archives of General Psychiatry, 58*, 503–8.

Huang, Q. and Tang, J. (2010) Age-related hearing loss or presbycusis. *European Archives of Otorhinolaryngology, 267*, 1179–91.

Hubert, H.B., Bloch, D.A., Oehlert, J.W. and Fries, J.F. (2002) Lifestyle habits and compression of morbidity. *The Journals of Gerontology Series A: Biological Sciences and Medical Sciences, 57*, 347–51.

Hudson, L. (1987) Creativity. In R.L. Gregory and O. Zangwill (eds) *The Oxford Companion to the Mind.* Oxford: Oxford University Press.

Hughes, P., Bath, P., Ahmed, N. and Noble, B. (2010) What progress has been made towards implementing national guidance on end of life care? A national survey of UK general practices. *Palliative Medicine, 24*, 68–78.

Hui, V., Bond, M. and Ng, I. (2007) General beliefs about the world as defensive mechanisms against death anxiety. *Omega: Journal of Death and Dying, 54*, 199–214.

Hull, R.H. and Kerschen, S.R. (2010) The influence of cardiovascular health on peripheral and central auditory function in adults: A research review. *American Journal of Audiology, 19*, 9–16.

Hulme, C., Lee, G. and Brown, G.D. (1993) Short-term memory impairments in Alzheimer-type dementia: Evidence for separable impairments of articulatory rehearsal and long-term memory. *Neuropsychologia, 31*, 161–72.

Hult, C., Stattin, M., Janlert, U. and Jarvholm, B. (2010) Timing of retirement and mortality – A cohort study of Swedish construction workers. *Social Science and Medicine, 70*, 1480–6.

Hultsch, D.F., Hertzog, C., Small, B.J., McDonald-Miszczak, L. and Dixon, R.A. (1992) Short-term longitudinal change in cognitive performance in later life. *Psychology and Aging, 7*, 571–84.

Hultsch , D.F., MacDonald, S.W.S. and Dixon, R.A. (2002) Variability in reaction time performance of younger and older adults. *The Journals of Gerontology Series B: Psychological Sciences and Social Sciences, 57*, 101–15.

Hummert, M.L., Garstka, T.A., O'Brien, L.T., Greenwald, A.G. and Mellott, D.S. (2002) Using the implicit association test to measure age differences in implicit social cognitions. *Psychology and Aging, 17*, 482–95.

Hummert, M.L., Garstka, T.A. and Shaner, J.L. (1997) Stereotyping of older adults: The role of target facial cues and perceiver characteristics. *Psychology and Aging, 12*, 107–14.

Huntgeburth, M., Ten Freyhaus, H. and Rosenkranz, S. (2005) Alcohol consumption and hypertension. *Current Hypertension Reports, 7*, 180–5.

Huntley, J. and Howard, R. (2010) Working memory in early Alzheimer's disease: A neuropsychological review. *International Journal of Geriatric Psychiatry, 25*, 121–32.

Hutchinson, K.M. (1989) Influence of sentence context on speech perception in young and older adults. *The Journals of Gerontology Series B: Psychological Sciences and Social Sciences, 44*, 36–44.

Hybertson, E.D., Perdue, J. and Hybertson, D. (1982) Age differences in information acquisition strategies. *Experimental Aging Research, 8*, 109–113.

Hyman, B.T., Arriagada, P.V., Van Housen, G.W. and Damasio, A.R. (1993) Memory impairment in Alzheimer's disease: An anatomical perspective. In R.W. Parks, R.F. Zec and R.S. Wilson (eds) *Neuropsychology of Alzheimer's Disease and Other Dementias*. New York: Oxford University Press, 138–50.

Iachine, I.A., Holm, N.V., Harris, J.R., Begun, A.Z. *et al.* (1998) How heritable is individual susceptibility to death? The results of an analysis of survival data on Danish, Swedish and Finnish twins. *Twin Research, 1*, 196–205.

Idler, E.L., Kasl, S.V. and Hays, J.C. (2001) Patterns of religious practice and belief in the last year of life. *The Journals of Gerontology Series B: Psychological Sciences and Social Sciences, 56*, 326–34.

Igier, V. and Mullet, E. (2003) Application of the five-factor model of personality to intergenerational perception. *The Journals of Gerontology Series B: Psychological Sciences and Social Sciences, 58*, 177–86.

Ihara, M., Polvikoski, T., Hall, R., Slade, J. *et al.* (2010) Quantification of myelin loss in frontal lobe white matter in vascular dementia, Alzheimer's disease, and dementia with Lewy bodies. *Acta Neuropathologica, 119*, 579–89.

Ingersoll-Dayton, B. and Saengtienchai, C. (1999) Respect for the elderly in Asia: Stability and change. *International Journal of Aging and Human Development, 48*, 113–30.

Irish, M., Cunningham, C., Walsh, J., Coakley, D. *et al.* (2006) Investigating the enhancing effect of music on autobiographical memory in mild Alzheimer's disease. *Dementia and Geriatric Cognitive Disorders, 22*, 108–20.

Irish, M., Lawlor, B., O'Mara, S. and Coen, R. (2011) Impaired capacity for autonoetic reliving during autobiographical event recall in mild Alzheimer disease. *Cortex, 47*, 236–49.

Ishimatsu, I., Miura, T. and Shinohara, K. (2010) Age influences visual attention characteristics among accident-free and accident-involved drivers. *Japanese Psychological Research, 52*, 186–200.

Isingrini, M. and Vazou, F. (1997) Relation between fluid intelligence and frontal lobe functioning in older adults. *International Journal of Aging and Human Development, 45*, 99–109.

Iwasa, H., Masui, Y., Gondo, Y., Yoshida, Y. *et al.* (2009) Personality and participation in mass health checkups among Japanese community-dwelling elderly. *Journal of Psychosomatic Research, 66*, 155–9.

Izquierdo-Porrera, A.M. and Waldstein, S.R. (2002) Cardiovascular risk factors and cognitive function in African Americans. *The Journals of Gerontology Series B: Psychological Sciences and Social Sciences, 57*, 377–80.

Jack, C.R., Petersen, R.C., Xu, Y.G., Obrien, P.C. *et al.* (1997) Medial temporal atrophy on MRI in normal aging and very mild Alzheimer's disease. *Neurology, 49*, 786–94.

Jackovitch, K.G. (1979) Sex, visitors from the grave, psychic healing: Kübler-Ross is a public storm center again. *People, 12*, 29 October.

Jackson, G.R. and Owsley, C. (2003) Visual dysfunction, neurodegenerative diseases, and aging. *Neurologic Clinics, 21*, 709–28.

Jackson, J., Bogg, T., Walton, K., Wood, D. *et al.* (2009) Not all conscientiousness scales change alike: A multimethod, multisample study of age differences in the facets of conscientiousness. *Journal of Personal and Social Psychology, 96*, 446–59.

Jackson, J.L., Bogers, H. and Kersthold, J. (1988) Do memory aids aid the elderly in their day to day remembering? In M.M. Gruneberg, P.E. Morris and R.N. Sykes (eds) *Practical Aspects of Memory: Current Research and Issues, Volume 2.* Chichester: Wiley.

Jackson, J.S., Antonucci, T.C. and Gibson, R.C. (1990) Cultural, racial and ethnic minority influences on aging. In J.E. Birren and K.W. Schaie (eds) *Handbook of the Psychology of Aging.* 3rd edition. San Diego, CA: Academic Press.

Jacobs, J., Hammerman-Rozenberg, R., Cohen, A. and Stessman, J. (2008) Reading daily predicts reduced mortality among men from a cohort of community-dwelling 70-year-olds. *The Journals of Gerontology Series B: Psychological Sciences and Social Sciences, 63*, 73–80.

Jacobs, R. and Kane, M. (2011) Psychosocial predictors of self-esteem in a multi-ethnic sample of women over 50 at risk for HIV. *Journal of Women and Aging, 23*, 23–39.

Jaffe, G.J., Alvarado, J.A. and Juster, R.P. (1986) Age-related changes of the normal visual field. *Archives of Ophthalmology, 104*, 1021–5.

Jahn, D., Cukrowicz, K., Linton, K. and Prabhu, F. (2011) The mediating effect of perceived burdensomeness on the relation between depressive symptom and suicide ideation in a community sample of older adults. *Aging and Mental Health, 15*, 214–20.

James, C. (1983) *Falling Towards England.* London: Jonathan Cape.

James, J. and Haley, W. (1995). Age and health bias in practising clinical psychologists. *Psychology and Ageing, 10*, 610–16.

James, L.E. (2004) Meeting Mr. Farmer versus meeting a farmer: Specific effects of aging on learning proper names. *Psychology and Aging, 19*, 515–22.

James, L.E, (2006) Specific effects of aging on proper name retrieval: Now you see them, now you don't. *The Journals of Gerontology Series B: Psychological Sciences and Social Sciences, 61*, 180–3.

Jansari, A. and Parkin, A.J. (1996) Things that go bump in your life: Explaining the reminiscence bump in autobiographical memory. *Psychology and Aging, 11*, 85–91.

Janssen, F., van der Heide, A., Kunst, A. and Mackenbach, J. (2006) End-of-life decisions and old-age mortality: A cross-country analysis. *Journal of the American Geriatrics Society, 54*, 1951–3.

Jarvik, L.F. (1983) Age is in – is the wit out? In D. Samuel, S. Alegri, S. Gershon, V.E. Grimm and G. Toffanl (eds) *Aging of the Brain.* New York: Raven Press, 1–7.

Jarvik, L.F. and Falek, A. (1963) Intellectual stability and survival in the aged. *Journal of Gerontology, 18*, 173–6.

Jelenec, P. and Steffens, M. (2002) Implicit attitudes towards elderly women and men. *Current Research in Social Psychology, 7*, 275–91.

Jellinger, K.A. (2006) Clinicopathological analysis of dementia disorders in the elderly – an update. *Journal of Alzheimer's Disease, 9*, 61–70.

Jenike, M. (1988) Depression and other psychiatric disorders. In M.S. Albert and M.B. Moss (eds) *Geriatric Neuropsychology.* New York: Guilford.

Jenkins, L., Myerson, J., Joerding, J.A. and Hale, S. (2000) Converging evidence that visuospatial cognition is more age-sensitive than verbal cognition. *Psychology and Aging, 15*, 157–75.

Jeong, H. and Kim, H. (2009) Aging and text comprehension: Interpretation and domain knowledge advantage. *Educational Gerontology, 35*, 906–28.

Jerant, A., Chapman, B., Duberstein, P., Robbins, J. and Franks, P. (2011) Personality and medication non-adherence among older adults enrolled in a six-year trial. *British Journal of Health Psychology, 16*, 151–69.

Jerram, K.L. and Coleman, P.G. (1999) The big five personality traits and reporting of health problems and health behaviour in old age. *British Journal of Health Psychology, 4*, 181–92.

Johansson, B., Hofer, S.M., Allaire, J.C., Maldonado-Molina, M.M. *et al.* (2004) Change in cognitive capabilities in the oldest old: The effects of proximity to death in genetically related individuals over a 6-year period. *Psychology and Aging, 19*, 145–56.

Johnson, K., Kuchibhatia, M. and Tulsky, J. (2008) What explains racial differences in the use of advance directives and attitudes toward hospice care? *Journal of the American Geriatrics Society, 56*, 1953–8.

Johnson, P. and Sung, H. (2009) Substance abuse among aging baby boomers: Health and treatment implications. *Journal of Addictions Nursing, 20*, 124–6.

Johnston, M. and Walker, M. (1996) Suicide in the elderly: Recognizing the signs. *General Hospital Psychiatry, 18*, 257–60.

Jones, E. and Pittman, T. (1982) Toward a general theory of strategic self presentation. In J.M. Suls (ed.) *Psychological Perspectives of the Self.* Hillsdale, NJ: Erlbaum, 231–62.

Jones, R.N. and Gallo, J.J. (2002) Education and sex differences in the mini-mental state examination: Effects of differential item functioning. *The Journals of Gerontology Series B: Psychological Sciences and Social Sciences, 57*, 548–58.

Juncos-Rabadan, O., Facal, D., Rodriguez, M. and Pereiro, A. (2010) Lexical knowledge and lexical retrieval in ageing: insights from a tip of the tongue (TOT) study. *Language and Cognitive Processes, 25*, 1301–34.

Jung-Hwa, H., Carr, D., Utz, R. and Nesse, R. (2006) Older adults' perceptions of intergenerational support after widowhood: How do men and women differ? *Journal of Family Issues, 27*, 3–30.

Kahana, M.J., Dolan E.D., Sauder, C.L. and Wingfield, A. (2005) Intrusions in episodic recall: Age differences in editing of overt responses. *The Journals of Gerontology Series B: Psychological Sciences and Social Sciences, 60*, 92–7.

Kahn, R.L., Goldfarb, A.I., Pollack, M. and Peck, A. (1960) Brief objective measures for determination of mental status in the aged. *American Journal of Psychiatry, 117*, 326–8.

Kail, R. (1997) The neural noise hypothesis: Evidence from processing speed in adults with multiple sclerosis. *Aging, Neuropsychology and Cognition, 4*, 157–65.

Kail, R. and Pelligrino, J.W. (1985) *Human Intelligence: Perspectives and Prospects.* San Francisco, CA: Freeman.

Kaplan, R. and Kronick, R. (2006) Marital status and longevity in the United States population. *Journal of Epidemiology and Community Health, 60*, 760–5.

Kapur, N. (1995) Memory aids in the rehabilitation of memory disordered patients. In A.D. Baddeley, B.A. Wilson and F.N. Watts (eds) *Handbook of Memory Disorders.* Chichester: Wiley, 533–56.

Karakus, M. and Patton, L. (2011) Depression and the onset of chronic illness in older adults: A 12-year prospective study. *Journal of Behavioral Health Services and Research, 38*, 373–82.

Karayanidis, F., Andrews, S., Ward, P.B. and McConaghy, N. (1993) Event-related potentials and repetition priming in young, middle-aged and elderly normal subjects. *Cognitive Brain Research, 1*, 123–34.

Karon, B.P. and VandenBos, G.R. (1998) Schizophrenia and psychosis in elderly populations. In I.H. Nordhus, G.R. VandenBos, S. Berg and P. Fromholt (eds) *Clinical Geropsychology.* Washington, DC: American Psychological Association, 219–27.

Karpel, M.E., Hoyer, W.J. and Toglia, M.P. (2001) Accuracy and qualities of real and suggested memories: Nonspecific age differences. *The Journals of Gerontology Series B: Psychological Sciences and Social Sciences, 56*, 103–10.

Kaskie, B. and Storandt, M. (1995) Visuospatial deficit in dementia of the Alzheimer type. *Archives of Neurology, 52,* 422–5.

Kasl-Godley, J.E., Gatz, M. and Fiske, A. (1998) Depression and depressive symptoms in old age. In I.H. Nordhus, G.R. VandenBos, S. Berg and P. Fromholt (eds) *Clinical Geropsychology.* Washington, DC: American Psychological Association, 211–7.

Kastenbaum, R. (1985) Death and dying: A life-span approach. In J. Birren and K. Schaie (eds) *Handbook of the Psychology of Aging.* 2nd edition. New York: Van Nostrand Reinhold.

Katz, S., Branch, L.G., Branson, M.H., Papsidero, J.A., Beck, M.D. and Greer, M.D. (1983) Active life expectancy. *New England Journal of Medicine, 309,* 1218–24.

Katzman, R., Terry, R., Deteresa, R., Brown, T. *et al.* (1988) Clinical, pathological and neurochemical changes in dementia: A subgroup with preserved mental status on numerous neocortical plaques. *Annals of Neurology, 23,* 138–44.

Kaufman, A.S. and Horn, J.L. (1996) Age changes on tests of fluid and crystallised ability for women and men on the Adolescent and Adult Intelligence Test (KAIT) at ages 17–94 years. *Archives of Clinical Neuropsychology, 11,* 97–121.

Kaufman, G. and Taniguchi, H. (2006) Gender and marital happiness in later life. *Journal of Family Issues, 27,* 735–57.

Kawachi, I. and Kennedy, B.P. (1997) Socioeconomic determinants of health: health and social cohesion: Why care about income inequality? *British Medical Journal, 314,* 1037–40.

Kaye, J.A., Swihart, T., Howieson, D., Dame, A. *et al.* (1997) Volume loss of the hippocampus and temporal lobe in healthy elderly persons destined to develop dementia. *Neurology, 48,* 1297–304.

Keilp, J.G., Gorlyn, M., Alexander, G.E., Stern, Y. and Prohovnik, I. (1999) Cerebral blood flow patterns underlying the differential impairment in category vs letter fluency in Alzheimer's disease. *Neuropsychologia, 37,* 1251–61.

Kellehear, A. (1984) Are we a 'death-denying' society? A sociological review. *Social Science and Medicine, 18,* 713–21.

Kelley, C.L., Morrell, R.W., Park, D.C. and Mayhorn, C.B. (1999) Predictors of electronic bulletin board system use in older adults. *Educational Gerontology, 25,* 19–35.

Kelly, F. (2010) Recognising and supporting self in dementia: A new way to facilitate a person-centred approach to dementia care. *Ageing and Society, 30,* 103–24.

Kempen, G.I.J.M., Jelicic, M. and Ormel, J. (1997) Personality, chronic medical morbidity and health-related quality of life among older persons. *Health Psychology, 16,* 539–46.

Kempen, G.I.J.M., Scaf-Klomp, W., Ranchor, A.V., Sanderman, R. and Ormel, J. (2001) Social predictors of recovery in late middle-aged and older persons after injury to the extremities: A prospective study. *The Journals of Gerontology Series B: Psychological Sciences and Social Sciences, 56,* 229–36.

Kemper, S. (1986) Limitation of complex syntactic construction by elderly adults. *Applied Psycholinguistics, 7,* 277–87.

Kemper, S. (1987a) Adults' diaries: Changes to written narratives across the life span. *Conference on Social Psychology and Language.* 20–24 July.

Kemper, S. (1987b) Life-span changes in syntactic complexity. *Journal of Gerontology, 42,* 3232–328.

Kemper, S. (1992) Adults' sentence fragments: Who, what, when, where and why. *Communication Research, 19,* 444–58.

Kemper, S. and Anagnopoulos, C. (1993) Adult use of discourse constraints on syntactic processing. In J. Cerella, J. Rybash, W. Hoyer and M.L. Commons (eds) *Adult Information Processing: Limits on Loss.* San Diego, CA: Academic Press, 489–507.

Kemper, S., Crow, A. and Kemtes, K. (2004) Eye-fixation patterns of high- and low-span young and older adults: Down the garden path and back again. *Psychology and Aging, 19,* 157–70.

Kemper, S., Herman, R. and Lian, C. (2003) The costs of doing two things at once for younger and older adults: Talking while walking, finger tapping and ignoring speech of noise. *Psychology and Aging, 18*, 181–92.

Kemper, S., Herman, R.E. and Liu, C.J. (2004) Sentence production by young and older adults in controlled contexts. *The Journals of Gerontology Series B: Psychological Sciences and Social Sciences, 59*, 220–4.

Kemper, S., McDowd, J. and Kramer, A. (2006) Eye movements of young and older adults while reading with distraction. *Psychology and Aging, 21*, 32–9.

Kemper, S. and Rush, S.J. (1988) Speech and writing across the life span. In M.M. Gruneberg, P.E. Morris and R.N. Sykes (eds) *Practical Aspects of Memory, Current Research and Issues.* Chichester: Wiley.

Kemper, S., Schmalzried, R., Hoffman, L. and Herman, R. (2010) Aging and the vulnerability of speech to dual task demands. *Psychology and Aging, 25*, 949–62.

Kemper, S. and Sumner, A. (2001) The structure of verbal abilities in young and older adults. *Psychology and Aging, 16*, 312–22.

Kemper, S., Thompson, M. and Marquis, J. (2001) Longitudinal change in language production: Effects of aging and dementia on grammatical complexity and propositional content. *Psychology and Aging, 16*, 600–14.

Kemtes, K.A. and Kemper, S. (1997) Younger and older adults' on-line processing of syntactically ambiguous sentences. *Psychology and Aging, 12*, 362–71.

Kennedy, G.J. (2010) Now neuroscience explains age-related changes in cognition: Implications for the early diagnosis of dementia. *Primary Psychiatry, 17*, 30–3.

Kennedy, S., Kiecolt-Glaser, J.K. and Glaser, R. (1988) Immunological consequences of acute and chronic stressors: Mediating role of interpersonal relationships. *British Journal of Medical Psychology, 61*, 77–85.

Kensinger, E.A. and Schachter, D.L. (1999) When true memories suppress false memories: Effects of ageing. *Cognitive Neuropsychology, 16*, 399–415.

Kenyon, C.J. (2010) The genetics of ageing. *Nature, 464*, 504–12.

Keranen, A., Savolainen, M., Raponen, A., Kujari, M. *et al.* (2009) The effect of eating behaviour on weight loss and maintenance during a lifestyle intervention. *Preventive Medicine, 49*, 32–8.

Kerfoot, K., Petrakis, I. and Rosenheck, R. (2011) Dual diagnosis in an aging population: Prevalence of psychiatric disorders, comorbid substance abuse, and mental health service utilization in the Department of Veterans Affairs. *Journal of Dual Diagnosis, 7*, 4–13.

Kermis, M.D. (1983) *The Psychology of Human Aging: Theory, Research and Practice.* Boston, MA: Allyn and Bacon.

Kermis, M.D. (1986) *Mental Health in Later Life. The Adaptive Process.* Boston, MA: Jones and Bartlett.

Kerr, D. (2007) *Understanding Learning Disability and Dementia.* London: Jessica Kingsley Publishers.

Kessels, R., van den Berg, E., Ruis, C. and Brands, A. (2008) The backward span of the Corsi Block-Tapping Task and its association with the WAIS-III Digit Span. *Assessment, 15*, 426–34.

Kiloh, L. (1961) Pseudodementia. *Acta Psychiatrica Scandanavica, 37*, 336–51.

Kim, J.E. and Moen, P. (2002) Retirement transitions, gender and psychological well-being: A life-course, ecological model. *The Journals of Gerontology Series B: Psychological Sciences and Social Sciences, 57*, 212–22.

Kim, K. (2007) Religion, weight perception, and weight control behaviour. *Eating Behaviors, 8*, 121–31.

Kim, S. and Yu, X. (2010) The mediating effect of self-efficacy on the relationship between health literacy and health status in Korean older adults: A short report. *Aging and Mental Health, 14*, 870–3.

Kirby, S.E., Coleman. P.G. and Daley, D. (2004) Spirituality and well-being in frail and nonfrail older adults. *The Journals of Gerontology Series B: Psychological Sciences and Social Sciences, 59,* 123–9.

Kirk, L.J., Hick, R. and Laraway, A. (2006) Assessing dementia in people with learning disabilities: The relationship between two screening measures. *Journal of Intellectual Disabilities, 10,* 357–64.

Kirkwood, T.B.L. (1988) The nature and causes of ageing. In *Research and the Ageing Population.* CIBA Foundation Symposium 134. Chichester: Wiley, 193–207.

Kitwood, T. (1993) Towards a theory of dementia care: the interpersonal process, *Ageing and Society, 13,* 51–67.

Kitwood, T. (1997) *Dementia Reconsidered: The Person Comes First.* Buckingham: Open University Press.

Kjølseth, I., Ekeberg, Ø. and Steihaug, S. (2010) Elderly people who committed suicide – their contact with the health service. What did they expect, and what did they get? *Aging and Mental Health, 14,* 938–46.

Klaczynski, P.A. and Robinson, B. (2000) Personal theories, intellectual ability and epistemological beliefs: Adult age differences in everyday reasoning biases. *Psychology and Aging, 15,* 400–16.

Kleemeier, R.W. (1962) Intellectual changes in the senium. *Proceedings of the Social Statistics Section of the American Statistical Association, 1,* 290–95.

Klessig, J. (1992) The effect of values and culture on life-support decisions. *Western Journal of Medicine, 157,* 316–22.

Kliegel, M., Jager, T. and Phillips, L. (2008) Adult age differences in event-based prospective memory: A meta-analysis on the role of focal versus nonfocal cues. *Psychology and Aging, 23,* 203–8.

Knapp, J.L., Beaver, L.M. and Reed, T.D. (2002) Perceptions of the elderly among ministers and ministry students: Implications for seminary curricula. *Educational Gerontology, 28,* 313–24.

Knight, R., Nicholls, J. and Titov, N. (2008) The effects of old age and distraction on the assessment of prospective memory in a simulated naturalistic environment. *International Psychogeriatrics, 20,* 124–34.

Kodama, H., Izumo, Y., Takahashi, R., Suda, Y. *et al.* (2009) Family relationships of self-care-dependent older people and institutionalized rate to nursing homes. *Geriatrics and Gerontology International, 9,* 320–5.

Kodama, H., Suda, Y., Takahashi, R., Nishimura, M. *et al.* (2007) Family relationships for self-care-dependent older people at home. *Geriatrics and Gerontology International, 7,* 252–7.

Koedam, E., Pijnenburg, Y., Deeg, D., Baak, M. *et al.* (2008) Early-onset dementia is associated with higher mortality. *Dementia and Geriatric Cognitive Disorders, 26,* 147–52.

Koenig, B. and Gates-Williams, J. (1995) Understanding cultural difference in caring for dying patients. *West Journal of Medicine, 163,* 244–9.

Koepsell, T., Kurland, B., Harel, O., Johnson, E. *et al.* (2008) Education, cognitive function, and severity of neuropathology in Alzheimer disease. *Neurology, 70,* 1732–9.

Kogan, N. (1990) Personality and aging. In J.E. Birren and K.W. Schaie (eds) *Handbook of the Psychology of Aging.* 3rd edition. San Diego, CA: Academic Press.

Kong, E., Evans, L. and Guevara, J. (2009) Nonpharmacological intervention for agitation in dementia: A systematic review and meta-analysis. *Aging and Mental Health, 13,* 512–20.

Konigsberg, R. (2011) *The Truth About Grief: The Myth of its Five Stages and the New Science of Loss.* New York: Simon & Schuster.

Kooij, D. and Van De Voorde, K. (2011) How changes in subjective general health predict future time perspective, and development and generativity motives over the lifespan. *Journal of Occupational and Organizational Psychology, 84,* 228–47.

Kopelman, M.D. (1985) Rates of forgetting in Alzheimer-type dementia and Korsakoff's syndrome. *Neuropsychologia, 23,* 623–38.

Korinek, K., Zimmer, Z. and Gu, D. (2011) Transitions in marital status and functional health and patterns of intergenerational coresidence among China's elderly population. *The Journals of Gerontology Series B: Psychological Sciences and Social Sciences, 66,* 260–70.

Korkeila, J., Oksanen, T., Virtanen, M., Salo, P. *et al.* (2011) Early retirement from work among employees with a diagnosis of personality disorder compared to anxiety and depression disorders. *European Psychiatry, 26,* 18–22.

Korpelainen, H. (1999) Genetic maternal effects on human life span through inheritance of mitochondrial DNA. *Human Heredity, 49,* 183–5.

Kossioni, A. and Bellou, O. (2011) Eating habits in older people in Greece: The role of age, dental status and chewing difficulties. *Archives of Gerontology and Geriatrics, 52,* 197–201.

Kosslyn, S.M., Brown, H.D. and Dror, I.E. (1999) Aging and the scope of visual attention. *Gerontology, 45,* 102–9.

Kott, A. (2011) Drug use and loneliness are linked to unprotected sex in older adults with HIV. *Perspectives on Sexual and Reproductive Health, 43,* 69–74.

Kovach, S.S. and Robinson, J.D. (1996) The roommate relationship for the elderly nursing home resident. *Journal of Social and Personal Relationships, 13,* 627–34.

Kozora, E. and Cullum, C.M. (1995) Generative naming in normal aging: Total output and qualitative changes using phonemic and semantic constraints. *Clinical Neuropsychologist, 9,* 313–20.

Kramer, A.F., Humphrey, D.G., Larish, J.F. and Logan, G.D. (1995) Aging and inhibition: Beyond a unitary view of inhibitory processing in attention. *Psychology and Aging, 9,* 491–512.

Kramer, A.F. and Madden, D.J. (2008) Attention. In F. Craik, F. and T.A. Salthouse (eds) *The Handbook of Aging and Cognition.* 3rd edition. New York: Psychology Press.

Kramer, A.F. and Strayer, D.L. (2001) Influence of stimulus repetition on negative priming. *Psychology and Aging, 16,* 580–7.

Kramer, B., Kavanaugh, M., Tentham-Beitx, A., Walsh, M. and Yonker, J. (2010) Predictors of family conflict at the end of life: The experience of spouses and adult children of persons with lung cancer. *The Gerontologist, 50,* 215–25.

Krause, N. (2002) Church-based social support and health in old age: Exploring variations by race. *The Journals of Gerontology Series B: Psychological Sciences and Social Sciences, 57,* 332–47.

Krause, N. (2010) Assessing coping responses within specific faith traditions: Suffering in silence, stress, and depressive symptoms among older Catholics. *Mental Health, Religion* and *Culture, 13,* 513–29.

Krause, N. (2011) Neighbourhood conditions and helping behaviour in late life. *Journal of Environmental Psychology, 31,* 62–9.

Krause, N., Jay, G. and Liang, J. (1991) Financial strain and psychological well-being among the American and Japanese elderly. *Psychology and Aging, 6,* 170–81.

Krause, N., Liang, J., Shaw, B.A., Sugisawa, H., Kim, H.K. and Sugihara, Y. (2002) Religion, death of a loved one and hypertension among older adults in Japan. *The Journals of Gerontology Series B: Psychological Sciences and Social Sciences, 57,* 96–107.

Krause, N., Shaw, B.A. and Cairney, J. (2004) A descriptive epidemiology of lifetime trauma and the physical health status of older adults. *Psychology and Aging, 19,* 637–48.

Krauss Whitbourne, S. and Whitbourne, S. (2011) *Adult Development and Ageing: Biopsychosocial Perspectives.* 4th edition. Hoboken, NJ: John Wiley.

Kübler-Ross, E. (1969) *On Death and Dying.* New York: McMillan.

Kübler-Ross, E. (2005) *On Grief and Grieving.* New York: Simon & Schuster.

Kumar, A. and Foster, T.C. (2007) Neurophysiology of old neurons and synapses. In D.R. Riddle (ed.) *Brain Aging: Models, Methods, and Mechanisms.* Boca Raton: CRC Press.

Kunz, M., Mylius, V., Schepelmann, K. and Lautenbacher, S. (2008) Impact of pain on the facial expression of pain. *Journal of Psychosomatic Research, 64,* 311–18.

Kunzmann, U. (2007) Wisdom: Adult development and emotional-motivational dynamics. In R. Fernandez-Ballesteros (ed.) *Geropsychology: European Perspectives for an Aging World*. Ashland: Hogrefe and Huber Publishers.

Kunzmann, U., Little, T.D. and Smith, J. (2000) Is age-related stability of subjective well-being a paradox? Cross-sectional and longitudinal evidence from the Berlin Aging Study. *Psychology and Aging, 15*, 511–26.

Kvavilashvili, L. (1987) Remembering intention as a distinct form of memory. *British Journal of Psychology, 78*, 507–18.

Kvavilashvili, L., Kornbrot, D., Mash, V., Cockburn, J. and Milne, A. (2009) Differential effects of age on prospective and retrospective memory tasks in young, young-old and old-old adults. *Memory, 17*, 180–96.

Kwong See, S.T., Hoffman, H.G. and Wood, T.L. (2001) Perceptions of an old female eyewitness: Is the older eyewitness believable? *Psychology and Aging, 16*, 346–50.

Kynette, D. and Kemper, S. (1986) Aging and the loss of grammatical form: A cross-sectional study of language performance. *Language and Communication, 6*, 65–72.

Labouvie-Vief, G. (1992) A neo-Piagetian perspective on adult cognitive development. In R.J. Sternberg and C.A. Berg (eds) *Intellectual Development*. Cambridge: Cambridge University Press.

Lachman, M., Agrigoroaei, S., Murphy, C. and Tun, P. (2010) Frequent cognitive activity compensates for education differences in episodic memory. *American Journal of Geriatric Psychiatry, 18*, 4–10.

Lacro, J.P., Harris, M.J. and Jeste, D.V. (1995) Late-life psychosis. In E. Murphy and G. Alexopoulos (ed.) *Geriatric Psychiatry: Key Research Topics for Clinicians*. Chichester: Wiley, 231–44.

Laditka, S.B., Fischer, M., Laditka, J.N. and Segal, D.R. (2004) Attitudes about aging and gender among young, middle age and older college-based students. *Educational Gerontology, 30*, 403–21.

Laditka, S.B. and Laditka, J.N. (2002) Recent perspectives on active life expectancy for older women. *Journal of Women and Aging, 14*, 163–84.

Laguna, K. and Babcock, R.L. (1997) Computer anxiety in young and older adults: Implications for human-computer interactions in older populations. *Computers in Human Behavior, 13*, 317–26.

Lahar, C.J., Tun, P.A. and Wingfield, A. (2004) Sentence–final word completion norms for young, middle-aged and older adults. *The Journals of Gerontology Series B: Psychological Sciences and Social Sciences, 59*, 7–10.

Lajoie, Y., Teasdale, N., Bard, C. and Fleury, M. (1996) Upright standing and gait: Are there changes in attentional requirements related to normal aging? *Experimental Aging Research, 22*, 185–98.

Lalande, K. and Bonanno, G. (2006) Culture and continuing bonds: A prospective comparison of bereavement in the United States and the People's Republic of China. *Death Studies, 30*, 303–24.

Lalitha, K. and Jamuna, D. (2006) Remote memory and well-being in the older men and women. *Psychological Studies, 51*, 275–9.

Lamberg, T., Virtanen, P., Vahtera, J., Luukkaala, T. and Koskenvuo, M. (2010) Unemployment, depressiveness and disability retirement: A follow-up study of the Finnish HeSSup population sample. *Social Psychiatry and Psychiatric Epidemiology, 45*, 259–64.

Lang, E., Arnold, K. and Kupfer, P. (1994) Women live longer–biological, medical and sociologic causes. *Zeitschrift fuer Gerontologie, 27*, 10–15.

Lannutti, P. (2011) Security, recognition, and misgivings: Exploring older same-sex couples' experiences of legally recognized same-sex marriage. *Journal of Social and Personal Relationships, 28*, 64–82.

Larson, R. (1978) Thirty years of research on the subjective well-being of older Americans. *Journal of Gerontology, 33*, 109–25.

LaRue, A. (1992) *Aging and Neuropsychological Assessment.* New York: Plenum.

Lasch, H., Castell, D.O. and Castell, J.A. (1997) Evidence for diminished visceral pain with aging: Studies using graded intraesophageal balloon distension. *American Journal of Physiology, 272,* 1–3.

Lasisi, A.O., Abiona, T., Gureje, O. (2010) Tinnitus in the elderly: Profile, correlates, and impact in the Nigerian Study of Ageing. *Otolaryngology, Head and Neck Surgery, 143,* 510–5.

Laslett, P. (1976) Societal development and aging. In R.H. Binstock and E. Shanas (eds) *Handbook of Aging and the Social Sciences.* New York: Reinhold.

Latimer, J. (1963) The status of aging in intelligence. *Journal of Genetic Psychology, 102,* 175–88.

Laurence, M.W. and Arrowood, A.J. (1982) Classification style differences in the elderly. In F.I.M. Craik and S. Trehub (eds) *Aging and Cognitive Processes.* New York: Plenum.

Lauver, S.C. and Johnson, J.L. (1997) The role of neuroticism and social support in older adults with chronic pain behavior. *Personality and Individual Differences, 23,* 165–7.

Laver, G.D. and Burke, D.M. (1993) Why do semantic priming effects increase in old age? A meta-analysis. *Psychology and Aging, 8,* 34–43.

LaVole, D., Mertz, H. and Richmond, T. (2007) False memory susceptibility in older adults: Implications for the elderly eyewitness. In M. Toglia, J. Read, D. Ross and R. Lindsay (eds) *The Handbook of Eyewitness Psychology, Vol 1: Memory for Events.* Mahwah: Lawrence Erlbaum.

Law, R. and O'Carroll, R.E. (1998) A comparison of three measures of estimating premorbid intellectual level in dementia of the Alzheimer type. *International Journal of Geriatric Psychiatry, 13,* 727–30.

Lawton, M.P. (2001) Quality of life and the end of life. In J.E. Birren and K.W. Schaie (eds) *Handbook of the Psychology of Aging.* San Diego: Academic Press.

Lawton, M.P. and Salthouse, T.A. (eds) (1998) *Essential Papers on the Psychology of Aging.* New York: New York University Press.

Leader, D. and Corfield, D. (2007) *Why do people get ill?* London: Hamish Hamilton.

Lee, E. (2007) Religion and spirituality as predictors of well-being among Chinese-American and Korean American older adults. *Journal of Religion, Spirituality and Aging, 19,* 77–100.

Lee, G.R., DeMaris, A., Bavin, S. and Sullivan, R. (2001) Gender differences in the depressive effect of widowhood in later life. *The Journals of Gerontology Series B: Psychological Sciences and Social Sciences, 56,* 56–61.

Lee, H., Hanner, J., Yokley, J., Appleby, B. *et al.* (2007) Clozapine for treatment-resistant agitation in dementia. *Journal of Geriatric Psychiatry and Neurology, 20,* 178–82.

Lee, I.M. and Paffenbarger, R.S. (1998) Physical activity and stroke incidence: The Havard Alumni Health Study. *Stroke, 29,* 2049–54.

Lee, I.M. and Paffenbarger, R.S. (2000) Associations of light, moderate and vigorous intensity physical activity with longevity. The Harvard Alumni Health Study. *American Journal of Epidemiology, 151,* 293–9.

Lee, I.M., Sesso, H.D., Oguma, Y. and Paffenbarger, R.S. (2004) The 'weekend warrior' and risk of mortality. *American Journal of Epidemiology, 160,* 636–41.

Lee, Y. and Kim, S. (2008) Effects of indoor gardening on sleep, agitation, and cognition in dementia patients – A pilot study. *International Journal of Geriatric Psychiatry, 23,* 485–9.

Leenaars, A.A. and Lester, D. (1998) Predicting suicide rate among elderly persons in Canadian provinces. *Psychological Reports, 82,* 1202.

Leentjens, A.F.G. and van der Mast, R.C. (2005) Delirium in elderly people: An update. *Current Opinion in Psychiatry, 18,* 325–30.

Leino, E.V., Romelsjoe, A., Shoemaker, C., Ager, C.R. *et al.* (1998) Alcohol consumption and mortality. II. Studies of male populations. *Addiction, 93,* 205–18.

Leist, A., Ferring, S. and Filipp, S. (2010) Remembering positive and negative life events: Associations with future time perspective and functions of autobiographical memory. *GeroPsych: The Journal of Gerontopsychology and Geriatric Psychiatry, 23*, 137–47.

Lemaire, P. (2010) Cognitive strategy variations during aging. *Current Directions in Psychological Science, 19*, 363–9.

Lennartsson, C. and Silverstein, M. (2001) Does engagement with life enhance survival of elderly people in Sweden? The role of social and leisure activities. *The Journals of Gerontology Series B: Psychological Sciences and Social Sciences, 56*, 335–42.

Lepowsky, M. (1985) Gender, aging, and dying in an egalitarian society. In D.A. Counts and D.R. Counts (eds) *Aging and its Transformations: Moving Toward Death in Pacific Societies.* Lanham: University Press of America, 157–78.

Levenson, R.W., Cartensen, L.L. and Gottman, J.M. (1993) Long-term marriage: Age, gender and satisfaction. *Psychology and Aging, 8*, 310–3.

Levesque, L., Ducharme, F. and Lachance, L. (1999) Is there a difference between family caregiving of institutionalized elders with or without dementia? *Western Journal of Nursing Research, 21*, 472–97.

Levine, B., Stuss, D.T. and Milberg, W.P. (1995) Concept generation: Validation of a test of executive functioning in a normal aging population. *Journal of Clinical and Experimental Neuropsychology, 17*, 740–58.

Levine, B., Svoboda, E., Hay, J.F., Winocur, G. and Moscovitch, M. (2002) Aging and autobiographical memory: Dissociating episodic from semantic retrieval. *Psychology and Aging, 17*, 677–89.

Levine, D., Neidecker, M., Kiefe, C., Karve, S. *et al.* (2011) Racial/ethnic disparities in access to physician care and medications among US stroke survivors. *Neurology, 76*, 53–61.

Levinson, D. (1980) Conception of the adult life course. In N. Smelser and E. Erikson (eds) *Themes of Work and Love in Adulthood.* Cambridge, MA: Harvard University Press.

Levy, B.R. (1999) The inner self of the Japanese elderly: A defense against negative stereotypes of aging. *International Journal of Aging and Human Development, 48*, 131–44.

Levy, B.R. and Banaji, M. (2002) Implicit Ageism. In T.D. Nelson (ed.) *Ageism: Stereotyping and Prejudice against Older Persons.* Cambridge, MA: The MIT Press.

Levy, B.R., Hausdorff, J.M., Hencke, R. and Wei, J.Y. (2000) Reducing cardiovascular stress with positive self-stereotypes of aging. *The Journals of Gerontology Series B: Psychological Sciences and Social Sciences, 55*, 205–13.

Levy, J.A. and Anderson, T. (2005) The drug career of the older injector. *Addiction Research and Theory, 13*, 245–58.

Leyhe, T., Muller, S., Milian, M., Eschweiler, G. and Saur, R. (2009) Impairment of episodic and semantic autobiographical memory in patients with mild cognitive impairment and early Alzheimer's disease. *Neuropsychologia, 47*, 2464–9.

Lezak, M.D. (1995) *Neuropsychological Assessment.* New York: Oxford University Press.

Li, F., Fisher, K.J., Harmer, P. and McAuley, E. (2005) Falls self-efficacy as a mediator of fear of falling in an exercise intervention for older adults. *The Journals of Gerontology Series B: Psychological Sciences and Social Sciences, 60*, 34–40.

Li, F., Fisher, K.J., Harmer, P., McAuley, E. and Wilson, N.L. (2003) Fear of falling in elderly persons: Association with falls, functional ability and quality of life. *The Journals of Gerontology Series B: Psychological Sciences and Social Sciences, 58*, 283–90.

Li, K.Z.H. and Lindenberger, U. (2002) Relations between aging sensory/sensorimotor and cognitive functions. *Neuroscience and Biobehavioral Reviews, 26*, 777–83.

Licinio, J. (2009) Update on molecular psychiatry: New publication guidelines and new ways to stay current. *Molecular Psychiatry, 14*, 463–4.

Lienert, G.A. and Crott, H.W. (1964) Studies on the factor structure of intelligence in children, adolescents and adults. *Vita Humana, 7*, 147–63.

Light, L.L. and Albertson, S.A. (1988) Comprehension of pragmatic implications in young and older adults. In L.L. Light and D.M. Burke (eds) *Language, Memory and Aging.* New York: Cambridge University Press.

Light, L.L. and Albertson, S.A. (1989) Direct and indirect tests of memory for category exemplars in young and older adults. *Psychology and Aging, 4*, 487–92.

Light, L.L. and Anderson, P.A. (1985) Working memory capacity, age and memory for discourse. *Journal of Gerontology, 40*, 737–47.

Light, L.L. and Burke, D. (eds) (1988) *Language, Memory and Aging.* New York: Cambridge University Press.

Lin, J., Lin, L., Sung, C. and Wu, J. (2011) Aged and dependency ratios among autism, intellectual disability and other disabilities: 10-year trend analysis. *Research in Autism Spectrum Disorders, 5*, 523–8.

Lin, L., Yang, M., Kao, C., Wu, S., Tang, S. and Lin, J. (2009) Using acupressure and Montessori-based activities to decrease agitation for residents with dementia: a cross-over trial. *Journal of American Geriatrics Society, 57*, 1022–9.

Lin, R., Heacock, L., Bhargave, G. and Fogel, J. (2010) Clinical associations of delirium in hospitalized older adult patients and the role of admission presentation. *International Journal of Geriatric Psychiatry, 25*, 1022–9.

Lindeman, E. (1944) Symptomatology and management of acute grief. *American Journal of Psychiatry, 101*, 141–9.

Lindenberger, U. and Baltes, P. (1994) Sensory functioning and intelligence in old age: A strong connection. *Psychology and Aging, 9*, 339–55.

Lindenberger, U. and Baltes, P. (1997) Intellectual functioning in old and very old age: Cross-sectional results from the Berlin Aging Study. *Psychology and Aging, 12*, 410–32.

Lindenberger, U., Brehmer, Y., Kliegl, R. and Baltes, P. (2008) Benefits of graphic design expertise in old age: Compensatory effects of a graphical lexicon? In C. Lange-Küttner and A. Vintner (eds) *Drawing and the Non-Verbal Mind: A Life-Span Perspective.* New York: Cambridge University Press.

Lindenberger, U. and Ghisletta, P. (2009) Cognitive and sensory decline in old age: Gauging the evidence for a common cause. *Psychology and Aging, 24*, 1–16.

Lindenberger, U., Kliegl, R. and Baltes, P.B. (1992) Professional expertise does not eliminate age differences in imagery-based memory performance during adulthood. *Psychology and Aging, 7*, 585–93.

Lindenberger, U., Marsiske, M. and Baltes, P.B. (2000) Memorizing while walking: Increase in dual-task costs from young adulthood to old age. *Psychology and Aging, 15*, 417–36.

Lindenberger, U., Mayr, U. and Kliegl, R. (1993) Speed and intelligence in old age. *Psychology and Aging, 8*, 207–20.

Lindenberger, U., Scherer, H. and Baltes, P.B. (2001) The strong connection between sensory and cognitive performance in old age: Not due to sensory acuity reductions operating during cognitive assessment. *Psychology and Aging, 16*, 196–205.

Lindesay, J., Briggs, K. and Murphy, E. (1989) The Guy's/Age Concern survey: Prevalence rates of cognitive impairment, depression and anxiety in an urban elderly community. *British Journal of Psychiatry, 155*, 317–29.

Litwin, H. and Shiovitz-Ezra, S. (2006) The association between activity and wellbeing in later life: What really matters? *Ageing and Society, 26*, 225–42.

Liu, C., Kemper, S. and Bovaird, J. (2009) Comprehension of health-related written materials by older adults. *Educational Gerontology, 35*, 653–68.

Liu, H., Wang, P., Wang, H., Lin, K. *et al.* (2007) Conversion to dementia from questionable dementia in an ethnic Chinese population. *Journal of Geriatric Psychiatry and Neurology, 20,* 76–83.

Livingston, M. and Room, R. (2009) Variations by age and sex in alcohol-related problematic behaviour per drinking volume and heavier drinking occasion. *Drug and Alcohol Dependence, 101,* 169–75.

Livner, A., Wahlin, A. and Backman, L. (2009) Thyroid stimulating hormone and prospective memory functioning in old age. *Psychoneuroendocrinology, 34,* 1554–9.

Lofland, L. (1978) *The Craft of Dying: The Modern Face of Death.* Beverly Hills, CA: Sage.

Lofwall, M.R., Brooner, R.K., Bigelow, G.E., Kindbom, K. and Strain, E.C. (2005) Characteristics of older opioid maintenance patients. *Journal of Substance Abuse Treatment, 28,* 265–72.

Logan, J.M. and Balota, D.A. (2003) Conscious and unconscious lexical retrieval blocking in younger and older adults. *Psychology and Aging, 18,* 537–50.

Logie, R. and Maylor, E. (2009) An Internet study of prospective memory across adulthood. *Psychology and Aging, 24,* 767–74.

Long, L.L. and Shaw, R.J. (2000) Adult age differences in vocabulary acquisition. *Educational Gerontology, 26,* 651–64.

Long, S. (2003) Cultural scripts for a good death in Japan and the United States: Similarities and differences. *Social Science and Medicine, 58,* 913–28.

Lopata, H. (1973) *Widowhood in an American City.* Cambridge: Schenkman.

Lopez, A.D., Mathers, C.D., Ezzati, M., Jamison, D., Murray, C. (2006) Global and regional burden of disease and risk factors, 2001: systematic analysis of population health data. *Lancet, 367,* 1747–57.

Lopez, L.M., Mullen, W., Zurbig, P., Harris, S.E. *et al.* (2011) A pilot study of urinary peptides as biomarkers for intelligence in old age. *Intelligence, 39,* 46–53.

Löppönen, M., Räihä, I., Isoaho, R., Vahlberg, T. and Kivela, S.L. (2003) Diagnosing cognitive impairment and dementia in primary health care – a more active approach is needed. *Age and Ageing, 32,* 606–12.

Lord, S.R., Smith, R.T. and Menant, J.C. (2010) Vision and falls in older people: Risk factors and intervention strategies. *Clinical and Geriatric Medicine, 26,* 569–81.

Lövdén, M., Bodammer, N., Kuhn, S., Kaufmann, J. *et al.* (2010) Experience-dependent plasticity of white-matter microstructure extends into old age. *Neuropsychologia, 48,* 3878–83.

Lövdén, M., Rönnlund, M., Wahlin, A., Bäckman, L., Nyberg, L. and Nilsson, L.G. (2004) The extent of stability and change in episodic and semantic memory in old age: Demographic predictors of level and change. *The Journals of Gerontology Series B: Psychological Sciences and Social Sciences, 59,* 130–4.

Lövdén, M. and Wahlin, A. (2005) The sensory-cognition association in adulthood: Different magnitudes for processing speed, inhibition, episodic memory and false memory? *Scandinavian Journal of Psychology, 46,* 253–62.

Lovie, K.J. and Whittaker, S. (1998) Relative size magnification versus relative distance magnification: Effect on the reading performance of adults with normal and low vision. *Journal of Visual Impairment and Blindness, 92,* 433–46.

Lowenstein, A. (2009) Elder abuse and neglect – 'old phenomenon': New directions for research, legislation, and service developments. *Journal of Elder Abuse and Neglect, 21,* 278–87.

Lucas, R. and Donnellan, M. (2009) Age differences in personality: Evidence from a nationally representative Australian sample. *Developmental Psychology, 45,* 1353–63.

Lucchetti, M., Corsonello, A., Fabbietti, P., Greco, C. *et al.* (2009) Relationship between socio-economic features and health status in elderly hospitalized patients. *Archives of Gerontology and Geriatrics, 49,* 163–72.

Luijendijk, H., van den Berg, J., Dekker, M., van Tuijl, H. *et al.* (2008) Incidence and recurrence of late-life depression. *Archives of General Psychiatry, 65,* 1394–1401.

Lun, M. (2011) Student knowledge and attitudes toward older people and their impact on pursuing aging careers. *Educational Gerontology, 37*, 1–11.

Luo, L. and Craik, F. (2008) Aging and memory: A cognitive approach. *Canadian Journal of Psychiatry, 53*, 346–53.

Luo, Y. and Waite, L.J. (2005) The impact of childhood and adult SES on physical, mental and cognitive well-being in later life. *The Journals of Gerontology Series B: Psychological Sciences and Social Sciences, 60*, 93–101.

Lupton, M., Stahl, D., Archer, N., Foy, C., Poppe, M., Hollingworth, P. *et al.* (2010) Education, occupation and retirement age effects on the age of onset of Alzheimer's disease. *International Journal of Geriatric Psychiatry, 25*, 30–6.

Luquet, G. (1927) *Children's Drawings*. London: Free Association Books.

Lynn, T.N., Duncan, R., Naughton, J.P., Brandt, E.N. *et al.* (1967) Prevalence of evidence of prior myocardial infarction, hypertension, diabetes and obesity in three neighboring communities in Pennsylvania. *American Journal of Medical Science, 254*, 4, 385–391.

Maas, M.S. and Kuypers, J.A. (1974) *From Thirty to Seventy*. San Francisco: Jossey-Bass.

MacDonald, M., Aneja, A., Martin, P., Margrett, J. and Poon, L. (2010) Distal and proximal resource influences on economic dependency among the oldest old. *Gerontology, 56*, 100–5.

MacDonald, S.W.S., Hultsch, D.F., Strauss, E. and Dixon, R.A. (2003) Age-related slowing of digit symbol substitution revisited: What do longitudinal age changes reflect? *The Journals of Gerontology Series B: Psychological Sciences and Social Sciences, 58*, 187–94.

MacDonell, G., Marsh, N., Hine, D. and Bhullar, N. (2010) Development and psychometric evaluation of a measure to assess distress in partners of Australian combat veterans. *Australian and New Zealand Journal of Psychiatry, 44*, 839–45.

Mace, J. (2004) Involuntary autobiographical memories are highly dependent on abstract cuing: The Proustian view is incorrect. *Applied Cognitive Psychology, 18*, 893–9.

Macintyre, S. (1994) Understanding the social patterning of health: The role of the social sciences. *Journal of Public Health Medicine, 16*, 53–9.

MacKay, D.G. and Abrams, L. (1998) Age-linked declines in retrieving orthographic knowledge: Empirical, practical and theoretical implications. *Psychology and Aging, 13*, 647–62.

MacKay, D.G., Abrams, L. and Pedroza, M.J. (1999) Aging on the input versus output side: Theoretical implications of age-linked assymetries between detecting versus retrieving orthographic information. *Psychology and Aging, 14*, 3–17.

MacKay, D.G. and Burke, D.M. (1990) Cognition and aging: A theory of new learning and the use of old connections. In T.M. Hess (ed.) *Aging and Cognition: Organization and Utilization*. Amsterdam: North-Holland, 1–51.

Mackenbach, J.P., Stirbu, I., Roskam, A.J., Schaap, M.M. *et al.* (2008) Socioeconomic inequalities in morbidity and mortality in western Europe. *New England Journal of Medicine, 358*, 2468–81.

MacPherson, S., Sala, S., Logie, R. and Wilcox, G. (2007) Specific AD impairment in concurrent performance of two memory tasks. *Cortex, 43*, 858–65.

MacPherson, S.E., Phillips, L.H. and Della Sala, S. (2002) Age, executive function and social decision making: A dorsolateral prefrontal theory of cognitive aging. *Psychology and Aging, 17*, 598–609.

Madden, C. and Dijkstra, K. (2010) Contextual constraints in situation model construction: An investigation of age and reading span. *Aging, Neuropsychology, and Cognition, 17*, 19–34.

Madden, D.J. (1992) Four to ten milliseconds per year: Age-related slowing of visual word identification. *Journals of Gerontology, 47*, 59–68.

Madden, D.J. and Langley, L.K. (2003) Age-related changes in selective attention and perceptual load during visual search. *Psychology and Aging, 18*, 54–67.

Madden, D.J., Whiting, W.L., Cabeza, R. and Huettel, S.A. (2004) Age-related preservation of top-down attentional guidance during visual search. *Psychology and Aging, 19*, 304–9.

Maddox, G.I. (1970a) Persistence of life style among the elderly. In E. Palmore (ed.) *Normal Aging*. Durham: Duke University Press.

Maddox, G.I. (1970b) Themes and issues in sociological theories of human aging. *Human Development, 13*, 17–27.

Maddox, W., Pacheco, J., Reeves, M., Zhu, B. and Schnyer, D. (2010) Rule-based and information-integration category learning in normal aging. *Neuropsychologia, 48*, 2998–3008.

Madigan, M.J., Mise, D.H. and Maynard, M. (1996) Life satisfaction and level of activity of male elderly in institutional and community settings. *Activities, Adaptation and Aging, 21*, 21–36.

Maentylae, T. and Nilsson, L.G. (1997) Remembering to remember in adulthood: A population-based study on aging and prospective memory. *Aging, Neuropsychology and Cognition, 4*, 81–92.

Magai, C., Cohen, C., Milburn, N., Thorpe, B., McPherson, R. and Peralta, D. (2001) Attachment styles in older European American and African American adults. *The Journals of Gerontology Series B: Psychological Sciences and Social Sciences, 56*, 28–45.

Maguire, E. and Frith, C. (2003) Aging affects the engagement of the hippocampus during autobiographical memory retrieval. *Brain, 126*, 1511FH-23.

Mahay, J. and Lewin, A. (2007) Age and the desire to marry. *Journal of Family Issues, 28*, 706–23.

Mahley, R. and Huang, Y. (2009) Alzheimer disease: Multiple causes, multiple effects of apolipoprotein E4, and multiple therapeutic approaches. *Annals of Neurology, 65*, 623–5.

Mahncke, H.W., Bronstone, A. and Merzenich, M.M. (2006) Brain plasticity and functional losses in the aged: Scientific bases for a novel intervention. *Progresses in Brain Research, 157*, 87–109.

Majeres, R. (2005) Phonological and orthographic coding skills in adult readers. *Journal of General Psychology, 132*, 267–80.

Mak, W. and Carpenter, B. (2007) Humor comprehension in older adults. *Journal of the International Neuropsychological Society, 13*, 606–14.

Maki, Y., Yoshida, H. and Yamaguchi, H. (2010) Computerized visuo-spatial memory test as a supplementary screening test for dementia. *Psychogeriatrics, 10*, 77–82.

Mallery, L. and Moorhouse, P. (2011) Respecting frailty. *Journal of Medical Ethics, 37*, 126–8.

Mallick, M. (1982) Gerontological social work practice in long-term care: Understanding illness and aging. *Journal of Gerontological Social Work, 5*, 113–26.

Maltby, J., Lewis, C., Freeman, A., Day, L. *et al.* (2010) Religion and health: The application of a cognitive-behavioural framework. *Mental Health, Religion and Culture, 13*, 749–59.

Malvern, J. (2011) Landscapes: Hockney's got an app for that. *The Times*, 8 September, 2011.

Mandel, R.G. and Johnson, N.S. (1984) A developmental analysis of story recall and comprehension in adulthood. *Journal of Verbal Learning and Verbal Behavior, 23*, 643–59.

Mandic, N. and Barkic, J. (1996) Psychosocial and cultural characteristics of personality disorders. *Psychiatrica Danubina, 8*, 29–33.

Mani, T., Bedwell, J. and Miller, L.S. (2005) Age-related decrements in performance on a brief continuous performance test. *Archives of Clinical Neuropsychology, 20*, 575–86.

Manthorpe, J. and Iliffe, S. (2005) *Depression in Later Life*. London: Jessica Kingsley Publishers.

Manthorpe, J. and Iliffe, S. (2011) Social work with older people – reducing suicide risk: A critical review of practice and prevention. *British Journal of Social Work, 41*, 131–40.

Manton, K.G., Gu, X. and Lamb, V.L. (2006) Long-term trends in life expectancy and active life expectancy in the United States. *Population and Development Review, 32*, 81–105.

Manton, K.G., Gu, X. and Lowrimore, G. (2008) Cohort changes in active life expectancy in the U.S. elderly population: Experience from the 1982–2004 National Long-Term Care Survey. *The Journals of Gerontology Series B: Psychological Sciences and Social Sciences 63*, 269–81.

Marengoni, A., Calíbrese, A.P. and Cossi, S. (2004) Hospital admissions for acute onset of behavioral symptoms in demented patients: What do they want to say? *International Psychogeriatrics, 16*, 491–3.

Margolin, S. and Abrams, L. (2007) Individual differences in young and older adults' spelling: Do good spellers age better than poor spellers? *Aging, Neuropsychology, and Cognition, 14,* 529–44.

Margolin, S. and Abrams, L. (2009) Not may be too difficult: The effects of negation on older adults' sentence comprehension. *Educational Gerontology, 35,* 306–20.

Marianetti, M., Izzo, C., Fratino, M. and Mina, C. (2010) Single strategic infarct dementia mimicking dementia with Lewy bodies. *Journal of the American Geriatrics Society, 58,* 2432–33.

Mariani, C., Defendi, S., Mailland, E. and Pomati, S. (2006) Frontotemporal dementia. *Neurological Sciences, 27,* S35–S36.

Marmot, M. (2001) Inequalities in health. *New England Journal of Medicine, 345,* 134–6.

Marmot, M. and Feeney, A. (1997) General explanations for social inequalities in health. *IARC Scientific Publications, 138,* 207–28.

Marquié, J.C. and Huet, N. (2000) Age differences in feeling-of-knowing and confidence judgments as a function of knowledge domain. *Psychology and Aging, 15,* 451–61.

Marsden, C.D. and Harrison, M.J.G. (1972) Outcome of investigation of patients with presenile dementia. *British Medical Journal, 2,* 249–52.

Marsh, G.A. (1980) Perceptual changes with aging. In E.W. Busse and D.G. Blazer (eds) *Handbook of Geriatric Psychiatry.* New York: Van Nostrand Reinhold.

Marsiske, M., Klumb, P. and Baltes, M. (1997) Everyday activity patterns and sensory functioning in old age. *Psychology and Aging, 12,* 444–57.

Martin, C.E. (1981) Factors affecting sexual functioning in 60–79 year old married males. *Archives of Sexual Behavior, 10,* 339–420.

Martin, S.B., Smith, C.D., Collins, H.R., Schmitt, F.A. and Gold, B.T. (2010) Evidence that volume of anterior medial temporal lobe is reduced in seniors destined for mild cognitive impairment. *Neurobiology of Aging, 31,* 1099–106.

Martone, M., Butlers, N., Payne, M., Becker, J.T. and Sax, D.S. (1984) Dissociation between skill learning and verbal recognition in amnesia and dementia. *Archives of Neurology, 41,* 965–70.

Marty, M., Segal, D. and Coolidge, F. (2010) Relationships among dispositional coping strategies, suicidal ideation, and protective factors against suicide in older adults. *Aging and Mental Health, 14,* 1015–23.

Masoro, E.J. (1988) Food restriction in rodents: An evaluation of its role in the study of aging. *Journal of Gerontology, 43,* 59–64.

Masoro, E.J. (1992) Retardation of aging processes by food restriction: An experimental tool. *American Journal of Clinical Nutrition, 55,* 1250–2.

Massimi, M., Berry, E., Browne, G., Smyth, G. *et al.* (2008) An exploratory case study of the impact of ambient biographical displays on identity in a patient with Alzheimer's disease. *Neuropsychological Rehabilitation, 18,* 742–65.

Mast, B., Zimmerman, J. and Rowe, S. (2009) What do we know about the aging brain? Implications for learning in late life. In M. Smith and N. DeFrates-Dentsch (eds) *Handbook of Research on Adult Learning and Development.* New York: Routledge.

Masters, W.H. and Johnson, V.E. (1966) *Human Sexual Response.* Boston, MA: Little, Brown.

Masunaga, H. and Horn, J. (2001) Expertise and age-related changes in components of intelligence. *Psychology and Aging, 16,* 293–311.

Matilainen, L., Talvitie, S., Pekkonen, E., Alku, P., May, P. and Tiitinen, H. (2010) The effects of healthy aging on auditory processing in humans as indexed by transient brain responses. *Clinical Neurophysiology, 121,* 902–11.

Matthias, R.E., Lubben, J.E., Atchison, K.A. and Schweitzer, S.O. (1997) Sexual activity and satisfaction among very old adults: Results from a community-dwelling medicare population survey. *Gerontologist, 37,* 6–14.

Mayers, K.S. and McBride, D. (1998) Sexuality training for caretakers of geriatric residents in long term care facilities. *Sexuality and Disability, 16,* 227–36.

Maylor, E.A. (1990a) Age and prospective memory. *Quarterly Journal of Experimental Psychology,* *42A,* 471–93.

Maylor, E.A. (1990b) Age, blocking and tip of the tongue state. *British Journal of Psychology, 81,* 123–34.

Maylor, E.A. (1997) Proper name retrieval in old age: Converging evidence against disproportionate impairment. *Aging, Neuropsychology and Cognition, 4,* 211–26.

Maylor, E.A. (1998) Changes in event-based prospective memory across adulthood. *Aging, Neuropsychology and Cognition, 5,* 107–28.

Maylor, E.A., Carter, S.M. and Hallett, E.L. (2002) Preserved olfactory cuing of autobiographical memories in old age. *The Journals of Gerontology Series B: Psychological Sciences and Social Sciences, 57,* 41–6.

Maylor, E.A. and Henson, R. (2000) Ranschburg effect: No evidence of reduced response suppression in old age. *Psychology and Aging, 15,* 657–70.

Maylor, E.A. and Lavie, N. (1998) The influence of perceptual load on age differences in selective attention. *Psychology and Aging, 13,* 563–73.

Maylor, E.A. and Rabbitt, P.M.A. (1994) Applying Brinley plots to individuals: Effect of aging on performance distributions in two speeded tasks. *Psychology and Aging, 9,* 224–30.

Maylor, E.A., Schlaghecken, F. and Watson, D. (2005) Aging and inhibitory processes in memory, attentional, and motor tasks. In R.W. Engle, G. Sedek, U. von Hecker and D. McIntosh (eds) *Cognitive Limitations in Aging and Psychopathology.* New York: Cambridge University Press.

Maylor, E.A., Vousden, J.I. and Brown, G.D.A. (1999) Adult age differences in short-term memory for serial order: Data and model. *Psychology and Aging, 14,* 572–94.

Mayr, U. and Kliegl, R. (2000) Complex semantic processing in old age: Does it stay or does it go? *Psychology and Aging, 15,* 29–43.

McArdle, J.J., Hamgami, F., Jones, K., Jolesz, F. *et al.* (2004) Structural modeling of dynamic changes in memory and brain structure using longitudinal data from the normative aging study. *The Journals of Gerontology Series B: Psychological Sciences and Social Sciences 59,* 294–304.

McCabe, J. and Hartman, M. (2008) An analysis of age differences in perceptual speed. *Memory and Cognition, 36,* 1495–508.

McCallion, P. and McCarron, M. (2004) Ageing and intellectual disabilities: A review of the recent literature. *Current Opinion in Psychiatry, 17,* 349–52.

McCaul, K., Almeida, O., Hankey, G., Jamrozik, K. *et al.* (2010) Alcohol use and mortality in older men and women. *Addiction, 105,* 1391–400.

McConatha, J.T., McConatha, D., Jackson, J.A. and Bergen, A. (1998) The control factor: Life satisfaction in later adulthood. *Journal of Clinical Geropsychology, 4,* 159–68.

McCrae, C.S. and Abrams, R.A. (2001) Age-related differences in object- and location-based inhibition of return of attention. *Psychology and Aging, 16,* 437–49.

McCrae, R.R., Arenberg, D. and Costa, P.T. (1987) Declines in divergent thinking with age: Cross-sectional, longitudinal and cross-sequential analyses. *Psychology and Aging, 2,* 130–7.

McCubbin, H.I. and Patterson, J.M. (1982) Family adaptation to crises. In H.I. McCubbin, A.E. Cauble and J.M. Patterson (eds) *Family Stress, Coping and Social Support.* Springfield, IL: Thomas.

McDermott, K. and Berk, A. (2010) *William Shakespeare: His Life and Times.* New York: Templar.

McDonald, L. (2011) Retirement. In I. Stuart-Hamilton (ed.) *Introduction to Gerontology.* Cambridge: Cambridge University Press.

McDonald, L. and Stuart-Hamilton, I. (1996) Older and more moral? Age related changes in performance on Piagetian moral reasoning tasks. *Age and Ageing, 25,* 402–04.

McDonald, L. and Stuart-Hamilton, I. (2000) The meaning of life: Animism in the classificatory skills of older adults. *International Journal of Aging and Human Development, 51,* 231–42.

McDonald, L. and Stuart-Hamilton, I. (2002) Egocentrism in older adults – Piaget's three mountains task revisited. *Educational Gerontology, 28,* 35–43.

McDowd, J.M. and Filion, D.L. (1992) Aging, selective attention and inhibitory processes: A psychophysiological approach. *Psychology and Aging, 7*, 65–71.

McEvoy, C.L., Nelson, D.L., Holley, P.E. and Stelnicki, G.S. (1992) Implicit processing in the cued recall of young and old adults. *Psychology and Aging, 7*, 401–8.

McFarland, C.P. and Glisky, E.L. (2009) Frontal lobe involvement in a task of time-based prospective memory. *Neuropsychologia, 47*, 1660–9.

McFarland, M. (2010) Religion and mental health among older adults: Do the effects of religious involvement vary by gender? *The Journals of Gerontology Series B: Psychological Sciences and Social Sciences, 65*, 621–30.

McFarland, R.A. and Fisher, M.B. (1955) Alterations in dark adaptation as a function of age. *Journal of Gerontology, 10*, 424–8.

McGinnis, D. (2009) Text comprehension products and processes in young, young-old and old-old adults. *The Journals of Gerontology Series B: Psychological Sciences and Social Sciences, 64*, 202–11.

McGinnis, D. and Zelinski, E.M. (2000) Understanding unfamiliar words: The influence of processing resources, vocabulary knowledge and age. *Psychology and Aging, 15*, 335–50.

McGinnis, D. and Zelinski, E.M. (2003) Understanding unfamiliar words in young, young-old and old-old adults: Inferential processing and the abstraction-deficit hypothesis. *Psychology and Aging, 18*, 497–509.

McGrath, A.M. and Jackson, G.A. (1996) Survey of neuroleptic prescribing in residents of nursing homes in Glasgow. *British Medical Journal, 312*, 611–12.

McGue, M. and Christensen, K. (2001) The heritability of cognitive functioning in very old adults: Evidence from Danish twins aged 75 years and older. *Psychology and Aging, 16*, 272–80.

McIntyre, J.S. and Craik, F.I.M. (1987) Age differences in memory for item and source information. *Canadian Journal of Psychology, 41*, 175–92.

McKhann, G., Drachman, D., Folstein, M., Katzman, R. *et al.* (2011) Clinical diagnosis of Alzheimer's disease: Report of the NINCDS-ADRDA work group under the auspices of department of health and human services task force on Alzheimer's disease. *Neurology, 77*, 333–45.

McKinnon, M., Nica, E., Sengdy, P., Kovacevic, N. *et al.* (2008) Autobiographical memory and patterns of brain atrophy in frontotemporal lobar degeneration. *Journal of Cognitive Neuroscience, 20*, 1839–53.

McLaren, S., Gomez, R., Bailey, M. and Van Der Horst, R. (2007) The association of depression and sense of belonging with suicidal ideation among older adults: Applicability of resiliency models. *Suicide and Life-Threatening Behavior, 37*, 89–102.

McLaughlin, P.M., Szostak, C., Binns, M., Craik, F.I.M., Tipper, S. and Stuss, D. (2010) The effects of age and task demands on visual selective attention. *Canadian Journal of Experimental Psychology, 64*, 197–207.

McMamish-Svensson, C., Samuelsson, G., Hagberg, G. and Dehlin, O. (1999) Social relationships and health as predictors of life satisfaction in advanced old age: Results from a Swedish longitudinal study. *International Journal of Aging and Human Development, 48*, 301–45.

McMasters, J.H. (1989) The flight of the bumblebee and related myths of entomological engineering. *American Scientist, 77*, 164–9.

McMurtray, A., Clark, D., Christine, D. and Mendez, M. (2006) Early-onset dementia: Frequency and causes compared to late-onset dementia. *Dementia and Geriatric Cognitive Disorders, 21*, 59–64.

McMurtray, A., Ringman, J., Chao, S., Lichet, E. *et al.* (2006) Family history of dementia in early-onset versus very late-onset alzheimer's disease. *International Journal of Geriatric Psychiatry, 21*, 597–8.

McNeilly, D.P. and Burke, W.J. (2001) Gambling as a social activity of older adults. *International Journal of Aging and Human Development, 52*, 19–28.

McNeilly, D.P. and Burke, W.J. (2002) Disposable time and disposable income: Problem casino gambling behavior in older adults. *Journal of Clinical Geropsychology, 8,* 75–85.

McShane, R., Keene, J., Gedling, K., Fairburn, C., Jacoby, R. and Hope, T. (1997) Do neuroleptic drugs hasten cognitive decline in dementia? Prospective study with necropsy follow up. *British Medical Journal, 314,* 266–7.

Meacham, J.A. (1990) The loss of wisdom. In R.J. Sternberg (ed.) *Wisdom: Its Nature, Origins and Development.* Cambridge: Cambridge University Press.

Medawar, P.B. (1952) *An Unsolved Problem of Biology.* London: H.K. Lewis.

Medvedev, Z.A. (1990) An attempt at a rational classification of theories of ageing. *Biological Review, 65,* 375–98.

Meesters, C.M.G., Muris, P. and Backus, I.P.G. (1996) Dimensions of hostility and myocardial infarction in adult males. *Journal of Psychosomatic Research, 40,* 21–8.

Meeter, M., Eijsackers, E. and Mulder, J. (2006) Retrograde amnesia for autobiographical memories and public events in mild and moderate Alzheimer's disease. *Journal of Clinical and Experimental Neuropsychology, 28,* 914–27.

Meier, D., Isaacs, S. and Hughes, R. (2010) *Palliative Care: Transforming the Care of Serious Illness.* San Francisco, CA: Jossey-Bass.

Meier-Ruge, W. Gygax, P. and Wiernsperger, N. (1980) A synoptic view of pathophysiology and experimental pharmacology in gerontological brain research. In C. Einsedorfer and W.E. Fann (eds) *Psychopharmacology of Aging.* New York: S.P. Medical and Scientific Books, 65–98.

Mein, G., Martikainen, P., Stansfeld, S.A., Brunner, E.J., Fuhrer, R. and Marmot, M.G. (2000) Predictors of early retirement in British civil servants. *Age and Ageing, 29,* 529–36.

Melzer, D., Izmirlian, G., Leveille, S.G. and Guralnik, J.M. (2001) Educational differences in the prevalence of mobility disability in old age: The dynamics of incidence, mortality and recovery. *The Journals of Gerontology Series B: Psychological Sciences and Social Sciences, 56,* 294–301.

Mendes-Chiloff, C., Torres, A., Lima, M. and de Abreu Ramos-Cerqueira, A. (2009) Prevalence and correlates of cognitive impairment among the elderly in a general hospital. *Dementia and Geriatric Cognitive Disorders, 28,* 433–41.

Menec, V.H. and Chipperfield, J.G. (1997) Remaining active in later life: The role of locus of control in senior's leisure activity participation, health and life satisfaction. *Journal of Aging and Health, 9,* 105–25.

Merriman, A. (1984) Social customs affecting the role of elderly women in Indian society. In D.B. Bromley (ed.) *Gerontology: Social and Behavioural Perspectives.* London: Croom Helm.

Metter, E.J. and Wilson, R.S. (1993) Vascular dementias. In R.W. Parks, R.F. Zec and R.S. Wilson (eds) *Neuropsychology of Alzheimer's Disease and Other Dementias.* New York: Oxford University Press, 416–37.

Meyer, B.J.F. (1987) Reading comprehension and aging. In K.W. Schaie (ed.) *Annual Review of Gerontology and Geriatrics, 7.* New York: Springer.

Meynen, G., van Stralen, H., Smit, J., Kamphorst, W., Swaab, D. (2010) Relation between neuritic plaques and depressive state in Alzheimer's disease. *Acta Neuropsychiatrica, 22,* 14–20.

Miccinesi, G., Fischer, S., Paci, E., Onwuteaka-Philipsen, B. *et al.* (2005) Physicians' attitudes towards end-of-life decisions: A comparison between seven countries. *Social Science and Medicine, 60,* 1961–74.

Midlov, P., Eriksson, T. and Kragh, A. (2009) *Drug-Related Problems in the Elderly.* Dordrecht: Springer.

Midwinter, E. (1991) *The British Gas Report on Attitudes to Ageing.* London: British Gas.

Millard, P.H, Cole, A., Hargreaves, P., Hill, D. *et al.* (2009) Dying patients. Letter to *The Telegraph,* 3 September.

Miller, E. (1975) Impaired recall and the memory disturbance in presenile dementia. *British Journal of Social and Clinical Psychology, 14,* 73–9.

Miller, E. and Lewis, P. (1977) Recognition memory in elderly patients with depression and dementia: A signal detection analysis. *Journal of Abnormal Psychology, 86,* 84–6.

Miller, K., Finney, G., Meador, K. and Loring, D. (2010) Auditory responsive naming versus visual confrontation naming in dementia. *Clincial Neuropsychologist, 24,* 103–18.

Miller, L.J., Myers, A., Prinzi, L. and Mittenberg, W. (2009) Changes in intellectual functioning associated with normal aging. *Archives of Clincial Neuropsychology, 24,* 681–88.

Miller, L.S. (1987) Forensic examination of arthritic impaired writings. *Journal of Police Science and Administration, 15,* 51–5.

Miller, M. (1979) Suicides on a southwestern American Indian reservation. *White Cloud Journal, 1,* 14–18.

Milne, G.G. (1956) Deterioration and over-learning. *Australian Journal of Psychology, 8,* 163–72.

Minois, G. (1989) *History of Old Age.* Cambridge: Polity Press.

Mireles, D.E. and Charness, N. (2002) Computational explorations of the influence of structured knowledge on age-related cognitive decline. *Psychology and Aging, 17,* 245–59.

Mitchell, D.B. and Bruss, P.J. (2003) Age differences in implicit memory: Conceptual, perceptual, or methodological? *Psychology and Aging, 18,* 807–22.

Mitchell, D.B. and Schmitt, F.A. (2006) Short and long term implicit memory in aging and Alzheimer's disease. *Aging, Neuropsychology and Cognition, 13,* 611–35.

Mitchell, K.J., Johnson, M.K., Raye, C.L., Mather, M. and D'Esposito, M. (2000) Aging and reflective processes of working memory: Binding and test load deficits. *Psychology and Aging, 15,* 527–41.

Mitford, E., Reay, R., McCabe, K., Paxton, R., Turkington, D. (2010) Ageism in first episode psychosis. *International Journal of Geriatric Psychiatry, 25,* 1112–8.

Miyoshi, K. (2009) What is 'early onset dementia'? *Psychogeriatrics, 9,* 67–72.

Moberg, P.J., Doty, R.L., Turetsky, B.I. and Arnold, S.E. (1997) Olfactory identification in elderly schizophrenia and Alzheimer's disease. *Neurobiology of Aging, 18,* 163–7.

Mockler, D., Riordan, J. and Sharma, T. (1996) A comparison of the NART (restandardized) and the NART-R (revised). *British Journal of Clinical Psychology, 35,* 567–72.

Moen, P. (1996) A life course perspective on retirement, gender and well-being. *Journal of Occupational Health Psychology, 1,* 131–44.

Mojet, J., Heidema, J. and Christ-Hazelhof, E. (2003) Taste perception with age: Generic or specific losses in supra-threshold intensities of five taste qualities? *Chemical Senses, 28,* 397–413.

Moller, D. (1987) On the value of suffering in the shadow of death. *Loss, Grief and Care, 1,* 127–36.

Monastero, R., Palmer, K., Qiu, C., Winblad, B. and Fratiglioni, L. (2007) Heterogeneity in risk factors for cognitive impairment, no dementia: Population-based longitudinal study from the Kungsholmen Project. *American Journal of Geriatric Psychiatry, 15,* 60–9.

Mondragon-Rodriguez, S., Basurto-Islas, G., Lee, H., Perry, G. *et al.* (2010) Causes versus effects: The increasing complexities of Alzheimer's disease pathogenesis. *Expert Review of Neurotherapeutics, 10,* 683–91.

Moon, C.N. and Hahn, M.J. (1981) Primary malleus fixation: Diagnosis and treatment. *Laryngoscope, 91,* 1298–307.

Moore, A. and Stratton, D. (2003) *Resilient Widowers: Older Men Adjusting to a New Life.* London: Prometheus Books.

Moorman, S. (2011) Older adults' preferences for independent or delegated end-of-life medical decision making. *Journal of Aging and Health, 23,* 135–57.

Morgan, D.L., Neal, M.B. and Carder, P.C. (1997) Both what and when: The effects of positive and negative aspects of relationships on depression during the first three years of widowhood. *Journal of Clinical Geropsychology, 3,* 73–91.

Morris, R.G. (1984) Dementia and the functioning of the articulatory loop system. *Cognitive Neuropsychology, 1,* 143–57.

Morris, R.G. (1986) Short-term forgetting in senile dementia of the Alzheimer's type. *Cognitive Neuropsychology, 3*, 77–97.

Morris, R.G. (1994) Working memory in Alzheimer-type dementia. *Neuropsychology, 8*, 544–54.

Morris, R.G., Craik, F.I.M. and Gick, M.L. (1990) Age differences in working memory tasks. The role of secondary memory and the central executive system. *Quarterly Journal of Experimental Psychology, 42A*, 67–86.

Morris, R.G., Gick, M.L. and Craik, F.I.M. (1988) Processing resources and age differences in working memory. *Memory and Cognition, 16*, 362–6.

Morris, R.G. and Kopelman, M.D. (1986) The memory deficit in Alzheimer-type dementia: A review. *Quarterly Journal of Experimental Psychology, 38A*, 57–602.

Morrisey, E., Becker, J. and Rubert, M.P. (1990) Coping resources and depression in the caregiving spouses of Alzheimers patients. *British Journal of Medical Psychology, 63*, 161–71.

Morrone, I., Declercq, C., Novella, J. and Besche, C. (2010) Aging and inhibition processes: The case of metaphor treatment. *Psychology and Aging, 25*, 697–701.

Morse, C.K. (1993) Does variability increase with age? An archival study of cognitive measures. *Psychology and Aging, 8*, 156–64.

Moscovitch, M. (1982) A neuropsychological approach to memory and perception in normal and pathological aging. In F.I.M. Craik and S. Trehub (eds) *Aging and Cognitive Processes.* New York: Plenum.

Moss, M.B. and Albert, M.S. (1988) Alzheimer's disease and other dementing disorders. In M.S. Albert and M.B. Moss (eds) *Geriatric Neuropsychology.* New York: Guilford.

Moss, S.C., Goldberg, D., Patel, D. and Wilkin, D. (1993) Psychiatric morbidity in older people with moderate and severe learning disability (mental retardation). Part I: Development and reliability of the patient interview (the PAS-ADD). *British Journal of Psychiatry, 163*, 471–80.

Moulin, C., Thompson, R., Wright, D. and Conway, M. (2007) Eyewitness memory in older adults. In M. Toglia, J. Read, D. Ross and R. Lindsay (eds) *The Handbook of Eyewitness Psychology, Vol 1: Memory for Events.* Mahwah: Lawrence Erlbaum.

Mrak, R. and Griffin, W. (2007) Dementia with Lewy bodies: Definition, diagnosis, and pathogenic relationship to Alzheimer's disease. *Neuropsychiatric Disease and Treatment, 3*, 619–25.

Mroczek, D.K. and Kolarz, C.M (1998) The effect of age on positive and negative affect: A developmental perspective on happiness. *Journal of Personality and Social Psychology, 75*, 1333–49.

Mroczek, D.K. and Spiro, A. (2003) Modeling intraindividual change in personality traits: Findings from the Normative Aging Study. *The Journals of Gerontology Series B: Psychological Sciences and Social Sciences, 58*, 3, 153–65.

Mroczek, D.K., Spiro, A. and Turiano, N. (2009) Do health behaviors explain the effect of neuroticism on mortality? Longitudinal findings from the VA Normative Aging Study. *Journal of Research in Personality, 43*, 653–9.

Mueller-Johnson, K. and Ceci, S. (2007) The elderly eyewitness: A review and prospectus. In M. Toglia, J. Read, D. Ross and R. Lindsay (eds) *The Handbook of Eyewitness Psychology, Vol 1: Memory for Events.* Mahwah: Lawrence Erlbaum.

Mullan, P. (2002) *The Imaginary Time Bomb: Why an Ageing Population is Not a Social Problem.* New York: I.B. Tauris.

Multhaup, K.S., Balota, D.A. and Cowan, N. (1996) Implications of aging, lexicality and item length for the mechanisms underlying memory span. *Psychonomic Bulletin and Review, 3*, 112–20.

Mund, I., Bell, R. and Buchner, A. (2010) Age differences in reading with distraction: Sensory or inhibitory deficits? *Psychology and Aging, 25*, 886–97.

Murayama, N., Iseki, E., Endo, T., Nagashima, K. *et al.* (2009) Risk factors for delusion of theft in patients with Alzheimer's disease showing mild dementia in Japan. *Aging and Mental Health, 13*, 563–8.

Murphy, C. (1985) Cognitive and chemosensory influences on age-related changes in the ability to identify blended foods. *Journal of Gerontology, 40*, 217–22.

Murphy, C. (1999) Loss of olfactory function in dementing disease. *Physiology and Behavior, 66*, 177–82.

Murphy, C. (2008) The chemical senses and nutrition in older adults. *Journal of Nutrition for the Elderly, 27*, 247–65.

Murphy, D.R., Craik, F.I.M., Li, K.Z.H. and Schneider, B.A. (2000) Comparing the effects of aging and background noise of short-term memory performance. *Psychology and Aging, 15*, 323–34.

Murphy, E.A. (1978) Genetics of longevity in man. In E.L. Schneider (ed.) *The Genetics of Aging.* New York: Plenum.

Myers, S.M. and Booth, A. (1996) Men's retirement and marital quality. *Journal of Family Issues, 17*, 336–57.

Myerson, J., Emery, L., White, D.A. and Hale, S. (2003) Effects of age, domain and processing demands on memory span: Evidence for differential decline. *Aging, Neuropsychology and Cognition, 10*, 20–27.

Myerson, J., Ferraro, F.R., Hale, S. and Lima, S.D. (1992) General slowing in semantic priming and word recognition. *Psychology and Aging, 7*, 257–70.

Myerson, J., Hale, S., Chen, J. and Lawrence, B. (1997) General lexical slowing and the semantic priming effect: The roles of age and ability. *Acta Psychologica, 96*, 83–101.

Nagdee, M. and O'Brien, G. (2009) Dementia in developmental disability. In G. O'Brien and L. Rosenbloom (eds) *Developmental Disability and Ageing.* London: MacKeith Press, 10–30.

Nair, A., Gavett, B., Damman, M., Dekker, W. *et al.* (2010) Clock Drawing Test ratings by dementia specialists: Interrater reliability and diagnostic accuracy. *Journal of Neuropsychiatry and Clinical Neurosciences, 22*, 85–92.

Namazi, K.H. and McClintic, M. (2003) Computer use among elderly persons in long-term care facilities. *Educational Gerontology, 29*, 535–50.

Nash, P., Stuart-Hamilton, I. and Mayer, P. (2009) The effects of specific education and direct experience on implicit and explicit measures of ageism. *Journal of Nutrition Health and Ageing, 13*, 683.

National Council on Aging (1975) *The Myth and Reality of Aging in America.* Washington, DC: National Council on Aging.

National Endowment for the Arts (2007) *To Read or Not to Read.* Washington: National Endowment for the Arts.

National Health Service (2011) Live Well. Available at www.nhs.uk/livewell/Pages/Livewellhub. aspx, accessed on 21 January 2011.

National Statistics Online. Available at www.statistics.gov.uk.

Naveh-Benjamin, M., Guez, J., Kilb, A. and Reedy, S. (2004) The associative memory deficit of older adults: Further support using face-name associations. *Psychology and Aging, 19*, 541–6.

Nay, R., McAuliffe, L. and Bauer, M. (2007) Sexuality: From stigma, stereotypes and secrecy to coming out, communication and choice. *International Journal of Older People Nursing, 2*, 76–80.

Naylor, E. and Clare, L. (2008) Awareness of memory functioning, autobiographical memory and identity in early-stage dementia. *Neuropsychological Rehabilitation, 18*, 590–606.

Neargarder, S.A., Stone, E.R., Cronin-Golomb, A. and Oross, S. (2003) The impact of acuity on performance of four clinical measures of contrast sensitivity in Alzheimer's disease. *The Journals of Gerontology Series B: Psychological Sciences and Social Sciences, 58*, 54–62.

Nebes, R.D. (1992) Cognitive dysfunction in Alzheimer's Disease. In F.I.M. Craik and T.A. Salthouse (eds) *The Handbook of Aging and Cognition.* Hillsdale, NJ: Lawrence Erlbaum.

Nebes, R.D. and Brady, C.B. (1990) Preserved organization of semantic attributes in Alzheimer's Disease. *Psychology and Aging, 5*, 574–9.

Neimeyer, R.A. (2001) *Meaning Reconstruction and the Experience of Loss.* Washington, D.C.: American Psychological Association.

Nelson, H.E. and McKenna, P. (1973) The use of current reading ability in the assessment of dementia. *British Journal of Social and Clinical Psychology, 14*, 259–67.

Nelson, H.E. and O'Connell, A. (1978) Dementia: The estimation of premorbid intelligence levels using the New Adult Reading Test. *Cortex, 14*, 234–44.

Nesselroade, J.R. and Salthouse, T.A. (2004) Methodological and theoretical implications of intraindividual variability in perceptual-motor performance. *The Journals of Gerontology Series B: Psychological Sciences and Social Sciences, 59*, 49–55.

Nestle, M. (1999) Animal v. plant foods in human diets and health: Is the historical record unequivocal? *Proceedings of the Nutrition Society, 58*, 211–18.

Nestor, P. (2010) Dementia in Lewy body syndromes: A battle between hearts and minds. *Neurology, 74*, 872–3.

Neugarten, B.L., Havinghurst, R.J. and Tobin, S.S. (1961) The measurement of life satisfaction. *Journal of Gerontology, 16*, 134–43.

Neugarten, B.L., Havinghurst, R.J. and Tobin, S.S. (1968) Personality and pattern of aging. In B.L. Neugarten (ed.) *Middle Age and Aging.* Chicago, IL: Chicago University Press.

Neundorfer, M.M., McClendon, M.J., Smyth, K.A., Stuckey, J.C., Strauss, M.E. and Patterson, M.B. (2001) A longitudinal study of the relationship between levels of depression among persons with Alzheimer's disease and levels of depression among their family caregivers. *The Journals of Gerontology Series B: Psychological Sciences and Social Sciences, 56*, 301–13.

Neupert, S., Mroczek, D. and Spiro, A. (2008) Neuroticism moderates the daily reaction between stressors and memory failures. *Psychology and Aging, 23*, 287–96.

Newman, L. (2004) Elisabeth Kübler-Ross obituary. *British Medical Journal, 329*, 627.

Newson, R.S. and Kemps, E.B. (2005) General lifestyle activities as a predictor of current cognition and cognitive change in older adults: A cross-sectional and longitudinal examination. *Journals of Gerontology Series B: Psychological Sciences and Social Sciences, 60*, 113–120.

Ng, K., Woo, J., Kwan, M. and Sea, M. (2004) Effect of age and disease on taste perception. *Journal of Pain and Symptom Management, 28*, 28–34.

Ngan, R. (2011) Social care and older people. In I. Stuart-Hamilton (ed.) *An Introduction to Gerontology.* Cambridge: Cambridge University Press.

Nicholas, M., Obler, L.K., Au, R. and Albert, M.L. (1996) On the nature of naming errors in aging and dementia: A study of semantic relatedness. *Brain and Language, 54*, 184–95.

Nielsen, T., Vogel, A., Phung, T., Gade, A. and Waldemar, G. (2011) Over- and under-diagnosis of dementia in ethnic minorities: A nationwide register-based study. *International Journal of Geriatric Psychiatry, 26*, 1128.

Nigro, G. and Neisser, U. (1983) Point of view in personal memories. *Cognitive Psychology, 15*, 465–82.

Nimrod, G. (2007) Expanding, reducing, concentrating and diffusing: Post retirement leisure behaviour and life satisfaction. *Leisure Sciences, 29*, 91–111.

Nissen, N.J. and Corkin, S. (1985) Effectiveness of attentional cueing in older and younger adults. *Journal of Gerontology, 40*, 185–191.

Nixon, A. and Narayanasamy, A. (2010) The spiritual needs of neuro-oncology patients from the patients' perspective. *Journal of Clinical Nursing, 19*, 15–6.

Noftie, E. and Fleeson, W. (2010) Age differences in big five behaviour averages and variabilities across the adult life span: Moving beyond retrospective, global summary accounts of personality. *Psychology and Aging, 25*, 95–107.

Nolen-Hoeksema, S. and Ahrens, C. (2002) Age differences and similarities in the correlates of depressive symptoms. *Psychology and Aging, 17,* 116–24.

Nordhus, I.H., VandenBos, G.R., Berg, S. and Fromholt, P. (1998) *Clinical Geropsychology.* Washington, DC: American Psychological Association.

Nordin, S. and Murphy, C. (1996) Impaired sensory and cognitive olfactory function in questionable Alzheimer's disease. *Neuropsychology, 10,* 113–19.

Nordin, S., Razani, L.J., Markison, S. and Murphy, C. (2003) Age-associated increases in intensity discrimination for taste. *Experimental Aging Research, 29,* 371–81.

Norman, A. (1985) *Triple Jeopardy: Growing Old in a Second Homeland.* London: Centre for Policy on Ageing.

Nyberg, L., Maitland, S.B., Rönnlund, M., Bäckman, L. *et al.* (2003) Selective adult age differences in an age-invariant multifactor model of declarative memory. *Psychology and Aging, 18,* 149–160.

O'Brien, G. and Rosenbloom, L. (2009) *Developmental Disability and Ageing.* Chichester: John Wiley.

O'Brien, R. and Wong, P. (2011) Amyloid precursor protein processing and Alzheimer's disease. *Annual Review of Neuroscience, 34,* 185–204.

O'Brien Cousins, S. (2000) 'My heart couldn't take it': Older women's beliefs about exercise benefits and risks. *The Journals of Gerontology Series B: Psychological Sciences and Social Sciences, 55,* 283–94.

O'Connell, H., Chin, A.V., Cunningham, C. and Lawlor, B. (2003) Alcohol use disorders in elderly people – redefining an age old problem in old age. *British Medical Journal, 327,* 664–7.

O'Neill, L. and Morrison, S. (2011) Palliative care for older adults. In I. Stuart-Hamilton (ed.) *An Introduction to Gerontology.* Cambridge: Cambridge University Press.

Obler, L.K., Fein, D., Nicholas, M. and Albert, M.L. (1991) Auditory comprehension and aging: Decline in syntactic processing. *Applied Psycholinguistics, 12,* 433–52.

Oboler, S.K. (1986) Brain death and persistent vegetative states. *Clinical and Geriatric Medicine, 2,* 547–76.

OECD (1988) *Ageing Populations: The Social Policy Implications.* Paris: OECD.

OECD (2004) *Ageing and Employment Policies: United Kingdom.* London: OECD.

Oeppen, J. and Vaupel, J.W. (2002) Broken limits to life expectancy. *Science, 296,* 1029–31.

Office for National Statistics (2010a) *Mid-year Population Estimates.* London: HMSO.

Office for National Statistics (2010b) *Life Expectancy at Birth and at Age 65 by Local Areas in the United Kingdom, 2007–9.* London: HMSO.

Office for National Statistics (2011) *Death Registrations Summary tables, England and Wales, 2010.* London: HMSO.

Ohlemiller, K.K. (2008) Recent findings and emerging questions in cochlear noise injury. *Hearing research, 245,* 5–17.

Oishi, S., Whitchurch, E., Miao, F., Kurtz, J. and Park, J. (2009) 'Would I be happier if I moved?' Retirement status and cultural variations in the anticipated and actual levels of happiness. *Journal of Positive Psychology, 4,* 437–46.

Ojha, H. and Pramanick, M. (2010) Do personality characteristics change with advancement of age? *Journal of the Indian Academy of Applied Psychology, 36,* 55–68.

Okamoto, K. and Tanaka, Y. (2004) Subjective usefulness and 6-year mortality risks among elderly persons in Japan. *The Journals of Gerontology Series B: Psychological Sciences and Social Sciences, 59,* 246–9.

Okun, M., Pugliese, J. and Rook, K. (2007) Unpacking the relation between extraversion and volunteering in later life: The role of social capital. *Personality and Individual Differences, 42,* 1467–77.

Old, S.R. and Naveh-Benjamin, M. (2008) Age-related changes in memory: Experimental approaches. In S. Hofer and D. Alwin (eds) *Handbook of Cognitive Aging: Interdisciplinary Perspectives.* Thousand Oaks: Sage.

Olichney, J.M., Iragui, V.J., Kutas, M., Nowacki, R., Morris, S. and Jeste, D.V. (1998) Relationship between auditory P300 amplitude and age of onset of schizophrenia in older patients. *Psychiatry Research, 79,* 241–54.

Oliver, C., Adams, D. and Kaisy, S. (2008) Ageing, dementia and people with intellectual disability. In R. Woods, and L. Clare (eds) *Handbook of the Clinical Psychology of Ageing.* 2nd edition. New York: John Wiley and Sons, 341–9.

Olsen, D.R., Torrance, N. and Hildyard, A. (eds) (1985) *Literacy, Language and Learning.* Cambridge: Cambridge University Press.

Olshansky, S.J., Carnes, B.A., Hershow, R., Passaro, D. *et al.* (2005) Misdirection on the road to Shangri-La. *Science of Aging Knowledge Environment, 1,* 15.

Oltmanns, T. and Balsis, S. (2011) Personality disorders in later life: Questions about the measurement, course, and impact of disorders. *Annual Review of Clinical Psychology, 7,* 321–49.

Onwuteaka-Philipsen, B., Rurup, M., Pasman, H., Roeline, W. and van der Heide, A. (2010) The last phase of life: Who requests and who receives euthanasia or physician-assisted suicide? *Medical Care, 48,* 596–603.

Orbelo, D.M., Grim, M.A., Talbot, R.E. and Ross, E.D. (2005) Impaired comprehension of affective prosody in elderly subjects is not predicted by age-related hearing loss or age-related cognitive decline. *Journal of Geriatric Psychiatry and Neurology, 18,* 25–32.

Orbuch, T.L., House, J.S., Mero, R.P. and Webster, P.S. (1996) Marital quality over the life course. *Social Psychology Quarterly, 59,* 162–71.

Ordovas, J.M. (2010) Nutrition and cognitive health. In C.L. Cooper, U. Goswami and B. Sahakian (eds) *Mental Capital and Wellbeing.* London: Wiley-Blackwell.

Osborn, D.P.J., Fletcher, A.E., Smeeth, L. Stirling, S. *et al.* (2003) Factors associated with depression in a representative sample of 14,217 people aged 75 and over in the United Kingdom: Results from the MRC trial of assessment and management of older people in the community. *International Journal of Geriatric Psychiatry, 18,* 623–30.

Ostir, G.V., Ottenbacher, K.J. and Markides, K.S. (2004) Onset of frailty in older adults and the protective role of positive affect. *Psychology and Aging, 19,* 402–8.

Ostwald, S. and Dyer, C. (2011) Fostering resilience, promoting health and preventing disease in older adults. In I. Stuart-Hamilton (ed) *An Introduction to Gerontology.* Cambridge: Cambridge University Press.

Oswald, F., Jopp, D., Rott, C. and Wahl, H. (2011) Is ageing in place a resource for or risk to life satisfaction? *The Gerontologist, 51,* 238–47.

Owens, W.A. (1959) Is age kinder to the initially more able? *Journal of Gerontology, 14,* 334–7.

Oyer, H.J. and Deal, L.V. (1989) Temporal aspects of speech and the aging process. *Folia-Phoniatrica, 37,* 109–112.

Pache, M., Smeets, C.H.W., Gasio, P.F., Savaskan, E. *et al.* (2003) Colour vision deficiencies in Alzheimer's disease. *Age and Ageing, 32,* 422–6.

Paganini-Hill, A. and Clark, L. (2007) Preliminary assessment of cognitive function in older adults by clock drawing, box copying and narrative writing. *Dementia and Geriatric Cognitive Disorders, 23,* 74–81.

Palacios, S., Tobar, A.C. and Menendez, C. (2002) Sexuality in the climacteric years. *Maturitas, 43,* 69–77.

Palinkas, L.A., Wingard, D.L. and Barrett-Connor, E. (1996) Depressive symptoms in overweight and obese older adults: A test of the 'jolly fat' hypothesis. *Journal of Psychosomatic Research, 40,* 59–66.

Palmore, E. and Cleveland, W. (1976) Aging, terminal decline and terminal drop. *Journal of Gerontology, 31,* 76–81.

Papalia, D.E. (1972) The status of several conservation abilities across the life-span. *Human Development, 15,* 229–43.

Park, D.C., Hertzog, C., Kidder, D.P., Morrell, R. and Mayhorn, C. (1997) Effect of age on event-based and time-based prospective memory. *Psychology and Aging, 12,* 314–27.

Park, D.C. and Reuter-Lorenz, P.A. (2009) The adaptive brain: Aging and neurocognitive scaffolding. *Annual Review of Psychology, 60,* 173–96.

Park, D.C. and Shaw, R.J. (1992) Effect of environmental support on implicit and explicit memory in younger and older adults. *Psychology and Aging, 7,* 632–42.

Park, J., Carp, J., Hebrank, A., Park, D.C. and Polk, T. (2010) Neural specificity predicts fluid processing ability in older adults. *Journal of Neuroscience, 30,* 9253–9.

Park, N. (2009) The relationship of social engagement to psychological well-being of older adults in assisted living facilities. *Journal of Applied Gerontology, 28,* 461–81.

Park, S.N., Back, S.A., Park, K.H., Kim, D.K. *et al.* (2010) Comparison of cochlear morphology and apoptosis in mouse models of presbycusis. *Clinical and Experimental Otorhinolaryngology, 3,* 126–35.

Park, Y., Song, M., Cho, B., Lim, J. *et al.* (2011) The effects of an integrated health education and exercise program in community-dwelling older adults with hypertension: A randomized controlled trial. *Patient Education and Counselling, 82,* 133–7.

Parker, L.D., Cantrell, C. and Demi, A.S. (1997) Older adults' attitudes toward suicide: Are there race and gender differences? *Death Studies, 21,* 289–98.

Parkes, C. (2000) Comments on Dennis Klass's article 'Developing a cross-cultural model of grief'. *Omega: Journal of Death and Dying, 41,* 323–6.

Parkin, A.J. and Java, R. (1999) Deterioration of frontal lobe function in normal aging: Influences of fluid intelligence versus perceptual speed. *Neuropsychology, 13,* 539–45.

Parnes, H. (1981) *Work and Retirement: A Longitudinal Study of Men.* Cambridge, MA: MIT Press.

Parry, R. and Stuart-Hamilton, I. (2009) Animism begins at forty: Evidence that animism and other naïve beliefs are established before the onset of old age. *Educational Gerontology, 36,* 1043–50.

Partington, L. (2006) The challenges in adopting care pathways for the dying for use in care homes. *International Journal of Older People Nursing, 1,* 51–5.

Pasupathi, M. and Carstensen, L.L. (2003) Age and emotional experience during mutual reminiscing. *Psychology and Aging, 18,* 430–42.

Pasupathi, M., Henry, R.M. and Carstensen, L.L. (2002) Age and ethnicity differences in storytelling to young children: Emotionality, relationality and socialization. *Psychology and Aging, 17,* 610–21.

Patel, D., Goldberg, D. and Moss, S. (1993) Psychiatric morbidity in older people with moderate and severe learning disability. II: The prevalence study. *British Journal of Psychiatry, 163,* 481–91.

Pattison, E. (1977) Death through the life cycle. In E. Pattison (ed.) *The Experience of Dying.* Englewood Cliffs, NJ: Prentice-Hall.

Paukert, A., Phillips, L., Cully, J., Loboprabhu, S. *et al.* (2009) Integration of religion into cognitive-behavioral therapy for geriatric anxiety and depression. *Journal of Psychiatric Practice, 15,* 103–12.

Paz, J. and Aleman, S. (1998) The Yaqui elderly of Old Pascua. *Journal of Gerontological Social Work, 30,* 47–59.

Peake, M.D. and Thompson, S. (2003) Ageism in the management of lung cancer. *Age and Ageing, 32,* 171–7.

Pearman, A., Andreoletti, C. and Isaacowitz, D. (2010) Sadness prediction and response: Effects of age and agreeableness. *Aging and Mental Health, 14,* 355–63.

Pearson, J.D., Morrell, C.H., Gordon-Salant, S., Brant, L.J. *et al.* (1995) Gender differences in a longitudinal study of age-associated hearing loss. *Journal of the Acoustical Society of America, 97,* 1196–205.

Peck, R.C. (1968) Psychological developments in the second half of life. In B.L. Neugarten (ed.) *Middle Age and Aging: A Reader in Social Psychology.* Chicago, IL: University of Chicago Press.

Peelle, J., Troiani, V., Wingfield, A. and Grossman, M. (2010) Neural processing during older adults' comprehension of spoken sentences. Age differences in resource allocation and connectivity. *Cerebral Cortex, 20,* 773–82.

Pelletier, A.L., Thomas, J. and Shaw, F.R. (2009) Vision loss in older persons. *American Family Physician, 79,* 963–70.

Penninx, B.W., Beekman, A.T.F., Ormel, J., Kriegsman, D.M.W. *et al.* (1996) Psychological status among elderly people with chronic diseases: Does type of disease play a part? *Journal of Psychosomatic Research, 40,* 521–34.

Penninx, B.W.J.H., Rejeski, W.J., Pandya, J., Miller, M.E. *et al.* (2002) Exercise and depressive symptoms: A comparison of aerobic and resistance exercise effects on emotional and physical function in older persons with high and low depressive symptomatology. *The Journals of Gerontology Series B: Psychological Sciences and Social Sciences, 57,* 124–32.

Peraita, H. (2007) Semantic memory in healthy aging. In R. Fernandez-Ballesteros (ed.) (2007) *Geropsychology: European Perspectives for an Aging World.* Ashland: Hogrefe and Huber.

Peretz, J.A. and Cummings, J.L. (1988) Subcortical dementia. In U. Holden (ed.) *Neuropsychology and Ageing.* London: Croom Helm.

Perez-Achaiga, N., Nelson, S. and Hassiotis, A. (2009) Instruments for the detection of depressive symptoms in people with intellectual disabilities: A systematic approach. *Journal of Intellectual Disabilities, 13,* 55–76.

Perfect, T.J. (1994) What can Brinley plots tell us about cognitive aging? *Journal of Gerontology: Psychological Sciences, 49,* 60–4.

Perfect, T.J. and Hollins, T.S. (1999) Feeling-of-knowing judgments do not predict subsequent recognition performance for eyewitness memory. *Journal of Experimental Psychology: Applied, 5,* 250–64.

Perfect, T.J. and Maylor, E.A. (eds) (2000) *Models of Cognitive Aging.* Oxford: Oxford University Press.

Perkins, E.A. and Small, B.J. (2006) Aspects of cognitive functioning in adults with intellectual disabilities. *Journal of Policy and Practice in Intellectual Disabilities, 3,* 181–94.

Perlmutter, L.C. and Monty, R.A. (1989) Motivation and aging. In L.W. Poon, D.C. Rubin and B.A. Wilson (eds) *Everyday Cognition in Adulthood and Later Life.* Cambridge: Cambridge University Press.

Perlmutter, M. (1978) What is memory aging the aging of? *Developmental Psychology, 14,* 330–45.

Perlmutter, M., Adams, C., Berry, S., Kaplan, M. and Person, D. (1987) Aging and memory. In K.W. Schaie (ed.) *Annual Review of Gerontology and Geriatrics, 7.* New York: Springer, 57–92.

Perlmutter, M. and Hall, E. (1992) *Adult Development and Aging.* New York: Wiley.

Perlow, E. (2010) Accessibility: Global gateway to health literacy. *Health Promotion Practice, 11,* 123–31.

Perneczky, R., Drzezga, A., Boecker, H., Cebalios-Baumann, A. *et al.* (2010) Metabolic alterations associated with impaired clock drawing in Lewy body dementia. *Psychiatry Research: Neuroimaging, 181,* 85–9.

Perneczky, R., Wagenpfeil, S., Lunetta, K., Cupples, L. *et al.* (2009) Education attenuates the effect of medial temporal lobe atrophy on cognitive function in Alzheimer's disease: The MIRAGE study. *Journal of Alzheimer's Disease, 17,* 855–62.

Perrotin, A., Isingrini, M., Souchay, C., Clarys, D. and Taconnat, L. (2006) Episodic feeling of knowing accuracy and cued recall in the elderly: Evidence for double dissociation involving executive functioning and processing speed. *Acta Psychologia, 122,* 58–73.

Persad, C.C., Abeles, N., Zacks, R.T. and Denburg, N.L. (2002) Inhibitory changes after age 60 and their relationship to measures of attention and memory. *The Journals of Gerontology Series B: Psychological Sciences and Social Sciences, 57,* 223–32.

Persey, C. and Schmitter-Edgecombe, M. (2011) Quantitative and qualitative analyses of the clock drawing test in mild cognitive impairment and Alzheimer disease: Evaluation of a modified scoring system. *Journal of Geriatric Psychiatry and Neurology, 24,* 108–18.

Peterson, L. and Litaker, D. (2010) County-level poverty is equally associated with unmet health care needs in rural and urban settings. *Journal of Rural Health, 26,* 373–82.

Petit, T.L. (1982) Neuroanatomical and clinical neuropsychological changes in aging and senile dementia. In F.I.M. Craik and S. Trehbub (eds) *Aging and Cognitive Processes.* New York: Plenum.

Petros, T., Tabar, L., Cooney, T. and Chabot, R.J. (1983) Adult age differences in sensitivity to semantic structure of prose. *Developmental Psychology, 19,* 907–14.

Pevey, C., Jones, T. and Yarber, A. (2009) How religion comforts the dying: A qualitative inquiry. *Omega: Journal of Death and Dying, 58,* 41–59.

Pew Research Center (2010) Americans spending more time following the news. Washington: Pew News Center. Available at http://people-press.org/reports/pdf/652.pdf, accessed on 21 January 2012.

Phillips, L. (2005) Both specific functions and general ability can be useful: But it depends on what type of research question you ask. *Cortex, 41,* 236–7.

Phillips, L.H. (1999) Age and individual differences in letter fluency. *Developmental Neuropsychology, 15,* 249–67.

Phillips, L.H. and Andres, P. (2010) The cognitive neuroscience of aging: New findings on compensation and connectivity. *Cortex, 46,* 421–4.

Phillips, L.H. and Della Sala, S. (1998) Aging, intelligence and anatomical segregation in the frontal lobes. *Learning and Individual Differences, 10,* 217–43.

Phillips, N.A. and Lesperance, D. (2003) Breaking the waves: Age differences in electrical brain activity when reading text with distractors. *Psychology and Aging, 18,* 126–39.

Phillips, S. and Williams, J.M.G. (1997) Cognitive impairment, depression and the specificity of autobiographical memory in the elderly. *British Journal of Clinical Psychology, 36,* 341–7.

Pichora-Fuller, M.K., Schneider, B.A. and Daneman, M. (1995) How young and old adults listen to and remember speech in noise. *Journal of the Acoustical Society of America, 97,* 593–608.

Pijnappels, M., Delbaere, K., Sturnieks, D.L. and Lord, S.R. (2010) The association between stepping reaction time and falls in older adults – a path analysis model. *Age and Ageing, 39,* 99–104.

Pinazo-Hernandis, S. (2010) Family reciprocity and caring relationships in ageing societies. *Journal of Intergenerational Relationships, 8,* 421–4.

Pinquart, M. (2001) Correlates of subjective health in older adults: A meta-analysis. *Psychology and Aging, 16,* 414–26.

Pinquart, M. and Sörensen, S. (2000) Influences of socioeconomic status, social network and competence on subjective well-being in later life: A meta-analysis. *Psychology and Aging, 15,* 187–224.

Pinquart., M. and Sörensen, S. (2001) Gender differences in self-concept and psychological well-being in old age: a meta-analysis. *The Journals of Gerontology Series B: Psychological Sciences and Social Sciences, 56,* 195–213.

Piolino, P., Coste, C., Martinelli, P., Mace, A. *et al.* (2010) Reduced specificity of autobiographical memory and aging: Do the executive and feature binding functions of working memory have a role? *Neuropsychologia, 48,* 429–40.

Piquado, T., Isaacowitz, D. and Wingfield, A. (2010) Pupillometry as a measure of cognitive effort in younger and older adults. *Psychophysiology, 47,* 560–9.

Pitkala, K.H., Laurila, J.V., Strandberg, T.E. and Tilvis, R.S. (2005) Prognostic significance of delirium in frail older people. *Dementia and Geriatric Cognitive Disorders, 19*, 158–63.

Plancher, G., Gyselinck, V., Nicolas, S. and Piolino, P. (2010) Age effect on components of episodic memory and feature binding: A virtual reality study. *Neuropsychology, 24*, 379–90.

Plassman, B., Langa, K., McCammon, R., Fisher, G. *et al.* (2011) Incidence of dementia and cognitive impairment, not dementia in the United States. *Annals of Neurology, 70*, 418–26.

Plassman, B.L., Welsh, K.A., Helms, M., Brandt, J., Page, W.F. and Breitner, J.C. (1995) Intelligence and education as predictors of cognitive state in late life: A 50-year follow-up. *Neurology, 45*, 1446–50.

Plemons, J.K., Willis, S.L. and Baltes, P.B. (1978) Modifiability of fluid intelligence in aging: A short-term longitudinal training approach. *Journal of Gerontology, 33*, 224–31.

Polizzi, K.G. and Millikin, R.J. (2002) Attitudes toward the elderly: Identifying problematic usage of ageist and overextended terminology in research instructions. *Educational Gerontology, 28*, 367–77.

Pollard, A.J. and Prendergast, M. (2004) Depressive pseudodementia in a child with autism. *Developmental Medicine and Child Neurology, 46*, 485–89.

Poon, L.W., Fozard, J.L., Paushock, D.R. and Thomas, J.C. (1979) A questionnaire assessment of age differences in retention of recent and remote events. *Experimental Age Research, 5*, 401–11.

Poon, L.W. and Schaffer, G. (1982) Prospective memory in young and elderly adults. Paper presented at meeting of American Psychological Association, Washington, DC. Cited in West (1988).

Popova, S., Rehm, J., Patra, J. and Zatonski, W. (2007) Comparing alcohol consumption in central and eastern Europe to the other countries? *Alcohol and Alcoholism, 42*, 465–73.

Population Reference Bureau (2010) *World Population Data Sheet.* Washington, DC: Population Reference Bureau.

Post, S.G. and Binstock, R.H. (2004) *The Fountain of Youth: Cultural, Scientific and Ethical Perspectives on a Biomedical Goal.* Oxford: Oxford University Press.

Potter, G., Helms, M. and Plassman, B. (2008) Associations of job demands and intelligence with cognitive performance among men in later life. *Neurology, 70*, 1803–8.

Potts, M. (2002) Fear has basis in reason. *British Medical Journal, 325*, 598.

Powell, R.R. (1974) Psychological effects of exercise therapy upon institutionalized geriatric mental patients. *Journal of Gerontology, 29*, 157–61.

Pratt, M.W., Diessner, R., Hunsberger, B., Pancer, S.M. and Savoy, K. (1991) Four pathways in the analysis of adult development and aging. *Psychology and Aging, 6*, 666–75.

Pratt, M.W. and Norris, J.E. (1994) *The Social Psychology of Aging: A Cognitive Perspective.* Cambridge, MA: Blackwells.

Preston, F., Shapiro, P. and Keene, J. (2007) Successful aging and gambling. Predictors of gambling risk among older adults in Las Vegas. *American Behavioral Scientist, 51*, 102–21.

Preston, M. (2007) The LCP for the dying patient: A guide to implementation. *End of Life Care, 1*, 61–8.

Price, C. and Balaswamy, S. (2009) Beyond health and wealth: Predictors of women's retirement satisfaction. *International Journal of Aging and Human Development, 68*, 195–214.

Priest, L., Nayak, U.S.L and Stuart-Hamilton, I. (2006) Website task performance by older adults. *Journal of Behaviour and Information Technology, 26*, 189–95.

Prigerson, H., Horowitz, M., Jacobs, S., Parkes, C. *et al.* (2009) Prolonged grief disorder: Psychometric validation of criteria proposed for DSM-V and ICD-11. *Public Library of Science Medicine, 6*. Available at: www.plosmedicine.org/article/info%3Adoi%2F10.1371%2Fjournal.pmed.1000121, accessed on 21 January 2012.

Pritchard, J. (1995) *The Abuse of Older People: A Training Manual for Detection and Prevention.* 2nd edition. London: Jessica Kingsley Publishers.

Purdue, U. (1966) Age and mental abilities: A second adult follow-up. *Journal of Educational Psychology, 57*, 311–25.

Purohit, D.P., Perl, D.P., Haroutunian, V., Powchik, P., Davidson, M. and Davis, K.L. (1998) Alzheimer disease and related neurodegenerative diseases in elderly patients with schizophrenia. A postmortem neuropathologic study of 100 cases. *Archives of General Psychiatry, 55*, 205–11.

Pushkar, D., Basevitz, P., Arbuckle, T., Nohara-LeClair, M., Lapidus, S. and Peled, M. (2000) Social behavior and off-target verbosity in elderly people. *Psychology and Aging, 15*, 361–74.

Qiu, C., Xu, W., Winblad, B. and Fratiglioni, L. (2010) Vascular risk profiles for dementia and Alzheimer's disease in very old people: A population-based study. *Journal of Alzheimer's Disease, 20*, 293–300.

Quandt, S.A. and Chao, D. (2000) Gender differences in nutritional risk among older rural adults. *Journal of Applied Gerontology, 19*, 138–50.

Quental, N., Brucki, S, and Bueno, O. (2009) Visuospatial function in early Alzheimer's disease: Preliminary study. *Dementia* and *Neuropsychologia, 3*, 234–40.

Quetelet, A. (1836) *Sur L'Homme et le Développement de ses Facultés*. Brussels: Haumann.

Quillan, D.A. (1999) Common causes of vision loss in elderly patients. *American Family Physician, 60*, 99–108.

Quin, R., Clare, L., Ryan, P. and Jackson, M. (2009) 'Not of this world': The subjective experience of late-onset psychosis. *Aging* and *Mental Health, 13*, 779–87.

Quinn, M.E., Johnson, M.A., Poon, L.W. and Martin, P. (1997) Factors of nutritional health-seeking behaviors. *Journal of Aging and Health, 9*, 90–104.

Qureshi, H. and Walker, A. (1989) *The Caring Relationship: Elderly People and Their Families*. London: Macmillan.

Rabbitt, P. (1979) Some experiments and a model for changes in attentional selectivity with old age. In F. Hoffmeister and C. Muller (eds) *Bayer Symposium VII. Evaluation of Change*. Bonn: Springer.

Rabbitt, P. (1980) A fresh look at reaction times in old age. In D.G. Stein (ed.) *The Psychology of Ageing: Problems and Perspectives*. New York: Elsevier.

Rabbitt, P. (1982) How do the old know what to do next? In F.I.M.Craik and S. Trehub (eds) *Aging and Cognitive Processes*. New York: Plenum.

Rabbitt, P. (1984) Memory impairment in the elderly. In P.E. Bebbington and R. Jacoby (eds) *Psychiatric Disorders in the Elderly*. London: Mental Health Foundation. 101–19.

Rabbitt, P. (1988) The faster the better? Some comments on the use of information processing rate as an index of change in individual differences in performance. In I. Hindmarch, B. Aufdembrinke and H. Ott (eds) *Psychopharmacology and Reaction Time*. London: Wiley.

Rabbitt, P. (1989) Secondary central effects on memory and attention of mild hearing loss in the elderly. *Acta Neurologica Scandanavica, 40A*, 167–87.

Rabbitt, P. (1990) Applied cognitive gerontology: Some problems, methodologies and data. *Applied Cogntiive Psychology, 4*, 225–46.

Rabbitt, P. (1993) Does it all go together when it goes? *Quarterly Journal of Experimental Psychology, 46A*, 385–434.

Rabbitt, P. (1996) Speed of processing and ageing. In R. Woods (ed.) *Handbook of the Clinical Psychology of Ageing*. Chichester: Wiley, 59–72.

Rabbitt, P. (ed.) (1997) *Methodology of Frontal and Executive Function*. Hove: Taylor and Francis.

Rabbitt, P. (1998) Aging of memory. In R.C. Tallis, S.H.M. Fillit and B.J.C. Brocklehurst (eds) *Brocklehurst's Textbook of Geriatric Medicine and Gerontology*. Edinburgh: Churchill Livingstone, 123–52.

Rabbitt, P., Diggle, P., Holland, F. and McInnes, L. (2004) Practice and drop-out effects during a 17-year longitudinal study of cognitive aging. *The Journals of Gerontology Series B: Psychological Sciences and Social Sciences, 59*, 84–97.

Rabbitt, P. and Goward, L. (1986) Effects of age and raw IQ test scores on mean correct and mean error reaction times in serial choice tasks: A reply to Smith and Brewer. *British Journal of Psychology, 77*, 69–73.

Rabbitt, P., Ibrahim, S., Lunn, M., Scott, M. *et al.* (2008) Age-associate losses of brain volume predict longitudinal cognitive decline over 8 to 20 years. *Neuropsychology, 22*, 3–9.

Rabbitt, P., Lowe, C. and Shilling, V. (2001) Frontal tests and models for cognitive ageing. *European Journal of Cognitive Psychology, 13*, 5–28.

Rabbitt, P., Mogapi, O., Scott, M., Thacker, N. *et al.* (2008) Effects of global atrophy, white matter lesions, and cerebral blood flow on age-related changes in speed, memory, intelligence, vocabulary, and frontal function. *Neuropsychology, 21*, 684–95.

Rabbitt, P., Osman, O., Moore, B. and Stollery, B. (2001) There are stable individual differences in performance variability, both from moment to moment and from day to day. *Quarterly Journal of Experimental Psychology: Human Experimental Psychology, 54*, 981–1003.

Rabbitt, P., Scott, M., Lunn, M., Thacker, N. *et al.* (2007) Matter lesions account for all age-related declines in speed but not in intelligence. *Neuropsychology, 21*, 363–70.

Rabbitt, P., Watson, P., Donlan, C., McInnes, L. *et al.* (2002) Effects of death within 11 years on cognitive performance in old age. *Psychology and Aging, 17*, 468–81.

Rabbitt, P. and Winthorpe, C. (1988) What do old people remember? The Galton paradigm reconsidered. In M.M. Gruneberg, P.E. Morris and R.N. Sykes (eds) *Practical Aspects of Memory, Volume 2*. Chichester: Wiley.

Rabbitt, P.M.A., Lunn, M. and Wong, D. (2008a) Death, dropout, and longitudinal measurements of cognitive change in old age. *The Journals of Gerontology Series B: Psychological Sciences and Social Sciences, 63B*, 271–8.

Rabbitt, P.M.A., Lunn, M., Wong, D. and Cobain, M. (2008b) Age and ability affect practice gains in longitudinal studies of cognitive change. *The Journals of Gerontology Series B: Psychological Sciences and Social Sciences, 63B*, 235–40.

Radermacher, H., Feldman, S., Lorains, F. and Bird, S. (2010) Exploring the role of family and older people's access to food in different cultures: Will the children be there to help? *Journal of Intergenerational Relationships, 8*, 354–68.

Raguet, M.L., Campbell, D.A., Berry, D.T.R., Schmitt, F.A. *et al.* (1996) Stability of intelligence and intellectual predictors in older persons. *Psychological Assessment, 8*, 154–60.

Rahhal, T.A., Hasher, L. and Colcombe, S.J. (2001) Instructional manipulations and age differences in memory: Now you see them, now you don't. *Psychology and Aging, 16*, 697–706.

Rakerd, B., Van der Velde, T.J. and Hartmann, W.M. (1998) Sound localization in the median sagittal plane by listeners with presbyacusis. *Journal of American Academy of Audiology, 9*, 466–497.

Rana, A., Kabir, Z., Lundborg, C. and Wahlin, A. (2010) Health education improves both arthritis-related illness and self-rated health: An intervention study among older people in rural Bangladesh. *Public Health, 124*, 705–12.

Ranchor, A.V., Sanderman, R., Bouma, J., Buunk, B.P. and van de Heuvel, W.J. (1997) An exploration of the relation between hostility and disease. *Journal of Behavioral Medicine, 20*, 223–40.

Rank, M. and Williams, J. (2010) A life course approach to understanding poverty among older American adults. *Families in Society, 91*, 337–41.

Rapp, A. and Wild, B. (2011) Nonliteral language in Alzheimer dementia: A review. *Journal of the International Neuropsychological Society, 17*, 207–18.

Raskin, A. (1979) Signs and symptoms of psychopathology in the elderly. In A. Raskin and L.F. Jarvik (eds) *Psychiatric Symptoms and Cognitive Loss in the Elderly*. Washington, DC: Hemisphere.

Ratcliff, R., Thapar, A., Gomez, P. and McKoon, G. (2004). A diffusion model analysis of the effects of aging in the lexical-decision task. *Psychology and Aging, 19*, 278–89.

Ratcliff, R., Thapar, A. and McKoon, G. (2001) The effects of aging on reaction time in a signal detection task. *Psychology and Aging, 16*, 323–41.

Ratner, H.H., Schell, D.A., Crimmins, A., Mittelman, D. and Baldinelli, L. (1987) Changes in adults' prose recall: Aging or cognitive demands? *Developmental Psychology, 23*, 521–5.

Rayburn, T.M. and Stonecypher, J.F. (1996) Diagnostic differences related to age and race of involuntarily committed psychiatric patients. *Psychological Reports, 79*, 881–2.

Raymer, A.M. and Berndt, R.S. (1996) Reading lexically without semantics: Evidence from patients with probable Alzheimer's disease. *Journal of the International Neuropsychological Society, 2*, 340–9.

Rayner, K., Reichie, E., Stroud, M., Williams, C. and Pollatsek, A. (2006) The effect of word frequency, word predictability, and font difficulty on the eye movements of young and older readers. *Psychology and Aging, 21*, 448–65.

Raz, N. and Lindenberger, U. (2010) News of cognitive cure for age-related brain shrinkage is premature: A comment on Burgmans *et al.* (2009) *Neuropsychology, 24*, 255–7.

Raz, N., Rodrigue, K.M., Kennedy, K.M. and Land, S. (2009) Genetic and vascular modifiers of age-sensitive cognitive skills: Effects of COMT, BDNF, ApoE, and hypertension. *Neuropsychology, 23*, 105–16.

Razani, J., Kakos, B., Orieta-Barbalace, C., Wong, J. *et al.* (2007) Predicting caregiver burden from daily functional abilities of patients with mild dementia. *Journal of the American Geriatrics Society, 55*, 1415–20.

Ready, R., Vaidya, J., Watson, D., Latzman, R. *et al.* (2011) Age-group differences in facets of positive and negative affect. *Aging and Mental Health, 15*, 784–95.

Rebok, G.W. (1987) *Life-Span Cognitive Development.* New York: Holt, Rinehart and Winston.

Receputo, G., Mazzoleni, G., Di Fazio, I., Alessandria, I. *et al.* (1996) Study on the sense of taste in a group of Sicilian centenarians. *Archives of Gerontology and Geriatrics, 5*, 411–14.

Reding, M., Haycox, J. and Blas, J. (1985) Depression in patients referred to a dementia clinic: A three-year prospective study. *Archives of Neurology, 42*, 894–6.

Reed, I.C. (2005) Creativity: Self-perceptions over time. *International Journal of Aging and Human Development, 60*, 1–18.

Reese, C. and Cherry, K. (2006) Effects of age and ability on self-reported memory functioning and knowledge of memory aging. *Journal of Genetic Psychology, 167*, 221–40.

Reichard, S., Livson, F. and Peterson, P.G. (1962) *Aging and Personality: A Study of 87 Older Men.* New York: Wiley.

Reicher-Roessler, A., Loeffler, W. and Munk-Jorgensen, P. (1997) What do we really know about late-onset schizophrenia? *European Archives of Psychiatry and Clinical Neuroscience, 247*, 195–208.

Reid, M.C., Boutros, N.N., O'Connor, P.G., Cadariu, A. and Concato, J. (2002) The health-related effects of alcohol use in older persons: A systematic review. *Substance Abuse, 23*, 149–64.

Reilly, J. and Peelie, J. (2008) Effects of semantic impairment on language processing in semantic dementia. *Seminars in Speech and Language, 29*, 32–43.

Reimanis, G. and Green, R.F. (1971) Imminence of death and intellectual decrement in the aged. *Developmental Psychology, 5*, 270–2.

Reisberg, B., Ferris, S.H., de Leon, M.J., Kluger, A. *et al.* (1989) The stage specific temporal course of Alzheimer's disease. In K. Iqbal, H.M. Wisniewski and B. Winblad (eds) *Alzheimer's Disease and Related Disorders.* New York: Alan R. Liss.

Reiss, S. (1988) *Reiss Screen for Maladaptive Behaviors Test Manual.* 2nd edition. Worthington, OH: IDS Publishing.

Renaud, M., Bherer, L. and Maquestiaux, F. (2010) A high level of physical fitness is associated with more efficient response preparation in older adults. *The Journals of Gerontology Series B: Psychological Sciences and Social Sciences, 65*, 317–22.

Reuter-Lorenz, P. and Lustig, C. (2005) Brain aging: Reorganizing discoveries about the aging mind. *Current Opinion in Neurobiology, 15*, 245–51.

Reuter-Lorenz, P.A. and Cappell, K.A. (2008) Neurocognitive aging and the compensation hypothesis. *Current Directions in Psychological Science, 17,* 177–82.

Reuter-Lorenz, P.A. and Park, D. (2010) Human neuroscience and the aging mind: A new look at old problems. *The Journals of Gerontology Series B: Psychological Sciences and Social Sciences, 65,* 405–15.

Revuelta, G. and Lippa, C. (2009) Dementia with Lewy bodies and Parkinson's disease dementia may best be viewed as two distinct entities. *International Psychogeriatrics, 21,* 213–6.

Ribot, T. (1882) *Diseases of Memory.* London: Kegan, Paul, Tench and Co.

Ribovich, J.K. and Erikson, L. (1980) A study of lifelong reading with implications for instructional programs. *Journal of Reading, 24,* 20–6.

Riby, L.M., Meikle, A. and Glover, C. (2004) The effects of age, glucose ingestion and gluco-regulatory control on episodic memory. *Age and Ageing, 33,* 483–7.

Rice, G.E. (1986a) The everyday activities of adults: Implications for prose recall. Part I. *Educational Gerontology, 12,* 173–86.

Rice, G.E. (1986b) The everyday activities of adults: Implications for prose recall. Part II. *Educational Gerontology, 12,* 187–98.

Richards, M., Hardy, R. and Wadsworth, M.E.J. (2005) Alcohol consumption and midlife cognitive change in the British 1946 birth cohort study. *Alcohol and Alcoholism, 40,* 112–17.

Richardson, F., Thomas, M., Filippi, R., Harth, H. and Price, C. (2010) Contrasting effects of vocabulary knowledge on temporal and parietal brain structure across the lifespan. *Journal of Cognitive Neurosciences, 22,* 943–54.

Riddle, D.R., Sonntag, W.E. and Lichtenwalner, R.J. (2004) Microvascular plasticity in aging. *Ageing Research Review, 2,* 149–68.

Riddle, T. (2001) I am Lord Voldemort. *If You're Reading This You've Too Much Time on Your Hands, 4,* 920–70.

Riegel, K.F. and Reigel, R.M. (1972) Development, drop and death. *Developmental Psychology, 6,* 306–19.

Rioux, L. and Werner, C. (2011) Residential satisfaction among aging people living in place. *Journal of Environmental Psychology, 31,* 158–69.

Ritchie, C., King, M., Nolan, F., O'Connor, S. *et al.* (2011) The association between personality disorder and an act of deliberate self harm in the older person. *International Psychogeriatrics, 23,* 299–307.

Ritchie, L. and Tuokko, H. (2010) Clinical decision trees for predicting conversion from cognitive impairment no dementia (CIND) to dementia in a longitudinal population-based study. *Archives of Clinical Neuorpsychology, 26,* 16–25.

Robbins, T.W., James, M., Owen, A.M., Sahakian, B.J. *et al.* (1998) A study of performance on tests from the CANTAB battery sensitive to frontal lobe dysfunction in a large sample of normal volunteers: Implications for theories of executive functioning and cognitive aging. *Journal of the International Neuropsychological Society, 4,* 474–90.

Roberge, R., Berthelot, J.M. and Wolfson, M. (1995) The Health Utility Index: Measuring health differences in Ontario by socioeconomic status. *Health Report, 7,* 29–37.

Robert, C. and Mathey, S. (2007) Aging and lexical inhibition: The effect of orthographic neighborhood frequency in young and older adults. *The Journals of Gerontology Series B: Psychological Sciences and Social Sciences, 62,* 340–2.

Roberts, B.W. and DelVecchio, W.F. (2000) The rank-order consistency of personality from childhood to old age: A quantitative review of longitudinal studies. *Psychological Bulletin, 126,* 3–25.

Roberts, B.W., Walton, K. and Viechtbauer, W. (2006) Patterns of mean-level change in personality traits across the life course: A meta-analysis of longitudinal studies. *Psychological Bulletin, 132,* 1–25.

Robertson, J. (1977) Grandmotherhood: A study of role conceptions. *Journal of Marriage and the Family, 39,* 165–74.

Robertson, S., Myerson, J. and Hale, S. (2006) Are there age differences in intraindividual variability in working memory performance? *The Journals of Gerontology: Series B: Psychological Sciences and Social Sciences, 61,* 18–24.

Robins, R.W., Trzesniewski, K.H., Tracy, J.L., Gosling, D.S. and Potter, J. (2002) Global self-esteem across the life span. *Psychology and Aging, 17,* 423–34.

Robinson, O., Demetre, J. and Corney, R. (2010) Personality and retirement: Exploring the links between the big five personality traits, reasons for retirement and the experience of being retired. *Personality and Individual Differences, 48,* 792–7.

Rocca, W., Petersen, R., Knopman, D., Hebert, L. *et al.* (2011) Trends in the incidence and prevalence of Alzheimer's disease, dementia, and cognitive impairment in the United States. *Alzheimer's and Dementia, 7,* 80–93.

Rodin, G., Lo, C., Mikulincer, M., Donner, A. *et al.* (2009) Pathways to distress: The multiple determinants of depression, hopelessness, and the desire for hastened death in metastatic cancer patients. *Social Science and Medicine, 68,* 562–9.

Roe, B., Beynon, C., Pickering, L. and Duffy, P. (2010) Experiences of drug use and ageing: Health, quality of life, relationship and service implications. *Journal of Advanced Nursing, 66,* 1968–79.

Roe, C., Xiong, C., Grant, E., Miller, P. and Morris, J. (2008) Education and reported onset of symptoms among individuals with Alzheimer disease. *Archives of Neurology, 65,* 108–11.

Roe, C., Xiong, C., Miller, P. and Morris, J. (2007) Education and Alzheimer disease without dementia: Support for the cognitive reserve hypothesis. *Neurology, 68,* 223–8.

Roediger, H. and Geraci, L. (2007) Aging and the misinformation effect: A neuropsychological analysis. *Journal of Experimental Psychology: Learning, Memory and Cognition, 33,* 321–34.

Rogers, W.A. (2000) Attention and aging. In D.C. Park and N. Schwarz (eds) *Cognitive Aging: A Primer.* Philadelphia: Taylor and Francis, 57–74.

Ronnemaa, E., Zethelius, B., Lannfelt, L. and Kilander, L. (2011) Vascular risk factors and dementia: 40-year follow-up of a population-based cohort. *Dementia and Geriatric Cognitive Disorders, 31,* 460–6.

Rook, K.S. (2003) Exposure and reactivity to negative social exchanges: A preliminary investigation using daily diary data. *The Journals of Gerontology Series B: Psychological Sciences and Social Sciences, 58,* 100–11.

Rose, M.R. (1984) Laboratory evolution of postponed senescence in Drosophila-Melanogaster. *Evolution, 38,* 1004–10.

Rose, M.R. (1999) Can human aging be postponed? *Scientific American, 281,* 6, 68–73.

Rosen, D. (2004) Factors associated with illegal drug use among older methadone clients. *The Gerontologist, 44,* 543–8.

Rosenberg, H. (1997) Use and abuse of illicit drugs among older people. In A. Gurnack, A. (ed.) *Older Adults' Misuse of Alcohol, Medicines, and Other Drugs: Research and Practice Issues.* New York: Springer.

Rosenstein, R. and Glickman, A.S. (1994) Type size and performance of the elderly on the Wonderlic Personnel Test. *Journal of Applied Gerontology, 13,* 185–92.

Rosenthal, C.J. (1986) Family supports in later life: Does ethnicity make a difference? *The Gerontologist, 26,* 19–24.

Ross, B., Snyder, J., Aalto, M., McDonald, K. *et al.* (2009) Neural encoding of sound duration persists in older adults. *Neuroimage, 47,* 678–87.

Rossor, M. and Iversen, L.L. (1986) Non-cholinergic neurotransmitter abnormalities in Alzheimer's disease. *British Medical Bulletin, 42,* 70–4.

Roth, D.L., Stevens, A.B., Burgio, L.D. and Burgio, K.L. (2002) Timed-event sequential analysis of agitation in nursing home residents during personal care interactions with nursing assistants. *The Journals of Gerontology Series B: Psychological Sciences and Social Sciences, 57,* 461–8.

Roth, M. (1979) The early diagnosis of Alzheimer's disease: An introduction. In A.I.M. Glen and L. Whalley (eds) *Alzheimer's Disease: Early Recognition of Potentially Reversible Deficits*. Edinburgh: Churchill Livingstone.

Rothermund, K. and Brandstädter, J. (2003) Coping with deficits and losses in later life: From compensatory action to accommodation. *Psychology and Aging, 18*, 896–905.

Rousseau, G.K. and Rogers, W.A. (2002) Effects of processing style and age on schema acquisition. *The Journals of Gerontology Series B: Psychological Sciences and Social Sciences, 57*, 11–18.

Rovio, S., Spulber, G., Nieminen, L., Niskanen, E. *et al.* (2010) The effect of midlife physical activity on structural brain changes in the elderly. *Neurobiology of Aging, 31*, 1927–36.

Rovner, B.W. (2006) The Charles Bonnet syndrome: A review of recent research. *Current Opinions in Ophthalmology, 17*, 275–7.

Rowe, G., Valderrama, S., Hasher, L. and Lenartowicz, A. (2006) Attentional disregulation: A benefit for implicit memory. *Psychology and Aging, 21*, 826–30.

Royal National Institute for the Blind (RNIB) (2011) *Key Information and Statistics Fact Sheet*. London: RNIB.

Rubin, D.C., Rahhal, T.A. and Poon, L.W. (1998) Things learned in early adulthood are remembered best. *Memory and Cognition, 26*, 3–19.

Rubin, D.C. and Schulkind, M.D. (1997a) The distribution of autobiographical memories across the lifespan. *Memory and Cognition, 25*, 859–66.

Rubin, D.C. and Schulkind, M.D. (1997b) Properties of word cues for autobiographical memory. *Psychological Reports, 81*, 47–50.

Rundinger, G. and Lantermann, E.D. (1980) Social determinants of intelligence in old age [English translation]. *Zeitschrift fuer Gerontologie, 13*, 433–41.

Rurup, M., Deeg, D., Poppelaars, J., Kerkhof, A. and Onwuteaka-Philipsen, B. (2011) Wishes to die in older people: A quantitative study of prevalence and associated factors. *Crisis: The Journal of Crisis Intervention and Suicide Prevention, 32*, 194–203.

Russell, D.W. and Catrona, C.E. (1991) Social support, stress and depressive symptoms among the elderly: Test of a process model. *Psychology and Aging, 6*, 190–201.

Ryan, J.J., Lopez, S.J. and Paolo, A.M. (1996) Temporal stability of digit span forward, backward and forward minus backward in persons aged 75–87 years. *Nursopsychiatry, Neuropsychology and Behavioral Neurology, 9*, 206–8.

Ryan, W.J. (1972) Acoustic aspects of the aging voice. *Journal of Gerontology, 27*, 265–8.

Ryff, C.D. (1991) Possible selves in adulthood and old age: A tale of shifting horizons. *Psychology and Aging, 6*, 286–95.

Rypma, B., Prabhakaran, V., Desmond, J.E. and Gabrieli, J.D.E. (2001) Age differences in prefrontal cortical activity in working memory. *Psychology and Aging, 16*, 371–84.

Sabate, J. (1999) Nut consumption, vegetarian diets, ischemic heart disease risk and all-cause mortality: Evidence from epidemiologic studies. *American Journal of Clinical Nutrition, 70*, 500–3.

Sabbagh, M. and Cummings, J. (2011) Progressive cholinergic decline in Alzheimer's Disease: Consideration for treatment with donepezil 23 mg in patients with moderate to severe symptomatology. *BMC Neurology, 11*, 21–7.

Saculu, S., Gustafson, D., Johansson, B., Thorvaldsson, V. *et al.* (2009) The pattern of cognitive symptoms predicts time to dementia onset. *Alzheimer's and Dementia, 5*, 199–206.

Sadavoy, J. (1996) Personality disorder in old age: Symptom expression. *Clinical Gerontologist, 16*, 19–36.

Sadavoy, J., Smith, I., Conn, D.K. and Richards, B. (1995) In E. Murphy and G. Alexopoulos (eds) *Geriatric Psychiatry: Key Research Topics for Clinicians*. Chichester: Wiley, 191–9.

Saizano, F.A., Guastini, L., Mora, R., Dellepiane, M. *et al.* (2010) Nasal tactile sensitivity in the elderly. *Acta Otolaryngology, 130*, 1389–93.

Salib, E. (1997) Elderly suicide and weather conditions: Is there a link? *International Journal of Geriatric Psychiatry, 12*, 937–41.

Salthouse, T. (1982) *Adult Cognition.* New York: Springer.

Salthouse, T. (1985) *A Theory of Cognitive Aging.* Amsterdam: North-Holland.

Salthouse, T. (1991a) Mediation of age differences in cognition by reductions in working memory and speed of processing. *Psychological Science, 2*, 179–83.

Salthouse, T. (1991b) *Theoretical Perspectives on Cognitive Aging.* Hillsdale, NJ: Lawrence Erlbaum.

Salthouse, T. (1992a) Reasoning and spatial abilities. In F.I.M. Craik and T. Salthouse (eds) *The Handbook of Aging and Cognition.* Hillsdale, NJ: Lawrence Erlbaum.

Salthouse, T. (1992b) *Mechanisms of Age-Cognition Relations in Adulthood.* Hillsdale, NJ: Lawrence Erlbaum.

Salthouse, T. (1996) The processing-speed theory of adult age differences in cognition. *Psychological Review, 103*, 403–28.

Salthouse, T. (2000) Item analysis of age relations on reasoning tasks. *Psychology and Aging, 15*, 3–8.

Salthouse, T. (2001) Attempted decomposition of age-related influences on two tests of reasoning. *Psychology and Aging, 16*, 251–63.

Salthouse, T., Berish, D.E. and Miles, J.D. (2002) The role of cognitive stimulation on the relations between age and cognitive functioning. *Psychology and Aging, 17*, 548–57.

Salthouse, T. and Czaja, S.J. (2000) Structural constraints on process explanations in cognitive aging. *Psychology and Aging, 15*, 44–55.

Salthouse, T. and Ferrer-Caja, E. (2003) What needs to be explained to account for age-related effects on multiple cognitive variables? *Psychology and Aging, 18*, 91–110.

Salthouse, T., Fristoe, N. and Rhee, S.H. (1996) How localized are age-related effects on neuropsychological measures? *Neuropsychology, 10*, 272–85.

Salthouse, T.A. (2006) Mental exercise and mental aging: Evaluating the validity of the 'use it or lose it' hypothesis. *Perspectives on Psychological Science, 1*, 68–87.

Salthouse, T.A. (2009) When does age-related cognitive decline begin? *Neurobiology of Aging, 30*, 507–14.

Salthouse, T.A. (2010) *Major Issues in Cognitive Aging.* New York: Oxford University Press.

Samaras, T.T. and Elrick, H. (1999) Height, body size and longevity. *Acta Medica Okayama, 53*, 149–69.

Sanchez-Benavides, G., Gomez-Anson, B., Quintana, M., Vives, Y. *et al.* (2010) Problem-solving abilities and frontal lobe cortical thickness in health aging and mild cognitive impairment. *Journal of the International Neurological Society, 16*, 836–45.

Sanderson, W. and Scherbov, S. (2010) Remeasuring aging. *Science, 329*, 1287–8.

Sando, S., Melquist, S., Cannon, A., Hutton, M. *et al.* (2008a) Risk-reducing effect of education in Alzheimer's disease. *International Journal of Geriatric Psychiatry, 23*, 1156–62.

Sando, S., Melquist, S., Cannon, A., Hutton, M. *et al.* (2008b) APOE e4 lowers age at onset and is a high risk factor for Alzheimer's disease: A case control study from central Norway. *BMC Neurology, 16*, 8–9.

Sasser-Coen, J.R. (1993) Qualitative changes in creativity in the second half of life: A life-span developmental perspective. *Journal of Creative Behavior, 27*, 18–27.

Satre, D.D., Knight, B.G., Dickson-Fuhrmann, E. and Jarvik, L.F. (2004) Substance abuse treatment initiation among older adults in the GET SMART program: Effects of depression and cognitive status. *Aging and Mental Health, 8*, 346–54.

Scaf-Klomp, W., Sanderman, R., Ormel, J. and Kempen, G.I.J.M. (2003) Depression in older people after fall-related injuries: A prospective study. *Age and Ageing, 32*, 88–94.

Scalmati, A. and Kennedy, G. (2009) Psychotherapy as end-of-life care: Special consideration for the older patient. *Psychiatric Annals, 39*, 833–7.

Scazufca, M., Almeida, O. and Menezes, P. (2010) The role of literacy, occupation and income in dementia prevention: The Sao Paulo Aging and Health Study (SPAH) *International Psychogeriatrics, 22,* 1209–15.

Schadlu, A.P., Schadlu, R. and Shepherd, J.B. (2009) Charles Bonnet syndrome: A review. *Current Opinions in Ophthalmology, 20,* 219–22.

Schaie, K.W. (1983) The Seattle Longitudinal Study: A 21-year exploration of psychometric intelligence in adulthood. In K.W. Schaie (ed.) *Longitudinal Studies of Adult Psychological Development.* New York, Guilford Press, 64–135.

Schaie, K.W. (1989a) Individual differences in rate of cognitive change in adulthood. In V.L. Bengtson and K.W. Schaie (eds) *The Course of Later Life: Research and Reflections.* New York: Springer.

Schaie, K.W. (1989b) Perceptual speed in adulthood: Cross-sectional studies and longitudinal studies. *Psychology and Aging, 4,* 443–53.

Schaie, K.W. (1994) The course of adult intellectual development. *American Psychologist, 49,* 304–13.

Schaie, K.W. (2005) What can we learn from longitudinal studies of adult intellectual development? *Research in Human Development, 2,* 133–58.

Schaie, K.W. (2008) Historical processes and patterns of cognitive ageing. In S.M. Hofer and D.F. Alwin (eds) *Handbook of Cognitive Aging: Interdisciplinary Perspectives.* Thousand Oaks, CA: Sage.

Schaie, K.W. and Hertzog, C. (1986) Toward a comprehensive model of adult intellectual development: Contributions of the Seattle Longitudinal Study. In R.J. Sternberg (ed.) *Advances in Human Intelligence, 3.* Hillsdale, NJ: Erlbaum, 79–118.

Schaie, K.W. and Willis, S.L. (1991) *Adult Development and Aging.* New York: HarperCollins.

Schatzman, M. (2004) Elisabeth Kübler-Ross obituary. *The Independent,* 28 August.

Scheinin, N., Aalto, S., Kaprio, J., Kozkenvuo, M. *et al.* (2011) Early detection of Alzheimer disease: 11C-PiB PET in twins discordant for cognitive impairment. *Neurology, 77,* 453–60.

Scherder, E., Bogen, T., Eggermont, L., Hamers, J. and Swaab, D. (2010) The more physical inactivity, the more agitation in dementia. *International Psychogeriatrics, 22,* 1203–8.

Scherger, S., Nazroo, J. and Higgs, P. (2011) Leisure activities and retirement: Do structures of inequality change in old age? *Ageing and Society, 31,* 146–72.

Scherrer, K. (2009) Images of sexuality and aging in gerontological literature. *Sexuality Research and Social Policy, 6,* 5–12.

Schiffman, S. (1977) Food recognition by the elderly. *Journal of Gerontology, 32,* 586–92.

Schiffman, S.S., Gatlin, L.A., Frey, A.E., Heiman, S.A., Stagner, W.C. and Cooper, D.C. (1995) Taste perception of bitter compounds in young and elderly persons: Relation to lipophilicity of bitter compounds. *Neurobiology of Aging, 15,* 743–50.

Schildmann, J., Hoetzel, J., Baumann, A., Mueller-Busch, C. and Vollmann, J. (2011) Limitation of treatment at the end of life: An empirical-ethical analysis regarding the practices of physician members of the German Society for Palliative Medicine. *Journal of Medical Ethics, 37,* 327–32.

Schlagman, S., Kvavilashvill, L. and Schulz, J. (2007) Effects of age on involuntary autobiographical memories. In J. Mace (ed.) (2007) *Involuntary Memory. New Perspectives in Cognitive Psychology.* Malden: Blackwell Publishing.

Schlehofer, M., Omoto, A. and Adelman, J. (2008) How do 'religion' and 'spirituality' differ? Lay definitions among older adults. *Journal for the Scientific Study of Religion, 47,* 411–25.

Schlesinger, B. (1996) The sexless years or sex rediscovered. *Journal of Gerontological Social Work, 26,* 117–31.

Schliemann, A.D. (2000) Informal learning. In A.E. Kazdin (ed.) *Encyclopaedia of Psychology, Volume 4.* Washington, DC: American Psychological Association, 288–90.

Schlotterer, G., Moscovitch, M., Crapper, M. and McLachlan, D. (1984) Visual processing deficits as assessed by spatial frequency contrast sensitivity and backward masking in normal ageing and Alzheimer's disease. *Brain, 107*, 309–25.

Schmiedek, F. and Li, S.C. (2004) Toward an alternative representation for disentangling age-associated differences in general and specific cognitive abilities. *Psychology and Aging, 19*, 40–56.

Schneck, M.E., Haegerstrom-Portnoy, G., Lott, L.A. Braby, J.A. and Gildengorin, G. (2004) Low contrast vision function predicts subsequent acuity loss in an aged population: The SKI study. *Vision Research, 44*, 2317–25.

Schneider, B. (1997) Psychoacoustics and aging: Implications for everyday listening. *Journal of Speech Language Pathology and Audiology, 21*, 111–24.

Schneider, B., Daneman, M. and Murphy, D. (2005) Speech comprehension difficulties in older adults: Cognitive slowing or age-related changes in hearing? *Psychology and Aging, 20*, 261–71.

Schneider, B.A., Daneman, M., Murphy, D.R. and See, S.K. (2000) Listening to discourse in distracting settings: The effects of aging. *Psychology and Aging, 15*, 110–25.

Schneider, B., Speranza, F. and Pichora-Fuller, M.K. (1998) Age-related changes in temporal resolution: Envelope and intensity effects. *Canadian Journal of Experimental Psychology, 52*, 184–91.

Schneider-Garces, N.J., Gordon, B.A., Brumback-Peltz, C.R., Shin, E. *et al.* (2010) Span, CRUNCH, and beyond: Working memory capacity and the aging brain. *Journal of Cognitive Neuroscience, 22*, 655–69.

Schonfeld, L., Rohrer, G.E., Zima, M. and Spiegel, T. (1993) Alcohol abuse and medication misuse in older adults as estimated by service providers. *Journal of Gerontological Social Work, 21*, 113–25.

Schooler, C. and Mulatu, M.S. (2001) The reciprocal effects of leisure time activities and intellectual functioning in older people: A longitudinal analysis. *Psychology and Aging, 16*, 466–82.

Schott, L., Kamarck, T., Matthews, K., Brockwell, S. and Sutton-Tyrell, K. (2009) Is brachial artery flow-mediated dilation associated with negative affect? *International Journal of Behavioral Medicine, 16*, 241–7.

Schram, L.L., Rubert, M. and Loewenstein, D.A. (1995) A qualitative analysis of semantic intrusive errors in Alzheimer's Disease. *Archives of Clinical Neuropsychology, 10*, 255–63.

Schuff, N., Tosun, D., Insel, P.S., Chiang, G.C., *et al.* (2010) Nonlinear time course of brain volume loss in cognitively normal and impaired elders. *Neurobiology of Aging, 31*, 1340–54.

Schuknecht, H.F. (1974) *Pathology of the Ear.* Cambridge, MA: Harvard University Press.

Schulz, R., McGinnis, K., Zhang, S., Martire, L. *et al.* (2008) Dementia patient suffering and caregiver depression. *Alzheimer's Disease and Associated Disorders, 22*, 170–6.

Schwartz, B. and Frazier, L. (2005) Tip of the tongue states and aging: Contrasting psycholinguistic and metacognitive perspectives. *Journal of General Psychology, 132*, 377–91.

Schwartz, J.E., Friedman, H.S., Tucker, J.S., Tomlinson-Keasey, C. Wingard, D.L. and Criqui, M.H. (1995) Childhood sociodemographic and psychosocial factors as predictors of longevity across the life-span. *American Journal of Public Health*, 85, 1237–45.

Schwartz, L.K. and Simmons, J.P. (2001) Contact quality and attitudes toward the elderly. *Educational Gerontology, 27*, 127–37.

Schweber, M.S. (1989a) Down Syndrome and the measurement of chromosome 21 DNA amounts in Alzheimer's Disease. In G. Miner, L. Miner, R. Richter and J.L. Valentine (eds) *Familial Alzheimer's Disease: Molecular Genetics and Clinical Prospects.* New York: Marcel Dekker.

Schweber, M.S. (1989b) Alzheimer's Disease and Down Syndrome. In K. Iqbal, H.M. Wisniewski and B. Winblad (eds) *Alzheimer's Disease and Related Disorders.* New York: Alan R. Liss.

Scialfa, C.T. (2002) The role of sensory factors in cognitive aging research. *Canadian Journal of Experimental Psychology, 56*, Ottawa: September, 153–64.

Scogin, F.R. (1998) Anxiety in old age. In I.H. Nordhus, G.R. VandenBos, S. Berg and P. Fromholt (eds) *Clinical Geropsychology.* Washington, DC: American Psychological Association, 205–209.

Searcy, J.H., Bartlett, J.C. and Memon, A. (1999) Age differences in accuracy and choosing in eyewitness identification and face recognition. *Memory and Cognition, 27,* 538–52.

Sebastian, M., Menor, J. and Elosua, M. (2006) Attentional dysfunction of the central executive in AD: Evidence from dual task and perseveration errors. *Cortex, 42,* 1015–20.

Seeman, T.E., Huang, M.H., Bretsky, P., Crimmins, E., Launer, L. and Guralnik, J.M. (2005) Education and APOE-e4 in longitudinal cognitive decline: MacArthur studies of successful aging. *The Journals of Gerontology Series B: Psychological Sciences and Social Sciences, 60,* 74–83.

Segraves, R.T. and Segraves, K.B. (1995) Human sexuality and aging. *Journal of Sex Education and Therapy, 21,* 88–102.

Sekuler, R. and Blake, R. (1985) *Perception.* New York: Random House.

Seltzer, B. and Sherwin, I. (1983) A comparison of clinical features in early- and late-onset primary degenerative dementia: One entity or two? *Archives of Neurology, 40,* 143–6.

Selzman, C., Jeste, D., Meyer, Cohen-Mansfield, J. *et al.* (2008) Elderly patients with dementia-related symptoms of severe agitation and aggression: Consensus statement on treatment options, clinical trials methodology, and policy. *Journal of Clinical Psychiatry, 69,* 889–98.

Sener, A., Oztop, H., Dogan, N. and Guven, S. (2008) Family, close relatives, friends: Life satisfaction among older people. *Educational Gerontology, 34,* 890–906.

Serra, L., Fadda, L., Perri, R., Caltagirone, C. and Carlesimo, G. (2009) The closing-in phenomenon in the drawing performance of Alzheimer's disease patients: A compensation account. *Cortex, 46,* 1031–6.

Serrano, J.P., Latorre, J.M., Gatz, M. and Montanes, J. (2004) Life review therapy using autobiographical retrieval practice for older adults with depressive symptomatology. *Psychology and Aging, 19,* 272–7.

Seshamani, M. and Gray, A. (2004) Time to death and health expenditure: An improved model for the impact of demographic change on health care costs. *Age and Ageing, 33,* 571–6.

Sesso, H.D., Paffenbarger, R.S. and Lee, I.M. (2000) Physical activity and coronary heart disease in men: The Harvard Alumni Health Study. *Circulation, 102,* 975–80.

Settersen, R.A. (1998) Time, age and the transition to retirement: New evidence on life-course flexibility? *International Journal of Aging and Human Development, 47,* 177–203.

Settersen, R.A. and Haegestad, G.O. (1996) What's the latest? Cultural age deadlines for family transitions. *Gerontologist, 36,* 178–88.

Settlage, C.F. (1996) Transcending old age: Creativity, development and psychoanalysis in the life of a centenarian. *International Journal of Psycho-Analysis, 77,* 549–64.

Shafto, M. (2010) Orthographic error monitoring in old age: Lexical and sublexical availability during perception and production. *Psychology and Aging, 25,* 991–1001.

Shafto, M., Burke, D., Stamatakis, E., Tam, P. and Tyler, L. (2007) On the tip of the tongue: Neural correlates of increased word finding failures in normal aging. *Journal of Cognitive Neuroscience, 19,* 2060–70.

Shafto, M., Burke, D., Stamatakis, E., Tam, P. and Tyler, L. (2010) Word retrieval failures in old age: The relationship between structure and function. *Journal of Cognitive Neuroscience, 22,* 1530–40.

Shah, A. (2011a) Are elderly dependency ratios associated with general population suicide rates? *International Journal of Social Psychiatry, 57,* 277–83.

Shah, A. (2011b) Elderly suicide rates: A replication of cross-national comparisons and association with sex and elderly age-bands using five year suicide data. *Journal of Injury and Violence Research, 3,* 80–4.

Shah, A. (2011c) Further evidence for epidemiological transition hypothesis for elderly suicides. *Journal of Injury and Violence Research, 3,* 29–34.

Shah, A. and Buckley, L. (2011) The current status of methods used by the elderly for suicides in England and Wales. *Journal of Injury and Violence Research, 3*, 68–73.

Shan, Z., Liu, J., Sahgai, V., Wang, B. and Yiu, G. (2005) Selective atrophy of left hemisphere and frontal lobe of the brain in old men. *The Journals of Gerontology Series A: Biological Sciences and Medical Sciences, 60*, 165–74.

Sharpe, T.H. (2004) Introduction to sexuality in late life. *Family Journal: Counseling and Therapy for Couples and Families, 12*, 199–205.

Sharpley, C.F. (1997) Psychometric properties of the self-perceived stress in retirement scale. *Psychological Reports, 81*, 319–22.

Sharps, M.J. (1998) Age-related change in visual information processing: Toward a unified theory of aging and visual memory. *Current Psychology, 16*, 284–307.

Shaw, C. (2004). Interim 2003-based national population projections for the United Kingdom and constituent countries. *Population Trends 118*, 6–16.

Shea, P. (1995) Ageing and wisdom. In F. Glendenning and I. Stuart-Hamilton (eds) *Learning and Cognition in Later Life*. Aldershot: Arena.

Sheikh, A. and Sheikh, K. (eds) (2007) *Healing with Death Imagery*. Amityville, Baywood Publishing.

Sheppard, L.D. and Vernon, P.A. (2008) Intelligence and speed of information-processing: A review of 50 years of research. *Personality and Individual Differences, 44*, 535–51.

Sherer, M. (1996) The impact of using personal computers on the lives of nursing home residents. *Physical and Occupational Therapy in Geriatrics, 14*, 13–31.

Shewmon, D. (1998) 'Brainstem death', 'brain death', and death: A critical re-evaluation of the purported equivalence. *Issues in Law and Medicine, 14*, 125–45.

Shimamura, A.P., Berry, J.M., Mangels, J.A., Rusting, C.L. and Jurica, P.J. (1995) Memory and cognitive abilities in university professors: Evidence for successful aging. *Psychological Science, 6*, 271–7.

Shimonaka, Y. and Nakazato, K. (2007) Creativity and factors affecting creative ability in adulthood and old age. *Japanese Journal of Educational Psychology, 55*, 231–43.

Shimonaka, Y., Nakazato, K. and Homma, A. (1996) Personality, longevity and successful aging among Tokyo metropolitan centenarians. *International Journal of Aging and Human Development, 42*, 173–87.

Shing, Y., Werkle-Bergner, M., Li, S. and Lindenberger, U. (2009) Committing memory errors with high confidence: Older adults do but children don't. *Memory, 17*, 169–79.

Shipley, B., Weiss, A., Der, G., Taylor, M. and Deary, I. (2007) Neuroticism, extraversion, and mortality in the UK Health and Lifestyle Survey: A 21-year prospective cohort study. *Psychosomatic Medicine, 69*, 923–31.

Shock, N.W. (1977) Biological theories of aging. In J.E. Birren and K.W. Schaie (eds) *Handbook of the Psychology of Aging*. 1st edition. New York: Van Nostrand Reinhold.

Shore, D. and Wyatt, R.J. (1983) Aluminium and Alzheimer's disease. *Journal of Nervous and Mental Disorders, 171*, 553–8.

Siedlecki, K., Tucker-Drob, E., Oishi, S. and Salthouse, T. (2008) Life satisfaction across adulthood: Different determinants at different ages? *Journal of Positive Psychology, 3*, 153–64.

Siegler, I.C. and Botwinick, J. (1979) A long-term longitudinal study of intellectual ability of older adults: The matter of selective subject attrition. *Journal of Gerontology, 34*, 242–5.

Siegler, I.C., McCarty, S.M. and Logue, P.E. (1982) Wechsler Memory Scale scores, selective attention and distance from death. *Journal of Gerontology, 37*, 176–81.

Silveira, M., Kim, S. and Langa, K. (2010) Advance directives and outcomes of surrogate decision making before death. *New England Journal of Medicine, 362*, 1211–8.

Simoni-Wastila, L. and Yang, H. (2006) Psychoactive drug abuse in older adults. *American Journal of Geriatric Pharmacotherapy, 4*, 380–94.

Simons, J.S., Dodson, C.S., Bell, D. and Schacter, D.L. (2004) Specific- and partial-source memory: Effects of aging. *Psychology and Aging, 19,* 689–94.

Simonton, D.K. (1990) Creativity and wisdom in aging. In J.W. Birren and K.W. Schaie (eds) *Handbook of the Psychology of Aging.* 3rd edition. San Diego, CA: Academic Press.

Sims, R.V., Allaire, J.C., Gamaldo, A.A., Edwards, C.L. and Whitfield, K. E. (2009) An examination of dedifferentiation in cognition among African-American older adults. *Journal of Cross-Cultural Gerontology, 24,* 193–208.

Sinforiani, E., Zucchella, C., Pasotti, C., Caroni, F. *et al.* (2011) The effects of alcohol on cognition in the elderly: From protection to neurodegeneration. *Functional Neurology, 26,* 103–6.

Singer, T., Lindenberger, U. and Baltes, P.B. (2003a) Plasticity of memory for new learning in very old age: A story of major loss? *Psychology and Aging, 18,* 306–17.

Singer, T., Verhaeghen, P., Ghisletta, P., Lindenberger, U. and Baltes, P.B. (2003b) The fate of cognition in very old age: Six-year longitudinal findings in the Berlin Aging Study (BASE). *Psychology and Aging, 18,* 318–31.

Singh, G.K. and Siapush, M. (2006) Widening socioeconomic inequalities in US life expectancy, 1980–2000. *International Journal of Epidemiology, 35,* 969–79.

Sjobeck, M. and Englund, E. (2003) Glial levels determine severity of white matter disease in Alzheimer's disease: A neuropathological study of glial changes. *Neuropathology and Applied Neurobiology, 29,* 159–69.

Skoog, I. (1996) Sex and Swedish 85-year-olds. *New England Journal of Medicine, 334,* 1140–1.

Slavin, M.J., Phillips, J.C. and Bradshaw, J.L. (1996) Visual cues and the handwriting of older adults: A kinematic analysis. *Psychology and Aging, 11,* 521–6.

Slavin, M.J., Phillips, J.C., Bradshaw, J.L., Hall, K.A. and Presnell, I. (1999) Consistency of handwriting movements in dementia of the Alzheimer's type: A comparison with Huntington's and Parkinson's diseases. *Journal of the International Neuropsychological Society, 5,* 20–5.

Sliwinski, M. (1997) Aging and counting speed: Evidence for process-specific slowing. *Psychology and Aging, 12,* 38–49.

Sliwinski, M., Buschke, H., Kuslansky, G., Senior, G. and Scarisbrick, D. (1994) Proportional slowing and addition speed in old and young adults. *Psychology and Aging, 9,* 72–80.

Sliwinski, M. and Hall, C.B. (1998) Constraints on general slowing: A meta-analysis using hierarchical linear models with random coefficients. *Psychology and Aging, 13,* 164–75.

Sliwinski, M.J., Hofer, S.M., Hall, C., Buschke, H. and Lipton, R.B. (2003) Modeling memory decline in older adults: The importance of preclinical dementia, attrition and chronological age. *Psychology and Aging, 18,* 658–71.

Small, B.J., Fratiglioni, L., von Strauss, E. and Bäckman, L. (2003) Terminal decline and cognitive performance in very old age: Does cause of death matter? *Psychology and Aging, 18,* 193–202.

Small, B.J., Rosnick, C.B., Fratiglioni, L. and Bäckman, L. (2004) Apolipoprotein E and cognitive performance: A meta-analysis. *Psychology and Aging, 19,* 592–600.

Smiler, A., Gagne, D.D. and Stine-Morrow, E.A.L. (2004) Aging, memory load and resource allocation during reading. *Psychology and Aging, 18,* 203–9.

Smiley, E. (2005) Epidemiology of mental health problems in adults with learning disability: An update. *Advances in Psychiatric Treatment, 11,* 214–22.

Smith, A. (1998) Breakfast consumption and intelligence in elderly persons. *Psychological Reports, 82,* 424–6.

Smith, G.A. and Brewer, N. (1995) Slowness and age: Speed-accuracy mechanisms. *Psychology and Aging, 10,* 238–47.

Smith, J., Heckhausen, J., Kilegl, R. and Baltes, P.B. (1984) Cognitive reserve capacity, expertise and aging. *Meeting of Gerontological Society of America, San Antonio.* Cited in Rebok (1987).

Smith, R. (2006) Adult age differences in episodic memory: Item-specific, relational, and distinctive processing. In R. Hunt and J. Worthen (eds) (2006) *Distinctiveness and Memory*. New York: Oxford University Press.

Smith, S.W., Rebok, G.W., Smith, W.R., Hall, S.E. and Alvin, M. (1989) Adult age differences in the use of story structure in delayed free recall. *Experimental Aging Research, 9*, 191–5.

Smyer, M.A. and Qualls, S.H. (1999) *Aging and Mental Health*. Oxford: Blackwells.

Snowdon, D.A., Kemper, S.J., Mortimer, J.A., Greiner, L.H., Wekstein, D.R. and Markesbury, W.R. (1996) Linguistic ability in early life and cognitive function and Alzheimer's disease in late life: Findings from the Nun Study. *Journal of the American Medical Association, 275*, 528–32.

Sobieszczyk, T., Knodel, J. and Chavoyan, N. (2003) Gender and wellbeing among older people: evidence from Thailand. *Ageing and Society, 23*, 701–35.

Soederberg Miller, L.M. (2003) The effects of age and domain knowledge on text processing. *The Journals of Gerontology Series B: Psychological Sciences and Social Sciences, 58*, 217–23.

Soederberg Miller, L.M. (2009) Age differences in the effects of domain knowledge on reading efficiency. *Psychology and Aging, 24*, 63–74.

Someya, S. and Prolla, T.A. (2010) Mitochondrial oxidative damage and apoptosis in age-related hearing loss. *Mechanisms of Ageing Development, 131*, 480–6.

Someya, S., Tanokura, M., Weindruch, R., Prolla, T.A. and Yamasoba, T. (2010) Effects of caloric restriction on age-related hearing loss in rodents and rhesus monkeys. *Current Ageing Science, 3*, 20–5.

Sonnenschein, E. and Brody, J.A. (2005) Effect of population aging on proportionate mortality from heart disease and cancer, U.S. 2000–2050. *The Journals of Gerontology Series B: Psychological Sciences and Social Sciences 60*, 110–12.

Sorce, P. (1995) Cognitive competence of older consumers. *Psychology and Marketing, 12*, 467–80.

Sorensen, S., Duberstein, P., Chapman, B., Lyness, J. and Pinquart, M. (2008) How are personality traits related to preparation for future care needs in older adults? *The Journals of Gerontology Series B: Psychological Sciences and Social Sciences, 63*, 328–36.

Souchay, C., Moulin, C., Clarys, D., Tacconat, L. and Isingrini, M. (2007) Diminished episodic memory awareness in older adults: Evidence from feeling of knowing and recollection. *Consciousness and Cognition, 16*, 769–84.

Souter, S. and Keller, C.S. (2002) Food choice in the rural dwelling older adult. *Southern Online Journal of Nursing Research, 5*, 3. Available at www.resourcenter.net/images/SNRS/Files/SOJNR_articles/iss05vol03.pdf, accessed on 21 January 2012.

Southwell, J., Boreham, P. and Laffan, W. (2008) Problem gambling and the circumstances facing older people. *Journal of Gambling Studies, 24*, 151–74.

Spaan, P. and Raaljmakers, J. (2011) Priming effects from young-old to very old age on a word-stem completion task: Minimizing explicit contamination. *Aging, Neuropsychology and Cognition, 18*, 86–107.

Specht, J., Egloff, B. and Schmukle, S. (2011) Stability and change of personality across the life course: The impact of age and major life events on mean-level and rank-order stability of the Big Five. *Journal of Personality and Social Psychology, 101*, 862–82.

Speranza, F., Daneman, M. and Schneider, B.A. (2000) How aging affects the reading of words in noisy backgrounds. *Psychology and Aging, 15*, 253–8.

Spieler, D.H. and Balota, D.A. (2000) Factors influencing word naming in younger and older adults. *Psychology and Aging, 15*, 225–31.

Spiro, A., Aldwin, C.M., Ward, K.D. and Mroczek, D.K. (1995) Personality and the incidence of hypertension among older men: Longitudinal findings from the Normative Aging Study. *Health Psychology, 14*, 563–9.

Sponheim, S., Jung, R., Seidman, L., Mesholam-Gately, R. *et al.* (2010) Cognitive deficits in recent-onset and chronic schizophrenia. *Journal of Psychiatric Research, 44*, 421–8.

Sprinzi, G.M. and Riechelmann, H. (2010) Current trends in treating hearing loss in elderly people: A review of the technology and treatment options – a mini-review. *Gerontology, 56,* 351–8.

Sreerupa, S. and Rajan,, S. (2010) Gender and widowhood: Disparity in health status and health care utilization among the aged in India. *Journal of Ethnic and Cultural Diversity in Social Work, 19,* 287–98.

St George-Hyslop, P.H., Tanzi, R.E., Polinsky, R.J., Haines, J.L. *et al.* (1987) The genetic defect causing familial Alzheimer's Disease maps on chromosome 21. *Science, 325,* 885–90.

St John, P. and Montgomery, P. (2009) Marital status, partner satisfaction, and depressive symptoms in older men and women. *Canadian Journal of Psychiatry, 54,* 487–92.

St John, P., Montgomery, P. and Tyas, S. (2009) Alcohol misuse, gender and depressive symptoms in community-dwelling seniors. *International Journal of Geriatric Psychiatry, 24,* 369–75.

Stalker, G. (2011) Leisure diversity as an indicator of cultural capital. *Leisure Sciences, 33,* 88–102.

Stallings, M.C., Dunham, C.C., Gatz, M., Baker, L. and Bengston, V.L. (1997) Relationships among life events and psychological well-being: More evidence for a two-factor theory of well-being. *Journal of Applied Gerontology, 16,* 104–19.

Stankov, L. (2005) Reductionism versus charting: Ways of examining the role of lower-order cognitive processes in intelligence. In R.J. Sternberg and J.E. Pretz (eds) *Cognition and Intelligence: Identifying the Mechanisms of the Mind.* New York: Cambridge University Press, 51–67.

Starr, J. and Lonie, J. (2007) The influence of pre-morbid IQ on Mini-Mental State Examination score at time of dementia presentation. *International Journal of Geriatric Psychiatry, 22,* 382–4.

Starr, J.M., Deary, I.J., Lemmon, H. and Whalley, L.J. (2000) Mental ability age 11 years and health status age 77 years. *Age and Ageing, 29,* 523–8.

States, R., Susman, W., Riquelme, L., Godwin, E. and Greer, E. (2006) Community health education: Reaching ethnically diverse elders. *Journal of Allied Health, 35,* 215–22.

Staudinger, U.M., Bluck, S. and Herzberg, P.Y. (2003) Looking back and looking ahead: Adult age differences in consistency of diachronous ratings of subjective well-being. *Psychology and Aging, 18,* 13–24.

Staudinger, U.M., Kessler, E. and Dorner, J. (2006) Wisdom in social context. In K.W. Schaie and L.L. Carstensen (eds) (2006) *Social structures, aging, and self-regulation in the elderly.* New York: Springer.

Staudinger, U.M., Lopez, D.F. and Baltes, P.B. (1997) The psychometric location of wisdom-related performance: Intelligence, personality and more? *Personality and Social Psychology Bulletin, 23,* 1200–14.

Staudinger, U.M., Maciel, A.G., Smith, J. and Baltes, P.B. (1998) What predicts wisdom-related performance? A first look at personality, intelligence and facilitative experiential contexts. *European Journal of Personality, 12,* 1–17.

Steadman, P., Tremont, G. and Davis, J. (2007) Premorbid relationship satisfaction and caregiver burden in dementia caregivers. *Journal of Geriatric Psychiatry and Neurology, 20,* 115–9.

Stebbins, G.T., Carrillo, M.C., Dorfman, J., Dirksen, C. *et al.* (2002) Aging effects on memory encoding in the frontal lobes. *Psychology and Aging, 17,* 44–55.

Steinberg, J. (2011) *Bismarck: A Life* Oxford: Oxford University Press

Stel, V.S., Smit, J.H., Plujm, S.M.F. and Lips, P. (2004) Consequences of falling in older men and women and risk factors for health service use and functional decline. *Age and Ageing, 33,* 58–65.

Stephan, B. and Brayne, C. (2008) Vascular factors and prevention of dementia. *International Review of Psychiatry, 20,* 344–56.

Stephan, Y., Fouquereau, E. and Fernandez, A. (2008a) Body satisfaction and retirement satisfaction: The meditational role of subjective health. *Aging and Mental Health, 12,* 374–81.

Stephan, Y., Fouquereau, E. and Fernandez, A. (2008b) The relation between self-determination and retirement satisfaction among active retired individuals. *International Journal of Aging and Human Development, 66,* 329–45.

Stephens, S. (1982) Some historical aspects of ototoxicity. *British Journal of Audiology, 16,* 76–80.

Stern, Y. (2009). Cognitive reserve. *Neuropsychologia, 47,* 2015–28.

Sternberg, R.J. (1996) *Cognitive Psychology.* Fort Worth: Harcourt Brace.

Sternberg, R.J. (1998) A balance theory of wisdom. *Review of General Psychology, 2,* 347–65.

Steunenberg, B., Beekman, A., Deeg, D., Bremner, M. and Kerkhof, A. (2007) Mastery and neuroticism predict recovery of depression in later life. *American Journal of Geriatric Psychiatry, 15,* 234–42.

Steunenberg, B., Twisk, J.W.R., Beekman, A.T.F., Deeg, D.J.H. and Kerkhof, A.J.F.M. (2005) Stability and change of neuroticism in aging. *The Journals of Gerontology Series B: Psychological Sciences and Social Sciences, 60,* 27–33.

Stevens, J.C. (1996) Detection of tastes in mixture with other tastes: Issues of masking and aging. *Chemical Senses, 21,* 211–21.

Stevens, J.C. and Patterson, M.Q. (1996) Dimensions of spatial acuity in the touch test: Changes over the life span. *Somatosensory and Motor Research, 12,* 29–47.

Stevens, M. (1979) Famous personality test. A test for measuring remote memory. *Bulletin of the British Psychological Society, 32,* 211.

Stewart, D. and Oslin, D.W. (2001) Recognition and treatment of late-life addictions in medical settings. *Journal of Clinical Geropsychology, 7,* 145–58.

Stine-Morrow, E.A., Loveless, M.K. and Soederberg, L.M. (1996) Resource allocation in on-line reading by younger and older adults. *Psychology and Aging, 11,* 475–86.

Stine-Morrow, E.A.L., Milinder, L.-A., Pullara, O. and Herman, B. (2001) Patterns of resource allocation are reliable among younger and older readers. *Psychology and Aging, 16,* 69 84.

Stine-Morrow, E., Shake, M., Miles, J., Lee, K., Gao, X. and McConkie, G. (2010) Pay now or pay later: Aging and the role of boundary salience in self-regulation of conceptual integration in sentence processing. *Psychology and Aging, 25,* 168–76.

Stine-Morrow, E., Soederberg Miller, L., Gagne, D. and Hertzog, C. (2008) Self-regulated reading in adulthood. *Psychology and Aging, 23,* 131–53.

Stine-Morrow, E., Soederberg Miller, L. and Hertzog, C. (2006) Aging and self-regulated language processing. *Psychological Bulletin, 132,* 582–606.

Stitt, B.G., Giacopassi, D. and Nichols, M. (2003) Gambling among older adults: A comparative analysis. *Experimental Aging Research, 29,* 189–203.

Stoddard, C.E. and Thompson, D.L. (1996) Alcohol and the elderly: Special concerns for counseling professionals. *Alcoholism Treatment Quarterly, 14,* 59–69.

Stokes, G. (1992) *On Being Old. The Psychology of Later Life.* London: The Falmer Press.

Stopford, C., Snowden, J., Thompson, J. and Neary, D. (2008) Variability in cognitive presentation of Alzheimer's disease. *Cortex, 44,* 185–95.

Storandt, M. (1976) Speed and coding effects in relation to age and ability level. *Developmental Psychology, 2,* 177–8.

Storandt, M. (1977) Age, ability level and scoring the WAIS. *Journal of Gerontology, 32,* 175–8.

Storandt, M. and Futterman, A. (1982) Stimulus size and performance on two subtests of the Wechsler Adult Intelligence Scale by younger and older adults. *Journal of Gerontology, 37,* 602–3.

Storandt, M., Kaskie, B. and Von Dras, D.D. (1998) Temporal memory for remote events in healthy aging and dementia. *Psychology and Aging, 13,* 4–7.

Strawbridge, W., Wallhagen, M. and Shema, S. (2011) Spousal interrelations in self-reports of cognition in the context of marital problems. *Gerontology, 57,* 148–52.

Strouse, A., Ashmead, D.H., Ohde, R.N. and Grantham, D.W. (1998) Temporal processing in the aging auditory system. *Journal of the Acoustical Society of America, 104*, 2385–99.

Strube, M.J., Berry, J.M., Goza, B.K. and Fennimore, D. (1985) Type A behavior, age and psychological well-being. *Journal of Personality and Social Psychology, 49*, 203–18.

Strydom, A., Hassiotis, A., King, M. and Livingston, G. (2009) The relationship of dementia prevalence in older adults with intellectual disability (ID) to age and severity of ID. *Psychological Medicine, 39*, 13–21.

Stuart-Hamilton, I. (1995) Problems with the assessment of intellectual change in elderly people. In F. Glendenning and I. Stuart-Hamilton (eds) *Learning and Cognition in Later Life*. Aldershot: Arena. 22–42.

Stuart-Hamilton, I. (1998) Women's attitudes to ageing: Some factors of relevance to educational gerontology. *Education and Ageing, 13*, 67–88.

Stuart-Hamilton, I. (1999a) *Key Ideas in Psychology*. London: Jessica Kingsley Publishers.

Stuart-Hamilton, I. (1999b) Intellectual changes in late life. In R.T. Woods (ed.) *Psychological Problems of Ageing*. Chichester: Wiley, 27–47.

Stuart-Hamilton, I. (2000) Attitudes to aging questionnaires: Some evidence for potential bias in their design. *Educational Gerontology, 26*, 1–11.

Stuart-Hamilton, I. (2003) Normal cognitive aging. In R. Tallis and H. Fillit (eds) *Brocklehurst's Textbook of Geriatric Medicine and Gerontology*. London: Churchill Livingstone.

Stuart-Hamilton, I. (2006) *The Psychology of Ageing: An Introduction*. 4th edition. London: Jessica Kingsley Publishers.

Stuart-Hamilton, I. (2010) Autism spectrum disorder in later life: The hidden problems. Closing address delivered to the conference *I Jornadas de Investigacion en Psicogrontgologia*, University of Santiago de Compostela, 3 July.

Stuart-Hamilton, I. (ed.) (2011) *An Introduction to Gerontology*. Cambridge: Cambridge University Press.

Stuart-Hamilton, I. and Mahoney, B. (2003) The effect of ageing awareness training on knowledge of and attitudes towards, older adults. *Educational Psychology 29*, 251–60.

Stuart-Hamilton, I. and McDonald, L. (1996) Age and a possible regression to childhood thinking patterns. *British Psychological Society Psychologists Special Interest Group in the Elderly Newsletter, 58*, 13–6.

Stuart-Hamilton, I. and McDonald, L. (1999) Limits to the use of *g*. Paper presented at the International Conference on Lifelong Learning, University College Worcester, July.

Stuart-Hamilton, I. and McDonald, L. (2001) Do we need intelligence? Some reflections on the importance of *G*. *Educational Gerontology, 27*, 399–407.

Stuart-Hamilton, I. and Morgan, H. (2011) What happens to people with autism spectrum disorders in middle age and beyond? Report of a preliminary on-line study. *Advances in Mental Health and Intellectual Disabilities, 5*, 22–8.

Stuart-Hamilton, I., Perfect, T. and Rabbitt, P. (1988) Remembering who was who. In M.M. Gruneberg, P.E. Morris and R.N. Sykes (eds) *Practical Aspects of Memory, Volume 2*. Chichester: Wiley.

Stuart-Hamilton, I. and Rabbitt, P. (1997a) Age-related decline in spelling ability: A link with fluid intelligence? *Educational Gerontology, 23*, 437–41.

Stuart-Hamilton, I. and Rabbitt, P. (1997b) The decline of eye-voice span in elderly readers. *Educational Gerontology, 23*, 389–400.

Sudore, R., Mehta, K., Simonsick, E., Harris, T. *et al.* (2006) Limited literacy in older people and disparities in health and healthcare access. *Journal of the American Geriatrics Society, 54*, 770–6.

Sulkava, R. (1982) Alzheimer's disease and senile dementia of the Alzheimer type: A comparative study. *Acta Neurologica Scandanavica, 65*, 636–50.

Sulkava, R. and Amberia, K. (1982) Alzheimer's disease and senile dementia of Alzheimer type: A neuropsychological study. *Acta Neurologica Scandanavica, 65,* 651–60.

Sullivan, A. (2010) Mortality differentials and religion in the United States: Religious affiliation and attendance. *Journal for the Scientific Study of Religion, 49,* 740–53.

Sunness, J.S., Gonzalez-Brown, J., Applegate, C.A., Bressler, N.M. *et al.* (1999) Enlargement of atrophy and visual acuity loss in geographic atrophy form of age-related macular degeneration. *Ophthalmology, 106,* 1768–79.

Sutin, A., Beason-Held, L., Resnick, S. and Costa, P. (2009) Sex differences in resting-state neural correlates of openness to experience among older adults. *Cerebral Cortex, 19,* 2797–802.

Swan, G.E. and Carmelli, D. (2002) Impaired olfaction predicts cognitive decline in nondemented older adults. *Neuroepidemology, 21,* 58–67.

Swan, G.E., Dame, A. and Carmelli, D. (1991) Involuntary retirement, Type A behavior and current functioning in elderly men: 27-year follow-up of the Western Collaborative Group Study. *Psychology and Aging, 6,* 384–91.

Szabo, J. (2010) *Death and Dying: An Annotated Bibliography of the Thanatological Literature.* Latham: Scarecrow Press.

Szinovacz, M. (1996) Couple's employment/retirement patterns and perceptions of marital quality. *Research on Aging, 18,* 243–68.

Szinovacz, M.E. and Davey, A. (2004) Retirement transitions and spouse disability: Effects on depressive symptoms. *The Journals of Gerontology Series B: Psychological Sciences and Social Sciences, 59,* 333–42.

Takashima, A. (2007) Study of aluminum on the pathology of Alzheimer's disease: *In vitro* versus *in vivo* evidence. *Journal of Alzheimer's Disease, 12,* 317–8.

Taki, Y., Kinomura, S., Sato, K., Goto, R. *et al.* (2011) Correlation between gray/white matter volume and cognition in healthy elderly people. *Brain and Cognition, 75,* 170–6.

Talarico, J. and Mace, J. (2010) Involuntary and voluntary memory sequencing phenomena: An interesting puzzle for the study of autobiographical memory organization and retrieval. In J. Mace (ed) *The Act of Remembering: Toward an Understanding of How we Recall the Past.* Malden: Wiley-Blackwell.

Tallis, R.C. and Fillit, H.M. (eds) (2003) *Brocklehurst's Textbook of Geriatric Medicine and Gerontology.* 6th edition. London: Churchill Livingstone.

Taub, H.A. (1979) Comprehension and memory of prose materials by young and old adults. *Experimental Aging Research, 5,* 3–13.

Taub, H.A., Baker, M.T. and Kline, G.E. (1982) Perceived choice of prose materials by young and elderly adults. *Educational Gerontology, 8,* 447–53.

Taub, H.A. and Kline, G. (1978) Recall of prose as a function of age and input modality. *Journal of Gerontology, 33,* 725–30.

Taylor, E. (1957) *Angel.* London: Peter Davies.

Taylor, J.K. and Burke, D.M. (2002) Asymmetric aging effects on semantic and phonological processes: Naming in the picture–word interference task. *Psychology and Aging, 17,* 662–76.

Taylor, M.G. and Lynch, S.M. (2004) Trajectories of impairment, social support and depressive symptoms in later life. *The Journals of Gerontology Series B: Psychological Sciences and Social Sciences, 59,* 238–46.

Tays, W., Dywan, J., Mathewson, K. and Segalowitz, S. (2008) Age differences in target detection and interference resolution in working memory: An event-related potential study. *Journal of Cognitive Neuroscience, 20,* 2250–62.

Teachman, B. (2006) Aging and negative affect: The rise and fall and rise of anxiety and depression syndromes. *Psychology and Aging, 21,* 201–7.

Teno, J.M., Clarridge, B.R., Casey, V., Welch, L.C. *et al.* (2004) Family perspectives on end-of-life care at the last place of care. *Journal of the American Medical Association, 291,* 88–93.

Terracciano, A., Lockenhoff, C., Zonderman, A., Ferrucci, L. and Costa, P. (2008) Personality predictors of longevity: Activity, emotional stability and conscientiousness. *Psychosomatic Medicine*, 70, 621–7.

Terracciano, A., Tanaka, T., Sutin, A., Deiana, B. *et al.* (2010) BDNF Val66Met is associated with introversion and interacts with 5-HTTLPR to influence neuroticism. *Neuropsychopharmacology*, 35, 1083–9.

Terry, A., Callahan, P., Brandon, W. and Webster, S. (2011) Alzheimer's disease and age-related memory decline (preclinical). *Pharmacology, Biochemistry and Behavior*, 99, 190–210.

Teunisse, R.J., Cruysberg, J.R., Verbeek, A. and Zitman, F.G. (1995) The Charles Bonnet syndrome: A large prospective study in The Netherlands. *British Journal of Psychiatry*, 166, 254–7.

Thane, P. (2000) *Old Age in English History*. Oxford: Oxford University Press.

Thane, P. and Parkin, T. (2005) *The Long History of Old Age*. London: Thames and Hudson.

Thimm, C., Rademacher, U. and Kruse, L. (1998) Age stereotypes and patronizing messages: Features of age-adapted speech in technical instructions to the elderly. *Journal of Applied Communication Research*, 26, 66–82.

Thogersen-Ntoumani, C. and Ntoumanis, N. (2006) The role of self-determined motivation in the understanding of exercise-related behaviours, cognitions and physical self-evaluations. *Journal of Sports Sciences*, 24, 393–404.

Thomas, A. and Bulevich, J. (2006) Effective cue utilization reduces memory errors in older adults. *Psychology and Aging*, 21, 379–89.

Thomas, A., Bulevich, J. and Dubois, S. (2011) Context affects feeling of knowing accuracy in younger and older adults. *Journal of Experimental Psychology: Learning, Memory and Cognition*, 37, 96–108.

Thompson, D.N. (1997) Contributions to the history of psychology: CVIII. On aging and intelligence: History teaches a different lesson. *Perception and Motor Skills*, 85, 28–30.

Thompson, I.M. (1988) Communication changes in normal and abnormal ageing. In U. Holden (ed.) *Neuropsychology and Aging*. London: Croom Helm.

Thompson, L.W., Gallagher-Thompson, D.G., Futterman, A., Gilewski, M.J. and Peterson, J. (1991) The effects of late-life spousal bereavement over a 30-month interval. *Psychology and Aging*, 6, 434–41.

Thompson, M.D., Knee, K. and Golden, C.J. (1998) Olfaction in persons with Alzheimer's disease. *Neuropsychology Review*, 8, 11–23.

Thompson-Schill, S.L., Jondies, J., Marshietz, C., Smith, E.E. *et al.* (2002) Effects of frontal lobe damage on interference effects in working memory. *Cognitive, Affective and Behavioral Neuroscience*, 2, 109–20.

Thornbury, J.M. and Mistretta, C.M. (1981) Tactile sensitivity as a function of age. *Journal of Gerontology*, 36, 34–39.

Thorvaldsson, V., Hofer, S. M., Berg, S., Skoog, I., Sacuiu, S. and Johansson, B. (2008) Onset of terminal decline in cognitive abilities in individuals without dementia. *Neurology*, 71, 882–7.

Time Magazine (1979) Behavior: The conversion of K. 12 November.

Titz, C. and Verhaeghen, P. (2010) Aging and directed forgetting in episodic memory: A meta-analysis. *Psychology and Aging*, 25, 405–11.

Tomijenovic, L. (2011) Aluminum and Alzheimer's disease: After a century of controversy, is there a plausible link? *Journal of Alzheimer's Disease*, 23, 567–98.

Tomimoto, H. (2011) Subcortical vascular dementia. *Neuroscience Research*, 71, 193–9.

Tomlinson, B.E., Blessed, G. and Roth, M. (1968) Observations on the brains of nondemented old people. *Journal of Neurological Science*, 7, 331–56.

Topolski, J.M., Gotham, H.J., Klinkenberg, W.D., O'Neill, D.L. and Brooks, A.R. (2002) Older adults, substance use and HIV/AIDS: Preparing for a future crisis. *Journal of Mental Health and Aging*, 8, 349–63.

Tornstam, L. (1997) Gerotranscendence in a broad cross-sectional perspective. *Journal of Aging and Identity, 2,* 17–36.

Tornstam, L. (1999) Late-life transcendence: A new developmental perspective on aging. In L.E. Thomas and S.A. Eisendandler (eds) *Religion, Belief, and Spirituality in Late Life.* New York: Springer.

Tornstam, L. and Tornqvist, M. (2000) Nursing staff's interpretations of 'gerotranscendental behavior' in the elderly. *Journal of Aging and Identity, 5,* 15–29.

Torr, J. (2009) Assessment of dementia in people with learning disabilities. *Advances in Mental Health and Learning Disabilities, 3,* 3–9.

Tran, U.S. and Formann, A.K. (2008) Piaget's water-level tasks: Performance across the lifespan with emphasis on the elderly. *Personality and Individual Differences, 45,* 232–7.

Tranter, L.J. and Koustaal, W. (2008) Age and flexible thinking: An experimental demonstration of the beneficial effects of increased cognitively stimulating activity on fluid intelligence in healthy older adults. *Aging, Neuropsychology and Cognition, 15,* 184–207.

Trill, M. and Holland, J. (1993) Cross-cultural differences in the care of patients with cancer: A review. *General Hospital Psychiatry, 15,* 21–30.

Tsai, H.K., Chou, F.S. and Cheng, T.J. (1958) On changes in ear size with age, as found among Taiwanese-Formosans of the Fukiense extraction. *Journal of the Formosan Medical Association, 57,* 105–11.

Tsiouris, J.A. and Patti, P.J. (1997) Drug treatment of depression associated with dementia or presented as 'pseudodementia' in older adults with Down syndrome. *Journal of Applied Research in Intellectual Disabilities, 10,* 312–22.

Tsuchiya, A. and Williams, A. (2005) A 'fair innings' between the sexes: Are men being treated inequitably? *Social Science and Medicine, 60,* 2, 277–86.

Tucker, J.S. Klein, D.J. and Elliott, M.N. (2004) Social control of health behaviors: A comparison of young, middle-aged and older adults. *The Journals of Gerontology Series B: Psychological Sciences and Social Sciences, 59,* 147–50.

Tucker-Drob, E.M. (2009) Differentiation of cognitive abilities across the life span. *Developmental Psychology, 45,* 1097–118.

Tucker-Drob, E.M. and Salthouse, T.A. (2008) Adult age trends in the relations among cognitive abilities. *Psychology and Aging, 23,* 453–60.

Tulving, E. (1972) Episodic and semantic memory. In E. Tulving and D.L. Horton (eds) *Verbal Behavior and General Behavior Theory.* New Jersey: Prentice-Hall.

Tun, P., Benichov, J. and Wingfield, A. (2010) Response latencies in auditory sentence comprehension: Effects of linguistic versus perceptual challenge. *Psychology and Aging, 25,* 730–5.

Tun, P.A., McCoy, S. and Wingfield, A. (2009) Aging, hearing acuity, and the attentional costs of effortful listening. *Psychology and Aging, 24,* 761–6.

Tun, P.A., Wingfield, A. and Lindfield, K.C. (1997) Motor-speed baseline for the digit–symbol substitution test. *Clinical Gerontologist, 18,* 47–51.

Tun, P.A., Wingfield, A., Stine, E.A. and Mecsas, C. (1992) Rapid speech processing and divided attention: Processing rate versus processing resources as an explanation of age effects. *Psychology and Aging, 7,* 546–50.

Tun, S., Murman, D. and Colenda, C. (2008) Concurrent validity of neuropsychiatric subgroups on caregiver burden in Alzheimer disease patients. *American Journal of Geriatric Psychiatry, 16,* 594–602.

Tuokko, H., Garrett, D. D., McDowell, I., Silverberg, N. and Kristjansson, B. (2003) Cognitive decline in high-functioning older adults: Reserve or ascertainment bias? *Aging and Mental Health, 7,* 259–70.

Turner, J.S. and Helms, D.B. (1987) *Lifespan Development.* 3rd edition. New York: Holt, Rinehart and Winston.

Turner, R. and Crisp, R. (2010) Imagining intergroup contact reduced implicit prejudice. *British Journal of Social Psychology, 49,* 129–42.

Tyler, L., Shafto, M., Randall, B., Wright, P., Marsien-Wilson, W. and Stamatakis, E. (2010) Preserving syntactic processing across the adult life span: The modulation of the frontotemporal language system in the context of age-related atrophy. *Cerebral Cortex, 20,* 352–64.

Uekermann, J., Channon, S. and Daum, I. (2006) Humor processing, mentalizing, and executive functioning in normal aging. *Journal of the International Neuropsychological Society, 12,* 184–91.

Uekermann, J., Thoma, P. and Daum, I. (2008) Proverb interpretation changes in aging. *Brain and Cognition, 67,* 51–7.

Unger, R. (2006) Trends in active life expectancy in Germany between 1984 and 2003 – a cohort analysis with different health indicators. *Journal of Public Health, 14,* 155–63.

United Nations Economic and Social Council (2006) Major developments in the area of ageing since the Second World Assembly on Ageing. Report of the Secretary-General. Geneva: 21 November.

United Nations Population Division (2009) *World Population Prospects: The 2008 Revision.* Geneva: United Nations Population Division.

US Department of Health and Human Services (2000) Healthy people 2010: Understanding and improving health. Available at www. healthypeople.gov, accessed on 21 January, 2012.

Vaarama, M., Pieper, R. and Sixsmith, A. (2008) *Care-Related Quality of Life in Old Age: Concepts, Models and Empirical Findings.* New York: Springer.

Vahia, I.V., Cain, A. and Depp, C.A. (2010) Cognitive interventions: Traditional and novel approaches. In C.A. Depp and D.V. Jeste (eds) *Successful Cognitive and Emotional Aging.* Arlington: American Psychiatric Publishing.

Vaillant, G.E. (1992) *Ego Mechanisms of Defense: A Guide.* Washington: American Psychiatric Association.

Valentijn, S., Hill, R., Van Hooren, S., Bosma, H. *et al.* (2006) Memory self-efficacy predicts memory performance: Results from a 6-year follow up study. *Psychology and Aging, 21,* 165–72.

Valimaki, T., Vehvilainen-Julkunen, K., Pietila, A. and Pirttila, T. (2009) Caregiver depression is associated with a low sense of coherence and health-related quality of life. *Aging and Mental Health, 13,* 799–807.

van Baarsen, B. (2002) Theories on coping with loss: The impact of social support and self-esteem on adjustment to emotional and social loneliness following a partner's death in later life. *The Journals of Gerontology Series B: Psychological Sciences and Social Sciences, 57,* 33–42.

van den Berg, T., Elders, L. and Burdorf, A. (2010) Influence of health and work on early retirement. *Journal of Occupational and Environmental Medicine, 52,* 576–83.

van den Hoonaard, D. (2010) *By Himself: The Older Man's Experience of Widowhood.* Toronto: University of Toronto Press.

van der Vlies, A., Pijnenburg, Y., Koene, T., Klein, M. *et al.* (2007) Cognitive impairment in Alzheimer's disease is modified by APOE genotype. *Dementia and Geriatric Cognitive Disorders, 24,* 98–103.

Van Dussen, D. and Morgan, L. (2009) Gender and informal caregiving in CCRCs: Primary caregivers or support networks? *Journal of Women and Aging, 21,* 251–7.

Van Eyken, E., Van Camp, G. and Van Laer, L. (2007) The complexity of age-related hearing impairment: Contributing environmental and genetic factors. *Audiological Neurootology, 12,* 345–58.

van Gelder, B.M., Tijhuis, M.A.R., Kalmijn, S., Giampaoli, S. and Krumhout, D. (2007) Decline in cognitive functioning is associated with a higher mortality risk. *Psychosomatic Medicine, 28,* 93–100.

van Oijen, M., de Jong, F., Hofman, A., Koudstaal, P. and Breteler, M. (2007) Subjective memory complaints, education, and risk of Alzheimer's disease. *Alzheimer's and Dementia, 3,* 92–7.

van Oorschot, W. and Jensen, P. (2009) Early retirement differences between Denmark and the Netherlands: A cross-national comparison of push and pull factors in two small European welfare states. *Journal of Aging Studies, 23*, 267–78.

van Rooij, M., Lusardi, A. and Alessie, R. (2011) Financial literacy and retirement planning in the Netherlands. *Journal of Economic Psychology, 32*, 593–608.

van Solinge, H. (2007) Health change in retirement: A longitudinal study among older workers in the Netherlands. *Research on Aging, 29*, 225–56.

van Solinge, H. and Henkens, K. (2005) Couples' adjustment to retirement: A multi-actor panel study. *The Journals of Gerontology Series B: Psychological Sciences and Social Sciences, 60*, 11–20.

van Solinge, H. and Henkens, K. (2007) Involuntary retirement: The role of restrictive circumstances, timing, and social embeddedness. *The Journals of Gerontology Series B: Psychological Sciences and Social Sciences, 62*, 295–303.

Vance, D.E. (2009) Speed of processing in older adults: A cognitive overview for nursing. *Journal of Neuroscience Nursing, 41*, 290–7.

Vance, D.E., Burgio, L.D., Roth, D.L., Stevens, A.B., Fairchild, J.K. and Yurick, A. (2003) Predictors of agitation in nursing home residents. *The Journals of Gerontology Series B: Psychological Sciences and Social Sciences, 58*, 129–37.

Vance, D.E., Heaton, K., Fazell, P.L. and Ackerman, M.L. (2010) Aging, speed of processing training, and everyday functioning: implications for practice and research. *Activities, Adaptation and Aging, 34*, 276–91.

Vander Bilt, J., Dodge, H.H., Pandav, R., Shaffer, H.J. and Ganguli, M. (2004) Gambling participation and social support among older adults: A longitudinal community study. *Journal of Gambling Studies, 20*, 373–90.

Vanderplas, J.M. and Vanderplas, J.H. (1980) Some factors affecting legibility of printed materials for older adults. *Perceptual and Motor Skills, 50*, 923–32.

Vaneste, S. and Pouthas, V. (1999) Timing in aging: The role of attention. *Experimental Aging Research, 25*, 49–67.

Vassallo, M., Sharma, J.C., Briggs, R.S.J. and Allen, S.C. (2003) Characteristics of early fallers on elderly patient rehabilitation wards. *Age and Ageing, 32*, 338–42.

Veerbeek, L., van der Heide, A., de Vogel-Voogt, E., de Bakker, R. *et al.* (2008) Using the LCP: Bereaved relatives' assessments of communication and bereavement. *American Journal of Hospice and Palliative Medicine, 25*, 207–14.

Veerbeek, L., van Zuylen, L., Swart, S., van der Maas, P. *et al.* (2008) The effect of the Liverpool Care Pathway for the dying: A multi-centre study. *Palliative Medicine, 22*, 145–51.

Venneri, A., McGeown, W., Hietanen, H., Guerrini, C. *et al.* (2008) The anatomical bases of semantic retrieval deficits in early Alzheimer's disease. *Neuropsychologia, 46*, 497–510.

Verghese, J., Lipton, R., Katz, M., Hall, C. *et al.* (2003) Leisure activities and the risk of dementia in the elderly. *New England Journal of Medicine, 348*, 2508–16.

Verhaeghen, P. (2006) Reaction time. In G.L. Maddox (ed.) *The Encyclopedia of Aging.* 4th edition. New York: Springer.

Verhaeghen, P. (2011) Cognitive processes and ageing. In I. Stuart-Hamilton (ed.) *Introduction to Gerontology.* Cambridge: Cambridge University Press.

Verhaeghen, P., Cerella, J., Semenec, S.C., Leo, M.A., Bopp, K.L. and Steitz, D.W. (2002) Cognitive efficiency modes in old age: Performance on sequential and coordinative verbal and visuospatial tasks. *Psychology and Aging, 17*, 558–70.

Verhaeghen, P. and De Meersman, L. (1998) Aging and the Stroop effect:A meta-analysis. *Psychology and Aging, 13*, 120–6.

Verhaeghen, P., Marcoen, A. and Goossens, L. (1992) Improving memory performance in the aged through mnemonic training: A meta-analytic study *Psychology and Aging, 7*, 242–51.

Vetter, P.H., Krauss, S., Steiner, O., Kropp, P. *et al.* (1999) Vascular dementia versus dementia of Alzheimer's type: Do they have differential effects on caregiver's burden? *The Journals of Gerontology B: Psychological Sciences and Social Sciences, 54,* 93–8.

Viard, A., Lebreton, K., Chetelat, G., Desgranges, B. *et al.* (2010) Patterns of hippocampal-neocortical interactions in the retrieval of episodic autobiographical memories across the entire life span of aged adults. *Hippocampus, 20,* 153–65.

Viard, A., Piolino, P., Desgranges, B., Chetelat, G. *et al.* (2007) *Cerebral Cortex, 17,* 2453–67.

Vink, D., Aartsen, M., Comijs, H., Heymans, M., Penninx, B. (2009) Onset of anxiety and depression in the ageing population: Comparison of risk factors in a 9-year prospective study. *American Journal of Geriatric Psychiatry, 17,* 642–52.

Vinkers, D.J., Gussekloo, J., Stek, M. L., Westendrop, R.G.J. *et al.* (2004) Temporal relation between depression and cognitive impairment in old age: Prospective population-based study. *British Medical Journal, 329,* 881–3.

Virta, J., Karrasch, M., Kaprio, J., Koskenvuo, M. *et al.* (2008) Cerebral glucose metabolism in dizygotic twin pairs discordant for Alzheimer's disease. *Dementia and Geriatric Cognitive Disorders, 25,* 9–16.

Viskontas, I.V., Morrison, R.G., Holyoak, K.J., Hummel, J.E. and Knowlton, B.J. (2004) Relational integration, inhibition and analogical reasoning in older adults. *Psychology and Aging, 19,* 581–91.

Vogt Yuan, A. (2011) Black-white differences in aging out of substance use and abuse. *Sociological Spectrum, 31,* 3–31.

Voyer, P., Richard, S., Doucet, L. and Carmichael, P. (2011) Factors associated with delirium severity among older persons with dementia. *Journal of Neuroscience Nursing, 43,* 62–9.

Wachelke, J. and Contarello, A. (2010) Social representations on ageing: Structural differences concerning age group and cultural context. *Revista Latinoamericana de Psicologia, 42,* 367–80.

Wadensten, B. (2010) Changes in nursing home residents during an innovation based on the theory of gerotranscendence. *International Journal of Older People Nursing, 5,* 108–15.

Wagner, N., Hassanein, K. and Head, M. (2010) Computer use by older adults: A multi-disciplinary review. *Computers in Human Behavior, 26,* 870–82.

Wahrendorf, M. and Siegrist, J. (2010) Are changes in productive activities of older people associated with changes in their well-being? Results of a longitudinal European study. *European Journal of Ageing, 7,* 59–68.

Wait, S. (2011) Policies on ageing. In I. Stuart-Hamilton (ed.) *Introduction to Gerontology.* Cambridge: Cambridge University Press.

Waite, L., Laumann, E., Das, A. and Schumm, P. (2009) Sexuality: Measures of partnerships, practices, attitudes, and problems in National Social Life, Health, and Aging Study. *The Journals of Gerontology Series B: Psychological Sciences and Social Sciences, 64,* 156–66.

Wajman, J. and Bertolucci, P. (2010) Intellectual demand and formal education as cognitive protection factors in Alzheimer's disease. *Dementia and Neuropsychologia, 4,* 320–4.

Walker, N., Fain, W.B., Fisk, A.D. and McGuire, C.L. (1997) Aging and decision making: Driving-related problem solving. *Human Factors, 39,* 438–44.

Walker, R., Luszcz, M., Gerstorf, D. and Hoppmann, C. (2011) Subjective wellbeing dynamics in couples from the Australian Longitudinal Study of Aging. *Gerontology, 57,* 153–60.

Walmsley, S.A., Scott, K.M. and Lehrer, R. (1981) Effects of document simplification on the reading comprehension of the elderly. *Journal of Reading Behavior, 12,* 236–48.

Walsh, D.A. (1982) The development of visual information processes in adulthood and old age. In F.I.M. Craik and S. Trehub (eds) *Aging and Cognitive Processes.* New York: Plenum.

Walsh, D.A., Williams, M.V. and Hertzog, C.K. (1979) Age-related differences in two stages of central perceptual processes. *Journal of Gerontology, 34,* 234–41.

Walton, J. (2010) Evidence for participation of aluminum in neurofibrillary tangle formation and growth in Alzheimer's disease. *Journal of Alzheimer's Disease*, 22, 65–72.

Walz, T. (2002) Crones, dirty old men, sexy seniors: Representations of sexuality of older persons. *Journal of Aging and Identity*, 7, 99–112.

Wambacq, I., Koehnke, J., Besing, J., Romei, L., DePierro, A. and Cooper, D. (2009) Processing interaural cues in sound segregation by young and middle-aged brains. *Journal of the American Academy of Audiology*, 20, 453–8.

Wancata, J., Borjesson-Hanson, A., Ostling, S., Sjogren, K. and Skoog, I. (2007) Diagnostic criteria influence dementia prevalence. *American Journal of Geriatric Psychiatry*, 15, 1034–45.

Ward, R. (1977) The impact of subjective age and stigma on older persons. *Journal of Gerontology*, 32, 227–32.

Ward, R. (1984) *The Aging Experience*. Cambridge: Harper and Row.

Warner, D. and Brown, T. (2011) Understanding how race/ethnicity and gender define age-trajectories of disability: An intersectionality approach. *Social Science and Medicine*, 72, 1236–48.

Warren, C.A.B. (1998) Aging and identity in premodern times. *Research on Aging*, 20, 11–35.

Watanabe, M., Kudo, H., Fukuoka, Y., Hatakeyama, A. *et al.* (2008) Salt taste perception and salt intake in older people. *Geriatrics and Gerontology International*, 8, 62–4.

Waters, G. and Caplan, D. (2002) Working memory and online syntactic processing in Alzheimer's disease: Studies with auditory moving window presentation. *The Journals of Gerontology Series B: Psychological Sciences and Social Sciences*, 57, 298–311.

Waters, G.S. and Caplan, D. (2001) Age, working memory and on-line syntactic processing in sentence comprehension. *Psychology and Aging*, 16, 128–44.

Waters, L., Galichet, B., Owen, N. and Eakin, E. (2011) Who participates in physical activity intervention trials? *Journal of Physical Activity and Health*, 8, 85–103.

Watson, D.G. and Maylor, E.A. (2002) Aging and visual marking: Selective deficits for moving stimuli. *Psychology and Aging*, 17, 321–39.

Watson, D.G., Maylor, E.A. and Manson, N.J. (2002) Aging and enumeration: A selective deficit for the subitization of targets among distractors. *Psychology and Aging*, 17, 496–504.

Webster, J. and Gould, O. (2007) Reminiscence and vivid personal memories across adulthood. *International Journal of Aging and Human Development*, 64, 149–70.

Weg, R.B. (1983) Changing physiology of aging: Normal and pathological. In D.S. Woodruff and J.E. Birren (eds) *Aging: Scientific Perspectives and Social Issues*. Monterey, CA: Brooks-Cole.

Weiffenbach, J.M., Baum, B.J. and Berghauser, R. (1982) Taste thresholds: Quality specific variation with human aging. *Journal of Gerontology*, 37, 372–7.

Weilge-Lüssen, A. (2009) Ageing, neurodegeneration, and olfactory and gustatory loss. *B-ENT*, 5, 129–32.

Weisberg, N. and Wilder, R. (eds) (2001) *Expressive Arts with Elders: A Resource*. 2nd edition. London: Jessica Kingsley Publishers.

Wells, Y., Foreman, P., Gething, L. and Petralia, W. (2004) Nurses' attitudes toward aging and older adults – Examining attitudes and practices among health services providers in Australia. *Journal of Gerontological Nursing*, 30, 5–13.

Wells, Y.D. and Kendig, H.L. (1997) Health and well-being of spouse caregivers and the widowed. *Gerontologist*, 37, 666–74.

Welsh, J., Fallon, M. and Keeley, P. (2003) Palliative care. In R.C. Tallis and H. Fillit (eds) *Brocklehurst's Textbook of Geriatric Medicine and Gerontology*. 6th edition. London: Churchill Livingstone.

Wenger, G.C. (1997) Review of findings on support networks of older Europeans. *Journal of Cross-Cultural Gerontology*, 12, 1–21.

West, C.G., Reed, D.M. and Gildengorin, G.L. (1998) Can money buy happiness? Depressive symptoms in an affluent older population. *Journal of the American Geriatrics Society*, 46, 49–57.

West, R. and Bowry, R. (2005) Effects of aging and working memory demands on prospective memory. *Psychophysiology, 42,* 698–712.

West, R., Murphy, K.J., Armilio, M.L., Craik, F.I.M. and Stuss, D.T. (2002) Effects of time of day on age differences in working memory. *The Journals of Gerontology Series B: Psychological Sciences and Social Sciences, 57,* 3–10.

West, R.L. (1988) Prospective memory and aging. In M.M. Gruneberg, P.E. Morris and R.N. Sykes (eds) *Practical Aspects of Memory: Current Research and Issues, Volume 2; Clinical and Educational Implications.* Chichester: Wiley, 119–225.

Westerman, S.J., Davies, D.R., Glendon, A.I., Stammers, R.B. and Matthews, G. (1998) Ageing and word processing competence: Compensation or compilation? *British Journal of Psychology, 89,* 579–97.

Westlye, L.T., Walhovd, K., Dale, A., Bjornerud, A. *et al.* (2010) Life-span changes of the human brain white matter: Diffusion tensor imaging (DTI) and volumetry. *Cerebral Cortex, 20,* 2055–68.

Wetherell, J.L., Gatz, M. and Pedersen, N.L. (2001) A longitudinal analysis of anxiety and depressive symptoms. *Psychology and Aging, 16,* 187–95.

Wetherell, J.L., Le Roux, H. and Gatz, M. (2003) DSM-IV criteria for generalized anxiety disorder in older adults: Distinguishing the worried from the well. *Psychology and Aging, 18,* 622–7.

Weyerer, S., Schaufele, M., Eiffaender-Gorfer, S., Kohler, L. *et al.* (2009) At-risk alcohol drinking in primary care patients aged 75 years and older. *International Journal of Geriatric Psychiatry, 24,* 1376–85.

Whelihan, W.M., Thompson, J.A., Piatt, A.L., Caron, M.D. and Chung, T. (1997) The relation of neuropsychological measures to levels of cognitive functioning in elderly individuals: A discriminant analysis approach. *Applied Neuropsychology, 4,* 160–4.

Whitbourne, S.K. (1987) Personality development in adulthood and old age. In K.W. Schaie (ed.) *Annual Review of Gerontology and Geriatrics, 7.* New York: Springer.

Whitbourne, S.K. (2010) *The Search for Fulfillment.* New York: Ballantine.

Whitbourne, S.K. and Whitbourne, S.B. (2011) *Adult Development and Aging: Biopsychosocial Perspectives.* 4th edition. Hoboken: John Wiley.

White, K.K. and Abrams, L. (2002) Does priming specific syllables during tip-of-the-tongue states facilitate word retrieval in older adults? *Psychology and Aging, 17,* 226–35.

White, L.R., Cartwright, W.S., Cornoni-Huntley, J. and Brock, D.B. (1986) Geriatric epidemiology. In C. Einsdorfer (ed.) *Annual Review of Gerontology and Geriatrics, 6.* New York: Springer.

White, N. and Cunningham, W.R. (1988) Is terminal drop pervasive or specific? *Journal of Gerontology, 43,* 141–4.

White-Means, S.I. (2000) Racial patterns in disabled elderly persons' use of medical services. *The Journals of Gerontology Series B: Psychological Sciences and Social Sciences, 55,* 76–89.

Whitfield, K., Jonassaint, C., Brandon, D., Stanton, M. *et al.* (2010) Does coping mediate the relationship between personality and cardiovascular health in African Americans? *Journal of the National Medical Association, 102,* 95–100.

Whitfield, K.E. and Baker-Thomas, T. (1999) Individual differences in aging minorities. *International Journal of Aging and Human Development, 48,* 73–9.

Whitwell, J., Przybelski, S., Weigand, S., Ivnik, R. *et al.* (2009) Distinct anatomical subtypes of the behavioural variant of frontotemporal dementia: A cluster analysis study. *Brain, 132,* 2932–46.

Whitworth, R. and Larson, C. (1988) Differential diagnosis and staging of Alzheimer's disease with an aphasia battery. *Neuropsychiatry, Neuropsychology and Behavioral Neurology, 1,* 255–65.

Wiebe, J.M.D. and Cox, B.J. (2005) Problem and probable pathological gambling among older adults assessed by the SOGS-R. *Journal of Gambling Studies, 21,* 205–21.

Wilcox, S., Bopp, M., Oberrecht. L., Kammermann, S.K. and McElmurray, C.T. (2003) Psychosocial and perceived environmental correlates of physical activity in rural and older African American and white women. *The Journals of Gerontology Series B: Psychological Sciences and Social Sciences, 58*, 329–37.

Wilcox, S. and King, A.C. (2000) Alcohol consumption in older adults: A comparison of two assessment methods. *Journal of Applied Gerontology, 19*, 170–80.

Wilkins, A. and Baddeley, A. (1978) Remembering to recall in everyday life: An approach to absent-mindedness. In M.M. Gruneberg, P.E. Morris and R.N. Sykes (eds) *Practical Aspects of Memory, Current Research and Issues, Volume 2*. Chichester: Wiley.

Wilkins, R. and Adams, O.B. (1983) Health expectancy in Canada, late 1970s: Demographic, regional and social dimensions. *American Journal of Public Health, 73*, 1073–80.

Williams, A., While, D., Windfuhr, K., Bickley, H. *et al.* (2011) Birthday blues: Examining the association between birthday and suicide in a national sample. *Crisis: The Journal of Crisis Intervention and Suicide Prevention, 32*, 134–42.

Williams, G.C. (1957) Pleiotropy, natural selection and the evolution of senescence. *Evolution, 11*, 398–411.

Williams, K. (2004) The transition to widowhood and the social regulation of health: Consequences for health and health risk behavior. *The Journals of Gerontology Series B: Psychological Sciences and Social Sciences, 59*, 343–49.

Williams, K., Holmes, F., Kemper, S. and Marquis, J. (2003) Written language clues to cognitive changes of aging: An analysis of the letters of King James VI/I. *The Journals of Gerontology Series B: Psychological Sciences and Social Sciences, 58*, 42–4.

Williams, P., Suchy, Y, and Kraybill, M. (2010) Five-factor model personality traits and executive functioning among older adults. *Journal of Research in Personality, 44*, 485–91.

Williamson, G.M. and Schulz, R. (1992) Physical illness and symptoms of depression among elderly outpatients. *Psychology and Aging, 7*, 343–51.

Williamson, G.M. and Schulz, R. (1995) Activity restriction mediates the association between pain and depressed affect: A study of younger and older adult cancer patients. *Psychology and Aging, 10*, 369–78.

Willis, L., Goodwin, J., Lee, K-O., Mosqueda, L. *et al.* (1997) Impact of psychosocial factors on health outcomes in the elderly: A prospective study. *Journal of Aging and Health, 9*, 396–414.

Willis, R. (2008) Advantageous inequality or disadvantageous equality? Ethnicity and family support among older people in Britain. *Ethnicity and Inequalities in Health and Social Care, 1*, 18–23.

Wilson, R., Schneider, J., Arnold, S., Bienias, J. and Bennett, D. (2007) Conscientiousness and the incidence of Alzheimer disease and mild cognitive impairment. *Archives of General Psychiatry, 64*, 1204–12.

Wilson, R., Weir, D., Leurgans, S., Evans, D. *et al.* (2011) Sources of variability in estimates of the prevalence of Alzheimer's disease in the United States. *Alzheimer's and Dementia, 7*, 74–9.

Wilson, R.S., Arnold, S.E., Tang, Y. and Bennett, D.A. (2006) Odor identification and decline in different cognitive domains in old age. *Neuroepidemiology, 26*, 61–7.

Wilson, R.S., Beck, T., Bienias, J. and Bennett, D. (2007) Terminal cognitive decline: Accelerated loss of cognition in the last years of life. *Psychosomatic Medicine, 69*, 131–7.

Wilson, R.S., Beckett, L.A., Barnes, L.L., Schneider, J.A. *et al.* (2002) Individual differences in rates of change in cognitive abilities of older persons. *Psychology and Aging, 17*, 179–93.

Wilson, R.S., Gilley, D.W., Bennett, D.A., Beckett, L.A. and Evans, D.A. (2000) Person-specific paths of cognitive decline in Alzheimer's disease and their relation to age. *Psychology and Aging, 15*, 18–28.

Wilson, R.S., Mendes de Leon, C.F., Bienias, J.L., Evans, D.A. and Bennett, D.A. (2004) Personality and mortality in old age. *The Journals of Gerontology Series B: Psychological Sciences and Social Sciences, 59*, 110–16.

Wilson, S. (2006) The validation of the Texas Revised Inventory of Grief on an older Latino sample. *Journal of Social Work in End of Life and Palliative Care, 2*, 33–60.

Wingfield, A. (1996) Cognitive factors in auditory performance: Context, speed of processing, and constraints of memory. *Journal of the American Academy of Audiology, 7*, 175–82.

Wingfield, A. and Grossman, M. (2006) Language and the aging brain: Patterns of neural compensation revealed by functional brain imaging. *Journal of Neuropsychology, 96*, 2830–9.

Wink, P. and Dillon, M. (2003) Religiousness, spirituality and psychosocial functioning in late adulthood: Findings from a longitudinal study. *Psychology and Aging, 18*, 916–24.

Wisdom, N., Callahan, J. and Hawkins, K. (2011) The effects of apolipoprotein E on non-impaired cognitive functioning: A meta-analysis. *Neurobiology of Aging, 32*, 63–74.

Wishart, L.R., Lee, T.D., Murdoch, J.E. and Hodges, N.J. (2000) Effects of aging on automatic and effortful processes in bimanual coordination. *The Journals of Gerontology Series B: Psychological Sciences and Social Sciences 55*, 85–94.

Witte, K.L. and Freund, J.S. (1995) Anagram solutions as related to adult age, anagram difficulty and experience in solving crossword puzzles. *Aging and Cognition, 2*, 146–55.

Wolf, E.S. (1997) Self psychology and the aging self through the life curve. *Annual of Psychoanalysis, 25*, 201–15.

Wolff, J.L. and Agree, E.M. (2004) Depression among recipients of informal care: The effects of reciprocity, respect and adequacy of support. *The Journals of Gerontology Series B: Psychological Sciences and Social Sciences, 59*, 173–80.

Wong, C., Holroyd-Leduc, J., Simel, D. and Strauss, S. (2010) Does this patient have delirium? Value of bedside instruments. *Journal of the American Medical Association, 304*, 779–86.

Wong, P. and Tomer, A. (2011) Beyond terror and denial: The positive psychology of death acceptance. *Death Studies, 35*, 99–106.

Wong, P., Jin, J., Gunasekera, G., Abel, R., Lee, E. and Dhar, S. (2009) Aging and cortical mechanisms of speech perception in noise. *Neuropsychologia, 47*, 693–703.

Woo, J., Lo, R., Cheng, J., Wong, F. and Mak, B. (2011) Quality of end-of-life care for non-cancer patients in a non-acute hospital. *Journal of Clinical Nursing, 20*, 1834–41.

Wood, E., Whitfield, E. and Christie, A. (1995) Changes in survival in demented hospital inpatients 1957–1987. In E. Murphy and G. Alexopoulos (eds) *Geriatric Psychiatry: Key Research Topics for Clinicians*. Chichester: Wiley, 85–93.

Woodruff-Pak, D. (1988) *Psychology and Aging.* Englewood Cliffs: Prentice Hall.

Woodruff-Pak, D.S. (1997) *The Neuropsychology of Aging.* Oxford: Blackwells.

Woods, R. (2011) The psychology of atypical ageing. In I. Stuart-Hamilton (ed.) *An Introduction to Gerontology*. Cambridge: Cambridge University Press.

Woods, R.T. (1996) *Handbook of the Clinical Psychology of Ageing.* Chichester: Wiley.

Woods, R.T. (1999) Mental health problems in late life. In R.T. Woods (ed.) *Psychological Problems of Ageing*. Chichester: Wiley, 73–110.

Woodward, K. (1991) *Aging and its Discontents. Freud and Other Fictions.* Bloomington, IN: Indiana University Press.

World Health Organization (2004) *World Health Report 2000.* Geneva: World Health Organization.

World Health Organization (2011) Palliative care definition. Available at www.who.int/en, accessed on 7 September 2011.

Wyndham, J. (1960) *Trouble With Lichen.* London: Michael Joseph.

Xue, S.A. and Deliyski, D. (2001) Effects of aging on selected acoustic voice parameters: Preliminary normative data and educational implications. *Educational Gerontology, 27*, 159–68.

Yaffe, K., Lindquist, K., Vittinghoff, E., Barnes, D. *et al.* (2010) The effect of maintaining cognition on risk of disability and death. *Journal of the American Geriatrics Society, 58*, 889–94.

Yamada, M., Mimori, Y., Kasagi, F., Miyachi, T. *et al.* (2008) Incidence of dementia, Alzheimer disease, and vascular dementia in a Japanese population: Radiation Effects Research Foundation Adult Health Study. *Neuroepidemiology, 30*, 152–60.

Yan, E., Wu, A., Ho, P. and Pearson, V. (2011) Older Chinese men and women's experiences and understanding of sexuality. *Culture, Health and Sexuality, 13*, 983–99.

Yang, Z., Norton, E.C. and Stearns, S.C. (2003) Longevity and health care expenditures: The real reasons older people spend more. *The Journals of Gerontology Series B: Psychological Sciences and Social Science, 58*, 2–10.

Yarmey, A.D. and Yarmey, M.J. (1997) Eyewitness recall and duration estimates in field settings. *Journal of Applied Social Psychology, 27*, 330–44.

Yashin, A.I., De Benedictis, G., Vaupel, J.W., Tan, Q. *et al.* (1999) Genes, demography and life span: The contribution of demographic data in genetic studies on aging and longevity. *American Human Genetics, 65*, 1178–93.

Yong, H.H., Gibson, S.J., Horne, D. and Helme, R.D. (2001) Development of a pain attitudes questionnaire to assess stoicism and cautiousness for possible age differences. *The Journals of Gerontology Series B: Psychological Sciences and Social Sciences, 56*, 279–84.

Yoon, C., Hasher, L., Feinberg, F., Rahhal, T.A. and Winocur, G. (2000) Cross-cultural differences in memory: The role of culture-based stereotypes about aging. *Psychology and Aging, 15*, 694–704.

You, J., Fung, H. and Isaacowitz, D. (2009) Age differences in dispositional optimism: A cross-cultural study. *European Journal of Ageing, 6*, 247–52.

Ystad, M., Eichele, T., Lundervald, A. and Lundervald, A. (2010) Subcortical functional connectivity and verbal episodic memory in healthy elderly – a resting state fMRI study. *Neuroimage, 52*, 379–88.

Yur'yev, A., Leppik, L., Tooding, L., Sisask, M.M. *et al.* (2010) Social inclusion affects elderly suicide mortality. *International Psychogeriatrics, 22*, 1337–43.

Zacks, R.T., Hasher, L., Doren, B., Hamm, V. and Attig, M.S. (1987) Encoding and memory of explicit and implicit information. *Journal of Gerontology, 42*, 418–22.

Zamarian, L., Weiss, E, and Delazer, M. (2011) The impact of mild cognitive impairment on decision making in two gambling tasks. *Journals of Gerontology, 66*, 23–31.

Zappala, S., Depolo, M., Fraccaroli, F. and Guglieimi, D. (2008) Postponing job retirement? Psychosocial influences on the preference for early or late retirement. *Career Development International, 13*, 150–67.

Zebrowitz, L. and Montepare, J. (2000) Too young, too old: Stigmatizing adolescents and elders. In T. Heatherton, R. Kleck, M. Hebl and J. Hull (eds.) *The Psychology of Stigma*. London: Guildford Press, 334–73.

Zeevl, N., Pachter, J., McCullough, L.D., Wolfson, L. and Kuchel, G.A. (2010) The blood-brain barrier: Geriatric relevance of a critical brain-body interface. *Journal of the American Geriatrics Society, 58*, 1532–54.

Zeintl, M. and Kliegel, M. (2010) Proactive and coactive interference in age-related performance in a recognition-based operation span task. *Gerontology, 56*, 421–9.

Zelinski, E.M and Stewart, S.T. (1998) Individual differences in 16-year memory changes. *Psychology and Aging, 13*, 622–30.

Zelinski, E.M. and Burnight, K.P. (1997) Sixteen-year longitudinal and time lag changes in memory and cognition in older adults. *Psychology and Aging, 12*, 503–13.

Zelinski, E.M. and Hyde, J.C. (1996) Old words, new meanings: Aging and sense creation. *Journal of Memory and Language, 35*, 689–707.

Zettel, L.A. and Rook, K.S. (2004) Substitution and compensation in the social networks of older widowed women. *Psychology and Aging, 19*, 433–43.

Zhang, A.Y., Yu, L.C., Yuan, J., Tong, Z., Yang, C. and Foreman, S.E. (1997) Family and cultural correlates of depression among Chinese elderly. *International Journal of Social Psychiatry, 43,* 199–212.

Zhang, X.H., Sasaki, S. and Kesteloot, H. (1995) The sex ratio of mortality and its secular trends. *International Journal of Epidemiology, 24,* 720–9.

Zhang, Z. and Hayward, M.D. (2001) Childlessness and the psychological well-being of older persons. *The Journals of Gerontology Series B: Psychological Sciences and Social Sciences, 56,* 311–20.

Zhihao, L., Moore, A.B., Tyner, C. and Hu, X. (2009) Asymetric connectivity and its relationship to 'HAROLD' in aging brain. *Brain Research, 1295,* 149–58.

Ziegler-Graham, K., Brookmeyer, R., Johnson, E. and Arrighi, H. (2008) Worldwide variation in the doubling time of Alzheimer's disease incidence rates. *Alzheimer's and Dementia, 4,* 316–23.

Zimmerman, C. (2004) Denial of impending death: A discourse analysis of the palliative care literature. *Social Science and Medicine, 59,* 1769–80.

Zimprich, D. and Martin, M. (2002) Can longitudinal changes in processing speed explain longitudinal age changes in fluid intelligence? *Psychology and Aging, 17,* 690–5.

Zollig, J., Martin, M. and Kliegel, M. (2010) Forming intentions successfully: Differential compensational mechanisms of adolesecents and old adults. *Cortex, 46,* 575–89.

Zwaan, B.J. (1999) The evolutionary genetics of ageing and longevity. *Heredity, 82,* 589–97.

Zwakhalen, S.M.G., Hamers, J.P.H., Peijnenburg, R.H.A. and Berger, M.P.F. (2007) Nursing staff knowledge and beliefs about pain in elderly nursing home residents with dementia. *Pain Research and Management, 12,* 177–84.

Subject Index

Some subjects, such as functional ageing, intelligence (fluid, crystallised or general) appear on practically every page of the book, and so obviously indexing every example would be counterproductive. Therefore, terms with such widespread applicability are indexed only where they are explicitly mentioned in the text.

Author Index